92

1962

Judy — Merry X-mas & I hope 1963 is even bet[illegible], Fred & Julie.

[illegible]ave

THE PHILOSOPHY OF CIVILIZATION

THE MACMILLAN COMPANY
NEW YORK • CHICAGO
DALLAS • ATLANTA • SAN FRANCISCO
LONDON • MANILA

IN CANADA
BRETT-MACMILLAN LTD.
GALT, ONTARIO

THE PHILOSOPHY

of CIVILIZATION

By ALBERT SCHWEITZER

TRANSLATED BY C. T. CAMPION

PART I *The Decay and the Restoration of Civilization*

PART II *Civilization and Ethics*

FIRST AMERICAN EDITION

THE MACMILLAN COMPANY

NEW YORK 1959

Published in the United States of America
BY THE MACMILLAN COMPANY

PRINTED IN THE UNITED STATES OF AMERICA

Ninth Printing, 1959

CONTENTS

PART I
THE DECAY AND THE RESTORATION OF CIVILIZATION

PART II
CIVILIZATION AND ETHICS

Part I

☼

THE DECAY AND THE RESTORATION OF CIVILIZATION

TO

Annie Fischer

IN DEEPEST GRATITUDE

AUTHOR'S PREFACE TO THE FIRST ENGLISH EDITION

"THE DECAY AND THE RESTORATION OF CIVILIZATION" IS THE FIRST part of a complete philosophy of civilization with which I have been occupied since the year 1900.

The second part, entitled "Civilization and Ethics," will appear immediately. The third is called "The World-View * of Reverence for Life." The fourth has to do with the civilized State.

That over which I have toiled since 1900 has been finally ripened in the stillness of the primeval forest of Equatorial Africa. There, during the years 1914–17, the clear and definite lines of this philosophy of civilization have been developed.

The first part, "The Decay and the Restoration of Civilization," is a kind of introduction to the philosophy of civilization. It states the problem of civilization.

Entering on the question as to what is the real essential nature of civilization, I come to the pronouncement that this is ultimately ethical. I know that in thus stating the problem as a moral one I shall surprise and even disgust the spirit of our times, which is accustomed to move amidst æsthetic, historical and material considerations. I imagine, however, that I am myself enough of an artist and also of an historian to be able to comprehend the æsthetic and historical elements in civilization, and that, as a modern physician and surgeon, I am sufficiently modern to appreciate the glamour of the technical and material attainments of our age.

Notwithstanding this, I have come to the conviction that the æsthetic and the historical elements, and the magnificent extension of our material knowledge and power, do not themselves

* *Weltanschauung*. See Translator's note on p. xvii.

form the essence of civilization, but that this depends on the mental disposition of the individuals and nations who exist in the world. All other things are merely accompanying circumstances of civilization, which have nothing to do with its real essence.

Creative, artistic, intellectual, and material attainments can only show their full and true effects when the continued existence and development of civilization have been secured by founding civilization itself on a mental disposition which is truly ethical. It is only in his struggle to become ethical that man comes to possess real value as a personality; it is only under the influence of ethical convictions that the various relations of human society are formed in such a way that individuals and people can develop in an ideal manner. If the ethical foundation is lacking, then civilization collapses, even when in other directions creative and intellectual forces of the strongest nature are at work.

This moral conception of civilization, which makes me almost a stranger amidst the intellectual life of my time, I express clearly and unhesitatingly, in order to arouse amongst my contemporaries reflection as to what civilization really is. We shall not succeed in re-establishing our civilization on an enduring basis until we rid ourselves completely of the superficial concept of civilization which now holds us in thrall, and give ourselves up again to the ethical view which obtained in the eighteenth century.

The second point which I desire should obtain currency is that of the connection between civilization and our theory of the universe. At the present time no regard is paid to this connection. In fact, the period in which we are living altogether misses the significance of having a theory of the universe. It is the common conviction nowadays, of educated and uneducated alike, that humanity will progress quite satisfactorily without any theory of the universe at all.

The real fact is that all human progress depends on progress in its theory of the universe, whilst, conversely, decadence is conditioned by a similar decadence in this theory. Our loss of real civilization is due to our lack of a theory of the universe.

Only as we again succeed in attaining a strong and worthy

theory of the universe, and find in it strong and worthy convictions, shall we again become capable of producing a new civilization. It is this apparently abstract and paradoxical truth of which I proclaim myself the champion.

Civilization, put quite simply, consists in our giving ourselves, as human beings, to the effort to attain the perfecting of the human race and the actualization of progress of every sort in the circumstances of humanity and of the objective world. This mental attitude, however, involves a double predisposition: firstly, we must be prepared to act affirmatively toward the world and life; secondly, we must become ethical.

Only when we are able to attribute a real meaning to the world and to life shall we be able also to give ourselves to such action as will produce results of real value. As long as we look on our existence in the world as meaningless, there is no point whatever in desiring to effect anything in the world. We become workers for that universal spiritual and material progress which we call civilization only in so far as we affirm that the world and life possess some sort of meaning, or, which is the same thing, only in so far as we think optimistically.

Civilization originates when men become inspired by a strong and clear determination to attain progress, and consecrate themselves, as a result of this determination, to the service of life and of the world. It is only in ethics that we can find the driving force for such action, transcending, as it does, the limits of our own existence.

Nothing of real value in the world is ever accomplished without enthusiasm and self-sacrifice.

But it is impossible to convince men of the truth of world- and life-affirmation and of the real value of ethics by mere declamation. The affirmative and ethical mentality which characterizes these beliefs must orginate in man himself as the result of an inner spiritual relation to the world. Only then will they accompany him as strong, clear, and constant convictions, and condition his every thought and action.

To put it in another way: World- and life-affirmation must be the products of thought about the world and life. Only as the majority of individuals attain to this result of thought and continue under its influence will a true and enduring civilization make progress in the world. Should the mental disposition toward world- and life-affirmation and toward ethics begin to wane, or become dim and obscured, we shall be incapable of working for true civilization, nay, more, we shall be unable even to form a correct concept of what such civilization ought to be.

And this is the fate which has befallen us. We are bereft of any theory of the universe. Therefore, instead of being inspired by a profound and powerful spirit of affirmation of the world and of life, we allow ourselves, both as individuals and as nations, to be driven hither and thither by a type of such affirmation which is both confused and superficial. Instead of adopting a determined ethical attitude, we exist in an atmosphere of mere ethical phrases or declare ourselves ethical sceptics.

How is it that we have got into this state of lacking a theory of the universe? It is because hitherto the world- and life-affirming and ethical theory of the universe had no convincing and permanent foundation in thought. We thought again and again that we had found such a basis for it; but it lost power again and again without our being aware that it was doing so, until, finally, we have been obliged, for more than a generation past, to resign ourselves more and more to a complete lack of any world-theory at all.

Thus, in this introductory part of my work, I proclaim two truths and conclude with a great note of interrogation. The truths are the following: The basic ethical character of civilization, and the connection between civilization and our theories of the universe. The question with which I conclude is this: Is it at all possible to find a real and permanent foundation in thought for a theory of the universe which shall be both ethical and affirmative of the world and of life?

The future of civilization depends on our overcoming the meaninglessness and hopelessness which characterize the thoughts and convictions of men to-day, and reaching a state of fresh hope and fresh determination. We shall be capable of this, however, only when the majority of individuals discover for themselves both an ethic and a profound and steadfast attitude of world- and life-affirmation, in a theory of the universe at once convincing and based on reflection.

Without such a general spiritual experience there is no possibility of holding our world back from the ruin and disintegration toward which it is being hastened. It is our duty then to rouse ourselves to fresh reflection about the world and life.

In "Civilization and Ethics," the second part of this philosophy of civilization, I describe the road along which thought has led me to world- and life-affirmation and to ethics. The root-idea of my theory of the universe is that my relation to my own being and to the objective world is determined by reverence for life. This reverence for life is given as an element of my will-to-live, and becomes clearly conscious of itself as I reflect about my life and about the world. In the mental attitude of reverence for life which should characterize my contact with all forms of life, both ethics and world- and life-affirmation are involved. It is not any kind of insight into the essential nature of the world which determines my relation to my own existence and to the existence which I encounter in the world, but rather only and solely my own will-to-live which has developed the power of reflection about itself and the world.

The theory of the universe characterized by reverence for life is a type of mysticism arrived at by self-consistent thought when persisted in to its ultimate conclusion. Surrendering himself to the guidance of this mysticism, man finds a meaning for his life in that he strives to accomplish his own spiritual and ethical self-fulfilment, and, simultaneously and in the same act, helps forward all the processes of spiritual and material progress which have to be actualized in the world.

I do not know how many, or how few, will allow themselves to be persuaded to travel with me on the road indicated above. What I desire above all things—and this is the crux of the whole affair—is that we should all recognize fully that our present entire lack of any theory of the universe is the ultimate source of all the catastrophes and misery of our times, and that we should work together for a theory of the universe and of life, in order that thus we may arrive at a mental disposition which shall make us really and truly civilized men.

It was a great joy to me to be afforded the opportunity of putting forward, in the *Dale Lectures,* delivered in Oxford, the views on which this philosophy of civilization is based.

I would tender my deepest thanks to my friends, Mr. C. T. Campion, M.A., now of Grahamstown, South Africa, and Dr. J. P. Naish, of Oxford. Mr. Campion is the translator of this first part of the "Philosophy of Civilization." Dr. Naish has seen the book through the press and translated this preface.

Strasbourg, Alsace
February, 1923

ALBERT SCHWEITZER

TRANSLATOR'S NOTE

The compound word *Weltanschauung* may be translated "theory of the universe," "world-theory," "world-conception," or "world-view." The first is misleading as suggesting, wrongly, a scientific explanation of the universe; the second and third as suggesting, less ambitiously but still wrongly, an explanation of how and why our human world is what it is. The last indicates a sufficiently wide knowledge of our corner of the universe to allow all factors to be taken into consideration which bear on the question at issue.

There may be passages in which it is desirable to vary the translation, and others in which it is possible to give the meaning in more elegant English, for good English style does not take kindly to such compound words. But this latter consideration can only be a secondary one in the translation of a philosophical work, the first object of which must be to ensure that the author's meaning is reproduced as clearly as possible.

The translator would now, nine years later, like to replace "theory of the universe" by "world-view," but such a change would involve too costly an amount of alteration in the pages of this second edition, which already accommodates a number of verbal revisions. If in the future there should be a complete resetting of the volume he will, if possible, make the change.

1932. *C. T. C.*

Chapter I

HOW PHILOSOPHY IS RESPONSIBLE FOR THE COLLAPSE OF CIVILIZATION

Our self-deception as to the real conditions of our civilization.

The collapse of the world-view on which our ideals were based.

The superficial character of modern philosophizing.

WE ARE LIVING TO-DAY UNDER THE SIGN OF THE COLLAPSE OF civilization. The situation has not been produced by the war; the latter is only a manifestation of it. The spiritual atmosphere has solidified into actual facts, which again react on it with disastrous results in every respect. This interaction of material and spiritual has assumed a most unhealthy character. Just below a mighty cataract we are driving along in a current full of formidable eddies, and it will need the most gigantic efforts to rescue the vessel of our fate from the dangerous side channel into which we have allowed it to drift, and bring it back into the main stream, if, indeed, we can hope to do so at all.

We have drifted out of the stream of civilization because there was amongst us no real reflection upon what civilization is. It is true that at the end of the last century and the beginning of this there appeared a number of works on civilization with the most varied titles; but, as though in obedience to some secret order, they made no attempt to settle and make clear the conditions of our intellectual life, but devoted themselves exclusively to its origin and history. They gave us a relief map of civilization marked with roads which men had observed or invented, and which led us over hill and dale through the fields of history from the Renaissance to the twentieth century. It was a triumph for the historical sense of the authors. The crowds whom these works instructed were filled with satisfied contentment when they understood that their civilization was the organic product of so many centuries of the working of spiritual and social forces, but no one worked out and described the content of our spiritual life. No one tested its value from the point of view of the nobility of its ideas, and its ability to produce real progress.

Thus we crossed the threshold of the twentieth century with an unshakable conceit of ourselves, and whatever was written at that time about our civilization only confirmed us in our ingenuous belief in its high value. Anyone who expressed doubt was regarded with astonishment. Many, indeed, who were on the road to error, stopped and returned to the main road again because they were afraid of the path which led off to the side. Others continued along the main road, but in silence; the understanding and insight which were at work in them only condemned them to isolation.

It is clear now to everyone that the suicide of civilization is in progress. What yet remains of it is no longer safe. It is still standing, indeed, because it was not exposed to the destructive pressure which overwhelmed the rest, but, like the rest, it is built upon rubble, and the next landslide will very likely carry it away.

But what was it that preceded and led up to this loss of power in the innate forces of civilization?

The age of the Illuminati and of rationalism had put forward ethical ideals, based on reason, concerning the development of the individual to true manhood, his position in society, the material and spiritual problems which arose out of society, the relations of the different nations to each other, and their issue in a humanity which should be united in the pursuit of the highest moral and spiritual objects. These ideals had begun, both in philosophy and in general thought, to get into contact with reality and to alter the general environment. In the course of three or four generations there had been such progress made, both in the ideas underlying civilization and in their material embodiment, that the age of true civilization seemed to have dawned upon the world and to be assured of an uninterrupted development.

But about the middle of the nineteenth century this mutual understanding and co-operation between ethical ideals and reality began to break down, and in the course of the next few decades it disappeared more and more completely. Without resistance, without complaint, civilization abdicated. Its ideas lagged behind, as though they were too exhausted to keep pace with it. How did this come about?

* * *

The decisive element in the production of this result was philosophy's renunciation of her duty.

In the eighteenth century and the early part of the nineteenth it was philosophy which led and guided thought in general. She had busied herself with the questions which presented themselves to mankind at each successive period, and had kept the thought of civilized man actively reflecting upon them. Philosophy at that time included within herself an elementary philosophizing about man, society, race, humanity and civilization, which produced in a perfectly natural way a living popular philosophy that controlled the general thought, and maintained the enthusiasm for civilization.

But that ethical, and at the same time optimistic, view of things in which the Illuminati and rationalism had laid the foundations of this healthy popular philosophy, was unable in the long run to meet the criticism levelled at it by pure thought. Its naïve dogmatism raised more and more prejudice against it. Kant tried to provide the tottering building with new foundations, undertaking to alter the rationalistic view of things in accordance with the demands of a deeper theory of knowledge, without, however, making any change in its essential spiritual elements. Goethe, Schiller and other intellectual heroes of the age, showed, by means of criticism both kindly and malicious, that rationalism was rather popular philosophy than real philosophy, but they were not in a position to put into the place of what they destroyed anything new which could give the same effective support to the ideas about civilization which were current in the general thought of the time.

Fichte, Hegel, and other philosophers, who, for all their criticism of rationalism, paid homage to its ethical ideals, attempted to establish a similar ethical and optimistic view of things by speculative methods, that is by logical and metaphysical discussion of pure being and its development into a universe. For three or four decades they succeeded in deceiving themselves and others with this supposedly creative and inspiring illusion, and in doing violence to reality in the interests of their theory of the universe. But at last the natural sciences, which all this time had been growing stronger and stronger, rose up against them, and, with a plebeian enthusiasm for the truth of reality, reduced to ruins the magnificent creations of their imagination.

Since that time the ethical ideas on which civilization rests have been wandering about the world, poverty-stricken and homeless. No theory of the universe has been advanced which can give them a solid foundation; in fact, not one has made its appearance which can claim for itself solidity and inner consistency. The age of philosophic dogmatism had come definitely to an end, and after that nothing was recognized as truth except the science which described reality. Complete theories of the universe no longer appeared as fixed stars; they were regarded as resting on hypothesis, and ranked no higher than comets.

The same weapon which struck down the dogmatism of knowledge about the universe struck down also the dogmatic enunciation of spiritual ideas. The early simple rationalism, the critical rationalism of Kant, and the speculative rationalism of the great philosophers of the nineteenth century had all alike done violence to reality in two ways. They had given a position above that of the facts of science to the views which they had arrived at by pure thought, and they had also preached a series of ethical ideals which were meant to replace by new ones the various existing relations in the ideas and the material environment of mankind. When the first of these two forms of violence was proved to be a mistaken one, it became questionable whether the second could still be allowed the justification which it had hitherto enjoyed. The doctrinaire methods of thought which made the existing world nothing but material for the production of a purely theoretical sketch of a better future were replaced by sympathetic attempts to understand the historical origin of existing things for which Hegel's philosophy had prepared the way.

With a general mentality of this description, a real combination of ethical ideals with reality was no longer possible; there was not the freedom from prejudice which that required, and so there came a weakening of the convictions which were the driving power of civilization. So, too, an end was put to that justifiable violence to human convictions and circumstances without which the reforming work of civilization can make no advance, because it was bound up with that other unjustifiable violence to reality. That is the tragic element in the psychological development of our spiritual life during the latter half of the nineteenth century.

Rationalism, then, had been dismissed; but with it went also the optimistic convictions as to the moral meaning of the universe and of humanity, of society and of man, to which it had given birth, though the conviction still exerted so much influence that no attention was paid to the catastrophe which had really begun.

* * *

Philosophy did not realize that the power of the ideas about civilization which had been entrusted to it was becoming a doubtful quantity. At the end of one of the most brilliant works on the history of philosophy which appeared at the close of the nineteenth century philosophy is defined as the process "by which there comes to completion, step by step, and with ever clearer and surer consciousness, that conviction about the value of civilization the universal validity of which it is the object of philosophy itself to affirm." But the author has forgotten the essential point, viz., that there was a time when philosophy did not merely convince itself of the value of civilization, but also let its convictions go forth as fruitful ideas destined to influence the general thought, while from the middle of the nineteenth century onwards these convictions had become more and more of the nature of hoarded and unproductive capital.

Once philosophy had been an active worker producing universal convictions about civilization. Now, after the collapse in the middle of the nineteenth century, this same philosophy had become a mere drawer of dividends, concentrating her activities far from the world on what she had managed to save. She had become a mere science, which sifted the results of the historical and natural sciences, and collected from them material for a future theory of the universe, carrying on with this object in view a learned activity in all branches of knowledge. At the same time she became more and more absorbed in the study of her own past. Philosophy came to mean practically the history of philosophy. The creative spirit had left her. She became more and more a philosophy which contained no real thought. She reflected, indeed, on the results achieved by the individual sciences, but she lost the power of elemental thought.

She looked back with condescending pity on the rationalism which she had outstripped. She prided herself on having got beyond the ideas of Kant, on having been shown by Hegel the inner meaning of history, and on being at work to-day in close sympathy with the natural sciences. But for all that she was poorer than the poorest rationalism, because she now carried on in imagination only, and not in reality, the recognized work of philosophy, which the latter had practised so zealously. Rationalism, for all its simplicity, had been a working philosophy, but philosophy herself had now become, for all her insight, merely a pedantic philosophy of degenerates. She still played, indeed, some sort of *rôle* in schools and universities, but she had no longer any message for the great world.

In spite of all her learning, she had become a stranger to the world, and the problems of life which occupied men and the whole thought of the age had no part in her activities. Her way lay apart from the general spiritual life, and just as she derived no stimulus from the latter, so she gave none back. Refusing to concern herself with elemental problems, she contained no elemental philosophy which could become a philosophy of the people.

From this impotence came the aversion to all generally intelligible philosophizing which is so characteristic of her. Popular philosophy was for her merely a review, prepared for the use of the crowd, simplified, and therefore rendered inferior, of the results given by the individual sciences which she had herself sifted and put together in view of a future theory of the universe. She was wholly unconscious of several things, viz., that there is a popular philosophy which arises out of such a review; that it is just the province of philosophy to deal with the elemental, inward questions about which individuals and the crowd are thinking, or ought to be thinking, to apply to them more comprehensive and more thorough methods of thought, and then restore them to general currency; and, finally, that the value of any philosophy is in the last resort to be measured by its capacity, or incapacity, to transform itself into a living philosophy of the people.

Whatever is deep is also simple, and can be reproduced as such, if only its relation to the whole of reality is preserved. It is then something abstract, which secures for itself a many-sided life as soon as it comes into contact with facts.

Whatever of inquiring thought there was among the general public was therefore compelled to languish, because our philosophy refused either to acknowledge or to help it. It found in front of it a deep chasm which it could not cross.

Of gold coinage, minted in the past, philosophy had abundance; hypotheses about a soon to be developed theoretical theory of the universe filled her vaults like unminted bullion; but food with which to appease the spiritual hunger of the present she did not possess. Deceived by her own riches, she had neglected to plant any ground with nourishing crops, and therefore, ignoring the hunger of the age, she left the latter to its fate.

That pure thought never managed to construct a theory of the universe of an optimistic, ethical character, and to build up on that for a foundation the ideals which go to produce civilization, was not the fault of philosophy; it was a fact which became evident as thought developed. But philosophy was guilty of a wrong to our age in that it did not admit the fact, but remained wrapped up in its illusion, as though this were really a help to the progress of civilization.

The ultimate vocation of philosophy is to be the guide and guardian of the general reason, and it was her duty, in the circumstances of the time, to confess to our world that ethical ideals were no longer supported by any general theory of the universe, but were, till further notice, left to themselves, and must make their way in the world by their own innate power. She ought to have shown us that we have to fight on behalf of the ideals on which our civilization rests. She ought to have tried to give these ideals an independent existence by virtue of their own inner value and inner truth, and so to keep them alive and active without any extraneous help from a corresponding theory of the universe. No effort should have been spared to direct the attention of the cultured and the uncultured alike to the problem of the ideals of civilization.

But philosophy philosophized about everything except civilization. She went on working undeviatingly at the establishment of a theoretical view of the universe, as though by means of it everything could be restored, and did not reflect that this theory, even if it were completed, would be constructed only out of history and science, and would accordingly be unoptimistic and unethical, and would remain for ever an "impotent theory of the universe," which could never call forth the energies needed for the establishment and maintenance of the ideals of civilization.

So little did philosophy philosophize about civilization that she did not even notice that she herself and the age along with her were losing more and more of it. In the hour of peril the watchman who ought to have kept us awake was himself asleep, and the result was that we put up no fight at all on behalf of our civilization.

Chapter 2

HINDRANCES TO CIVILIZATION

IN OUR ECONOMIC AND SPIRITUAL LIFE

The unfree economic position of the modern man.

His overwork and incapacity for self-collectedness.

The undeveloped condition of the modern man and his lack of humanity.

The lack of spiritual independence in the man of to-day.

EVEN IF THE ABDICATION OF THOUGHT HAS BEEN, AS WE HAVE SEEN, the decisive factor in the collapse of our civilization, there are yet a number of other causes which combine with it to hinder our progress in this regard. They are to be found in the field of spiritual as well as in that of economic activity, and depend, above all, on the interaction between the two, an interaction which is unsatisfactory and continually becoming more so.

The capacity of the modern man for progress in civilization is diminished because the circumstances in which he finds himself placed injure him psychically and stunt his personality.

The development of civilization comes about—to put it quite generally—by individual men thinking out ideals which aim at the progress of the whole, and then so fitting them to the realities of life that they assume the shape in which they can influence most effectively the circumstances of the time. A man's ability to be a pioneer of progress, that is, to understand what civilization is and to work for it, depends, therefore, on his being a thinker and on his being free. He must be the former if he is to be capable of comprehending his ideals and putting them into shape. He must be free in order to be in a position to launch his ideals out into the general life. The more completely his activities are taken up in any way by the struggle for existence, the more strongly will the impulse to improve his own condition find expression in the ideals of his thought. Ideals of self-interest then get mixed up with and spoil his ideals of civilization.

Material and spiritual freedom are closely bound up with one another. Civilization presupposes free men, for only by free men can it be thought out and brought to realization.

But among mankind to-day both freedom and the capacity for thought have been sadly diminished.

If society had so developed that a continually widening circle of the population could enjoy a modest, but well-assured, condition of comfort, civilization would have been much more helped than it has been by all the material conquests which are lauded in its name. These do, indeed, make mankind as a whole less dependent upon nature, but at the same time they diminish the number of free and independent lives. The artisan who was his own master becomes the factory hand through the compulsion of machinery. Because in the complicated business world of to-day only undertakings with abundant capital behind them can maintain their existence, the place of the small, independent dealer is being taken more and more completely by the employee. Even the classes which still possess a larger or smaller amount of property or maintain a more or less independent activity get drawn more and more completely into the struggle for existence because of the insecurity of present conditions under the economic system of to-day.

The lack of freedom which results is made worse still because the factory system creates continually growing agglomerations of people who are thereby compulsorily separated from the soil which feeds them, from their own homes and from nature. Hence comes serious psychical injury. There is only too much truth in the paradoxical saying that abnormal life begins with the loss of one's own field and dwelling-place.

Civilization is, it is true, furthered to a certain extent by the self-regarding ideals produced by the groups of people who unite and co-operate in defence of their similarly threatened interests in so far as they seek to obtain an improvement in their material, and thereby also in their spiritual, environment. But these ideals are a danger to the idea of civilization as such, because the form which they assume is either not at all, or very imperfectly, determined by the really universal interests of the community. The consideration of civilization as such is held back by the competition between the various self-regarding ideals which go under its name.

To the want of freedom we have to add the evil of overstrain. For two or three generations numbers of individuals have been living as workers merely, not as human beings. Whatever can be said in a general way about the moral and spiritual significance of labour has no bearing on what they have to do. An excessive amount of labour is the rule to-day in every circle of society, with the result that the labourer's spiritual element cannot possibly thrive. This overwork hits him indirectly even in his childhood, for his parents, caught in the inexorable toils of work, cannot devote themselves to his up-bringing as they should. Thus his development is robbed of something which can never be made good, and later in life, when he himself is the slave of over-long hours, he feels more and more the need of external distractions. To spend the time left to him for leisure in self-cultivation, or in serious intercourse with his fellows or with books, requires a mental collectedness and a self-control which he finds very difficult. Complete idleness, forgetfulness, and diversion from his usual activities are a physical necessity. He does not want to think, and seeks not self-improvement, but entertainment, that kind of entertainment, moreover, which makes least demand upon his spiritual faculties.

The mentality of this mass of individuals, spiritually relaxed and incapable of self-collectedness, reacts upon all those institutions which ought to serve the cause of culture, and therewith of civilization. The theater takes a second place behind the pleasure resort or the picture show, and the instructive book behind the diverting one. An ever increasing proportion of periodicals and newspapers have to accommodate themselves to the necessity of putting their matter before their readers in the shape which lets it be assimilated most easily. A comparison of the average newspapers of to-day with those of fifty or sixty years ago shows how thoroughly such publications have had to change their methods in this respect.

When once the spirit of superficiality has penetrated into the institutions which ought to sustain the spiritual life, these exercise on their part a reflex influence on the society which they have brought to this condition, and force on all alike this state of mental vacuity.

How completely this want of thinking power has become a second nature in men to-day is shown by the kind of sociability which it produces. When two of them meet for a conversation each is careful to see that their talk does not go beyond generalities or develop into a real exchange of ideas. No one has anything of his own to give out, and everyone is haunted by a sort of terror lest anything original should be demanded from him.

The spirit produced in such a society of never-concentrated minds is rising among us as an ever growing force, and it results in a lowered conception of what man should be. In ourselves, as in others, we look for nothing but vigour in productive work, and resign ourselves to the abandonment of any higher ideal.

When we consider this want of freedom and of mental concentration, we see that the conditions of life for the inhabitants of our big cities are as unfavourable as they could be. Naturally, then, those inhabitants are in most danger on their spiritual side. It is doubtful whether big cities have ever been foci of civilization in the sense that in them there has arisen the ideal of a man well and truly developed as a spiritual personality; to-day, at any rate, the condition of things is such that true civilization needs to be rescued from the spirit that issues from them and their inhabitants.

* * *

But, besides the hindrance caused to civilization by the modern man's lack of freedom and of the power of mental concentration, there is a further hindrance caused by his imperfect development. The enormous increase of human knowledge and power, in specialized thoroughness as well as in extent, necessarily leads to individual activities being limited more and more

to well-defined departments. Human labour is organized and co-ordinated so that specialization may enable individuals to make the highest and most effective possible contribution. The results obtained are amazing, but the spiritual significance of the work for the worker suffers. There is no call upon the whole man, only upon some of his faculties, and this has a reflex effect upon his nature as a whole. The faculties which build up personality and are called out by comprehensive and varied tasks are ousted by the less comprehensive ones, which from this point of view are, in the general sense of the word, less spiritual. The artisan of to-day does not understand his trade as a whole in the way in which his predecessor did. He no longer learns, like the latter, to work the wood or the metal through all the stages of manufacture; many of these stages have already been carried out by men and machines before the material comes into his hands. Consequently his reflectiveness, his imagination, and his skill are no longer called out by ever varying difficulties in the work, and his creative and artistic powers are atrophied. In place of the normal self-consciousness which is promoted by work into the doing of which he must put his whole power of thought and his whole personality, there comes a self-satisfaction which is content with a fragmentary ability which, it may be admitted, is perfect, and this self-satisfaction is persuaded by its perfection in mastering details to overlook its imperfection in dealing with the whole.

In all professions, most clearly perhaps in the pursuit of science, we can recognize the spiritual danger with which specialization threatens not only individuals, but the spiritual life of the community. It is already noticeable, too, that education is carried on now by teachers who have not a wide enough outlook to make their scholars understand the interconnection of the individual sciences, and to be able to give them a mental horizon as wide as it should be.

Then, as if specialization and the organization of work, where it is unavoidable, were not already injurious enough to the soul of the modern man, it is pursued and built up where it could be dispensed with. In administration, in education, and in every kind of calling the natural sphere of activity is narrowed as far as possible by rules and superintendence. How much less free in many countries is the elementary school teacher of to-day compared with what he was once! How lifeless and impersonal has his teaching become as a result of all these limitations!

Thus through our methods of work we have suffered loss spiritually and as individuals just in proportion as the material output of our collective activity has increased. Here, too, is an illustration of that tragic law which says that every gain brings with it, somehow or other, a corresponding loss.

* * *

But man to-day is in danger not only through his lack of freedom, of the power of mental concentration, and of the opportunity for all-round development: he is in danger of losing his humanity.

The normal attitude of man to man is made very difficult for us. Owing to the hurry in which we live, to the increased facilities for intercourse, and to the necessity for living and working with many others in an overcrowded locality, we meet each other continually, and in the most varied relations, as strangers. Our circumstances do not allow us to deal with each other as man to man, for the limitations placed upon the activities of the natural man are so general and so unbroken that we get accustomed to them, and no longer feel our mechanical, impersonal intercourse to be something that is unnatural. We no longer feel uncomfortable that in such a number of situations we can no longer be men among men, and at last we give up trying to be so, even when it would be possible and proper.

In this respect, too, the soul of the townsman is influenced most unfavourably by his circumstances, and that influence, in its turn, works most unfavourably on the mentality of society.

Thus we tend to forget our relationship with our fellows, and are on the path towards inhumanity. Wherever there is lost the consciousness that every man is an object of concern for us just because he is man, civilization and morals are shaken, and the advance to fully developed inhumanity is only a question of time.

As a matter of fact, the most utterly inhuman thoughts have been current among us for two generations past in all the ugly clearness of language and with the authority of logical principles. There has been created a social mentality which discourages humanity in individuals. The courtesy produced by natural feeling disappears, and in its place comes a behaviour which shows entire indifference, even though it is decked out more or less thoroughly in a code of manners. The standoffishness and want of sympathy which are shown so clearly in every way to strangers are no longer felt as being really rudeness, but pass for the behaviour of the man of the world. Our society has also ceased to allow to all men, as such, a human value and a human dignity; many sections of the human race have become merely raw material and property in human form. We have talked for decades with ever increasing light-mindedness about war and conquest, as if these were merely operations on a chess-board; how was this possible save as the result of a tone of mind which no longer pictured to itself the fate of individuals, but thought of them only as figures or objects belonging to the material world? When the war broke out the inhumanity within us had a free course. And what an amount of insulting stuff, some decently veiled, some openly coarse, about the coloured races, has made its appearance during the last decades, and passed for truth and reason, in our colonial literature and our parliaments, and so become an element in general public opinion! Twenty years ago there was a discussion in one of our Continental parliaments about some deported Negroes who had been allowed to die of hunger and disease; and there was no protest or comment when, in a statement from the tribune, it was said that they "had been lost" (*"eingegangen"* or *"crêvé"*), as though it were a question of cattle!

In the education and the school books of to-day the duty of humanity is relegated to an obscure corner, as though it were no longer true that it is the first thing necessary in the training of personality, and as if it were not a matter of great importance to maintain it as a strong influence in our human race against the influence of outer circumstances. It has not been so always. There was a time when it was a ruling influence not only in schools, but in literature, even down to the book of adventures. Defoe's hero, Robinson Crusoe, is continually reflecting on the subject of humane conduct, and he feels himself so responsible for loyalty to this duty that when defending himself he is continually thinking how he can sacrifice the smallest number of human lives; he is so faithful, indeed, to this duty of humanity, that the story of his adventures acquires thereby quite a peculiar character. Is there among works of this kind to-day a single one in which we shall find anything like it?

* * *

Another hindrance to civilization to-day is the over-organization of our public life.

While it is certain that a properly ordered environment is the condition and, at the same time, the result of civilization, it is also undeniable that, after a certain point has been reached, external organization is developed at the expense of spiritual life. Personality and ideas are then subordinated to institutions, when it is really these which ought to influence the latter and keep them inwardly alive.

If a comprehensive organization is established in any department of social life, the results are at first magnificent, but after a time they fall off. It is the already existing resources which are realized at the start, but later on the destructive influence of such organization on what is living and original is clearly seen in its natural results, and the more consistently the organization is enlarged, the more strongly its effect is felt in the repression of creative and spiritual activity. There are modern States which cannot recover either economically or spiritually from the effects of over-centralization of government dating from a very early period of their history.

The conversion of a wood into a park and its maintenance as such may be a step toward carrying out several different objects, but it is all over then with the rich vegetation which would assure its future condition in nature's own way.

Political, religious and economic associations aim to-day at forming themselves in such a way as will combine the greatest possible inner cohesion with the highest possible degree of external activity. Constitution, discipline, and everything that belongs to administration are brought to a perfection hitherto unknown. They attain their object, but just in proportion as they do so these centres of activity cease to work as living organizations, and come more and more to resemble perfected machines. Their inner life loses in richness and variety because the personalities of which they are composed must needs become impoverished.

Our whole spiritual life nowadays has its course within organizations. From childhood up the man of to-day has his mind so full of the thought of discipline that he loses the sense of his own individuality and can only see himself as thinking in the spirit of some group or other of his fellows. A thorough discussion between one idea and another or between one man and another, such as constituted the greatness of the eighteenth century, is never met with now. But at that time fear of public opinion was a thing unknown. All ideas had then to justify themselves to the individual reason. To-day it is the rule—and no one questions it—always to take into account the views which prevail in organized society. The individual starts by taking it for granted that both for himself and his neighbours there are certain views already established which they cannot hope to alter, views which are determined by nationality, creed, political party, social position, and other elements in one's surroundings. These views are protected by a kind of taboo, and are not only kept sacred from criticism, but are not a legitimate subject of conversation. This kind of intercourse, in which we mutually abjure our natural quality as thinking beings, is euphemistically described as respect for other people's convictions, as if there could be any convictions at all where there is no thought.

The modern man is lost in the mass in a way which is without precedent in history, and this is perhaps the most characteristic trait in him. His diminished concern about his own nature makes him as it is susceptible, to an extent that is almost pathological, to the views which society and its organs of expression have put, ready made, into circulation. Since, over and above this, society, with its well-constructed organization, has become a power of as yet unknown strength in the spiritual life, man's want of independence in the face of it has become so serious that he is almost ceasing to claim a spiritual existence of his own. He is like a rubber ball which has lost its elasticity, and preserves indefinitely every impression that is made upon it. He is under the thumb of the mass, and he draws from it the opinions on which he lives, whether the question at issue is national or political or one of his own belief or unbelief.

Yet this abnormal subjection to external influences does not strike him as being a weakness. He looks upon it as an achievement, and in his unlimited spiritual devotion to the interests of the community he thinks he is preserving the greatness of the modern man. He intentionally exaggerates our natural social instincts into something fantastically great.

It is just because we thus renounce the indefeasible rights of the individual that our race can neither produce new ideas nor make current ones serviceable for new objects; its only experience is that prevailing ideas obtain more and more authority, take on a more and more one-sided development, and live on till they have produced their last and most dangerous consequences.

Thus we have entered on a new mediæval period. The general determination of society has put freedom of thought out of fashion, because the majority renounce the privilege of thinking as free personalities, and let themselves be guided in everything by those who belong to the various groups and cliques.

Spiritual freedom, then, we shall recover only when the majority of individuals become once more spiritually independent and self-reliant, and discover their natural and proper relation to those organizations in which their souls have been entangled. But liberation from the Middle Ages of to-day will be a much more difficult process than that which freed the peoples of Europe from the first Middle Ages. The struggle then was against external authority established in the course of history. To-day the task is to get the mass of individuals to work themselves out of the condition of spiritual weakness and dependence to which they have brought themselves. Could there be a harder task?

Moreover, no one as yet clearly perceives what a condition of spiritual poverty is ours to-day. Every year the spread of opinions which have no thought behind them is carried further by the masses, and the methods of this process have been so perfected, and have met with such a ready welcome, that our confidence in being able to raise to the dignity of public opinion the silliest of statements, wherever it seems expedient to get them currently accepted, has no need to justify itself before acting.

During the war the control of thought was made complete. Propaganda definitely took the place of truth.

With independence of thought thrown overboard, we have, as was inevitable, lost our faith in truth. Our spiritual life is disorganized, for the over-organization of our external environment leads to the organization of our absence of thought.

Not only in the intellectual sphere, but in the moral also, the relation between the individual and the community has been upset. With the surrender of his own personal opinion the modern man surrenders also his personal moral judgment. In order that he may find good what the mass declares to be such, whether in word or deed, and may condemn what it declares to be bad, he suppresses the scruples which stir in him. He does not allow them to find utterance either with others or with himself. There are no stumbling-blocks which his feeling of unity with the herd does not enable him to surmount, and thus he loses his judgment in that of the mass, and his own morality in theirs.

Above all, he is thus made capable of excusing everything that is meaningless, cruel, unjust, or bad in the behaviour of his nation. Unconsciously to themselves, the majority of the members of our barbarian civilized States give less and less time to reflection as moral personalities, so that they may not be continually coming into inner conflict with their fellows as a body, and continually having to get over things which they feel to be wrong.

Public opinion helps them by popularizing the idea that the actions of the community are not to be judged so much by the standards of morality as by those of expediency. But they suffer injury to their souls. If we find among men of to-day only too few whose human and moral sensibility is still undamaged, the chief reason is that the majority have offered up their personal morality on the altar of their country, instead of remaining at variance with the mass and acting as a force which impels the latter along the road to perfection.

Not only between the economic and the spiritual, then, but also between the mass of men and individuals, there has developed a condition of unfavourable action and reaction. In the days of rationalism and serious philosophy the individual got help and support from society through the general confidence in the victory of the rational and moral, which society never failed to acknowledge as something which explained and justified itself. Individuals were then carried along by the mass; we are stifled by it. The bankruptcy of the civilized State, which becomes more manifest every decade, is ruining the man of to-day. The demoralization of the individual by the mass is in full swing.

The man of to-day pursues his dark journey in a time of darkness, as one who has no freedom, no mental collectedness, no all-round development, as one who loses himself in an atmosphere of inhumanity, who surrenders his spiritual independence and his moral judgment to the organized society in which he lives, and who finds himself in every direction up against hindrances to the temper of true civilization. Of the dangerous position in which he is placed philosophy has no understanding, and therefore makes no attempt to help him. She does not even urge him to reflection on what is happening to himself.

The terrible truth that with the progress of history and the economic development of the world it is becoming not easier, but harder, to develop true civilization, has never found utterance.

Chapter 3

CIVILIZATION ESSENTIALLY ETHICAL IN CHARACTER

What is civilization?

Origin of the unethical conception of civilization.

Our sense of reality. Our historical sense. Nationalism as a product of these.

National civilization. Our misleading trust in facts and organization.

The true sense for reality.

WHAT IS CIVILIZATION? This question ought to have been pressing itself on the attention of all men who consider themselves civilized, but it is remarkable that in the world's literature generally one hardly finds that it has been put at all until to-day, and still more rarely is any answer given. It was supposed that there was no need for a definition of civilization, since we already possessed the thing itself. If the question was ever touched upon, it was considered to be sufficiently settled with references to history and the present day. But now, when events are bringing us inexorably to the consciousness that we live in a dangerous medley of civilization and barbarism, we must, whether we wish to or not, try to determine the nature of true civilization.

For a quite general definition we may say that civilization is progress, material and spiritual progress, on the part of individuals as of the mass.

In what does it consist? First of all in a lessening of the strain imposed on individuals and on the mass by the struggle for existence. The establishment of as favourable conditions of living as possible for all is a demand which must be made partly for its own sake, partly with a view to the spiritual and moral perfecting of individuals, which is the ultimate object of civilization.

The struggle for existence is a double one: man has to assert himself in nature and against nature, and similarly also among his fellow-men and against them.

A diminution of the struggle is secured by strengthening the supremacy of reason over both external nature and human nature, and making it subserve as accurately as possible the ends proposed.

Civilization is then twofold in its nature: it realizes itself in the supremacy of reason, first, over the forces of nature, and, secondly, over the dispositions of men.

Which of these kinds of progress is most truly progress in civilization? The latter, though it is the least open to observation. Why? For two reasons. First, the supremacy which we secure by reason over external nature represents not unqualified progress, but a progress which brings with its advantages also disadvantages which may work in the direction of barbarism. The reason why the economic circumstances of our time endanger our civilization is to be sought for partly in the fact that we have pressed into our service natural forces which can be embodied in machines. But with that there must be such a supremacy of reason over the dispositions of men that they, and the nations which they form, will not use against one another the power which the control of these forces gives them, and thus plunge one another into a struggle for existence which is far more terrible than that between men in a state of nature.

A normal claim to be civilized can, then, only be reckoned as valid when it recognizes this distinction between what is essential in civilization and what is not.

Both kinds of progress can, indeed, be called spiritual in the sense that they both rest upon a spiritual activity in man, yet we may call the supremacy over natural forces material progress because in it material objects are mastered and turned to man's use. The supremacy of reason over human dispositions, on the other hand, is a spiritual achievement in another sense, in that it means the working of spirit upon spirit, *i.e.*, of one section of the power of reflexion upon another section of it.

And what is meant by the supremacy of the reason over human dispositions? It means that both individuals and the mass let their willing be determined by the material and spiritual good of the whole and the individuals that compose it; that is to say, their actions are ethical. Ethical progress is, then, that which is truly of the essence of civilization, and has only one significance; material progress is that which is much less essential and may have a good or bad effect on the development of civilization. This moral conception of civilization will strike some people as rationalistic and old-fashioned. It accords better with the spirit of our times to conceive of civilization as a natural manifestation of life in the course of human evolution, but one with most interesting complications. We are concerned, however, not with what is ingenious, but with what is true. In this case the simple is the true—the inconvenient truth with which it is our laborious task to deal.

* * *

The attempts to distinguish between civilization as what the Germans call "Kultur" and civilization as mere material progress aim at making the world familiar with the idea of an unethical form of civilization side by side with the ethical, and at clothing the former with a word of historical meaning. But nothing in the history of the word "civilization" justifies such attempts. The word, as commonly used hitherto, means the same as the German "Kultur", viz., the development of man to a state of higher organization and a higher moral standard. Some languages prefer one word: others prefer the other. The German usually speaks of "Kultur", the Frenchman usually of "civilisation", but the establishment of a difference between them is justified neither philologically nor historically. We can speak of ethical and unethical "Kultur" or of ethical and unethical "civilisation", but not of "Kultur" and "civilisation".

But how did it come about that we lost the idea that the ethical has a decisive meaning and value as part of civilization?

All attempts at civilization hitherto have been a matter of processes in which the forces of progress were at work in almost every department of life. Great achievements in art, architecture, administration, economics, industry, commerce, and colonization succeeded each other with a spiritual impetus which produced a higher conception of the universe. Any ebb of the tide of civilization made itself felt in the material sphere as well as in the ethical and spiritual, earlier, as a rule, in the former than in the latter. Thus in Greek civilization there set in as early as the time of Aristotle an incomprehensible arrest of science and political achievement, whereas the ethical movement only reached its completion in the following centuries in that great work of education which was undertaken in the ancient world by the Stoic philosophy. In the Chinese, Indian and Jewish civilizations ability in dealing with material things was from the start, and always remained, at a lower level than the spiritual and ethical efforts of these races.

In the movement of civilization which began with the Renaissance, there were both material and spiritual-ethical forces of progress at work side by side, as though in rivalry with each other, and this continued down to the beginning of the nineteenth century. Then, however, something unprecedented happened: man's ethical energy died away, while the conquests achieved by his spirit in the material sphere increased by leaps and bounds. Thus for several decades our civilization enjoyed the great advantages of its material progress while as yet it hardly felt the consequences of the dying down of the ethical movement. People lived on in the conditions produced by that movement without seeing clearly that their position was no longer a tenable one and preparing to face the storm that was brewing in the relations between the nations and within the nations themselves. In this way our own age, having never taken the trouble to reflect, arrived at the opinion that civilization consists primarily in scientific, technical and artistic achievements, and that it can reach its goal without ethics, or, at any rate, with a minimum of them.

Public opinion bowed down before this merely external conception of civilization because it was exclusively represented by persons whose position in society and scientific culture seemed to show them to be competent to judge in matters of the spiritual life.

* * *

What was the result of our giving up the ethical conception of civilization, and therewith all attempts to bring reasoned ethical ideals into effective relation with reality? It was that instead of using thought to produce ideals which fitted in with reality, we left reality without any ideals at all. Instead of discussing together the essential elements, such as population, State, Church, society, progress, which decide the character of our social development and that of mankind generally, we contented ourselves with starting from what is given by experience. Only forces and tendencies which were already at work were to be considered. Fundamental truths and convictions which ought to produce logical or ethical compulsion we would no longer acknowledge. We refused to believe that any ideas could be applicable to reality except those derived from experience. Thus ideals which had been knowingly and intentionally lowered dominated our spiritual life and the whole world.

How we glorified our practical common-sense, which was to give us such power in dealing with the world! Yet we were behaving, really, like boys who give themselves up exultingly to the forces of nature and whizz down a hill on their toboggan without asking themselves whether they will be able to steer their vehicle successfully when they come to the next bend or the next unexpected obstacle.

It is only a conviction which is based upon reasoned ethical ideals that is capable of producing free activity, *i.e.*, activity deliberately planned with a view to its object. In proportion as ideals taken from the workaday world are combined with it, reality influences reality. But then the human soul acts merely as an agent of debasing change.

Events which are to produce practical results within us are worked upon and moulded by our mentality. This mentality has a certain character, and on that character depends the nature of those value-judgments which rule our relation to facts.

Normally this character is to be found in the reasoned ideas which our reflexion upon reality brings into existence. If these disappear there is not left a void in which "events in themselves" can affect us, but the control of our mentality passes now to the opinions and feelings which hitherto have been ruled and kept under by our reasoned ideas. When the virgin forest is cut down, brushwood springs up where the big trees were formerly. Whenever our great convictions are destroyed their place is taken by smaller ones which carry out in inferior fashion the functions of the former.

With the giving up of ethical ideals which accompanies our passion for reality our practical efficiency is not, therefore, improved, but diminished. It does not make the man of to-day a cool observer and calculator such as he supposes himself to be, for he is under the influence of opinions and emotions which are created in him by facts. All unconsciously he mixes with what is the work of his reason so much of what is emotional that the one spoils the other. Within this circle move the judgments and impulses of our society, whether we deal with the largest questions or the smallest. Individuals and nations alike, we deal indiscriminately with real and imaginary values, and it is just this confused medley of real and unreal, of sober thought and capacity for enthusiasm for the unmeaning, that makes the mentality of the modern man so puzzling and so dangerous.

Our sense of reality, then, means this, that, as a result of emotional and short-sighted calculations of advantage, we let one fact issue immediately in another, and so on indefinitely. As we are not consciously aiming at any definitely planned goal, our activity may really be described as a kind of natural happening.

We react to facts in the most irrational way. Without plan or foundations we build our future into the circumstances of the time and leave it exposed to the destructive effects of the chaotic jostling that goes on amongst them. "Firm ground at last"! we cry, and sink helpless in the stream of events.

* * *

The blindness with which we endure this fate is made worse by our belief in our historical sense, which, in this connection, is nothing else than our sense of reality prolonged backwards.

We believe ourselves to be a critical generation which, thanks to its thorough knowledge of the past, is in a position to understand the direction which events are destined to take from the present to the future. We add to the ideals which have been taken from existing reality others which we borrow from history.

The achievements of historical science reached by the nineteenth century do, indeed, deserve our admiration, but it is another question whether our generation, for all its possession of an historical science, possesses a true historical sense.

Historical sense, in the full meaning of the term, implies a critical objectivity in the face of far-off and recent events alike. To keep this faculty free from the bias of opinions and interests when we are estimating facts is a power which even our historians do not possess. As long as they are dealing with a period so remote that it has no bearing on the present they are critical so far as the views of the school to which they belong allow it. But if the past stands in any real connection with "to-day", we can perceive at once in their estimate the influence of their particular standpoint, rational, religious, social or economic.

It is significant that while during the last few decades the learning of our historians has, no doubt, increased, their critical objectivity has not. Previous investigators kept this ideal before their eyes in much greater purity than have those of to-day; we have gone so far that we no longer seriously make the demand that in scientific dealings with the past there shall be a suppression of all prejudices which spring from nationality or creed. It is quite common nowadays to see the greatest learning bound up with the strongest bias. In our historical literature the highest positions are occupied by works written with propagandist aims.

So little educative influence has science had on our historians that they have often espoused as passionately as anyone the opinions of their own people instead of calling the latter to a thoughtful estimate of the facts, as was their duty to their profession; they have remained nothing but men of learning. They have not even started on the task for which they entered the service of civilization, and the hopes of civilization, which in the middle of the nineteenth century rested on the rise of a science of history, have been as little fulfilled as those which were bound up with the demand for national States and democratic forms of government.

The generation that has been brought up by teachers such as these has naturally not much idea of an elevated practical conception of events. Accurately viewed, its characteristic feature is not so much that we understand our past better than earlier generations understood theirs, but rather that we attribute to the past an extraordinarily increased meaning for the present. Now and again we actually substitute it for the latter. It is not enough for us that what has been is present in its results in what now is; we want to have it always with us, and to feel ourselves determined by it.

In this effort to be continually experiencing our historical process of becoming, and to acknowledge it, we replace our normal relation to the past by an artificial one, and wishing to find within the past the whole of our present, we misuse it in order to deduce from it, and to legitimize by an appeal to it, our claims, our opinions, our feelings and our passions. Under the very eyes of our historical learning there springs up a manufactured history for popular use, in which the current national and confessional ideas are unreservedly approved and upheld, and our school history books become regular culture beds of historical lies.

This misuse of history is a necessity for us. The ideas and dispositions which rule us cannot be justified by reason; nothing is left for us but to give them foundations in history.

It is significant that we have no real interest in what is valuable in the past. Its great spiritual achievements are mechanically registered, but we do not let ourselves be touched by them. Still less do we accept them as a heritage; nothing has any value for us except what can be squared with our plans, passions, feelings, and æsthetic moods of to-day. With these we live ourselves by lies into the past, and then assert with unshaken assurance that we have our roots in it.

This is the character of the reverence we pay to history. The fascination exercised upon us by earlier events is elevated to a religion. Blinded by what we consider or declare to be past and done with, we lose all sense for what is to happen. Nothing is any longer past for us; nothing is done and finished with. Again and again we let what is past rise up artificially in what is present, and endow bygone facts with a persistence of being which makes wholly impossible the normal development of our peoples. Just as our sense of reality makes us lose ourselves in present-day events, so does our historical sense compel us to do the same in those of the past.

* * *

From these two things, our sense of reality and historical sense, is born the nationalism to which we must refer the external catastrophe in which the decadence of our civilization finds its completion.

What is nationalism? It is an ignoble patriotism, exaggerated till it has lost all meaning, which bears the same relation to the noble and healthy kind as the fixed idea of an imbecile does to normal conviction.

How does it develop among us?

About the beginning of the nineteenth century the course of thought gave the national State its rightful position, starting for this from the axiom that it, as a natural and homogeneous organism, was better calculated than any other to make the ideal of the civilized State a working reality. In Fichte's addresses to the German nation the nation-State is summoned to the bar of the moral reason and learns that it has to submit in all things to the latter. It gives the necessary promise and straightway receives a commission to bring the civilized State into existence. It is given emphatically to understand that it must recognize as its highest task the continuous and steady development of the purely human element in the nation's life. It is to seek greatness by representing the ideas which can bring healing to the nations. Its citizens are urged to show their membership of it not through the lower, but through the higher, patriotism, that is, not to overvalue its external greatness and power, but to be careful to take for their aim "the unfolding of what is eternal and Godlike in the world", and to see that their objects coincide with the highest aims of humanity. Thus national feeling is placed under the guardianship of reason, morality and civilization. The cult of patriotism as such is to be considered as barbarism; it does, indeed, announce itself to be such by the purposeless wars which it necessarily brings in its train.

In this way the idea of nationality was raised to the level of a valuable ideal of civilization. When civilization began to decline, its other ideals all fell also, but the idea of nationality maintained itself because it had transferred itself to the sphere of reality. It incorporated henceforward all that remained of civilization, and became the ideal which summed up all others. Here, then, we have the explanation of the mentality of our age, which concentrates all the enthusiasm of which it is capable on the idea of nationality, and believes itself to possess in that all moral and spiritual good things.

But with the decay of civilization the character of the idea of nationality changed. The guardianship exercised over it by the other moral ideals to which it had hitherto been subordinate now ceased, since these were themselves on trial, and the nationalist idea began a career of independence. It asserted, of course, that it was working in the service of civilization, but it was, in truth, only an idea of reality with a halo of civilization round it, and it was guided by no ethical ideals, but only by the instincts which deal with reality.

That reason and morality shall not be allowed to contribute a word to the formation of nationalist ideas and aspirations is demanded by the mass of men to-day as a sparing of their holiest feelings.

If in earlier times the decay of civilization did not produce any such confusion in the sentiments of the various nations, this was because the idea of nationality had not then been raised in the same way to be the ideal of civilization. It was, therefore, impossible that it should insinuate itself into the place of the true ideals of civilization, and through abnormal nationalist conceptions and dispositions bring into active existence an elaborate system of uncivilization.

That in nationalism we have to do not so much with things as with the unhealthy way in which they are dealt with in the imagination of the crowd, is clear from its whole behaviour. It claims to be following a policy of practical results (Realpolitik);

in reality it by no means represents the uncompromisingly businesslike view of all the questions of home and foreign policy, but side by side with its egoism displays a certain amount of enthusiasm. Its practical policy is an over-valuation of certain questions of territorial economic interests, an over-valuation which has been elevated to a dogma and idealized, and is now supported by popular sentiment. It fights for its demands without having established any properly thought-out calculation of their real value. In order to be able to dispute the possession of millions of value, the modern State loaded itself with armaments costing hundreds of millions. Meaning to care for the protection and extension of its trade, it loaded the latter with imposts which imperilled its power of competing with its rivals much more than did any of the measures taken by those rivals.

Its practical politics were, therefore, in truth impracticable politics, because they allowed popular passion to come in, and thereby made the simplest questions insoluble. This style of politics put economic interests in the shop window, while it kept in the warehouse the ideas about greatness and conquest which belong to nationalism.

Every civilized State, in order to increase its power, gathered allies wherever it could. Thus half-civilized and uncivilized races were summoned by civilized ones to fight against the civilized neighbours of the latter, and these helpers were not content with the subordinate *rôle* which had been assigned to them. They acquired more and more influence on the course of events, till they were at last in a position to decide when the civilized nations of Europe should begin to fight each other about them. Thus has Nemesis come upon us for abandoning our dignity and betraying to the uncivilized world all that we still possessed of things that were of universal value.

It was significant of the unhealthy character of nationalism's "practical" politics that it tried in every possible way to deck itself out with a tinsel imitation of idealism. The struggle for power became one for right and civilization; the alliances for the promotion of their selfish interests which various nations made with one another against all the rest were made to appear to be friendships and spiritual affinities. As such they were dated back into the past, even though history had a great deal more to say about hereditary quarrels than about spiritual relationships.

* * *

Finally, nationalism was not content with putting aside, in the sphere of politics generally, all attempts to bring into existence a really civilized humanity; it distorted the very idea of civilization itself and talked of national civilization.

Once there was what was known just simply as civilization, and every civilized nation strove to possess it in its purest and most fully developed form. In this respect nationality had in the idea of civilization at that time something much more original and less spoilt than it has in the same idea to-day. If, in spite of this, there was no impulse among the nations to separate the spiritual life of each from that of its neighbours, we have a proof that nationality is not in itself the strong element in the people that demanded this. Such a claim as is made to-day to have a *national civilization* is an unhealthy phenomenon. It presupposes that the civilized peoples of to-day have lost their healthy nature, and no longer follow instincts, but theories. They percuss and sound their souls to such an extent that these are no longer capable of any natural action. They analyse and describe them so continuously that in thinking of what they ought to be they forget what they actually are. Questions of spiritual differences between races are discussed so subtly, and with such obstinacy and dogmatism, that the talk works like an obsession, and the peculiarities that are said to exist make their appearance like imaginary diseases.

In every department of life more and more effort is devoted to making clearly visible in the results which follow from them the emotions, the ideas, and the reasonings of the mass of the people. Any peculiarity preserved and fostered in this way shows that its natural counterpart has perished. The individual element in the personality of a people no longer, as something unconscious or half conscious, plays with varying lights on the totality of the nation's spiritual life. It becomes an artifice, a fashion, a self-advertisement, a mania. There is bred in the nation a mass of thought, the serious results of which in every department become more evident year by year. The spiritual life of some of the leading civilized nations has already, in comparison with earlier days, taken on a monotonous tone such as makes an observer feel anxious.

The unnatural character of this development shows itself not only in its results, but in the part which it allows to be played by conceit, self-importance, and self-deception. Anything valuable in a personality or a successful undertaking is attributed to some special excellence in the national character. Foreign soil is assumed to be incapable of producing the same or anything similar, and in most countries this vanity has grown to such a height that the greatest follies are no longer beyond its reach.

It goes without saying that there follows a serious decline of the spiritual element in the national civilization. The spirituality is, moreover, only a kind of disguise; it has in reality an avowedly materialist character. It is a distillation from all the external achievements of the nation in question and appears in partnership with its economic and political demands. While alleged to be grounded in the national peculiarities, nationalist civilization will not, as we should normally expect, remain limited to the nation itself; it feels called upon to impose itself upon others and make them happy! Modern nations seek markets for their civilization, as they do for their manufactures!

National civilization, therefore, is matter for propaganda and for export, and the necessary publicity is secured by liberal expenditure. The necessary phrases can be obtained ready-made and need only be strung together. Thus the world has inflicted on it a competition between national civilizations, and between these civilization itself comes off badly.

The nations of Europe entered the Middle Ages side by side as the heirs of the Greco-Roman world, and lived side by side with the freest mutual intercourse through the Renaissance, the period of the Illuminati, and of the philosophy of more recent times. But we no longer believe that they, with their offshoots in the other continents, form an indivisible unit of civilization. If, however, in this latest age, the differences in their spiritual life have begun to stand out more distinctly, the cause of it is that the level of civilization has sunk. When the tide ebbs, shallows which separate bodies of deep water become visible; while the tide is flowing they are out of sight.

How closely the nations which form the great body of civilized humanity are still interrelated spiritually is shown by the fact that they have all side by side suffered the same decadence.

* * *

With our sense of reality is bound up, further, the false confidence which we have in facts. We live in an atmosphere of optimism, as if the contradictions which show themselves in the world arranged themselves automatically so as to promote well-thought-out progress, and reconciled themselves in syntheses in which the valuable parts of the thesis and the antithesis coalesced.

In justification of this optimism appeal is made, both rightly and wrongly, to Hegel. It cannot be denied that he is the spiritual father of our sense of reality; he is the first thinker who tried to be just to things as they exist. We have been trained by him to realize the method of progress in thesis, antithesis, and synthesis as they show themselves in the course of events. But his optimism was not a simple optimism about facts, as ours is. He lived still in the spiritual world of rationalism, and believed in the power of ethical ideas worked out by reason; that was why he believed also in the certainty of uninterrupted spiritual progress. And it was because this was something upon which he could rely that he undertook to show how it was to be seen in the successive phases of events, and at the same time how it made itself a reality in the stream of outward facts. By emphasizing, however, the progressive purpose, which he finds immanent in the course of events, so strongly that it is possible to forget the ethical-spiritual presuppositions of his belief in progress, he is preparing the way for the despiritualized optimism about reality which has for decades been misleading us. Between the facts themselves there is nothing but an endless series of contradictions. The fresh mediating fact in which they counteract each other so as to make progress possible they cannot of themselves produce. This fact can only assert itself if the contradictions resolve themselves in a reasoned view in which there are ethical ideas about the condition of things which it is sought to realize. These are the formative principles for the new element which is to arise out of the contradictories, and it is only in this reasoned ethical view that the latter cease to be blind.

It was because we assumed the existence of principles, of progress, in the facts, that we viewed the advance of history, in which our future was being prepared, as progress in civilization, even though evolution condemned our optimism. And even now, when facts of the most terrible character cry out loudly against it, we shrink from giving up our creed. It no longer, indeed, gives us any real enlightenment, but the alternative, which bases optimism on belief in the ethical spirit, means such a revolution in our mode of thought that we find it difficult to take it into consideration.

With our reliance upon facts is bound up our reliance on organizations. The activities and the aims of our time are penetrated by a kind of obsession that if we could only succeed in perfecting or reforming in one direction or another the institutions of our public and social life, the progress demanded by civilization would begin of itself. We are, indeed, far enough from unanimity as to the plan needed for the reform of our arrangements: one section sketches out an anti-democratic plan; others believe that our mistake lies in the fact that democratic principles have not yet been applied consistently; others, again, see salvation only in a Socialist or Communist organization of society. But all agree in attributing our present condition, with its absence of true civilization, to a failure of our institutions; all look for the attainment of such civilization to a new organization of society; all unite in thinking that with new institutions there would arise a new spirit.

* * *

In this terrible confusion are entangled not only the unreflecting masses, but also many of the most earnest amongst us. The materialism of our age has reversed the relation between the spiritual and the actual. It believes that something with spiritual value can result from the working of facts. It was even expected that the war would bring us a spiritual regeneration! In reality, however, the relation between them works in the opposite direction. A spiritual element of real value can, if it is present, influence the moulding of reality so as to bring about desired results, and can thus produce facts in support of itself. All institutions and organizations have only a relative significance. With the most diverse social and political arrangements, the various civilized nations have all sunk to the same depth of barbarism. What we have experienced, and are still experiencing, must surely convince us that the spirit is everything and that institutions count for very little. Our institutions are a failure because the spirit of barbarism is at work in them. The best planned improvements in the organization of our society (though we are quite right in trying to secure them) cannot help us at all until we become at the same time capable of imparting a new spirit to our age.

The difficult problems with which we have to deal, even those which lie entirely in the material and economic sphere, are in the last resort only to be solved by an inner change of character. The wisest reforms in organization can only carry them a little nearer solution, never to the goal. The only conceivable way of bringing about a reconstruction of our world on new lines is first of all to become new men ourselves under the old circumstances, and then as a society in a new frame of mind so to smooth out the opposition between nations that a condition of true civilization may again become possible. Everything else is more or less wasted labour, because we are thereby building not on the spirit, but on what is merely external.

In the sphere of human events which decide the future of mankind reality consists in an inner conviction, not in given outward facts. Firm ground for our feet we find in reasoned ethical ideals. Are we going to draw from the spirit strength to create new conditions and turn our faces again to civilization, or are we going to continue to draw our spirit from our surroundings and go down with it to ruin? That is the fateful question with which we are confronted.

The true sense for reality is that insight which tells us that only through reasoned ethical ideals can we arrive at a normal relation to reality. Only so can man and society win all the power over events that they are able to use. Without that power we are, whatever we may choose to do, delivered over into bondage to them.

What is going on to-day between nations and within them throws a glaring illumination upon this truth. The history of our time is characterized by a lack of reason which has no parallel in the past. Future historians will one day analyse this history in detail, and test by means of it their learning and their freedom from prejudice. But for all future times there will be, as there is for to-day, only one explanation, viz., that we sought to live and to carry on with a civilization which had no ethical principle behind it.

Chapter 4

THE WAY TO THE RESTORATION OF CIVILIZATION

Civilization-ideals have become powerless.

Ups and downs in the history of civilization.

The reform of institutions and the reform of convictions.

The individual as the sole agent of the renewal of civilization.

Difficulties which beset the renewal of civilization.

THE ETHICAL CONCEPTION OF CIVILIZATION, THEN, IS THE ONLY one that can be justified.

But where is the road that can bring us back from barbarism to civilization? Is there such a road at all?

The unethical conception of civilization answers: "No." To it all symptoms of decay are symptoms of old age, and civilization, just like any other natural process of growth, must after a certain period of time reach its final end. There is nothing, therefore, for us to do, so it says, but to take the causes of this as quite natural, and do our best at any rate to find interesting the unedifying phenomena of its senility, which testify to the gradual loss of the ethical character of civilization.

In the thinking then which surrenders itself to our sense of reality, optimism and pessimism are inextricably intermingled.

If our optimism about reality is proved untenable, the optimism which thinks that continuous progress evolves itself among the facts as such, then the spirit which from above contemplates and analyses the situation turns without much concern to the mild pessimistic supposition that civilization has reached its Indian summer.

The ethical spirit cannot join in this little game of "Optimism or pessimism?" It sees the symptoms of decay as what they really are, viz., something terrible. It asks itself with a shudder what will become of the world if this dying process really goes on unchecked. The condition of civilization is a source of pain to it, for civilization is not an object which it is interesting to analyse, but the hope on which its thoughts fly out over the future existence of the race. Belief in the possibility of a renewal of civilization is an actual part of its life; that is why it can no longer quiet itself with what contents the sense of reality as it hovers between optimism and pessimism.

Those who regard the decay of civilization as something quite normal and natural console themselves with the thought that it is not civilization, but *a* civilization, which is falling a prey to dissolution; that there will be a new age and a new race in which there will blossom a new civilization. But that is a mistake. The earth no longer has in reserve, as it had once, gifted peoples as yet unused, who can relieve us and take our place in some distant future as leaders of the spiritual life. We already know all those which the earth has to dispose of. There is not one among them which is not already taking such a part in our civilization that its spiritual fate is determined by our own. All of them, the gifted and the ungifted, the distant and the near, have felt the influence of those forces of barbarism which are at work among us. All of them are, like ourselves, diseased, and only as we recover can they recover.

It is not the civilization of a race, but that of mankind, present and future alike, that we must give up as lost, if belief in a rebirth of our civilization is a vain thing.

But it need not be so given up. If the ethical is the essential element in civilization, decadence changes into renaissance as soon as ethical activities are set to work again in our convictions and in the ideas which we undertake to stamp upon reality. The attempt to bring this about is well worth making, and it should be world-wide.

It is true that the difficulties that have to be reckoned with in this undertaking are so great that only the strongest faith in the power of the ethical spirit will let us venture on it.

First among them towers up the inability of our generation to understand what is and must be. The men of the Renaissance and the Illuminati of the eighteenth century drew courage to desire the renewal of the world through ideas from their conviction of the absolute indefensibility of the material and spiritual conditions under which they lived. Unless with us, too, the many come to some such conviction, we must continue incapable of taking in hand this work, in which we must imitate them. But the many obstinately refuse to see things as they are, and hold with all their might to the most optimistic view of them that is possible. For this power, however, of idealizing with continually lowering ideals the reality which is felt to be ever less and less satisfying, pessimism also is partly responsible. Our generation, though so proud of its many achievements, no longer believes in the one thing which is all-essential: the spiritual advance of mankind. Having given up the expectation of this, it can put up with the present age without feeling such suffering as would compel it, for very pain, to long for a new one. What a task it will be to break the fetters of unthinking optimism and unthinking pessimism which hold us prisoners, and so to do what will pave the way for the renewal of civilization!

A second difficulty besetting the work which lies before us is that it is a piece of reconstruction. The ideals of civilization which our age needs are not new and strange to it. They have been in the possession of mankind already, and are to be found in many an antiquated formula. We have fundamentally nothing else to do than to restore to them the respect in which they were once held, and again regard them seriously as we bring them into relation with the reality which lies before us for treatment.

To make what is used up usable—is there a harder task? "It is an impossible one," says history. "Never hitherto have worn-out ideas risen to new power among the peoples who have worn them out. Their disappearance has always been a final one."

That is true. In the history of civilization we find nothing but discouragement for our task. Anyone who finds history speaking optimistically lends her a language which is not her own.

Yet from the history of the past we can infer only what has been, not what will be. Even if it proves that no single people has ever lived through the decay of its civilization and a rebirth of it, we know at once that this, which has never happened yet, must happen with us, and therefore we cannot be content to say that the reasoned ethical ideals on which civilization rests get worn out in the course of history, and console ourselves with the reflection that this is exactly in accordance with the ordinary processes of nature. We require to know why it has so happened hitherto, and to draw an explanation, not from the analogy of nature, but from the laws of spiritual life. We want to get into our hands the key of the secret, so that we may with it unlock the new age, the age in which the worn out becomes again unworn and the spiritual and ethical can no longer get worn out. We must study the history of civilization otherwise than as our predecessors did, or we shall be finally lost.

Why do not thoughts which contribute to civilization retain the convincing power which they once had, and which they deserve on account of their content? Why do they lose the evidential force of their moral and rational character? Why do traditional truths cease to be realities and pass from mouth to mouth as mere phrases?

* * *

Is this an unavoidable fate, or is the well drying up because our thinking did not go down to the permanent level of the water?

Moreover, it is not merely that the past survives among us as something valueless; it may cast a poisonous shade over us. There are thoughts on which we have never let our minds work directly because we found them ready formulated in history. Ideas which we have inherited do not let the truth which is in them come out into active service. but show it through a kind of dead mask. The worn-out achievements which pass over from a decadent civilization into the current of a new age often become like rejected products of metabolism, and act as poisons.

Granted that the Teutonic nations received a powerful stimulus to civilization at the Renaissance by reverting to the ideas of Greco-Roman thinkers, not less true is it that for many centuries they had been kept by that same Greco-Roman civilization in a condition of spiritual dependence which was wholly in contradiction to their native character. They took over from it decadent ideas which were for a long time a hindrance to their normal spiritual life, and thence came that strange mixture of strength and weakness which is the chief characteristic of the Middle Ages. The dangerous elements in the Greco-Roman civilization of the past still show themselves in our spiritual life. It is because Oriental and Greek conceptions which have had their day are still current among us that we bleed to death over problems which otherwise would have no existence for us. How much we suffer from the one fact that to-day and for several centuries past our thoughts about religion have been under the hereditary foreign domination of Jewish transcendentalism and Greek metaphysics, and, instead of being able to express themselves naturally, have suffered continual torture and distortion!

Because ideas get worn out in this way, and in this condition hinder the thinking of later generations, there is no continuity in the spiritual progress of mankind, but only a confused succession of ups and downs. The threads get broken, or knotted, or lost, or when tied up again get tied wrongly. Hitherto it has been thought possible to interpret this up-and-down movement optimistically because it was universally held that the Renaissance and the age of the Illuminati were quite natural successors of the Greco-Roman civilization, and it was assumed further that, as a permanent result of this, renewed civilizations would spring up in the place of exhausted ones, and thus continual progress be assured. But this generalization cannot justifiably be drawn from such observations. It was because new peoples came on the scene, who had been only superficially touched by the decadent civilizations and now produced others of their own, that it was possible to see this succession of ups and downs ending in an ascent. As a matter of fact, however, our newer civilization was not in any organic connection with the Greco-Roman, even if it did take its first steps with the help of the crutches which the latter provided; it may be described more truly as the reaction of a healthy spirit against the worn-out ideas which were thus offered to it. The essential element in the process was the contact of what was worn out with the fresh thought of young peoples.

To-day, however, all our thought is losing its power in its contact with the worn-out ideas of our expiring civilization, or —in the case of the Hindus and the Chinese—of our own and other expiring civilizations. The up-and-down movement will end, therefore, not in slow progress, but in unbroken descent— unless we can succeed in giving the worn-out ideas a renewal of their youth.

* * *

Another great difficulty in the way of the regeneration of our civilization lies in the fact that it must be an internal process, and not an external as well, and that, therefore, there is no place for healthy co-operation between the material and the spiritual. From the Renaissance to the middle of the nineteenth century the men who carried on the work of civilization could expect help toward spiritual progress from achievements in the sphere of external organization. Demands in each of these spheres stood side by side in their programme and were pushed on simultaneously. They were convinced that while working to transform the institutions of public life they were producing results which would call forth the development of the new spiritual life. Success in one sphere strengthened at once the hopes and the energies that were at work in the other. They laboured for the progressive democratization of the State with the idea of thereby spreading through the world the rule of grace and justice.

We, who have lived to see the spiritual bankruptcy of all the institutions which they created, can no longer work in this way simultaneously at the reform of institutions and the revival of the spiritual element. The help which such co-operation would give is denied us. We cannot even reckon any longer on the old co-operation between knowledge and thought. Once these two were allies. The latter fought for freedom and in so doing made a road for the former, and, on the other hand, all the results attained by knowledge worked for the general good of the spiritual life in that the reign of law in nature was more and more clearly demonstrated, and the reign of prejudice was becoming continually more restricted. The alliance also strengthened the thought that the well-being of mankind must be based upon spiritual laws. Thus knowledge and thought joined in establishing the authority of reason and the rational tone of mind.

To-day thought gets no help from science, and the latter stands facing it independent and unconcerned. The newest scientific knowledge may be allied with an entirely unreflecting view of the universe. It maintains that it is concerned only with the establishment of individual facts, since it is only by means of these that scientific knowledge can maintain its practical character; the co-ordination of the different branches of knowledge and the utilization of the results to form a theory of the universe are, it says, not its business. Once every man of science was also a thinker who counted for something in the general spiritual life of his generation. Our age has discovered how to divorce knowledge from thought, with the result that we have, indeed, a science which is free, but hardly any science left which reflects.

Thus we no longer have available for the renewal of our spiritual life any of the natural external helps which we used to have. We are called upon for a single kind of effort only, and have to work like men who are rebuilding the damaged foundations of a cathedral under the weight of the massive building. There is no progress in the world of phenomena to encourage us to persevere; an immense revolution has to be brought about without revolutionary action.

* * *

Again, the renewal of civilization is hindered by the fact that it is so exclusively the individual personality which must be looked to as the agent in the new movement.

The renewal of civilization has nothing to do with movements which bear the character of experiences of the crowd; these are never anything but reactions to external happenings.

But civilization can only revive when there shall come into being in a number of individuals a new tone of mind independent of the one prevalent among the crowd and in opposition to it, a tone of mind which will gradually win influence over the collective one, and in the end determine its character. It is only an ethical movement which can rescue us from the slough of barbarism, and the ethical comes into existence only in individuals.

The final decision as to what the future of a society shall be depends not on how near its organization is to perfection, but on the degrees of worthiness in its individual members. The most important, and yet the least easily determinable, element in history is the series of unobtrusive general changes which take place in the individual dispositions of the many. These are what precede and cause the happenings, and this is why it is so difficult to understand thoroughly the men and the events of past times. The character and worth of individuals among the mass and the way they work themselves into membership of the whole body, receiving influences from it and giving others back, we can even to-day only partially and uncertainly understand.

One thing, however, is clear. Where the collective body works more strongly on the individual than the latter does upon it, the result is deterioration, because the noble element on which everything depends, viz., the spiritual and moral worthiness of the individual, is thereby necessarily constricted and hampered. Decay of the spiritual and moral life then sets in, which renders society incapable of understanding and solving the problems which it has to face. Therefore, sooner or later, it is involved in catastrophe.

That is the condition in which we are now, and that is why it is the duty of individuals to rise to a higher conception of their capabilities and undertake again the function which only the individual can perform, that of producing new spiritual-ethical ideas. If this does not come about in a multitude of cases nothing can save us.

A new public opinion must be created privately and unobtrusively. The existing one is maintained by the Press, by propaganda, by organization, and by financial and other influences which are at its disposal. This unnatural way of spreading ideas must be opposed by the natural one, which goes from man to man and relies solely on the truth of the thoughts and the hearer's receptiveness for new truth. Unarmed, and following the human spirit's primitive and natural fighting method, it must attack the other, which faces it, as Goliath faced David, in the mighty armour of the age.

About the struggle which must needs ensue no historical analogy can tell us much. The past has, no doubt, seen the struggle of the free-thinking individual against the fettered spirit of a whole society, but the problem has never presented itself on the scale on which it does to-day, because the fettering of the collective spirit as it is fettered to-day by modern organizations, modern unreflectiveness, and modern popular passions, is a phenomenon without precedent in history.

* * *

Will the man of to-day have strength to carry out what the spirit demands from him, and what the age would like to make impossible?

In the over-organized societies which in a hundred ways have him in their power, he must somehow become once more an independent personality and so exert influence back upon them. They will use every means to keep him in that condition of impersonality which suits them. They fear personality because the spirit and the truth, which they would like to muzzle, find in it a means of expressing themselves. And their power is, unfortunately, as great as their fear.

There is a tragic alliance between society as a whole and its economic conditions. With a grim relentlessness those conditions tend to bring up the man of to-day as a being without freedom, without self-collectedness, without independence, in short as a human being so full of deficiencies that he lacks the qualities of humanity. And they are the last things that we can change. Even if it should be granted us that the spirit should begin its work, we shall only slowly and incompletely gain power over these forces. There is, in fact, being demanded from the will that which our conditions of life refuse to allow.

And how heavy the tasks that the spirit has to take in hand! It has to create the power of understanding the truth that is really true where at present nothing is current but propagandist truth. It has to depose ignoble patriotism, and enthrone the noble kind of patriotism which aims at ends that are worthy of the whole of mankind, in circles where the hopeless issues of past and present political activities keep nationalist passions aglow even among those who in their hearts would fain be free from them. It has to get the fact that civilization is an interest of all men and of humanity as a whole recognized again in places where national civilization is to-day worshipped as an idol, and the notion of a humanity with a common civilization lies broken to fragments. It has to maintain our faith in the civilized State, even though our modern States, spiritually and economically ruined by the war, have no time to think about the tasks of civilization, and dare not devote their attention to anything but how to use every possible means, even those which undermine the conception of justice, to collect money with which to prolong their own existence. It has to unite us by giving us a single ideal of civilized man, and this in a world where one nation has robbed its neighbour of all faith in humanity, idealism, righteousness, reasonableness, and truthfulness, and all alike have come under the domination of powers which are plunging us ever deeper into barbarism. It has to get attention concentrated on civilization while the growing difficulty of making a living absorbs the masses more and more in material cares, and makes all other things seem to them to be mere shadows. It has to give us faith in the possibility of progress while the reaction of the economic on the spiritual becomes more pernicious every day and contributes to an ever growing demoralization. It has to provide us with reasons for hope at a time when not only secular and religious institutions and associations, but the men, too, who are looked upon as leaders, continually fail us, when artists and men of learning show themselves as supporters of barbarism, and notabilities who pass for thinkers, and behave outwardly as such, are revealed, when crises come, as being nothing more than writers and members of academies.

All these hindrances stand in the path of the will to civilization. A dull despair hovers about us. How well we now understand the men of the Greco-Roman decadence, who stood before events incapable of resistance, and, leaving the world to its fate, withdrew upon their inner selves! Like them, we are bewildered by our experience of life. Like them, we hear enticing voices which say to us that the one thing which can still make life tolerable is to live for the day. We must, we are told, renounce every wish to think or hope about anything beyond our own fate. We must find rest in resignation.

The recognition that civilization is founded on some sort of theory of the universe, and can be restored only through a spiritual awakening and a will for ethical good in the mass of mankind, compels us to make clear to ourselves those difficulties in the way of a rebirth of civilization which ordinary reflection would overlook. But at the same time it raises us above all considerations of possibility or impossibility. If the ethical spirit provides a sufficient standing ground in the sphere of events for making civilization a reality, then we shall get back to civilization, if we return to a suitable theory of the universe and the convictions to which this properly gives birth.

The history of our decadence preaches the truth that when hope is dead the spirit becomes the deciding court of appeal, and this truth must in the future find in us a sublime and noble fulfilment.

Chapter 5

CIVILIZATION AND WORLD-VIEW

Renewal of world-view, and re-birth of civilization.

A thinking world-view. Rationalism and mysticism.

The optimistic-ethical world-view as the civilization world-view.

The renewal of our ideas by thinking about the meaning of life.

THE GREATEST OF ALL THE SPIRIT'S TASKS IS TO PRODUCE A THEORY of the universe *(Weltanschauung*[1]*).*

In that all the ideas, convictions and activities of an age have their roots, and it is only when we have arrived at one which is compatible with civilization that we are capable of holding the ideas and convictions which are the conditions of civilization at all.

What is meant by a theory of the universe? It is the content of the thoughts of society and the individuals which compose it about the nature and object of the world in which they live, and the position and the destiny of mankind and of individual men within it. What significance have the society in which I live and I myself in the world? What do we want to do in the world, what do we hope to get from it? What is our duty to it? The answer given by the majority to these fundamental questions about existence decides what the spirit is in which they and their age live.

[1] Translated "world-view" throughout the second part of these Lectures.

Is not this putting too high the value of a theory of the universe?

At present, certainly, the majority do not, as a rule, attain to any properly thought-out theory, nor do they feel the need of deriving their ideas and convictions from such a source. They are in tune, more or less, with all the tones which pervade the age in which they live.

But who are the musicians who have produced these tones? They are the personalities who have thought out theories of the universe, and drawn from them the ideas, more or less valuable, which are current amongst us to-day. In this way all thoughts, whether those of individuals or those of society, go back ultimately, in some way or other, to a theory of the universe. Every age lives in the consciousness of what has been provided for it by the thinkers under whose influence it stands.

Plato was wrong in holding that the philosophers of a State should also be its governors. Their supremacy is a different and a higher one than that which consists in framing and issuing laws and ordinances and giving effect to official authority. They are the officers of the general staff who sit in the background thinking out, with more or less clearness of vision, the details of the battle which is to be fought. Those who play their part in the public eye are the subordinate officers who, for their variously sized units, convert the general directions of the staff into orders of the day: namely, that the forces will start at such and such a time, move in this or that direction, and occupy this or that point. Kant and Hegel have commanded millions who had never read a line of their writings, and who did not even know that they were obeying their orders.

Those who command, whether it be in a large or a small sphere, can only carry out what is already in the thought of the age. They do not build the instrument on which they have to play, but are merely given a seat at it. Nor do they compose the piece they have to play; it is simply put before them, and they cannot alter it; they can only reproduce it with more or less skill and success. If it is meaningless, they cannot do much to improve it, but neither, if it is good, can they damage it seriously.

To the question, then, whether it is personalities or ideas

which decide the fate of an age, the answer is that the age gets its ideas from personalities. If the thinkers of a certain period produce a worthy theory of the universe, then ideas pass into currency which guarantee progress; if they are not capable of such production, then decadence sets in in some form or other. Every theory of the universe draws after it its own special results in history.

The fall of the Roman Empire in spite of that empire's having over it so many rulers of conspicuous ability, may be traced ultimately to the fact that ancient philosophy produced no theory of the universe with ideas which tended to that empire's preservation. With the rise of Stoicism, as the definitive result of the philosophic thought of antiquity, the fate of the Mediterranean peoples was decided. Thinking based on resignation, magnificent as it was, could not ensure progress in a world-wide empire. The efforts of its strongest emperors were useless. The yarn with which they had to weave was rotten.

In the eighteenth century, under the rule, in most places, of insignificant rococo-sovereigns and rococo-ministers, a progressive movement began among the nations of Europe which was unique in the history of the world. Why? The thinkers of the Aufklärung and of rationalism produced a worthy theory of the universe from which valuable ideas spread among mankind.

But when history began to shape itself in accordance with these ideas, the thought which had produced the progress came to a halt, and we have now a generation which is squandering the precious heritage it has received from the past, and is living in a world of ruins, because it cannot complete the building which that past began. Even had our rulers and statesmen been less short-sighted than they actually were, they would not in the long run have been able to avert the catastrophe which burst upon us. Both the inner and the outer collapse of civilization were latent in the circumstances produced by the prevalent view of the universe. The rulers, small and great alike, did not act in accordance with the spirit of the age.

With the disappearance of the influence exerted by the *Aufklärung*, rationalism, and the great philosophy of the early nineteenth century, the seeds were sown of the world-war to come. Then began to disappear also the ideas and convictions which would have made possible a solution on right lines of the controversies which arise between nations.

Thus the course of events brought us into a position in which we had to get along without any real theory of the universe. The collapse of philosophy and the rise and influence of scientific modes of thought made it impossible to arrive at an idealist theory which should satisfy thought. Moreover, our age is poorer in deep thinkers than perhaps any preceding one. There were a few strong spirits who, with varied knowledge and with devoted efforts, offered the world some patchwork thought; there were some dazzling comets; but that was all that was granted us. Their products in the way of world theories were good enough to interest a circle of academic culture, or to delight a few believing followers, but the people as a whole were entirely untouched.

We began, therefore, to persuade ourselves that it was, after all, possible to get through without any theory of the universe. The feeling that we needed to stir ourselves up to ask questions about the world and life, and to come to a decision upon them, gradually died away. In the unreflective condition to which we had surrendered ourselves, we took, to meet the claims of our own life and the nation's life, the chance ideas provided by our feeling for reality. During more than a generation and a half we had proof enough and to spare that the theory which consists in the result of absence of theory is the most worthless of all, involving not only ruin to the spiritual life, but ruin universal. For where there is no general staff to think out its plan of campaign for any generation its subordinate officers lead it, as in actual warfare so in the sphere of ideas, from one profitless adventure to another.

The reconstruction of our age, then, can begin only with a reconstruction of its theory of the universe. There is hardly anything more urgent in its claim on us than this which seems to be so far off and abstract. Only when we have made ourselves at home again in the solid thought-building of a theory which can support a civilization, and when we take from it, all of us in co-operation, ideas which can stimulate our life and work, only then can there again arise a society which can possess ideals with magnificent aims and be able to bring these into effective agreement with reality. It is from new ideas that we must build history anew.

For individuals as for the community, life without a theory of things is a pathological disturbance of the higher capacity for self-direction.

* * *

What conditions must a theory of the universe fulfil to enable it to create a civilization?

First, and defined generally, it must be the product of thought. Nothing but what is born of thought and addresses itself to thought can be a spiritual power affecting the whole of mankind. Only what has been well turned over in the thought of the many, and thus recognized as truth, possesses a natural power of conviction which will work on other minds and will continue to be effective. Only where there is a constant appeal to the need of a reflective view of things are all man's spiritual capacities called into activity.

Our age has an almost artistic prejudice against a reflective theory of the universe. We are still children of the Romantic movement to a greater extent than we realize. What that movement produced in opposition to the *Aufklärung* and to rationalism seems to us valid for all ages against any theory that would found itself solely on thought. In such a theory of the universe we can see beforehand the world dominated by a barren intellectualism, convictions governed by mere utility, and a shallow optimism, which together rob mankind of all human genius and enthusiasm.

In a great deal of the opposition which it offered to rationalism the reaction of the early nineteenth century was right. Nevertheless it remains true that it despised and distorted what was, in spite of all its imperfections, the greatest and most valuable manifestation of the spiritual life of man that the world has yet seen. Down through all circles of cultured and uncultured alike there prevailed at that time a belief in thought and a reverence for truth. For that reason alone that age stands higher than any which preceded it, and much higher than our own.

At no price must the feelings and phrases of Romanticism be

allowed to prevent our generation from forming a clear conception of what reason really is. It is no dry intellectualism which would suppress all the manifold movements of our inner life, but the totality of all the functions of our spirit in their living action and interaction. In it our intellect and our will hold that mysterious intercourse which determines the character of our spiritual being. The ideas about the world which it produces contain all that we can feel or imagine about our destiny and that of mankind, and give our whole being its direction and its value. The enthusiasm which comes from thought has the same relation to that which is produced by mere random feeling as the wind which sweeps the heights has to that which eddies about between the hills. If we venture once more to seek help from the light of reason, we shall no longer keep ourselves down at the level of a generation which has ceased to be capable of enthusiasm, but shall rise to the deep and noble passion inspired by great and sublime ideals. These will so fill and expand our being that that by which we now live will seem to be merely a poor kind of excitement, and will disappear.

Rationalism is more than a movement of thought which realized itself at the end of the eighteenth and the beginning of the nineteenth centuries. It is a necessary phenomenon in all normal spiritual life. All real progress in the world is in the last analysis produced by rationalism.

It is true that the intellectual productions of the period which we designate historically as the rationalistic are incomplete and unsatisfactory, but the principle, which was then established, of basing our views of the universe on thought and thought alone, is valid for all time. Even if the tree's earliest fruit did not ripen perfectly, the tree itself remains, nevertheless, the tree of life for the life of our spirit.

All the movements that have claimed to take the place of rationalism stand far below it in the matter of achievement. From speculative thought, from history, from feeling, from æsthetics, from science, they tried to obtain something like a world-view, grubbing at haphazard in the world around them instead of excavating scientifically. Rationalism alone chose the right place for its digging, and dug systematically, according to plan. If it found only metal of small value, that was because, with the means at its disposal, it could not go deep enough. Impoverished and ruined as we are because we sought as mere adventurers, we must make up our minds to sink another shaft in the ground where rationalism worked, and to go down through all the strata to see whether we cannot find the gold which must certainly be there.

To think out to the end a theory of the universe which has been produced by thought—that is the only possible way of finding our bearings amid the confusion of the world of thought to-day.

Philosophical, historical, and scientific questions with which it was not capable of dealing overwhelmed the earlier rationalism like an avalanche, and buried it in the middle of its journey. The new rational theory of the universe must work its way out of this chaos. Leaving itself freely open to the whole influence of the world of fact, it must explore every path offered by reflection and knowledge in its effort to reach the ultimate meaning of being and life, and to see whether it can solve some of the riddles which they present.

The ultimate knowledge, in which man recognizes his own being as a part of the All, belongs, they say, to the realm of mysticism, by which is meant that he does not reach it by the method of ordinary reflection, but somehow or other lives himself into it.

But why assume that the road of thought must suddenly stop at the frontier of mysticism? It is true that pure reason has hitherto called a halt whenever it came into that neighbourhood, for it was unwilling to go beyond the point at which it could still exhibit everything as part of a smooth, logical plan. Mysticism, on its side, always depreciated pure reason as much as it could, to prevent at all costs the idea from gaining currency that it was in any way bound to give an account to reason. And yet, although they refuse to recognize each other, the two belong to each other.

It is in reason that intellect and will, which in our nature are mysteriously bound up together, seek to come to a mutual understanding. The ultimate knowledge that we strive to acquire is knowledge of life, which intellect looks at from without, will from within. Since life is the ultimate object of knowledge, our ultimate knowledge is necessarily our thinking experience of life. But this does not lie outside the sphere of reason, but within reason itself. Only when the will has thought out its relation to the intellect, has come, as far as it can, into line with it, has penetrated it, and in it become logical, is it in a position to comprehend itself, so far as its nature allows this, as a part of the universal will-to-live and a part of being in general. If it merely leaves the intellect on one side, it loses itself in confused imaginings, while the intellect, which, like the rationalism of the past, will not allow that in order to understand life it must finally lose itself in thinking experience, renounces all hope of constructing a deep and firmly based theory of the universe.

Thus reflection, when pursued to the end, leads somewhere and somehow to a living mysticism, which is for all men everywhere a necessary element of thought.

Doubts whether the mass of men can ever attain to that level of reflection about themselves and the world which is demanded by a reflective theory of the universe, are quite justifiable if the man of to-day is taken as an example of the race. But he, with his diminished need of thought, is a pathological phenomenon.

In reality there is given in the mental endowment of the average man a capacity for thought which to the individual makes the creation of a reflective theory of things of his own not only possible, but under normal conditions even a necessity. The great movements of illumination in ancient and modern times help to maintain the confident belief that there is in the mass of mankind a power of thought on fundamentals which can be roused to activity. This belief is strengthened by observation of mankind and intercourse with the young. A fundamental impulse to reflect about the universe stirs us during those years in which we begin to think independently. Later on we let it languish, even though feeling clearly that we thereby impoverish ourselves and become less capable of what is good. We are like springs of water which no longer run because they have not been watched and have gradually become choked with rubbish.

More than any other age has our own neglected to watch the thousand springs of thought; hence the drought in which we are pining. But if we only go on to remove the rubbish which conceals the water, the sands will be irrigated again, and life will spring up where hitherto there has been only a desert.

Certainly there are guides and the guided in the department of world-theories, as in others. So far the independence of the mass of men remains a relative one. The question is only whether the influence of the guides leads to dependence or independence. The latter brings with it a development in the direction of truthfulness; the former means the death of that virtue.

Every being who calls himself a man is meant to develop into a real personality within a reflective theory of the universe which he has created for himself.

* * *

But of what character must the theory be if ideas and convictions about civilization are to be based on it?

It must be optimistic and ethical.

That theory of the universe is optimistic which gives existence the preference as against non-existence and thus affirms life as something possessing value in itself. From this attitude to the universe and to life results the impulse to raise existence, in so far as our influence can affect it, to its highest level of value. Thence originates activity directed to the improvement of the living conditions of individuals, of society, of nations and of humanity, and from it spring the external achievements of civilization, the lordship of spirit over the powers of nature, and the higher social organization.

Ethics is the activity of man directed to secure the inner perfection of his own personality. In itself it is quite independent of whether the theory of the universe is pessimistic or optimistic. But its sphere of action is contracted or widened according as it appears in connection with a theory of the first or the second type.

In the consistently pessimistic theory of the universe, as we have it in the thought of the Brāhmans or of Schopenhauer, ethics has nothing whatever to do with the objective world. It aims solely at securing the self-perfection of the individual as this comes to pass in inner freedom and disconnection from the world and the spirit of the world.

But the scope of ethics is extended in proportion as it develops and strengthens a connection with a theory of the universe which is affirmative toward the world and life. Its aim is now the inner perfection of the individual and at the same time the direction of his activity so as to take effect on other men and on the objective world. This freedom with its release from the world and its spirit ethics no longer holds up to man as an aim in itself. By its means man is to become capable of acting among men and in the world as a higher and purer force, and thus to do his part toward the actualization of the ideal of general progress.

Thus the optimistic-ethical theory of the universe works in partnership with ethics to produce civilization. Neither is capable of doing so by itself. Optimism supplies confidence that the world-process has somehow or other a spiritual and real aim, and that the improvement of the general relations of the world and of society promotes the spiritual-moral perfection of the individual. From the ethical comes ability to develop the purposive state of mind necessary to produce action on the world and society and to cause the co-operation of all our achievements to secure the spiritual and moral perfection of the individual which is the final end of civilization.

Once we have recognized that the energies which spring out of a theory of the universe, and impel us to create a civilization, are rooted in the ethical and the optimistic, we get light on the question why and how our ideals of civilization got worn out. This question is not to be answered by good or bad analogies from nature. The decisive answer is that they got worn out because we had not succeeded in establishing the ethical and optimistic elements on a sufficiently firm foundation.

If we should analyse the process in which the ideas and convictions that produce civilization reveal themselves, it would be found that whenever an advance has been registered, either the optimist or the ethical element in the theory of the universe has proved more attractive than usual, and has had as its consequence a progressive development. When civilization is decaying there is the same chain of causation, but it works negatively. The building is damaged or falls in because the optimist element or the ethical, or both, give way like a weak foundation.

No amount of inquiry will give any other reason for the changes. All imaginable ideas and convictions of that character spring from optimism and the ethical impulse. If these two pillars are strong enough, we need have no fears about the building.

The future of civilization depends, therefore, on whether it is possible for thought to reach a theory of the universe which will have a more secure and fundamental hold on optimism and the ethical impulse than its predecessors have had.

* * *

We Westerners dream of a theory of the universe which corresponds to our impulse to action and at the same time clarifies it. We have not been able to formulate such a theory definitely. At present we are in the state of possessing merely an impulse without any definite orientation. The spirit of the age drives us into action without allowing us to attain any clear view of the objective world and of life. It claims our toil inexorably in the service of this or that end, this or that achievement. It keeps us in a sort of intoxication of activity so that we may never have time to reflect and to ask ourselves what this restless sacrifice of ourselves to ends and achievements really has to do with the meaning of the world and of our lives. And so we wander hither and thither in the gathering dusk formed by lack of any definite theory of the universe like homeless, drunken mercenaries, and enlist indifferently in the service of the common and the great without distinguishing between them. And the more hopeless becomes the condition of the world in which this adventurous impulse to action and progress ranges to and fro, the more bewildered becomes our whole conception of things and the more purposeless and irrational the doings of those who have enlisted under the banner of such an impulse.

How little reflection is present in the Western impulse to action becomes evident when this tries to square its ideas with those of the Far East. For thought in the Far East has been constantly occupied in its search for the meaning of life, and forces us to consider the problem of the meaning of our own restlessness, the problem which we Westerners shirk so persistently. We are utterly at a loss when we contemplate the ideas which are presented to us in Indian thought. We turn away from the intellectual presumption which we find there. We are conscious of the unsatisfying and incomplete elements in the ideal of cessation from action. We feel instinctively that the will-to-progress is justified not only in its aspect as directed to the spiritual perfecting of personality, but also in that which looks toward the general and material.

For ourselves we dare to allege that we adventurers, who take up an affirmative attitude toward the world and toward life, however great and even ghastly our mistakes may be, can yet show not only greater material, but also greater spiritual and ethical, achievements than can those who lie under the ban of a theory of the universe which leads to cessation from action.

And yet, all the same, we cannot feel ourselves completely justified in the face of these strange Eastern theories. They have in them something full of nobility which retains its hold on us, even fascinates us. This tinge of nobility comes from the fact that these convictions are born of a search for a theory of the universe and for the meaning of life. With us, on the other hand, activist instincts and impulses take the place of a theory of the universe. We have no theory affirming the world and life to oppose to the negative theory of these thinkers, no thought which has found a basis for an optimistic conception of existence to oppose to this other, which has arrived at a pessimistic conception.

The reawakening of the Western spirit must thus begin by our people, educated and simple alike, becoming conscious of their lack of a theory of the universe and feeling the horror of their consequent position. We can no longer be satisfied to make shift with substitutes for such a theory. What is the basis of the will-to-activity and progress which impels both to great actions and to terrible deeds, and which tries to keep us from reflection? We must bend all our energies to the solution of this problem.

There is only one way in which we can hope to emerge from the meaningless state in which we are now held captive into one informed with meaning. Each one of us must turn to contemplate his own being, and we must all give ourselves to co-operative reflection so as to discover how our will to action and to progress may be intellectually based on the way in which we interpret our own lives and the life around us, and the meaning which we give to these.

The great revision of the convictions and ideals in which and for which we live cannot be brought about by preaching to our contemporaries ideas and thoughts other and better than those by which they are dominated at the moment. It can start if the many come to reflect about the meaning of life and to re-orientate, revise and make over again their ideals of action and of progress, asking themselves whether these have a meaning in accord with that which we attribute to life itself. This personal reflection about final and elemental things is the one and only reliable way of measuring values. My willing and doing have real meaning and value only in proportion as the aims which action sets before itself can be justified as being in direct accord with my interpretation of my own and of other life. All else, however much it may pass current as approved by tradition, usage, and public opinion, is vain and dangerous.

It seems, indeed, little better than mockery that we should urge men to anything so remote as a return to reflection about the meaning of life at a time when the passions and the follies of the nations have become so intense and so extended, when unemployment and poverty and starvation are rife, when power is being used on the powerless in the most shameless and senseless way, and when organized human life is dislocated in every direction. But only when the general population begins to reflect in this way will forces come into being which will be able to effect something to counterbalance all this chaos and misery. Whatever other measures it is attempted to carry out will have doubtful and altogether inadequate results.

When in the spring the withered grey of the pastures gives place to green, this is due to the millions of young shoots which sprout up freshly from the old roots. In like manner the revival of thought which is essential for our time can only come through a transformation of the opinions and ideals of the many brought about by individual and universal reflection about the meaning of life and of the world.

But are we sure of being able to think out that affirmation of the world and of life, which is such a powerful impulse in us, into a theory of the world and of life from which a stream of energy productive of intelligible life and action may convincingly and constantly proceed? How are we to succeed in doing what the spirit of the Western world during past generations has in vain toiled to accomplish?

Even if thought, once more awakened, should only attain to an incomplete and unsatisfying theory of the universe, yet this, as the truth to which we have ourselves worked through, would be of more value than a complete lack of any theory at all, or, alternatively, than any sort of authoritative theory to which, neglecting the demands of true thought, we cling on account of its supposed intrinsic value without having any real and thorough belief in it.

The beginning of all spiritual life of any real value is courageous faith in truth and open confession of the same. The most profound religious experience, too, is not alien to thought, but must be capable of derivation from this if it is to be given a true and deep basis. Mere reflection about the meaning of life has already value in itself. If such reflection should again come into being amongst us, the ideals, born of vanity and of suffering, which now flourish in rank profusion like evil weeds among the convictions of the generality of people, would infallibly wither away and die. How much would already be accomplished toward the improvement of our present circumstances if only we would all give up three minutes every evening to gazing up into the infinite world of the starry heavens and meditating on it, or if in taking part in a funeral procession we would reflect on the enigma of life and death, instead of engaging in thoughtless conversation as we follow behind the coffin! The ideals, born of folly and passion, of those who make public opinion and direct public events, would have no more power over men if they once began to reflect about infinity and the finite, existence and dissolution, and thus learnt to distinguish between true and false standards, between those which possess real value and those which do not. The old-time rabbis used to teach that the kingdom of God would come if only the whole of Israel would really keep a single Sabbath simultaneously! How much more is it true that the injustice and violence and untruth, which are now bringing so much disaster on the human race, would lose their power if only a single real trace of reflection about the meaning of the world and of life should appear amongst us!

But is there not a danger in challenging men with this question about the meaning of life and in demanding that our impulse to action should justify and clarify itself in such reflection as that of which we have spoken? Shall we not lose, in acceding to this demand, some irreplaceable element of naïve enthusiasm?

We need not thus be anxious as to how strong or how weak our impulse to action will prove to be when it shall have arrived, as the result of intellectual reflection, at an interpretation of life. The impulse to action is meaningless apart from the meaning which we can find and feel in our own life. It is not the quantity, but the quality, of activity that really matters. What is needed is that our will-to-action should become conscious of itself and should cease to work blindly.

But perhaps, it may be objected, we shall end in the resignation of agnosticism, and shall be obliged to confess that we cannot discover any meaning in the universe or in life.

If thought is to set out on its journey unhampered, it must be prepared for anything, even for arrival at intellectual agnosticism. But even if our will-to-action is destined to wrestle endlessly and unavailingly with an agnostic view of the universe and of life, still this painful disenchantment is better for it than persistent refusal to think out its position at all. For this disenchantment does, at any rate, mean that we are clear as to what we are doing.

There is, however, no necessity whatever for such an attitude of resignation. We feel that a position of affirmation regarding the world and life is something which is in itself both necessary and valuable. Therefore it is at least likely that a foundation can be found for it in thought. Since it is an innate element of our will-to-live, it must be possible to comprehend it as a necessary corollary to our interpretation of life. Perhaps we shall have to look elsewhere than we have done hitherto for the real basis of that theory of the universe which carries with it affirmation of the world and of life. Previous thought imagined that it could deduce the meaning of life from its interpretation of the universe. It may be that we shall be obliged to resign ourselves to abandon the problem of the interpretation of the universe and to find the meaning of our life in the will-to-live as this exists in ourselves.

The ways along which we have to struggle toward the goal may be veiled in darkness, yet the direction in which we must travel is clear. We must reflect together about the meaning of life; we must strive together to attain to a theory of the universe affirmative of the world and of life, in which the impulse to action which we experience as a necessary and valuable element of our being may find justification, orientation, clarity and depth, may receive a fresh access of moral strength, and be retempered, and thus become capable of formulating, and of acting on, definite ideals of civilization, inspired by the spirit of true humanitarianism.

Part II

CIVILIZATION AND ETHICS

TO

MY WIFE

THE MOST LOYAL OF COMRADES

REVISER'S NOTE

THOUGH HE IS SO COMPLETELY BI-LINGUAL THAT ONE OF HIS WORKS was first written in French, Dr. Schweitzer, being an Alsatian, habitually writes in German, a dialect of which, interspersed with a few French words, is the common tongue of his country. For those who are totally unacquainted with the German language, it may make what follows easier to grasp if I explain a few of the expressions which Dr. Schweitzer frequently uses, expressions which, familiar and simple in the original—for he avoids the technical phrases of the philosophers—have in English no exact equivalent.

DIE ETHIK. Very simple in German. But some critics have said that in English the use of the word "ethics" to denote anything but "the science of morality" is wrong, and that it is impossible to speak of "an ethic." Then, again, there is divergence of opinion in dictionaries as to whether the word is singular or plural, so that writers have a habit of avoiding its use when a verb must follow.

The *Oxford English Dictionary* among its meanings adds to "the science of morality":

"The moral principles or system of a particular leader or school of thought";

"The moral principles by which a person is guided";

"The rules of conduct recognized in certain associations or departments of human life";

"The whole field of moral science," and quotes Bentham (1789):

"Ethics at large may be defined as the art of directing men's actions to the production of the greatest possible quantity of happiness."

As for "an ethic," the same authority gives its meaning as "The science of morals"; "A scheme of moral science," and quotes its use from Spencer's *Data of Ethics* in the words, "an attempt to construct an ethic apart from theology . . ."

AUSEINANDERSETZUNG and its verb. This is a very favourite word with Dr. Schweitzer and occurs very frequently throughout the original of this volume. No single English word can give its meaning, which is, roughly, the taking of a subject to pieces, the spreading out of the details for thorough examination and discussion, and following on this the arrival at some kind of agreement or compromise. It has been translated as "trying conclusions," "discussion," "conflict," "agreement," etc., as best suits the context.

WELTANSCHAUUNG. Many writers, for want of an English word that conveys exactly the same very wide meaning, use the German word to express what it stands for. But to the general reader unfamiliar with a foreign language nothing is more annoying than to be constantly encountering a word he cannot even pronounce. Dr. Schweitzer himself defines "Weltanschauung" as the sum-total of the thoughts which the community or the individual think about the nature and purpose of the universe and about the place and destiny of mankind within the world.

Mr. Campion, for reasons which he explains in a footnote, has invariably translated the word as "world-view." I have ventured to vary the monotony of this in English rather odd-sounding word, by the use of "outlook on life," "conception of the universe," "philosophy," etc. It should be noted that the one German word "Welt" does duty for our two words, universe and world.

GEIST and GEISTIG. Here again the Germans have only one word where we have two. We say mind and spirit, mental and spiritual, where they say only spirit and spiritual. The translator almost always uses the latter terms, comprising both senses in the one word, but it must be remembered that the meaning is wider than that we often attach to spiritual, and the word may therefore sometimes appear not quite appropriate.

WORLD- AND LIFE-AFFIRMATION. This means that man has an inner conviction that life is a real thing, that the world in itself and life in itself have great value, that life is for each individual infinitely worth while, that the human spirit can dominate nature, and that man must never admit defeatism. It is the characteristic European attitude to human life.

WORLD- AND LIFE-NEGATION is the contrary belief, that life is an illusion, that nothing really matters because all is vanity, that the individual in his short span of life can achieve nothing of value, that the supreme good is to make an end of it. This is the characteristic Indian attitude to life.

CIVILIZATION. The exceptionally wide and comprehensive meaning attached to this word should also be kept in mind throughout. Dr. Schweitzer defines it as the sum-total of all progress made by mankind in every sphere of action and from every point of view, in so far as this progress is serviceable for the spiritual perfecting of the individual. Its essential element is, he says, the ethical perfecting of the individual and of the community.

REVERENCE FOR LIFE. This phrase too is immensely wide in its meaning, embracing as it does the whole span and the whole scale, in all its degrees, of a single and constant attitude toward all life as such, including even those forms of life which are injurious to our lives.

L.M.R.

1945.

PREFACE

MY SUBJECT IS THE TRAGEDY OF THE WESTERN WORLD-VIEW.[1]

While still a student I was surprised to find the history of thought always written merely as a history of philosophical systems, never as the history of man's effort to arrive at a conception of the universe. Later, when reflecting on the current of civilization in which I found myself living, I was struck by the strange and inexorable connections which exist between civilization and our view of the world as a whole. Next I felt a still stronger compulsion to put to Western thought the question what it has been aiming at, and what result it has reached in the matter of a philosophy of life. What is there left of the achievements of our philosophy when it is stripped of its tinsel of learning? What has it to offer when we demand from it those elemental ideas which we need, if we are to take our position in life as men who are growing in character through the experience given by work?

So I came to an unsparing effort to come to an understanding with Western thought. I recognized and admitted that it has sought for that outlook on life from which alone a deep and

[1] [*Translator's Note*—Weltanschauung. This compound word may be translated "theory of the universe," "world-theory," "world-conception," or "world-view." The first is misleading as suggesting, wrongly, a scientific explanation of the universe; the second and third as suggesting, less ambitiously but still wrongly, an explanation of how and why our human world is what it is. The last indicates a sufficiently wide knowledge and consideration of our corner of the universe to allow all factors to be taken into consideration which bear on the question at issue.

There may be passages in which it is desirable to vary the translation, and others in which it is possible to give the meaning in more elegant English, for good English style does not take kindly to such compound words. But this latter consideration can be only a secondary one in the translation of a philosophical work, the first object of which must be to ensure that the author's meaning shall be reproduced as clearly as possible.]

comprehensive civilization can come. It has wanted to reach a position of world- and life-affirmation and with that as a foundation decree that it is our duty to be active, to strive for progress of all kinds, and to create values. It has wanted to reach an ethical system and on that foundation establish that for the sake of serviceable activity we have to place our life at the service of ideas and of the other life around us.

But it did not succeed in grounding its world- and life-affirming ethical world-view convincingly and permanently in thought. Our philosophy did nothing more than produce again and again unstable fragments of the serviceable outlook on life which hovered before its mind's eye. Consequently our civilization also has remained fragmentary and insecure.

It was a fatal mistake that Western thought never admitted to itself the unsatisfying result of its search for a stable and serviceable outlook on the universe. Our philosophizing became less and less elemental, losing all connection with the elementary questions which man must ask of life and of the world. More and more it found satisfaction in the handling of philosophic questions that were merely academic, and in expert mastery of philosophical technique. It became more and more the captive of secondary things. Instead of real music it produced again and again mere bandmaster's music, often magnificent of its kind, but still only bandmaster's music.

Through this philosophy which did nothing but philosophize instead of struggling for a world-view founded on thought and serviceable for life, we came to be without any world-view at all, and therefore lacking in civilization.

Signs of an awakening of thought on this point are beginning to be visible. It is admitted here and there that philosophy must again try to offer a conception of the universe. This is generally expressed by saying that people are encouraging it to venture once more on "metaphysics," that is to say, to put forward definitive views about the spiritual nature of the world, whereas hitherto it has been occupied with the classification of scientific facts and the emission of cautious hypotheses.

Not only in philosophy, but in thought generally, this awakening of the need for a world-view expresses itself as a need for "metaphysics." Fantastic systems of "metaphysics" are sought for and offered. Individuals who believe that they have at their disposal peculiar psychic experiences, and assert that with their aid they can look behind the actual nature of phenomena, come forward as producers of a world-view.

But neither the cautious academic, nor the much-claiming fantastic, "metaphysics," can really give us a world-view. That the road to this leads through "metaphysics" is a fatal error which has already enjoyed too long a span of life in our Western thought. It would be tragic if we renewed its vigour just now, when we are faced by the necessity of working our way out of that shortage of a philosophy of life in which our misery, both spiritual and material, is grounded. No further wandering along the traditional roads that lead nowhere can save us, whether we advance as the successors of our fathers or on adventurous lines of our own. Only in a deep conception of, and experience in, the problems of world-view lies for us any possibility of advance.

That is why I am undertaking what has never been attempted in this way before, namely, so to pose the problem of Western philosophy as to make the Western search for a world-view come to a halt and take account of itself. There are two points on which it must be clear before it proceeds to further exertion. The first is the overwhelming importance in the search for a world-view of the quality of that which is sought. What is it we want? We want to find the world- and life-affirmation, and the ethical system which we need for that serviceable activity which gives our life a meaning, based on such thought about the world and life as finds a meaning in them also. If our search for a world-view is once thoroughly permeated by the recognition that everything turns upon these two fundamental questions, it is thereby saved from betaking itself to by-paths, thinking that by some happy disposition of fortune it can reach its goal along them. It will then not search for a "metaphysic," thinking by means of it to reach a world-view, but it will search for a world-view and accept with it anything "metaphysical" that may turn up. From every point of view it will remain elemental.

The second task which the conscious search for a conception of the universe must not shirk, is the consideration of what is the real and ultimate nature of the process by which it has hitherto attempted to secure that serviceable world-view which hovered before it. Reflection on this is necessary that it may make up its mind whether further advance along the road it has hitherto followed gives any prospect of success. Our philosophy ought to have been philosophizing long ago about the road along which it was going in search of a world-view. It never did so, and therefore was always running uselessly round and round in a circle.

The process by which Western thought has hitherto sought for a world-view is doomed to be fruitless. It has consisted simply in interpreting the world in the sense of world- and life-affirmation, that is to say, in attributing to the world a meaning which allowed it to conceive the aims of mankind and of individual men as having a meaning within that world. This interpretation is acted upon by all Western philosophy. A few thinkers who venture to be un-Western, and resolutely allow world- and life-negation and ethics to be made subjects of discussion, are side-currents which do not affect the main course of the river.

That this process followed by Western thought consists in adopting an optimistic-ethical interpretation of the world will not be clear without further explanation, for it is, indeed, not always openly followed. The optimistic-ethical interpretation is often found imbedded in the results of investigations into the nature of knowledge; it often appears beneath a veil of "metaphysics"; it is often so delicately shaded that it produces none of its usual effects. It is only when one has clearly grasped the fact that Western thought has nothing else in mind than to establish for itself a world-view based on world- and life-affirmation and ethical in character, that one can realize how in its theory of knowledge, in its metaphysics, and in all its movements generally in the game of life, it is guided, consciously or unconsciously, by the effort to interpret the world in some way or other, and in some measure, in the sense of world- and life-affirmation and ethics. Whether in this attempt it goes to work openly or secretly, skilfully or unskilfully, honourably or craftily, does not matter. Western thought needs this interpretation in order that it may be able to give a meaning to human life. Its view of life is to be a result of its view of the world. It has never considered any other course.

But this awakening of Western thought will not be complete until that thought steps outside itself and comes to an understanding with the search for a world-view as this manifests itself in the thought of mankind as a whole. We have too long been occupied with the developing series of our own philosophical systems, and have taken no notice of the fact that there is a world-philosophy of which our Western philosophy is only a part. If, however, one conceives philosophy as being a struggle to reach a view of the world as a whole, and seeks out the elementary convictions which are to deepen it and give it a sure foundation, one cannot avoid setting our own thought face to face with that of the Hindus, and of the Chinese in the Far East. The latter looks strange to us because in much it has remained till now naïve and embodied in myth, while on the other hand it has spontaneously advanced to refinements of criticism and to artificialities. But this does not matter. The essential thing is that it is a struggle for a philosophy of life: the form it takes is a secondary matter. Our Western philosophy, if judged by its own latest pronouncements, is much naïver than we admit to ourselves, and we fail to perceive this only because we have acquired the art of expressing what is simple in a pedantic way.

Among the Hindus we encounter the world-view which is based on world- and life-negation, and the way in which it has laid its foundations in thought is calculated to leave us not knowing what to make of our prejudice in favour of world- and life-affirmation, which, as Westerners, we are inclined to assume to be more or less self-evident.

The attraction and tension which in Hindu thought govern the relations between world- and life-negation and ethics afford us glimpses into the problem of ethics for which Western thought offers us no comparable opportunities.

Nowhere, again, has the problem of world- and life-affirmation, both in itself and in its relation to ethics, been felt in so elemental and comprehensive a fashion as in Chinese thought. Lao-tse, Chwang-tse, Kung-tse (Confucius), Meng-tse, Lie-tse and the rest are thinkers in whom the problems of world-view with which our Western thought is wrestling encounter us in a form, strange indeed, but compelling our attention. Discussing these problems with them means that we ourselves are wrestling with them as well.

That is why I bade our search for a world-view seek to reach clear ideas about itself, and come to a halt in order to fix its attention on the thought of mankind as a whole.

My solution of the problem is that we must make up our minds to renounce completely the optimistic-ethical interpretation of the world. If we take the world as it is, it is impossible to attribute to it a meaning in which the aims and objects of mankind and of individual men have a meaning also. Neither world- and life-affirmation nor ethics can be founded on what our knowledge of the world can tell us about the world. In the world we can discover nothing of any purposive evolution in which our activities can acquire a meaning. Nor is the ethical to be discovered in any form in the world-process. The only advance in knowledge that we can make is to describe more and more minutely the phenomena which make up the world and their implications. To understand the meaning of the whole—and that is what a world-view demands!—is for us an impossibility. The last fact which knowledge can discover is that the world is a manifestation, and in every way a puzzling manifestation, of the universal will to live.

I believe I am the first among Western thinkers who has ventured to recognize this crushing result of knowledge, and the first to be absolutely sceptical about our knowledge of the world without at the same time renouncing belief in world- and life-affirmation and ethics. Resignation as to knowledge of the world is for me not an irretrievable plunge into a scepticism which leaves us to drift about in life like a derelict vessel. I see in it that effort of honesty which we must venture to make in order to arrive at the serviceable world-view which hovers within sight. Every world-view which fails to start from resignation in regard to knowledge is artificial and a mere fabrication, for it rests upon an inadmissible interpretation of the universe.

When once thought has become clear about the relation in which world-view and life-view stand to each other, it is in a position to reconcile resignation as to knowledge with adherence to world- and life-affirmation and ethics. Our view of life is not dependent on our view of the world in the way that uncritical thought imagines. It does not wither away if it cannot send its roots down into a corresponding world-view, for it does not originate in knowledge although it would like to base itself thereon. It can safely depend upon itself alone, for it is rooted in our will-to-live.

World- and life-affirmation and ethics are given in our will-to-live, and they come to be clearly discerned in it in proportion as it learns to think about itself and its relation to the world. The rational thought of other times aimed at getting to know the world, and at being able in that knowledge to conceive of the highest impulses of our will-to-live as purposive in view of the universe and its evolution. But that aim was unattainable. We are not meant to unite the world and ourselves in such harmony with one another. We were naïve enough to assume that our view of life must be contained in our view of the world, but the facts do not justify this assumption. The result is that our thought finds itself involved in a dualism with which it can never be reconciled. It is the dualism of world-view and life-view, of knowing and willing.

To this dualism all the problems with which human thought has busied itself ultimately go back. Every fragment of the thought of mankind which has any bearing on man's conception of the universe—whether in the world-religious or in philosophy—is an attempt to resolve this dualism. It is sometimes softened down, but only to let a unitary, monistic world-view be adopted in its place; at other times it is left standing, but is transformed into a drama with a monistic issue.

Innumerable are the expedients which thought has used in trying to get rid of dualism. Everything it has undertaken commands respect, even the staggering *naïvetés* and the meaningless acts of violence to which it committed itself, for it has always been acting under the compulsion of inner necessity: it wanted to rescue a serviceable world-view from the abyss of dualism.

But from this continuous mishandling of the problem there could issue no solution capable of satisfying thought. We were to be taken over the abyss on tottering bridges of snow.

Instead of going on bridging this abyss with forced logic and imaginative ideas, we must make up our minds to get to the root of the problem and let it bring its influence to bear as it directly encounters us in the facts. The solution is, not to try to get rid of dualism from the world, but to realize that it can no longer do us any harm. This is possible, if we leave behind us all the artifices and unveracities of thought and bow to the fact that, as we cannot harmonize our life-view and our world-view, we must make up our minds to put the former above the latter. The volition which is given in our will-to-live reaches beyond our knowledge of the world. What is decisive for our life-view is not our knowledge of the world but the certainty of the volition which is given in our will-to-live. The eternal spirit meets us in nature as mysterious creative power. In our will-to-live we experience it within us as volition which is both world- and life-affirming and ethical.

Our relation to the world as it is given in the positive certainty of our will-to-live, when this seeks to comprehend itself in thought: that is our world-view. World-view is a product of life-view, not vice versa.

The rational thought of to-day, therefore, does not pursue the phantom of getting to know the world. It leaves knowledge of the world on one side as something for us unattainable, and tries to arrive at clear ideas about the will-to-live which is within us.

The problem of world-view, then, brought back to facts and tackled by rational thought without formulating any hypothesis, may be put thus: "What is the relation of my will-to-live, when it begins to think, to itself and to the world?" And the answer is: "From an inner compulsion to be true to itself and to remain consistent with itself, our will-to-live enters into relations with our own individual being, and with all manifestations of the will-to-live which surround it, that are determined by the sentiment of reverence for life."

Reverence for life, *veneratio vitæ,* is the most direct and at the same time the profoundest achievement of my will-to-live.

In reverence for life my knowledge passes into experience. The simple world- and life-affirmation which is within me just because I am will-to-live has, therefore, no need to enter into controversy with itself, if my will-to-live learns to think and yet does not understand the meaning of the world. In spite of the negative results of knowledge, I have to hold fast to world-

and life-affirmation and deepen it. My life carries its own meaning in itself. This meaning lies in my living out the highest idea which shows itself in my will-to-live, the idea of reverence for life. With that for a starting-point I give value to my own life and to all the will-to-live which surrounds me, I persevere in activity, and I produce values.

Ethics grow out of the same root as world- and life-affirmation, for ethics, too, are nothing but reverence for life. That is what gives me the fundamental principle of morality, namely, that good consists in maintaining, promoting, and enhancing life, and that destroying, injuring, and limiting life are evil. Affirmation of the world, which means affirmation of the will-to-live that manifests itself around me, is only possible if I devote myself to other life. From an inner necessity, I exert myself in producing values and practising ethics in the world and on the world even though I do not understand the meaning of the world. For in world- and life-affirmation and in ethics I carry out the will of the universal will-to-live which reveals itself in me. I live my life in God, in the mysterious divine personality which I do not know as such in the world, but only experience as mysterious Will within myself.

Rational thinking which is free from assumptions ends therefore in mysticism. To relate oneself in the spirit of reverence for life to the multiform manifestations of the will-to-live which together constitute the world is ethical mysticism. All profound world-view is mysticism, the essence of which is just this: that out of my unsophisticated and naïve existence in the world there comes, as a result of thought about self and the world, spiritual self-devotion to the mysterious infinite Will which is continuously manifested in the universe.

This world-affirming, ethical, active mysticism has always been hovering as a vision before Western thought, but the latter could never adopt it because in its search for a world-view it always turned into the wrong road of optimistic-ethical interpretation of the world, instead of reflecting directly on the relation which man assumes to the world under the inner compulsion of the profoundest certainty of his will-to-live.

From my youth onwards, I have felt sure that all thought

which thinks itself out to an issue ends in mysticism. In the stillness of the African jungle I have been able to work out this thought and give it expression.

I come forward therefore with confidence as a restorer of that rational thought which refuses to make assumptions. I know indeed that our time will have absolutely no connection with anything that is in any way rationalistic, and would like to know it renounced as an aberration of the eighteenth century. But the time will come when it will be seen that we must start again where that century came to a stop. What lies between that time and to-day is an intermezzo of thought, an intermezzo with extraordinarily interesting and valuable moments, but nevertheless unhappy and fatal. Its inevitable end was our sinking into a condition in which we had neither a philosophy of life nor civilization, a condition which contains in itself all that spiritual and material misery in which we languish.

The restoration of our world-view can come only as a result of inexorably truth-loving and recklessly courageous thought. Such thinking alone is mature enough to learn by experience how the rational, when it thinks itself out to a conclusion, passes necessarily over into the non-rational. World- and life-affirmation and ethics are non-rational. They are not justified by any corresponding knowledge of the nature of the world, but are the disposition in which, through the inner compulsion of our will-to-live, we determine our relation to the world.

What the activity of this disposition of ours means in the evolution of the world, we do not know. Nor can we regulate this activity from outside; we must leave entirely to each individual its shaping and its extension. From every point of view, then, world- and life-affirmation and ethics are non-rational, and we must have the courage to admit it.

If rational thought thinks itself out to a conclusion, it arrives at something non-rational which, nevertheless, is a necessity of thought. This is the paradox which dominates our spiritual life. If we try to get on without this non-rational element, there result views of the world and of life which have neither vitality nor value.

All valuable conviction is non-rational and has an emotional character, because it cannot be derived from knowledge of the world but arises out of the thinking experience of our will-to-live, in which we stride out beyond all knowledge of the world. This fact it is which the rational thought that thinks itself out to a conclusion comprehends as the truth by which we must live. The way to true mysticism leads up through rational thought to deep experience of the world and of our will-to-live. We must all venture once more to be "thinkers," so as to reach mysticism, which is the only direct and the only profound world-view. We must all wander in the field of knowledge to the point where knowledge passes over into experience of the world. We must all, through thought, become religious.

This rational thought must become the prevailing force among us, for all the valuable ideas that we need develop out of it. In no other fire than that of the mysticism of reverence for life can the broken sword of idealism be forged anew.

In the disposition to reverence for life lies enclosed an elementary conception of responsibility to which we must surrender ourselves; in it there are forces at work which drive us to revision and ennoblement of our individual social and political disposition.

It is the disposition to reverence for life, too, which alone is capable of creating a new consciousness of law. The misery prevailing under our political and social condition is due to a great extent to the fact that neither jurists nor laity have in their minds a living and direct conception of law. During the age of rational thought there was a search made for such a conception, and effort was made to establish fundamental laws which were held to be given in the nature of man, and to get them generally recognized. Later on, however, this endeavour was given up, and laws passed at definite dates displaced natural law. Finally we got to the stage of being satisfied with purely technical law. This was the intermezzo which followed the period of rational thought in the sphere of law.

We have entered on a period in which the feeling for law is hopelessly bereft of force, of soul, and of sense of moral obligation. It is a period of lawlessness. Parliaments produce with easy readiness statutes which contradict the idea of law. States deal arbitrarily with their subjects without regard to the maintenance of any feeling for law. Those, indeed, who fall into the power of a foreign nation are outlaws. No respect is shown for their natural right to a fatherland, or freedom, or dwelling-place, or property, or industry, or food, or anything else. Belief in law is to-day an utter ruin.

This state of things was in preparation from the moment when the search for the natural conception of law, grounded on rational thought, was given up.

The only thing to be done, then, is to make a new connection in the sphere of law also, at the point where the thread of the rational thought of the eighteenth century got broken. We must search for a conception of law that is founded on an idea which grows directly and independently out of a world-view. We have to re-establish human rights which cannot be infringed, human rights which guarantee to each person the greatest possible freedom for his personality within the entity of his own nation, human rights which protect his existence and his human dignity against any foreign violence to which he may be subjected.

Jurists have allowed law and the feeling for law to be ruined. They could not help it, however, for there was no idea provided by the thought of the time to which a living conception of law could have anchored itself. In the complete absence of any world-view, law collapsed entirely, and it is only out of a new world-view that it can be built up again. It is from a fundamental idea about our relation to all that lives, as such, that it must flow in future, as from a spring which can never dry up and never become a swamp. That spring is reverence for life.

Law and ethics spring up together from the same idea. Law is so much of the principle of respect for life as can be embodied in an external code; ethics are what cannot be so embodied. The foundation of law is humanity. It is folly to wish to put out of action the links between law and world-view.

In this way a world-view is the germ of all ideas and dispositions which are determinative for the conduct of individuals and of society.

Aeroplanes carry men to-day through the air over a world in which hunger and brigandage have a place. It is not in China only that one recognizes the grotesque character of such progress: it is almost typical for mankind generally, and such grotesque progress cannot be changed to the normal until there prevails a general disposition capable of bringing order again into the chaos of human life through ethics. In the last resort the practical can be realized only through the ethical.

What a remarkable circle! Rational thought which thinks itself out arrives at something non-rational and subjective which is a necessity of thought, namely the ethical affirmation of world and life. On the other hand, what for the purpose of moulding the conditions of existence for individual men and mankind as a whole is rational, that is to say, what is objectively practical in this regard, can only be brought about by individuals perseveringly putting into action the above-mentioned non-rational and subjective. The non-rational principle underlying our activity, a principle which is provided for us by rational thought, is the sole rational and practical principle underlying all the happenings which are to be produced through human action. Thus the rational and the non-rational, the objective and the subjective, proceed each from the other, and return each into the other again. Only when the play of this mutual interchange is in full activity do normal conditions of existence arise for men and mankind. Let it be disturbed, and the abnormal develops.

So in this book I have written the tragedy of the search for a world-view, and have myself trodden a new path to the same goal. Whereas Western thought has not arrived at any goal because it would not venture resolutely into the desert of scepticism about knowledge of the world, I make my way through this desert with calm confidence. It is, after all, only a narrow strip, and it lies in front of the ever-green oasis of an elemental philosophy of life which grows out of thought about the will-to-live. In my attempt, however, to reach a philosophy of life by this new method, I am conscious of having done no more than put together and think out to conclusions many gropings after this new method which were made by other seekers during the period covered.

But I also put into this book my conviction that mankind must renew itself in a new temper of mind, if it is not to be ruined. I entrust to it, further, my belief that this revolution will come about, if only we can make up our minds to become thinking men.

A new Renaissance must come, and a much greater one than that in which we stepped out of the Middle Ages; a great Renaissance in which mankind discovers that the ethical is the highest truth and the highest practicality, and experiences at the same time its liberation from that miserable obsession by what it calls reality, in which it has hitherto dragged itself along.

I would be a humble pioneer of this Renaissance, and throw the belief in a new humanity, like a torch, into our dark age. I make bold to do this because I believe I have given to the disposition to humanity, which hitherto has ranked only as a noble feeling, a firm foundation in a philosophy of life which is a product of elementary thinking and can be made intelligible to everyone. Moreover, it has gained thereby a power of attracting and convincing which it has not had hitherto; and is capable now of trying conclusions in energetic and consistent fashion with reality, and of proving its full value within it.

ALBERT SCHWEITZER

July 1923

The two instalments of my Philosophy of Civilization which are now ready—*The Decay and Restoration of Civilization* and *Civilization and Ethics*—will be followed by two others. In the next, which will be entitled *The World-view of Reverence for Life,* I elaborate this world-view, which so far I have only sketched for a conclusion to my discussion of the search for a world-view, as carried on down to the present day. The fourth and last will treat of the Civilized State.

Chapter 6

THE CRISIS IN CIVILIZATION AND ITS SPIRITUAL CAUSE

The material and spiritual elements in civilization. Civilization and world-view.

OUR CIVILIZATION IS GOING THROUGH A SEVERE CRISIS. Most people think that the crisis is due to the war,[1] but they are wrong. The war, with everything connected with it, is only a phenomenon of the condition of uncivilization in which we find ourselves. Even in States which took no part in the war, and on which the war had no direct influence, civilization is shaken, only the fact is not so clearly evident in them as in those which were hard hit by the consequences of its peculiarly cruel spiritual and material happenings.

Now, is there any real, live thought going on among us about this collapse of civilization, and about possible ways of working our way up out of it? Scarcely any! Clever men stumble about in seven-league boots in the history of civilization and try to make us understand that civilization is some kind of natural growth which blossoms in definite peoples at definite times and then of necessity withers, so that new peoples with new civilizations must keep replacing those which are worn out. When they are called upon, indeed, to complete their theory by telling us what peoples are destined to be our heirs, they are somewhat embarrassed. There are, in fact, no peoples to be seen whom one could imagine to be capable of even a portion of such a task. All the peoples of the earth have been in large measure under

[1] I.e. the war of 1914–18.

the influence both of our civilization and of our lack of it, so that they more or less share our fate. Among none of them are to be found thoughts which can lead to any considerable original movement of civilization.

Let us put on one side ingenious theories and interesting surveys of the history of civilization, and busy ourselves in a practical way with the problem of our own endangered civilization. What is the nature of this degeneration in our civilization, and why has it come about?

To begin with, there is one elementary fact which is quite obvious. The disastrous feature of our civilization is that it is far more developed materially than spiritually. Its balance is disturbed. Through the discoveries which now place the forces of Nature at our disposal in such an unprecedented way, the relations to each other of individuals, of social groups, and of States have undergone a revolutionary change. Our knowledge and our power have been enriched and increased to an extent that no one would have thought possible. We have thereby been enabled to make the conditions of human existence incomparably more favourable in numerous respects, but in our enthusiasm over our progress in knowledge and power we have arrived at a defective conception of civilization itself. We value too highly its material achievements, and no longer keep in mind as vividly as is necessary the importance of the spiritual element in life. Now come the facts to summon us to reflect. They tell us in terribly harsh language, that a civilization which develops only on its material side, and not in corresponding measure in the sphere of the spirit, is like a ship with defective steering gear which gets out of control at a constantly accelerating pace, and thereby heads for catastrophe.

The essential nature of civilization does not lie in its material achievements, but in the fact that individuals keep in mind the ideals of the perfecting of man, and the improvement of the social and political conditions of peoples, and of mankind as a whole, and that their habit of thought is determined in living and constant fashion by such ideals. Only when individuals work in this way as spiritual forces brought to bear on themselves and on society is the possibility given of solving the problems which have been produced by the facts of life, and of attaining to a general progress which is valuable in every respect. Whether there is rather more or rather less of material achievement to record is not what is decisive for civilization. Its fate depends on whether or not thought keeps control over facts. The issue of a voyage does not depend on whether the vessel's speed is a little faster or a little slower, but on whether it follows the right course, and its steering gear keeps in good condition.

Revolutions in the relations of life between individuals, society, and peoples, as they follow in the train of our great material achievements, if they are to show real progress in the sense of valuable civilization, make higher demands on the habit of thought of civilized people, just as the increased speed of a ship presupposes greater reliability in rudder and steering gear. Advances in knowledge and power work out their effects on us almost as if they were natural occurrences. It is not within our power so to direct them that in every respect they influence favourably the relations in which we live, but they produce for individuals, for society, and for nations, difficult and still more difficult problems, and bring with them dangers which it is quite impossible to estimate in advance. Paradoxical as it may seem, our progress in knowledge and power makes true civilization not easier but more difficult. Judging by the events of our own and the two preceding generations, one might even say that we are almost entitled to doubt whether in view of the way in which these material achievements have been showered upon us, true civilization is still possible.

The most widespread danger which material achievements bring with them for civilization consists in the fact that through the revolutions in the conditions of life men become in greater numbers unfree, instead of free. The type of man who once cultivated his own bit of land becomes a worker who tends a machine in a factory; manual workers and independent tradespeople become employees. They lose the elementary freedom of the man who lives in his own house and finds himself in immediate connection with Mother Earth. Further, they no longer have the extensive and unbroken consciousness of responsibility of those who live by their own independent labour. The conditions of their existence are therefore unnatural. They no longer carry on the struggle for existence in comparatively normal relations in which each one can by his own ability make good his position whether against Nature or against the competition of his fellows, but they see themselves compelled to combine together and create a force which can extort better living conditions. They acquire thereby the mentality of unfree men, in which ideals of civilization can no longer be contemplated with the needful clarity, but become distorted to correspond with the surrounding atmosphere of struggle.

To a certain extent we have all of us, under modern conditions, become unfree men. In every rank of life we have from decade to decade, if not from year to year, to carry on a harder struggle for existence. Overwork, physical or mental or both, is our lot. We can no longer find time to collect and order our thoughts. Our spiritual dependence increases at the same rate as our material dependence. In every direction we are the victims of conditions of dependence which in former times were never known in such universality and such strength. Economic, social, and political organizations, which are steadily becoming more and more complete, are getting us more and more into their power. The State with its increasingly rigid organization holds us under a control which is growing more and more decisive and inclusive. In every respect, therefore, our individual existence is depreciated. It is becoming ever more difficult to be a personality.

Thus it is that the progress of our external civilization brings with it the result that individuals, in spite of all the advantages they get, are thereby in many respects injured both materially and spiritually in their capacity for civilization.

It is our progress in material civilization, too, which intensifies in so disastrous a way our social and political problems. Modern social problems involve us in a class struggle which shakes and shatters economic and national relations. If we go down to rock-bottom, it was machinery and world commerce which brought about the world war, and the inventions which put into our hands such mighty power of destruction made the war of such a devastating character that conquered and conquerors alike are ruined for a period of which no one can see the end. It was also our technical achievements which put us in a position to kill at such a distance, and to annihilate men in such masses, that we sank so low as to push aside any last impulse to humanity, and were mere blind wills which made use of perfected lethal weapons of such destructive capacity that we were unable to maintain the distinction between combatants and non-combatants.

Material achievements, then, are not civilization, but become civilization only so far as the mental habit of civilized peoples is capable of allowing them to aim at the perfecting of the individual and the community. Fooled, however, by our advances in knowledge and power, we did not reflect on the danger to which we were exposing ourselves by the diminished value we put on the spiritual elements in civilization. We surrendered completely to a naïve satisfaction at our magnificent material achievements, and went astray into an incredibly superficial conception of civilization. We believed in a progress which was a matter of course, because contained in the facts themselves. Instead of harbouring in our thought ideals approved by reason, and undertaking to mould reality into accordance with them, we were deluded by a vain conception of reality, and wanted to live with lowered ideals borrowed from it. By taking this course we lost all control over the facts.

Accordingly, just when it was necessary that the spiritual element in civilization should be present in unparalleled strength, we allowed it to waste away.

* * *

But how could it come about that the spiritual element in civilization became so lost to us?

To understand that, we must return to the time when it was at work among us in a direct and living way, and this leads us back into the eighteenth century. Among the Rationalists, who approach everything through reason, and would regulate everything in life by rational considerations, we find expression given in elemental strength to the conviction that the essential element in civilization is a habit of thought. It is true that they are already impressed by modern achievements in discovery and invention, and do allow to the material side of civilization a corresponding importance. But they nevertheless regard it as self-evident that the essential and valuable element in civilization is the spiritual. Their interest is focused first of all on the spiritual progress of men and humanity, and in this they believe with vigorous optimism.

The greatness of these men of the period of the "Aufklärung" lies in the fact that they set up as ideals the perfecting of the individual, of society, and of mankind, and devote themselves to these ideals with enthusiasm. The force on which they count for realizing them is the general habit of thought; they demand of the human spirit that it shall transform men and the relations in which they live, and they trust to it to prove itself stronger than the facts of life.

But whence came the impulse to set up such high ideals of civilization, and their confidence that they would be able to realize them? It came from their conception of the world—from their Weltanschauung.

The Rationalist world-view is optimistic and ethical. Its optimism consists in that it assumes as ruling in the world a general purpose directed to the achievement of perfection, and that from this purposiveness the efforts of individual men and of mankind in general to secure material and spiritual progress derive meaning and importance, and in addition a guarantee of success.

This conception is ethical because it regards the ethical as something in accordance with reason, and on that ground demands from man that, putting egoistic interests behind him, he shall devote himself to all ideals that are waiting for realization, taking the ethical as in everything the standard by which to judge. A habit of humane thought is for the Rationalist an ideal which they can by no consideration be induced to resign.

When, at the close of the eighteenth century and the beginning of the nineteenth, the reaction against rationalism set in and criticism began to play upon it, its optimism was reproached as superficial and its ethics as sentimental. But the spiritual movements which criticize it and take its place cannot develop on the same lines what it accomplished, in spite of its manifold imperfections, by inspiring men with ideals of civilization grounded in reason. The energy of thought about civilization dwindles imperceptibly but steadily. In proportion as the world-view of rationalism is left behind, the feeling for actuality makes its influence felt, until at last, from the middle of the nineteenth century onwards, ideals are borrowed no longer from reason but from actuality, and we therewith sink still further into a state of uncivilization and lack of humanity. This is the clearest and the most important of all the facts which can be established in the history of our civilization.

What has it to tell us? It tells us that there is a close connection between civilization and world-view. Civilization is the product of an optimistic-ethical conception of the world. Only in proportion as the prevalent philosophy is world- and life-affirming and at the same time ethical, do we find ideals of civilization put forward and kept influential in the habits of thought of individuals and of society.

That this inner relation between civilization and the world-view of civilized peoples has never received the attention that it deserves, is the result of there having been among us so little real meditation on the essential nature of civilization.

What then is civilization? It is the sum total of all progress made by men and the individual man in every sphere of action and from every point of view, in so far as this progress helps towards the spiritual perfecting of individuals as the progress of all progress.

The impulse to strive for progress in all spheres of action and from every point of view comes to men from an optimistic philosophy which affirms the world and life to be valuable in themselves, and consequently bears within itself a compulsion to raise to its highest possible value all that exists in so far as it can be influenced by us. Hence come will and hope, and effort directed to the improvement of the condition of individuals and of society, of peoples and of mankind. This leads to a lordship of the spirit over the powers of Nature, to the perfecting of the religious, social, economic, and practical association of men, and the spiritual perfecting of individuals and of the community.

Just as the world- and life-affirming, that is to say, the optimistic philosophy of life, is alone capable of stirring men to effort aimed at promoting civilization, so in an ethical world-view alone is there latent the power to make men, after renouncing altogether their selfish interests, persevere in such effort, and to keep them always bent on the spiritual and moral perfecting of the individual as the essential object of civilization. Bound the one to the other, then, world- and life-affirming world-view and ethics think out in harmony the ideals of true, complete civilization and set to work at realizing them.

If civilization remains incomplete or its level falls, this rests in the last resort on the fact that either the world- and life-affirmation of the world-view, or its ethics, or both, have remained undeveloped or have declined. And that is the case with us. It is evident that the ethics required for civilization have gone out of use.

For decades we have been accustoming ourselves increasingly to measure with relative ethical standards, and no longer to allow ethics to have their say in all questions alike. We regard this renunciation of consistent ethical judgment as an advance in practicality.

But our world- and life-affirmation also have become shaky. The modern man no longer feels under any compulsion to think about and to will ideals of progress. To a large extent he has come to terms with actuality. He is much more resigned than he admits to himself, and in one respect he is even outspokenly pessimistic. For he really no longer believes in the spiritual and ethical progress of men and of mankind, which is nevertheless the essential element in civilization.

This stunting of our world- and life-affirmation and of our ethics has its cause in the character of our world-view, in regard to which we have been going through a crisis since the middle of the nineteenth century. It is no longer possible for us to arrive at a conception of the universe in which the meaning of the existence of men and of mankind can be recognized, and in which, therefore, there are also contained the ideals which flow from thoughtful world- and life-affirmation and from ethical volition. We are falling more and more into a condition of having no world-view at all, and from this deficiency comes our lack of civilization.

The great question for us is, therefore, whether we have to renounce permanently the world-view which carries within it in all their strength the ideal of the perfecting of individual men and of mankind, and the ideal of ethical effort. If we succeed in re-establishing a world-view in which world- and life-affirmation is given in convincing fashion, we shall master the decay of civilization which is in progress, and reach again a true and living civilization. Otherwise we are condemned to see the wreck of all attempts to arrest the degeneration. Only when the truth that renewal of civilization can only come by a renewal of our outlook on life becomes a universal conviction, and when a new longing for a world-view sets in, shall we find ourselves on the right path. But this is not yet in prospect. The modern man is still without any correct feeling for the full significance of the fact, that he is living with an unsatisfactory philosophy, or without any at all. The unnatural and dangerous character of this condition must first be brought home to his consciousness, just as those persons who exhibit disturbances of the stability of their nervous system have to be clearly told that their vitality is threatened although they feel no pain. Similarly, we have to stir up the men of to-day to elementary meditation upon what man is in the world, and what he wants to make of his life. Only when they are impressed once more with the necessity of giving meaning and value to their existence, and thus come once more to hunger and thirst for a satisfying world-view, are the preliminaries given for a spiritual condition in which we again become capable of civilization.

But in order to learn the way to a satisfactory philosophy of life, we must see clearly why the struggle undertaken by the European spirit to secure it was for a time successful, but during the second half of the nineteenth century came to an unfortunate end.

Because our thinking is too little occupied with civilization, it has been insufficiently noticed that the essential aspect of the history of philosophy is the history of man's struggle for a satisfactory world-view. Thus regarded, this history unrolls itself like a tragic drama.

Chapter 7

THE PROBLEM OF THE OPTIMISTIC WORLD-VIEW

The Western and the Indian conceptions of civilization.

The struggle for the optimistic world-view.

Optimism and pessimism.

Optimism, pessimism and ethics.

FOR US WESTERNERS CIVILIZATION CONSISTS IN THIS: THAT WE WORK simultaneously for the perfecting of ourselves and of the world.

But do the activities that are directed outwards and inwards necessarily belong together? Cannot the spiritual and moral perfecting of the individual, which is the ultimate aim of civilization, also be secured if he works for himself alone, and leaves the world and its circumstances to themselves? Who gives us any guarantee that the course of the world can be influenced so as to promote the special aim of civilization, the perfecting of the individual? Who tells us that it has any meaning at all which can be further developed? Is not any action of mine which is directed on the world a diversion of what could be directed on myself, on whom finally everything depends?

Moved by these doubts, the pessimism of the Hindus and of Schopenhauer refuses to allow any importance to the material and social achievements which form the outward and visible part of civilization. About society, nation, mankind, the individual is not to trouble himself; he is only to strive to experience in himself the sovereignty of spirit over matter.

This, too, is civilization, in that it pursues its own final object, namely, the spiritual and ethical perfecting of the individual. If we Westerners pronounce it incomplete, we must not do so too confidently. Do the outward progress of mankind and the moral and spiritual perfecting of the individual really belong together as we imagine? Are we not, under an illusion, forcing together things which are different in kind? Does the victory of the spirit in one kind of action actually bring about some gain for the other?

What we set up as our ideal, we have not realized. We have lost ourselves in outward progress, allowing all advance in the moral life and inwardness of the individual to come to a standstill. So we have not been able to produce practical proof of the correctness of our view of what civilization is. We cannot, therefore, simply put aside that other narrower conception, but must come to terms with it.

There will come a time—it is already being prepared for—when pessimistic and optimistic thought, which have hitherto talked past each other almost as strangers, will have to meet for practical discussion. World-philosophy is just dawning. It will shape itself in a struggle as to whether its philosophy of life shall be optimistic or pessimistic.

* * *

The history of Western philosophy is the history of the struggle for an optimistic outlook on life. If in antiquity and in modern times the peoples of Europe have managed to produce a civilization, it is because the optimistic world-view was dominant in their thought, and held the pessimistic permanently in subjection, although it was not able to suppress it altogether.

The accessions of knowledge which have come in the course of our philosophy have been nothing in themselves: they always stand in the service of one world-view or the other, and only in it attain to their real significance.

But the characteristic thing about the way in which the dispute is conducted on each occasion is that it never is settled in the open. The two world-views are never brought face to face and the case of each heard. That the optimistic alone is in the right is a conviction which is accepted as more or less self-evident. The only thing felt as a problem is how to marshal all possible knowledge in the triumphal procession of proof to defeat the other, and how to knock on the head anything that may still wish to rise in its defence.

Since the pessimistic world-view has never made its presence properly felt, Western thought manifests a lofty unwillingness to understand it, though it has a splendid flair for detecting it. Where it finds, as in Spinoza, too little interest for activity directed upon the world, it reacts immediately by rejecting it. Yet all objectively thinking investigation of the reality of nature is disliked in the West because it may lead to the central position of the human spirit in the universe being insufficiently emphasized. It is because materialism seems likely to be the last ally of pessimism, that Western thought carries on so embittered a struggle against it.

In the discussion of the problem of the theory of knowledge from Descartes to Kant and beyond him, it is really the cause of the optimistic world-view which is being maintained. That is why the theoretical possibility of a depreciation or a denial of the world of sense is attacked with such obstinacy. By proving the ideality of space and time, Kant hopes to make finally secure the optimistic world-view of rationalism with all its ideals and demands. Only thus can it be explained that the most penetrating examinations of the theory of knowledge are carried through with the most naïve conclusions about world-view. The great post-Kantian systems of thought, however much they differ from one another in their subject-matter and the process of the speculation with which they deal with it, are all united in this, that in their cloud-castles they crown the optimistic world-view as the ruler of the universe.

To fit in the aims of mankind with those of the universe in a logically convincing fashion: that is the endeavour in which European philosophy serves the optimistic world-view. Anyone who does not help, or who is indifferent about it, is an enemy.

In its prejudice against scientific materialism philosophy was right. Materialism has done much more to shake the position of the optimistic world-view than has Schopenhauer, although it never proceeded against it with outspoken hostility. When, after the collapse of the great systems, it was allowed to seat itself at table with philosophy, which had now become more modest, it even exerted itself to find out in what tone the latter would like the conversation to be carried on. In dealing with Darwin and others, philosophizing natural science made touchingly naïve attempts so to extend and stretch out the history of zoological development which led up to man, that mankind and with it the spiritual should appear again as the goal of the world-process, as in the speculative systems. But in spite of these well-meant efforts of materialism, the proletarian guest, the conversation could no longer be carried on in the old spirit. Of what use was it for this guest to try to be better than his reputation? He brought with him more respect for nature and facts than was consistent with the convincing establishment of the optimistic world-view. He therefore shook it, even when he did not intend to.

To such a disregard of nature and science as was shown by the earlier philosophy we can never return. Nor can we expect the return of a system of thought which makes it possible to discover in any convincing way in the universe the aims and objects of mankind, as was allowed by the old methods. The optimistic world-view ceases, therefore, to be self-evident to us, or to be demonstrable by the arts of philosophy. It must renounce the attempt to find for itself a solid foundation.

* * *

Confusion is caused by the fact that in the history of human thought the optimistic and pessimistic world-views seldom come forward pure and unadulterated. Their relations are usually such that the one is predominant, while the other has a voice in the matter without being officially recognized. In India a tolerated world- and life-affirmation maintains for pessimism something of interest in the external civilization which pessimism nominally denies. With us it slips in and gnaws at the civilizing energies of the optimistic view, with the result that belief in the spiritual progress of mankind has left us. From pessimism, too, comes the fact that we everywhere conduct the business of life with lowered ideals.

Pessimism is depreciated will-to-live, and is to be found wherever man and society are no longer under the pressure of all those ideals of progress which must be thought out by a will-to-live that is consistent with itself, but have sunk to the level of letting actuality be, over wide stretches of life, nothing but actuality.

It is where pessimism is at work in this anonymous fashion, that it is most dangerous to civilization. It attacks then the most valuable ideas belonging to life-affirmation, leaving the less valuable untouched. Like some concealed source of magnetic power, it disturbs the world-view's compass, so that it takes a wrong course without suspecting it. Thus the unavowed mixture of optimism and pessimism in our thought has the result that we continue to approve the external blessings given us by civilization, things which to thinking pessimism are a matter of indifference, while we abandon that which alone it holds to be valuable, the pursuit of inner perfection. The desire for progress which is directed to objects of sense, goes on functioning because it is nourished by actuality, while that which reaches after the spiritual becomes exhausted, because it is thrown back upon the inner stimulus which comes from the thinking will-to-live. As the tide ebbs, objects which reach deep down are left stranded, while flat ones remain afloat.

Our degeneration, then, traced back to our world-view and what resulted from it, is due to the fact that true optimism, without our noticing it, has disappeared from among us. We are by no means a race weakened and decadent through excessive enjoyment of life, and needing to pull ourselves together to show vigour and idealism amid the thunderstorms of history. But although we have retained our vigour in most departments of the direct activities of life, we are spiritually stunted. Our conception of life with all that depends on it has been lowered both for individuals and for the community. The higher forces of volition and influence are impotent in us, because the optimism from which they ought to draw their strength has become imperceptibly permeated with pessimism.

A characteristic feature of the presence at the same time of optimism and pessimism as lodgers in "Thoughtless House" is that each goes about in the other's clothes, so that what is really pessimism gives itself out among us as optimism, and vice versa. What passes for optimism with the mass of people is the natural or acquired faculty of seeing things in the best possible light, this being the result of lowered ideals for the future no less than for the present. A person ill with consumption is brought by the poison of the disease into the condition which is called Euphoria, so that he experiences an imaginary feeling of health and strength. Similarly there is an external optimism present in individuals and in society just in proportion as they are, without realizing it, infected with pessimism.

True optimism has nothing to do with any sort of lenient judgment. It consists in contemplating and willing the ideal in the light of a deep and self-consistent affirmation of life and the world. Because the spirit which is so directed proceeds with clear vision and impartial judgment in the valuing of all that is given, it wears to ordinary people the appearance of pessimism. That it wishes to pull down the old temples in order to build them again more magnificently, is by vulgar optimism put down to its discredit as sacrilege.

The reason, then, why the only legitimate optimism, that of volition inspired by imagination, has to carry on such a hard struggle with pessimism is that it always has first to track the latter down in vulgar optimism and unmask it. That is a task which optimism has never finished. Never must it think it is at an end. For so long as it allows the enemy to emerge in any shape whatever, there is danger for civilization. When that happens, activity in promoting the special aims of civilization always diminishes, even if satisfaction with its material achievements remains as strong as before.

Optimism and pessimism, therefore, do not consist in counting with more or less confidence on a future for the existing state of things, but in what the will desires the future to be. They are qualities not of the judgment, but of the will. The fact that up to now the inadmissible definition of optimism and pessimism was current side by side with the correct one, so that there were four items to deal with instead of two, made the game easier for the unthinking by deceiving us about what true optimism is. Pessimism of the will they passed off as optimism of the judgment, and optimism of the will they put aside as pessimism of the judgment. These false cards must be taken from them, so that they may not continue to deceive the world in such a fashion.

* * *

In what relation do optimism and pessimism stand to ethics?

That close and peculiar relations do exist between them is clear from the fact that in the thought of mankind the two struggles, that for optimistic or pessimistic world-view and that about ethics, are usually involved in each other. It is the general belief that when the one issue is being fought out the other is being fought as well.

This mutual connection is very convenient for thought. When a foundation for ethics is being laid, optimistic or pessimistic arguments are unconsciously pressed into the service, as are ethical arguments when optimism or pessimism have to be established. In this process Western thought lays most stress on justifying a life-affirming—that is to say an activist—ethical system and thinks that merely by doing so it has proved the case for optimism in its world-view. For Indian thought the most important thing is to find a logical foundation for pessimism; and the justifying of a life-denying—that is to say a passivist—ethical system, is rather a derivative from that.

The confusion which resulted from the struggles for optimism and pessimism and for ethics not being kept distinct, has contributed almost more than anything else to prevent the thought of mankind from attaining to clarity.

It was an easy mistake to make. For the question whether it is to be affirmation or negation of life and the world, crops up in ethics in the same way as in the dispute between optimism and pessimism. Things which by their nature belong together feel themselves drawn together, so that optimism naturally thinks it can support itself on an affirmative ethical system, and pessimism thinks the same about a negative one. Nevertheless, the result has hitherto always been that neither of these two closely-related entities could stand firm, because neither of them chose to depend on itself alone.

Chapter 8

THE ETHICAL PROBLEM

The difficulties of ethical perception.

The importance of thought about ethics.

The search for a basic principle of morality.

Religious and philosophical ethics.

HOW CAME MANKIND TO REFLECT ON MORALITY AND TO MAKE progress in that sphere of thought?

It is a picture of confusion that unrolls itself before the eyes of anyone who undertakes a journey through the history of man's search for the ethical. Progress in moral thought is inexplicably slow and uncertain. That the scientific view of the world could be delayed in its rise and development is to a certain extent intelligible, for its advance depended more or less on the chance of there existing gifted observers, whose discoveries in the realm of the exact sciences and the knowledge of nature was needed, to begin with, to provide new horizons and to point out new paths for thought.

But in ethics thought is thrown back entirely on itself: it has to do only with man himself and his self-development, which goes on by a process of causation from within. Why, then, does it not make better progress? Just because man himself is the material which has to be investigated and moulded.

Ethics and æsthetics are the step-children of philosophy. They both deal with a subject which is coy about submitting itself to reflection, for they both treat of spheres in which man exercises his purely creative activities. In science man observes and describes the course of nature, and tries to penetrate its mysteries. In practical matters he uses and moulds it by applying what he has grasped of it outside his own person. But in his moral and artistic activities he uses knowledge and obeys impulses, perceptions, and laws which originate in himself. To establish these firmly and from them to create ideals, is an undertaking which can be successful to a certain extent only. Thought lags behind the material on which it exercises itself.

This is evident from the fact that the examples with which ethics and æsthetics try to work upon reality are usually not quite consistent and are often foolish. And how far from simple are their assertions! How they contradict each other! The guidance that an artist can get for his activities from the best works on æsthetics is but small. Similarly, a business man who seeks in a work on ethics advice as to how, in any given case, he is to bring the demands of his business into harmony with those of ethics, can seldom find any satisfactory information.

The inadequacy of æsthetics is not of great importance for the spiritual life of mankind. Artistic activity is always the peculiar affair of individuals, whose natural gifts are developed more by the study of actual works of art than by consideration of the conclusions arrived at by æsthetic theorizing.

With ethics, however, it is a matter of the creative activity of the mass of men, an activity which is largely determined by the principles which are current in the general thought of the time. The absence of that progress which is still possible in ethics is tragic.

Ethics and æsthetics are not sciences. Science, as the description of objective facts, the establishment of their connection with one another, and the drawing of inferences from them, is only possible when there is a succession of similar facts to be dealt with, or a single fact in a succession of phenomena, when, that is to say, there is subject matter which can be reduced to order under a recognized law. But there is no science of human willing and doing, and there never can be. Here there are only subjective and infinitely various facts to be studied, and their mutual connection lies within the mysterious human ego.

It is only the history of ethics that can be regarded as a science, and that only in so far as a history of man's spiritual life is scientifically possible.

* * *

There is, therefore, no such thing as a scientific system of ethics; there can only be a thinking one. Philosophy must give up the illusion which it has cherished even down to the present day. As to what is good and what is bad, and about the considerations in which we find strength to do the one and avoid the other, no one can speak to his neighbour as an expert. All that one can do is to impart to him so much as one finds in oneself of that which ought to influence everybody, though better thought out perhaps, and stronger and clearer, so that noise has become a musical note.

Is there, however, any sense in ploughing for the thousand and second time a field which has already been ploughed a thousand and one times? Has not everything which can be said about ethics already been said by Lao-tse, Confucius, the Buddha, and Zarathustra; by Amos and Isaiah; by Socrates, Plato, and Aristotle; by Epicurus and the Stoics; by Jesus and Paul; by the thinkers of the Renaissance, of the "Aufklärung," and of Rationalism; by Locke, Shaftesbury, and Hume; by Spinoza and Kant; by Fichte and Hegel; by Schopenhauer, Nietzsche, and others? Is there a possibility of getting beyond all these contradictory convictions of the past to new beliefs which will have a stronger and more lasting influence? Can the ethical kernel of the thoughts of all these men be collected into an idea of the ethical, which will unite all the energies to which they appeal? We must hope so, if we are not to despair of the fate of the human race.

Does thought about ethics bring more ethics into the world? The confused picture offered us by the history of ethics is enough to make one sceptical. On the other hand, it is clear that ethical thinkers like Socrates, Kant, or Fichte had a moralizing influence on many of their contemporaries. From every revival of ethical reflection there went forth ethical movements which made the contemporary generation fitter for its tasks. If any age lacks the minds which force it to reflect about the ethical, the level of its morality sinks, and with it its capacity for answering the questions which present themselves.

In the history of ethical thought we wander in the innermost circles of world-history. Of all the forces which mould reality, morality is the first and foremost. It is the determining knowledge which we must wring from thought. Everything else is more or less secondary.

For this reason everyone who believes that he can contribute something to help forward the ethical self-consciousness of society and of individuals has the right to speak now, although it is political and economic questions that the present day prescribes for study. For what is inopportune is really opportune. We can accomplish something lasting in the problems of political and economic life only if we approach them as men who are trying to think ethically. All those who in any way help forward our thought about ethics are working for the coming of peace and prosperity in the world. They are engaged in the higher politics, and the higher national economics, and even if all they can do is nothing more than to bring ethical thinking to the fore, they have nevertheless done something valuable. All reflection about ethics has as one result a raising and rousing of the general disposition to morality.

* * *

But however certain it is that every age lives by the energies which have sprung from its thought about ethics, it is equally certain that up to now the ethical thoughts which have become current after a longer or shorter period have lost their power of convincing. Why has the establishment of an ethical system never met with more than a partial and temporary success, and never become a permanency? Why is the history of the ethical thinking of mankind the history of inexplicable stoppages and retrogressions? Why has there been no organic progress to allow one period to build upon the achievements of preceding ones? Why in the sphere of ethics do we live in a city of ruins, in which, to provide for its barest needs, one generation builds for itself here, and another there.

"To preach morality is easy, to give it a foundation is hard," says Schopenhauer, and that saying shows the nature of the problem.

In every effort of thought about ethics there is to be seen, distinctly or indistinctly, the search for a basic principle of morality, which needs no support outside itself, and unites in itself the sum total of all moral demands. But no one has ever succeeded in really formulating this principle. Only elements of it have been brought to light and given out to be the whole, until the difficulties which emerged destroyed the illusion. The tree, however finely it sprouted, did not live to grow old, because it was unable to send its roots down into the permanently nourishing and moisture-giving earth.

The chaos of ethical views becomes to some extent intelligible as soon as one sees that we are concerned with differing and mutually contradictory opinions about fragments of the basic principle. The contradiction lies in their incompleteness. There is ethical matter in what Kant objects to in the ethics of rationalism, as also in what he puts in its place; in that part of Kant's writings where his conception of the moral is opposed by Schopenhauer, as also in what is to take its place in the ethical system of the latter. Schopenhauer is ethical in the points on which Nietzsche attacks him, and Nietzsche is ethical in his opposition to Schopenhauer. What is wanted is to find the fundamental chord in which the dissonances of these varied and contradictory ethical ideas unite in producing harmony.

The ethical problem, then, is the problem of a basic principle of morality founded in thought. What is the common element of good in the manifold things which we feel to be good? Is there such a universally valid conception of the good? If there is, in what does it consist, and how far is it real and necessary for me? What influence has it over my general disposition and my actions? Into what relations with the world does it bring me?

It is, then, on the basic principle of the moral that the attention of thought has to be fixed. The mere giving of a list of virtues and duties is like striking notes at random on the piano and thinking it is music. And when we come to discuss the works of earlier moralists, it is only the elements in them which can help the establishment of an ethical system that will interest us, not the way in which any system has been advocated.

Otherwise there can be no success for any attempt to bring order into chaos. How utterly at sea is Friedrich Jodl[1] in his history of ethics, the most important existing work in this de-

[1] Friedrich Jodl: *A History of Ethics as Philosophical Science,* 2nd ed., 2 vols. (Vol. I., 1906; Vol. II., 1912). It treats of the ethics of Western philosophy only.

partment, when he tries to estimate the relative values of the various ethical standpoints! Failing to judge them directly by their distance from an initial basic principle of morality, he is unable to establish a standard of comparison. He gives us, therefore, only a survey of ethical views, not a history of the ethical problem.

* * *

In the search for the fundamental principle of morality, are we concerned only with the direct attempts of philosophy to find it? No, we are concerned with every attempt of the kind, those of religion as well as others. We must pass through the whole experience of mankind in its search for the ethical.

The raising of a dividing wall between philosophical ethics and religious ethics is based on the mistaken idea that the former are scientific and the latter non-scientific. But neither of them is either: they are both alike simply thought; only the one has freed itself from acceptance of the traditional religious world-view, while the other still maintains its connection with it.

The difference, however, is merely relative. Religious ethics appeal, indeed, to a supernatural authority, but that is rather the form which they assume. As a matter of fact, however high they rise, they will seek to find an independent basic principle of morality. In every religious genius there lives an ethical thinker, and every really deep philosophical moralist is in some way or other religious.

How indeterminate is the border-line, is shown by Indian ethics. Are they religious, or are they philosophical? Originating in the thought of the priests, they claim to be a deeper exposition of the demands of religion, but in essential nature they are philosophical. With the Buddha and others, they venture to make the step from pantheism to atheism, but without giving up their claim to be religious. Spinoza and Kant, however, who are counted among philosophical moralists, do, if we judge by the general direction of their thought, belong at the same time to the realm of religious ethics.

It all depends on a relative difference in methods of thought. The one group works towards the basic principle of ethics by a more intuitive process, the other by a process which is more analytical. It is the depth, not the method of the thought, which decides the matter. The more intuitive thinker produces his ethical thought like an artist who with the production of an important work of art opens up new horizons. In deep-reaching moral sayings, like the beatitudes of Jesus, the basic principle of morality shines out. There comes progress in the recognition of what is moral, even if the provision of a foundation for it fails to advance in the same way.

On the other hand, the search for the basic principle of the moral by a process of critical analysis may lead to an impoverished system of ethics, because there runs through it the effort to take into account only what is connected with the idea that seems to be what is being sought for. That is why philosophical ethics are as a rule so far behind practical ethics, and have so little direct influence. While religious moralists with one mighty word can get down to the waters flowing far below the surface, philosophical ethics often dig out nothing but a slight hollow in which a puddle forms.

Nevertheless, it is rational thinking alone which is able to pursue the search for the basic principle with perseverance and hope of success. It must find it at last, if it only goes deep enough, and is sufficiently simple.

The weakness of all ethics hitherto, whether philosophical or religious, has lain in this, that they have not shown individuals how to deal directly and naturally with reality. To a large extent they merely talk "about it and about." They do not touch a man's daily experience, and therefore they exert no permanent pressure upon him. The result is lack of ethical thought, and mere platitudes about ethics.

The true basic principle of the ethical must be not only something universally valid, but something absolutely elementary and inward, which, once it has dawned upon a man, never relinquishes its hold, which as a matter of course runs like a thread through all his meditation, which never lets itself be thrust aside, and which continually challenges him to try conclusions with reality.

For centuries men who navigated the seas guided themselves by the stars. In time they rose above this imperfect method through the discovery of the magnetic needle, which by its natural principle of activity pointed them to the north. Now they can tell where they are in the darkest night on the most distant sea. That is the kind of progress that we have to seek in ethics. So long as we have nothing but an ethical system of ethical sayings, we direct our course by stars, which, however brilliant their radiance, give us only more or less reliable guidance, and can be hidden from us by rising mist. During a stormy night, as we know by recent experiences, they leave mankind in the lurch. If, however, we have in our possession a system of ethics which is a necessity of thought and a principle which comes to clearness within ourselves, there begins a far-reaching ethical deepening of the consciousness of individuals, and steady ethical progress in mankind.

Chapter 9

RELIGIOUS AND PHILOSOPHICAL WORLD-VIEWS

The world-views of the world-religions.

The world-views of the world-religions and that of Western thought.

IN THE WORLD-RELIGIONS WE CAN SEE POWERFUL ATTEMPTS TO establish an ethical world-view.

The religious thinkers of China, Lao-tse (born 604 B.C.), Kung-tse (Confucius, 551–479 B.C.), Meng-tse (372–289 B.C.), and Chwang-tse (fourth century B.C.), all try to base the ethical on a world- and life-affirming nature-philosophy. In so doing they arrive at a world-view which, because it is optimistic-ethical, contains incentives to inward and outward civilization.

The religious thinkers of India also, the Brahmans, the Buddha (560–480 B.C.), and the Hindus, start, like the Chinese, from reflection on existence, that is to say, from nature-philosophy. They do not, however, take a world- and life-affirming, but a world- and life-denying, view of it. Their world-view is pessimistic-ethical, and contains, therefore, incentives only to the inward civilization of the heart, not to outward civilization as well.

Chinese and Indian piety recognize but a single world-principle. They are monistic and pantheistic. Their world-view has to solve the problem of how far we can recognize the original source of the world as ethical, and how far, correspondingly, we become ethical by the surrender to it of our will.

In contrast to these monistic-pantheistic world-views, we find a dualistic outlook on life in the religion of Zarathustra (sixth century B.C.), in that of the Jewish prophets (from the eighth century B.C. onwards), and in those of Jesus and Mohammed, this last, however, showing itself to be in all points unoriginal and decadent. These religious thinkers do not start from an investigation of the existence which manifests itself in the universe, but from a view of the ethical which is quite independent. They put it in opposition to natural happenings. Accordingly they assume the existence of two world-principles, the natural and the ethical. The first is in the world, and has to be overcome; the other is incorporated in an ethical personality which is outside the world and endowed with final authority.

If among the Chinese and the Hindus the basic principle of morality was life in harmony with the world-will, so among dualists it is an attempt to be different from the world in harmony with an ethical divine personality outside and above the world.

The weakness of dualistic religions is that their world-view, because it rejects every kind of nature-philosophy, is always naïve. Their strength lies in the fact that they have the ethical within themselves, directly present and with undiminished force. They have no need to strain it and explain it, as must the monists, in order to be able to conceive it as an effluence from the world-will which reveals itself in nature.

The world-views of the dualistic world-religions, taken as a whole, are optimistic. They live in the confident belief that ethical force will prove superior to natural, and so raise the world and mankind to true perfection. Zarathustra and the older Jewish prophets represent this process as a kind of world-reform. The optimistic element in their world-view asserts itself in a quite natural way. They have the will, and the hope, of being able to transform human society and make the races of the world fit for their higher destiny. Progress in any department of life means for them something gained, for they think of inward and outward civilization together.

With Jesus the value of the optimistic element in his world-view is impaired by the fact, that he looks forward to the perfected world as the result of a catastrophic end to the natural one, and while with Zarathustra and the older Jewish prophets the Divine intervention is to a certain extent only the completion of the human activities which have been directed to the perfecting of the world, it is with Jesus the only thing which has to be taken into account. The kingdom of God is to appear in a supernatural way; it is not prepared for by any effort made by mankind to attain to civilization.

The world-view of Jesus, because it is fundamentally optimistic, accepts the ends aimed at by outward civilization. But biased by the expectation of the end of the world, it is indifferent to all attempts made to improve the temporal, natural world by a civilization which organizes itself on lines of outward progress, and concerns itself only with the inward ethical perfecting of individuals.

Just in proportion, however, as the Christian world-view realizes the consequences of the fact that the world has not come to an end, and accepts the idea that the kingdom of God must be established by a process of development which transforms the natural world, it begins to understand and be interested in the completing of social organization, and in all such progress in outward civilization as contributes to it. The optimistic element in the world-view can again work unhindered side by side with the ethical. Thus we get an explanation of the fact that Christianity, which in the ancient world showed itself hostile to civilization, seeks in modern times with more or less success to conduct itself as the world-view of true progress in every sphere of activity.

* * *

The questions which press for an answer from the world-religions in their struggle to reach an ethical and an optimistic-ethical world-view, are the same as those which present themselves also to Western philosophy. The great problem is to think out a connection between the universe and ethics.

The three types of world-view which show themselves in the world-religions, recur also in Western philosophy. The latter, too, attempts to find an ethical code either in a world- and life-affirming, or in a world- and life-denying, nature-philosophy, or it attempts, more or less completely setting aside all nature-philosophy, to reach a world-view which is in itself ethical. Only, it at the same time does its best to avoid acknowledging, and indeed to conceal, the naïve and dualistic element which is inevitably encountered when this last method of procedure is followed.

The world-views, then, of the world-religions, and of Western philosophy, do not belong to different worlds, but stand in close inward relations to one another. After all, the distinction between a religious world-view and a philosophical is quite superficial. The religious world-view which seeks to comprehend itself in thought becomes philosophical, as is the case among the Chinese and the Hindus. On the other hand a philosophical world-view, if it is really profound, assumes a religious character.

Although Western thought does, in principle, approach the problem of world-view without any presuppositions, it has not been able to keep itself entirely uninfluenced by religious conceptions of the universe. From Christianity it has received impulses of a decisive character, and the attempt to transform the naïve-ethical world-view of Jesus into a philosophical system has cost it more attention and effort than it admits to itself. With Schopenhauer and his successors the pessimistic monism of India finds expression, and it enriches their reflection upon the nature of the ethical.

Thus the energies of all the great world-views stream into Western thought. Through the co-operation of these varied forms of thought and energy it is enabled to exalt into a universal conviction the optimistic-ethical concept which hovers before its mind, and that too in a strength which it has never displayed in any previous age or in any other part of the world. And that is why the West has advanced farthest both in inward and outward civilization.

To give a real foundation to the optimistic-ethical world-view, Western thought is indeed as little able as were any of the world-religions. Because the West experiences the problem of world-view in its most universal and most pressing form, it is the scene of the greatest advances made by the civilized mind, but also of its greatest catastrophes. It experiences portentous changes in its world-view, and is familiar, too, with terrible periods when it has no philosophy of life at all.

It is because Western thought is so sensitive in all directions, that it reveals most clearly the questions and difficulties amid which the search for an optimistic world-view moves.

To what extent does the history of our thought give to us Westerners the explanation of our fate? What road does it indicate to us as the best for our future search for a world-view in which the individual can find inwardness and strength, and mankind progress and peace?

Chapter 10

CIVILIZATION AND ETHICS IN THE GRÆCO-ROMAN PHILOSOPHY

The beginnings: Socrates.
Epicureanism and Stoicism. The ethic of resignation.
Plato's abstract basic principle of the ethical. The ethic of world-negation.
Aristotle. Instruction about virtue in place of ethics.
The ideal of the civilized state in Plato and Aristotle.
Seneca, Epictetus and Marcus Aurelius.
The optimistic-ethical world-view of the later Stoicism.

IN THE SEVENTH CENTURY BEFORE CHRIST THE GREEK SPIRIT BEGINS to free itself from the conception of the universe which underlay the traditional religion, and undertakes to base its world-view on a foundation of knowledge and thought.

First there comes a nature-philosophy, the result of investigation of Being and reflection upon what it really is. Then criticism begins its work. Belief in the gods is found unsatisfying, not only because the course of nature is not made intelligible by the rule of dwellers in Olympus, but also because these personalities no longer answer to the demands of feeling which is thoughtful and moral. These two elements, nature-philosophy and criticism, are found united in Xenophanes and Heraclitus in the sixth century B.C.

In the course of the fifth century B.C. the Sophists appear, and begin to concern themselves critically with the accepted standards of value current for social life and individual activities.[1] The result is annihilating. The more moderate of these "Enlighteners" proclaim the overwhelming majority of these standards which pass for moral to be merely claims made by society on its members, leaving open thereby the possibility that a small remainder may be able to prove themselves to rational consideration as moral in themselves. But the younger radical Sophists maintain the position that all morality, like all current law, has been invented by organized society in its own interest. Hence the thinking man who is freeing himself from this tutelage will make his own moral standards, and will follow in them nothing but his own pleasure and his own interests. Thus Western philosophical thought about the problem of ethics and civilization starts with shrill dissonance.

What was Socrates (470–399 B.C.) able to contribute, when he came forward to oppose this tendency?

In the place of the simply pleasurable he put the rationally pleasurable.

By rational consideration, he asserts, it is possible to establish a standard of action in which the happiness of the individual, rightly understood, is in harmony with the interests of society. Virtue consists in right knowledge.

That the rationally moral is that which procures for the person concerned true pleasure, or, what means the same thing, true profit, Socrates draws out into the most diverse applications in the simple everyday discussions which Xenophon has transmitted to us in his *Memorabilia*.[2] The dialogues of Plato show

[1] Very important for our knowledge of the old philosophy and ethics are the ten books entitled *The Lives and Teaching of Famous Philosophers*, composed by Diogenes Laertius in the third century after Christ. Just because they are purely anecdotal, they have preserved for us much information and many views which otherwise—for the works of the philosophers treated of have all been lost—we should not possess.

[2] Xenophon, one of the generals who led the ten thousand back from Asia, wrote down his recollections of Socrates after the latter's death. By his report of the simple conversations of the Master, he seeks to render impotent for all time the accusation that he corrupted youth and taught atheism, for even after his

him going beyond this primitive utilitarianism, and seeking a conception of the good which has been made inward and aims at the well-being of the soul; which stands, too, in relationship with the beautiful.[3] How much of this more advanced view is actually the Master's own, and how much of his own thoughts his pupil has in this way put into his mouth, cannot now be decided.

That Socrates spoke of an inner, mysterious voice, the "daimonion," as being the highest moral authority in man is indeed certain, for it is mentioned in his indictment. His utilitarian rationalism is therefore completed by a kind of mysticism. An empirical ethic—that is to say, an ethic founded on past experience and with future experience in view—and an intuitive ethic live in him side by side and undistinguished from one another, to be separated later and developed in contrast to one another in his pupils, the Cynics and Cyrenaics on the one hand, and Plato on the other.

Was Socrates at all conscious that with the bringing back of the moral to that which is rationally pleasurable he builds the road only a short way further, and stops exactly at the point where the real difficulty makes its appearance, namely, that of defining the most general content of the moral as given by reason? Or was he so naïve as to regard the general formula he had arrived at as the solution of the difficulty?

The confidence which he displays in all his public life leads us to suppose the latter. In his unaffected simplicity lies his strength. In that perilous hour when Western thought comes to the point of having to philosophize about the moral in order to arrest the dissolution of Greek society which has been begun by a body of unstable and disputatious teachers, the wise man of Athens shatters all scepticism by the mighty earnestness of his conviction that what is moral can be determined by thought. Beyond that general statement he does not go, but he is the

---

death teachers of rhetoric did in fact draw up formal complaints against him. Xenophon's straightforward, realistic portrait of Socrates is extraordinarily valuable.

3 The most important dialogues in this connection are the *Protagoras*, the *Gorgias*, the *Phædrus*, the *Symposium*, the *Phædo*, and the *Philebus*.

course of that serious spirit in which antiquity after his day busied itself with the problem. What would that ancient world have become without him?

Characteristic for this prologue to Western philosophizing about the moral is the indifference with which Socrates stands aloof from the philosophic endeavour to reach a complete world-view. He troubles himself neither about the results of natural science, nor about inquiries into the nature of knowledge, but is busied simply with man in his relation to himself and to society. Lao-tse, Confucius, the Indian philosophers, the Jewish prophets, and Jesus seek to comprehend ethics as somehow or other derived from, or forming part of, a world-view. Socrates gives them no foundation but themselves. On this stage, which has no scenery to form a background, there will appear in succession to him the utilitarians of every age.

And here a remarkable prospect opens before us. To all efforts to determine the content of the moral, more help is afforded by the ethic which keeps clear of all connection with a complete world-view than by any other. Such an ethic is the most practical. And yet this isolation is unnatural. The idea that ethics are rooted in a complete world-view, or must find their completion in one—that is, the idea that one's relations to one's fellowmen and to society are in the last resort rooted in some relation to the world—never loses its natural claim. Hence again and again—already in Plato, then in Epicurus and in the Stoic philosophy—ethics have felt the need of resuming connection with world-view, and the same process continues in modern thought. But the practical search for the content of the ethical remains the prerogative of those who are busied with ethics as such.

In Socrates the ethical mysticism of devotion to the inner voice takes the place of the complete world-view, which was in future to be the foundation of the ethical destiny of man.

* * *

Three tasks were left by Socrates to his successors: to determine more exactly the content of the rationally useful; to give the world the most universal general notion of the good; and to think ethics into a complete world-view.

What conclusions are come to by those who concern themselves with the first question, and seek to determine the rationally useful from a corresponding experience of pleasure?

As soon as the notion of pleasure is brought into connection with ethics, it shows disturbances, as does the magnetic needle in the neighbourhood of the poles. Pleasure as such shows itself incapable in every respect of being reconciled with the demands of ethics, and it is therefore given up. Enduring pleasure is called on to take its place, but this retreat does not suffice, for lasting pleasure, interpreted seriously, can be nothing but pleasure of the mind. Even this position, however, is not tenable. Reflection upon the ethic which is to produce happiness is compelled at last to give up the positive notion of pleasure in any form. It has to reconcile itself to the negative notion which conceives pleasure as somehow or other a liberation from the need of pleasure. Thus the individualistic, utilitarian ethic, also called Eudæmonism, destroys itself as soon as it ventures to be consistent. This is the paradox which reveals itself in the ethics of antiquity.

Instead of coming to maturity in the following generations, the ethically-rational life-ideal put forward by Socrates succumbs to an incurable decline, because the notion of pleasure, which lives in it, denies itself as soon as it makes any attempt to think itself out.

Aristippus (*c.* 435–355 B.C.), the founder of the Cyrenaic school, Democritus of Abdera (*c.* 450–360 B.C.), the author of the atomic theory, and Epicurus (341–270 B.C.) seek to retain as much as possible of the positive notion of pleasure. The Cynic school of Antisthenes (born *c.* 440 B.C.), and the Stoicism which originated with Zeno, a native of Kittium in Cyprus (*c.* 336–264 B.C.), withdraw from the very beginning to the negative notion.[4] But the final result is the same in both cases. Epicurus sees him-

4 Of the writings of the Cyrenaics and the Cynics, of Democritus, Epicurus, Zeno, and the older Stoics hardly anything has come down to us. Our knowledge of them is derived mostly from Diogenes Laertius.

The Cyrenaics were known as the philosophers of pleasure because Aristippus, the first preacher of the world-wisdom of joy, hailed from Cyrene. The Cynics, or dog-philosophers, derived their name from the fact that they despised the amenities of life and often delighted in a coarse naturalness. The best known of them is Diogenes of Sinope (died 323 B.C.).

Zeno's philosophy was called Stoicism because he taught at Athens in a colonnaded portico (Stoa).

self compelled at last to exalt the absence of desire for pleasure as being itself the purest pleasure, landing thereby on the shore of resignation where the Stoics take their exercise. The fundamental difference between the two great philosophical schools of antiquity does not lie in what they offer to men as ethical. About what the "wise man" does and leaves undone, they both frequently express themselves almost in the same way. What separates them is the world-view with which their ethic is combined. Epicureanism accepts the atomistic materialism of Democritus, is atheistic, asserts that the soul perishes, and is in every respect irreligious. Stoicism is pantheistic.

With Epicurus and Zeno ethics no longer trust themselves, as with Socrates, to maintain an independent existence. They see the necessity of attaching themselves to some sort of world-view. Travelling along this road, Epicurus is guided solely by the effort to retain veracity. He leaves the last word to the purely scientific knowledge of the world, not allowing ethics to join in the investigation of Being and introduce into it what might be of advantage to itself. How poor, or how rich, it will finally become is to him a matter of indifference. The one thing he is concerned about is that the world-view be a true one, and therein lies the greatness of Epicurus and his claim to our respect.

Stoicism seeks to satisfy the need for an inward, stable philosophy of life; like the Chinese monists it tries to find a meaning in the world. It tries to widen out the ethical rationalism of Socrates into cosmic rationalism. The moral is to show itself to be conduct agreeable to the pronouncements of world-reason.

Stoicism has a vision of an optimistic-ethical affirmation of life, grounded in the nature of the cosmos, but it fails to reach it.

It is not untutored enough to acquiesce in the ethical simplicity of a nature-philosophy such as can be seen in Lao-tse and in the older philosophical Taoism. It is ever struggling to discover in world-reason the notion of purposive activity, and is ever mercilessly thrust back upon that of activity pure and simple. Hence the ethic with which it is operating never has a sufficiently universalist character to let it form a natural connection with world-reason. As might be expected from its origin, it is dominated by the problem of pleasure and not-pleasure, and therefore no longer possesses any efficacious instinct for effort. Its horizons, because still determined by the questions arising out of ancient citizenship and the ancient city-state, are narrow. It is, therefore, not advanced enough to engage in thought on scientific lines, concerned with both the world and man, although it does feel the inner necessity for doing so.

The vacillation which is characteristic of Stoicism comes, then, from the fact that the results it attains do not match its aspirations, but are much poorer than these. The spirit of antiquity tries to find an optimistic-ethical life-affirmation in nature-philosophy, and to find in it also the justification of those instincts for reliable activity which it has possessed since the days when it was entirely unsophisticated, but it cannot do so. Whenever it acknowledges what has happened, it sees clearly that thinking about the universe leads only to resignation, and that a life in harmony with the world means quiet surrender to being carried along in the flood of world-happenings, and, when the hour comes, sinking into it without a murmur.

Stoicism talks, it is true, with deep earnestness of responsibility and duty, but since it cannot draw either from nature-philosophy or from ethics a well-established and living notion of activity, it lays out in these words nothing but beautiful corpses. It is impotent to command anything whatever that is bound up with voluntary activity which is conscious of its aim. Again and again evidence breaks through that its thinking has been pushed aside on to the track of passivity. Nature-philosophy only provides the cosmic background for the resignation to which ethics have come. The ideal, which gives life to Chinese Monism, of the perfecting of a world through ethical and ethically organized mankind, is not really discerned, much less securely grasped.

One watches with dismay the shaping of the fate of ancient ethics in Epicureanism and Stoicism. In place of the vigorous life-affirming ethic which Socrates expects from rational thinking, resignation steps in. An inconceivable impoverishment takes place in the representation of the moral. The notion of action cannot be worked out to completion. Even so much of it as, thanks to tradition, still survives in the simple thought-methods of the Greek world in general, is lost.

The ancient Greek was more citizen than man. Active devotion to the cause of the community was to him a matter of course. Socrates takes it for granted. In the conversations which

Xenophon hands down to us in the *Memorabilia,* he is ever insisting that the individual must make himself fit in order to become an active citizen. The natural course would have been that the thought which originated with him should deepen this mentality by setting before it the highest social aims. It was, however, never at all in a position to maintain the mentality as it received it. More and more it leads the individual to withdraw himself from the world and from all that goes on in it.

By a never-ceasing process of change, the ethics of Greek thought become in Epicureanism and Stoicism ethics of decadence. Not being capable of producing ideals of progressive development for collective bodies, they are also impotent to become really ethics of civilization. In place of the ideal of the man who works for civilization they set the ideal of the "wise man." It is only the inward individual civilization of refined and reflective self-liberation from the world that now floats before their eyes, but this in all its depth.

It is true that there is power in the preaching of resignation which ancient thought, no longer ignorant about life, allows to go forth to mankind. Resignation is the lofty porch through which one enters upon ethics. But Epicurus and the Stoics stay on in this porch. Resignation becomes for them an ethical world-view. Hence they are incapable of leading ancient society from its ingenuous life- and world-affirmation to a philosophy based on thought.

The conception of the rationally pleasurable, which was the legacy of Socrates, is not productive enough to keep a world alive. It is impossible to develop from it the ideas of a utilitarianism directed to the welfare of the community, although he believed he found them in it. Ethical thought remains confined within the circle of the *ego.* Every attempt to ennoble the rationally pleasurable ends in life-affirmation changing into life-negation. On this logical fact was wrecked the ancient West, which, after the critical awakening of the Greek spirit, could have been saved only by means of a reflective optimistic-ethical outlook on life. It was able to take seriously what Socrates gave it, but not to make it capable of producing life and civilization.

* * *

Plato, too (427–347 B.C.), and Aristotle (384–322 B.C.), the two great independent thinkers of antiquity, are incapable of producing an ethic of action, and so giving civilization a firm foundation.

Plato seeks the general notion of the Good, but he abandons the path which was pointed out, even if not followed to the end, by Socrates, namely the determination of the Good by a process of induction. He gives up trying to arrive at the nature of the Good by considerations of the kind, the object, and the results of action, that is to say, by its content. He wants to establish it by a purely formal process, by abstract logical thinking.

In order to arrive at an ethic he uses a detour through the theory of ideas. All similar phenomena, he says, are to be conceived of as varying copies of an original—to express which he uses the word "idea." In trees there is to be seen the idea of tree, in horses, that of horse. The idea does not come to us, as we are inclined to think, by our abstracting from trees the idea of tree, and from horses that of horse. We have it within us already. It originates, not in our experience of the empirical world, but in the recollection which our soul brought with it from the supra-sensuous, pure world of ideas, when it began its existence in a body. In the same way we have brought with us the idea of the Good.

Thus in a tortured doctrine which is disfigured everywhere with fancies and obscurities, Plato tries to found ethics on a theory about the character of our knowledge of the world of sense, and he is encouraged to this undertaking by the consideration, that it is not from reflection that we obtain our conception of the Beautiful, which is closely allied with that of the Good: that conception also we bring with us, ready made.

Plato is the first of all thinkers who feels that the presence of the ethical idea in man is what it is: something profoundly mysterious. That is his great distinction. Hence he cannot profess to be satisfied with the attempt of the historic Socrates to explain the Good as that which is rationally pleasure-giving. It is clear to him that it must be something absolute, with a compelling force of its own, and to preserve for it this character seems to him, as later to Kant, to be the great task of thought.

But what is the result of his undertaking? A fundamental

principle of ethics which is devoid of content. In order to secure its lofty character, it is supposed to be born of abstract considerations in the country of the supra-sensuous. It can, therefore, never find itself at home in reality or become familiar with it, nor can any rules for concrete ethical conduct be developed from it. Thus Plato, when he treats of ethics on practical lines, is compelled to abide by the chief virtues as popularly conceived. In the *Republic* he names four of them: wisdom, courage, temperance, and justice, and he founds them, not on his general idea of the Good, but on psychology.

But the characteristic ethic of Plato has nothing whatever to do with such virtues. If the conception of the Good is suprasensible and the immaterial world is the only real one, then it is only thought and conduct which deal with the immaterial that can have any ethical character. In the world of appearance there is nothing of value to be made actual. Man is simply compelled to be an impotent spectator of its shadow-play. All willing must be directed to enabling oneself to turn away from this, and discover that true activity which goes on in the light.

The true ethic, then, is world-negation. To this view Plato was committed the moment he allowed the ethical to find its home in the world of pure Being. Thoughts of ascetic inactivity find expression in him side by side with the Greek feeling for reality, and it is confusing that he does not recognize the conflict between them, but speaks now in one sense, now in the other. His ethic is a chaos, and he himself an expert in inconsistency.

Plato's ethic of world-negation is not an original creation; he takes it over in the Indian setting in which it is offered to him by Orphism and Pythagoreanism. By what route there found its way into Greek thought this pessimism which had been thought out to a system and equipped with the doctrine of re-incarnation, we do not know, and shall probably never learn. The presence side by side in Greek thought of an artless optimism and a mature pessimism will always remain for us the great puzzle of Greek civilization. But if the pessimism had not been there, Plato must have introduced it. The abstract basic principle of morality, which he adopts in order to preserve the absolute character of morality which he was the first to pronounce a necessity, precludes any other content than the denial of the world of the senses and of natural life.

* * *

Plato's fate alarms Aristotle. He refuses to soar to the heights where Plato lost himself. How then does he fare?

His object is the establishment of a serviceable ethic which is in harmony both as to extent and content with reality. What he accomplished lies before us in the so-called *Nicomachean Ethics,* the comprehensive work which he composed for the benefit of his son, Nicomachus. The general thought of Socrates, that ethics are a striving after happiness, he acknowledges. But at the same time he is clear that activity plays a much greater part in ethics than is given to it by Plato or the other post-Socratics. Aristotle feels that the crux of the question is the conception of activity, and this he wants to save. He therefore avoids Plato's paths of abstract thinking, and rejects the ethic of pleasure and not-pleasure over which the Cyrenaics and Cynics work so hard. In his ethical thinking the vitality of the ancient world tries to find expression.

In magnificent fashion he lays down the hypotheses which are necessary for the accomplishment of his undertaking. He finds the motive to activity in the conception of pleasure, a thing he can do because his whole philosophy has indeed for its aim and object the conceiving of Being as formative activity. Hence the essential element in human nature also is activity. Happiness is to be defined as activity in accordance with the law of excellence. Rational pleasure is experience of the perfecting of activity.

Starting from the conception of pleasure which experiences itself as activity, Aristotle is on the way to comprehend ethics as deepened life-affirmation, and to attack the problem of leading the ancient world up from a naïve to a reflecting world-affirmation. But on the way he diverges from the high-road.

When he has to ask the decisive question as to what makes activity moral, he shrinks from discussing the problem of the basic principle of the moral. Ethics are not some sort of knowledge which gives a content to activity, he says in opposition to Socrates. The content of the will is already given. No reflection and no knowledge can put anything new into it, or alter it.

Ethics consist, then, not in a guiding of the will by aims and objects which knowledge puts before it, but in the will's own regulation of itself. The right thing to do is to establish the correct balance between the different elements in the given contents of the will. Left to itself, the will rushes to extremes. Rational reflection keeps it in the correct middle path. Thus brought to a state of harmony, human activity can be conceived as motived and ethical. Virtue, therefore, is readiness to observe the correct mean which is to be acquired by practice.

Instead of creating an ethic, Aristotle contents himself with a doctrine of virtue. This depreciation of the ethical is the price he pays in order to reach an ethic which ends neither in the abstract nor in resignation. While he shirks the problem of the basic principle of the moral, he still remains able to establish an ethic of activity, though the latter contains indeed no live forces, only dead ones.

Aristotle's ethic is therefore an æsthetic of the impulses of the will. It consists in a catalogue of virtues and in the demonstration that they are to be conceived as a mean. Thus courage lies between rashness and cowardice, temperance between sensuality and insensibility, modesty between boastfulness and bashfulness, liberality between prodigality and avarice, high-mindedness between conceit and small-mindedness, gentleness between quarrelsomeness and characterless good-nature.

On this excursion through the field of the ethical, there open up many interesting views. In an acute and living discussion, Aristotle lets his readers survey the questions of the relations of man to his fellow-men and to society. How much that is deep and true there is in the chapter on moral excellence and in that on friendship! How he wrestles with the problem of justice!

No one can fail to feel the charm of the *Nicomachean Ethics.* There is revealed in them a noble personality with abundant experience of life, depicted with a magnificent simplicity. But just in proportion as the method followed is technically advantageous, it is valueless in itself. The ethical tries conclusions with reality without having first endeavoured to come to clear understanding of itself. It is in the course of this disputation that understanding is to be found, Aristotle thinks, but he is mistaken. His mind is seduced through his having observed that some virtues—but even these more or less under compulsion—allow themselves to be conceived as real means between two extremes, and he is misled into developing on these lines the whole of his ethical system.

But a more or less natural quality, which in ordinary speech is called a virtue, is one thing; virtue in the really ethical sense is another. The middle quality between prodigality and avarice is not the ethical virtue of liberality, but the quality of rational economy. The middle quality between rashness and cowardice is not the ethical virtue of courage, but the quality of rational prudence. The combination of two qualities only produces a single one. But virtue, in the ethical sense, means a quality guided by an ideal of self-perfection, and serviceable for some object which looks towards the universal. Liberality as an ethical virtue means a process of spending which serves some object recognized by the person practising it as valuable in principle, and serving it in such a way that any natural tendency to prodigality, should there be such in the giver, plays no part, while the tendency to avarice is paralysed.

Courage is daring to risk my life for an object I recognize as altogether valuable: the natural disposition to foolhardiness which I possibly possess plays no part in it, and natural timidity is invalidated.

Devotion of one's property or one's life to an object which is valuable in principle is under all circumstances ethical, while prodigality and avarice, rashness and cowardice, being simple qualities not inspired by any higher aim, have never any ethical character; they are merely natural. Whether the devotion of one's property or of one's life for an object valuable in principle is made more completely than need be, or exactly to the extent required by the circumstances, does not alter in any way the ethical character of the determination and the action. Such excess or defect only shows how much or how little the ethical will has allowed itself to be influenced by considerations of prudence.

Aristotle's representation, then, rests on the fact that he allows virtue in the ordinary sense and virtue in the ethical sense to get mixed up. He smuggles in the really ethical, and then offers it as the resultant of two natural qualities, each of which is an extreme.

In the chapter on temperance—in the third Book of the *Nicomachean Ethics*—he has to admit that the theory which makes the ethical a mean between two extremes cannot be completely developed. The love of beauty, he says plainly, however strong it becomes, remains what it is; there can never be any question of excess. He throws out this admission without seeing that he thereby undermines his feeble definition of the ethical as the appropriate relative mean, and, like Socrates and Plato, acknowledges that there can be something which its content allows to be reckoned as good in itself.

Aristotle is so firmly resolved not to have anything to do with the problem of the basic principle of ethics, that he will allow nothing to lead him to discuss it. He means to voyage along the coast, keep to facts, and deal with ethics as if they were a branch of natural science. Only he forgets that in science we can confine ourselves to venturing from definite given happenings through hypotheses to the nature of the Being which lies behind them, while in ethics, on the contrary, we have to establish a basic principle through the application of which we secure our happenings.

It is because he misunderstands their nature that Aristotle cannot help ethics forward. Plato goes beyond Socrates and loses himself in abstractions. Aristotle, in order to maintain the connection with reality, aims lower than Socrates. He brings together material for a monumental building, and runs up a wooden shack. Among teachers of virtue he is one of the greatest. Nevertheless, the least of those who venture on the search for the basic principle of the ethical is greater than he.

Ethical theory is no more ethics than cartilage is bone. But how strange is this inability to establish the basic principle of ethical action which Socrates regarded as from the outset the certain product of thoughtful reflection on the ethical! Why do all the ancient thinkers who in succession to Socrates search for it, always miss it? Why does Aristotle cease to concern himself with it, and so condemn himself to a doctrine of virtue in which, as a matter of fact, there is hardly any more living ethical force than there is in the abstract ethical system of Plato or in the ethics of resignation of other thinkers?

* * *

How little Plato and Aristotle are capable of establishing an ethic of action can be seen from the way in which they sketch their ideal of the civilized State. Plato develops his in the *Republic,* Aristotle his in the *Politics.* At this very time, Mencius (Meng-tse) is putting before the princes of China a doctrine of the civilized State.

That the State must be something more than a union which regulates in the most practical way the common life of a number of persons whom natural conditions compel to depend upon one another, is quite clear to both of them. They also agree in demanding that the State shall promote the true prosperity of its citizens. This is, however, unthinkable and impossible without virtue, so the State must develop into an ethical institution. "Honourable and virtuous conduct is the object at which the political community aims," is the way Aristotle puts it.

The State, evolved by history, is therefore to come under the influence of a representation of its nature as a political body which is both ethical and rational. In the *Republic* Plato puts in the mouth of Socrates the following sentiment: "Unless it happen that either philosophers acquire the kingly power in States, or those who are to-day called kings and potentates cultivate philosophy truly and sufficiently, and thus political power and philosophy become as one . . . there can be no deliverance from evil for States, nor even, I think, for the human race."

When, however, it comes to a more detailed carrying out of the ideal of the civilized State, Plato and Aristotle betray remarkable embarrassment. To begin with, their vision of the State of the future is not that of a community which embraces a whole nation, but is always just a copy of the Greek city-republic with appropriate improvements. That they think out their ideal within such narrow limits is historically intelligible, but for the development of the philosophical idea of the civilized State it is deplorable.

One result of these narrow limits is that both are anxiously concerned to provide that the well-being of the city-republic shall not be endangered by the increase of the population. The number of the inhabitants is to be kept as far as possible always near the same figure. Aristotle is not alarmed by the proposal that weakly children shall be allowed to die of hunger, and that unborn children shall be disposed of by intentional abortion. That the Spartan State, on the contrary, regards the increase of the population as desirable, and exempts a citizen from all imposts as soon as he has four children, does not seem to him reasonable.

Again, just as these two thinkers cannot rise to a general idea of a national State, so they are unable to reach the idea of mankind. They draw a strict line of division between the unfree on the one side, and the free on the other. The former they regard merely as creatures made for work, who are to maintain the material well-being of the State. What becomes of them as human beings is to them a matter of very little interest. Such beings as they, are not meant to have any share in the growth towards perfection which is to be brought about by means of the civilized State.

Slavery was, indeed, attacked now and again by the Sophists from their point of view, not, however, on the ground of humanity, but from a desire to raise doubts about the accepted justification of existing institutions. Aristotle defends it as a natural arrangement, but recommends kindly treatment.

Artisans, and in general all who earn their living by the labour of their hands, are not to be allowed to be citizens. "One cannot practise virtue, if one leads the life of an artisan, or of one who labours for wages," says Aristotle. An ethical valuation of labour as such is still a thing unknown to him, even though he conceives of happiness as "activity in accordance with the law of excellence." Plato and he are still entirely under the influence of the ancient opinion that only the "free" man can have full value as a man.

In details of the ideal of the State, however, the two part company, and Aristotle argues against Plato. Unfortunately, just those parts of the *Politics* in which he sketches his ideal State have not come down to us complete. The main difference is that Aristotle keeps closer than Plato to the historically given. He builds his State upon the family; Plato makes the State into a family. In his *Republic* the free men live with property, wives, and children owned in common. They are to possess nothing as their own, so that they may not by private interests be held back from working for the general welfare. Moreover, the general welfare allows the State to breed its citizens systematically. He prescribes the connections which men and women are to form, and permits only such as allow the expectation of a new generation which is sound both in body and mind. The offspring of unions not approved by the authorities are either to be killed before birth, or removed from the world by starvation.

Aristotle contents himself with guaranteeing the quality of the offspring by legal regulation of the age for marriage. Women may marry at eighteen, men not till they are thirty-seven. Moreover, marriages are to take place preferably in winter, and as far as possible, when the wind is in the north.

In what, then, does the good consist which is to be realized by the civilized State? To this decisive question Aristotle and Plato have in reality only the answer that it is meant to make it possible for a number of its members, namely the "free" men, released from material cares, to devote themselves entirely to their own bodily and mental culture, and to take the lead in public affairs. The State is not established with a view to the production of anything ethical in any deeper sense, nor for the sake of an ideal of progress on lines which could be described as great and noble. Nowhere do the characteristic limitations of ancient ethics reveal themselves so clearly as in the inadequacy of the ideal of the State.

The ethical valuation of man as man has not yet been reached. Hence the State has for its object, not the growth to perfection of all, but only that of a particular class.

The nation, too, is not yet recognized as a great natural and ethical entity, and therefore no consideration is given to the question of uniting the various city communities for the joint pursuit of higher objects. Each remains isolated. Plato thinks he has satisfied the claims arising from membership of the same nation by requiring that in wars waged by Greek cities against one another the houses shall not be destroyed nor the fields laid waste, as would be done if the war were against barbarians.

The idea of humanity as a whole has not yet come in sight. It is, therefore, not possible for Plato and Aristotle to make their State work in coo-poration with others to promote the general progress of mankind.

So they establish their civilized State on a political organism which is hemmed in in every direction by narrow horizons. Moreover, the political community which they adopt as the typical State at the very time when they are writing is already a dying entity. While Aristotle is writing the *Politics*, his pupil, Alexander the Great, is founding an empire, and Rome is beginning to subject Italy to her rule.

More important still than all external faults in their ideal of the civilized State, is the fact that these two thinkers are unable to introduce into the community the energies which are needed for its maintenance. The idea of the civilized State is present with the vitality needed only when the individual is by the impulse contained in his world-view moved so far as to devote himself to organized society with enthusiastic activity. Without civic idealism no civilized State! But to assume anything of that kind in the members of their State is impossible for Plato and Aristotle, since both have already arrived at the ideal of the wise man who withdraws himself prudently and gracefully from the world.

Plato admits this. His wise citizens who are destined to be rulers devote themselves to the service of the State only when their turn comes, and are glad when they are relieved and in retirement can once more concern themselves, as wise men among wise men, with the world of pure Being.

When Aristotle raises in the *Politics* the question whether the contemplative life is not to be preferred to that of political activity, he decides in theory in favor of the latter. "It is a mistake," he says, "to value inactivity higher than activity, since happiness consists in activity." But in the doctrine of virtue in the *Nicomachean Ethics* there is nothing which could lead the individual to place his life at the service of the community.

Plato and Aristotle undoubtedly cherish the ancient conviction that the individual ought to devote himself to the State, but they cannot find a foundation for it in their philosophy. Like Epicurus and the adherents of the Porch, they are under the spell of an ethic in which there is present no will to attempt a transformation of the world.

How much greater than the two Greeks is Meng-tse (Mencius), when he is thinking out the ideal of the civilized State! He can make it as large as he likes and take men into its service with their best thoughts, because it results in the most natural way from a large-scale philosophy of ethical activity.

Plato and Aristotle, lacking such a world-view, can do no more than guess at the nature of a civilized State, and invent one for themselves. Plato's *Republic* is a mere curiosity. Aristotle's *Politics* is valuable, not on account of the theory of the civilized State which is there presented, but only for his magnificent practical analysis of the advantages and disadvantages of the various State-constitutions, and of their economic problems.

The decadence of antiquity does not begin, then, with the suppression of the individual by the Empire, and its destruction of the normal mutual relations between the individual and the community. It sets in immediately after Socrates, because the ethical thinking which started with him cannot really lead the individual beyond himself, and set him as an effective force in the service of the moralization and the perfecting of social relations.

There is no middle term between the ethic of enthusiasm and the ethic of resignation. But an ethic of resignation cannot think out, much less bring into existence, a system of social relations which can be called really civilized.

* * *

"In imperial times Stoicism shrivels up into a moralizing popular philosophy" is what we are usually told in works on ancient philosophy. As a matter of fact there is by no means a shrivelling up, but a serious struggle for a living ethic which begins unexpectedly in the later period of Græco-Roman thought, and leads to an optimistic-ethical nature-philosophy.

The pillars of this movement are L. Annæus Seneca (4 B.C.–A.D. 65), Nero's teacher, who at the command of his pupil had to open his veins; the Phrygian slave, Epictetus (born *c.* A.D. 50), who in A.D. 94 was banished from Rome by Domitian with all the other philosophers; the Emperor Marcus Aurelius (A.D. 121–180) who, brought up by pupils of Epictetus, defended the Empire at a time of great danger, and wrote his philosophical *Meditations* in camp.[5]

In their classical period Greek ethics offer us either egoistic considerations of advantage, or cold doctrines of virtue, or ascetic renunciation of the world, or resignation. In whichever direction they turn, they never really lead men out beyond themselves.

In Seneca, Epictetus, and Marcus Aurelius, ethics lose this self-regarding character. Renouncing the spirit of the earlier time, they develop to an ethic of universal brotherhood, and are concerned with the direct, altruistic relations of man to man.

Whence comes this understanding for humanity, which is never seen in classical antiquity?

The older Greek moralists are concerned with the State. Their interest is absorbed in the maintenance of the organization of society which is embodied in the city-republic, so that the free citizens can continue to live the life of freedom. The type of complete manhood is to be realized. All around are toiling men who receive no consideration except in so far as they are means to this end.

But amid the mighty political and social revolutions which lead to the creation of the Empire, this mentality ceases to be accepted as a matter of course. The fearful experiences it goes through cause feeling to become more humane, and the horizons of ethics are widened. The city-republic, on which ethical thinking had been focused, has disappeared, but an empire now oppresses the lives of all men alike. Thus the individual man as such becomes the object of reflection and of ethics. The concep-

[5] Of Seneca quite a series of ethical treatises have come down to us. We mention here: *On Clemency (De Clementia,* addressed to Nero); *On Benefits (De Beneficiis); On Tranquillity of Soul (De Tranquillitate Animi); On Anger (De Ira).*

Our knowledge of the teachings of Epictetus we owe to his pupil, Flavius Arrianus, the historian. The latter has recorded a number of his master's lectures in eight books, of which four have survived. In addition to these he collected and published a number of his sayings on morality in the *Enchiridion.*

In the popular philosophizings of Cicero (106–43 B.C.) as well, we can see an attempt to produce a new ethic which is really living.

tion of the brotherhood of all men appears. A disposition to humanity makes itself heard, and Seneca condemns the gladiatorial shows. Nay more: even the inner relationship between mankind and the animal world is recognized.

So now, when mankind as a whole and man as such have come into view, ethics reach such a depth and breadth as allows them to be comprehended in a universal world-will. Henceforth nature-philosophy and ethics can work together. Stoicism from the very beginning had a vision of this, but had not been able to make it a reality, since it had not at its disposal the living and universal ethic which was needed.

But there is another reason why optimism and ethics can now in nature-philosophy come into power. The old school of the Porch was crushed down into resignation just in proportion as it submitted to the necessity for critical thinking. But as time goes on, the practical and religious instincts which were always present in its world-view, gain in strength. The antiquity which is passing away is no longer critical, but either sceptical or religious, and therefore the later school of the Porch can submit it to the guidance of the ethical demands of its world-view much more completely than could the old one. It becomes at once deeper and more simple than the latter, and, like Chinese ethical monism, rises to such freedom from limitations as to be able to interpret the world-will as ethical. So now Stoics appear who, like Confucius, like Mencius, and like Chwang-tse, and indeed, like the Rationalists of the eighteenth century, preach ethics as grounded in the nature of the universe and the nature of mankind. They cannot prove the truth of this world-view any better than could Zeno and his pupils, who also resorted to it, but they announce it with an inner conviction which these could not command, and produce their results by means of an enthusiasm which was denied to their predecessors.

When the later school of the Porch reaches the stage of exalting the world-principle more and more to the status of a personal and ethical god, it is following laws which are at work also in Hinduism.

Yet it never succeeds in rendering entirely impotent the world-view of resignation, which it had inherited from the older school. In Seneca and Epictetus this is still strongly maintained side by side with the ethical conception of the universe. It is only in Marcus Aurelius that the optimistic motives victoriously ring out.

Stoicism was from the beginning a multiform elemental philosophy, and it is because it ventured to be this in such comprehensive measure that the Later Stoicism is so rich and so full of life.

Moral Sayings of Seneca

No man is nobler than his fellow, even if it happen that his spiritual nature is better constituted and he is more capable of higher learning. The world is the one mother of us all, and the ultimate origin of each one of us can be traced back to her, whether the steps in the ladder of descent be noble or humble. To no one is virtue forbidden; she is accessible to all; she admits everyone, she invites everyone in: free men and freedmen, slaves, kings, and exiles. She regards neither birth nor fortune; the man alone is all she wants.

It is a mistake to think that the status of a slave affects the whole of a person's nature; the nobler part of it is not touched thereby.

Every single person, even if there is nothing else to recommend him, I must hold in regard, because he bears the name of man.

In the treatment of a slave we have to consider not how much we can do to him without being liable to punishment, but how much the nature of right and of justice allows us to do, seeing that these bid us treat gently even prisoners and purchased slaves. Although in the treatment of a slave everything is allowed, there is nevertheless something which through the common right of every living being is stigmatized as not permissible in the treatment of a man, because he is of the same nature as thyself.

This, in fact, is the demand which is laid upon each man, namely that he works, when possible, for the welfare of many; if that is impracticable, that he works for the welfare of a few; failing that, for the welfare of his neighbours, and if that is impossible, for his own.

It is through untiring benevolence that the bad are won over, and there is no disposition so hard and so hostile to loving treatment . . . as to refuse love to the good people whom it will in the end have to thank again for something more. "Not a word of thanks did I get! What am I now to begin to do?" What the gods do, . . . who begin to shower benefits on us before we are aware of it, and continue them even though we do not thank them.

Moral Sayings of Epictetus

Nature is wonderful, and full of love for all creatures.

Wait upon God, ye men. When He calls you, and releases you from service, then go to Him; but for the present remain quietly in the position in which He has placed you.

You carry a god about with you, and do not know it, unhappy one! You have him within yourself, and do not notice it when you defile him with unclean thoughts or foul deeds.

Cultivate the will to satisfy yourself, and to stand right before God. Strive to become pure, one with yourself and one with God.

Think silence best; say only what is necessary, and say it shortly. Above all, do not talk about thy fellow-men, either to praise them, or to blame them, or to compare them with others. Do not swear; never, if possible, or at any rate as seldom as possible. Your bodily wants—food, drink, clothing, housing, service—satisfy in the simplest way. Avoid unseemly joking, for there is always a danger of becoming vulgar, and joking away the respect of your fellow-men.

As you are careful when walking not to tread on a nail or to sprain your ankle, so take care not to let your soul get hurt.

Moral Sayings from the Meditations *of Marcus Aurelius*

Everything that happens, happens right, and if you can observe things carefully, you will recognize that it is so. I do not mean only in accordance with the course of nature, but much more that they happen in accordance with the law of righteousness, and as if controlled by a Being who orders all things according to merit.

If I am active, I am so with due regard to the general welfare. If anything happens to me, I accept it and consider it in relation to the gods and the universal source from which, in close connection, come all our happenings.

He who commits unrighteousness is godless, for universal nature created rational beings for one another; to help each other where there is need, but never to injure one another.

Love mankind; obey the godhead.

If thou art unwilling to get up in the morning, reflect thus: I am waking in order to go and work as a man.

Seek all thy joy and contentment in advancing, mindful always of God, from one generally useful deed to another.

The best way to avenge oneself on anyone is to avoid returning evil for evil.

It is a privilege of man to love even those who do him wrong. One can reach this level by reflecting that all men are of one family with oneself; that their shortcomings are due to ignorance, and against their will; that in a short time both of you will be dead.

What is good is necessarily useful, and that is why the good and noble man must be concerned about it.

Nobody gets tired of seeking his own advantage. But doing so procures us an activity which is natural. Never get tired, then, of seeking thine own advantage, provided thou procurest thus the advantage of others also.

Treat as befits a man endowed with reason, that is magnanimously and nobly, the animals which are not so endowed, and indeed all creatures whatever that can feel but have no reason. But other men, since they are endowed with reason, treat with friendly affection.

Thou has existed till now as a fragment of the universe, and wilt some day be absorbed in thy creator, or rather, thou wilt suffer a transformation and reappear as a new germ of life.

Many grains of incense are destined for the same altar. Some fall soon into the flame, others later, but that makes no difference.

* * *

In their optimistic-ethical world-view the Later Stoics find those impulses to effort which were not available for the ancient ethics of the classical age. Marcus Aurelius is an enthusiastic utilitarian like the Rationalists of the eighteenth century, because, like them, he is convinced that nature itself has bound up together what is ethical and what is advantageous both to the individual and to the community.

That being so, the classical question of ancient ethics, whether the thinking man is to busy himself with public affairs or not must again be discussed. Epicurus taught that "the wise man has nothing to do with State affairs unless exceptional circumstances arise." Zeno's decision was that "he will take part in the business of the State unless obstacles prevent it." Both schools leave the retirement into oneself to the decision of the wise man, only one lets the grounds for the decision be given somewhat earlier, the other somewhat later. The thought of a devotion to the general good which is to be kept active for its own sake and under all circumstances is beyond the horizon of their ethic.

With the Later Stoics it emerges, because the conception of "mankind" has come in sight. Man, as Seneca works out in his treatise on Leisure (*De Otio*), belongs to two republics. One is large and universal, extends as far as the sun shines, and embraces both gods and men; the other is that into which through the fate assigned us by our birth, we have been adopted as citizens. Circumstances may bring it about that the wise man cannot dedicate himself to the service of the State, but, to escape the storm, must "take refuge in the harbour." It may happen—and Seneca has in mind his own time—that not one of the existing States is of such a character as to tolerate the activity of the wise man. Nevertheless, the latter does not wholly withdraw into himself, but serves the great republic by working to improve the general outlook of mankind and hasten the coming of a new age.

In Epictetus also this deepened and widened conception of duty is to be found. Marcus Aurelius does not even consider that it might be impossible to take part in public life. In him there speaks the ruler who feels himself to be the servant of the State. His ideal is the citizen who "from one activity which makes his fellow-citizens happier goes on to another, and undertakes with alacrity anything whatever that the State lays upon him." "Do what is needed, and what is bidden by the reason of a being who is destined by nature to membership of a State, and do it as it is bidden."

In the middle of the second century A.D. ancient thought arrives at an optimistic-ethical world-view which offers living ideals of civilization, and therefore anticipates that which later on in the eighteenth century will bring into activity so mighty and universal a movement of civilization. But for the men of the Græco-Roman world it comes too late. It does not permeate the masses, but remains the private possession of an *élite*.

It cannot permeate the masses, because there are forces at work among them with which it cannot combine. It is true, indeed, that the ethic of the later Stoicism is so near akin to the universal charity of the Christian ethic, that by the tradition of later times Seneca is declared to be a Christian, and that the

Church father, Augustine, holds up the life of the heathen emperor, Marcus Aurelius, as an example for Christians.

Yet the two movements cannot amalgamate, but have to oppose each other. Marcus Aurelius is responsible for most terrible persecutions of Christians, and Christianity on its side declares war to the death against the Porch.

Why this strange fatality? Because Christianity is dualistic and pessimistic, whilst the ethic of Stoicism is monistic and optimistic. Christianity abandons the natural world as evil, the later Stoics idealize it. It helps not at all that their ethical teaching is almost identical. Each appears as part of a philosophy which is irreconcilable with that of the other. All contradictions in the world may be concealed, but not that between two world-views, and the struggle ends with the annihilation of the optimistic-ethical philosophy of the Stoics, which is defended by officers without an army. The attempt that was undertaken as the ancient world was coming to an end, to restore the Empire and make it embrace the whole of mankind, was a failure.

The horizons of the philosophy of the ancient world had remained narrow too long. No ethical thinkers had appeared who at the right time might have led that world to an ethical optimism about reality. It was a calamity, too, that the natural sciences, which had made such a promising start, came to a standstill, partly through the fault of fate, partly because philosophy turned away from them, before mankind discovered the laws governing the forces of nature, and thereby obtained control over them. Hence the men of antiquity never acquired that self-consciousness which in their descendants of modern times has kept alive, even through the darkest periods of history, the belief in progress—even though it be sometimes progress of the most superficial kind. This psychological factor is of great importance.

It is true that artistic ability, which in the Greek spirit meets us in such abundant measure, is also control over the material, but this creative power was unable to draw the man of antiquity up to a higher life-affirmation and to belief in progress. It served only to let him express himself, in words and in form, in the antagonism between unsophisticated world- and life-affirmation, and reflective world- and life-negation. It is the mysterious intermixture of serenity and melancholy which constitutes the tragic charm of Hellenic art.

From every point of view, vigorous ethical world- and life-affirmation is made difficult for the ancient world. That is why it falls more and more a prey to pessimistic conceptions of the universe, which draw its thoughts away from reality, and celebrate the liberation of the spiritual from its bondage to the material in a succession of cosmic dramas. Gnosticism, Oriental and Christian, Neo-Pythagoreanism, which arose as early as the first century B.C., the Neo-Platonism which originated with Plotinus (A.D. 204–269), and the great Mystery-religions, all come to meet the religious, world-shunning disposition of the masses during the break-up of antiquity, and offer it that deliverance from the world of which it is in search. In this chaos of ideas Christianity emerges victorious because it is the most robust religion of redemption, because as a community it possesses the strongest organization, and because beneath its pessimistic world-view it has at its disposal living ethical ideas.

The optimistic-ethical monism of the later Stoics is like a sunbeam breaking through in the evening of the long, gloomy day of antiquity while the darkness of the middle ages is already drawing on, but it has no power to waken any civilization to life. The time for that is past. The spirit of antiquity, having failed to reach an ethical nature-philosophy, has become the prey of a pessimistic dualism in which no ethic of action is any longer possible; there can only be an ethic of purification.

The thoughts of Seneca, Epictetus, and Marcus Aurelius are the winter seed of a coming civilization.

Chapter II

OPTIMISTIC WORLD-VIEW AND ETHICS IN THE RENAISSANCE AND POST-RENAISSANCE PERIODS

Belief in progress and ethics.

Christian and Stoic elements in modern ethics.

THE ESSENTIAL CHARACTERISTIC OF THE MODERN AGE IS THAT IT thinks and acts in the spirit of a world- and life-affirmation which has never before appeared in such active strength.

This world-view breaks through in the Renaissance, beginning at the end of the fourteenth century, and it arises as a protest against the mediæval enslavement of the human spirit. The movement is helped to victory by the increasing knowledge of Greek philosophy in its original form, which is the result of the migration to Italy about the middle of the fifteenth century of learned Greeks from Constantinople. Among the thinking men of that time there arises the belief that philosophy must be something more elemental and more living than Scholasticism taught.

But the thought of antiquity would not have been sufficient by itself to keep alive this new world- and life-affirmation which appealed to it as a precedent. It had not, in truth, the mentality required. But another kind of fuel is in time brought for the fire. Taking refuge from book-learning in nature, the men of that time discover the world. As mariners they reach countries whose very existence was not suspected, and they measure the size of the earth. As inquirers they press on into the infinite and the secrets of the universe, and learn by experience that forces governed by uniform laws are at work, and that man has power to make them serviceable to himself. The knowledge and power won by Leonardo da Vinci (1452–1519), Corpernicus (1473–1543), Kepler (1571–1630), Galileo (1564–1642), and others are decisive for the current world-view.

As a movement which draws its life solely from spiritual forces, the Renaissance passes its blossoming-time comparatively quickly, and without forming much fruit. With Paracelsus (1493–1541), Bernardino Telesio (1508–1588), Giordano Bruno (1548–1600), and others, an enthusiastic nature-philosophy is announced. But it does not reach full growth. The Renaissance has not strength enough to bring to birth a world- and life-affirming philosophy which can rise to the height of these men's intellects. Here and there their thought surges for a time, like a rough sea, against the world-denying philosophy of the Church. Then all is still. What we know definitely as the philosophy of modern times begins almost without any reference to the Renaissance. It springs, not from any nature-philosophy, but from the problem of the theory of knowledge which was raised by Descartes, and from that starting-point philosophy has once more had laboriously to seek its way to a nature-philosophy.

It is not, then, because it was enlarged during the Renaissance into a fully thought out theory of the universe that world- and life-affirmation made good its position in the modern age. If it was able to hold out right into the eighteenth century, when it triumphs against the world- and life-negation which mediæval thought and Christianity kept in action in opposition to it, it owed this to the circumstance that progress in knowledge and power never ceased. In them the new mentality had a support which never wavered, but became continually stronger. Since the new scientific knowledge cannot be suppressed nor its progress arrested, belief in the sovereignty of truth becomes firmly established. Since it becomes more and more evident that nature works with a uniformity which never misses its aim, there grows up a confidence that the circumstances of society and of mankind can also be so organized as to secure definite objects. Since man is ever obtaining greater power over nature, he takes it more and more as self-evident that the reaching of perfection in other spheres is only a question of a sufficiency of will-power and a no less correct method of grappling with problems.

Under the steadily active influence of the new mentality, the world-view of Christianity changes, and becomes leavened with the yeast of world- and life-affirmation. It gradually begins to be accepted as self-evident that the spirit of Jesus does not renounce the world, but aims at transforming it. The early Christain conception of the Kingdom of God, which was born of pessimism and, thanks to Augustine, prevailed through the Middle Ages, is rendered impotent, and its place is taken by a conception which is the offspring of modern optimism. This new orientation of the Christian world-view, which is accomplished by a slow and often interrupted process of change between the fifteenth century and the end of the eighteenth, is the decisive spiritual event of the modern age. During this period Christianity takes no account of what is happening to itself. It believes that it is remaining unaltered, whereas in reality, by this change from pessimism to optimism, it is surrendering its original character.

The modern man, then, becomes optimistic, not because deepened thought has made him understand the world in the sense of world- and life-affirmation, but because discovery and invention have given him power over the world. This enhancement of his self-reliance and the consequent strengthening of his will and his hopes, determine his will-to-live in a correspondingly pronounced and positive sense.

In the ancient world, man's natural disposition to world- and life-affirmation could not be worked out to a complete world-view, because at that time deep thought about the world and life pressed resignation upon him as a necessity of thought. In the man of the modern age the mentality produced by discovery and invention unites with his natural disposition to world- and life-affirmation, and establishes him in an optimistic world-view without leading him to deeper thought about the world and life.

The spirit of the modern age is not the work of any one great thinker. It wins its way gradually by reason of the unbroken series of triumphs won by discovery and invention. Hence it is not a result of chance that an almost unphilosophic and moreover somewhat worm-eaten personality like Francis Bacon, Lord Verulam (1561–1626), is the man who drafts the programme of the modern world-view. He founds it upon the sentence: "Knowledge is power." He develops his picture of the future in his *New Atlantis,* in which he describes how the inhabitants of an island, through the practical application of all known discoveries and inventions and all possible rational reflection on the purposive organization of society, find themselves in a position to lead the happiest possible lives.[1]

* * *

What is the relation between ethics and the mentality of belief in progress, and how were ethics influenced by this belief?

When the ethical thought of antiquity wanted to come to clearness about itself, it fell a victim to resignation, because it tried to determine the moral as that which is rationally profitable and pleasurable to the individual. It remained shut up within the circle of the egoistic, and never reached the idea of social utilitarianism. From such a fate modern ethics are protected in advance. They have no need to produce from their own resources the thought that the ethical is action directed to promoting the welfare of others, for they find it already accepted as true. That is the gift of Christianity. The thought of Jesus that the ethical is the individual's active self-devotion to others has won its way to acceptance. Ethics, whilst becoming independent of religion, as a result of their passage through Christianity, retain a pronouncedly active and altruistic mode of thought. All they have to do is to provide this possession with a rational foundation.

It is extraordinarily significant that in the Later Stoicism there comes to meet modern ethics a philosophical ethical system in which, as the result of rational thinking, there appear thoughts which closely approach Christian morality. There is now coming up for the benefit of modern times the seed sown

[1] Bacon was Lord Chancellor under James I. of England, but was in 1621 deprived of his office because found guilty of corruption. His two chief works are the *Novum Organum Scientiarum* (1620) and *De Dignitate et Augmentis Scientiarum* (1623). Of the *New Atlantis* only a fragment has survived.

by Seneca, Epictetus, and Marcus Aurelius. Cicero, too, counts for so much, because modern thinkers find in his writings noble morality based upon thought. The discovery of Late Stoicism's ethic of humanity is for them as important as their discovery of nature. They identify it with the true Christian ethic, and contrast it with the scholastic ethic, in which Jesus is expounded according to Aristotle. It is through Late Stoicism that modern times become aware of morality as an independent value. Because Seneca, Epictetus, and Marcus Aurelius speak to such an extent just as Jesus did, they help to spread the conviction that the truly rational ethic and the ethic of the Gospels coincide with one another.

By the time antiquity came to an end, Late Stoicism and Christianity, in spite of the identity of their moral teaching, had torn each other to pieces. In modern times they unite to produce together an ethical outlook on life. Why is it that now possible which before was impossible? Because the chasm which lay between their respective world-views has been bridged. Christianity now treats world- and life-affirmation as valid.

But how could this volte-face of Christianity be brought about? Because of the fact that in spite of its pessimistic world-view it upholds an ethic which, so far as it touches the relation of man to man, is activist. The pessimistic world-view, if it is thought out to a consistent conclusion, must end as in Indian philosophy with a purely world-denying ethic, divorced from action. The unique character, however, of the world-view of Jesus, which is determined by the expectation of the end of the world and the coming of a supernatural kingdom of God, and the directness of his ethical feeling, entail that, in spite of his pessimistic attitude towards the natural world, he proclaims an ethic of active devotion to one's neighbour. This activist ethic is what is wanted to provide the cardinal-point of an evolution from a Christian-pessimistic to a Christian-optimistic philosophy. The modern age, following its instinct, assumes as self-evident that an ethic which deals with the active relations of man to man is pre-supposed to be an ethic which assigns a positive value to action as such, and, further, that such an ethic of action belongs to a world-view which is optimistic and which wills and hopes for a purposive reorganization of relationships.

It is, then, the ethic of active self-devotion taught by Jesus which makes it possible for Christianity, inspired by the spirit of the modern age, to modulate from the pessimistic to the optimistic world-view. This result finds expression in the way the new conception of Christianity, when it has to come to an understanding with the old, rebels against "the Christianity of dogma" under the banner of "the religion of Jesus."

A way is prepared in Erasmus and individual representatives of the Reformation, shyly at first but then more and more clearly, for an interpretation of the teaching of Jesus which corresponds to the spirit of modern times, an interpretation which conceives the teaching as a religion of action in the world. Historically and in actual fact this is a wrong interpretation, for the world-view of Jesus is thoroughly pessimistic so far as concerns the future of the natural world. His religion is not a religion of world-transforming effort, but the religion of awaiting the end of the world. His ethic is characterized by activity only so far as it commands men to practise unbounded devotion to their fellow-men, if they would attain to that inner perfection which is needed for entrance into the supernatural kingdom of God. An ethic of enthusiasm, seemingly focused upon an optimistic world-view, forms part of a pessimistic world-view! That is the magnificent paradox in the teaching of Jesus.

But the modern age was right in overlooking this paradox, and assuming in Jesus an optimistic world-view which corresponded to an ethic of enthusiasm and met with a welcome the spirit of Late Stoicism and that of modern times. For the progress of the spiritual life of Europe this mistake was a necessity. What crises the latter must have gone through, if it had not been able without embarrassment to place the new outlook on the universe under the authority of the great personality of Jesus!

The mistake was such a natural one that till the end of the nineteenth century it was never seriously shaken. When historical criticism, at the beginning of the twentieth century, proclaimed its discovery that Jesus, in spite if his activist ethic, thought and acted under the influence of a pessimistic world-view dominated by the expectation of the end of the world, it aroused indignation. It was accused of degrading Jesus to a mere enthusiast, while after all it was only putting an end to the false modernizing of his personality.[2] What we at the present time have to do is to go through the critical experience of being obliged to think as modern men with a world-view of world- and life-affirmation, and yet let the ethic of Jesus speak to us from out of a pessimistic world-view.

Of this problem, which is disclosing itself to-day, the early period of the modern age suspects nothing. Jesus and the moralists of Late Stoicism together are its authorities for an ethical world- and life-affirmation.

What the Late-Stoic ethic is for the modern age is shown by Erasmus of Rotterdam (1466–1536), Michel de Montaigne (1533–1592), Pierre Charron (1541–1603), Jean Bodin (1530–1596), and Hugo Grotius (1583–1645), and that whether their ideas run predominantly on Christian or on freethinking lines. To the Later Stoics Erasmus owes it that he can understand the simple gospel of Jesus, discovered behind the dogmas of the Church, as the essence of all ethical philosophizing. It is by finding support in them that Montaigne in his *Essays* (1580) is saved from falling into complete ethical scepticism. Because he is inspired by the Later Stoics, Bodin in his work *De la république* (1577), puts forward an ethical ideal of the State to combat the ideas of Machiavelli's *Principe* (1515). Because he draws from the same source, Pierre Charron in his work *De la sagesse* (1601), ventures to assert that ethics are higher than revealed religion, and can maintain themselves in an independent position in face of it without losing anything of their essential nature or of their depth. Because the work of Marcus Aurelius has preceded him, Hugo Grotius is able in his famous work, *De jure belli ac pacis* (1625) to lay so securely the foundations of natural and international law, and thereby to champion the claims of reason and humanity in the domain of jurisprudence.

Other considerations apart, it would have been the first task of the rising power of natural science to restore to currency the

[2] See the writer's books: *Das Messianitats- und Leidensgeheimniss–Eine Skizze des Lebens Jesu* (1901). English version: *The Mystery of the Kingdom of God* (1914 A. & C. Black). *Geschichte der Leben-Jesu Forschung* (1906; new edition, 1922). English version: *The Quest of the Historical Jesus* (1911; 3rd impression, 1922, A. & C. Black).

world-view of Epicurus. Pierre Gassendi (1592–1655)[3] attempts it but fails to accomplish his purpose. By its inward belief in progress the mentality of the modern age is driven in elemental fashion beyond scepticism and sceptical ethics. What is great in Epicurus, namely that in obedience to the deepest demands of truth he tries to think ethically within a nature-philosophy which does not interpret nature as embodying any purpose, can neither be comprehended nor be put before his own age by the philosopher's all too clever modern prophet.

For the weighty questions of absolute truth, that time is by no means ripe. Its capacity is only that of the uncritical. Typical for its spirit is Isaac Newton (1643–1727), who in his investigation of nature is purely empirical, and in his world-view remains simply Christian.

Against the difficulties which crop up for ethics and world- and life-affirmation from a nature-philosophy which works without any presuppositions, the Renaissance and the Post-Renaissance are secure. The belief in progress which arises from the achievements of discovery and invention, and the joy felt in action itself constitute their philosophy of life.

Thanks to belief in progress, new life streams into ethics. The inner relations between ethics and world- and life-affirmation begin to take effect. The elementary impulses to activity which are embodied in the Christian ethic are set free, and belief in progress gives them an aim: the transformation of the circumstances of society and of mankind.

It is not any really deeper ethical thinking that brings on the modern age, but the influence exerted by the belief in progress, which arose out of the achievements of discovery and invention, on the ethic which drew its life from Stoic and Christian thought. The cart is drawn by the belief in progress, and at first ethics have only to run along beside it. But as the cart gets heavier and the road more difficult, so that ethics ought to lend their strength to help, they refuse, because they have no strength of their own. The cart begins to run backward, and carries belief in progress, and ethics with it, down the hill.

The task before philosophy was to change the world- and

[3] Gassendi: *De vita, moribus, et doctrina Epicuri* (1647) and *Syntagma philosophiæ Epicuri* (1649).

life-affirmation which arose from enthusiasm over the attainments of discovery and invention into a deeper, inner world- and life-affirmation arising out of thought about the universe and the life of man, and on that same foundation to build up an ethical system. But philosophy could do neither.

About the middle of the nineteenth century, when it has become perfectly clear that we are living with a world- and life-affirmation which has its source merely in our confidence in discovery and invention and not in any profounder thought about the world and life, our fate is sealed. The modern optimistic-ethical world-view, after doing so much for the material development of civilization, has to collapse like a building erected already to a considerable height but on rotten foundations.

Chapter 12

LAYING THE FOUNDATION OF ETHICS IN THE SEVENTEENTH AND EIGHTEENTH CENTURIES

Hartley, Holbach. Devotion as enlightened egoism.

Hobbes, Locke, Helvetius, Bentham.

Altruism as a natural quality. Hume, Adam Smith.

The English ethic of self-perfecting.

Shaftesbury. An optimistic-ethical nature-philosophy.

THE MODERN AGE FINDS WORLD- AND LIFE-AFFIRMATION SO SELF-evident that it feels no need to give them a sure foundation and deepen them by thought about the world and life. It brushes pessimism aside as reactionary folly, without suspecting how deep down into thought it has sent its roots.

But it does see the necessity of establishing the nature of the ethical. How does it proceed to do this?

That the ethical means action directed to promoting the common good is its firm belief from the first, and it is safe from the fate of ancient thought, that is to say, sticking fast in the mud of resignation while trying to give the ethical a proper foundation. Instead of that it has to answer the question how the unegoistic makes its appearance beside the egoistic, and in what inner relation they stand to each other.

Now begins a process like that which went on after the appearance of Socrates, only the task is proposed this time, not by an individual, but by the spirit of the time. Another attempt is made to consider the ethical problem in isolation, as if it consisted in reflections on the relation of the individual to himself and to society, these having no need to settle their position with regard to ultimate questions of the meaning of the world and of life. The ethical problem seems, too, to be much simpler than it was, because world-affirmation and activity directed toward the general welfare no longer have to be proved, but appear among the hypotheses which are taken for granted.

There are three ways in which the relations between the egoistic and the altruistic can be made clear. Either one assumes that the egoistic in the thought of the individual is automatically converted into the altruistic by consistent meditation. Or one supposes the altruistic to have its beginning in the thought of society and thence to pass over into the convictions of the individual. Or one retires to the position that egoism and altruism are both among the original endowments of human nature. All three explanations are attempted, each with most varied arguments. They are not always carried to a conclusion without intermixture, and with many thinkers there is interplay of one with another.

The attempt to deduce devotion to the common welfare from egoism by psychological considerations is made with the greatest consciousness of the end in view by David Hartley (1705–1757) [1] and Dietrich von Holbach (1723–1789).[2]

Hartley, a theologian who betook himself to the practice of medicine, claims to see in altruism a purposive ennoblement of original selfishness which comes into play under the influence of rational thought. The much-reviled Holbach ascribes its origin to the fact that the individual, if he rightly understands his own interest, will always form his conception of it in connection with the interest of society, and will therefore direct his activities to the latter as well.

Both attempt to erect their building, so far as it goes, with materialistic considerations and then proceed to roof it with idealistic views. But neither with the coarser nor with the finer considerations, nor with both together, can the psychological

[1] D. Hartley: *Observations on Man, his Frame, his Duty, and his Expectations* (1749; 6th ed., 1834).

[2] D. von Holbach: *Systéme de la nature ou des lois du monde physique et du monde moral* (1770).

derivation of altruism from egoism produce any convincing result.

The coarser ones do not carry us very far. It is acknowledged, of course, that the prosperity of society depends upon the moral disposition of its members, and that the better the moral condition of society the better is the individual's expectation of prosperity. But it does not follow that the individual becomes more moral the better he understands his own interests. The mutual relation between him and society is not of such a character that he derives benefit from the latter just in proportion as he himself by his moral conduct helps to establish its prosperity. If the majority of its members, with short-sighted egoism, are intent only on their own good, then the man who acts with wider outlook makes sacrifices from which there is no prospect of gain for himself, even if the best happens and they are not lost without benefiting the community. If, on the other hand, through the moral conduct of the majority of its members the condition of society is favourable, the individual profits by it, even if he fails to behave towards it as morality demands. By conduct which disregards both past and future, he will carve for himself an unduly big share of personal prosperity out of the prosperity of the community, milking the cow which the rest provide with fodder. The influence of the individual on the prosperity of the community, and the reaction of social prosperity on that of the individual, do not stand in a simple reciprocal relationship to each other. The consideration, therefore, that egoism, rightly understood, will oblige the individual to resolve on activity which is directed to promoting the common good, is a ship which sails well, but leaks.

The psychological derivation of altruism from egoism must, in some way or other, make an appeal to the self-sacrifice of the individual. This it does by inducing him to consider that in happiness there is a spiritual as well as a material element. Man needs not only external prosperity, but to be respected by others and to be satisfied with himself, and he can have this double experience only when he concerns himself about the prosperity of others. Even Holbach, who tries to be inexorably matter-of-fact, lets these considerations raise their voices.

The attempt is made, therefore, to modulate into the spiritualized conception of happiness above the prolonged bass note of that conception which is derived from ordinary egoism.

The path which this attempt has to follow runs parallel to that which led the successors of Socrates into the abyss of the paradoxical. In order to get from egoism into altruism, and so think out to a conclusion the ethic of the rationally-pleasurable, the Epicureans wished to use the same scale of values for spiritual and material pleasure alike. The only result was that their ethic was transformed into resignation. Now again, in the modern age, and again for the sake of ethics, spiritual happiness is to be regarded as happiness in the same way as is material happiness. Here again the result is a paradox.

Material and spiritual happiness are not so related that the one can find its continuation in the other. If, for the sake of ethics, the second is called in with the first, it does not strengthen the first, but paralyses it. The man who does earnestly try to guide himself by the light of spiritual as well as material happiness, ends by finding that the recognition accorded him by his fellow-men, which at first seemed to make almost the whole of spiritual happiness, becomes more and more meaningless. It is to him a miserable lump of solder which drops down between material and spiritual happiness without being able to unite them. More and more exclusively, he experiences spiritual happiness as the condition in which he is at one with himself and therefore can justifiably accord himself a certain amount of self-approbation.

Spiritual happiness is sufficient unto itself. Either the man is led to resolve on ethical conduct because he expects from it a moulding of the outward circumstances of his being which will bring him profit and pleasure; or he chooses it because he finds his happiness in obeying the inner compulsion to ethical action. In the latter case he has left far behind him all calculations about the interdependence of his morality and his material happiness. The fact that he is a moral man is in itself his happiness, even though it land him in the most disadvantageous situations.

But if spiritual and material happiness can never be welded together, it is useless endeavour to try to depict altruism as an ennobling of egoism.

If the ordinary conception of pleasure, that it may be brought into union with ethics, is submitted to a process of refining, it ends by being refined away. In ancient ethics, in which the refining is done under the influence of an ethical system which is definitely egoistic, it transforms itself into the pleasure of being without pleasure, and allows ethics to end in resignation. In modern ethics, in which the pleasure to be refined is under the influence of altruism, it works itself up into an irrational and immaterialistic enthusiasm. In both cases there is the same paradoxical proceeding, only that in one case it goes in the negative direction, in the other in the positive.

Whenever, then, thought wishes to conceive ethics as springing from pleasure or happiness, it arrives at resignation or enthusiasm, at spiritualized egoistic or at spiritualized expansive conduct.

Where thought is profound there is no way in which natural pleasure can be brought into connection with ethics.

* * *

The explanation that altruism is a principle of action which the individual derives from society is to be found expressed in characteristic ways by Thomas Hobbes (1588–1679),[3] John Locke (1632–1704),[4] Adrien Helvetius (1715–1771)[5] and Jeremy Bentham (1748–1832).[6]

Hobbes represents the State as commissioned and empowered by the majority of the individual citizens to employ them to the general advantage. In this way alone, he asserts, is it possible to realize the common good in which the egoism of individuals finds the highest possible degree of prosperity. Left to themselves, men would never be able to get free from their short-sighted egoism, and would, therefore, miss prosperity. Their

3 Thomas Hobbes: *Elementa philosophica de cive* (1642); *Leviathan, or the Matter, Form, and Authority of Government* (1651); *De homine.*

4 John Locke: *An Essay concerning Human Understanding* (2 vols., 1690).

5 Adrien Helvetius: *Traité de l'Esprit* (1758).

6 Jeremy Bentham: *An introduction to the Principles of Morals and Legislation* (1780). E. Dumont (1759–1828) of Geneva, an admirer of Bentham who was domiciled in England, reproduced this work in French in a free abbreviation as *Traités de législation civile et pénale* (1802). Frederick Edward Beneke followed this abbreviation when he produced a German translation with the title: *Grundsätze der Civil- und Criminalgesetzgebung* (1830).

only possible course is to join in setting up an authority which will compel them to altruism.

With external means, however, organized society cannot employ the individual in all the activities which are needed for the common good. It must strive to ensure its power over him by means of spiritual conviction as well. Locke takes this need into consideration. According to him it is God and society together who force altruism upon the individual by appealing to his egoism. These two authorities have, that is to say (as our reason enables us to recognize), so ordered the course of things that actions beneficial to society are rewarded, and those injurious to it are punished. God has at his disposal rewards and punishments of endless duration. Society works in two different ways: through the power given to it by the criminal law, and through the law of public opinion which uses praise and blame as spiritual means of compulsion. Man, being guided both by pleasure and its opposite, manages to accommodate himself to those rules which so effectually defend the general good, and thereby becomes moral.

In spite of all their differences on single points, Hobbes and Locke agree in having this external conception of ethics. The essential point of distinction between them is that with Hobbes society alone plies the whip, while with Locke God and society wield it together.

Helvetius, who belonged to a family which had migrated from the Palatinate into France, is more refined and more inward. In his life as farmer-general of taxes and property-owner, he always tried, along with his noble-minded wife, to act with kindness and justice as he explains them in his book. It is clear to him that ethics mean somehow or other enthusiastic action, that is, action which springs from feeling.[7] Society cannot, therefore, force these virtues into the individual; it can only inculcate them, and it does in fact apply all the means and devices which are at its disposal to influence his egoism in their direction. Above all it makes good use of his striving to win recognition and fame. The praise which it pours on that which is "good" in

[7] *Translator's Note.*—German "enthusiastisches Handeln." The explanatory periphrasis is added once for all, since "enthusiastic" implies a kind and degree of feeling which is not implied in these philosophical passages.

its own sense of the word is for the mass of men the strongest inducement to work for its interests. Helvetius would perhaps have offered a less external conception of how ethical action is realized, if he had not, with the best intentions, taken so much trouble to depict ethics as a subject which can be taught.

In the view that morality is enthusiastic action to which the individual is roused by society, Bentham agrees entirely with Helvetius, but he develops it with far greater profundity. He turns the ballad into a hymn.

The part played by society in originating morality cannot, according to Bentham, be emphasized too strongly. In vehement words he opposes the view that the human conscience can decide between good and evil. Nothing can be left to subjective feeling. Man is truly moral only when he receives his ethics at the hand of society and executes their commands with ardour.

But if society is to decide about ethics, it must first bring order into its own ethical views, and therefore, says Bentham, must learn to combine clear and definite notions with its presentation of the general good. That done, it must make up its mind to apply this principle with absolute consistency as a foundation for legislation and the establishment of ethical standards, excluding all considerations of a different character. A "moral arithmetic" should be constructed to allow the calculating in correct utility values of all decisions that have to be made.

Dealing in a dry, practical way with all cases of penal legislation, and the establishment of standards by the moral law, Bentham then shows that the principle of the greatest good of the greatest number is applicable in all of them, and guides us safely and accurately in questions of good and evil.

"Moral philosophy, in its general meaning, is the theory underlying the art of so directing the actions of men that there is produced the greatest possible amount of happiness."

It is legislation that decides what moral actions the community can order to be performed. If it is to exert an educative influence it must be completely humane.

"But there are many actions which, though useful to the community, legislation may not command. There are even many injurious actions which it may not forbid, although moral philosophy does so. Legislation is, in a word, a circle with the same centre as moral philosophy, but its circumference is smaller."

Where the resources of the law come to an end, there is nothing that society can do except continually bring to the notice of the individual how greatly he contributes to his own welfare by furthering that of others. Bentham does not make it do this with pedagogic guile as does Helvetius. Society appeals to his feeling for truth. It throws itself at his feet and entreats him for the sake of the general welfare to listen to the voice of reason. Thus the dry way in which Bentham writes about ethics has in it something peculiarly impressive, and explains the powerful influence which this eccentric tenant of the house which looks across St. James's Park has exercised all over the world through the individuals who were inspired by him.

The most influential parts of his work are those in which he intensifies the seriousness of men, and sharpens their outlook, by leading them to reflect, not only on the immediate, but also on the more distant consequences of anything done or left undone, and, further, not only on the material, but on the spiritual, consequences. It is pleasant to note the courage with which this fanatic for utility ventures to represent material blessings as the foundation of those which are spiritual.

Bentham is one of the most powerful moralists who have ever lived, but his mistakes are as great as his insight. The latter is shown in the fact that he conceives morality as a kind of enthusiasm. His mistake is that he thinks he must guarantee the rightness of this enthusiasm by making it nothing higher than a judgment of society which is taken over by the individual.

This compels us to rank Bentham with Hobbes, Locke, and Helvetius, although in other respects he stands high above them. Like them, he makes morality originate outside the individual. Like them, in order to find this explanation of the altruistic, he puts out of action the ethical personality which is in man, and, to compensate for this, raises society to an ethical personality that he may then by a transmission of energy connect individuals with this central power-station. The difference is only that with those other commonplace moralists the individual is a marionette directed by society on ethical principles, whereas in Bentham he carries out with deep conviction the movements suggested to him.

Ethical thought falls from one paradox into another. If, as in antiquity, it thinks out a system in which the activity that must be directed to the common good is not sufficiently represented, it arrives at ethics which are no longer ethics, and ends in resignation. If it assumes and starts from such an activity directed to the common good, it arrives at an ethic in which there is no ethical personality. Strange to say, it is unable to mark out the middle course and let an activity which is directed to the promotion of the common good spring from the ethical personality itself.

* * *

The explanations of altruism as an ennobling of egoism which has a spontaneous origin through the activity of reason, or as brought into existence through the influence of society, are obviously unsatisfying both psychologically and ethically. Utilitarianism must therefore necessarily come to admit that altruism is somehow or other given independently in human nature side by side with egoism. It is true that it always appears there as the backward twin-brother who can be reared only with the most careful nursing, and therefore the upholders of the third alternative appeal to the considerations used for the first two. They continually allow the capacity for altruistic feeling to be exposed to the influence of considerations which seem calculated to let egoism flow into altruism. The first two views are taken into service as wet-nurses for the third.

David Hume (1711–1776) [8] and Adam Smith (1723–1790) [9] must be named here.

Hume agrees with the other utilitarians in allowing that the principle of seeking to promote the common good must be

[8] David Hume: *A Treatise of Human Nature: Being an Attempt to introduce the Experimental Method of Reasoning into Moral Subjects* (1740). German translation by Heinrich Jacob (2 vols., 1791): *Inquiry Concerning the Principles of Morals* (1751).

[9] Adam Smith: *The Theory of Moral Sentiments* (1759); *Inquiry into the Nature and Causes of the Wealth of Nations* (1770). German translation of *The Theory of Moral Sentiments* by L. Th. Kosegarten (1791). Adam Smith was Professor of Moral Philosophy at Glasgow.

accepted as the dominant principle of morality. Whether actions are good or bad is decided solely by whether or not they are directed towards the production of general happiness. There is nothing which is in itself ethical or unethical.

To the idea that ethics can have as their object the self-perfecting of the individual, as little weight is given by Hume as by the other utilitarians. Like them, he opposes asceticism and other life-denying demands of Christian ethics, because he cannot discover in them anything profitable for the general welfare.

But what makes men decide to work together for the common good? Consistent utilitarians answer: Reflection about what the common good means. Of this one-sidedness Hume is not guilty, because he does not find it in accord with psychological facts. It is not in high-minded reflection, he asserts, but in direct sympathy that the emotions and actions of benevolence have their source. The virtues which serve the common good have their origin in feeling. We can resolve on acts of love only because there is in us an elementary feeling for the happiness of men, and a dislike of seeing them in misery. We become moral through sympathy.

It would not have been a big step further to explain this sympathy as a form of the egoistic need of happiness, more or less through the assumption that in order to be really happy a man must see happiness around him. But that is not Hume's way. He does not aim at constructive thought but at stating facts, and it is enough for him that direct sympathy with other men be proved to be a principle inherent in human nature. We have to stop somewhere or other, he says, in our search for causes. In every science there are certain general principles beyond which there is no still more general principle for us to discover.

Among the elements which are effective in developing moral feeling, Hume attributes great importance to the love of fame. This keeps us considering ourselves in the light in which we wish to appear in the eyes of others, for the effort to secure the respect of others is the great teacher of virtue. On this point he thinks like Frederick the Great, from whom comes the sentence: "L'amour de la gloire est inné dans les belles âmes: il n'y a qu'à l'animer, il n'y a que l'exciter, et des hommes qui végétaient jusqu'alors, enflammés par ce heureux instinct, vous paraîtront changés en demi-dieux." (*Œuvres de Frédéric le Grand*, vol. ix., p. 98.) [10]

Adam Smith wishes to trace out the idea of sympathy in all its manifestations, and in doing so he discovers that our capacity for sympathy covers more than participation in the weal or woe of others. It brings us, he says, to a community of thought with those who are actively engaged. We feel ourselves directly attracted or repelled by the actions of others and the motives that inspire those actions. Our ethics are the product of these sympathetic experiences. We come in time to take care that an impartial third party can justify and sympathize with the mainspring and the tendency of our actions. Innate sympathy, not only with the actions but also with the experience of others, is thus the beneficent regulator of the behaviour of men to one another. God has implanted this feeling in human nature that it may keep men faithful to work for the common good.

How far this somewhat artificial extension of the notion of sympathy through the doctrine of the impartial third party really means a step forward beyond Hume, we may leave undiscussed.

In his famous work, *An Inquiry into the Nature and Causes of the Wealth of Nations* (1776), Adam Smith founds this prosperity purely upon the entirely free and rational activity of egoism. He says nothing about the part to be played by ethics in economic questions, but leaves economic development to be determined by its own internal laws, confident that, if these are left a free course, the result will be favourable. Adam Smith, the moral philosopher, because he is endowed with a rationalistic optimism, is also the founder of the *laissez-faire* form of economic doctrine, that of the Manchester school. He led industry and commerce in their struggle for liberation from the petty and injurious tutelage of authority. To-day, when economic life among all peoples is again delivered over to the most shortsighted ideas of authorities who never think in terms of economics, we can measure the greatness of his achievement.

10 "The love of fame is innate in noble souls; you have only to arouse it and urge it on, and men who till then merely vegetated, will seem to you, when inflamed by this happy instinct, to be changed into demi-gods."

Like Adam Smith, Bentham is an adherent of the principle of freedom in economic life. At the same time he has an ethical conception of society, and demands from it that in a spirit of progress it shall help to level out as far as possible the differences between rich and poor.

What, then, do Hume and Adam Smith mean for ethics? They introduce the element of empirical psychology. They believe that through the value they give to the significance of sympathy they are giving a natural foundation to utilitarianism, though in reality psychology begins to correct it and to undermine its position. There hovers before the mind of utilitarianism the great conception that ethics are a result of reflection. It thinks to make men moral by keeping their attention fixed on the profound nature of ethics and the necessity of the aims in view.

This conception draws its life from the conviction that thought has been given complete control over the will. The absolute rationality of the ethical is the foundation on which it builds, and if it is not to get quite bewildered about its own nature, it cannot allow itself to recognize, as presuppositions of the ethical, facts which are given it by psychology and cannot be verified independently.

With Hume and Adam Smith, who trace ethics back to something inherent in human nature which resembles instinct, there crops up the problem how ethics can be natural, and at the same time serve as a basis for thought, for that they do form the groundwork of thought must be assumed even by the champions of this psychological utilitarianism. If they were nothing but the exercise of an instinct, they would not be capable of widening and deepening, nor could they be imparted to all and sundry with convincing force. Yet how is it conceivable that thought influences the sympathetic instinct? What have the two in common that the work of one can be carried further by the other?

If Hume and Adam Smith had suspected the far-reaching character of this great problem of ethics which they brought into the field of discussion, they would have had to go on and settle the extent and the depth of this sympathy which they adopted in their scheme, in order to understand how it continues to function in the domain of thought.

But they fail to notice the full importance of what they establish, and believe they have done nothing but give by means of psychology an explanation of altruism which is superior to that commonly approved. The spirit of the time, with its wonderful capacity for holding various ideas side by side, takes possession of their view, and popular utilitarianism now confidently declares that altruism is to be conceived as a rational ennobling of egoism, as a result of the influence of society, and in addition as a manifestation of a natural instinct.

It is, really, only in appearance that the psychological conception of ethics imparts new life to utilitarianism. It is rather a consumption germ which the latter absorbs. The establishment of a natural element in ethics, when the consequences begin to make themselves felt, can only end in its devouring rationalist utilitarianism, as becomes evident in the nineteenth century when biological thought becomes influential in ethics.

The funeral procession of rationalist utilitarianism begins to assemble with Hume and Adam Smith, though it is a long time before the coffin is carried to the cemetery.

* * *

Against the utilitarians, who from the content of the moral would derive both its essential nature and the obligation to morality, the "Intellectualists" and the "Intuitionists" enter the lists. The empirical derivation of ethics seems to them to be an endangering of the majesty of the moral. Morality—this is the thought before their minds—is a striving after perfection, and this develops in us because it is implanted in our hearts by nature. Action for the common advantage does not by any means constitute ethics; it is only a manifestation of the struggle for self-perfection.

To this deeper and more comprehensive conception of ethics, however, the Intellectualists and Intuitionists do not give correct expression. For that they are still too much involved in a lifeless and semi-scholastic philosophizing.

Their chief strength lies in their showing up of the weaknesses of the foundation which Hobbes and Locke give to ethics, and to these they principally devote themselves, bringing to their task a great deal that is correct about the directly and absolutely binding character of the moral law. That the meaning of the moral is not to be found merely in the useful character of the actions it inspires, but also in the self-perfecting of the human being which those actions bring about, and, further, that morality presupposes a moral personality, is emphasized by them in many happy turns of expression.

When, however, the task before them is to describe exactly in what way men carry in them the idea of the good as a force which works effectively upon their character, the Intellectualists and the Intuitionists land themselves in a psychologizing which is sometimes ingenious, but often artificial and commonplace. They occupy themselves with logical distinctions instead of investigating in a practical fashion the nature of man. Instead of really developing the problem in answer to the innovators, they work at it with data taken from bygone philosophy. They hark back largely to Plato, and on many points argue consciously or unconsciously, not as philosophers, but as theologians.

They diverge from each other on the details, and attack each other's positions according as they would have the foundations of the ethical more intellectualist, or more sentimental and mystical, or more theological.

The majority of these anti-utilitarians belong to the school of the Cambridge Platonists. We must name here Ralph Cudworth (1617–1688),[11] Henry More (1614–1687),[12] the Rev. Samuel Clarke (1675–1729),[13] Bishop Richard Cumberland (1632–1718),[14] and William Wollaston (1659–1724).[15]

According to Cudworth, the truths of morality are just as evident as these of mathematics. For More the ethical is an intellectual power of the soul meant for the control of natural impulses. Cumberland finds the moral law given in the reason which has been bestowed upon man by God. Clarke, living in the thought world of Isaac Newton, sees it as the spiritual

[11] R. Cudworth: *Intellectual System of the Universe* (1678); *Treatise concerning Eternal and Immutable Morality* (posthumous, 1731).

[12] H. More: *Enchiridium Ethicum* (1667).

[13] S. Clarke: *A Discourse concerning the Unchangeable Obligations of Natural Religion, and the Truth and Certainty of the Christian Revelation* (1706).

[14] R. Cumberland: *De legibus naturæ disquisitio philosophica* (1672).

[15] W. Wollaston: *The Religion of Nature Delineated* (1722).

phenomenon which corresponds to the law of nature. Wollaston defines it as that which is logically right.

When all is said, these thinkers do nothing but amplify the statement that the ethical is ethical. They assert that the utilitarian view of ethics is pitched too low, but they do not succeed in establishing, in contrast to it, a more exalted principle in such a way that a higher and more comprehensive content of ethics can be derived from it. As to content, their ethic does not really differ from that of the utilitarians. Only it lacks the great enthusiastic driving-force which is seen in the latter. To establish a living ethic of self-perfecting is beyond the capacity of the Intellectualists and the Intuitionists.

What is the inner connection between the struggle for self-perfecting and action for the common advantage? This is the weighty question of ethics which crops up in the discussion between the utilitarians and their conservative opponents. At first it remains veiled, and it does not come to clear expression till we reach Kant.

* * *

A singular position in the ethical thought of the eighteenth century is held by Anthony Ashley-Cooper, Earl of Shaftesbury (1671–1713).[16] He opposes not only the utilitarians, but the Intellectualists and the Intuitionists as well, and tries to secure a mediating position between them. That the content of ethics is utilitarian he openly admits, but he derives the ethical neither from considerations of usefulness nor from the intellect; he places its origin in feeling. At the same time he emphasizes, as does Adam Smith a few years later, its relationship to the æsthetic.

But the important thing is that he puts forward a living philosophy of nature in combination with ethics. He is convinced that harmony reigns in the universe and that man is meant to experience this harmony in himself. Æsthetic feeling and ethical thinking are for him forms of union with that divine life which

16 *Characteristics of Men, Manners, Opinions, Times* (3 vols., 1711). In the second volume there is included his ethical treatise entitled, *Inquiry concerning Virtue or Merit,* which appeared first, in 1699, independently. It was published in French in 1745 by Denis Diderot.

struggles to find expression in the spiritual being of man as it does in nature.

With Shaftesbury ethics descend from a rocky mountain range into a luxuriant plain. The utilitarians as yet know nothing of a world. Their ethic is restricted to considerations about the relation of the individual to society. The anti-utilitarians have some idea of a world, but not a correct one. They elaborate ethics with a formal theology and a formal philosophizing about the All, but Shaftesbury plants ethical thought in the universe of reality, which he himself contemplates through an idealising optimism, reaching thereby a direct and universal notion of the moral.

A mysticism based on a philosophy of nature begins to spin its magic threads through European thought. The spirit of the Renaissance rules again, this time, however, not like a raging storm, as in Giordano Bruno, but as a gentle breeze. Shaftesbury thinks pantheistically, more pantheistically than he confesses to himself, but his is not a pantheism which throws his age into struggles about world-views, and comes into conflict with theism. It is the harmless pantheism which rules in Hinduism and also in Late Stoicism; pantheism which raises no question of principle, but desires only to be regarded as a vivifying of belief in God.

Shaftesbury also exerts a liberating influence on the spiritual life of his time by according ethics a much freer attitude toward religion than anyone had hitherto ventured to give. Religion, according to him, has not to make decisions about ethics, but on the contrary must prove its own claims to be true by its relation to pure ethical ideas. He even ventures to represent the Christian teaching about rewards and punishment as not consistent with pure ethical considerations. Morality, he says, is pure only when good has been done simply because it is good.

His optimistic-ethical philosophy of nature is offered by Shaftesbury only as a sketch. He throws out his ideas without proving that they are well founded, and without feeling any necessity for thinking them out to a conclusion. He steps with an easy stride across all problems. What a difference between his philosophy of nature and Spinoza's! Yet his meets the needs of the time. He offers what is new to it, and inspires it: ethics bound up with a philosophy of life that is full of vitality.

The belief in progress now clothes itself in a living philosophy which really suits it. This is the process which, thanks to Shaftesbury, began in the first decades of the eighteenth century and went on developing till its end. Hence the appearance of his writings, which were immediately spread abroad through the whole of Europe, is the great event for the spiritual life of the eighteenth century. Voltaire, Diderot, Lessing, Condorcet, Moses Mendelssohn, Wieland, Herder, and Goethe too, are under his influence, and he dominates popular thought completely. Hardly ever has any man had so direct and so powerful an influence on the formation of the world-view of his time as the invalid whose life ended at Naples when he was only forty-two.

Direct continuators of Shaftesbury's ethic are found in Francis Hutcheson (1694–1747)[17] and Bishop Joseph Butler (1692–1752),[18] but they take from it just that fluid indefiniteness which gives it its charm and its strength. Hutcheson, who strongly emphasizes ethics' independence of theology, the relationship of the former to the æsthetic, and their utilitarian content, stands nearer to his teacher than does Butler, who does not go as far in his welcome of utilitarianism, and also opposes, from the Christian standpoint, the optimism of Shaftesbury's world-view.

But Shaftesbury's true successor is J. G. Herder (1744–1803). In his *Ideas on the Philosophy of Human History* (4 vols., 1784–1791), he carries the optimistic-ethical nature-philosophy on into a corresponding philosophy of history.

[17] F. Hutcheson: *An Inquiry into the Original of our Ideas of Beauty and Virtue* (1725); *A System of Moral Philosophy* (1755, posthumous).

[18] Joseph Butler: *Fifteen Sermons upon Human Nature, or Man considered as a Moral Agent* (1726).

Chapter 13

LAYING THE FOUNDATIONS OF CIVILIZATION IN THE AGE OF RATIONALISM

The mentality and the achievements of the ethical belief in progress.

Obstacles to the reform movement. The French Revolution.

The undermining of the rationalistic world-view.

THANKS TO THE FULLY WORKED OUT OPTIMISTIC-ETHICAL WORLD-view with which the belief in progress is environed in the course of the eighteenth century, these generations prove capable of thinking out the ideals of civilization and advancing towards their realization. The fact that all attempts to give ethics a foundation in reason have proved to be more than unsatisfactory does not move them, if indeed they give the point any consideration at all. By the conviction that they have formed a rational conception of the world which gives it an optimistic-ethical meaning, they surmount all the inner problems of ethics. The alliance which belief-in-progress and ethics have in the course of modern times contracted with one another is sealed by means of their outlook on the world, and now they set to work together. Rational ideals are to be realized.

The ethical and the optimistic come into power, therefore, in the philosophy of the eighteenth century, although they have not yet received any real foundation. Scepticism and materialism range around the fortress like hordes of unconquered enemies, though at first without being dangerous; as a rule they have themselves absorbed no small amount of belief-in-progress and of ethical enthusiasm. Voltaire is an example of the sceptic who stands under the restraint exercised by the prevalent optimistic and ethical thought.

So far as its elements are concerned, the world-view of rationalism hides under the optimistic-ethical monism of Kung-tse (Confucius) and the Later Stoics, but the enthusiasm which supports it is incomparably stronger than any felt by them. The circumstances, too, amid which it appears are far more favourable. So it becomes an elemental and popular force.

In a world-view which springs from a noble faith, but is remarkable also for the extent of its knowledge, the men of the eighteenth century begin to think out ideals of civilization and to realize them in such measure that the greatest epoch in the history of human civilization now dawns.

The characteristic feature of the mentality of this belief in progress which is ever showing itself in works is its magnificent want of respect for reality, whether the past or the present. In all its various forms reality is the imperfect value, which is destined to be replaced by perfection.

The eighteenth century is thoroughly unhistoric. In what is good, as in what is bad, it cuts itself loose from whatever was or is, and is confident of being able to put in its place something that is more valuable, because more ethical or more in accordance with reason. In this conviction the age feels itself so creative that it has no understanding for the creations of original genius. Gothic buildings, early painting, J. S. Bach's music, and the poetry of earlier ages, are regarded by these generations as art which was produced at a time when taste had not yet been purified. Activity which follows rules in accordance with right reason will, they think, introduce a new art which will be superior in every respect to any that has preceded it. Full of this self-confidence, a mediocre musician like Zelter in Berlin works over the scores of Bach's Cantatas. Full of this self-confidence, respectable poetasters re-write the texts of the wonderful old German chorales and replace the originals in the hymn books with their own wretched productions.

That they so naïvely push forward right into the sphere of art the bounds of the creative faculties with which nature endowed them, is a mistake made by these men for which they have often been laughed at. But mockery cannot do them much harm. In those departments of life in which the important matter is the shaping of thought according to ideals given by reason—and such work means for the establishment of civilization very much more than any work accomplished in the promotion of art—they are as creative as any generation ever has been, and as scarcely any will be in the future. They are dismayed by nothing which has to be undertaken in this sphere, and in every department they make the most astonishing advance.

They venture also to deal with religion. That religion should be split up into various antagonistic confessional bodies is to them an offence against reasonable reflection. Only relative, not absolute, authority, they maintain, can be allowed to the belief which is handed down in historical formulas. Finding expression in so many and such varied forms it can, of course, be nothing but a more or less imperfect expression of the ethical religion taught by reason, which must be equally intelligible to all men. The right thing is, therefore, to strive after the religion of reason, and to accept as true only such parts of the various confessions as are in harmony with it.

The churches, naturally, put themselves on the defensive against this spirit, but they are unable in the long run to hold out against the strong general convictions of the age. Protestantism succumbs first, because the elements already within it allow such considerations to find easy access. It carries within itself impulses to rationalism, inherited from Humanism, from Huldreich Zwingli (1484–1531) and from the Italians Lælius (1525–1562) and Faustus Socinus (1539–1604), and these impulses, hitherto suppressed, are now set free.[1]

Catholicism shows itself more capable of resistance. Nothing in its past makes it attuned to the spirit of the age: its strong organization serves as a protection against this. Yet it, too, has to yield considerably, and to allow its doctrines to pass, so far as may be, for a symbolic expression of the religion of reason.

[1] The free-thinking, anti-dogmatic religiousness of Socinianism had been maintained chiefly in Poland, Holland, Hungary, England, and North America. Its closer adherents called themselves also Latitudinarians, the more distant ones Unitarians. The fact that religious rationalism had already existed in a literary form facilitated its appearnce in the eighteenth century.

While utilitarian ethics are on the whole the product of the English spirit, the whole of Europe takes part in establishing the religion of reason. Herbert of Cherbury (1582–1648), John Toland (1669–1722), Anthony Collins (1676–1729), Matthew Tindal (1655–1733), David Hume (1711–1776), Pierre Bayle (1647–1706), Jean-Jacques Rousseau (1712–1778), Voltaire (1694–1778), Denis Diderot (1713–1784), Hermann Samuel Reimarus (1694–1768), Gottfried Wilhelm Leibniz (1646–1716), Christian Wolff (1679–1754), Gotthold Ephraim Lessing (1729–1781), Moses Mendelssohn (1729–1786), and a host of others, whether standing nearer to or further from the Church, and whether or not going further than others in systematic criticism, all bring stones for the erection of the great building in which the piety of illuminated mankind is to live.[2] The researches in the history of religion made by the Germans, like Johann Salomo Semler (1725–1791), Johann David Michaelis (1717–1791), and Johann August Ernesti (1707–1781), provide scientific data which throw light upon the division between eternal truths and the time-conditioned convictions of religion.

The creed of the religion of reason is simply the optimistic-ethical world-view reproduced in a Christian phraseology, that is to say, preserving within it the Christian theism, and the belief in immortality. An all-wise and wholly benevolent Creator has produced the world, and upholds it in corresponding fashion. Man is endowed with free will, and discovers in his reason and his heart the moral law which is meant to lead individuals and mankind to perfection, and to accomplish in the world God's highest purposes. Every man has within him an indestructible soul, which feels his moral life to be the highest happiness, and after death enters a state of pure, spiritual existence.

This belief in God, in virtue, and in immortality was held to have been taught in its purest form in previous ages in the teaching of Jesus. But it was acknowledged that elements of the same beliefs were to be found in all the higher religions.[3]

2 Tindal's work bears the title *Christianity as Old as the Creation* (1730). Pierre Bayle's famous *Dictionnaire historique et critique* appeared for the first time in two volumes in 1695.

3 The most impressive, and perhaps the most profound document of the religion of reason is the confession of faith which Rousseau in his novel *Emile* (1762) puts into the mouth of a country minister in Savoy.

If the eighteenth century attained to an optimistic-ethical world-view which was preached so confidently and was so widely accepted, the reason is that it was able to re-interpret Christianity —which had by that time eliminated the world- and life-negation that was originally inherent in it—in that sense. Jesus was to it a teacher who even in his own age and then through all the intervening centuries had been misunderstood, and was now first rightly accepted as a revealer of the religion of reason. Let anyone read a rationalistic Life of Jesus, such as those of Franz Volkmar Reinhard (1753–1812) or Karl Heinrich Venturini (1768–1849).[4] They hold Jesus up to admiration as the champion of enlightenment and of blessings for the common people. This transformation of the historical picture is made easier for them by the fact that the chief component element of the Gospel narrative is ethical teaching, while hardly a hint is given of the late-Jewish pessimistic world-view which it presupposes.

As an immediate result of the obliteration of confessional differences, the middle of the eighteenth century sees the beginning of a period of tolerance in place of the persecution of the unorthodox which had been common only a short time before. The last serious act of confessional intolerance was the expulsion of all evangelicals from the Salzburg district by the Archbishop of that town, Count von Firmian, in the years 1731 and 1732.

About the middle of the century there begins also the movement of opposition to the Jesuits, who were recognized as the enemies of tolerance, and this led to the suppression of the order in 1773 by Pope Clement XIV.[5]

But the religion of reason fought superstition as well as intolerance. In 1704 the philosopher and jurist of Halle, Christian Thomasius (1655–1728), published his essays condemning trial for witchcraft,[6] and about the middle of the century the law courts in most of the States of Europe refused to concern them-

[4] F. V. Reinhard: *Essay concerning the Plan which the Founder of the Christian Religion drew up for the Benefit of Mankind* (1781; 4th ed., 1798). K. H. Venturini: *Natural History of the Great Prophet of Nazareth* (1800–1802). See for an account of them the writer's work: *The Quest of the Historical Jesus* (1906; 4th ed., 1922 (German); 1st English ed., 1910; 3rd, 1922).

[5] Expulsion of the Jesuits from Portugal, 1759; from France, 1764; from Spain and Naples, 1767; from Parma, 1768.

[6] *Short Theses upon the Sin of Witchcraft and the Practice of Trial Therefor.*

selves any longer with the crime of magic. The last death sentence on a witch was passed in 1782 at Glarus, in Switzerland.

About the end of the century it became good form to detest anything which had even a remote connection with superstitious convictions.

Again, the will-to-progress of the eighteenth century makes a clean sweep of nationalist as of religious prejudices. Above and beyond individual nations it points to mankind as the great object towards which ideals are to be directed. Educated people accustom themselves to see in the State not so much an organ of national feeling as a mere organization for legal and economic purposes. Cabinets may carry on war with each other, but in the thought of the common people there grows up a recognition of the brotherhood of nations.

In the sphere of law, too, the will-to-progress acquires strength. The ideas of Hugo Grotius find acceptance. The law of reason is exalted in the convictions of the men of the eighteenth century to a position above all traditional maxims of jurisprudence. It alone is allowed to have permanent authority, and legal decisions have to be in harmony with it. Fundamental principles of law, principles everywhere equally beyond dispute, have to be deduced from human nature. To protect these and thus ensure to every human being a human value with an inviolable measure of freedom of which he can never be robbed, is the first task of the State. The proclamation of "the Rights of Man" by the States of North America and the French Revolution, do no more than give recognition and sanction to what, in the convictions of the time, had already been won.

The first State in which torture was abolished was Prussia, and this was secured by an administrative order of Frederick the Great in 1740. In France a certain amount of torture was practised down to the Revolution—and somewhat later. The thumb-screw was used under the Directory during the examination which the royalist conspirators had to undergo.[7]

Side by side with the fight against absence of law and the existence of inhuman laws, go efforts to adapt law to circum-

[7] See G. Lenôtre: "Les Agents Royalistes sous la Révolution" (*Revue des Deux Mondes,* 1922).

stances. Bentham raises his voice against laws which tolerate usury, against senseless customs duties, and against inhuman methods of colonization.

There dawns an age in which the purposive and the moral are the ruling authorities. Officialdom acquires during these generations familiarity with the notions of duty and honour, which later become natural to it. Without any fuss, far-reaching beneficial reforms are introduced into administration.

The education of mankind in citizenship makes splendid progress. The general good becomes the criterion of excellence both for the commands of rulers and the obedience of their subjects, while at the same time a beginning is made towards securing that everyone shall be educated in a manner corresponding to his human dignity and the needs of his personal welfare. The war against ignorance is begun.

The way is prepared, too, for a more rational method of living. More comfortable houses are built and the land is better cultivated. Even the pulpit uses its influence to promote improvements of this kind. The theory that reason has been given to man to be used consistently and in every department of life plays at this time an important and beneficent part in the preaching of the Gospel, even if the way in which this is done often seems queer. Sermons, for example, frequently treated incidentally of the best methods of manuring, irrigating, and draining the fields. That Jenner's discovery of vaccination was so readily adopted in many districts was due to the enlightenment which was spread abroad by the clergy.

Characteristic of the age of rationalism are the secret societies formed to promote the moral and utilitarian progress of mankind. In 1717 members of the higher ranks of society in London reorganize as "The Order of Freemasons" the brotherhood which in earlier times had been built up by the union in a single body of the members of the mediæval building-lodges, but was now in a state of decay, and to this new organization was assigned the duty of labouring to build up a new humanity. About the middle of the century this order spread all over Europe, and reached the zenith of its success. Princes, officials, and scholars alike joined it in great numbers, and were inspired by it to the achievement of a huge amount of reform.

Similar aims were pursued by the "Order of the Illuminati" (or enlightened) which was founded in Bavaria in 1776, but was suppressed in 1784 by the reactionary Bavarian Government, which was still under the influence of the Jesuits. It is said to have been the intellectual counterpart of the Jesuit order, on the model of whose organization it was formed.

That private societies aiming at the rational and moral perfecting of mankind should work effectively seemed to the men of the eighteenth century so much a matter of course that they assumed them to have existed in earlier times. In a series of rationalist descriptions of the life of Jesus it is assumed that the sect of the Essenes, near the Dead Sea, of which we learn from Josephus, the Jewish writer of the first century A.D., was such an order, and that it was in touch with similar brotherhoods in Egypt and India. Jesus, it is said, was trained by the Essenes, and then helped by them to carry through the *rôle* of the Messiah, in order that with the authority given by a holy yet popular personality he might work to spread true illumination. The famous *Life of Jesus* by Karl Venturini develops this theory in complete detail. According to him, the miracles of Jesus were staged by brothers of this secret association.

At any rate, the fact that the will-to-progress of the eighteenth century created for itself in these private societies organizations which spread throughout Europe, contributed much to its ability to influence the age.

It must be admitted indeed that the men of the rationalistic period were not so great as their achievements. True, they all possessed personality, but it did not reach very deep. It was produced by the enthusiasm which they found in the mentality of the time and shared with many of their contemporaries. The individual acquired personality by taking over a ready-made philosophy which gave him firm standing-ground together with ideals. His own contribution was really nothing more than the capacity for enthusiasm. That is why the men of this age are so remarkably like one another. They all graze side by side in the same nourishing pasture.

Nevertheless, the ideas of the purposive and the ethical have never exercised so much influence over reality as they did among these men of shallow optimism and emotional morale.

No book has been written yet which fully describes their achievements, doing justice to their origin, their character, their number and their significance. We only really comprehend what they accomplished, because we experience the tragic fact that the most valuable part of it is lost to us, while we do not feel in ourselves any ability to reproduce it. They were masters of the facts of life to an extent which we are to-day quite unable to realize.

Only a world-view which accomplishes all that rationalism did has a right to condemn rationalism. The greatness of that philosophy is that its hands are blistered.

* * *

The great work of reform is never completed, partly because external circumstances arise to check it, but also because the world-view of rationalism becomes convulsed from within. In its confidence in the enlightening power of all that is in accordance with reason, the will-to-progress was inclined to underestimate the resistant power of the traditional, and to aim at carrying through reforms where minds had not been sufficiently prepared for their reception. On these unsuccessful advances followed reaction which permanently injured the work. This was the case in southeastern Europe. Joseph II. of Austria, who was emperor from 1764 to 1790, is the type of the reforming prince. He discontinued the use of torture, opposed the infliction of the death penalty, abolished serfdom, gave the Jews full civic rights, introduced a new method of legislation and a new system of legal administration, took away all class privileges, contended for the equality of all before the law, protected the oppressed, founded schools and hospitals, guaranteed the freedom of the press and freedom of domicile, abolished all State monopolies, and promoted the development of agriculture and industry.

But he was a ruler on the wrong throne. He decreed these reforms and further caused similar shocks, one after another, in countries which, being in spiritual matters still wholly under the dominion of the Catholic Church of that time, were not prepared for them, and moreover in other things as well displayed a specially backward attitude, because they belonged to the zone in which the Europe of that day passed over into Asia.

The Emperor was therefore unable to count upon either any willingness to make sacrifices in the classes which were to give up their privileges, or upon any understanding of his ideas among the common people. In his attempts to organize the monarchy as a unity, and in an effective way for practical purposes, he came into conflict with the nationalities of which it was composed. The reduction in the number of the religious houses, which he undertook from economic considerations, along with the introduction of the freedom of the press and of a system of State education, brought on him the hostility of the Church. Finally, because he is a ruler in the wrong place, this noble reforming emperor dies of a broken heart, while Europe, because the will-to-progress in Austria, owing to unfavorable circumstances, can accomplish nothing even at the time of its greatest strength, is condemned to a period of the deepest misery over the problems of that huge State, which have in this way been rendered insoluble, and over the portion of Asia which continues along the southern bank of the Danube.

In France, too, the wrong men are on the throne. There the spread of the new ideas prepares the way splendidly for reform, but the reforms are not undertaken, because its rulers cannot understand the signs of the times, and allow the State to fall into decay. Consequently the reform movement has to take the road of violence, whereby it slips away from the guidance of the educated, and falls into the hands of the mob, from which it is taken by the powerful genius of Napoleon. Native of an island in which the Europe of that day passed over into Africa, and lacking all but a superficial education, he is uninfluenced by the valuable convictions of his time. Guided solely by the force of his own personality, he decides what is to happen in Europe, and hurls it into wars through which it sinks into misery. Thus from East and from West alike disaster overtakes the work of the will-to-progress.

The French Revolution is a snowstorm falling upon trees in blossom. A transformation which promises great things is in progress, but everywhere silently and slowly. Extraordinarily valuable results are being prepared in the thoughts of men. Provided that circumstances remain even tolerably near the normal, humanity in Europe faces an amazingly beneficial development.

But in place of this there sets in a chaotic period of history in which the will-to-progress has to cease more or less completely from its task, and becomes a bewildered spectator. The first surge of the advance of reforming thought, thought bent with full consciousness of its aims on securing the practical and the ethical, comes to a complete stop.

An experience for which it was in no wise prepared now falls to the lot of the will-to-progress. Up to this time it had always been a more or less worn out reality with which it had had to endeavour to come to terms. In the French Revolution, however, and in the following period, it becomes familiar with a reality which has at its disposal elemental forces. Until now the only factor to be reckoned with had been the force exercised by rational thought. In Napoleon it has to learn to recognize as power a personality with creative genius of its own.

By his reorganization of France, a magnificent work but concerned only with the technical matters of administration, Napoleon creates a new State. His achievement, too, has had the way prepared for it by the work of rationalism, in so far as this upset the equilibrium of the old order and made current the idea of something novel but necessary. But the new State which now comes into existence is not the State which is ethical and in harmony with reason, but merely the State which works well. Its achievements compel our admiration. In the garden which the will-to-progress was laying out in order to plant it with lovely flowers, an individual ploughs for himself a piece of ordinary arable land which at once produces an excellent crop. With the elemental creative forces of reality revealing their power in so imposing a fashion, the noble but unoriginal spirit of the age, with all its higher aims, finds itself in a state of instability from which it never completely recovers. Hegel, who saw Napoleon ride past after the Battle of Jena, tells us that he then saw the World-spirit on horseback. In these words we can hear the expression of the confused spiritual experience of the time.

* * *

There now sets in a development which works against the spirit of the age. The hitherto unopposed authority of the rational ideal is undermined. Forces of reality which are not guided by it obtain recognition.

While the will-to-progress remains an amazed spectator of events, respect for what is historical revives, though it seemed to have been banished for ever. In religion, in art, and in law, men begin, though at first only quite shyly, to look again with other eyes on the traditional. It is no longer reckoned as merely something which is to be replaced, but men venture to admit to themselves that it conceals within itself original values. The forces of reality, which had been taken by surprise, everywhere act on the defensive, and a guerilla warfare against the will-to-progress begins.

The various religious bodies revoke the abdications which they had made in presence of the religion of reason. The traditional law begins to set itself in opposition to the law laid down by reason. In the atmosphere of passion produced by the Napoleonic wars, the idea of the nation takes on a new character, directing on itself, and beginning to absorb, the universal enthusiasm for ideals. The struggles carried on, no longer by chancelleries but by peoples, are fatal to the ideals of cosmopolitanism and the brotherhood of nations. By this reawakening of national thought a whole series of political problems affecting the whole of Europe are rendered insoluble. Just as the organization of Austria as a unified modern State has now become impossible, so also has the civilizing of Russia, and that it is the destiny of Europe to be ruined on account of territories which are in it but not of it, begins to become apparent.

At the close of the Napoleonic era the whole of Europe is in a condition of misery. Far-seeing ideas of reform can be neither thought out nor worked out; only extemporized palliative measures suit the time. The will-to-progress is therefore unable to recover its former vigour.

It is fatally affected, too, by the fact that everybody with any capacity for independent thought feels himself attracted by this new valuation of reality, and consequently irritated at the one-sided, doctrinaire character of the rationalist way of looking at life.

Nevertheless, the position of the will-to-progress is far from being critical. The first attacks are made by Romanticism and the feeling for reality, but are mere outpost-skirmishes, and for a long time yet the will-to-progress remains master of the field. Bentham remains still the great authority. Alexander II. of Russia, Tsar from 1801 to 1825, instructs the legislative commission which he sets up, to obtain the opinion of the great Englishman on all doubtful points. Madame de Staël expresses the opinion that the fateful period she has lived through will one day be called by posterity not the Napoleonic but the Benthamite age.[8]

The noblest men of the period still live in the unshaken confidence that nothing can delay the speedy and conclusive victory of the purposive and moral. The philosophically minded mathematician and astronomer, the Marquis Marie Jean de Condorcet (1743–1794), though put by the Jacobins upon the list of the proscribed, writes, while living in concealment in Paris in a dismal room in the Rue des Fossoyeurs, his *Historical Sketch of the Progress of the Human Spirit.*[9] Then, betrayed, he wanders about the Clamart quarries, is recognized by the labourers, in spite of his disguise, as an aristocrat, and while confined in the prison of Bourg la Reine, puts an end to his life by poison. The document in which he gave his exposition of the ethical belief in progress concludes with a forward glance at the time, now soon to appear, when reason, having attained a position of permanent sovereignty, will put every human being in possession of the rights which belong to man as man, and will establish purposive and ethical relations in every department of life.

There is one thing, it must be admitted, which Condorcet and those who share his views overlook. Their belief that the final result will be good might be considered justifiable, if the will-to-progress had been endangered only through unfavourable outward circumstances, the revival, that is, of the higher estimation of reality, and the romantic idealizing of the past. But it is far more seriously threatened. The assurance displayed by rationalism rests on the fact that it regards the optimistic-ethical

[8] Her dictum is given in the English periodical, *The Atlas,* in its issue of January 27th, 1828.

[9] *Esquisse d'un tableau historique des progrès de l'esprit humain.* It was published in 1795, after the author's death, at the expense of the National Convention.

world-view as proved. But it is not, for it rests, like the world-views of Confucius and the Later Stoics, on a naïve interpretation of the world. All deeper thought, therefore, even if it is not directed against rationalism, or even if it aims at strengthening its position, must in the long run have a disintegrating effect upon it. Hence Kant and Spinoza spell its doom. Kant undermines it by his attempt to provide a deeper foundation for the essence of the ethical. Spinoza, the thinker of the seventeenth century, brings it to confusion when, a hundred years after his death, his nature-philosophy begins to occupy people's attention.

It is about the beginning of the new century, the nineteenth, just when the pressure exerted by material and spiritual circumstances alike begins to make itself felt, that the optimistic-ethical world-view begins to suspect the existence of the serious problems which are arising within it.

Chapter 14

THE OPTIMISTIC-ETHICAL WORLD-VIEW IN KANT

Kant's ethics, deepened, but lacking content.
Kant's attempt to reach an ethical world-view.

SO FAR AS CONCERNS THE GENERAL TENDENCY OF HIS THOUGHT, Immanuel Kant (1724–1804) lives entirely in the optimistic-ethical world-view of rationalism.[1] He has, however, a feeling that its foundations are not sufficiently deep and firm, and he regards it as his task to give them an altogether securer basis. For this purpose profounder ethics and a less naïve positiveness in assertions about philosophy which touch upon the supra-sensible, seem to him desirable.

Like the English intellectualists and intuitionists, Kant is offended by the idea that the ethics in which the modern age finds satisfaction and its impulse to activity is rooted merely in considerations of the universal advantage of morally good actions. Like them, he feels that ethics is something more than this, and that in the ultimate analysis it has its origin in the compulsion which men experience to strive for self-perfection. But while his predecessors stick fast in the matter provided by semi-scholastic philosophy and theology, he attacks the problem along the lines of pure ethical thought. It follows for him that the fundamental origin and the exalted character of the moral

[1] Immanuel Kant: *Kritik der reinen Vernunft* (1781); *Grundlegung zur Metaphysik der Sitten* (1785); *Kritik der praktischen Vernunft* (1788); *Kritik der Urteilskraft* (1790); *Die Religion innerhalb der Grenzen der blossen Vernunft* (1793); *Metaphysik der Sitten* (1797).

can be preserved only if we always consciously make it an end in itself, and never merely a means to an end. Even if moral conduct prove itself to be always advantageous and practical, our motive to it must nevertheless always be a purely inward compulsion. Utilitarian ethics must abdicate before the ethics of immediate and sovereign duty. That is the meaning of the doctrine of the Categorical Imperative.

The English anti-utilitarians had in common with the utilitarians the thought that the moral law was related in essence to empirical natural law. Kant, however, asserts that it has nothing to do with the order of nature, but has its origin in supra-natural impulses. He is the first since Plato to feel, like him, that the ethical is the mysterious fact within us. In powerful language he proves in the *Critique of the Practical Reason* that ethics is a volition which raises us above ourselves, frees us from the natural order of the world of the senses, and attaches us to a higher world-order. That is his great discovery.

In the development of it, however, he falls short of success. Whoever asserts the absoluteness of moral duty, must also give the moral an absolute and completely universal content. He must specify a principle of conduct which shows itself as absolutely binding, and as lying at the foundations of the most varied ethical duties. If he does not succeed in doing this, his work is only a fragment.

When Plato announces that ethics is supra-natural and mysterious, his world-view provides him with a basic principle of the ethical which corresponds to these qualities, and also has a definite content. He is in a position to define ethics as a process of becoming pure and free from the world of sense. This, his own special form of ethics, he develops in the passages where he is consistent with himself. Then, when he cannot complete his argument without active ethics, he has recourse to the popular theory of virtue.

Kant, however, as a child of the modern spirit, cannot let world- and life-negation rank as ethics. Since he can go only a part of the way with Plato, he sees himself faced with the confusing task of letting purposive, activist ethics directed on the empirical world originate in impulses which are not determined by any adaptation to the empirical.

He can find no solution of the problem thus set. In the form which he gives it, it is in fact insoluble. But he never even realises that he has arrived at the problem of finding a basic principle of the moral which is a necessity of thought. He is content with formally characterizing ethical duty as absolutely binding. That duty, unless a content is at once given to it, remains an empty concept, he is unwilling to admit. For the exalted character of his basic principle of the moral, he pays the price of having it devoid of all content.

Beginnings of an attempt to establish a basic moral principle with a content are to be found in his treatise, *Prolegomena to a Metaphysic of Morals* (1785), and again later in *A Metaphysic of Morals* (1797).[2] In the 1785 volume he arrives at the dictum: "Act in such a way that you use human nature both in your own person and in everyone else's always as an end, never merely as a means." But instead of seeing how far the totality of ethical duties can be developed out of this principle, in the 1797 treatise he prefers to set before ethics two ends to be aimed at, the perfecting of oneself and the happiness of others, and to enlarge upon the virtues which promote them.

In his investigation of the ethics which aim at personal perfection, he drives his gallery [3] with sure instinct towards the recognition that all virtues which contribute thereto must be conceived as manifestations of sincerity and or reverence for one's own spiritual being. He does not, however, go the length of comprehending these two as a unity. Just as little does he concern himself to make clear the inner connection between effort directed to self-perfecting and effort directed to the common good, and in that way to dig down to the roots of the ethical as such.

How far Kant is from understanding the problem of finding a basic moral principle which has a definite content can be seen from the fact that he never gets beyond an utterly limited conception of the ethical. He obstinately persists in drawing the boundary of his ethics as narrow as possible, making them concerned with no duties beyond those of man to man. He does

[2] "Grundlegung zur Metaphysik der Sitten" (1785). "Metaphysik der Sitten" (1797)

[3] "Treibt den Stollen"—The metaphor is drawn from mining.

not include the relations of man to non-human existence. It is only indirectly that he finds room for the prohibition of cruelty to animals, putting this among the duties of man to himself. By inhuman treatment of animals, he says, sympathy with their sufferings is blunted in us, and thereby "comes a weakening of a natural disposition which is very helpful to our morality in relation to other men, and it gradually dies out."

Again, the vandalism of the destruction of beautiful, natural objects, which are viewed as entirely without feeling, is said to be unethical only because it violates the duty of man to himself by undermining the desire—itself a support to morality—of having something to love without regard to utility.

If the sphere of the ethical is limited to the relations of man to man, then all attempts to reach a basic principle of the moral with an absolutely binding content are rendered hopeless in advance. The absolute demands the universal. If there really is a basic principle for the moral, it must be concerned in some way or other with the relations between man and life as such in all its manifestations.

Kant, then, does not essay the task of developing a system of ethics which corresponds to his deepened conception of the ethical. On the whole he does nothing more than put the current utilitarian ethics under the protectorate of the Categorical Imperative. Behind a magnificent façade he constructs a block of tenements.

His influence on the ethics of his time is twofold. He furthers them by his challenge to profounder reflection on the nature of the ethical and the ethical destiny of man. At the same time he is a danger in that he robs ethics of their simplicity. The strength of the ethics of the age of reason lies in their naïve utilitarian enthusiasm. They directly enlist men in their service by offering them good aims and objects. Kant makes ethics insecure by bringing this directness in question and calling for ethics derived from much less elementary considerations. Profundity is gained at the cost of vitality, because he fails to establish at the same time a basic moral principle with a content, a principle which shall compel acceptance from deep and yet elementary considerations.

Often Kant actually makes it his object to block the natural sources of morality. He will not, for example, allow direct sympathy to be regarded as ethical. The inner feeling for the suffering of another as if it were one's own is not to count as duty in the real sense of the word, but only as a weakness by which the evil in the world is doubled. All help to others must have its source in a reasoned consideration of the duty of contributing to the happiness of mankind.

By taking from ethics their simplicity and directness, Kant also loosens the connection which ethics and the belief in progress had formed with one another, with the result that the two together had proved so productive of good. The disastrous separation between them which later on, in the course of the nineteenth century, became complete, was partly due to him.

He endangers the ethics of his time by wishing to drive out the naïve rationalistic conception of the ethical in favour of a deepened interpretation, without at the same time being in a position to establish for it a basic principle which has been correspondingly deepened, has a definite content of its own, and is directly convincing. He labours at the provision of new foundations without remembering that a house that is not adequately shored up will develop cracks.

* * *

Kant passes by the problem of finding a basic principle of the moral with a definite content, because, while attempting to deepen the concept of the ethical, he pursues an object which lies outside ethics. He wishes to bring ethical idealism into connection with an idealistic representation of the world which has its source in a theory of knowledge. From that source he hopes there will come an ethical philosophy capable of satisfying critical thought.

Why has Kant, with a rigorism which intentionally depreciates ordinary moral experience, ventured forward to the discovery that the moral law has nothing to do with the natural world-order, but is super-sensible? Because he refuses, similarly, to let the world of the senses which is experienced by us in space and time be accepted as anything more than a manifestation of the non-sensible which makes up true reality. The concept of the moral which contains none but inward and spiritual duties is for him the extending ladder which he draws out so as to mount by it to the region of pure Being. He has no feeling of dizziness when, in company with ethics, he climbs above all empirical experience and all empirical aims. He is determined to go right up with ethics, which can never be sufficiently *a priori* for him, because he sets up another ladder of the same length, that of epistemological idealism, and tries to lean one against the other, so that they may give mutual support.

How does it come about that the theoretical assumption that the world of sensible phenomena has a non-sensible world of Being lying behind it, has any importance for philosophy? Because within the notion of absolute duty which man experiences at work within himself there lies a fact of the world-order of that same immaterial world. Hence arises the possibility, thinks Kant, of raising to certainty by means of ethics those great elements in the non-sensible world which are of value for the optimistic-ethical world-view: the ideas of God, of the ethical freedom of the will, and of immortality, which otherwise would always remain merely problematical.

So far as rationalism affirms unhesitatingly from the standpoint of theoretical knowledge the ideas of God, of the ethical freedom of the will (virtue), and of immortality, which make up its optimistic-ethical world-view, it builds upon a foundation which cannot bear the weight of critical thought. Kant wishes, therefore, to erect the optimistic-ethical conception of the universe as a lake-dwelling built upon piles rammed into place by ethics. These three ideas are to be able to claim real existence as necessary postulates of the ethical consciousness.

This plan, however, of thus securing the position of the optimistic-ethical world-view cannot be carried out. It is only the idea of the ethical freedom of the will that can be made a logical demand of the moral consciousness. To establish the ideas of God and immortality as equally "postulates," Kant has to abandon all respectable logic and argue with bold and ever bolder sophisms.

There is no way of uniting epistemological and ethical idealism, however enticing the undertaking looks at first sight. When they are set side by side, the happenings which take place according to a law of causation originating in freedom, and become conscious in man through the moral law, are seen to be identical with the happenings which are universal in the world of things in themselves. There ensues a disastrous confusion of the ethical with the intellectual. If the world of the senses is only a manifestation of an immaterial world, then all the happenings which come about in the space and time sphere of causation produced by necessity are only parallel appearances of the events which are brought about in the intellectual sphere of causation produced by freedom. All happenings, therefore, —human activity just as much as natural happenings—are, according to the point of view, at once immaterial and free, and also natural and necessary. If ethical activity produced by freedom is represented as analogous with the results of epistemological idealism, then either everything that happens in the world, conceived as intellectual happening, is ethical, or there is no such thing as an ethical event. Because he has chosen to put side by side these two things, human activity and natural happening, Kant has to renounce all ability to maintain the difference between them. But the very life of ethics depends on this difference being there and effective.

Epistemological idealism is a dangerous ally for ethical idealism. The world-order of immaterial happening has a supra-ethical character. From the setting side by side of ethical and epistemological idealism there can never result an ethical, but always only a supra-ethical, world-view.

From epistemological idealism, therefore, ethics have nothing to expect, but everything to fear. By its depreciation of the reality of the empirical world ethical philosophy is not helped; but injured.

Ethics have materialist instincts. They want to be concerned with empirical happenings and to transform the circumstances of the empirical world. But if that world is only "appearance," derived from an intellectual world which functions within it or behind it, ethics have nothing on which to act. To wish to influence a self-determined play of appearances has no sense. Ethics can therefore allow validity to the view that the empirical world is mere appearance only with the limitation that activity exerted upon the appearance does at the same time influence the reality lying behind it. But thereby they come into conflict with all epistemological idealism.

Kant is defeated by the same fate which rules in Stoic, Indian, and Chinese monism alike. As soon as thought tries in any way to comprehend ethics in connection with the world-process, it falls at once, consciously or unconsciously, into the supra-ethical manner of regarding it. Fully to shape ethics to an ethical world-view means making them come to terms with nature-philosophy. Ethics are thereupon, as a matter of fact, devoured in one way or another by that philosophy, even if they are verbally saved from such a fate. The coupling of ethical with epistemological idealism is only bringing ethics and nature-philosophy into relation with one another in a roundabout way by which it is hoped to outwit the logic of facts. But this logic cannot be outwitted. The tragical result lies in the ensuing identification of the ethical with the intellectual.

The ethical is not something irrational which becomes explicable when we betake ourselves from the world of appearance to the region of immaterial Being that lies behind it. Its spiritual character is of a peculiar kind, and rests upon the fact that the world-process, as such, comes in man into contradiction with itself. It follows that the ethical will and ethical freedom of the will are not explicable by any theory of knowledge, and cannot, moreover, serve as a support to any such theory.

As a result of conceiving the moral law and empirical obedience to natural law as in absolute opposition to each other, Kant finds himself on the road which leads to a dualistic world-view. Afterwards, however, in order to satisfy the claims of the unitary and optimistic world-view which the spirit of the age prescribes, he manages, with the stratagems which are provided for him by the combination of ethical and epistemological idealism, to work his way back on to the road which leads to the monistic point of view.

Kant is great as an ethical thinker, great too with his theory of knowledge, but as shaper of a world-view he is not in the first rank. By his deepened conception of the nature of the ethical, a conception which lands him in dualistic thought, the problem of the optimistic-ethical conception of life is unfolded in an entirely new way. Difficulties reveal themselves which till then no one could have imagined. But he does not deal with them. He is blinded by his ambition to be the Copernicus of the optimistic-ethical world-view, believing that he can show the difficulties inherent in that view to be misunderstandings which explain themselves away as soon as, by means of his epistemological idealism, actual relations take the place of these which are apparent but inexplicable. In reality he does nothing but replace the naïve optimistic-ethical interpretation of the world which was the basis of action for the rationalists by a fake explanation.

He does not take the trouble to ask himself in what the optimistic ethical world-view really consists, to what final items of knowledge and demands it leads, and how far these are confirmed by experience of the moral law. He takes it over without examination in the formula: "God, Freedom (or Virtue), and Immortality," which was supplied to it by rationalism, and determines to raise it in this naïve form to a certainty!

There is thus in Kant's philosophy the most terrible want of thought interwoven with the deepest thinking. Tremendous new truths, make their appearance in it. But they get only halfway on their journey. The absoluteness of ethical duty is grasped, but its content is not investigated. Experience of the ethical is recognized as the great secret by means of which we comprehend ourselves as "other than the world"; but the dualistic thinking which goes with it is not worked out any further. That the final perceptions of our world-view are assertions of the ethical will is admitted, but the consequences of this supremacy of the will over knowledge are not thought out to a conclusion.

Kant stimulates powerfully the men of his time, but is unable to make secure for them the optimistic-ethical philosophy of life in which they have been living. Although both he and they are content to deceive themselves in the matter, his mission is to deepen it, and . . . to make it become less secure than before.

Chapter 15

NATURE-PHILOSOPHY AND WORLD-VIEW IN SPINOZA AND LEIBNIZ

Spinoza's attempt to reach an optimistic-ethical nature-philosophy.

Leibniz's optimistic-ethical world-view side by side with nature-philosophy.

JUST WHEN KANT IS BEGINNING TO INFLUENCE MEN'S MINDS, THE entirely different ideas of a thinker who had now been dead for a century, Baruch Spinoza (1632–1677),[1] also begin to interest those who are searching for a world-view. The *Critique of Pure Reason* appears in 1781. In 1785 F. H. Jacobi in his letters addressed to Moses Mendelssohn, *Concerning the Teaching of Spinoza,* draws attention once more to the philosopher whom hitherto everyone had attacked without making any effort to understand him.

Spinoza wants to win ethics from a real nature-philosophy. He makes no attempt to give an optimistic-ethical interpretation of the universe, or to refashion it with any theory of knowledge. He accepts it just as it is in every respect. His philosophy is therefore elementary nature-philosophy, but his method of expounding it is by no means elementary. Acquiescing in the way Descartes puts the problem and the language he uses, he

1 *Tractatus theologico-politicus* (anonymous, 1670); *Ethica ordine geometrico demonstrata* (posthumous and anonymous, 1677); German translation by Johann Lorenz Schmidt, 1744); *Tractatus politicus* (posthumous and anonymous, 1677). First complete edition of Spinoza's works, 1802–3.

makes his own thought about the universe proceed "in geometrical fashion" in a series of axioms, definitions, precepts, and proofs. Nature-philosophy is embodied in his philosophizing in a magnificent way, but it is as rigid as an ice-bound landscape.

His chief work—only published after his death, for he dared not publish it himself—he called *Ethics*. The title is confusing, because the nature-philosophy in the work is developed almost as completely as the ethics. It is only when the reader has freed himself of all naïve conceptions in his thought about the universe that he can be permitted, according to Spinoza, to begin upon ethics. The fact that ethics too are broken up into precepts which are given as proved is very prejudicial to their exposition.

In his attempt to found ethics upon nature-philosophy, Spinoza proceeds as follows. Everything that exists, he says, is given in that infinite Being, which may be called either God or Nature. For us, and to us, it presents itself in two forms: as thought (spirit) and as corporeity (matter). Within this divine nature everything, human activity included, is determined by necessity. There is no such thing as doing, there are only happenings. The meaning of human life, therefore, cannot consist in action, but only in coming to an ever clearer understanding of man's relation to the universe. Man becomes happy when, besides belonging to the universe naturally, he also surrenders himself to it consciously and willingly, and loses himself spiritually within it.

Spinoza demands therefore a higher experience of life. With the Stoics and the thinkers of India and China, he belongs to the great family of the monistic and pantheistic nature-philosophers. Like them, he conceives of God merely as the sum-total of nature, and accepts as valid only the notion of God which makes him in this way an independent unity. The attempts, made in the interests of the ethical world-view, to allow God to be at the same time an ethical personality standing outside the universe, are to him an offence against thought. Their only object is of course to obtain with the help of a confessed or unconfessed dualism a starting-point for an optimistic-ethical world-view. They are striving to reach along naïve religious by-roads the goal for which the rationalistic optimistic-ethical interpretation of the universe is making along the direct, but not less naïve, main-road.

The tragic result of monistic thinking in the Stoic, the Indian, and the Chinese philosophies is that nature-philosophy, when consistent, arrives only at resignation, not at ethics. Has Spinoza escaped this fate?

Like Lao-tse, Chwang-tse, Lie-tse, and the Chinese thinkers in general, Spinoza is the representative of an optimistic monism without suspecting that under distant skies in a remote age, he had such great predecessors.[2] His resignation is of a world- and life-affirming character. He conceives of infinite Being not as something devoid of qualities, as do the Indians, but as life with a full content. The self-perfecting, therefore, for which man is to strive is not for him, as it is for them, in any way an anticipation of a state of death, but a living out of life guided by deep reflection. A dignified egoistic world- and life-affirmation speaks through him, as through Chwang-tse.

The efforts of the man who refuses to deceive himself about himself are not directed, therefore, to any sort of action which is recognized as serviceable, but are concerned with maintaining his own Being, and giving it the fullest possible experience of life. Whatever good he does to others he never does for their sakes, but always for his own.

Spinoza rejected the achievement of modern ethics as influenced by Christianity, that is to say, the regarding of altruism as something that belongs to the essence of ethics. He confined himself to the thought that in the last resort all ethical action aims at our own interests, though it may be at our highest spiritual interests. In order to avoid thinking anything which is not a necessity of thought, he went back of his own free will into the captivity in which ancient ethics had their homes.

If he could have let himself go, like Chwang-tse, he would have conducted a campaign against the morality of love and duty. But since he already had as thoroughgoing opponents the authorities, the theologians, whether Jewish or Christian, and almost every philosopher, he had to speak cautiously and offer

[2] Lao-tse (born, *circa*: 604 B.C.): *Taoteking;* Chwang-tse (fourth century B.C.): *The True Book of the Southern Flower Land;* Lie-tse (fourth century B.C.): *The True Book of the Primitive Water-spring.*

mankind without attracting notice the philosophy of life which advocates profound and thinking egoism.

Just as God, the totality of universal Being, acts not with any aim or object but from an inner necessity, so also does the man who has attained to insight. He does only what contributes to complete experience of life. Virtue is capacity for self-maintenance at the highest level, and this self-maintenance is attained when reason is the highest motive to action, and efforts after knowledge and freedom from passion take possession of the man and make him free, that is, allow his conduct to be determined by himself alone and on purely inward grounds. The ordinary man is unstable, moved hither and thither in all sorts of ways by outward causes, with no idea of his future fortune or his final fate, like a ship that is tossed about on a stormy sea. Ethics, therefore, consist in living our life more as manifested thought than in corporeal actuality.

Acting with a deep, enlightened egoism and purely from intellectual impulses, a man behaves nobly in every relation of life. In so far as he can, he strives to requite hatred, anger, and contempt with love and noble feeling, because he knows that hatred always arouses repugnance. He seeks at any price to create around him an atmosphere of peace. He never acts deceitfully, but always straight-forwardly. He has no need to feel sympathy. Since he lives entirely under the guidance of reason, he does good whenever the opportunity offers, and therefore does not deliberately need to be roused to noble feeling by any experience of aversion. In fact he avoids sympathy. Again and again he makes it clear to himself that everything that happens is brought about by some necessity in the divine nature and in obedience to eternal laws. Just as he finds nothing in the world which deserves hatred, mockery, and contempt, so he finds in it nothing to evoke sympathy. Man must be ever striving to be virtuous and happy, and if he is conscious of having done good within the limits of what is commanded him, he can with an easy mind leave his fellow-men and the world to their fate. Beyond the possibilities of his own immediate activities, he need have nothing to do with them.

The wise man who practises the higher life-affirmation possesses power. He has power over himself, power over his fellow-men, and power over circumstances. How very similar is the tone of Spinoza's thought to that of Lao-tse, Chwang-tse, and Lie-tse!

Spinoza lived out his own ethics. He passed his life in contented independence until consumption brought it to an early close. He had declined an invitation to be lecturer in philosophy at Heidelberg University. He was strict with himself, but his attitude of resignation was lighted up by a mild trait of deliberate benevolence. The persecutions to which he was exposed failed to embitter him.

Intent though he is on thinking only in accordance with pure nature-philosophy, Spinoza does not concern himself so exclusively with the two natural entities, nature and the individual man, as do many of his Chinese predecessors, but maintains an interest in organized society. He is convinced that it betokens progress when men change from the "natural" stage of society to the "civic." Being formed for living with his fellows, man is freer if he settles by general agreement what belongs to each, and what the relations are to be between himself and society. The State must, therefore, have power to issue general orders as to how people are to live, and to secure respect for its laws by means of penalties.

Spinoza appears to have found no place for genuine devotion to the community. According to him, the perfect human society appears automatically just in proportion as its individual members live according to reason. In contrast, therefore, to his contemporary, Hobbes, he looks for the progress of society, not to the measures taken by the authorities, but to a growth towards perfection in the dispositions of their subjects. The State is to educate its citizens not to submissiveness, but to the right use of freedom. In no way must it do any injury to their sincerity. Therefore it must tolerate all religious views.

Far as Spinoza goes to meet the spirit of the age, there is one point on which he cannot agree with it, namely, that there are ethical aims, aims practical and purposive, to be realized in the world.

Advancing far ahead of his contemporaries, he reaches a universal conception of ethics, and recognizes that from the standpoint of consistent thinking, all moral behaviour can be nothing but an expression of the relation of the individual to the universe. But when ethics have in this way become universal, the next question is how the relation of the individual to the universe is conceivable as producing an effect upon the universe. On the answer to this depends whether genuine activist ethics can be established, or whether the ethical is only so far present as resignation can be explained as ethical.

That is the reef which threatens danger to all nature-philosophy, and whenever a thinker imagines that with clever seamanship and a favourable wind he can sail round it without coming to grief, he is nevertheless finally driven upon it, as by hidden currents, and suffers the same fate as his predecessors. Like Lao-tse and Chwang-tse, like the Indians, the Stoics, and all self-consistent philosophic thinkers before him, Spinoza cannot satisfy the demand of ethics, that the relation of man to the universe shall be conceived of as not merely a spiritual relation, but, at the same time, as active devotion to it in the material world. The opponents of this solitary thinker are instinctively conscious that with the re-establishment of an independent nature-philosophy there appears something which means danger to the optimism and the ethics of their world-view. Hence it is that in the seventeenth and eighteenth centuries everything unites to suppress Spinoza's philosophy.

It is on behalf of optimism that the age is most troubled. The terrible earthquake which in 1755 destroyed Lisbon, set the mass of men asking whether the world is really ruled by a wise and kindly Creator. Voltaire, Kant, and many other thinkers of the age seized on the occurrence as a topic for discussion, partly confessing their perplexity, partly seeking new ways out of the difficulty for their optimism.

* * *

How little optimism and ethics have to expect from a genuine nature-philosophy is shown not only in Spinoza, but also in Gottfried Wilhelm Leibniz (1646–1716).[3] In his *Theodicée* (1710) he tries to be fair to the optimistic world-view. He is helped in this by the fact that his nature-philosophy is much

[3] G. W. Leibniz: *Système nouveau de la nature, et de la communication des substances* (1695); *Nouveaux Essais* (1704); *La Monadologie* (1714).

more living and adaptable than Spinoza's. He is also determined to employ every possible device to attach an optimistic meaning to reality. He nevertheless gets no further than a laborious establishment of the conclusion that the actually existing world is the best of all possible worlds.

Moreover, so much of optimism as he rescues is useless for his world-view because it contains no energies which can be directed to ethical action upon the world. When he is consistent with himself he remains, like Spinoza, a prisoner within nature-philosophy. All the difficulties for ethics which Spinoza's deterministic nature-philosophy contains within itself, are to be found also in his. Owing to the fact that he does not put the union of thought (spirit) and extension (matter) far away in the Absolute, but allows it to be realized in countless tiny individualities which in their totality constitute the universe—he calls them monads—his nature-philosophy corresponds to the multiform character of reality much better than does Spinoza's. He anticipates to a considerable extent the modern nature-philosophy which is based on the cell-theory of matter. Yet he, too, remains under the spell of the way the problem is put by Descartes. He does not allow the individualities in which thought and extension are united to enter into living relations with each other, but limits their existence to being merely forces with powers of imagination. Their essential nature consists in being conscious of the universe, more clearly some, more confusedly others, but each independent of the rest.

In Spinoza there is a possibility of reaching a system of ethics, inasmuch as an attempt can be made to give an ethical interpretation to the mystical relation between man and the Absolute. Leibniz bars this path against himself in that he does not recognize such an abstract Absolute as the content of the universe. So it is not the result of chance that he nowhere philosophizes searchingly about ethics. In no way can ethics be deduced from his nature-philosophy.

Instead of admitting this result and unfolding the problem of the relation between ethics and nature-philosophy, he weaves into his philosophy traditional dicta about ethics, and defines the Good as love to God and man.

In nature-philosophy Leibniz is greater than Spinoza, because he deals with living reality more thoroughly. But in the struggle for a correct outlook on the universe, he is far behind him, because Spinoza, a man with a simpler mental endowment, recognizes the reconciliation of ethics and nature-philosophy as the central problem of world-view, and proceeds to tackle the problem.

If Leibniz had remained consistent, he would have ended in atheism, as does the Indian Samkhya philosophy, which similarly makes the world consist of a multiplicity of eternal individualities. Instead of that, in order to preserve a satisfactory conception of life, he introduces into his nature-philosophy a theistic notion of God, and by giving it an optimistic, ethical, and theistic expression, makes it acceptable to the eighteenth century. His philosophy, popularized till it is almost unrecognizable by Christian Wolff (1679–1754), helps to lay the foundations of German rationalism.

But in spite of the treason of which he is thus, though with the best intentions, guilty against nature-philosophy, Leibniz cannot undo the fact that through him thought on the lines of nature-philosophy awoke at that time to activity. Without wishing it, he contributes to making Spinoza an influence.

But for the spirit of the time to let itself be mixed up with nature-philosophy is to step into the dangerous unknown. It therefore resists as long as possible. At last, however, since Kant and Spinoza together are undermining the optimistic-ethical world-view of rationalism which has been built upon the real world and so conveniently furnished, it has to make up its mind to rebuild, and attempt the process of arriving at a conception of optimism and ethics by direct thinking on the essential nature of the world. German speculative philosophy offers its services for the carrying out of this undertaking.

Chapter 16

J. G. FICHTE'S OPTIMISTIC-ETHICAL WORLD-VIEW

Speculative philosophy and Gnosticism.

Fichte's speculative founding of an ethic and of optimism.

Fichte's mysticism of activity incapable of being carried through.

THE VISION OF AN OPTIMISTIC-ETHICAL PHILOSOPHY CAST IN ONE mould hovers in front of speculative philosophy, which hopes to discover the meaning of the world by the most direct route. It will have nothing to do with analysing the phenomena of the universe in order to deduce its nature from them. It proceeds deductively, not inductively. In pure abstract thinking it hopes to learn how the real world has evolved out of the notion of Being. It is imaginative nature-philosophy dressed up as logic.

The right to deal with the world in this fashion is derived by speculative thought from the results of epistemological theory, according to which the world as we observe it is more or less our own idea of it. We have, somehow or other, a creative share in its coming into existence. It follows that the logic which is the rule with the finite ego is to be conceived as an emanation of that which holds good with the Absolute. The individual is therefore entitled to disclose in his own thinking the motives and the process of the emanation of the empirical world from the notion of Being. Speculation, or in other words constructive logic, is the key of the secret door to knowledge of the world.

By nature, speculative German philosophy is essentially related to the Græco-Oriental Gnosticism, which in the first centuries of the Christian era advances its views concerning the emergence of the world of the senses from the world of pure Being.[1] The Gnostic systems aim at establishing a philosophy of redemption. They concentrate on the question how the spiritual individualities which are found in the material world arrived there, and how they can return from it into the world of pure Being. Speculative German philosophy on the other hand tries to obtain such a knowledge of the world as shall give a meaning to the activities of the spiritual individualities in the world. Speculative thinking at the beginning of the Christian era is dualistic and pessimistic; at the beginning of the nineteenth century it is monistic and optimistic. In both cases, however, the method of obtaining the world-view is the same.

Among the representatives of the speculative philosophy the most eminent are: Johann Gottlieb Fichte (1762–1814), Friedrich Wilhelm Joseph Schelling (1775–1854), and Georg Wilhelm Friedrich Hegel (1770–1831). It is only Fichte and Hegel, however, who produce world-views with a characteristic stamp of their own. Schelling gets no further than a nature-philosophy, and stands almost completely aside from the struggle for an optimistic-ethical philosophy with which his age is occupied. Kept in a perpetual state of flux, his thinking makes use of all possible standpoints one after another and is now more concerned with natural science, now more akin to Spinoza's, and now to Christian, thought. He never makes a definite, conscious attempt to found a system of ethics.

* * *

Fichte begins as the antipodes of Spinoza.[2] By thinking Kant's

[1] The greatest representatives of Gnosticism are Basilides, Valentinus, and Marcion, all three living in the first half of the second century B.C. At the beginning of that century all sorts of Gnostic systems sprang up, as did speculative systems at the beginning of the nineteenth. The two great Christian teachers of Alexandria, Flavius Clemens at the end of the second century A.D., and Origen at the beginning of the third, try to bring the Gnostic speculations into harmony with the doctrine of the Church.

[2] J. G. Fichte: *The Foundations of All Scientific Theories* (1794); *The System of Moral Teaching According to the Principles of Science* (1798); *The Destiny of*

thoughts out to a conclusion he aims at extracting from the universe a confession that it is purely optimistic-ethical.

Kant, according to him, made the mistake of not bringing his two discoveries, epistemological idealism and the ethics of the categorical imperative, into that inward connection with one another in which they really stand.

What is the meaning of the fact that the moral law and the material world both become actual in me? That is the starting-point of Fichte's philosophizing.

Through the categorical imperative, I experience that my particular *ego* is a self-determined will to activity. Correspondingly, every "thing in itself" which I assume to exist behind phenomena as the reality on which they are based, is also a self-determined will to activity. The essential nature, too, of infinite Being can consist of nothing else. The universe is, therefore, the phenomenal form of an infinite, self-determined will to activity.

Why does the absolute *ego* appear as a phenomenon in a world of sense? Why is Being revealed as Becoming? If I understand this, I have comprehended the meaning of the world and of my own life.

Now the absolute *ego,* because it is infinite will to activity, cannot persist in being an *ego*. It establishes a non-*ego* to be a limit to itself in order that it may again and again overcome it, and thereby become conscious of itself as will to activity. This process takes place amid the multiplicity of finite rational beings. In their power of perception the world of the senses becomes actual. To overcome it they recognize as a duty which makes itself mysteriously felt within them and unites them with the world-spirit. This is the meaning of the philosophy of the identity of the *ego* and the non-*ego*.

It is not only, then, that the world exists merely in my idea of it: it is, further, only produced in me in order that I may have something on which my will to fulfilment of duty can

---

Man (1800); *How to Attain to the Happy Life* (1806); *Addresses to the German Nation* (1808).

A complete edition of J. G. Fichte's works was edited by his son, J. H. Fichte, in 1845 and the following years. A good selection has been published by F. Medicus (1908 to 1912).

exercise itself. The phenomena of becoming and disappearing which I project out of myself exist only that through them I may comprehend myself as an ethical being. In this way epistemological idealism and the categorical imperative, when they unite and one climbs on the shoulders of the other, can look behind the curtain which hides the secret of the world.

Kant protests against the idea that Fichte's system is to be considered the completion of his own philosophy. As a matter of fact, however, Fichte does with ingenious art continue the lines which were begun in the *Critique of Pure Reason* and the *Critique of the Practical Reason,* and think out the ideas of the philosopher of Königsberg to a self-contained world- and life-affirming ethical world-view. He presents them in a generally intelligible form in *The Destiny of Man,* published in 1800. This book is one of the most powerful documents produced by the struggle for an ethical outlook on life.

Fichte gives a content to the abstract, absolute duty of Kant, making it consist in man, as the instrument of the ever-active absolute Ego, assigning to himself the destiny of working with that Ego "to bring the whole world of the senses under the sovereignty of reason."

Since his fundamental moral principle possesses a content, Fichte is able to deduce particular demands from it, but that content is so general and so vague that the code of duty which is drawn out from it has but little vital force. Nothing can really be learnt from this fundamental principle beyond the demand that man shall in every situation of life fulfil the duties which from time to time fall to him as a result of his destined mission to help forward the sovereignty of reason over nature. Fichte therefore distinguishes between the general duties which man, as such, has to fulfil, and the special duties which are incumbent on him because of his natural gifts, his social position, and his profession. These are emphasized as specially important.

By defining ethics as activity which aims at subjecting the material world to reason, Fichte gives a cosmic formulation to the utilitarian ethics of rationalism, and thus supplies a comprehensive and deep foundation for the ethical enthusiasm which was a discovery of his time. Here too he develops what had hovered before the mind of Kant.

At the same time he opposes the representatives of the popular philosophy of the Illumination, and in a polemical pamphlet criticizes very severely Cristoph Friedrich Nicolai. At bottom, however, the only reproach he can level at them is that they wish to go on providing a place for ethics and belief in progress in the naïve world-view arrived at by the healthy human reason, instead of accepting both of them from the philosophy which results from the union of epistemological idealism and the categorical imperative. To persist in imperfect rationalism when the perfect has been made a reality by Kant and himself is, in his opinion, a crime against truth. To him the beginning of wisdom is insight into the paradox that "consciousness of the world of actuality springs from our need of action, not our need of action from our consciousness of the world."

The spirit of Fichte's philosophy is then completely that of rationalism, only that rationalism believes it has found itself with him in the real nature of Being, and now comes forward with still stronger conviction and a still more burning enthusiasm. In Fichte's writings, men are positively whipped up to work for the improvement of the world. With impressive pathos he teaches them to obey the inner voice which urges them on to activity, and indicates to them their definite duty whatever may be the special circumstances of their existence. And he teaches them to recognize that in so doing they are fulfilling the highest, and indeed the only, destiny of their lives.

It is as the result of this inner urge to activity that we long for a better world than the one which we see around us, and belief in that better world is what we live by. Fichte makes confession of unbounded optimism. "All those outbreaks of untamed force before which human power is annihilated, those devastating hurricanes, those earthquakes, those volcanic eruptions, can be nothing else than the last struggles of the wild mass of nature against the uniformly progressive, purposive and life-promoting course to which, in opposition to its own tendencies, it is being compelled." . . . "Nature is to become to us more and more transparent and capable of examination even to its innermost secret; and enlightened human power, armed with its own inventions, is destined to master it without trouble, and then to exploit peacefully its once for all made conquest."[3] Here Fichte gives us the triumphant pæan of the belief in progress which the spirit of the modern age, that lives on the achievements of its knowledge and power, has been composing since the Renaissance. He is as thoroughly convinced as the staunchest rationalist that nature is the buffalo which has remained refractory so long, but will at last be brought beneath the yoke.

That mankind will perfect itself and reach a condition of unbroken peace, is to him as certain as the perfection that nature will one day attain. At present, it is true, we are in a period of arrested progress with temporary setbacks, but when this is past, "and all useful things which have been discovered at one end of the world, get known to and distributed to all men, then mankind, using its powers in complete co-operation and marching forward in step, will raise itself uninterruptedly, without arrest of progress or setback, to a culture of which we can form no conception."

To the State Fichte assigns in his early writings a not very important *rôle,* but in his later works a great one. In *The Foundations of the Law of Nature (Grundlage des Naturrechts)* (1796), it is for him only the maintainer of law and order. In his work *The Complete Commercial State (Der geschlossene Handelsstaat),* which appeared in 1800, he allows it to organize industry and to take over social duties. In his *Address to the German Nation* (*Reden an die deutsche Nation,* 1808), he makes it a moral educator and a protector of the virtue of humanity.

The man who, with the help of epistemological idealism, has made his way through to the higher rationalism, is safe from losing his optimism, even though he goes through the cruellest experiences. He has grasped the fact that the material world is only the barrier which the infinitely active will has created on purpose that it may overcome it. This lends him inward independence in the face of all happenings. He has no need to understand them individually. He can let a large proportion of them be put aside as puzzling to his finite spirit. What is essential he knows: that what is real in the world is not matter, but spirit only.

[3] This and the following quotations are from *The Destiny of Man.*

Partaking of the eternally active spirit, man is raised above the world, and is eternal. The sufferings he meets with afflict only nature, "with which he is connected in a marvellous way," but not himself, the being who is exalted above the whole of nature. Of death he has no fear. He does not die for himself, but only for those who survive him. . . . "All death in nature is birth. . . . Nature is throughout nothing but life. It is not death which kills, but the living life which, concealed behind the old one, now begins and proceeds to develop. Death and birth are nothing but the struggle of life with itself in an effort to reveal itself more and more clearly and more and more like its real self." It is in similar words that the Chinese monist, Chwang-tse, announces that life is eternal and the dying of an individual only means that one existence is being re-cast to form another.

* * *

Fichte's philosophy of absolute activity is the expression of his own strong ethical personality, which with impetuosity and self-sacrifice takes problems in hand, and uses itself up in the strain involved. But even he is unable to make a genuine combination of epistemological and ethical idealism so as to produce an ethical world-view which is a necessity of thought. The impossibility of the undertaking reveals itself everywhere.

In order to conceive ethics as a part of the normal course of world-happenings, Fichte, like all others who make the same attempt, gives up as hopeless any differentiation between human action and world-happenings. The world-spirit's impulse to activity, he says, experiences itself in man as will to ethical action. But, indeed, the whole world is filled with this will to activity which is forever surging against the limitations it has set up for itself. Everything that happens is only an expression of it. What difference, then, is there between natural and ethical happenings? Between activity in itself and ethical activity? Purposive activity directed with knowledge and intention to the subjection of the world of the senses to reason is ethical, decides Fichte. But what does that mean, when closely examined? It means that the finite spirit becomes moral by entering into and taking seriously the play of the infinite spirit which aims at overcoming its own self-created limitations. Looking in this way at Fichte's thought, we see clearly that with the world-view which results from the combination of ethical and epistemological idealism, ethics have no longer any meaning.

Again, what is the meaning of "bringing the whole of the material world under the sovereignty of reason"? This conception of the ethical is not only too wide, but fantastic. To a limited extent man is able to harness the forces of nature for his service, and with a little stretching of language he can, with Fichte, describe such action as not merely purposive, but also in the widest sense ethical. He has some "influence" on the earth, but none at all upon the universe. That he gives names to the mighty heavenly bodies and can calculate the orbits of many, cannot mean that he brings them under the sovereignty of reason. Upon deep-sea life, too, he exercises no other influence than catching specimens of it and giving them names.

That he may be able to assert that there is such a thing as an ethical purpose in the world, Fichte falsifies its birth certificate, and gives it the categorical imperative for father and epistemological idealism for mother. But this is of no use. The ethical purpose thus produced cannot satisfy ethical thought.

By conceiving the infinite spirit, in which the finite spirit has a share, as will to activity, Fichte tries to make possible a philosophy of ethical world- and life-affirmation. In reality, however, this takes him no further than a more emphatic world- and life-affirmation, into which, with the help of speculative thought, he smuggles the idea of duty, thereupon proclaiming it to be ethical. It fares with him just as with the Chinese nature-philosophers, who similarly exert themselves in vain to produce ethics from world- and life-affirmation.

Absorption in the Absolute by means of action, as in the thought of Fichte, is a prodigious thing, but, like its counterpart, absorption in the Absolute effected by an act of thought, it is not ethical but supra-ethical. The element which is needed by the mysticism of absorption in the Absolute to make it ethical cannot be secured either by enhancing or by depreciating the will to activity.

Fichte's mysticism of activity in which man lets loose his energy in the world is related to the ethics of action, just as

Spinoza's mysticism of knowledge, in which man is absorbed in the world, is related to the ethics of self-perfecting. But it is only very incompletely that either can be developed into real ethics.

The absorption in the Absolute which comes into actuality in an act of thought lies nearer to nature-philosophy than that which completes itself in action. The Brahmans, the Buddha, Lao-tse, Chwang-tse, Spinoza, and the mystics of every age, have experienced the becoming one with the Absolute as a coming-to-rest in it. Fichte's mysticism of activity lies more in the path of dualistic thinking than in that of real nature-philosophy. It is something which has been extorted by enthusiasm, but Fichte is devoted to it, and rightly, because he has a feeling that the interests of the ethics of activity are better guarded by it than by the other. But since he thus once and for all decides for a nature-philosophy, dominated though he is by the ideal of active ethics, he comes more and more to the natural quietist consequences of such a philosophy. He goes through a process of evolution which brings him nearer to Spinoza's world-view. In his *Instruction Concerning the Blessed Life,* which appeared in 1806, six years later than *The Destiny of Man,* it is to him no longer what is ethical which in itself is the highest, but what is religious. The ultimate meaning of life, he now recognizes, is not to act in God, but to be merged in Him. "Self-annihilation is the gateway into the higher life." [4]

He believes, indeed, that he is thereby merely deepening his world-view without diminishing its ethical energy. Right to the end he remains the fiery spirit which consumes itself in activity for promoting the progress of the world. But his thought has bent under the weight of nature-philosophy. Without clearly admitting it to himself, he recognizes that from nature-philosophy there can be drawn only an intellectual, not an ethical, meaning for the world and life. Spinoza observes with a smile how he retires upon the thought beyond which a nature philosophy cannot advance by its own momentum.

Fichte is the first philosopher to declare plainly that no outlook on life is ethical which does not enable man to explain that an enthusiastic active devotion to the universe is grounded

4 "Anweisung zum seligen Leben."

in the nature of the world and of life. But the road he takes in order to develop this thought leads him astray. Instead of going more deeply into the question how ethical happenings, though coming from the world-spirit, and directed upon the world, are nevertheless different from world-happenings, and investigating the nature of this difference, he employs the trick, which had been made possible by Kant, of declaring, with the help of epistemological idealism, that the ethical world-view is a necessity of thought. Many of his contemporaries believe with him that it has thereby really reached a position of supremacy, and even those who cannot go with him the whole length of the philosophy of the *ego* and non-*ego,* are gripped by the force of the ethical personality which speaks from Fichte's writings.

The direct effect, then, of Fichte's philosophy is that the optimistic, ethical spirit of rationalism maintains its position and becomes stronger and deeper. This enthusiast gives a tremendous impetus to ethics and civilization. But the vessel in which, with a magnificent wind behind him, he starts with his companions on a voyage over the sea of knowledge is leaky. A catastrophe is only a question of time.

Fichte's belief that he has obtained from the nature of the universe the living compulsion to ethical duty and ethical action which he feels within himself, is an illusion. The manner, however, in which he conceives the problem of the optimistic-ethical world-view, and perceives that for its solution ordinary processes afford no help, so that more or less violent methods must be tried in turn, reveals him as a great thinker.

Chapter 17

SCHILLER; GOETHE; SCHLEIERMACHER

Schiller's ethical world-view: Goethe's world-view based on nature-philosophy.

Schleiermacher's attempt at a nature-philosophy.

IT IS A VERY IMPORTANT FACT THAT THE DEEPENED OPTIMISTIC-ethical world-view of Kant and Fichte finds a champion in Friedrich von Schiller (1759–1805), who brings it to the mass of the people with the force added by poetical language. He is himself philosophically gifted, and undertakes to develop it further, for he wishes to broaden the foundations of the ethical by showing its relation to the æsthetic.

In his *Letters Concerning the Æsthetic Education of Mankind* (1795), he works out the idea that art and ethics belong together as far as that in both man maintains with the material world a relation which is free and creative. "The transition from the passive condition of feeling to the active one of thinking and willing comes about in no other way than through an intermediate condition of æsthetic freedom. . . . There is no way of making the sentient man rational other than first making him æsthetic." In what way the capacity for freedom which is built up in man by æsthetic practice really disposes him to morality, Schiller does not work out in further detail. His treatise, in spite of all the notice it attracted and deserves, is more rhetorical than substantial. He has not gone to the bottom of the problem of the relations between the æsthetic and the ethical.

In contrast to Schiller, Johann Wolfgang von Goethe (1749–1832), stands in almost as alien an attitude to the philosophy of the deepened rationalism as he does to that of ordinary rationalism. He finds it impossible to share the confidence with which people around him regard optimistic and ethical convictions as well founded. What separates him from Kant and Fichte and Schiller is reverence for the reality of nature. Nature is to him something in herself, not merely something existing for the sake of mankind. He does not require from her that she shall fit herself completely into our optimistic-ethical designs. He does no violence to her either through epistemological and ethical idealism or through presumptuous speculation, but lives in her as a human being who looks at existence with wonder and knows not how to bring her relation to the world-spirit within any formula.

Descartes led modern philosophy astray by cutting the world up into objects which have extension and objects which think, and then refusing to each of them the possibility of influencing the other. Following in his steps, thinkers rack their brains over the problem of these two parallel kinds of existence, and try to comprehend the world in formulas. That the world is life, and that in life lies the riddle of riddles, never enters their minds. Hence they overlook in their philosophizing what is most important. Because Descartes preceded them, the two great spirits who adhere to nature-philosophy, Spinoza and Leibniz, cannot get further than a nature-philosophy which is more or less dead. Being in the line of descent from Descartes, Kant and Fichte renounce all philosophizing over the real world.

Descartes and the ethical belief-in-progress, therefore, agree in a common neglect of nature. Both alike overlook the fact that she is living, and that she exists for her own sake. It is because he cannot join them in this that Goethe dares to confess that he understands nothing about philosophy. His greatness is this: that in a time of abstract and speculative thought he had the courage to remain elemental.

Overwhelmed by the mysterious individual life in nature, he adheres to a magnificently unfinished world-view. With the spirit of an investigator he looks within into everything; in that of an inquirer he looks around upon everything. He wants to think optimistically. Shaftesbury's thoughts exercise their charm upon him also. But in the chorus of optimism which makes itself heard so loudly around him, he cannot join. World- and life-affirmation is for him not such a simple thing as it is for Fichte and Schiller. He strives to reach an ethical conception of the universe, but admits to himself that he cannot succeed. So he does not venture to attribute a meaning to nature. To life, however, he desires to attribute a meaning. He seeks it in serviceable activity. To give the world-view of activity a place in nature-philosophy is for him an inner necessity. To the conviction that activity provides the only real satisfaction in life, and that therein lies the mysterious meaning of existence, he gives expression in *Faust* as something which he has laboriously gained during his pilgrimage through existence and to which he will hold fast, without being able to explain it completely.

Goethe struggles to arrive at a conception of ethical activity, but cannot reach such a conception because nature-philosophy is unable to provide him with any criterion of what is ethical. What that philosophy had to refuse to the Chinese monists and to Spinoza, it cannot give to him either.

The range of this world-view of Goethe's, conditioned as it is by reality, remains hidden from his contemporaries. Its incompleteness alienates their sympathies and irritates them. For knowledge of the world and of life which cannot be reduced to a system, but sticks fast in facts, they have no understanding. They hold to their optimism and their ethics.

* * *

Daniel Ernst Schleiermacher (1768–1834), stands apart both from the ordinary and from the deepened rationalism because he cannot free himself from the influence of Spinoza.[1] His life-work is directed to preaching the Spinozan nature-philosophy as being, as far as he can make it so, both ethics and the Christian religion. Hence he always dresses it up as one or the other.

The accepted ethical code, in Schleiermacher's opinion, makes man merely run about on the earth as an ethical individual bent on improving the world. Living in this way, in a constant state

[1] D. E. Schleiermacher: *Discourses on Religion for the Educated among its Contemners* (1799); *Monologues* (1800); *Outlines of a Critique of Moral Philosophy down to the Present Day* (1803); *Christian Belief* (1821–23); *Draft of a System of Moral Philosophy* (posthumous, 1835).

of enthusiasm, he runs the risk of losing himself and becoming unpersonal. He forgets that it is his first duty to be alone with himself, to look within himself, and, instead of being a mere human creature, to become a personality.

This renunciation of rationalism's enthusiasm for activity is to be found in the Monologues, those splendid introspective meditations meant for the first New Year's Day of the nineteenth century. One seems to hear in them Lao-tse and Chwang-tse criticising the moralism and the fanaticism for progress of Confucius.

According to Schleiermacher man's first task is to realize his oneness with the Infinite and in the Infinite to see the universe. Only what results from this as action is really significant, and has importance for morality.

Spinoza's ethics consisted in keeping oneself at the highest level and living rather a life of thought than a life of corporeal existence. Schleiermacher's ethics have the same objective, except that he seeks to combine with it a more comprehensive interest in the world than is to be found in Spinoza. He is helped in this direction by his belief that progress is immanent.

We have, he says, no other perfecting to bring about in things than that which is inherent in them. Ethics, therefore, are not a setting up of laws, but the recognition and description of the tendencies working for perfection which appear in the world, together with behaviour in the same sense. The moral law is not distinct from the law of nature and pursues no different aims. It is only the law of nature arriving in man at the consciousness of itself.

So Schleiermacher's task was not, as was Fichte's, the bringing of the universe under the sovereignty of reason; it consisted solely in supporting the oneness of nature and reason in the sphere of human action, which is ever striving to realize itself within that universe. "All ethical knowledge is the expression of the ever-beginning but never completed efforts of reason to become nature." Ethics are a contemplative "science." They revolve around the two poles of natural science and human history.

The ethics which result from this fundamental conception, like those of Lao-tse and Chwang-tse, are so toned down that there is no longer any real power in them. However completely Schleiermacher may try to conceal this fact by the wonderful way he presents his theme, it plays only a subordinate *rôle.* What gives a meaning to human existence is something which is independent of deeds; it is the oneness with the Infinite which is experienced in feeling.

In clever dialectic, but not in reality, Schleiermacher's ethics surpass Spinoza's. His philosophy is the same as that of Spinoza, only enriched by his belief in the immanence of progress. Hence his ethics glow with somewhat more brilliant colours.

Thus do a living nature-philosophy in Goethe and a Spinozan nature-philosophy in Schleiermacher undermine the ground on which stand the men of the now beginning nineteenth century, whose thinking is so enthusiastically optimistic-ethical. The crowd pays no attention to their dangerous proceedings. It gazes at the fireworks of Kant and Fichte, while Schiller recites his poetry. And now there begin to rise bursts of rockets which throw a peculiarly brilliant light. The past-master in the art of firework display, Hegel, has come into action.

Chapter 18

HEGEL'S SUPRA-ETHICAL OPTIMISTIC WORLD-VIEW

Ethics in Hegel's nature-philosophy, and in his philosophy of history.

Hegel's supra-ethical world-view. His belief in progress.

IN HIS SPECULATIVE PHILOSOPHY FICHTE'S FIRST AND CHIEF interest was ethical. Hegel, a profounder and more objective thinker, aims at truth before everything.[1] While availing himself of any helpful considerations provided by facts, he endeavours to discover the meaning of Being. So he cannot join Fichte in the violent procedure, suggested by his ethics, of giving the world the categorical imperative for father and epistemological idealism for mother. Before going so far as to write out a birth-certificate for the world, he undertakes some essential investigations. He studies the laws which govern events, as they are revealed in history. He then lays these as the foundation for the constructive operations which are to explain the origin of the world from the notion of Being. His philosophy, therefore, is a philosophy of history become cosmic. The building, so far as one can measure it externally, is solidly constructed. That is why it is still convincing even where its lines lose themselves in infinity.

What, then, does Hegel discover to be the principle under-

[1] Friedrich Hegel *Phenomenology of the Spirit* (1807); *The Science of Logic* (3 vols., 1812–26); *Encyclopædia of the Philosophical Sciences* (1817); *The Philosophy of Law* (1821); *The Philosophy of History* (posthumous, 1840). Complete edition of his works in eighteen volumes, prepared by his pupils, 1832–45.

lying the course of events in history? He discovers that every process of becoming advances with natural progress, and that this progress realizes itself in the occurrence of a consecutive series of contradictions which invariably issue in reconciliation! In thoughts as in facts, every thesis evokes an antithesis. Then these unite in a synthesis which preserves what is valuable in both of them. Every synthesis that is reached becomes again a thesis for a new antithesis. From these there results again a new synthesis, and so on forever.

With the aid of this scheme, Hegel can expound the course of history. From it he is, at the same time, able to develop the basic principles of logic. Hence he is sure that with it also it must be possible to make intelligible how the conceptual world which can be logically developed out of the notion of Being passes over into being the world of reality. He carries this fancy through to its conclusion in such magnificent fashion, that even we, who are proof against its charm, can understand how it was possible to become intoxicated with it.

While Fichte seeks to give an ethical meaning to the expansion of pure Being into the world of reality, Hegel from the very outset takes his stand upon the assertion that in its ultimate analysis the meaning of the world can only be found in the realm of the spirit. The Absolute has no other object in bringing a world into existence than to become conscious of itself. It is infinitely creative spirit, but not, as in Fichte's thought, with the object of endless activity, but with that of returning into itself by the road of its own creations.

In nature the Absolute comprehends itself only very dimly. It is first in man that it really experiences itself, and that in three ascending stages. In the man who is concerned only with himself and nature it is still subjective spirit. In the communal spirit of men who co-operate for the legal and ethical organization of human society, it expands to objective spirit and at the same time, on a basis of concepts provided within this spirit, shows itself capable of being creative. In art, in religion, and in philosophy it becomes conscious of itself as absolute spirit, existing in and for itself, and having overcome the contradictions of subject and object, thought and being. In art it contemplates itself as such; in religious devotion it presents itself as such; in philosophy, which is pure thought, it comprehends itself as such. With the world represented as thought, the Absolute experiences itself.

Before the destiny to which Spinoza submits with a smile, against which Fichte and Schleiermacher rebel, Hegel bows in courageous reverence for truth. His world-view is supra-ethical mysticism. The ethical is to him only a phase in the development of the immaterial. Civilization he conceives not as ethical, but only as intellectual.

For proof that the ethical is nothing in itself, but only a phenomenon of the intellectual, Hegel appeals to French usage. "The moral," he says, "must be taken in the wider sense in which it signifies not the morally good alone. 'Le moral' in French is the antithesis of the physical, and means the spiritual, the intellectual, or the non-material in general." [2]

The notion of the ethical with which Hegel works is extraordinarily wide. It consists in "the will having for its objects not subjective, that is to say, selfish, interests, but a universal content." [3] It is the business of thought to define this universal content in particular instances.

If Hegel had fully explored the fact that the individual will comes to a point where it assigns itself universal objects, and had felt this fact to be the mystery that it is, he could not have passed as lightly as he does over the ethical problem. He would have had to admit to himself that the spiritual element which manifests itself in it is unique in character, and cannot be included in any higher form of spirituality, or classified under any other at all. The problem of the mutual relationship between the spiritual and the moral would have been clearly posed.

But Hegel is so anxious to find some sort of shelter for his speculative optimistic world-view that he estimates the birth of the ethical in man not by and for itself, but simply as a phenomenon of the rise of the supra-individual spirit. Instead of directing his thought to the question of how the individual spirit in each several person can be at the same time supra-individual and conscious of its oneness with the Absolute, Hegel sets out to make intelligible the higher experience of the indi-

[2] *The Encyclopædia,* Part III. (1845 ed.), p. 386.

[3] *The Encyclopædia of Philosophical Sciences,* Part III. (1845 ed.), p. 359.

vidual by means of the mutual relation between it and the universal spirit of the collective body to which it belongs. He says it is presumption for the individual spirit as such to seek, as it does in Indian thought, to comprehend its relation to the Absolute. Becoming one with the Absolute is an experience of the universal spirit of collective humanity when it has reached its loftiest height. Only when it stands in connection with this, as a river with the waters of a lake through which it has flowed, can the individual spirit obtain experience of the Absolute. This is the fatal turning towards the general and supra-personal at which the Hegelian philosophy becomes superficial.

Ethics, then, for Hegel have at bottom only the significance that they make possible the growth of a society in the collective spirit of which the absolute spirit can come to a consciousness of itself. Man becomes moral by submitting voluntarily to the demands which society recognizes as expedient with a view to the creation of the higher life of the spirit.

Hegel has no ethics for the individual. The deep problems of ethical self-perfecting and of the relations between man and man do not concern him. When he does discuss ethics, he at once turns to the family, society, and the State.

With Bentham ethics complete law. Hegel works the two in together. It is significant that he wrote no treatise on ethics. All that he does publish about ethics is to be found in his philosophy of law.

His first concern is to show that the State, correctly conceived, is not merely a legal, but a legal-ethical entity. Fichte had made it the ethical educator of the individual. For Hegel it is the essential element in all moral happenings, "the self-conscious moral substance," as he expresses it. What is most valuable in the moral is realized in it and through it. This overvaluing of the State is a natural consequence of his low valuation of the spiritual significance of individuality as such.

* * *

Hegel can have nothing to do with Fichte's idea—an idea which he found impossible to develop to a conclusion—of giving ethics a cosmic foundation in such a way that their content might be the bringing of the world under the sovereignty of reason. His feeling for reality debars him from anything so fantastic. But his complete abandonment of the cosmic conception of ethics is disastrous. Instead of allowing ethics and nature-philosophy to try conclusions together in his speculative thought, he makes a sacrifice of ethics from the start. He refuses them the liberty (which they enjoyed with Spinoza, Fichte, and Schleiermacher), of trying to be understood as the relation of the individual to the universe. They are forbidden, further, to try (as they can do with the Chinese monists), to get accepted as part of the meaning of the universe. They are restricted to being a standard for the regulation of the relations between individuals and society. They may not be active as a formative idea in the creation of a world-view upon a foundation of nature-philosophy. They are simply built into the edifice as an already shaped and dressed stone.

In consequence of Hegel's allowing ethics no significance beyond that of a preparatory motive to realizing the spiritual meaning of the world, his teaching becomes remarkably analogous to the Brahmanic. Hegel and the Brahmans are akin because, as consistent thinkers, they venture to admit that thought about the world and the Absolute which lies behind it can reach only an intellectual, not an ethical, meaning in the union of the finite spirit with the infinite, and therefore value ethics only as a preparatory motive thereto. With the Brahmans ethics prepare the individual for the intellectual act in which he experiences the Absolute in himself and in death passes into that Absolute. With Hegel they help in the formation of society, in whose communal spirit the Absolute first becomes capable of experiencing itself.

It is only a relative difference between Hegel and the Brahmans that the latter make their intellectualist mysticism individualist and world- and life-denying, while Hegel develops his as world- and life-affirming, and makes the intellectual act take place only when a society has produced the requisite spirituality. The inner similarity in character of the two world-views is not affected thereby. One is the complement of the other. Both give value to ethics only as a phase of intellectuality.

With Hegel, as with the Brahmans, a place is found for ethics, but this is not shown to be necessary. For the realization of the consciousness of oneness with the Absolute the decisive element for the Brahmans is, in the last resort, only a sufficient advance in world- and life-denial, and depth of meditation. With Hegel, society, which has to create the spirituality in which the absolute spirit experiences itself in the finite, could come into existence just as well by means of law alone, as by means of ethics and law together. His ethics are, in truth, only a species of law.

With the Brahmans ethics are a colouring which their world- and life-negation takes on for a certain distance; with Hegel they are a similar mode of manifestation of world- and life-affirmation. Hegel's world-view is in itself supra-ethical mysticism of world- and life-affirmation, just as that of the Brahmans is supra-ethical mysticism of world- and life-negation.

That his philosophy is this and nothing else, Hegel admits in the fit of brutal frankness under the influence of which he wrote on June 25th, 1820, the famous Preface to his *Philosophy of Law*. Our task, he there explains, is not to re-fashion reality in accordance with ideals which have arisen in our spirit, but only to listen to the way in which the real world affirms itself, and us within itself, in its own immanent impulse to progress. "What is rational is real, and what is real is rational." We must recognize the eternal which is present under the form of the temporal and transient and is developing within this, and thereby become reconciled with reality. It is not for philosophy to set up ideas about what is to be. Its task is to understand what is. It does not bring forth any new age, but is only "its own age comprehended in thought." It always arrives too late to teach us what the world ought to be, and begins to speak only when reality has completed its process of construction. "Minerva's owl does not begin its flight till darkness is closing in." Sincere recognition of reality will create beneficent peace in our hearts.

Rationalism is ethical belief in progress combined with ethical will-to-progress. It was as such that Kant and Fichte had undertaken to deepen it. After passing through Hegel's mind it is only a belief in progress—belief in immanent progress. It is this alone that this powerful speculative thinker believes himself able to place upon a cosmic foundation. Here he is in contact with Schleiermacher. On the whole, and reduced to the simplest possible expression, his world-view and Schleiermacher's lie not very far apart. The secret feud in which the two thinkers lived with one another had in reality no objective justification.

The extent of the strategical retreat on which Hegel starts remains hidden from his contemporaries. They rejoice unreservedly at the magnificent energy which his system displays, and the more ingenuously because he himself only once, in the Preface to his *Philosophy of Law,* expresses himself freely about the final results of his thinking. The fact that with him the moon of ethics is obscured does not evoke the excitement that might normally have been expected, because, in compensation, he makes the sun of the cosmically founded belief in progress shine all the brighter. Being still under the influences of rationalism, the men of that time are so accustomed to regard ethics and belief in progress as organically connected that they look on the strengthening of optimism effected by Hegel as being also a strengthening of ethics.

Hegel's formal assumption that progress comes about through a succession of antitheses which are always finally reconciled in valuable syntheses has kept optimism alive through most critical times right on to the present day. He is the creator of that confident feeling for reality with which Europe staggered into the second half of the nineteenth century without becoming aware that ethics have at some point or other been left behind. And that being so, he is able to hold his optimistic philosophy of history, from which springs his world-view, only because he lives in a period when a general temper which works with ethical energies of extraordinary strength is carrying humanity forward in an extraordinary way. Whence comes the progress which he experiences all around him, the great philosophic historian does not recognize. He explains what is ethical in origin as due to natural forces.

In Hegel's philosophy the connection between ethics and belief in progress, on which the spiritual energy of modern times has always rested, is broken, and with the separation both are ruined. Ethics languish, and the belief in progress, now left to itself, becomes spiritless and powerless because it is now only a belief in immanent progress, and no longer a belief in progress brought about by enthusiasm. With Hegel originates the spirit which borrows its ideals empirically from reality and believes in the progress of humanity more than it labours to promote it. He stands on the bridge of an ocean liner and explains to the passengers the wonders of the machinery in the vessel that is carrying them, and the mysteries of the calculation of its course. But he gives no thought to the necessary maintenance of the fires under the boilers. Hence the speed gradually diminishes until the vessel comes at last to a standstill. It no longer obeys the helm, and becomes a plaything of the gales.

Chapter 19

THE LATER UTILITARIANISM. BIOLOGICAL AND SOCIOLOGICAL ETHICS

Beneke, Feuerbach, Laas, Auguste Comte, John Stuart Mill. Darwin and Spencer.

The weak points in biological and sociological utilitarianism. Sociological ethics and socialism. Mechanical belief in progress.

THE FACT THAT SPECULATIVE PHILOSOPHY ALSO IS UNABLE TO establish the truth of the optimistic-ethical world-view upon a basis of nature-philosophy is not felt with all its weight in the intellectual life of Europe. In that philosophy we have a form of thought which flames out like a flash of lightning and vanishes as quickly, but it is confined to Germany. The rest of Europe takes hardly any notice of Fichte and Hegel, just as, indeed, it paid scarcely any attention to Kant. It does not understand that these adventurous advances in the struggle for the optimistic-ethical world-view have been undertaken by leaders who see clearly that the battle is not to be won on the usual lines. The universal conviction is, of course, that the victory was won long before, and can no longer be disputed. It is only later that people in France and England see what Kant, Fichte, and Hegel were aiming at and what their significance was in the struggle for a world-view.

For the intellectual life of Europe, then, the philosophy of rationalism still stands upright at a time when it has, in truth, already collapsed. Generally speaking a generation lives, of course, less by the world-view that has been produced within it than by that of the previous age. The light of a star is still visible to us when it has long ceased to exist. There is hardly anything in the world that clings so toughly to life as does a world-view.

It never becomes clear, then, to popular utilitarian ethics that in the course of the first half of the nineteenth century they are being gradually robbed of their philosophy of life by new modes of thought, those of historical science, romanticism, nature-philosophy, and natural science. Certain that they are still in favour with the healthy human reason, they remain unmoved at their post, and still do a considerable amount of work. Whenever, too, they consider their future prospects, they assume that if they should ever have to give up all connection with rationalism, they will be able to come to terms with positivism, the philosophy which has been sobered by the exact sciences. As a matter of fact, rationalism does merge imperceptibly into a kind of popular positivism. The optimistic-ethical interpretation of the universe is still relied on, but less unreservedly and less enthusiastically than before. In this weakened form rationalism is maintained till the end of the nineteenth century, and even later, always working to produce the temper that desires civilization, whether independently or accompanied by popular religiousness.

While, then, Kant, Fichte, and Schleiermacher are struggling with the ethical problem, Bentham supplies the world with a system of ethics. The periodical entitled *The Utilitarian* (*L'Utilitaire*) is started in Paris in 1829 to propagate his views. In England the *Westminster Review* works for him. In 1830 Friedrich Eduard Beneke's translation of his *Principles of Civil and Criminal Legislation* paves a way for him in Germany. At his death—which occurred in 1832, a year after Hegel's—Bentham could take to the grave with him the conviction that, thanks to him, ethics which provided enlightenment both for the reason and for the heart had proved victorious everywhere.

All the earlier methods followed to establish utilitarianism continue at work in the nineteenth century. Friedrich Eduard

Beneke (1798–1854),[1] the translator of Bentham, and Ludwig Andreas Feuerbach (1804–1872) [2] take up with confidence the attempts of David Hartley and Dietrich von Holbach to derive the unegoistic directly from the egoistic, and try hard to complete them in a deepened psychology. Beneke believes he can show how through the continuous influence of reason on the feelings of pleasure and non-pleasure, there develops in man a capacity for moral judgment which holds up before him as the highest goal for his activity the universal perfecting of human society. Feuerbach derives altruism from the possession by man of an impulse to think himself into the personality of others and to put himself in their place. Thereby, he says, his impulse to seek happiness loses its original independence, and suffers if the happiness of others is spoilt. At last, under the influence of habit, man forgets altogether that his helpful behaviour was originally meant to satisfy the impulse to seek his own happiness, and he conceives his own care for the welfare of his fellows as duty.

Ernst Laas (1837–1885),[3] repeats the view that ethics consist primarily in the individual's acceptance of the rules laid down by society, an acceptance which from being a matter of habit becomes at last unconscious and automatic.

In general, however, the mainstay of the utilitarianism of the nineteenth century is the assumption, first made by David Hume and Adam Smith, that from the very beginning the non-egoistic is given in human nature side by side with the egoistic.

Auguste Comte (1798–1857) [4] in his *Physiology of Society* praises as the greatest achievement of his time the then commencing recognition of the fundamental social tendency in

[1] F. E. Beneke: *Prolegomena to a Physiology of Morals* (1822); *The Natural System of Practical Philosophy* (3 vols., 1837–40). By his appearance as a champion of utilitarianism and his consequent attitude of hostility to Kant, Beneke drew upon himself the enmity of Hegel, and was compelled in 1822 to stop the course of lectures which he was giving as a *Privat-dozent* at Berlin University. After Hegel's death he filled a professorship at Berlin.

[2] L. A. Feuerbach: *What is Christianity?* (1841); *Divinity, Freedom, and Immortality from the Standpoint of Anthropology* (1866).

[3] Ernst Laas: *Idealism and Positivism* (3 vols., 1879–84).

[4] *The Physiology of Society* is the fourth volume of Comte's *Course of Positive Philosophy* (6 vols., 1830–42).

human nature. In his opinion the future of mankind depends on intelligence working correctly and perseveringly on this endowment and so rendering man's natural benevolence capable of achieving the noblest and most beneficial objects. If devotion to the universal good remains active in the multitude of individuals so as to provide the necessary complement to their natural egoism there will arise from the rational state of tension between the two a society which is ever drawing nearer to perfection in its economic and social relations.

A great defender and developer of utilitarianism in England was John Stuart Mill (1806–1873),[5] who thus followed in the footsteps of his father, James Mill (1773–1836).

* * *

Utilitarian ethics receive unexpected help from natural science. Biology declares itself able to explain by reference to its origin the altruism which thinkers had decided to accept as inherent in man by the side of the egoistic, but not further derivable from it. The unegoistic, so it teaches, does as a matter of fact grow out of the egoistic, only it does not issue from it afresh on every occasion as a result of conscious reflection by the individual. The change has taken place in the species by a long and slow process and is now revealed as an acquired faculty. The conviction that the welfare of the individual is best secured if the whole body of individuals is also active in promoting the common good has been established by experience in the struggle for existence. Action on this principle has thus become a characteristic of individuals which develops more and more in the course of generations. We possess this devotion to others as descendants of herds which maintained themselves in the struggle for existence while others succumbed, because the social impulses were developed in them the most strongly and the most universally.

This thought is developed by Charles Darwin (1869–1882)[6]

[5] John Stuart Mill: *Principles of Political Economy* (2 vols., 1848); *Utilitarianism* (1861). There is a German translation of his works by Th. Gomperz (12 vols., 1869–86). It was J. S. Mill who introduced into philosophy the word "utilitarian" as the descriptive title of this particular school of ethics.

[6] Charles Darwin: *The Descent of Man and Selection in Relation to Sex* (1871).

in his *Descent of Man,* and by Herbert Spencer (1820–1903)[7] in his *Principles of Ethics.* Each of these thinkers refers to the other.

Altruism therefore is now regarded as natural and at the same time as something which has come into existence through reflection, whilst the relation subsisting between it and egoism is understood as having obviously become rational. On this judgment is founded at the same time the conviction that the co-operation of these two impulses, as it developed in the past, will also be perfected in the future. More and more will these two impulses show clearly their mutual dependence on each other. From sporadic altruism, developing in the animal kingdom for the production and maintenance of new generations, we have advanced to a settled altruism which serves to maintain the family and society. To bring this to completion must now be our aim. We shall succeed if the compromise between egoism and altruism continues to grow better adjusted and more purposive. We must advance to the view which at first seems to be a paradox that (to use Spencer's language) the general prosperity can be reached mainly through an adequate struggle on the part of all individuals for their own prosperity, and that of individuals, on the other hand, partly through their struggle for the general prosperity.

Comte's *Physiology of Society* is thus given a foundation in natural science by Darwin and Spencer.

Utilitarianism now continues on its way full of satisfaction at having found itself accepted by modern biology and in the history of evolution as natural. But it has not thereby become either fresher or more capable. It advances more and more slowly. Its breath fails. What is the matter with it? Its ethical energy leaves it because it has conceived itself to be natural. The fatal fact that ethics cease to be ethics in proportion as they are brought into harmony with natural happenings, is fulfilled not only when ethics are developed from nature-philosophy but also when they are explained by biology.

Ethics consist in this: that natural happenings in man are seen, on the basis of conscious reflection, to carry within them

[7] Herbert Spencer: *Social Statistics* (1851); *The Data of Ethics* (1879); *The Principles of Ethics* (1892).

an inner contradiction. The more this contradiction is removed into the sphere of that which goes back to instinct, the weaker do ethics become.

Assuredly the origin of ethics is that something which is contained as instinct in our will-to-live is absorbed by conscious reflection and further developed. The great question is, however, what this last and most original element in the instinct of solidarity is,—this element which by thinking is developed far beyond everything instinctive—and in what way this development is accomplished. By proclaiming developed herd-mentality to be ethics, Darwin and Spencer show that they have not gone to the root of the problem of the relation between instinct and reflection in ethics. If nature wishes to have a perfect herd, she does not appeal to ethics, but gives the individuals, as in the ant- or the bee-kingdom, instincts by the force of which they are wholly merged in the society.

But ethics are the putting into practice of the principle of solidarity on a basis of free reflection, and this practice, moreover, directs itself not only to individuals of the same species, but to everything living in general. The ethics of Darwin and Spencer are a failure from the first, because they are too narrow and do not leave the irrational its rights. The social impulse which they put in the place of the sympathy which is assumed by Hume and Adam Smith is set at a lower pitch than the latter, and is correspondingly less calculated to explain real ethics.

The transition from egoism to altruism is then equally impracticable if one transfers the proceeding from the individual to the species. The fact that the process is thereby prolonged allows numerous series of most delicate transitions to be taken into account and their results summed up as inheritance of acquired characters. Nevertheless, that does not explain truly ethical altruism. The fruits of ethics are hung upon the bush of social impulse, but the bush itself did not bear them.

* * *

The strength of utilitarianism lies in its simplicity. Bentham and Adam Smith still show this quality. They have society in their minds as the sum of a number of individuals, not as an organized body. Their efforts are directed to inducing human beings to do as much good as they can to each other.

With John Stuart Mill this simplicity disappears. It occurs to him, and then in still stronger measure to Spencer and the others, that the ethics of the conduct of an individual to his fellows cannot be carried out as a matter of reasoning. Hence, they conclude, "scientific ethics" has to do only with the relations between individuals and organized society as such.

Bentham's simple utilitarianism puts before the individual an estimate of the manifold ways in which society needs his devotion, if it is to see all its members prosperous, and, further, it appeals to his enthusiasm. The utilitarianism which has become biological and sociological tries to reckon up for the individual the correct balance between egoism and altruism. It endeavours to be social-science transformed into sentiment.

Adam Smith keeps ethics and sociology still apart in such a way that he is not a sociologist when he speaks as a moralist, and not a moralist when he puts forward sociological theories. Now, however, the two points of view are worked in together, and indeed in such a way that ethics are merged in sociology.

The ethics of simple utilitarianism are concerned with actions due to enthusiasm, the biologico-sociological ethics with the conscientious employment of the complicated machinery of organized society. In the former an occasional piece of ineffective action means at worst a waste of power, in the latter a disturbance of the organism. Hence thorough-going utilitarianism comes to a depreciatory estimate of the morality of the individual which springs from ethical convictions in a single person and does not think biologically and sociologically.

The later utilitarians regard it as an established fact that in the sphere of individual ethics there are no more discoveries to make. They look on ethics as an uninteresting hinterland, to advance into which is not worth while. They therefore confine themselves to the fertile coast land of social ethics, perceiving, no doubt, that the streams which water this lower ground come from the hinterland of individual ethics. But instead of following them up to their sources their only care is to make the lower ground safe from occasional inundations which may be caused by them. They therefore lead the streams into such deep-lying channels that the land becomes arid.

Scientific ethics undertake the impossible, namely to regulate altruism from outside. They try to drive watermills without any head of water, and to shoot with a bow which is but half-bent.

How tortured are Spencer's disquisitions on absolute and relative ethics! For the natural, ethical point of view absolute ethics consist in a man experiencing directly in himself an absolute ethical "must." Because absolute ethics think of devotion without limits and would lead straight to self-sacrifice which would in some way or other suspend life and activity, they have to come to an understanding with reality and decide what measure of self-sacrifice is to be made, and how far that minimum of compromise can be allowed which is necessary to ensure a continuation of life and activity. In this origin from absolute ethics of applied, relative ethics, the scientific, biological point of view cannot acquiesce. Spencer transforms the conception of absolute ethics and turns it into the conduct of the perfect man in the perfect society. We have no need, he says, to picture to ourselves the ideal man except "as he would exist in ideal social surroundings." "According to the evolution hypothesis the two mutually condition each other, and only where both are to be found, is such ideal action also possible."

This form of ethics is then objective in origin. It is determined by the relation in which society and the individual stand to one another in their mutual state of imperfection. Into the place of the living conception of absolute ethics there steps a fiction. For the ethics of sociological utilitarianism provide for man only relative standards, subject to changes of time and circumstances. That means that they can only feebly rouse his will to the ethical. They even reduce him to a state of confusion because they take from him the elementary conviction that he has to exert himself to the utmost without regard to what the given situation is like, and must contend with circumstances from an inward compulsion, even without the certainty of any result at all.

Spencer is more biologist than moralist. A code of ethics is to him merely the setting in which the principle of utility comes to us after it has been worked up in the brain-cells together with the experiences it has produced, and after it has been passed on by heredity. Thus he gives up all the inward forces by which ethics live. The urge to attain to a perfecting of the personality which has to be reached through morality, and the longing for a spiritual bliss which is to be experienced within its bounds, are deprived of their functions.

The ethics of Jesus and of the religious thinkers of India completely withdraw from society to the individual. The utilitarianism which has become scientific ethics gives up individual ethics in order that social ethics alone may have currency. In the one case ethics can survive because they keep possession of the mother-country, and have sacrificed only its foreign possessions. In the other they strive to exert their authority in the foreign possessions while the mother-country belongs to them no more. Individual ethics without social ethics are imperfect, but they can be very profound and full of vitality. Social ethics without individual ethics are like a limb with a tourniquet round it, into which life no longer flows. They become so impoverished that they really cease to be ethics at all.

The reduction to impotence of scientific, biological ethics is seen not only in the fact that in the end all ethical standards become merely relative, but also in the fact that ethics can no longer uphold the duty of humanity as is necessary.

A sinister uniformity prevails in the evolution of ethics. The ethics of antiquity began to teach humanity after it had lost in the Later Stoicism its interest in organized society as it found it existing in the ancient State. Modern utilitarianism, again, loses its sensitiveness to the duty of humanity in proportion to the consistency with which it develops into the ethics of organized society. It cannot be otherwise. The essence of humanity consists in individuals never allowing themselves to think impersonally in terms of expediency as does society, or to sacrifice individual existences in order to attain their object. The outlook which seeks the welfare of organized society cannot do otherwise than compromise with the sacrifice of individuals or groups of individuals. In Bentham, with whom utilitarianism is still simple and concerns itself with the conduct of individuals to the multitude of other individuals, the idea of humanity has not been tampered with. Biological, sociological utilitarianism is obliged to abandon it as sentimentality which cannot be maintained in the face of matter-of-fact ethical reflection. Thus sociological ethics contribute not a little to the disappearance from the modern mind of any shrinking from inhumanity. They allow individuals to adopt the mentality of society instead of keeping them in a state of tension with regard to it.

Society cannot exist without sacrifice. The ethics which spring from individuals try to distribute this in such a way that through the devotion of individuals as many sacrifices as possible are voluntary, and that the individuals who are most severely hit are relieved of their burden by others in so far as is possible. This is the doctrine of self-sacrifice. The sociological morality which no longer reaches back to individual ethics can only decree that the progress of society advances according to inexorable laws at the price of the freedom and prosperity of individuals and groups of individuals. This is the doctrine of being sacrificed by others.

If followed out consistently, biological and sociological utilitarianism arrives finally, even if with hesitation, at the conviction that in reality it no longer has for its object the greatest possible happiness of the greatest possible number. To this object, formulated by Bentham, it must now assign, as being sentimental, a place behind one which corresponds more exactly to reality. What is to be realized in the ever more complete development of the reciprocal relations between the individual and society is not, if one dares to admit it, an increase in the welfare either of the individual or of society but . . . the enhancing and perfecting of life as such. However much it may struggle against it, utilitarianism, as soon as it has become biological and sociological, undergoes a change in its ethical character, and enters the service of supra-ethical aims. Spencer still fights to keep it in the path of a natural ethical feeling.

Developed utilitarianism, directed to the enhancing and perfecting of life, can no longer regard the claims of humanity as absolutely binding, but must make up its mind in certain cases to go outside them. Biology has become its master.

If it be granted that progress in the welfare of society depends on the application of the conclusions of biology and scientific sociology, it is not as a matter of course necessary to leave to the good pleasure of the individual the corresponding conduct which is to be ethical. It can be imposed upon him, if by economic measures and measures of organization the relation between the individual and society is determined in such a way that it automatically functions as is most expedient. Thus by the side of social ethics socialism makes its appearance. Henri de Saint-Simon (1760–1825),[8] Charles Fourier (1772–1837),[9] and P. J. Proudhon (1809–1865),[10] in France, Robert Owen the mill-owner (1771–1858),[11] in England, and Ferdinand Lassalle (1825–1864),[12] and others in Germany, prelude its appearance. Karl Marx (1818–1883) [13] and Friedrich Engels (1820–1895) put forward in *Das Kapital* its consistent programme, demanding the abolition of private property and the State-regulation both of labour and of the reward of labour.

Das Kapital is a doctrinaire book which works with definitions and tables, but never goes very deeply into questions of life and the conditions of life. The great influence it exerts rests on the fact that it preaches belief in a progress which is inherent in events and works itself out in them automatically. It undertakes to unveil the mechanism of history, and to show how the succession of different methods of social organization—slavery, feudalism, and bourgeois wage-system—tend towards the final replacement of private production by State-communistic production as the logical crown of the whole of evolution. Through Marx, Hegel's belief in inherent progress becomes, if with a

[8] Henri de Saint-Simon: *L'Organisateur* (1819–20); *Catéchisme des Industriels* (1823–24).

[9] Charles Fourier: *Le nouveau monde industriel et sociétaire* (1829).

[10] P. J. Proudhon: *Qu'est-ce que la Propriété?* (1840).

[11] Robert Owen: *A New View of Society* (1813); and *Book of the New Moral World* (7 parts, 1836–49).

[12] Ferdinand Lassalle: *Das System der erworbenen Rechte* (2 vols., 1861); *Offenes Antwortschreiben an das Centralkomitee zur Berufung eines allgemeinen deutschen Arbeiterkongresses* (1863).

[13] Karl Marx: *Manifesto of the Communist Party* (1848, in collaboration with Friedrich Engels); *Capital* (vol. i., 1867; the second and third volumes were published in 1884 and 1894 by Friedrich Engels).

somewhat different interpretation, the conviction of the masses. His optimistic feeling for reality takes the helm.

Through the rise of socialism ethical utilitarianism loses in importance. The hopes of the masses begin to centre no longer on what can be accomplished in the world by an ethical temper which is steadily growing stronger and working ever more and more effectively in social matters, but on what is reached when free course is secured for the laws of progress which are assumed to be inherent in things.

It is true that ethical utilitarianism is still maintained among the educated as an influential disposition to reform. In competition with socialism there even begins a vigorous movement which stirs individuals, society, and the State, alike, into effective action against social distress. One of its leaders is Friedrich Albert Lange (1828–1875), the author of *The History of Materialism* (1866). In his work *The Labour Question in its Significance for the Present and the Future* (1866) he discusses the social tasks of the time and the measures that will be effective for their accomplishment, and appeals for ethical idealism, without which, he says, nothing profitable can be accomplished.[14]

Christianity too supports the movement. In 1864 Bishop Ketteler, of Mainz, comes forward, demanding in his book *The Labour Question and Christianity* the creation of a Christian-social temper.[15]

In England it is the clergymen, Frederick Denison Maurice (1805–1872) and Charles Kingsley (1819–1875), who bid Christendom adopt a social way of thinking. Kingsley's famous sermon *The Message of the Church to Working Men* was preached on the evening of Sunday, June 22nd, 1851, to working men who had come to London to see the first International Exhibition. On account of the excitement it caused, the Bishop of London inhibited him from preaching.[16]

14 The same spirit pervades the work of the national economist, Gustav Schmoller of Berlin: *Concerning Some Questions of Law and National Economy* (1875). Schmoller was the leader of the so-called "Socialists of the Chair" (Kathedersozialisten).

15 The first to set before Christendom its duty to take part in the solution of the social question is Félicité de Lamennais (1782–1854) in his *Paroles d'un croyant* (1833). This book was condemned by the Pope in 1834.

16 The English public was made familiar with working-class misery by Kingsley's novel *Yeast* (which appeared in 1848 in *Fraser's Magazine,* and in 1851 was

In Russia, Count Leo Tolstoi (1828–1910)[17] let loose the force of the ethical thinking of Jesus. He did not, like others, interpret his words as teaching a social idealism focused on the service of systematic purposive effort, but made them the commands to the absolute, uncalculating devotion which their author meant them to be. In his *Confessions,* which in the eighties were read throughout the world, the lava of primitive Christianity is poured into the Christianity of modern times.

The social-ethical movement produced the greatest results in Germany, because in that country the State welcomed it in the person of the Hohenzollerns. In 1883 and 1884 the Reichstag, in spite of the disapproving attitude of the Social Democratic Party, passed laws for the protection of the worker which may be considered to be models of their kind.

In the bosom of socialism itself thoughtful spirits like Eduard Bernstein (b. 1850),[18] and others, came to see that even the most effective measures taken for the social organization of society cannot succeed unless there is a strong ethical idealism behind them as their driving force. This was a return to the spirit of Lassalle.

There exists, then, an active social ethical disposition. Nevertheless it is only a trickling stream of water in a big river-bed. That the reforms called for under the guidance of ethics can be realized is no longer a general conviction, as it was in the age of rationalism. The ethical temper which would work for the future of mankind becomes less and less appreciated. In the victory, so fateful for the development of civilized mankind, won by Marxian State-socialism over the social ideas of Lassalle

---

printed as a book), and by two articles of Henry Mayhew's in the *Morning Chronicle* (December 14th and 18th, 1849).

That Christian Socialism made its appearance first in England and France is connected with the fact that the industry which creates social problems developed earliest in these countries.

[17] Leo Tolstoi: *My Confessions*; German translation as *Worin besteht mein Glaube* (1884); French as *Ma Réligion* (1884); English as *Christ's Christianity* (1885). See also *What then shall we do?* (German, 1886). The fact that Tolstoi's ethical Christianity associates itself with contempt for civilization brings it near to primitive Christianity. But the all-important question, how the power of the ethical thoughts of Jesus are to work in the temper and the circumstances of modern times, it does not answer. Tolstoi is a great stimulator but no guide.

[18] Eduard Bernstein: *The Presuppositions of Socialism, and the Tasks of Social Democracy* (1899).

(which allow much more natural play to the forces of reality), we see an expression of the fact that in the mentality of the masses the belief-in-progress has been emancipated from ethics and has become mechanistic. Confusion in the conception of civilization and ruin of the civilized way of thinking are the consequence of this disastrous separation. The spirit of the modern age renounces thereby the very thing which had really constituted its strength.

How remarkable are the vicissitudes undergone by ethics! Utilitarianism refuses all contact with nature-philosophy. It wishes to be a form of ethics which is concerned only with the practical, but it does not on that account escape its fate, which is to be wrecked upon nature-philosophy. In its attempt to secure a basis for itself and to think itself out completely, it changes into biological-sociological utilitarianism. Next it loses its ethical character. Without becoming aware of it, it has, of course, at the same time become involved with nature and natural happenings, and has given cosmic problems a place within itself. Although it pretends to be only the practical ethics of human society, it has become a product of nature. It has been no good removing all the distaffs: the Sleeping Beauty pricks her finger nevertheless. No ethics can avoid trying conclusions with nature-philosophy.

Chapter 20

SCHOPENHAUER AND NIETZSCHE

Schopenhauer. An ethic of world- and life-denial.

Absorption of ethics in world- and life-denial.

Nietzsche's criticism of current ethics.

Nietzsche's ethic of higher life-affirmation.

AS BAD LUCK WILL HAVE IT, THE TWO MOST IMPORTANT ETHICAL thinkers of the second half of the nineteenth century, Schopenhauer and Nietzsche, do not help the age in the search for what it needs, namely, a system of social ethics which is also true ethics. Concerned only with individualist ethics from which no social ethics can be developed, they offer incitements which, however valuable in themselves, cannot arrest the demoralization in the general outlook on life which is in progress.

Common to both is the fact that they are elemental moralists. They pursue no abstract cosmic speculations. Ethics are for them an experience of the will-to-live. They are therefore, from their very core, cosmic.

In Schopenhauer the will-to-live tries to become ethical by turning to world- and life-negation; in Nietzsche by devoting itself to a deepened world- and life-affirmation.

From the standpoint of their own elemental ethics, these two thinkers, who stand in such deep contrast to each other, rise as judges of what they find accepted as ethics in their time.

Arthur Schopenhauer (1788–1860) begins to publish at the beginning of the century. His *The World as Will and Idea* appears in 1819.[1] But he first obtains a hearing about 1860 when speculative philosophy had definitely gone bankrupt, and the unsatisfactory nature of the ethics of popular utilitarianism, as also of that of Kant's successors, was generally acknowledged.

The most important among the earlier of these is Johann Friedrich Herbart (1776–1841). His importance lies in the department of psychological investigation. It is on a psychological foundation that he tries to establish ethics in his *General Practical Philosophy* (1808). He traces morality back to five direct and ultimate judgments, which cannot be derived from anything beyond themselves, and may be compared with æsthetic judgments. They are: the ideas of inward freedom, of perfection, of benevolence, of right, and of equity. By submitting itself to this mode of outlook, which starts from pure intuition and is confirmed as correct for human beings by the course of their experience, the will becomes ethical.

Instead, therefore, of seeking one basic principle for morality, Herbart accepts several ethical ideas which appear side by side. This anæmic ethical theory possesses no convincing power. But in his teaching about society and the State Herbart does produce something of solid value.

Among the earlier successors of Kant there belongs also Immanuel Hermann Fichte (1797–1879) a son of J. G. Fichte, the so-called Younger Fichte, with his *System of Ethics* (2 vols., 1850–1853), which in its time enjoyed considerable repute.

Schopenhauer is the first representative in Western thought of a consistent world- and life-denying system of ethics. The incentive came to him from the philosophy of India, which early in the nineteenth century began to be known in Europe.[2] For the exposition of his world-view he starts, like Fichte, from Kant's epistemological idealism. Like Fichte he defines the essence of things in themselves, which is to be accepted as underlying all phenomena, to be Will, not, however, like Fichte,

[1] What Schopenhauer wrote after this, his chief work, which was printed when he was thirty, are only appendices and popular explanations of it: *Concerning the Will in Nature* (1836), *The Two Fundamental Problems of Ethics* (1840), *Parerga and Paralipomena* (2 vols., 1851).

[2] In 1802–1804 Anquetil Duperron (1731–1805) published in two volumes, with a Latin translation, the *Oupnek'hat,* a collection of fifty Upanishads which he had brought back from India in a Persian text.

as will to action, but more directly and more correctly, as will-to-live. The world, he says, I can understand only by analogy with myself. Myself, looked at from outside, I conceive as a physical phenomenon in space and time, but looked at from within, as will-to-live. Everything, accordingly, which meets me in the world of phenomena is a manifestation of the will-to-live.

What is the meaning, then, of the world-process? Simply that countless individualities which are rooted in the universal will-to-live are continually seeking satisfaction, which is never gratified, in aims which they set before themselves in obedience to an inward impulse. Again and again they experience the disappointment that pleasure longed for, not pleasure attained, is real pleasure; they have continually to struggle against hindrances; their won will-to-live continually comes into conflict with other wills-to-live. The world is meaningless and all existence is suffering. The knowledge of this is attained by the will-to-live in the highest living creatures, who are gifted with the power of remaining always conscious that the totality of what is around them, outside themselves, is merely a world of appearances. Surveying in this way the totality of existence, the will is in a position to reach clarity of thought about itself and about existence.

That it must effect something worth while in the world is the obsession with which the will-to-live has befooled itself in European philosophy. When it has attained to knowledge of itself, it knows that optimistic world-affirmation is of no benefit to it. It can only hurry it on from unrest to unrest, from disappointment to disappointment. What it must try to do is to step out from the terrible game in which, bedazzled, it is taking part, and settle itself to rest in world- and life-negation.

For Spinoza the meaning of the world-process is that supreme individualities arise, who find their experience within the Absolute; for Fichte that the urge to activity of the Absolute comprehends itself in supreme individualities as ethical; for Hegel that the Absolute in supreme individualities arrives at adequate consciousness of itself; for Schopenhauer that in supreme individualities the Absolute attains to knowledge of itself, and finds deliverance from the blind urge to life-affirmation which is within it. The meaning of the world-process, therefore, is always found in this: that the Finite and the Infinite blend their experiences in one another. Spinoza, Fichte, and Hegel—and this is the weakness of their world-view—cannot make it properly intelligible how far this experience in the Finite has really a meaning for the Absolute. In Schopenhauer, however, it has such a meaning. In man the universal will-to-live begins to turn from the path of unrest and suffering into the path of peace.

The transition from Being to nothingness is introduced. This nothingness is nothingness, it is true, only for the will-to-live, which is still filled with an urge to life-affirmation and with its conception of the world. What it is in itself, this Nirvana of the Buddhists, cannot be defined by our conceptions, which come to us through our senses.

That Schopenhauer develops his pessimistic-ethical, as Fichte his optimistic-ethical, world-view, with the material provided by epistemological idealism has not the importance that he himself attributes to this fact. Indian predecessors have made this connection easier for him. In itself, pessimism can be developed just as well without epistemological idealism. The drama of the tragical experience of the will-to-live remains the same whatever the scenery and costumes with which it is played.

Although, therefore, it makes its appearance in the dress of Kant's theory of knowledge, Schopenhauer's philosophy is elemental nature-philosophy.

What then is the ethical content of his system?

Like the philosophy of the Indians it appears in a three-fold shape: as ethics of resignation, as ethics of universal pity, and as ethics of world-renunciation.

About resignation Schopenhauer speaks in forcible words. In language which rises to the level of poetry, he describes how the man who is intent on his own self-perfecting does not meet the destinies of his existence in childish resistance to what is hard, but feels them as incitements to become free from the world. In the disagreeable circumstances which poison his existence, and in the misfortune which threatens to crush him, he suddenly feels himself lifted out of everything on which he sets value, and brought to the triumphant feeling that nothing can any longer do him harm. The field of resignation, which the philosophical ethics of modern times had allowed to lie fallow for generations, is replanted by Schopenhauer.

Ethics are pity. All life is suffering. The will-to-live which has attained to knowledge is therefore seized with deep pity for all creatures. It experiences not only the woe of mankind, but that of all creatures with it. What is called in ordinary ethics "love" is in its real essence pity. In his overpowering feeling of pity the will-to-live is diverted from itself. Its purification begins.

How anxious Kant and Hegel and others are in their ethics to deprive direct pity of its rights, because it does not suit their theories! Schopenhauer takes the gag out of its mouth and bids it speak. Those who, like Fichte, Schleiermacher, and others, base ethics on a laboriously thought out world-scheme, expect man to run every time to the topmost attic of his reflections to fetch down his motives to moral action. According to the sociological utilitarians he should always first sit down and calculate what is ethical. Schopenhauer bids him do something never yet heard of in philosophical ethics—listen to his own heart. The elemental ethical which by the others has been pushed into the corner, can now, thanks to him, take its proper place again.

The others, in order not to get embarrassed with their theories, have to limit ethics exclusively to the conduct of man to man. They anxiously insist that pity for animals is not ethical in itself, but has importance only in view of the kindly disposition which must be maintained among men. Schopenhauer tears down these fences, and teaches love to the most insignificant being in creation.

The artificial and curious pleas, too, which the rest produce to put man into an ethical relation to organized society disappear in Schopenhauer. Fichte's and Hegel's ethical overvaluation of the State makes him smile. He himself is left free from the necessity of dragging into ethics worldly things which refuse to be fitted in. He can allow the conviction that ethics consist in being different from the world to flame up in dazzling clearness. He is pledged to no concessions, since he does not, like the others, represent a morality which has a purposive aim in the world. Because his philosophy is world- and life-denying he can be an elemental moralist when others have to renounce being that. Nor does he need, like them, to sever all connection with Jesus and religious ethics. He can appeal as often as he likes to the fact that his philosophy only establishes what has always been accepted by the piety of Christianity and of the Indians as the essential element in the moral. It is well known that Schopenhauer judged Christianity to have the Indian spirit, and to be probably, in some way or other, of Indian origin.[3]

Elemental morality now once more obtains its right place in a thinking conception of the universe, and this explains the enthusiasm which Schopenhauer arouses when he at last gets known. That it was possible to ignore for nearly forty years the very significant matter which he gave to the world remains one of the most remarkable facts in the history of European thought. The optimistic world-view passed at that time for so self-evident that the man who laid hands upon it, even in the directly illuminating thoughts upon ethics to which Schopenhauer gave utterance, could not obtain a hearing. At a later period also many attach themselves to Schopenhauer only because of his ethical maxims with their natural and attractive appeal, and refuse to accept his consistent world-view of world- and life-negation. It is a right feeling which guides them.

* * *

Schopenhauer's outlook on the universe, like that of the Brahmans, because it reveals itself as consistent world- and life-denial, is in the last resort not ethical but supra-ethical. Even though through several chapters of his ethics he can speak in more elemental fashion than Spinoza, Fichte, Schleiermacher, and Hegel, he is nevertheless in reality no more ethical than they are. He ends, as they do, in the frozen sea of the supra-ethical point of view, only at the South Pole instead of at the North. The price which he pays for being able to outbid them in elemental ethics is his philosophy of world- and life-negation. But the price is a ruinous one.

With Schopenhauer, as with the Indians, ethics are only a phase of world- and life-negation. They are nothing in them-

[3] *The World as Will and Idea,* vol. ii., chap. xli.

selves but merely what they are in the frame provided by that world-view. And everywhere there peeps through his ethically tinted world- and life-negation world- and life-negation as such. Like a ghostly sun in the sky it devours ethics, just as the real sun devours a mass of clouds from which men are vainly hoping to get a refreshing shower of rain.

On the assumption of world- and life-negation all ethical action is illusory. Schopenhauer's pity is merely deliberative. Of pity which brings help he can have no real knowledge any more than can the Indian thinkers. Like all will-to-action in the world, such pity has no sense. It has no power to lighten the misery of the rest of creation, since that misery lies in the will-to-live, which is irretrievably full of suffering. The one thing, therefore, that pity can do is to enlighten the will-to-live everywhere about the delusion in which it is held captive, and bring it to the apathy and peace offered by world- and life-negation. Schopenhauer's pity, like that of the Brahmans and the Buddha, is at bottom merely theoretical. It can use as its own the words of the religion of love, but it stands at a far lower level. As is the case with the thinkers of India, the ideal of inactivity obstructs the way to the real ethics of love.

The ethics also of self-perfecting are present in Schopenhauer more in word than in reality. The attainment of inward freedom from the world is really ethical only if the personality is thereby enabled to work as a more direct force in the world, but this thought is not to be found either in Schopenhauer or in the Indians. World- and life-negation is with them an end in itself, and it continues to assert itself when its ethical character has ceased. Higher than ethics, says Schopenhauer, stands asceticism. Everything which helps to deaden the will-to-live, is to him significant. Men and women who renounce love and the hope of offspring so that there may be less life in the world, are to him in the right. Those who deliberately choose religious suicide, and after employing every conceivable device for deadening the will-to-live allow the lamp of life to be extinguished, as the Brahmans do, by withholding all nourishment from the body, these similarly act as truly enlightened men. Only suicide as the outcome of despair is to be rejected. That is, of course, not a result of the true life-denial, but is, on the contrary, the act of a life-affirming will, which is simply discontented with the conditions in which it finds itself.[4]

With Schopenhauer, then, ethics reach only so far as world- and life-negation has willed and so far as that is in a position to be declared ethical. They are only an introduction to and a preparation for, liberation from the world. It is, at bottom, by an intellectual act that the suspension of the will-to-live is consummated. If I have won my way through to understanding that the whole phenomenal world is delusion and misery, and that my will-to-live has no need to take the world or itself seriously, then I am saved. How far and to what extent I then take part in the game of life with the consciousness that I am but a player, has no importance.

Schopenhauer does not think out the pessimistic world-view in the great and calm manner of the wise men of India. He behaves under its influence like a nervous and sickly European. While they, on the basis of the liberating knowledge they have reached, advance with majestic gait from the ethical to the supra-ethical, and leave good and evil behind them, as things over which they have equally triumphed, he reveals himself as a miserable Western sceptic.[5] Incapable of living out the world-view which he preaches, he clings to life as to money, appreciates the pleasures of the table as well as those of love, and has more contempt than pity for mankind. As though to justify himself in this, in *The World as Will and Idea,* where he has just been speaking about the deadening of the will-to-live, he rebels against the notion that anyone who teaches a saintly course of life must also live like a saint. "It is indeed," so runs the famous passage, "a strange demand to make of a moralist that he shall recommend no other virtue than those which he himself possesses. To sum up in a series of conceptions the whole essence of the world, in abstract terms, in general terms, and with clearness, and to offer it thus as a reflected copy in permanent rational conceptions which are always ready to hand: that and nothing else is philosophy."[6]

[4] *The World as Will and Idea,* vol. i., chap. lxix.

[5] That the man who has won through to complete world- and life-negation remains holy even if he commits actions which according to accepted ideas are unethical, is taught by the Bhagavadgita as well as by the Upanishads.

[6] *The World as Will and Idea,* vol. i., chap. lxviii.

With these sentences Schopenhauer's philosophy commits suicide. Hegel has a right to say that philosophy is only reflective, not imperative, thinking, for his own philosophy does not claim to be anything more. But *The World as Will and Idea* protests with illuminating language and in a tone of urgent entreaty against the will-to-live. It ought therefore to be the life-creed of the author.

The fact that Schopenhauer can for a moment so far forget himself as to express himself sceptically about ethics has its own deep-reaching explanation. It belongs to the essence of world- and life-negation, which he wishes to proclaim as ethics, that it cannot be thought out consistently to a conclusion, and cannot be consistently put into practice. Even with the Brahmans and the Buddha it keeps itself alive by inadmissible concessions to world- and life-affirmation. But with Schopenhauer it goes so far in that direction that he can no longer make any attempt to bring theory and practice into harmony, but must resolutely live in an atmosphere of mendacity.

He does succeed in making the ethical radiance which world- and life-negation can assume flash up in brilliant colours. But of really producing ethics from world- and life-negation he is as little capable as the Indians.

* * *

Friedrich Nietzsche (1844–1900) in the early period of his activity is under the spell of Schopenhauer.[7] One of his *Old-fashioned Reflections* bears the title: "Schopenhauer as Educator." Later on he goes through a development which leads him to recognize as the ideal a scientifically deepened Positivism and Utilitarianism. He is his real self first when, starting with *Joyous Science,* he tries to establish his world-view of the higher life-affirmation, and thereby becomes anti-Schopenhauer, anti-Christian, and anti-Utilitarian.

His criticism of current philosophical and religious ethics is passionate and malicious. But it goes deep. He casts at them

[7] Friedrich Nietzsche: *Old-fashioned Reflections* (4 parts, 1873–1876); *Human and All too Human* (3 vols., 1878–1880); *Joyous Science* (1882); *Thus spake Zarathustra* (4 parts, 1883–1885); *Beyond Good and Evil* (1886); *On the Genealogy of Morality* (1887); *The Will to Power* (posthumous, 1906).

two reproaches: that they have made a pact with unveracity, and that they do not allow a human being to become a personality. In this he says only what had long been due. Sceptics had already made public many such complaints. But he speaks as one who is searching for the truth, and concerned about the spiritual future of mankind, thus giving such complaints a new tone and a wider range. Whereas the current philosophy believed that it had in the main solved the ethical problem, and was united with biological and sociological utilitarianism in the conviction that in the department of individual ethics there were no more discoveries to be made, Nietzsche overthrows the whole game, and shows that all ethics rest upon the morals of the individual. The question about the essential nature of good and evil which was generally accepted as settled, he puts forward again in elemental fashion. The truth that ethics in their real nature are a process of self-perfecting shines out in his works, as in Kant's, although in a different light. Hence his place is in the first rank of the ethical thinkers of mankind. Those who were torn from their false certainty when his impassioned writings descended on the lowlands of the thought of the outgoing nineteenth century, as the south wind sweeps down from the high mountains in spring, can never forget the gratitude they owe to this upheaver of thought, with his preaching of veracity and personality.

According to Nietzsche, accepted ethics are deficient in veracity, because the conceptions of good and evil which they put into circulation do not spring out of man's reflection on the meaning of his life, but have been invented in order to keep individuals useful to the majority. The weak proclaim that sympathy and love are good, because that is to their advantage. Thus led astray, all men try to force themselves to the opinion that they fulfil the highest destiny of their existence by self-sacrifice and the devotion of their lives to others. But this opinion never becomes a real inward conviction. They live out their lives without any thought of their own as to what makes life valuable. They join the crowd in praising the morality of humility and self-sacrifice as the true morality, but they do not really believe in it. They feel self-assertion to be what is natural, and act accordingly without admitting the fact to themselves. They do not question the general ethical prestige of humility and self-sacrifice; they help to maintain it, from fear that individuals stronger than themselves might become dangerous to them, if this method of taming men were abandoned.

Current morality, then, is something with which mankind as a whole is deceived by means of traditional views, and with which individuals deceive themselves.

With indignant statements like these, Nietzsche is so far in the right, that the ethics of humility and self-sacrifice do as a matter of principle avoid engaging in a clear and practical discussion with reality. They exist by leaving quite undetermined the degree of life-denial involved. In theory they proclaim life-negation; in practice, however, they allow a life-affirmation which has thereby become unnatural and sickly to prevail. Stripped of all its passion, then, Nietzsche's criticism means that only that system of ethics deserves to be accepted which springs from independent reflection on the meaning of life, and arrives at a straightforward understanding with reality.

Individual morality comes before social morality. Not what it means for society, but what it means for the perfecting of the individual, is the first question which has to be put. Does it allow a man to become a personality or not? It is here, says Nietzsche, that current ethics fail. They do not allow men to grow straight up, but train them like stunted trees on espaliers. They put humility and self-surrender before men as the content of perfection, but for the ethical which consists in man being one with himself and thoroughly sincere, it has no understanding.

What does "noble" mean? shouts Nietzsche with harsh words to his age as being the ethical question which has been forgotten. Those who, when the question re-echoed everywhere, were touched by the truth which was stirring, and the anxiety which was quivering within it, have received from that solitary thinker all that he had to give to the world.

If life-negation brings with it so much that is unnatural and fraught with doubt, it cannot be ethics. Ethics, then, must consist of a higher life-affirmation.

But what is higher life-affirmation? Fichte and the speculative philosophers in general make it consist in this: that the will of man conceives itself within the infinite will, and in consequence of this no longer belongs to the universe in merely natural fashion, but to it surrenders itself consciously and willingly as an energy which acts in intelligent harmony with the infinite will. Nietzsche sees clearly that in this way they have not arrived at any convincing idea of the content of the higher life-affirmation, but are moving in the region of the abstract. He himself means to remain at all costs elemental, and he therefore avoids philosophizing about the universe, showing himself thereby to be a true moralist like Socrates. He jeers at those who, not content with belittling mankind, proceed further to profane the reality of the world by declaring that it exists merely in the human imagination. It is only on the essential nature of the will-to-live and the way to use it most completely in experience, that he wishes to reflect.

His original belief was that he could conceive the higher life-affirmation as the development to a higher spirituality of the will-to-live. But when he attempted to develop this idea in the course of his study, it took on another form. Higher spirituality means, of course, the repressing of natural impulses and natural claims on life, and is thereby in some way or other connected with life-negation. Higher life-affirmation, therefore, can only consist in the entire content of the will-to-live being raised to its highest conceivable power. Man fulfils the meaning of his life by affirming with the clearest consciousness of himself everything that is within him—even his impulses to secure power and pleasure.

But Nietzsche cannot get rid of the antagonism between the spiritual and the natural. Just in proportion as he emphasizes the natural does the spiritual shrink back. Gradually, under the visible influence of the mental disease which is threatening him, his ideal man becomes the "superman," who asserts himself triumphantly against all fate, and seeks his own ends without any consideration for the rest of mankind.

From the very outset Nietzsche is condemned, in his thinking out of what life-affirmation means, to arrive at the higher form of it by a more or less meaningless living out of life to the full.

He wants to listen to the highest efforts of the will-to-live without putting it in any relation to the universe. But the higher life-affirmation can be a living thing only when life-affirmation tries to understand itself in world-affirmation. Life-affirmation in itself, in whichever direction it turns, can only become enhanced life-affirmation never a higher form of it. Unable to follow any fixed course, it careers wildly in circles like a ship with its tiller firmly lashed.

Nietzsche, however, instinctively shrinks from fitting life-affirmation into world-affirmation, and bringing it by that method to development into a higher and ethical life-affirmation. Life-affirmation within world-affirmation means self-devotion to the world, but with that there follows somehow or other life-negation within the life-affirmation. But it is just this interplay of the two that Nietzsche wants to get rid of, because it is there that ordinary ethics come to grief. . . .

He was not the first to put forward in Western thought the theory of living one's own life to the full. Greek sophists and others after them anticipated him in this. There is a great difference, however, between him and his predecessors. They are for living a full life because it brings them enjoyment. He, on the other hand, brings to the theory the much deeper thought that by living one's own life victoriously to the full, life itself is honoured, and that by the enhancement of life the meaning of existence is realized. Men of genius and strong individuality, therefore, should be intent only on allowing the greatness that is in them to have free play.[8]

Nietzsche's true predecessors are unknown to him. They have their home, like those of Spinoza, in China. In that country life-affirmation made the attempt to come to clear ideas about itself. In Lao-tse and his pupils it is still naïvely ethical. In Chwang-tse it becomes cheerful resignation; in Lie-tse the will to secret power over things; in Yang-tse it ends in an all-round living

[8] Max Stirner (1806–1856), whose real name was Kaspar Schmidt, has recently been regarded as a predecessor of Nietzsche's on account of his book, *The Individual and His Property* (1845), in which he supports the theory of merciless egoism. But he is not. He has provided no deep philosophical background for his anarchistic egoism. He speaks as a mere logician, and does not rise above the level of the Greek sophists. A religious reverence for life, such as Nietzsche feels, is not to be found in him.

of life to the full. Nietzsche is a synthesis, appearing in European mentality, of Lie-tse and Yang-tse. It is only we Europeans who are capable of producing the philosophy of brutality.

Zarathustra is for him the symbol of the thoughts which are forming within him: Zarathustra the hero of veracity who dares to value natural life as a good thing, and Zarathustra the genius who is far removed from the Jewish-Christian mode of thought.

At bottom Nietzsche is no more unethical than Schopenhauer. He is misled by the ethical element which there is in life-affirmation into giving the status of ethics to life-affirmation as such. Thereby he falls into the absurdities which follow from an exclusive affirmation of life, just as Schopenhauer falls into those of an exclusive denial of life. Nietzsche's will-to-power should cause no more offence than Schopenhauer's will-to-self-annihilation, as it is explained in the passages in his works which deal with asceticism. It is interesting to note that neither of the two men lives in accordance with his view of life. Schopenhauer is no ascetic but a *bon vivant,* and Nietzsche does not lord it over his fellow men but lives in seclusion.

Life-affirmation and life-negation are both for a certain distance ethical; pursued to a conclusion they become unethical. This result, which was reached by the optimistic thought of China and the pessimistic thought of India, makes its appearance in Europe in Nietzsche and Schopenhauer because they are the only thinkers in this continent who philosophize in elemental fashion about the will-to-live, and venture to follow the paths of one-sidedness. Each completing the other, they pronounce sentence on the ethics of European philosophy by bringing into daylight again the elemental ethical thoughts contained in life-negation as in life-affirmation, thoughts which philosophy was keeping buried. Arriving as they do at the non-ethical by thinking out to a conclusion, one of them life-negation, the other life-affirmation, they corroborate together the statement that the ethical consists neither of life-negation nor of life-affirmation, but is a mysterious combination of the two.

Chapter 21

THE ISSUE OF THE WESTERN STRUGGLE FOR A WORLD-VIEW

Academic thinkers: Sidgwick, Stephen, Alexander, Wundt, Paulsen, Höffding.

The ethic of self-perfecting, Kant's successors: Cohen, Herrmann.

The ethic of self-perfecting: Martineau, Green, Bradley, Laurie, Seth, and Royce.

Nature-philosophy and ethics. Fouillée, Guyau, Lange, Stern.

Nature-philosophy and ethics in Eduard von Hartmann.

Nature-philosophy and ethics in Bergson, Chamberlain, Keyserling, Haeckel.

The death-agony of the optimistic-ethical world-view.

THE ATTEMPTS OF SPECULATIVE PHILOSOPHY TO FIND A FOUNDATION for ethics in knowledge of the nature of the world have come to grief. Ethics based on science and sociology are seen to be powerless. Schopenhauer and Nietzsche, although they bring back into general consideration some elementary questions of ethics, are unable, nevertheless, to establish an ethical system that can give satisfaction.

In the later decades of the nineteenth century, therefore, ethics find themselves in an unenviable position. But they remain of good courage being confident that they have at their disposal a sufficiency of "scientifically" recognized results to guarantee an assured existence.

This conviction is produced by a series of inter-related works —chiefly academic manuals of ethics. Their authors are of the opinion that ethics can be built, like the arch of a bridge, upon two piers. One of their piers is the natural ethical character of man; the other they find in those needs of society which influence the mental outlook of individuals. They consider their task to be the bringing into actual existence of the arch (the possibility of completing which they take for granted), building it with the solid material of modern psychology, biology, and sociology, and dividing the load in the best calculated way between the two piers. Fundamentally they do nothing beyond restoring with new means the standpoint of Hume.

The following writers try to carry through this adjustment of the morality which starts from the standpoint of ethical personality and that which starts from the standpoint of society: Henry Sidgwick (1838–1900),[1] Leslie Stephen (1832–1904),[2] Samuel Alexander (b. 1859),[3] Wilhelm Wundt (b. 1832),[4] Friedrich Paulsen (1846–1908),[5] Friedrich Jodl (b. 1849),[6] Georg von Gizyki (1851–1895),[7] Harald Höffding (b. 1843),[8] and others. Of these ethical writers who, in spite of the variety of experience they bring to bear on the subject, are essentially

1 H. Sidgwick: *The Method of Ethics* (1874). (German translation by C. Bauer, 1909.)

2 Leslie Stephen: *The Science of Ethics* (1882).

3 S. Alexander: *Moral Order and Progress: An Analysis of Ethical Conceptions* (1889).

4 Wm. Wundt: *Ethics: An Examination of the Facts and Laws of the Moral Life* (1887).

5 Friedrich Paulsen: *A System of Ethics* (1889).

6 Friedrich Jodl: *A History of Ethics as Philosophical Science* (2 vols., 2nd ed., 1906 and 1912).

7 Georg von Gizyki: *Moral Philosophy, expounded so as to be intelligible to all* (1888).

8 Harald Höffding (a Dane): *Ethics* (1887). (German translation, 1888.)

Georg Simmel (1858–1918) adopts a critical attitude towards modern "scientific" ethics in his *Introduction to Moral Science* (1892).

related to one another, the most original is Leslie Stephen, the scientifically soundest is Wilhelm Wundt, the most ethical is Harald Höffding.

Höffding makes the ethical originate partly out of a consideration which limits the sovereignty of the present moment. "An action (he says) is good which preserves the totality of life and gives fulness and life to its content; an action is bad which has a more or less decided tendency to break into and narrow the totality of life and its content." Supporting this consideration come also instincts of sympathy, which make us feel pleasure in the pleasure of others, and pain in their pain. The aim of ethics is general prosperity.

Of these ethical writers some put the chief emphasis on the ethical disposition of the individual, while others hold that ethics are constituted chiefly by their content, which aims at the good of society. What is common to them all is that they try to combine the ethics of ethical personality and the ethics of utilitarianism without having inquired into their higher unity. That is why the chapters in which they touch on the problem of the basic principle of the moral are always the least clear and the least living part of their works. One is conscious of how happy they feel when they have waded through this swamp, and can launch out into consideration of the different ethical standpoints which have emerged in history, or can face questions on single points in ethical practice. And when they handle practical questions, it is obvious that they are not in possession of any serviceable basic principle of the moral. Their coming to terms with reality is a mere groping here and there. The considerations on the strength of which they decide are set out now in this sense, now in that. Hence these ethical writers frequently offer very interesting discussions on ethical problems, but the conception of the moral never gets from them any real explanation or any deepening. The criterion of a real code of ethics is whether it allows their full rights to the problems of personal morality and of the relation of man to man, problems with which we are concerned every day and every hour, and by means of which we must become ethical personalities. These academical works do not do this. Therefore, although they may arrive at results which deserve attention, they are not capable of giving effective ethical impulses to the thought of their time.

* * *

This mediating form of ethics is not left uncriticized. In Germany inheritors of the Kantian spirit like Hermann Cohen (b. 1842)[9] and Wilhelm Herrmann (1846–1922)[10] oppose it, and in English-speaking countries successors of the Intuitionists like James Martineau (1805–1900),[11] F. H. Bradley (b. 1846),[12] T. H. Green (1836–1882),[13] Simon Laurie (1829–1909),[14] and James Seth (b. 1860).[15]

In spite of wide differences in detail, these thinkers agree in refusing to derive ethics either from the ethical disposition of man or from the claims of society. They represent ethics as produced entirely through the ethical personality. To become ethical personalities, they say, we step out of ourselves and work for the good of the community.

Cohen and Herrmann attempt to reach ethics which will form a consistent unity by using logic to put a content into the empty categorical imperative of Kant. They wish to make good what he missed in his *Grundlegung zur Metaphysik der Sitten* (Foundations for a Metaphysic of Morals) and in his *Metaphysik der Sitten* (A Metaphysic of Morals). Cohen finds the origin of ethics in the pure Will thinking out the idea of one's fellow-man and the idea of the associating of men to form a state, his ethical *ego* being brought into existence by this logical operation. The morality thus attained consists in honesty, modesty, loyalty, justice, and humanity, and culminates in the representation of the State as the highest creation of the moral

9 H. Cohen: *Kant's Foundation given to Ethics* (1877); *Ethics of the Pure Will* (1904).

10 W. Herrmann: *Ethics* (1901).

In France Charles Renouvier (1838–1903) tries, in his *Science of the Moral* (1869), to restore the Kantian system of ethics.

11 James Martineau: *Types of Ethical Theory* (2 vols., 1885).

12 F. H. Bradley: *Ethical Studies* (1876).

13 T. H. Green: *Prolegomena to Ethics* (posthumous, 1883).

14 Simon Laurie: *Ethica, or the Ethics of Reason* (1885). (A French translation by Georges Remack, 1902.)

15 James Seth: *Study of Ethical Principles* (3rd ed., 1894).

spirit. But that it is only the offspring of mental ability is betrayed by the whole story of its appearance. The "pure will" is an abstraction with which nothing can be set in motion.

Instead of obtaining ethics by deduction, using abstract logical methods, Wilhelm Herrmann opens the backdoor of experience. He does indeed make ethics consist in "the bowing of the individual before the power of a something which is universally valid in thought," but that content of ethics which is a necessity of thought we are to reach by seeing ourselves in each other as if in a mirror, and deciding what kind of conduct makes us mutually "reliable." The thought of the unconditional claim originates, therefore, spontaneously in us, but awakes to the fact that it is determined by its content "through experience of human intercourse, and in relations of mutual trust."

Herrmann did not complete this system of philosophic ethics. He sketched it as an introduction to a not less artificial theological system. His conception is allied to Adam Smith's theory of the impartial third party.[16]

* * *

Martineau, Green, Bradley, Laurie, and Seth try to reach ethics which can form a consistent unity by making the whole of ethics originate in the need for self-perfecting. Of these, Martineau goes more on the lines of the eighteenth century Cambridge Platonists. Ethics consist for him in thinking ourselves into the ideal of perfection which God gave us with our life, and letting ourselves be determined by it. T. H. Green, F. H. Bradley, Simon Laurie, and James Seth show more or less the influence of J. G. Fichte. The ethical is with them founded on the fact that man wishes to live out his life in the deepest way as an effective personality, and thereby attain to true union with the infinite spirit. This thought is expounded best by T. H. Green. He is also led at the same time to the relation between civilization and ethics, and determines that all the achievements of human activity, especially the political and social perfecting of society, are nothing in themselves, and have a real meaning only so far as they render attainable by individuals a more thorough perfection of heart. A spiritualized

[16] See page 160.

conception of civilization is therefore now struggling for acceptance. On American soil Josiah Royce (1855–1916) [17] was a representative of this ethic of self-perfecting.

In the effort to conceive of ethics as a whole as concerned with self-perfecting, that is to say, with conduct which springs from inward necessity, these thinkers express thoughts which are full of vitality. To be energetically occupied with the basic principle of the moral, even though it leads in the direction of the universal and apparently abstract, always brings with it results which are of practical value, even if the solution of the problem itself is not thereby advanced beyond a certain point.

These thinkers go so far on these lines as to understand ethics to be higher life-affirmation, consisting in our co-operation with the activity which the world-spirit wills for us. They represent the mysticism of activity taught by J. G. Fichte, but without its speculative foundation.

They leave unsolved, however, indeed they do not even put, the question, how the higher life-affirmation comes to give itself a content which stands in contradiction to the course of nature. They conceive of higher life-affirmation as altruism, that is to say as life-affirmation within which life-negation is active. But how does this paradox come about? How far is this direction of the will, which contradicts the natural will-to-live, a necessity of thought? Why must man become different from the world in order to exist and work in the world in true harmony with the world-spirit? And what meaning has this conduct of his for the happenings which take place in the universe?

* * *

The thought of Alfred Fouillée (1838–1913) [18] and Jean Marie Guyau (1854–1888) [19] also circles round the conception of ethics as higher life-affirmation. They too conceive of the ethical as self-devotion, that is to say, as life-affirmation within

[17] Josiah Royce: *The Spirit of Modern Philosophy* (1892); *Religious Aspects of Philosophy* (4th ed., 1892).

[18] A. Fouillée: *Critique des systèmes de morale contemporaine* (1883): *Evolutionisme des idées-forces* (1890; German translation, 1908); *La morale des idées-forces* (1907).

[19] Jean Marie Guyau: *La morale anglaise contemporaine* (1879); *Esquisse d'une morale sans obligation ni sanction* (1885); *L'irréligion de l'avenir* (1886). A German version of his works appeared in 6 vols. in 1912.

which life-negation is present, but they dig deeper than the English and American representatives of the ethics of self-perfecting in that they seek to conceive of ethics within a nature-philosophy. Hence questions come to be discussed which these had left unnoticed. The problems of the basic principle of the moral and that of the optimistic-ethical world-view are once more opened up and, for the first time, in a comprehensive and elemental way.

Fouillée philosophizes in a noble way about the will-to-live. The ideas directed towards ethical ideals which come into our minds, like all our ideas in general, are, he says, not simply thoughts, but the expression of forces which press within us towards making existence full and complete.[20] Speaking generally, we must in this matter clearly understand that the evolution which in the course of the world produces and maintains existence is the work of representative forces (*idées-forces*), and is therefore to be explained in the last analysis as psychic. It reaches its highest point in man's ideas, which will their ends with clear consciousness. In this highest being, man, reality gets so far as to produce ideals which go out beyond reality, and by their means is led on beyond itself. Ethics are therefore a result of the evolution of the world. The idea of self-perfecting through self-devotion, which we experience as the mysterious element within us, is after all a natural manifestation of the will-to-live. The *ego* which has reached the farthest height of willing and representing enlarges itself by over-lapping other human existences. Self-devotion is, therefore, not a surrender of the self, but a manifestation of its expansion.[21] The man who analyses himself more deeply learns by experience that the highest life-affirmation comes about, not by the natural will-to-live simply rising into will-to-power, but by its "expanding." "Act towards others as if you became conscious of them at the same time as you become conscious of yourself." [22]

20 "Toute idée enveloppe un élément impulsif; nulle idée n'est un état simplement représentatif." (Every idea contains an element of impulse; no idea is merely a condition of re-presenting something in thought.)

21 . . . "notre conscience de nous-même tendant à sa plénitude par son expansion en autrui." (. . . our consciousness of ourselves, which presses on to its full growth by expanding into others.)

22 "Agis envers les autres comme si tu avais conscience des autres en même temps que de toi."

Jean Marie Guyau, a pupil and friend of Fouillée, in his *"Esquisse d'une morale sans obligation ni sanction,"* tries to develop the thought of this ethical life-affirmation through expansion. Ordinary morality, he says, stands helpless before this insoluble cleft between the *ego* and other men, but living nature makes no stop at that point. The individual life is expansive because it is life. As in the physical sphere it carries within itself the impulse to produce fresh life like itself, so in the spiritual sphere also it wishes to widen its own existence by linking it on to other life like itself. Life is not only the intake of food, but also production and fruitfulness; real living consists not only in receiving, but in a giving out of oneself as well. Man is an organism which imparts itself to others; its perfection consists in the most complete imparting of itself. In this philosophizing, then, Hume's notion of sympathy is given more profound expression.

Fouillée and Guyau, both of them invalids, lived together at Nice and Mentone. Trying in one another's company to realize the ethical higher life-affirmation, they take their exercise on the very shore on which Nietzsche that same year thought out his heightened life-affirmation of *Beyond Good and Evil.* He knows their works, as they know his, but they remain personally unknown to each other.[23]

Fouillée and Guyau, because they think deeply, are led to nature-philosophy by their philosophizing about the way in which the will-to-live is to become ethical. They wish to conceive ethics, within a world- and life-affirming nature-philosophy, as a deepening of life-affirmation, and also as a necessity of thought. In this matter they join the procession of the Chinese monists. That which these, like Spinoza and Fichte, attempted and failed to do, they attempt again in the confidence that their nature-philosophy will be fairer to the conception of living existence than was that of the others.

Navigating the rushing stream of heightened life-affirmation, they try with mighty efforts at the oars to reach the bank of the ethical. They believe that they will be able to land there

23 Fouillée reveals his attitude towards Nietzsche in a work entitled *Nietzsche and Immoralism.* Notes on the works of Fouillée and Guyau have been preserved by Nietzsche.

. . . but the waves carry them past it, like all those who attempted the journey before them.

They fail to show convincingly that life-affirmation in its highest form, by a paradox which lies in the nature of things, becomes ethical altruism. This proposition by which they would change the world-view from natural to ethical, is truth only for the thought which dares to make the same leap because it sees no possibility otherwise of reaching land from the drifting boat.

The ethics of Fouillée and Guyau, then, are an enthusiastic conception of life to which man pulls himself up when coming to terms with reality, in order to assert and exert himself in the universe in accordance with a higher value which he feels he embodies.

So Fouillée and Guyau are elemental moralists like Schopenhauer and Nietzsche. They are not, however, like the latter, making a voyage with their rudder tightly lashed in the circle of world- and life-negation or world-negation and life-affirmation; they hold on their course with sure perception towards the mysterious union of world-affirmation, life-affirmation, and life-negation which constitutes ethical life-affirmation. . . . But this course takes them out over the boundless ocean. They never reach land.

In order to understand themselves as a direction of the will-to-live which is a necessity of thought, and to think themselves out to an ethical world-view, ethics must come to terms with nature-philosophy. We find them, then, attempting—as did the Rationalists, and Kant and the speculative philosophers—to read into the world, in simple or in detailed thought, an optimistic-ethical meaning, or at least, as with Spinoza, to give an ethical character in some way or other to the relation of the individual to the universe. These two men also, Fouillée and Guyau, wrestle with nature-philosophy in order from it to justify ethics and an ethical world-view as not without meaning. At the same time, however, they dare—and this is the new element which appears in them—to look straight in the face the possibility that it will perhaps be impossible to carry their undertaking through. What will then become of ethics and world-view? Although they really ought to collapse, they do nevertheless remain standing—so Fouillée and Guyau judge.

Whether the idea of the good can ultimately claim any objective validity cannot be asserted with complete certainty, says Fouillée in his *Morale des Idées-forces*. Man must finally be content to force himself to acceptance of the ethically expansive life-affirmation, merely because he feels it to be the only thing which is capable of making life valuable. Out of love for the ideal he triumphs over all doubt, and sacrifices himself to it, untroubled about whether or no anything results from his doing so.

Guyau's *"Esquisse d'une morale sans obligation ni sanction"* ends in similar thoughts. An inner force, he says, works upon us and drives us forward. Do we go forward alone, or will the idea eventually win for itself some influence upon nature? . . . Anyhow let us go forward! . . . "Perhaps the earth, perhaps mankind, will one day reach some as yet unknown goal which they themselves have created. There is no hand leading us, no eye watching on our behalf; the rudder was broken long ago, or rather there never was one at all; it has to be provided. That is a big task, and it is our task." . . . Ethical men are crossing the ocean of events on a rudderless and mastless derelict, hoping nevertheless that they will some day and somewhere reach land.

In these sentences there is announced from afar the disappearance of the optimistic-ethical interpretation of the world. Because they dare to abandon this, and proclaim in principle the sovereign independence of ethics, Fouillée and Guyau belong among the greatest thinkers who have had a share in shaping our conception of the universe.

They do not, however, follow to the end the path on which they have stumbled. While they make ethics independent of whether their activity can or cannot prove itself legitimate as significant and effective in the totality of world-happenings, they assume the existence of a conflict between world-view and life-view, which philosophy down to their day had actually not noticed. But they do not investigate its nature, and do not show how it is that life-view can venture to assert itself in opposition to world-view, and even to exalt itself as the more important. They are content to prophesy that ethics and ethical world-view will grow green again as mighty oases, fed by subterranean springs, even if the sand-storms of scepticism should have turned into a desert the broad territory of the optimistic-ethical knowledge of the world, in which we once wished to make our home. At bottom, however, they hope that nothing like this will happen. Their confidence that a nature-philosophy which deals in the proper way with the nature of Being will after all finally reach ethics and an ethical world-view, is not completely overthrown.

Since they at first claim only a hypothetical validity for their new outlook, and do not develop it as a matter of principle, Fouillée and Guyau do not exercise upon the thought of the end of the nineteenth century and the beginning of the twentieth the influence which they deserve to have. Their age indeed, was not ready for that renunciation of knowledge for which their writings were preparing the way.

A forerunner of their ethic is to be found in that which Friedrich Albert Lange sketches as his own at the end of his *History of Materialism* (1866). Ethics, he says, are an imaginative creation on which we determine, because we carry an ideal within ourselves. We rise above the actual because we find no satisfaction in it. We are ethical because our life thereby obtains a definite character such as we long for. . . . Ethics mean becoming free from the world.

Lange also, then, has already reached the view that from direct philosophizing about the world and life an ethical outlook on the universe results, not as a necessity of thought, but as a necessity for life. But like the two French thinkers he just throws out the thought instead of following it into all its presuppositions and consequences.

A peculiar supplement which completes the ethics of Fouillée, Guyau, and Lange, without actually going back to them, is provided by the Berlin physician, Wilhelm Stern, in an inquiry, which has attracted far too little notice, into the evolutionary origin of ethics.[24] The essential nature of the moral, he says, is the impulse to the maintenance of life by the repelling of all injurious attacks upon it, an impulse through which the individual being experiences a feeling of relationship to all other animate beings in face of nature's injurious attacks upon them.

24 Wilhelm Stern, *Foundation of Ethics as a Positive Science* (Berlin, 1897).

How has this mentality arisen in us? Through the fact that animate beings of the most varied kinds have been obliged through countless generations to fight side by side for existence against the forces of nature, and in their common distress have ceased to be hostile to one another, so that they might attempt a common resistance to the annihilation which threatened them, or perish in a common ruin. This experience, which began with their first and lowest stage of existence and has become through thousands of millions of generations more and more pronounced, has given its special character to the psychology of all living beings. All ethics are an affirmation of life, the character of which is determined by perception of the dangers to existence which living beings experience in common.

How much deeper does Wilhelm Stern go than did Darwin! According to Darwin, experience of the never-ceasing, universal danger to existence produces in the end nothing but the herd-instinct, which holds together creatures of the same species. According to Stern, there is developed by the same experience a kind of solidarity with everything that lives. The barriers fall. Man experiences sympathy with animals, as they experience it, only less completely, with him. Ethics are not merely something peculiar to man, but, in a less developed form, are to be seen also in the animal world as such. Self-devotion is an experience of the deepened impulse to self-preservation. In the active as well as in the passive meaning of the word the whole animate creation is to be included within the basic principle of the moral.

The fundamental commandment of ethics, then, is that we cause no suffering to any living creature, not even the lowest, unless it is to effect some necessary protection for ourselves, and that we be ready to undertake, whenever we can, positive action for the benefit of other creatures.

In Fouillée, Guyau, and Lange ethics try to come to terms with nature-philosophy, but without any advance towards becoming cosmic. They fall into the anachronism of regarding themselves still, even at that date, as nothing beyond the regulating of the disposition of man towards his fellow-men, instead of expanding so as to comprehend the conduct of man towards every living creature and towards Being in general. In Stern this obvious, further step is taken.

Only a system of ethics that has become universal and cosmic is capable of taking in hand the investigation of the basic principle of the moral; only such a system can really attempt to come to terms in intelligible fashion with nature-philosophy.

* * *

Eduard von Hartmann (1842–1906)[25] also endeavours to include ethics in nature-philosophy. His *Philosophy of the Unconscious* is largely in line with the thoughts of Fouillée, but in the matter of an outlook on the universe he takes a different course. Instead of allowing ethics, when coming to terms with nature-philosophy, to experience freedom from this, he compels their adjustment to such a philosophy. And his nature-philosophy is pessimistic. It confesses to being unable to discover in what happens in the world any principle which contains a meaning. Therefore, so Hartmann concludes, as do the Indians and Schopenhauer, the world-process is something which must come to a standstill. Everything that exists must gradually enter on the blessed condition of willlessness. Ethics are the state of mind which brings this development into action.

In language obscure enough, at the end of his *Phenomenology of the Moral Consciousness,* von Hartmann formulates his pessimistic-ethical philosophy as follows: "Existence in the world of matter is the incarnation of the Godhead; the world-process is the history of the passion of the incarnate God, and at the same time the way to the redemption of Him who is crucified in the flesh; but morality is co-operation for the shortening of this road of suffering and redemption."

Then, however, instead of unfolding what this ethic is, and how it is to come into force, he undertakes to show that all ethical standpoints which have ever made their appearance at all in history have their own justification. He wants to house them all within an evolution which necessarily leads to pessimistic ethics.

[25] Eduard von Hartmann: *Philosophy of the Unconscious* (1879); *Phenomenology of the Moral Consciousness* (1789).

Every moral principle which shows itself in history, von Hartmann asserts, changes when it searches for the completion which lies nearest to it. It lives itself out, and then makes way for the higher moral principle which logically issues from it. That is how the ethical consciousness in individuals and in mankind works itself up from one moral principle to another till it reaches the highest knowledge. From the primitive moral principle of aiming at individual pleasure it travels past the authoritarian, the æsthetic, the sentimental, and the intellectual moral systems, which are one and all subjective, to the objective morality of care for the general happiness. But still beyond this it is led to the evolutionary moral principle of the development of civilization, and here it learns to think on supra-moral lines. It grasps the notion that for moral consideration there is still something higher than the prosperity of individuals and of society, namely "contest and struggle for the maintenance and enhancing of civilization." This, according to usual ideas, unethical conception of ethics has to be developed completely, so that it may then be resolved into the ethics of world- and life-negation.

By this insight into the logic of the course of ethical evolution, von Hartmann is saved from protesting, as would an ordinary ethical thinker, against the unethical civilization-ethics of the close of the nineteenth century. He knows, on the contrary, that he is helping the cause of rightly understood ethical progress, if he treats that form of ethics with respect as a necessary phenomenon, and urges that it be allowed to live itself out with the utmost completeness. Accordingly he asserts that we have learnt to see through the ethic which aims at making men and peoples happy as being a piece of sentimentality, and ought now to make up our minds to deal seriously with the supra-ethical ethic of the enhancement of life and civilization. We must learn to regard as good whatever is necessary for the development of civilization, and we are no longer at liberty to condemn war in the name of ethics. "The principle of the development of civilization compels us to recognize all these protests as unsound, since wars are the chief means of carrying on the struggle between races, that is to say, the process of natural selection within mankind, and preparation for the effective waging of war has formed one of the most important means of education and training for mankind in every phase of the development of civilization, as it will also be, so far as we can see, in the future."[26] Economic misery too, and the conflicts which arise from it, are seen by the ethical spirit which looks further ahead to subserve a higher objective. The sufferings under the wage system, which are far greater than those under slavery, are necessary for the course of civilization. The struggle which they evoke calls forces into being and has an educative effect. The course of civilization needs a favoured minority to serve as bearers of its ideas. Beneficence and charity to the poor must therefore be practised with moderation. The need which spurs men on to active work must not be banished from the world.

Another element in the course of civilization is the taking into possession of the whole earth by the race with the highest civilization, which must therefore increase its numbers as much as possible. In order to make the female population zealous about the task which thus falls to them, women must be raised intellectually. This is done by inculcating as much as possible patriotism and national feeling, by arousing their historical sense, and by filling them with enthusiasm for the principle of civilization which underlies evolution. "To effect this object, the history of civilization must be made the foundation of all instruction in the upper classes of girls' schools."[27]

It is desirable, therefore, to make efforts to secure the "improvement of the human type," and the attainment of an enhancement of civilization in which "the world-spirit becomes in increasing measure conscious of itself."

In his nature-philosophy and his philosophy of history, then, Eduard von Hartmann reaches a supra-ethical conception of life in which Hegel and Nietzsche drink to brotherhood, and the principles of inhumanity and relativity, which underlie biologico-sociological ethics, sit at table with garlands on their heads.

How and when the supra-ethical ethics of enhanced world- and life-affirmation pass over into the highest ethics of world- and life-negation, and in what way this highest system of ethics,

[26] *Phenomenology,* p. 670.
[27] *Idem,* p. 700.

in which we function as redeemers of the absolute, is to be carried out in practice, von Hartmann is unable to make clear. The abstruse modulations with which, in the last chapters of his work, he tries to get from one to the other provide us with ample proof of the unnatural character of the undertaking. To produce a philosophy with Hegel for body and Schopenhauer for head, is an absurdity. By his resolve to attempt it, von Hartmann admits his inability to make enhanced life-affirmation become in a natural way ethical.

Eduard von Hartmann prefers to the profession of moralist that of philosopher of the history of morals. Instead of serving the world with an ethical system of morals, he makes it happy with the discovery of the principle of inherent progress in the history of morals, and thus helps to befool completely the thought of his age, which is living its life in an unethical and unspiritual optimism.

From the history of ethics nothing is to be gained except a certain amount of clearness about the problem of ethics. Anyone who discovers in it principles which promise automatic progress in the ethical development of mankind, has mendaciously read these principles into the facts as a result of his miserably faulty construction of that history.

* * *

Henri Bergson (b. 1860) [28] renounces altogether the attempt to bring together nature-philosophy and ethics. Houston Stewart Chamberlain (b. 1855) [29] and Count Hermann Keyserling (b. 1880) [30] make the attempt but without reaching any result.

In his philosophizing about nature, Bergson does not go beyond the *rôle* of the observing subject. He analyses in a masterly

[28] Henri Bergson: *Sur les données immédiates de la conscience* (1888). (English translation by F. L. Pogson, 1910: *Time and Freewill: An Essay on the Immediate Data of Consciousness.*) *Matière et memoire. Essai sur la relation du corps et de l'esprit* (1896). (English translation by N. M. Paul and W. S. Palmer: *Matter and Memory,* 1911.) L'*évolution créatrice* (1907). (English translation by A. Mitchell: *Creative Evolution,* 1911.)

[29] H. S. Chamberlain: *The Foundations of the Nineteenth Century* (1899). (14th German edition, 1922.) *Immanuel Kant* (1905); *Goethe* (1912).

[30] Count Hermann Keyserling: *The Structure of the World* (1906); *A Philosopher's Travel-Diary* (2 vols., 1919); *Philosophy as Art* (1920).

way the nature of the process of knowledge. His investigations into the origin of our conception of time and of the actions of our consciousness which are bound up with it, have taught us how to comprehend the course of nature in its living reality. Leading us on beyond the science which consists in external affirming and calculating, Bergson shows that the true knowledge of Being comes to us through a sort of intuition. Philosophizing means experiencing our consciousness as an emanation of the creative impulse which rules in the world. Bergson's nature-philosophy has therefore a close inward connection with that of Fouillée, but he does not find it necessary, as Fouillée does, to produce from it a world- and life-view. He limits himself to depicting it from the standpoint of the problem of the theory of knowledge. He does not attempt any analysis of the ethical consciousness. Year after year we have waited for him to complete his work, as he no doubt himself intended, with an attempt at producing an ethic based on nature-philosophy. But he has contented himself with developing in ever-new forms his theories about our inner knowledge of the real. He never comes to the recognition that all deepening of our knowledge of the world acquires its real significance only so far as it teaches us to understand what we ought to aim at in life. He lets the waves of events roll past us, as if we were seated on an island in the stream, whereas we are in reality obliged to exert ourselves in it as swimmers.

During the war the German cinema theatres were crammed. People went to see the pictures in order to forget their hunger. Bergson's philosophy brings before us as living events the world which Kant depicted in motionless wall-pictures. But to satisfy the hunger of to-day for ethics he does nothing. He has no world-view to offer us in which we can find a life-view. A quietistic, sceptical mood overshadows his philosophy.

Houston Stewart Chamberlain tries to find a world-view which is based on nature-philosophy and is at the same time ethical. His work entitled *Immanuel Kant* (1905), which is really a journey through the problems raised by philosophy and the attempts to solve them, ends in the thought that, if we wish to reach a real civilization, we have to combine Goethe's nature-philosophy, which conceives becoming as an eternal being, with

Kant's judgment about the nature of duty. But he finds himself unable to develop such a world-view to completion.

Stimulated by Chamberlain, Hermann Keyserling goes far beyond Bergson in the aims of his thinking. He wants to reach clear ideas not only about knowledge of the world, but also about life and work in the world. From the pinnacle, however, to which he mounts, he sees only the fields of wisdom; those of ethics are veiled in mist. The highest idea, so he declares at the conclusion of his work, *The Structure of the World,* is that of truth. We want to know, because knowledge, "whether it visibly serves life at present or not, already implies in itself a purposive reaction to the outer world." In correct knowledge the human spirit enters into reciprocal relations with the universe. Life carries within itself its own purposive character.

Keyserling finds it quite in order that the outlook on life of great men should be superior to ordinary moral standards. One must not reproach Leonardo da Vinci for working as willingly in the service of the French king, Francis I., as he had done previously in that of the Sforzas whom Francis expelled. "Almost every great spirit is a complete egoist." If anyone has experience of life in its full extent and depth and living force, and works in reciprocity with the universe, interest in the human race is a kind of specialization which is no longer incumbent on him.

In the Preface to the second edition of *The Structure of the World* (1920), Keyserling admits that he has not reached a decision about the ethical problem. In his *Philosophy as Art* (1920), he declares it to be the foremost duty of our time to "make the wise man a possible type, to draw him out by education, and give him all necessary publicity and scope for his activities."

The wise man is the one man who is capable of veracity, the man who lets all the tones of life sound within him, and seeks to be in tune with the fundamental key-note which is given in him. He has no universally valid conception of the universe to impart to others. Not even for himself has he a conception that is definite and final; he has only one which is liable to constant alteration for the better. He himself is unalterable only in this, that he wants to live his life in its entirety and in the most vital co-operation with the universe, and at the same time ever strives to be himself. Sincere and emphatic life-affirmation is therefore the last word of this philosophizing about the world and life. . . .

Thus does nature-philosophy admit that it cannot produce ethics.

With the lesser spirits self-deception goes further. The ordinary scientific monism, the greatness of which consists in its being an elemental movement towards veracity in an age which is weary of veracity, is still convinced that from its insight into the essential nature of life, into the development of lower life into higher, and into the inner connection of the individual life with the life of the universe, it can somehow or other arrive at ethics. But it is significant that its representatives take altogether different roads in the search for ethics. An incredible absence of thought and of plan reigns in the ethical philosophizing of the ordinary scientific nature-philosophy. Many of its representatives have before their mind's eye a conception of the moral as a becoming one with the universe, a conception which is related to that of the Stoics and Spinoza. Others, influenced by Nietzsche, entertain the thought that true ethics are an enhanced and aristocratic life-affirmation, and have nothing to do with the claims of the "democratic" social ethics.[31] Others again, like Johannes Unold in his work *Monism and Its Ideals* (1908), try to bring together nature-philosophy and ethics in such a way as to let them conceive of the human activity which is directed to social ends as the final result of the development of the organic world. There are also scientific nature-philosophers who are content to put together out of what is commonly regarded as moral a system of ethics which is universally accepted, and to exalt it, so far as they can, into a product of nature-philosophy. In Ernst Haeckel's (1834–1919) work *The Riddle of the Universe* (1899), an ethic of that character is built on to the palace of nature-philosophy like a kitchen. It is maintained that the basic principle of monistic ethical theory is the equal justification of egoism and altruism, and

[31] Thus Otto Braun in his essay "Monism and Ethics" in the volume entitled *Monism Expounded in Contributions from its Representatives* (edited by Arthur Drews; vol. i., 1908). The poverty of this form of ethics is clearly revealed when the editor tries to indicate its content.

supplies the equilibrium between them. Both are laws of nature. Egoism serves the preservation of the individual, altruism that of the species. That "golden rule of morality" is said to be of equal significance with the rule which Jesus and other ethical thinkers before him are said to have proclaimed in the demand that we shall love our neighbour as ourselves. Spencer and water is poured out under a Christian label.

* * *

An inexorable development of thought, then, brings it about that the philosophy of the end of the nineteenth century and the beginning of the twentieth, either advances to a supra-ethical world-view, or lives among ethical ruins. What happens in the great German speculative philosophy of the beginning of the nineteenth century is a prelude to the *dénouement* of the drama. In that philosophy an ethical world-view tries to find a foundation in speculative nature-philosophy, and in doing so becomes, as stands confessed in Hegel, supra-ethical. Later, ethics are believed capable of providing a "scientific" conception of themselves, thanks to the results reached by psychology, biology, and sociology, but in proportion as they effect this, their energy decreases. Later still, when, through the growth of science and the inward changes in thought, a nature-philosophy which is in harmony with scientific observation of nature becomes the only possible philosophy, ethics once more have to make a real attempt to find a basis in a nature-philosophy which is directed upon the universe. There is nothing, however, but the enhancement and perfecting of life which nature-philosophy can give as the meaning of life. Hence ethics must struggle to conceive the enhancement and perfecting of life as something which comes to pass within the field of ethical ideas, and it is this for which, without ever attaining its goal, the most modern thought is striving, on lines of development which are often apparently irreconcilable.

Whenever an ethic really relies in any way upon nature-philosophy for the production of the convincing, ethical world-view for which the age is longing, it gets wrecked upon it in one way or another. Either it actually attempts to give itself out to be somehow a natural enhancement of life, and thereby so alters its character that it ceases to be really and truly ethics. Or it abdicates; perhaps, as with Keyserling, leaving the field free to supra-ethical world-view; perhaps, as with Bergson, leaving nature-philosophy and ethical questions with it, to rest in peace.

Thus the sun of ethics becomes darkened for our generation. Nature-philosophy pushes itself forward like a wall of cloud. Just as an inundation overwhelms pastures and fields with its water-borne *débris,* so do the supra-ethical and the unethical ways of thinking break in upon our mentality. They bring about the most terrible devastations without anyone having any clear idea of what the catastrophe means, or indeed being conscious of anything wrong beyond that the spirit of the time is rendering all ethical standards powerless.

Everywhere there grows up an unethical conception of civilization. The masses reconcile themselves in an incomprehensible way to the theory of the relativity of all ethical standards and to thoughts of inhumanity. Freed from any obligation to the exercise of ethical will, the belief in progress suffers a process of externalization which increases from year to year, becoming finally nothing better than a wooden façade which conceals the pessimism behind it. That we have lapsed into pessimism is betrayed by the fact that the demand for the spiritual advance of society and mankind is no longer seriously made among us. We have now resigned ourselves, as if no explanation of it were needed, to the fate of being obliged to smile at the high-flying hopes of previous generations. There is no longer to be found among us the true world- and life-affirmation which reaches down to the depths of the spiritual nature of man. Unavowed pessimism has been consuming us for decades.

Delivered over to events in an attitude of mind which is powerless because it is entirely without any true and ethical ideals of progress, we are experiencing the collapse of material and spiritual civilization alike.

By its belief in an optimistic-ethical philosophy the modern age became capable of a mighty advance towards civilization. But as its thought has not been able to show this philosophy to be founded in the nature of things, we have sunk, consciously and unconsciously, into a condition in which we have no world-view at all, a condition of pessimism, too, and of absence of all ethical conviction, so that we are on the point of complete ruin.

The bankruptcy of the optimistic-ethical philosophy was announced beforehand as little as was the financial bankruptcy of the ruined states of Europe. But just as the latter was gradually revealed, by the constantly diminishing value of the paper-money that was issued, as having actually come about, so is the former being gradually revealed by the constantly diminishing power among us of the true and profound ideals of civilization.

Chapter 22

THE NEW WAY

Why the optimistic-ethical world-view cannot be carried through to the logical conclusion.

Life-view independent of world-view.

THE GREATNESS OF EUROPEAN PHILOSOPHY CONSISTS IN ITS HAVING chosen the optimistic-ethical world-view; its weakness in its having again and again imagined that it was putting that conception on a firm foundation, instead of making clear to itself the difficulties of doing so. The task before our generation is to strive with deepened thought to reach a truer and more valuable world-view, and thus bring to an end our living on and on without any philosophy of life at all.

Our age is striking out unmeaningly in every direction like a fallen horse in the traces. It is trying with external measures and new organization to solve the difficult problems with which it has to deal, but all in vain. The horse cannot get on its feet again till it is unharnessed and allowed to get its head up. Our world will not get upon its feet again till it lets the truth come home to it that salvation is not to be found in active measures but in new ways of thinking.

But new ways of thinking can arise only if a true and valuable conception of life casts its spell upon individuals.

The one serviceable world-view is the optimistic-ethical. Its renewal is a duty incumbent on us. Can we prove it to be true?

In the struggle of the thinkers who for centuries exerted themselves to demonstrate the truth of optimistic-ethical philosophy, and kept surrendering themselves comfortably to the illusion, always very soon shattered, that they had succeeded, the problem with which we are concerned reveals itself in outlines which become clearer and clearer. We are now in a position to reckon up why these or those paths, apparently so full of promise, have led to nothing, and can lead to nothing. By the insight into the problem thus won we shall be kept off impassable roads and forced to follow the only track which is practicable.

The most general result of the attempts made up to the present is this: that the optimistic-ethical interpretation of the world, by which it was hoped to put the optimistic-ethical world-view on a firm foundation, cannot be developed to a conclusion. Yet how logical and natural it seems to tune the meaning of life and the meaning of the world to the same key! How invitingly the path opens out to explaining our own existence from the nature and significance of the universe! It rises so naturally to the crest of the foothills that one can only believe it leads up to the highest point of knowledge. But high up in the ascent it breaks off with chasms ahead.

The consideration that the meaning of human life must be conceivable within the meaning of the universe is so obvious to thought, that it never lets itself be led from its path by the failure, one after another, of all attempts in that direction. It merely concludes that it has not tackled the problem in the right way. It therefore has resort to the whisperings of the theory of knowledge, and undertakes to depreciate the reality of the world in order to deal with it more successfully. In Kant, in the speculative philosophy, and in much "spiritualistic" popular philosophy which has been current almost down to our own day, it preserved its hope of reaching the goal by some sort of combination of epistemological with ethical idealism. Hence the philosophy of academic manuals declaims against the ingenuous thinking which tries to reach a world-view without first having been baptized by Kant with fire and the holy spirit. But this too is a vain proceeding. The crafty and fraudulent attempts to form a conception of the world with an optimistic-ethical meaning meet with no better success than the naïve ones. What our thinking tries to proclaim as knowledge is never anything but an unjustifiable interpretation of the world.

Against the admission of this, thought guards itself with the courage of despair, because it fears it will find itself in that case with no idea of what to do in face of the problem of life. What meaning can we give to human existence, if we must renounce all pretence of knowing the meaning of the world? Nevertheless there remains only one thing for thought to do, and that is to adapt itself to facts.

The hopelessness of the attempt to find the meaning of life within the meaning of the universe is shown first of all by the fact that in the course of nature there is no purposiveness to be seen in which the activities of men, and of mankind as a whole, could in any way intervene. On one of the smaller among the millions of heavenly bodies there have lived for a short space of time human beings. For how long will they continue so to live? Any lowering or raising of the temperature of the earth, any change in the inclination of the axis of their planet, a rise in the level of the ocean, or a change in the composition of the atmosphere, can put an end to their existence. Or the earth itself may fall, as so many other heavenly bodies have fallen, a victim to some cosmic catastrophe. We are entirely ignorant of what significance we have for the earth. How much less then may we presume to try to attribute to the infinite universe a meaning which has us for its object, or which can be explained in terms of our existence!

It is not, however, merely the huge disproportion between the universe and man which makes it impossible for us to give the aims and objects of mankind a logical place in those of the universe. Any such attempt is made useless beforehand by the fact that we fail to succeed in discovering any general purposiveness in the course of nature. Whatever we do find of purposiveness in the world is never anything but an isolated instance.

In the production and maintenance of some definite form of life, nature does sometimes act purposively in a magnificent way. But in no way does she ever seem intent on uniting these instances of purposiveness which are directed to single objects into a collective purpose. She never undertakes to let life coalesce with life to form a collective life. She is wonderfully creative force, and at the same time senselessly destructive force. We face her absolutely perplexed. What is full of meaning within the meaningless, the meaningless within what is full of meaning: that is the essential nature of the universe.

* * *

European thought has tried to ignore these elemental certainties. It can do so no longer, and it is of no use to try. The facts have silently produced their consequences. While the optimistic-ethical world-view is still current among us as a dogma, we no longer possess the ethical world- and life-affirmation which should result from it. Perplexity and pessimism have taken possession of us without our admitting the fact.

There remains, therefore, nothing for us to do but confess that we understand nothing of the world, and are surrounded by complete enigmas. Our knowledge is becoming sceptical.

Just as thought has hitherto allowed world-view and life-view to be mutually dependent on each other, so have we in consequence fallen a prey to a sceptical conception of life. But is it really the case that life-view is towed along by world-view, and when the latter can no longer be kept afloat must sink with it into the depths? Necessity bids us cut the tow-rope and try to let life-view continue its voyage independently.

This manœuvre is not so unexpected as it seems. While people still acted as though their life-view were taken from their world-view, the relationship between the two was really just the opposite, for their world-view was formed from their life-view. What they put forward as their view of the world was an interpretation of the world in the light of their life-view.

The life-view held by European thought being optimistic-ethical, the same character was attributed to world-view in defiance of facts. Wishful thinking, without admitting it, overpowered knowledge. Life-view prompted and world-view recited. So the belief that life-view was derived from world-view was only a fiction.

In Kant this overpowering of knowledge, which till then had been but naïvely practised, was worked out systematically. His doctrine of the "Postulates of the Practical Reason" means just this: that the will claims for itself the decisive word in the last pronouncements of the world-view. Only Kant manages to arrange the matter so cleverly that the will never forces its supremacy on knowledge, but receives it from the latter as a free gift, and then makes use of it in carefully chosen parliamentary phrases. It proceeds as if it had been invoked by the theoretical reason to provide possible truths with the reality belonging to truths which are necessities of thought.

In Fichte the will dictates its world-view to knowledge without any regard for the arts of diplomacy.

From the middle of the nineteenth century onward, there can be discerned in natural science a tendency no longer to claim that philosophy must be accommodated to scientifically established facts. The valuable convictions of the traditional world-view are to hold good, even if they cannot be brought into harmony with the accepted knowledge of the world. After the publication of Du Bois-Raymond's (1818–1896) lectures "On the Limits of Our Knowledge of Nature" (1872) with a certain school of natural science it begins to be considered almost a part of good manners to declare oneself incompetent in questions of world-view. There grows up gradually what one may call a modern doctrine of the two-fold nature of truth. To this movement expression is given by the "Keplerbund," which was founded in 1907 by representatives of natural science, and goes so far as to declare acceptable to natural science the valuable pronouncements of the current philosophy of life, even when given in formulas provided by ecclesiastical authority. This new doctrine of the two-fold nature of truth is brought to philosophical expression by the theory of the solidity of "value-judgments." By means of this theory Albrecht Ritschl (1822–1889) and his imitators try to uphold the validity of a religious, side by side with a scientific, conception of life. Almost the whole religious world, in so far as it tries to remain a thinking body, grasps at such expedients. Next, in William James's (1842–1910) philosophy of Pragmatism the will admits in half-naïve, half-cynical fashion that all the knowledge professed by its world-view has been produced by itself.

That the valuable assertions of philosophy are to be traced back to the will which has been determined by valuable convictions is therefore a fact, and since Kant's day a fact that has been admitted in the most varied directions. The shock given to the feeling for veracity, which accompanies this no longer naïve but half-conscious and insidiously employed interpretation of the world, plays a fatal part in the mentality of our time.

But why go on with this dirty business? Why keep knowledge in subservience to the will by means of a kind of infamous secret police? Any world-view deduced therefrom must ever be a miserable thing. Let us allow will and knowledge to come together in a relation honourable to both.

In what has hitherto been called world-view there are two things united: view of the world and life-view. So long as it was possible to cherish the illusion that the two were harmonious and each completed the other, there was nothing to be said against this combination. Now, however, when the divergence can no longer be concealed, the wider conception of world-view which includes life-view organically within itself, must be given up. It is no longer permissible to go on either naïvely believing that we get our conception of life from our conception of the world, or furtively elevating in some way or other our conception of life into a conception of the world. We are standing at a turning-point of thought. Critical action which clears away all prevailing *naïvetés* and dishonesties has become necessary. We must make up our minds to leave our conceptions of life and of the world mutually independent of each other, and see that a straightforward understanding between the two is reached. We have to admit that because our conception of life is made up of convictions which are given in our will-to-live but are not confirmed by knowledge of the world, we have allowed it to go beyond the varied knowledge which makes up our conception of the world.

This renunciation of world-view in the old sense, that is of a unitary world-view which is complete in itself, means a painful experience for our thought. We come hereby to a dualism against which we at every moment instinctively rebel. But we must surrender to facts. Our will to live has to accommodate itself to the inconceivable truth that it is unable with its own valuable convictions to discover itself again in the manifold will-to-live which is seen manifested in the world. We wanted to form a philosophy of life for ourselves out of items of knowledge gathered from the world. But it is our destiny to live by means of convictions which an inward necessity makes a part of our thought.

In the old rationalism reason undertook to investigate the world. In the new it has to take as its task the attaining to clarity about the will-to-live which is in us. Thus we return to an elemental philosophizing which is once more busied with questions of world- and life-view as they directly affect men, and seeks to give a safe foundation to, and to keep alive, the valuable ideas which we find in ourselves. It is in a conception of life which is dependent on itself alone, and seeks to come in a straightforward way to an understanding with world-knowledge, that we hope to find once more power to attain to ethical world- and life-affirmation.

Chapter 23

THE FOUNDATIONS OF OPTIMISM SECURED FROM THE WILL-TO-LIVE

The pessimistic result of knowledge.

The world- and life-affirmation of the will-to-live.

THERE ARE TWO THINGS WHICH THOUGHT HAS TO DO FOR US; IT must lead us from the naïve to a deepened world- and life-affirmation, and must let us go on from mere ethical impulses to an ethic which is a necessity of thought.

Deepened world- and life-affirmation consists in this: that we have the will to maintain our own life and every kind of existence that we can in any way influence, and to bring them to their highest value. It demands from us that we think out all ideals of the material and spiritual perfecting of individual men, of society, and of mankind as a whole, and let ourselves be determined by them to steady activity and constant hope. It does not allow us to withdraw into ourselves, but orders us to bring to bear a living, and so far as possible an active, interest on everything which happens around us. To endure a state of unrest through our relation to the world, when by withdrawing into ourselves we might enjoy rest: that is the burden which deeper world- and life-affirmation lays upon us.

We begin our life-course in an unsophisticated world- and life-affirmation. The will-to-live which is in us gives us that as natural. But later, when thought awakes, questions crop up which make a problem of what has hitherto been a matter of course. What meaning will you give your life? What do you mean to do in the world? When, along with these questions, we begin trying to reconcile knowledge and will-to-live, facts get in the way with confusing suggestions. Life attracts us, they say, with a thousand expectations, and fulfils hardly one of them. And the fulfilled expectation is almost a disappointment, for only anticipated pleasure is really pleasure; in pleasure which is fulfilled its opposite is already stirring. Unrest, disappointment and pain are our lot in the short span of time which lies between our entrance on life and our departure from it. What is spiritual is in a dreadful state of dependence on our bodily nature. Our existence is at the mercy of meaningless happenings and can be brought to an end by them at any moment. The will-to-live gives me an impulse to action, but the action is just as if I wanted to plough the sea, and sow in the furrows. What did those who worked before me effect? What significance in the endless chain of world-happenings have their efforts had? With all its illusive promises, the will-to-live only means to mislead me into prolonging my existence, and allowing to enter on existence other beings to whom the same miserable lot has been assigned as to myself, so that the game may go on and on without end.

The discoveries in the field of knowledge which the will-to-live encounters when it begins to think, are therefore altogether pessimistic. It is not by accident that all religious world-views, except the Chinese, have a more or less pessimistic tone and bid man expect nothing from his existence here.

Who will prevent us from making use of the freedom we are allowed, and casting existence from us? Every thinking human being makes acquaintance with this thought. We let it take a deeper hold of us than we suspect from one another, as indeed we are all more oppressed by the riddles of existence than we allow others to notice.

What determines us, so long as we are comparatively in our right mind, to reject the thought of putting an end to our existence? An instinctive feeling of repulsion from such a deed. The will-to-live is stronger than the pessimistic facts of knowledge. An instinctive reverence for life is within us, for we are will-to-live. . . .

Even the consistently pessimistic thought of Brahmanism makes to the will-to-live the concession that voluntary death may only come about when the individual has put behind him a considerable portion of life. The Buddha goes still further. He rejects any violent exit from existence and demands only that we mortify the will-to-live within us.

All pessimism, then, is inconsistent. It does not push open the door to freedom, but makes concessions to the obvious fact of existence. In Indian thought, with its pessimistic tendency, there is an attempt to make these concessions as small as possible, and to maintain the impossible fiction that merely bare life is being lived, with complete abstinence from any share in the happenings which are taking place here, there, and everywhere about it. With us the concessions are larger, since the conflict between the will-to-live and pessimistic recognition of facts is to a certain extent damped down and obscured by the optimistic outlook on the world which prevails in the general mode of thought. There arises an unthinking will-to-live which lives out its life trying to snatch possession of as much happiness as possible, and wishes to do something active without having made clear to itself what its intentions really are.

Whether somewhat more or somewhat less of world- and life-affirmation is retained matters little. Whenever the deepened world- and life-affirmation is not fully reached, there remains only a depreciated will-to-live, which is not equal to the tasks of life.

Thought usually deprives the will-to-live of the force lent it by its freedom from pre-conceptions, without being able to induce it to adopt a practice of reflection in which it would find new and higher force. Thus it still possesses energy enough to continue in life, but not enough to overcome pessimism. The stream becomes a swamp.

That is the experience which determines the character of men's existence, without their confessing it to themselves. They nourish themselves scantily on a little bit of happiness and many vain thoughts, which life puts in their manger. It is only by the pressure of necessity, exerted by elementary duties which throng upon them, that they are kept on the path of life.

Often their will-to-live is changed into a kind of intoxication. Spring sunshine, trees in flower, passing clouds, fields of waving corn provoke it. A will-to-live which announces itself in many forms in magnificent phenomena all around them, carries their own will-to-live along with it. Full of delight, they want to take part in the mighty symphony which they hear. They find the world beautiful. . . . But the transport passes. Horrid discords allow them once more to hear only noise, where they thought they perceived music. The beauty of nature is darkened by the suffering they discover everywhere within it. Now they see once more that they are drifting like shipwrecked men over a waste of waters, only that their boat is at one moment raised aloft on mountainous waves and the next sinks into the valleys between them, and that now sunbeams, and now heavy clouds, rest upon the heaving billows.

Now they would like to persuade themselves that there is land in the direction in which they are drifting. Their will-to-live befools their thinking, so that it makes efforts to see the world as it would like to see it. It compels it also to hand them a chart which confirms their hopes of land. Once more they bend to the oars, till once again their arms drop with fatigue, and their gaze wanders, disappointed, from billow to billow.

That is the voyage of the will-to-live which has abjured thought.

Is there, then, nothing that the will-to-live can do but drift along without thought, or sink in pessimistic knowledge? Yes, there is. It must indeed voyage across this boundless sea; but it can hoist sails, and steer a definite course.

* * *

The will-to-live which tries to know the world is a shipwrecked castaway; the will-to-live which gets to know itself is a bold mariner.

The will-to-live is not restricted to maintaining its existence on what the ever unsatisfying knowledge of the world offers it; it can feed on the life-forces which it finds in itself. The knowledge which I acquire from my will-to-live is richer than that which I win by observation of the world. There are given in it values and incitements bearing on my relation to the world and to life which find no justification in my reflection upon the world and existence. Why then tune down one's will-to-live to the pitch of one's knowledge of the world, or undertake the meaningless task of tuning up one's knowledge of the world to the higher pitch of one's will-to-live? The right and obvious course is to let the ideas which are given in our will-to-live be accepted as the higher and decisive kind of knowledge.

My knowledge of the world is a knowledge from outside, and remains for ever incomplete. The knowledge derived from my will-to-live is direct, and takes me back to the mysterious movements of life as it is in itself.

The highest knowledge, then, is to know that I must be true to the will-to-live. It is this knowledge that hands me the compass for the voyage I have to make in the night without the aid of a chart. To live out one's life in the direction of its course, to raise it to higher power, and to ennoble it, is natural. Every depreciation of the will-to-live is an act of insincerity towards myself, or a symptom of unhealthiness.

The essential nature of the will-to-live is determination to live itself to the full. It carries within it the impulse to realize itself in the highest possible perfection. In the flowering tree, in the strange forms of the medusa, in the blade of grass, in the crystal; everywhere it strives to reach the perfection with which it is endowed. In everything that exists there is at work an imaginative force, which is determined by ideals. In us beings who can move about freely and are capable of pre-considered, purposive activity, the craving for perfection is given in such a way that we aim at raising to their highest material and spiritual value both ourselves and every existing thing which is open to our influence.

How this striving originated within us, and how it has developed, we do not know, but it is given with our existence. We must act upon it, if we would not be unfaithful to the mysterious will-to-live which is within us.

When the will-to-live arrives at the critical point where its early unsophisticated world- and life-affirmation must be changed into a reflective philosophy, it is the part of thought to assist it by holding it to the thinking out of all the ideas which are given within it and to the surrender of itself to them. That the will-to-live within us becomes true to itself and remains so; that it experiences no degeneration but develops itself to complete vitality; that is what decides the fate of our existence.

When it comes to clearness about itself, the will-to-live knows that it is dependent on itself alone. Its destiny is to attain to freedom from the world. Its knowledge of the world can show that its striving to raise to their highest value its own life and every living thing which can be influenced by it must remain problematic when regarded in relation to the universe. This fact will not disturb it. Its world- and life-affirmation carries its meaning in itself. It follows from an inward necessity, and is sufficient for itself. By its means my existence joins in pursuing the aims of the mysterious universal will of which I am a manifestation. In my deepened world- and life-affirmation, I manifest reverence for life. With consciousness and with volition I devote myself to Being. I become of service to the ideas which it thinks out in me; I become imaginative force like that which works mysteriously in nature, and thus I give my existence a meaning from within outwards.

Reverence for life means to be in the grasp of the infinite, inexplicable, forward-urging Will in which all Being is grounded. It raises us above all knowledge of things and lets us become like a tree which is safe against drought, because it is planted among running streams. All living piety flows from reverence for life and the compulsion towards ideals which is given in it. In reverence for life lies piety in its most elemental and deepest form, in which it has not yet become involved with, or has abandoned the hope of, any explanation of the world. It is piety which comes from inward necessity, and therefore asks no questions about ends to be pursued.

The will-to-live, too, which has become reflective and has penetrated to deeper world- and life-affirmation, tries to secure happiness and success, for as will-to-live it is will to the realizing of ideals. But it does not live on happiness and success. What portion of these it obtains is a strengthening of itself which it thankfully accepts, though it is resolved on action, even if happiness and success should be denied it. It sows as one who does not count on living to reap the harvest.

The will-to-live is not a flame which burns only when events provide suitable fuel; it blazes up, and that with the purest light, when it is forced to feed on what it derives from itself. Then, too, when events seem to leave no future for it but suffering, it still holds out as an active will. In deep reverence for life it makes the existence which according to usual ideas is no longer in any way worth living, precious, because even in such an existence it experiences its own freedom from the world. Quiet and peace radiate from a being like that upon others, and cause them also to be touched by the secret that we must all, whether active or passive, preserve our freedom in order truly to live.

True resignation is not a becoming weary of the world, but the quiet triumph which the will-to-live celebrates at the hour of its greatest need over the circumstances of life. It flourishes only in the soil of deep world- and life-affirmation.

In this way our life is a coming to an understanding between our will-to-live and the world, along with which we have continually to be on our guard against allowing any deterioration in our will-to-live. The struggle between optimism and pessimism is never fought to a finish within us. We are ever wandering on slipping rubble above the abyss of pessimism. When that which we experience in our own existence, or learn from the history of mankind, falls oppressively upon our will-to-live and robs us of our freshness and our power of deliberation, we may lose hold, and be carried away with the moving boulders into the depths beneath. But knowing that what awaits us below is death, we work our way up to the path again. . . .

Or it may perhaps be that pessimism comes over us, like the bliss of complete rest over those who, tired out, sit down in the snow. No longer to be obliged to hope for and aim at what is commanded us by the ideals which are forced upon us by the deepened will-to-live! No longer to be in a state of unrest when by lessening our efforts we can have rest! . . . Gently comes the appeal from knowledge to our will to tune itself down to the facts. . . .

That is the fatal state of complete rest in which men, and civilized mankind as a whole, grow numb and die.

And when we think that the riddles by which we are surrounded can no longer harm us, there once more rises up before us somewhere or other the most terrifying of them all, the fact that the will-to-live can be shattered in suffering or in spiritual night. This enigma, too, before which our will-to-live shudders as before the most inexplicable of all inexplicable things, we must learn to leave unsolved.

Thus does pessimistic knowledge pursue us closely right on to our last breath. That is why it is so profoundly important that the will-to-live should rouse itself at last, and once for all insist on its freedom from having to understand the world, and that it should show itself capable of letting itself be determined solely by that which is given within itself. Then with humility and courage it can make its way through the endless chaos of enigmas, fulfilling its mysterious destiny by making a reality of its union with the infinite Will-to-live.

Chapter 24

THE PROBLEMS OF ETHICS, STARTING FROM THE HISTORY OF ETHICS

An ethic of self-devotion, or an ethic of self-perfecting?
Ethics and a theory of knowledge. Ethics and natural happenings. The enthusiastic element in ethics.
The ethic of ethical personality, and the ethic of society.
The problem of a complete ethic.

PROFOUND THOUGHT, THEN, ARRIVES AT UNSHAKEABLE WORLD- AND life-affirmation. Let it now try whether it can lead us to ethics. But that we may not wander, as so often happens, merely at random, we must gather from the thought which has hitherto been devoted to ethics all the guidance which is there to be found.

What does the history of ethics teach?

In general we learn from it, that the object of ethical enquiry is the discovery of the universal basic principle of the moral.

The basic principle of the moral must be recognized as a necessity of thought, and must bring man to an unceasing, living, and practical conflict and understanding with reality.

The principles of the moral which have hitherto been offered us are absolutely unsatisfying. This is clear from the fact that they cannot be thought out to a conclusion without either leading to paradoxes, or losing in ethical content.

Classical thought tried to conceive of the ethical as that which brings rational pleasure. It did not succeed, however, from that starting-point in arriving at an ethic of active devotion. Confined to the egoistic-utilitarian, it ended in an ethically-coloured resignation.

The ethical thought of modern times is from the outset social-utilitarian. It is to it a matter of course that the individual must devote himself in every respect to his fellow-individuals, and to society. But when it tries to give a firm foundation to the ethic of altruism which seems to it so much a matter of course, and to think that matter out to a conclusion, it is driven to the most remarkable consequences, consequences inconsistent with each other in the most varied directions. At one time it explains altruism as a refined egoism; at another as something which society forcibly imposes on individuals; at another as something which it develops in him by education; next, as in Bentham, as something which he adopts as one of his convictions on the ground of the urgent representations of society; or again, as an instinct which he obeys. The first assumption cannot be maintained; the second, third, and, fourth are unsatisfying because they make ethics reach men from the outside; the last leads to a *cul-de-sac*. If, for example, self-devotion is an instinct, it must, of course, be made conceivable how thought can influence it, and raise it to the level of a considered, widely inclusive, voluntary activity, at which level it first becomes ethical. This, which is its peculiar problem, utilitarianism does not recognize, much less solve. It is always in too much of a hurry to reach practical results. At last it sells its soul to biology and social science, which lead it to conceive itself as herd-mentality, wonderfully developed and capable of still further development. And with this it finally sinks far below the level of real ethics.

Strange to say, therefore, although starting from what is most elementary and essential in ethics, the ethics of altruism fail to take shape in a way which satisfies thought. It is as if the true basic principle of ethics were within their reach, yet these ethics of altruism always grasped to right or left of it.

Along with these two attempts to understand ethics either as effort to procure rational pleasure, or as devotion to one's neighbour and to society, there is a third method, which tries to explain ethics as effort for self-perfecting. This enterprise has in it something abstract and venturesome. It disdains to start from a universally acknowledged content of the ethical, as utilitarianism does, and in contrast to that sets before thought the task of deriving the whole content of ethics from the effort for self-perfecting.

Plato, the first representative in the West of the ethics of self-perfecting, and Schopenhauer try to solve the problem by setting up, as do the Indians, world- and life-negation as the basic principle of the ethical. That, however, is no solution. World- and life-negation, if consistently thought out and developed does not produce ethics but reduces ethics to impotence.

Kant, the modern restorer of the ethics of self-perfecting, sets up the conception of absolute duty, but without giving it any content. He thereby admits his inability to derive the content of ethics from the effort for self-perfecting.

If the ethic of self-perfecting tries really to acquire a content, it must allow that ethics consist either in world- and life-negation or in higher world- and life-affirmation. The first need not be considered; there remains, therefore, only the other.

Spinoza conceives the higher world- and life-affirmation as contemplative absorption in the universe. He does not, however, arrive thereby at real ethics, but only at an ethically-coloured resignation. Schleiermacher uses much art to lend this ethical colouring a more brilliant tone. Nietzsche avoids the paths of resignation, but reaches thereby a world- and life-affirmation which is ethical only in so far as it feels itself to be an effort for self-perfecting.

The only thinker who succeeds to some extent in giving to self-perfecting within world- and life-affirmation an ethical content is J. G. Fichte. The result, however, is valueless, because it presupposes an optimistic-ethical view of the nature of the universe and the position of man within it, which is based upon inadmissible speculation.

The ethic of self-perfecting is therefore not capable of so establishing the basic principle of the moral, that it has a content which is ethically satisfying; the ethic of altruism, on the other hand, starting from a pre-supposed content, cannot reach a basic principle of ethics which is founded on thought.

The attempt made by antiquity to conceive ethics as that which brings rational pleasure we need no longer consider. It is only too clear that it does not sufficiently take into account the enigma of self-sacrifice, and can never solve it. So there remain for consideration only the two undertakings, so strangely opposed to one another, one of which starts from altruism as a generally accepted content of the ethical in order to conceive it as belonging to the self-perfecting of man, while the other starts from self-perfecting and seeks to conceive altruism as an item in its content which is a necessity of thought.

Is there a synthesis of these two? In other words, do altruism and the perfecting of the self belong together in such a way that the one is contained in the other?

If this inward unity has not been visible hitherto, may not the cause be that reflection, whether upon devotion or upon self-perfecting, did not go deep enough and was not sufficiently comprehensive?

* * *

Before thought attempts to investigate more profoundly and completely the essential nature of altruism and of self-perfecting, it must proceed further to visualize what is offered in the way of different kinds of knowledge and other considerations on its journey through the Western search for ethics.

It may be accepted as fully recognized that ethics have nothing to expect from any theory of knowledge. Depreciation of the reality of the material world brings merely apparent profit. Thought believes it can draw from the possibility of a spiritualizing of the world some advantage for the optimistic-ethical interpretation of it. It has, however, been established by this time that ethics can no more be derived from an ethical interpretation of the world than world- and life-affirmation can be referred back to an optimistic interpretation of it, but that they must rather find their foundation in themselves in a world which is known to be absolutely mysterious. At once and for ever, then, all attempts to bring ethical and epistemological idealism into connection with one another must be recognized as useless for ethics. Ethics can let space and time go to the devil.

In epistemological investigations into the nature of space and time ethics feel a satisfaction which is strong but uninterested. They view them as efforts after knowledge which must be made, but know that the results can never touch what is essential in any conception of the world or of life. It suffices to know that the whole world of the senses is a manifestation of forces, that is to say of mysteriously manifold will-to-live. In this their thought is spiritualistic. It is materialistic, however, so far as it presupposes manifestation and force to be connected in such a way that any effect produced upon the former influences the force which lies behind it. Ethics feel that if it were not thus possible for one will-to-live to produce through its manifestations effects on another will-to-live, they would have no reason for existing. But to investigate how this relation between force and its manifestation is to be explained from the standpoint of epistemology, and whether it can be explained at all, ethics can leave undecided as being none of their business; they claim for themselves, just as does natural science, the right to remain free from preconceptions.

In this connection it is an interesting fact that it is among the representatives of scientific materialism that enthusiastic ethical idealism is often to be met with, while the adherents of spiritualistic philosophy are usually moralists with an unemotional temperament.

With renunciation of all help from epistemological idealism, it follows that ethics ask for nothing and expect nothing from speculative philosophy. They declare they have nothing to do with any kind of ethical interpretation of the world.

Thought gathers, further, from the history of ethics that ethics cannot be conceived as being merely a natural happening which continues itself in man. In the ethical man natural happenings come into contradiction with themselves. Nature knows only a blind affirmation of life. The will-to-live which animates natural forces and living beings is concerned to work itself out unhindered. But in man this natural effort is in a state of tension with a mysterious effort of a different kind. Life-affirmation exerts itself to take up life-negation into itself in order to serve other living beings by self-devotion, and to protect them, even, it may be, by self-sacrifice, from injury or destruction.

It is true that self-devotion plays a certain *rôle* in non-human living beings. As a sporadic instinct it rules in sexual love and in parental love; as a permanent instinct it is found in certain individual members of animal species (*e.g.*, ants, bees) which, because sexless, are incomplete individualities. These manifestations are in a certain way a prelude to the interplay of life-affirmation and life-negation which is at work in the ethical man. But they do not explain it. That which is active elsewhere only as a sporadic instinct, or as an instinct in incomplete individualities and that, too, always within special relations of solidarity with others, becomes now, in man, a steady, voluntary, unlimited form of action, a result of thought, in which individuals endeavour to realize the higher life-affirmation. How does this come about?

Here one is faced once more by the problem of the *rôle* which thought plays in the origin of ethics. It seizes on something of which a preliminary form is seen in an instinct, in order to extend it and bring it to perfection. It apprehends the content of an instinct, and tries to give it practical application in new and consistent action.

In some way or other the *rôle* of thought lies in the fulfilment of life-affirmation. It rouses the will-to-live, in analogy with the life-affirmation which shows itself in the manifold life which is everywhere around it, and to join in its experiences. On the foundation of this world-affirmation, life-negation takes its place as a means of helping forward this affirmation of other life than its own. It is not life-denial in itself that is ethical, but only such as stands in the service of world-affirmation and becomes purposive within it.

Ethics are a mysterious chord in which life-affirmation and world-affirmation are the key-note and the fifth; life-negation is the third.

It is important, further, to know what is to be gathered from ethical inquiry down to the present time about the intensity and the extension of the life-negation which stands in the service of world-affirmation. Again and again the attempt has been made to establish this objectively. In vain. It belongs to the nature of self-devotion that it must live itself out subjectively and without reservations.

In the history of ethics there is downright fear of what cannot be subjected to rules and regulations. Again and again thinkers have undertaken to define altruism in such a way that it remains rational. This, however, is never done except at the cost of the naturalness and living quality of ethics. Life-denial remains an irrational thing, even when it is placed at the service of a purposive aim. A universally applicable balance between life-affirmation and life-negation cannot be established. They remain in a state of continual tension. If any relaxation does take place, it is a sign that ethics are collapsing, for in their real nature they are unbounded enthusiasm. They originate indeed in thought, but they cannot be carried to a logical conclusion. Anyone who undertakes the voyage to true ethics must be prepared to be carried round and round in the whirlpool of the irrational.

* * *

Together with the subjectively enthusiastic nature of ethics goes the fact that it is impossible to succeed in developing the ethic of ethical personality into a serviceable ethic of society. It seems so obvious, that from right individual ethics right social ethics should result, the one system continuing itself into the other like a town into its suburbs. In reality, however, they cannot be so built that the streets of the one continue into those of the other. The plans of each are drawn on principles which take no account of that.

The ethic of ethical personality is personal, incapable of regulation, and absolute; the system established by society for its prosperous existence is supra-personal, regulated, and relative. Hence the ethical personality cannot surrender to it, but lives always in continuous conflict with it, obliged again and again to oppose it because it finds its focus too short.

In the last analysis, the antagonism between the two arises from their differing valuations of humaneness. Humaneness consists in never sacrificing a human being to a purpose. The ethic of ethical personality aims at preserving humaneness. The system established by society is impotent in that respect.

When the individual is faced with the alternative of having to sacrifice in some way or other the happiness or the existence of another, or else to bear the loss himself, he is in a position to obey the demands of ethics and to choose the latter. But society, thinking impersonally and pursuing its aims impersonally, does not allow the same weight to consideration for the happiness or existence of an individual. In principle humaneness is not an item in its ethics. But individuals come continually into the position of being in one way or another executive organs of society, and then the conflict between the two points of view becomes active. That this may always be decided in its own favour, society exerts itself as much as possible to limit the authority of the ethic of personality, although inwardly it has to acknowledge its superiority. It wants to have servants who will never oppose it.

Even a society whose ethical standard is relatively high, is dangerous to the ethics of its members. If those things which form precisely the defects of a social code of ethics develop strongly, and if society exercises, further, an excessively strong spiritual influence on individuals, then the ethic of ethical personality is ruined. This happens in present-day society, whose ethical conscience is becoming fatally stunted by a biologico-sociological ethic and this, moreover, finally corrupted by nationalism.

The great mistake of ethical thought down to the present time is that it fails to admit the essential difference between the morality of ethical personality and that which is established from the standpoint of society, and always thinks that it ought, and is able, to cast them in one piece. The result is that the ethic of personality is sacrificed to the ethic of society. An end must be put to this. What matters is to recognize that the two are engaged in a conflict which cannot be made less intense. Either the moral standard of personality raises the moral standard of society, so far as is possible, to its own level, or it is dragged down by it.

But to prevent such harm as has been caused up to the present, it is not enough to bring individuals to a consciousness that if they are not to suffer spiritual injury they must be in a state of continual conflict with the ethics of society. What matters is to establish a basic principle of the moral, which will put the ethic of personality in a position to try conclusions with the ethic of society with consistency and success. Hitherto there has been no possibility of putting this weapon into its hands.

Ethics have, as we know, always been regarded as the most thorough-going possible self-devotion to society.

The morality of ethical personality, then, and the morality which is established from the standpoint of society cannot be traced back the one to the other, and they are not of equal value. The first only is a real ethic; the other is improperly so called. Thought must aim at finding the basic principle of absolute ethics, if it is to reach ethics at all, and it was because it was not clear on this point that so little progress has been made. Ethical progress consists in making up our minds to think pessimistically of the ethics of society.

The system of ethics established from the standpoint of society consists in its essential nature in society appealing to the moral disposition of the individual in order to secure from him what cannot be forced upon him by compulsion and law. It only comes nearer to real ethics when it enters into discussion with the ethics of personality and tries to bring its own demands on the individual into harmony as far as possible with those of personal morality. In proportion as society takes on the character of an ethical personality, its code of morals becomes the code of ethical society.

* * *

In general, thought ought to have busied itself with the question of what is included in the whole field of ethics, and how the different elements within it are connected with each other.

In ethics are included the ethics of passive self-perfecting, effected by inward self-liberation from the world (resignation); the ethics of active self-perfecting, effected by means of the mutual relations between man and man; and the ethics of ethical society. Ethics thus form an extensive gamut of notes. It starts from the not yet ethical where the vibrations of resignation begin to be perceptible as notes of ethical resignation. With increasingly rapid vibrations it passes from the ethics of resignation into the ethics of active self-perfecting. Rising still higher it arrives at the notes of the ethics of society which are already becoming more or less harsh and noisy, and it dies away finally into the legal commands of society which are never more than conditionally ethical.

Up to now all ethical systems have been thoroughly fragmentary. They confine themselves to this or that octave of the gamut. The Indians and, following in their train, Schopenhauer, are, on the whole, concerned only with the ethic of passive self-perfecting; Zarathustra, the Jewish prophets, and the great moralists of China only with that of active self-perfecting. The interest of modern Western philosophy is fixed almost exclusively on the ethic of society. In consequence of the starting-point which they chose, the thinkers of antiquity in the West cannot get any further than an ethic of resignation. The deeper thinkers among our moderns—Kant, J. G. Fichte, Nietzsche, and others—have inklings of an ethic of active self-perfecting.

European thought is characterized by almost always playing in the upper octaves, and not in the lower ones. Its ethic has no bass because the ethic of resignation plays no part in it. An ethic of duty, that is to say, an activist ethic, appears to it to be complete. It is because he is a representative of the ethic of resignation that Spinoza remains such a stranger to his own age.

Inability to understand resignation and the relations prevailing between ethics and resignation, is the fatal weakness of modern European thought.

In what, then, does a complete code of ethics consist? In ethics of passive self-perfecting, combined with ethics of active self-perfecting. The ethics established from the standpoint of of society are supplementary and have to be corrected by the ethics of active self-perfecting.

In view of that fact, a complete system of ethics must be put forward in a shape which compels it to seek to come to terms with the ethics of society.

Chapter 25

THE ETHICS OF SELF-DEVOTION AND THE ETHICS OF SELF-PERFECTING

The widening of the ethic of self-devotion into a cosmic ethic.

The ethic of self-perfecting and mysticism.

Abstract mysticism and the mysticism of reality.

Supra-ethical and ethical mysticism.

BEING SUFFICIENTLY INFORMED ABOUT THE QUESTIONS WHICH have called for solution and the results attained in the search for ethics down to the present time, the ethics of altruism and the ethics of self-perfecting can now try to combine their ideas, with a view to establishing together the true basic principle of the moral.

Why do they not succeed in mutual interpenetration of thought?

On the side of the ethic of self-devotion the fault must somehow lie in the fact that it is too narrow. As a matter of principle, social utilitarianism is concerned only with the self-devotion of man to man and to human society. The ethic of self-perfecting on the other hand is universal. It has to do with the relation of man to the world. If the ethic of self-devotion, therefore, is to agree with the ethic of self-perfecting, it too must become universal, and let its devotion be directed not only towards man and society but somehow or other towards all life whatever in the world.

But ethics hitherto have been unwilling to take even the first step in this universalizing of altruism.

Just as the housewife who has scrubbed out the parlour takes care that the door is kept shut so that the dog may not get in and spoil the work she has done by the marks of his paws, so do European thinkers watch carefully that no animals run about in the fields of their ethics. The stupidities they are guilty of in trying to maintain the traditional narrow-mindedness and raise it to a principle border on the incredible. Either they leave out altogether all sympathy for animals, or they take care that it shrinks to a mere afterthought which means nothing. If they admit anything more than that, they think themselves obliged to produce elaborate justifications, or even excuses, for so doing.

It seems as if Descartes with his dictum that animals are mere machines had bewitched the whole of European philosophy.

So important a thinker as Wilhelm Wundt mars his ethics with the following sentences: "The only object for sympathy is man. . . . The animals are for us fellow-creatures, an expression by which language already hints at the fact that we acknowledge here a kind of co-ordination with ourselves only with reference to the ultimate ground of everything that happens, namely, creation. Towards animals also, then, there can arise within us stirrings which are to a certain extent related to sympathy, but as to true sympathy with them there is always wanting the fundamental condition of the inner unity of our will with theirs." To crown this wisdom he ends with the assertion that of rejoicing with animals there can at any rate be no question, as if he had never seen a thirsty ox enjoying a drink.

Kant emphasizes especially that ethics have to do only with duties of man towards men. The "human" treatment of animals he thinks himself obliged to justify by putting it forward as a practising of sensibility which helps to improve our sympathetic relations with other human beings.

Bentham, too, defends kindness to animals chiefly as a means of preventing the growth of heartless relations with other men, even though he here and there recognizes it as obviously right.

Darwin in his *Descent of Man* notices that the feeling of sympathy which is dominant in the social impulse, becomes at last so strong that it comes to include all men, and indeed even animals. But he does not pursue the problem and the significance of this fact any further, and contents himself with establishing the ethics of the human herd.

Thus it ranks with European thought as a dogma that ethics properly concerns only a man's relations to his fellows and to society. The motives which emanate from Schopenhauer, Stern, and others, for throwing down the antiquated ring-fence, are not understood.

This backward attitude is the more unintelligible seeing that Indian and Chinese thought, even when they have only scarcely begun to develop, make ethics consist in a kindly relation to all creatures. Moreover, they have come to this view quite independently of each other. The beautiful and far-reaching commands concerning regard for animals in the popular Chinese ethics of the book *Kan Yin Pien* (*Concerning Rewards and Punishments*) cannot be referred back, as is commonly supposed, to Buddhist influences.[1] They have no connection with metaphysical discussions about the mutual relationship of all beings, such as became effective as the ethical horizon widened in Indian thought, but originate in a living, ethical feeling which dares to draw the consequences which seem to it to be natural.

When European thought refuses to make self-devotion universal, the reason is that its efforts are directed to reaching a rational morality which deals with universally valid judgments, and it sees a prospect of that only when it can keep its feet upon the solid ground of discussion of the interests of human society. But ethics concerned with the relations of man to the whole creation quit that solid ground, being driven into discussions about existence as such. Willing or unwilling, ethics have to

1 This book dates from about the eleventh century A.D. It has been translated into English by James Legge (*Sacred Books of the East,* 1891) and by T. Susuki and P. Carus (Chicago, 1906); into French by M. A. Rémusat (*Le livre des récompenses et des peines,* 1816), and by Stanislas Julien (1835); into German by W. Schuler (*Zeitschrift für Missionskunde,* 1909).

"Be humane with animals, and do no harm to insects, plants, and trees," is the command of one saying in this book. The following acts are condemned: "Hunting men or animals to death; shooting with bow and arrow at birds; hunting quadrupeds; driving insects out of their holes; frightening birds which are asleep in the trees; blocking up the holes of insects, and destroying birds-nests." To delight in hunting is described as a serious moral perversion.

plunge into the adventure of trying to come to terms with nature-philosophy, and the outcome cannot be foreseen.

This is a correct conclusion. But it has already been shown that the objective, standard morality of society, supposing it can be drawn up in this way at all, is never a true code of ethics, but merely an appendix to ethics. It is certain further that true ethics are always subjective, that they have an irrational enthusiasm as the very breath of their life, and that they must be in conflict with nature-philosophy. The ethic of altruism has, therefore, no reason for shrinking from this in any case unavoidable adventure. Its house has been burnt down. It can go out into the world to seek its fortune.

Let ethics, then, venture to accept the thought that self-devotion has to be practised not only towards men but towards all living creatures, yes, towards all life whatever that exists in the world and is within the reach of man. Let them rise to the conception that the relation of men to each other is only an expression of that in which they all stand to Being and to the world in general. Having thus become cosmic, the ethic of self-devotion can hope to meet the ethic of self-perfecting, which is fundamentally cosmic, and unite with it.

* * *

But in order that the ethic of self-perfecting may combine with the ethic of self-devotion, it must first become cosmic in the right way.

It is indeed fundamentally cosmic, because self-perfecting can consist of nothing but man coming into his true relationship to the Being that is in him and outside him. His natural, outward connection with Being he strives to change into a spiritual, inward devotion, letting his passive and active relation to things be determined by this devotion.

In this effort, however, he has never yet advanced further than to a passive self-dedication to Being. He is always driven past active self-devotion to it. It is this one-sidedness which makes it impossible for the ethics of self-perfecting and of self-devotion to inter-penetrate each other, and produce together the complete ethics of passive and active self-perfecting.

But what is the reason that the ethic of self-perfecting, in spite of all efforts, cannot get out of the circle of the passive? It is that it allows the spiritual inward devotion to Being to be directed to an abstract totality of Being instead of to real Being. So nature-philosophy is approached in a wrong way.

Whence this error? It is a result of the difficulties which the ethic of self-perfecting meets when it attempts to be comprehended in nature-philosophy.

In a way which to us seems strange, but is really profound, Chinese thought undertakes to attempt to arrive at this agreement. It thinks that it is somehow or other in the "impersonal" element of the world's activity that the secret of the truly ethical lies. It accordingly makes spiritual devotion to Being consist in our looking away from the subjective stirrings within ourselves, and regulating our behaviour by the laws of objectivity which we discover in the course of nature.

It is with this deep "becoming like the world" that the thought of Lao-tse and that of Chwang-tse are concerned. The motifs of such an ethic ring out in a wonderful fashion in Lao-tse's *Taoteking;* but they cannot be made to produce a complete symphony. The meaning of what happens in the world is a thing we cannot investigate. What we do understand of it is only that all life tries to live itself out. The true ethics of life, therefore, "in the spirit of what happens" would seem to be that of Yang-tse and Friedrich Nietzsche. On the other hand the assumption of an objectivity, dominant in the course of nature, which can be a pattern for our activity is nothing but an attempt, undertaken with the palest of colours, to paint the world as ethical. Correspondingly, this existence in the spirit of the world means with Lao-tse and Chwang-tse an inward liberation from the rule of passion and from outward occurrences, which is accompanied by marked depreciation of all tendencies to activity. Whenever life in the spirit of the world leads to really activist ethics as with Kungtse (Confucius), Mitse (Mo-Di), and others, there has been a corresponding interpretation of the meaning of the world. Whenever, in general, human thinking raises being-like-the-world to the status of ethics, the ethical willing of mankind has somehow or other read into the world-spirit an ethical character in order to be able to find itself in it again.

Since no motives to ethical activity are to be discovered in the course of nature, the ethic of self-perfecting must allow both active and passive ethics to originate side by side in the bare fact of spiritual inward self-dedication to Being. Both must be derived from action as such, without any presupposition of any sort of moral quality in Being. Then only will thought have reached a complete system of ethics without having been guilty of any sort of naïve or tricky proceedings.

That is the problem at which the ethical searching of all peoples and all ages vainly toils, so far as it ventures to think in the spirit of true nature-philosophy. With the Chinese and the Indians, in Stoicism, with Spinoza, Schleiermacher, Fichte, and Hegel, and in all mysticism of union with the Absolute, it reaches only the ethics of resignation, consisting of inward liberation from the world, never at the same time the ethics of working in the world and upon the world.

It is true that it but seldom ventures honestly to admit to itself the unsatisfactory result. As a rule it seeks to widen it, and to maintain in some measure an activist morality in spite of it, letting this morality be combined in some form or other with the ethics of resignation. The more consistent the thinkers, the more modest is the space occupied by this appendage.

With Lao-tse and Chwang-tse, with the Brahmans and the Buddha, with the Stoics of antiquity, with Spinoza, Schleiermacher, and Hegel, and with the great monistic mystics, activist ethics is reduced to little more than nothing. With Confucius and Meng-tse (Mong Dei), with the Hindoo thinkers, with the representatives of the Later Stoicism, and with J. G. Fichte, ethics of this nature make strenuous efforts to stand their ground, but can do so only in so far as the help of either naïve or sophisticated thought is employed.

Every world-and-life-view which is to satisfy thought is mysticism. It must seek to give to the existence of man such a meaning as will prevent him from being satisfied with being a part of the infinite existence in merely natural fashion, but will make him determine to belong to it in soul and spirit also, through an act of his consciousness.

The ethic of self-perfecting is in inmost connection with mysticism. Its own destiny is decided in that of mysticism.

Thinking out the ethic of self-perfecting means nothing else than seeking to found ethics on mysticism. Mysticism, on its side, is a valuable world-and-life-view only in proportion as it is ethical.

And yet it finds it cannot succeed in being ethical. Experience of becoming one with the Absolute, of existence within the world-spirit, of absorption into God, or whatever one may choose to call the process, is not in itself ethical, but spiritual. Of this deep distinction Indian thought has become conscious. With the most varied phrasing it repeats the proposition: "Spirituality is not ethics." We Europeans have remained naïve in matters of mysticism. What appears among us as mysticism is usually mysticism with a more or less Christian, that is to say ethical, colouring. Hence we are inclined to deceive ourselves about the ethical content of mysticism.

If one analyses the mysticism of all peoples and all ages to find out its ethical content, we find that this is extraordinarily small. Even the ethic of resignation, which seems after all to belong naturally to mysticism, is in mysticism more or less afflicted with impotence. Through the absence of the activist ethic with which it should normally be bound up, it to a certain extent loses its hold, and pushes itself more and more into the region of resignation which is no longer ethical. There then arises a mysticism that ceases to help the effort for self-perfecting, which is the profound task to which it is called, but makes absorption into the Absolute become an aim in itself. The purer the mysticism, the further has this evolution developed. Mysticism becomes then a world- and life-view of the merging of the finite existence in the infinite, if indeed it does not get reversed, as with the Brahmans, into the lofty mysticism of the existence of infinite existence within the finite. The ethic of self-perfecting, which should arise out of mysticism, is always therefore in danger of perishing in mysticism.

The tendency of mysticism to become supra-ethical is quite natural. As a matter of fact its connection with an Absolute which has neither qualities nor needs has nothing more to do with self-perfecting. It becomes a pure act of consciousness, and leads to a spirituality which is just as bare of content as the hypothetical Absolute. Feeling its weakness, mysticism does all it can to be more ethical than it is, or at any rate to appear so. Even the Indian form of it makes efforts in this direction, although again on the other hand it has courage to be veracious enough to rank the spiritual above the ethical.

In order to judge what mysticism is worth ethically, one must reckon only with what it contains in itself in the way of ethics, not what it does or says beyond that. Then, however, the ethical content of even Christian mysticism is alarmingly small. Mysticism is not a friend of ethics but a foe. It devours ethics. And yet the ethic which is to satisfy thought must be born of mysticism. All profound philosophy, all deep religion, are ultimately a struggle for ethical mysticism and mystical ethics.

Dominated by efforts to secure an activist ethical conception of the world and of life, we Westerners do not allow mysticism to come into its own. It leads among us a furtive, intermittent existence. We feel instinctively that it stands in antagonism to activist ethics, and we have therefore no inward relationship to it.

Our great mistake, however, is thinking that without mysticism we can reach an ethical world- and life-view, which shall satisfy thought. Up to now we have done nothing but compose world- and life-views. They are good because they keep men up to activist ethics, but they are not true, and therefore they are always collapsing. Moreover they are shallow. Hence European thought makes men ethical indeed, but superficial, and the European, because he is surfeited with philosophy which has been fabricated with a view to activist ethics, has no equanimity and no inward personality, nor indeed any longer a feeling of need for these qualities.

It is indeed time for us to abandon this error. Depth and stability in thinking come to the world- and life-view of activist ethics only when this outlook springs from mysticism. The question of what we are to make of our life is not solved by our being driven out into the world with an impulse to activity, and never being allowed to come to our right senses. It can be really answered only by a philosophy which brings man into a spiritual inward relation to Being, from which there result of natural necessity ethics both passive and active.

The hitherto accepted mysticism cannot effect this because

it is supra-ethical. The struggle of thought must therefore be directed upon ethical mysticism. We must rise to a spirituality which is ethical, and to an ethic which includes all spirituality. Then only do we become profoundly qualified for life.

Ethics must originate in mysticism. Mysticism, for its part, must never be thought to exist for its own sake. It is not a flower, but only the calyx of a flower. Ethics are the flower. Mysticism which exists for itself alone is the salt which last lost its savour.

The hitherto accepted mysticism leads into the supra-ethical because it is abstract. Abstraction is the death of ethics, for ethics are a living relationship to living life. We must therefore abandon abstract mysticism, and turn to the mysticism which is alive.

* * *

The Essence of Being, the Absolute, the Spirit of the Universe, and all similar expressions denote nothing actual, but something conceived in abstractions which for that reason is also absolutely unimaginable. The only reality is the Being which manifests itself in phenomena.

How does thought come to such a meaningless proceeding as making man enter into a spiritual relation with an unreal creation of thought? By yielding to temptation in two ways, one general, one particular.

Thrown back upon the necessity of expressing itself in words, thought adopts as its own the abstractions and symbols which have been coined by language. But this coinage should have no more currency than allows it to represent things in an abbreviated way, instead of putting them forward with all the detail in which they are given. But in time it comes about that thought works with these abstractions and symbols as if they represented something which really exists. That is the general temptation.

The particular temptation lies in this case in this, that man's devotion to infinite Being with the help of abstractions and symbols is given expression in an enticingly simple way. It is taken to consist of entrance into relation with the totality of Being, that is to say, with its spiritual essence.

That looks very well in words and in thoughts. But reality

knows nothing about the individual being able to enter into connection with the totality of Being. As it knows of no Being except that which manifests itself in the existence of individual beings, so also it knows of no relations except these of one individual being to another. If mysticism, then, intends to be honest, there is nothing for it to do but to cast from it the usual abstractions, and to admit that it can do nothing rational with this imaginary essence of Being. The Absolute may be as meaningless to it as his fetish is to a converted Negro. It must in all seriousness go through the process of conversion to the mysticism of reality. Abandoning all stage decorations and declamation, let it try to get its experience in living nature.

There is no Essence of Being, but only infinite Being in infinite manifestations. It is only through the manifestations of Being, and only through those with which I enter into relations, that my being has any intercourse with infinite Being. The devotion of my being to infinite Being means devotion of my being to all the manifestations of Being which need my devotion, and to which I am able to devote myself.

Only an infinitely small part of infinite Being comes within my range. The rest of it passes me by, like distant ships to which I make signals they do not understand. But by devoting myself to that which comes within my sphere of influence and needs me, I make spiritual, inward devotion to infinite Being a reality and thereby give my own poor existence meaning and richness. The river has found its sea.

From self-devotion to the Absolute there comes only a dead spirituality. It is a purely intellectual act. No motives to activity are given in it. Even the ethics of resignation can only eke out a miserable existence on the soil of such an intellectualism. But in the mysticism of reality self-devotion is no longer a purely intellectual act, but one in which everything that is alive in man has its share. There is therefore dominant in it a spirituality which carries in itself in elemental form the impulse to action. The gruesome truth that spirituality and ethics are two different things no longer holds good. Here the two are one and the same.

Now, too, the ethics of self-perfecting and the ethics of altruism can interpenetrate each other. They now become cosmic in nature-philosophy, which leaves the world as it is. Hence they cannot but meet each other in a thought, which satisfies in every direction the laws of thinking, of living devotion to Being which lives. In this thought lie passive and active self-perfecting in mutual agreement and perfect union. They comprehend each other as the working out of one and the same inner compulsion. Having become one, they no longer need first of all to exert themselves to establish by joint efforts the completed ethics of influencing the world on the basis of liberation from the world. The completeness is now automatically attained. Now there ring out in wonderful harmonies all the notes in the gamut of ethics, from the vibrations in which resignation begins to be audible as ethics, up to the higher notes in which morality passes over into the harsh noises of the commands which are proclaimed by society to be ethical.

Subjective responsibility for all life which comes within his reach, responsibility which widens out extensively and intensively to the limitless, and which the man who has become inwardly free from the world experiences and tries to make a reality, that is ethics. It originates in world- and life-affirmation. It becomes a reality in life-negation. It is completely bound up with optimistic willing. Never again can the belief-in-progress get separated from ethics, like a badly-fastened wheel from a cart. The two turn inseparably on the same axle.

The basic principle of ethics, that principle which is a necessity of thought, which has a definite content, which is engaged in constant, living, and practical dispute with reality, is: Devotion to life resulting from reverence for life.

Chapter 26

THE ETHICS OF REVERENCE FOR LIFE

The basic principle of the moral.

The ethic of resignation. An ethic of veracity towards oneself, and an activist ethic.

Ethics and thoughtlessness. Ethics and self-assertion.

Man and other living creatures. The ethic of the relation of man to man.

Personal and supra-personal responsibility. Ethics and humanity.

COMPLICATED AND LABORIOUS ARE THE ROADS ALONG WHICH ethical thought, which has mistaken its way and taken too high a flight, must be brought back. Its course, however, maps itself out quite simply if, instead of taking apparently convenient short cuts, it keeps to its right direction from the very beginning. For this three things are necessary: It must have nothing to do with an ethical interpretation of the world; it must become cosmic and mystical, that is to say, it must seek to conceive all the self-devotion which rules in ethics as a manifestation of an inward, spiritual relation to the world; it must not lapse into abstract thinking, but must remain elemental, understanding self-devotion to the world to be self-devotion of human life to every form of living being with which it can come into relation.

The origin of ethics is that I think out the full meaning of the world-affirmation which, together with the life-affirmation in my will-to-live, is given by nature, and try to make it a reality.

To become ethical means to begin to think sincerely.

Thinking is the argument between willing and knowing which goes on within me. Its course is a naïve one, if the will demands of knowledge to be shown a world which corresponds to the impulses which it carries within itself, and if knowledge attempts to satisfy this requirement. This dialogue, which is doomed to produce no result, must give place to a debate of the right kind, in which the will demands from knowledge only what it really knows.

If knowledge answers solely with what it knows, it is always teaching the will one and the same fact, namely, that in and behind all phenomena there is will-to-live. Knowledge, though ever becoming deeper and more comprehensive, can do nothing except take us ever deeper and ever further into the mystery that all that is, is will-to-live. Progress in science consists only in increasingly accurate description of the phenomena in which life in its innumerable forms appears and passes, letting us discover life where we did not previously expect it, and putting us in a position to turn to our own use in this or that way what we have learnt of the course of the will-to-live in nature. But what life is, no science can tell us.

For our conception of the universe and of life, then, the gain derived from knowledge is only that it makes it harder for us to be thoughtless, because it ever more forcibly compels our attention to the mystery of the will-to-live which we see stirring everywhere. Hence the difference between learned and unlearned is entirely relative. The unlearned man who, at the sight of a tree in flower, is overpowered by the mystery of the will-to-live which is stirring all round him, knows more than the scientist who studies under the microscope or in physical and chemical activity a thousand forms of the will-to-live, but, with all his knowledge of the life-course of these manifestations of the will-to-live, is unmoved by the mystery that everything which exists is will-to-live, while he is puffed up with vanity at being able to describe exactly a fragment of the course of life.

All true knowledge passes on into experience. The nature of the manifestations I do not know, but I form a conception of it in analogy to the will-to-live which is within myself. Thus my knowledge of the world becomes experience of the world. The knowledge which is becoming experience does not allow me to remain in face of the world a man who merely knows, but forces upon me an inward relation to the world, and fills me with reverence for the mysterious will-to-live which is in all things. By making me think and wonder, it leads me ever upwards to the heights of reverence for life. There it lets my hand go. It cannot accompany me further. My will-to-live must now find its way about the world by itself.

It is not by informing me what this or that manifestation of life means in the sum-total of the world that knowledge brings me into connection with the world. It goes about with me not in outer circles, but in the inner ones. From within outwards it puts me in relation to the world by making my will-to-live feel everything around it as also will-to-live.

With Descartes, philosophy starts from the dogma: "I think, therefore I exist." With this paltry, arbitrarily chosen beginning, it is landed irretrievably on the road to the abstract. It never finds the right approach to ethics, and remains entangled in a dead world- and life-view. True philosophy must start from the most immediate and comprehensive fact of consciousness, which says: "I am life which wills to live, in the midst of life which wills to live." This is not an ingenious dogmatic formula. Day by day, hour by hour, I live and move in it. At every moment of reflection it stands fresh before me. There bursts forth from it again and again as from roots that can never dry up, a living world- and life-view which can deal with all the facts of Being. A mysticism of ethical union with Being grows out of it.

As in my own will-to-live there is a longing for wider life and for the mysterious exaltation of the will-to-live which we call pleasure, with dread of annihilation and of the mysterious depreciation of the will-to-live which we call pain; so is it also in the will-to-live all around me, whether it can express itself before me, or remains dumb.

Ethics consist, therefore, in my experiencing the compulsion to show to all will-to-live the same reverence as I do to my own. There we have given us that basic principle of the moral which is a necessity of thought. It is good to maintain and to encourage life; it is bad to destroy life or to obstruct it.

As a matter of fact, everything which in the ordinary ethical valuation of the relations of men to each other ranks as good can be brought under the description of material and spiritual maintenance or promotion of human life, and of effort to bring it to its highest value. Conversely, everything which ranks as bad in human relations is in the last analysis material or spiritual destruction or obstruction of human life, and negligence in the endeavour to bring it to its highest value. Separate individual categories of good and evil which lie far apart and have apparently no connection at all with one another fit together like the pieces of a jig-saw puzzle, as soon as they are comprehended and deepened in this the most universal definition of good and evil.

The basic principle of the moral which is a necessity of thought means, however, not only an ordering and deepening, but also a widening of the current views of good and evil. A man is truly ethical only when he obeys the compulsion to help all life which he is able to assist, and shrinks from injuring anything that lives. He does not ask how far this or that life deserves one's sympathy as being valuable, nor, beyond that, whether and to what degree it is capable of feeling. Life as such is sacred to him. He tears no leaf from a tree, plucks no flower, and takes care to crush no insect. If in summer he is working by lamplight, he prefers to keep the window shut and breathe a stuffy atmosphere rather than see one insect after another fall with singed wings upon his table.

If he walks on the road after a shower and sees an earthworm which has strayed on to it, he bethinks himself that it must get dried up in the sun, if it does not return soon enough to ground into which it can burrow, so he lifts it from the deadly stone surface, and puts it on the grass. If he comes across an insect which has fallen into a puddle, he stops a moment in order to hold out a leaf or a stalk on which it can save itself.

He is not afraid of being laughed at as sentimental. It is the fate of every truth to be a subject for laughter until it is generally recognized. Once it was considered folly to assume that men of colour were really men and ought to be treated as such, but the folly has become an accepted truth. To-day it is thought to be going too far to declare that constant regard for everything that lives, down to the lowest manifestations of life, is a demand made by rational ethics. The time is coming, however, when people will be astonished that mankind needed so long a time to learn to regard thoughtless injury to life as incompatible with ethics.

Ethics are responsibility without limit towards all that lives.

As a general proposition the definition of ethics as a relationship within a disposition to reverence for life, does not make a very moving impression. But it is the only complete one. Compassion is too narrow to rank as the total essence of the ethical. It denotes, of course, only interest in the suffering will-to-live. But ethics include also feeling as one's own all the circumstances and all the aspirations of the will-to-live, its pleasure, too, and its longing to live itself out to the full, as well as its urge to self-perfecting.

Love means more, since it includes fellowship in suffering, in joy, and in effort, but it shows the ethical only in a simile, although in a simile that is natural and profound. It makes the solidarity produced by ethics analogous to that which nature calls forth on the physical side, for more or less temporary purposes between two beings which complete each other sexually, or between them and their offspring.

Thought must strive to bring to expression the nature of the ethical in itself. To effect this it arrives at defining ethics as devotion to life inspired by reverence for life. Even if the phrase reverence for life sounds so general as to seem somewhat lifeless, what is meant by it is nevertheless something which never lets go of the man into whose thought it has made its way. Sympathy, and love, and every kind of valuable enthusiasm are given within it. With restless living force reverence for life works upon the mind into which it has entered, and throws it into the unrest of a feeling of responsibility which at no place and at no time ceases to affect it. Just as the screw which churns its way through the water drives the ship along, so does reverence for life drive the man.

Arising, as it does, from an inner compulsion, the ethic of reverence for life is not dependent on the extent to which it can be thought out to a satisfying conception of life. It need give no answer to the question of what significance the ethical man's work for the maintenance, promotion, and enhancement of life can be in the total happenings of the course of nature. It does not let itself be misled by the calculation that the maintaining and completing of life which it practises is hardly worth consideration beside the tremendous, unceasing destruction of life which goes on every moment through natural forces. Having the will to action, it can leave on one side all problems regarding the success of its work. The fact in itself that in the ethically developed man there has made its appearance in the world a will-to-live which is filled with reverence for life and devotion to life is full of importance for the world.

In my will-to-live the universal will-to-live experiences itself otherwise than in its other manifestations. In them it shows itself in a process of individualizing which, so far as I can see from the outside, is bent merely on living itself out to the full, and in no way on union with any other will-to-live. The world is a ghastly drama of will-to-live divided against itself. One existence makes its way at the cost of another; one destroys the other. One will-to-live merely exerts its will against the other, and has no knowledge of it. But in me the will-to-live has come to know about other wills-to-live. There is in it a yearning to arrive at unity with itself, to become universal.

Why does the will-to-live experience itself in this way in me alone? Is it because I have acquired the capacity of reflecting on the totality of Being? What is the goal of this evolution which has begun in me?

To these questions there is no answer. It remains a painful enigma for me that I must live with reverence for life in a world which is dominated by creative will which is also destructive will, and destructive will which is also creative.

I can do nothing but hold to the fact that the will-to-live in me manifests itself as will-to-live which desires to become one with other will-to-live. That is for me the light that shines in the darkness. The ignorance in which the world is wrapped has no existence for me; I have been saved from the world. I am thrown, indeed, by reverence for life into an unrest such as the world does not know, but I obtain from it a blessedness which the world cannot give. If in the tenderheartedness produced by being different from the world another person and I help each other in understanding and pardoning, when otherwise will would torment will, the division of the will-to-live is at an end. If I save an insect from a puddle, life has devoted itself to life, and the division of life against itself is ended. Whenever my life devotes itself in any way to life, my finite will-to-live experiences union with the infinite will in which all life is one, and I enjoy a feeling of refreshment which prevents me from pining away in the desert of life.

I therefore recognize it as the destiny of my existence to be obedient to this higher revelation of the will-to-live in me. I choose for my activity the removal of this division of the will-to-live against itself, so far as the influence of my existence can reach. Knowing now the one thing needful, I leave on one side the enigma of the universe and of my existence in it.

The surmisings and the longings of all deep religiousness are contained in the ethics of reverence for life. This religiousness, however, does not build up for itself a complete philosophy, but resigns itself to the necessity of leaving its cathedral unfinished. It finishes the chancel only, but in this chancel piety celebrates a living and never-ceasing divine service.

* * *

The ethic of reverence for life shows its truth also in that it includes in itself the different elements of ethics in their natural connection. Hitherto no system of ethics has been able to present in their parallelism and their interaction the effort after self-perfecting, in which man acts upon himself without outward deeds, and activist ethics. The ethics of reverence for life can do this, and indeed in such a way that they not only answer academic questions, but also produce a deepening of ethical insight.

Ethics are reverence for the will-to-live within me and without me. From the former comes first the profound life-affirmation of resignation. I apprehend my will-to-live as not only something which can live itself out in happy occurrences, but also something which has experience of itself. If I refuse to let this self-experience disappear in thoughtlessness, and persist in feeling it to be valuable, I begin to learn the secret of spiritual self-realization. I win an unsuspected freedom from the various destinies of life. At moments when I had expected to find myself shattered, I find myself exalted in an inexpressible and surprising happiness of freedom from the world, and I experience therein a clarification of my life-view. Resignation is the vestibule through which we enter ethics. Only he who in deepened devotion to his own will-to-live experiences inward freedom from outward occurrences, is capable of devoting himself in profound and steady fashion to the life of others.

Just as in reverence for my own will-to-live I struggle for freedom from the destinies of life, so I struggle too for freedom from myself. Not only in face of what happens to me, but also with regard to the way in which I concern myself with the world, I practise the higher self-maintenance. Out of reverence for my own existence I place myself under the compulsion of veracity towards myself. Everything I might acquire would be purchased too dearly by action in defiance of my convictions. I fear that if I were untrue to myself, I should be wounding my will-to-live with a poisoned spear.

The fact that Kant makes, as he does, sincerity towards oneself the central point of his ethics, testifies to the depth of his ethical feeling. But because in his search for the essential nature of the ethical he fails to find his way through to reverence for life, he cannot comprehend the connection between veracity towards oneself and activist ethics.

As a matter of fact, the ethics of sincerity towards oneself passes imperceptibly into that of devotion to others. Such sincerity compels me to actions which manifest themselves as self-devotion in such a way that ordinary ethics derive them from devotion.

Why do I forgive anyone? Ordinary ethics say, because I feel sympathy with him. They allow men, when they pardon others, to seem to themselves wonderfully good, and allow them to practise a style of pardoning which is not free from humiliation of the other. They thus make forgiveness a sweetened triumph of self-devotion.

The ethics of reverence for life do away with this crude point of view. All acts of forbearance and of pardon are for them acts forced from one by sincerity towards oneself. I must practise unlimited forgiveness because, if I did not, I should be wanting in sincerity to myself, for it would be acting as if I myself were not guilty in the same way as the other has been guilty towards me. Because my life is so liberally spotted with falsehood, I must forgive falsehood which has been practised upon me; because I myself have been in so many cases wanting in love, and guilty of hatred, slander, deceit, or arrogance, I must pardon any want of love, and all hatred, slander, deceit or arrogance which have been directed against myself. I must forgive quietly and unostentatiously; in fact I do not really pardon at all, for I do not let things develop to any such act of judgment. Nor is this any eccentric proceeding; it is only a necessary widening and refining of ordinary ethics.

We have to carry on the struggle against the evil that is in mankind, not by judging others, but by judging ourselves. Struggle with oneself and veracity towards oneself are the means by which we influence others. We quietly draw them into our efforts to attain the deep spiritual self-realization which springs from reverence for one's own life. Power makes no noise. It is there, and works. True ethics begin where the use of language ceases.

The innermost element then, in activist ethics, even if it appears as self-devotion, comes from the compulsion to sincerity towards oneself, and obtains therein its true value. The whole ethics of being other than the world flow pure only when they come from this source. It is not from kindness to others that I am gentle, peaceable, forbearing, and friendly, but because by such behaviour I prove my own profoundest self-realization to be true. Reverence for life which I apply to my own existence, and reverence for life which keeps me in a temper of devotion to other existence than my own, interpenetrate each other.

* * *

Because ordinary ethics possess no basic principle of the ethical, they must engage at once in the discussion of conflicting duties. The ethics of reverence for life have no such need for hurry. They take their own time to think out in all directions their own principle of the moral. Knowing themselves to be firmly established, they then settle their position with regard to these conflicts.

They have to try conclusions with three adversaries: these are thoughtlessness, egoistic self-assertion, and society.

To the first of these they usually pay insufficient attention, because no open conflicts arise between them. This adversary does, nevertheless, obstruct them imperceptibly.

There is, however, a wide field of which our ethics can take possession without any collision with the troops of egoism. Man can accomplish much that is good, without having to require of himself any sacrifice. And if there really goes with it a bit of his life, it is so insignificant that he feels it no more than if he were losing a hair or a flake of dead skin.

Over wide stretches of conduct the inward liberation from the world, the being true to oneself, the being different from the world, yes, and even self-devotion to other life, is only a matter of giving attention to this particular relationship. We fall short so much, because we do not keep ourselves up to it. We do not stand sufficiently under the pressure of any inward compulsion to be ethical. At all points the steam hisses out of the boiler that is not tightly closed. In ordinary ethics the resulting losses of energy are as high as they are because such ethics have at their disposal no single basic principle of the moral which acts upon thought. They cannot tighten the lid of the boiler, indeed, they do not ever even examine it. But reverence for life being something which is ever present to thought, penetrates unceasingly and in all directions a man's observation, reflection, and resolutions. He can keep himself clear of it as little as the water can prevent itself from being coloured by the dye-stuff which is dropped into it. The struggle with thoughtlessness is started, and is always going on.

But what is the position of the ethics of reverence for life in the conflicts which arise between inward compulsion to self-sacrifice, and the necessary upholding of the ego?

I too am subject to division of my will-to-live against itself. In a thousand ways my existence stands in conflict with that of others. The necessity to destroy and to injure life is imposed upon me. If I walk along an unfrequented path, my foot brings destruction and pain upon the tiny creatures which populate it. In order to preserve my own existence, I must defend myself against the existence which injures it. I become a persecutor of the little mouse which inhabits my house, a murderer of the insect which wants to have its nest there, a mass-murderer of the bacteria which may endanger my life. I get my food by destroying plants and animals. My happiness is built upon injury done to my fellow-men.

How can ethics be maintained in face of the horrible necessity to which I am subjected through the division of my will-to-live against itself?

Ordinary ethics seek compromises. They try to dictate how much of my existence and of my happiness I must sacrifice, and how much I may preserve at the cost of the existence and happiness of other lives. With these decisions they produce experimental, relative ethics. They offer as ethical what is in reality not ethical but a mixture of non-ethical necessity and ethics. They thereby bring about a huge confusion, and allow the starting of an ever-increasing obscuration of the conception of the ethical.

The ethics of reverence for life know nothing of a relative ethic. They make only the maintenance and promotion of life rank as good. All destruction of and injury to life, under whatever circumstances they take place, they condemn as evil. They do not keep in store adjustments between ethics and necessity all ready for use. Again and again and in ways that are always original they are trying to come to terms in man with reality. They do not abolish for him all ethical conflicts, but compel him to decide for himself in each case how far he can remain ethical and how far he must submit himself to the necessity for destruction of and injury to life, and therewith incur guilt. It is not by receiving instruction about agreement between ethical and necessary, that a man makes progress in ethics, but only by coming to hear more and more plainly the voice of the ethical, by becoming ruled more and more by the longing to preserve and promote life, and by becoming more and more obstinate in resistance to the necessity for destroying or injuring life.

In ethical conflicts man can arrive only at subjective decisions. No one can decide for him at what point, on each occasion, lies the extreme limit of possibility for his persistence in the preservation and furtherance of life. He alone has to judge this issue, by letting himself be guided by a feeling of the highest possible responsibility towards other life.

We must never let ourselves become blunted. We are living in truth, when we experience these conflicts more profoundly. The good conscience is an invention of the devil.

* * *

What does reverence for life say about the relations between man and the animal world?

Whenever I injure life of any sort, I must be quite clear whether it is necessary. Beyond the unavoidable, I must never go, not even with what seems insignificant. The farmer, who has mown down a thousand flowers in his meadow as fodder for his cows, must be careful on his way home not to strike off in wanton pastime the head of a single flower by the roadside, for he thereby commits a wrong against life without being under the pressure of necessity.

Those who experiment with operations or the use of drugs upon animals, or inoculate them with diseases, so as to be able to bring help to mankind with the results gained, must never quiet any misgivings they feel with the general reflection that their cruel proceedings aim at a valuable result. They must first have considered in each individual case whether there is a real necessity to force upon any animal this sacrifice for the sake of mankind. And they must take the most anxious care to mitigate as much as possible the pain inflicted. How much wrong is committed in scientific institutions through neglect of anæsthetics, which to save time or trouble are not administered! How much, too, through animals being subjected to torture merely to demonstrate to students generally known phenomena! By the very fact that animals have been subjected to experiments, and have by their pain won such valuable results for suffering humanity, a new and special relation of solidarity has been established between them and us. From that springs for each one of us a compulsion to do to every animal all the good we possibly can. By helping an insect when it is in difficulties, I am only attempting to cancel part of man's ever new debt to the animal world. Whenever an animal is in any way forced into the service of man, every one of us must be concerned with the sufferings which for that reason it has to undergo. None of us must allow to take place any suffering for which he himself is not responsible, if he can hinder it in any way. He must not soothe his conscience with the reflection that he would be mixing himself up in something which does not concern him. No one must shut his eyes and regard as non-existent the sufferings of which he spares himself the sight. Let no one regard as light the burden of his responsibility. While so much ill-treatment of animals goes on, while the moans of thirsty animals in railway trucks sound unheard, while so much brutality prevails in our slaughter-houses, while animals have to suffer in our kitchens painful death from unskilled hands, while animals have to endure intolerable treatment from heartless men, or are left to the cruel play of children, we all share the guilt.

We are afraid of making ourselves conspicuous if we let it be noticed how we feel for the sufferings which man brings upon the animals. At the same time we think that others have become more "rational" than we are, and regard what we are excited about as usual and a matter of course. Yet suddenly they will let slip a word which shows us that they too have not yet learnt to acquiesce. And now, though they were strangers, they are quite near us. The mask in which we deceived each other falls off. We know now, from one another, that we feel alike about being unable to escape from the gruesome proceedings that are taking place unceasingly around us. What a making of a new acquaintance!

The ethics of reverence for life guard us from letting each other believe through our silence that we no longer experience what, as thinking men, we must experience. They prompt us to keep each other sensitive to what distresses us, and to talk and act together, just as the responsibility we feel moves us, and without any feeling of shyness. They make us join in keeping on the look-out for opportunities of bringing some sort of help to animals, to make up for the great misery which men inflict on them, and thus to step for a moment out of the incomprehensible horror of existence.

In the matter also of our relation to other men, the ethics of reverence for life throw upon us a responsibility so unlimited as to be terrifying.

Here again they offer us no rules about the extent of the self-maintenance which is allowable; again, they bid us in each case to thrash the question out with the absolute ethics of self-devotion. I have to decide in accordance with the responsibility of which I am conscious, how much of my life, my possessions, my rights, my happiness, my time, and my rest I must devote to others, and how much I may keep for myself.

In the question of possessions, the ethics of reverence for life are outspokenly individualist in the sense that wealth acquired or inherited should be placed at the service of the community, not through any measures taken by society, but through the absolutely free decision of the individual. They expect everything from a general increase in the feeling of responsibility. Wealth they regard as the property of society left in the sovereign control of the individual. One man serves society by carrying on a business in which a number of employees earn their living; another by giving away his wealth in order to help his fellows. Between these two extreme kinds of service, let each decide according to the responsibility which he finds determined for him by the circumstances of his life. Let no man judge his neighbour. The one thing that matters is that each shall value what he possesses as means to action. Whether this is accomplished by his keeping and increasing his wealth, or by surrender of it, matters little. Wealth must reach the community in the most varied ways, if it is to be of the greatest benefit to all.

Those who possess little to call their own are most in danger of holding what they have in a purely selfish spirit. There is profound truth in the parable of Jesus which makes the servant who had received least the least loyal to his duty.

My rights too the ethics of reverence for life do not allow to belong to me. They forbid me to still my conscience with the reflection that, as the more efficient man, by quite legitimate means I am advancing myself at the cost of one who is less efficient than I. In what the law and public opinion allow me, they set a problem before me. They bid me think of others, and make me ponder whether I can allow myself the inward right to pluck all the fruit that my hand can reach. Thus it may happen that, in obedience to consideration for the existence of others, I do what seems to ordinary opinion to be folly. Yes, it may even show itself to be folly by the fact that my renunciation has not been any use to him for whom it was made. And yet I was right. Reverence for life is the highest court of appeal. What it commands has its own significance, even if it seems foolish or useless. We all look, of course, in one another, for the folly which indicates that we have higher responsibilities making themselves felt in our hearts. Yet it is only in proportion as we all become less rational, in the meaning given it by ordinary calculation, that the ethical disposition develops in us, and allows problems to become soluble which have hitherto been insoluble.

Nor will reverence for life grant me my happiness as my own. At the moments when I should like to enjoy myself without restraint, it wakes in me reflection about misery that I see or suspect, and it does not allow me to drive away the uneasiness I feel. Just as the wave cannot exist for itself, but is ever a part of the heaving surface of the ocean, so must I never live my life for itself, but always in the experience which is going on around me. It is an uncomfortable doctrine which the true ethics whisper into my ear. You are happy, they say; therefore you are called upon to give much. Whatever more than others you have received in health, natural gifts, working capacity, success, a beautiful childhood, harmonious family circumstances, you must not accept as being a matter of course. You must pay a price for them. You must show more than average devotion of life to life.

To the happy the voice of the true ethics is dangerous, if they venture to listen to it. When it calls to them, it never damps down the irrational which glows within it. It assails them to see whether it can get them off their smooth track and turn them into adventurers of self-devotion, people of whom the world has too few. . . .

Reverence for life is an inexorable creditor! If it finds anyone with nothing to pledge but a little time and a little leisure, it lays an attachment on these. But its hard-heartedness is good, and sees clearly. The many modern men who as industrial machines are engaged in callings in which they can in no way be active as men among men, are exposed to the danger of merely vegetating in an egoistic life. Many of them feel this danger, and suffer under the fact that their daily work has so little to do with spiritual and ideal aims and does not allow them to put into it anything of their human nature. Others acquiesce; the thought of having no duties outside their daily work suits them very well.

But that men should be so condemned or so favoured as to be released from responsibility for self-devotion as men to men, the ethics of reverence for life will not allow to be legitimate. They demand that every one of us in some way and with some object shall be a human being for human beings. To those who have no opportunity in their daily work of giving themselves in this way, and have nothing else that they can give, it suggests their sacrificing something of their time and leisure, even if of these they have but a scanty allowance. It says to them, find for yourselves some secondary activity, inconspicuous, perhaps secret. Open your eyes and look for a human being, or some work devoted to human welfare, which needs from someone a little time or friendliness, a little sympathy, or sociability, or labour. There may be a solitary or an embittered fellow-man, an invalid or an inefficient person to whom you can be something. Perhaps it is an old person or a child. Or some good work needs volunteers who can offer a free evening, or run errands. Who can enumerate the many ways in which that costly piece of working capital, a human being, can be employed? More of him is wanted everywhere! Search, then, for some investment for your humanity, and do not be frightened away if you have to wait, or to be taken on trial. And be prepared for disappointments. But in any case, do not be without some secondary work in which you give yourself as a man to men. It is marked out for you, if you only truly will to have it. . . .

Thus do the true ethics speak to those who have only a little time and a little human nature to give. Well will it be with them if they listen, and are preserved from becoming stunted natures because they have neglected this devotion of self to others.

But to everyone, in whatever state of life he finds himself, the ethics of reverence for life do this: they force him without cessation to be concerned at heart with all the human destinies and all the other life-destinies which are going through their life-course around him, and to give himself, as man, to the man who needs a fellow-man. They will not allow the scholar to live only for his learning, even if his learning makes him very useful, nor the artist to live only for his art, even if by means of it he gives something to many. They do not allow the very busy man to think that with his professional activities he has fulfilled every demand upon him. They demand from all that they devote a portion of their life to their fellows. In what way and to what extent this is prescribed for him, the individual must gather from the thoughts which arise in him, and from the destinies among which his life moves. One man's sacrifice is outwardly insignificant. He can accomplish it while continuing to live a normal life. Another is called to some conspicuous act of self-sacrifice, and must therefore put aside regard for his own progress. But let neither judge the other. The destinies of men have to be decided in a thousand ways in order that the good may become actual. What he has to bring as an offering is the secret of each individual. But one with another we have all to recognize that our existence reaches its true value only when we experience in ourselves something of the truth of the saying: "He that loseth his life shall find it."

* * *

The ethical conflicts between society and the individual arise out of the fact that the latter has to bear not only a personal, but also a supra-personal responsibility. When my own person only is concerned, I can always be patient, always forgive, always exercise forbearance, always be merciful. But each of us comes into a situation where he is responsible not for himself only, but also for a cause, and then is forced into decisions which conflict with personal morality.

The craftsman who manages a business, however small, and the musician who conducts public performances, cannot be men in the way they would like to be. The one has to dismiss a worker who is incapable or given to drink, in spite of any sympathy he has for him and his family; the other cannot let a singer whose voice is the worse for wear appear any longer, although he knows what distress he thus causes.

The more extensive a man's activities, the oftener he finds himself in the position of having to sacrifice something of his humanity to his supra-personal responsibility. From this conflict customary consideration leads to the decision that the general responsibility does, as a matter of principle, annul the personal. It is in this sense that society addresses the individual. For the soothing of consciences for which this decision is too categorical, it perhaps lays down a few principles which undertake to determine in a way that is valid for everybody, how far in any case personal morality can have a say in the matter.

No course remains open to current ethics but to sign this capitulation. They have no means of defending the fortress of personal morality, because it has not at its disposal any absolute notions of good and evil. Not so the ethics of reverence for life. These possess, as we can see, what the other lacks. They therefore never surrender the fortress, even if it is permanently invested. They feel themselves in a position to persevere in holding it, and by continual sorties to keep the besiegers on the *qui vive*.

Only the most universal and absolute purposiveness in the maintenance and furtherance of life, which is the objective aimed at by reverence for life, is ethical. All other necessity or expediency is not ethical, but only a more or less necessary necessity, or a more or less expedient expediency. In the conflict between the maintenance of my own existence and the destruction of, or injury to, that of another, I can never unite the ethical and the necessary to form a relative ethical; I must choose between ethical and necessary, and, if I choose the latter, must take it upon myself to incur guilt by an act of injury to life. Similarly I am not at liberty to think, that in the conflict between personal and supra-personal responsibility I can balance the ethical and the expedient to make a relative ethical, or even annul the ethical with the purposive; I must choose between the two. If, under the pressure of the supra-personal responsibility, I yield to the expedient, I become guilty in some way or other through failure in reverence for life.

The temptation to combine with the ethical into a relative

ethical the expedient which is commanded me by the supra-personal responsibility is especially strong, because it can be shown, in defence of it, that the person who complies with the demand of this supra-personal responsibility, acts unegoistically. It is not to his individual existence or his individual welfare that he sacrifices another existence or welfare, but he sacrifices an individual existence and welfare to what forces itself upon him as expedient in view of the existence or the welfare of a majority. But ethical is more than unegoistic. Only the reverence felt by my will-to-live for every other will-to-live is ethical. Whenever I in any way sacrifice or injure life, I am not within the sphere of the ethical, but I become guilty, whether it be egoistically guilty for the sake of maintaining my own existence or welfare, or unegoistically guilty for the sake of maintaining a greater number of other existences or their welfare.

This so easily made mistake of accepting as ethical a violation of reverence for life, if it is based upon unegoistic considerations, is the bridge by crossing which ethics enter unawares the territory of the non-ethical. The bridge must be broken down.

Ethics go only so far as does humanity, humanity meaning consideration for the existence and the happiness of individual human beings. Where humanity ends, pseudo-ethics begin. The day on which this boundary is once for all universally recognized, and marked out so as to be visible to everyone, will be one of the most important in the history of mankind. Thenceforward it can no longer happen that ethics which are not ethics at all are accepted as real ethics, and deceive and ruin individuals and peoples.

The system of ethics hitherto current has hindered us from becoming as earnest as we ought to be by the fact that it has utterly deceived us as to the many ways in which each one of us, whether through self-assertion, or by actions justified by supra-personal responsibility, becomes guilty again and again. True knowledge consists in being gripped by the secret that everything around us is will-to-live and in seeing clearly how again and again we incur guilt against life.

Fooled by pseudo-ethics, man stumbles about in his guilt like a drunkard. If he gains knowledge and becomes serious, he seeks the road which least leads him into guilt.

We are all exposed to the temptation of lessening the guilt of inhumanity, which comes from our working under supra-personal responsibility, by withdrawing as far as possible into ourselves. But such freedom from guilt is not honestly obtained. Because ethics start with world- and life-affirmation, they do not allow us this flight into negation. They forbid us to be like the housewife who leaves the killing of the eel to her cook, and compel us to undertake all duties involving supra-personal responsibility which fall to us, even if we should be in a position to decline them for reasons more or less satisfactory.

Each one of us, then, has to engage, in so far as he is brought to it by the circumstances of his life, in work which involves supra-personal responsibility. But we must do this not in the spirit of the collective body, but in that of the man who wishes to be ethical. In every individual case, therefore, we struggle to preserve as much humanity as is possible, and in doubtful cases we venture to make a mistake on the side of humanity rather than on that of the object in view. When we have become aware and earnest, we think of what is usually forgotten: that all public activity has to do not only with the facts which are to be made actual in the interests of the collective body, but also with the creation of the state of mind which promotes the welfare of that body. The creation of such a spirit and temper is more important than anything directly attained in the facts. Public activity in which the utmost possible effort is not made to preserve humanity ruins the character. He who under the influence of supra-personal responsibility simply sacrifices men and human happiness when it seems right, accomplishes something. But he has not reached the highest level. He has only outward, not spiritual influence. We have spiritual influence only when others notice that we do not decide coldly in accordance with principles laid down once and for all, but in each individual case fight for our sense of humanity. There is too little among us of this kind of struggle. From the most insignificant man who is engaged in the smallest business, right up to the political ruler who holds in his hands the decision for peace or war, we act too much as men who in any given case can prepare without effort to be no longer men, but merely the executive of general interests. Hence there is no longer among us any trust in a righteousness lighted up with human feeling. Nor have we any longer any real respect for one another. We all feel ourselves in the power of a mentality of cold, impersonal, and usually unintelligent opportunism, which stiffens itself with appeals to principle, and in order to realize the smallest interests is capable of the greatest inhumanity and the greatest folly. We therefore see among us one temper of impersonal opportunism confronting another, and all problems are resolved in a purposeless conflict of force against force because there is nowhere at hand such a spirit as will make them soluble.

It is only through our struggles for humanity that forces which work in the direction of the truly rational and expedient can become powerful while the present way of thinking prevails. Hence the man who works with supra-personal responsibilities has to feel himself answerable not only for the successful result which is to be realized through him, but for the general disposition which has to be created.

Thus we serve society without abandoning ourselves to it We do not allow it to be our guardian in the matter of ethics. That would be as if the solo violinist allowed his bowing to be regulated by that of the double-bass player. Never for a moment do we lay aside our mistrust of the ideals established by society, and of the convictions which are kept by it in circulation. We always know that society is full of folly and will deceive us in the matter of humanity. It is an unreliable horse, and blind into the bargain. Woe to the driver, if he falls asleep!

All this sounds too hard. Society serves ethics by giving legal sanction to its most elementary principles, and handing on the ethical principles of one generation to the next. That is much, and it claims our gratitude. But society is also something which checks the progress of ethics again and again, by arrogating to itself the dignity of an ethical teacher. To this, however, it has no right. The only ethical teacher is the man who thinks ethically, and struggles for ethics. The conceptions of good and evil which are put in circulation by society are paper-money, the value of which is to be calculated not by the figures printed upon it, but by its relation to its exchange value in the gold of the ethics of reverence for life. But so measured, the rate of exchange is revealed as that of the paper-money of a half-bankrupt state.

The collapse of civilization has come about through ethics being left to society. A renewal of it is possible only if ethics become once more the concern of thinking human beings, and if individuals seek to assert themselves in society as ethical personalities. In proportion as we secure this, society will become an ethical, instead of the purely natural, entity, which it is by origin. Previous generations have made the terrible mistake of idealizing society as ethical. We do our duty to it by judging it critically, and trying to make it, so far as is possible, more ethical. Being in possession of an absolute standard of the ethical, we no longer allow ourselves to make acceptable as ethics principles of expediency or of the vulgarest opportunism. Nor do we remain any longer at the low level of allowing to be current, as in any way ethical, meaningless ideals of power, of passion or of nationalism, which are set up by miserable politicians and maintained in some degree of respect by bewildering propaganda. All the principles, dispositions, and ideals which make their appearance among us we measure, in their showy pedantry, with a rule on which the measures are given by the absolute ethics of reverence for life. We allow currency only to what is consistent with the claims of humanity. We bring into honour again regard for life and for the happiness of the individual. Sacred human rights we again hold high; not those which political rulers exalt at banquets and tread underfoot in their actions, but the true rights. We call once more for justice, not that which imbecile authorities have elaborated in a legal scholasticism, nor that about which demagogues of all shades of colour shout themselves hoarse, but that which is filled to the full with the value of each single human existence. The foundation of law and right is humanity.

Thus we confront the principles, dispositions, and ideals of the collective body with humanity. At the same time we shape them in accordance with reason, for only what is ethical is truly rational. Only so far as the current disposition of men is animated by ethical convictions and ideals is it capable of truly purposive activity.

The ethics of reverence for life put in our hands weapons for fighting false ethics and false ideals, but we have strength to use them only so far as we—each one in his own life—preserve our humanity. Only when those men are numerous who in thought and in action bring humanity to terms with reality, will humanity cease to be current as a mere sentimental idea and become what it ought to be, a leaven in the minds of individuals and in the spirit of society.

Chapter 27

THE CIVILIZING POWER OF THE ETHICS OF REVERENCE FOR LIFE

Civilization as a product of reverence for life.
The four ideals of civilization. The struggle for a civilized mankind in the machine age.
Church and State as historical entities, and as ideals of civilization.
The moralizing of the religious and political community.

THE REVERENCE FOR LIFE WHICH HAS GROWN UP IN THE WILL-TO-live which has become reflective, contains world- and life-affirmation and ethics side by side and interpenetrating each other. It therefore cannot but continually think out and will all the ideals of ethical civilization, and strive to bring them into agreement with reality.

Reverence for life will not allow the validity of the purely individualistic and inward conception of civilization as it rules in Indian thought and in mysticism. That man should make efforts for self-perfecting by withdrawing into himself is to it a deep, but an incomplete, ideal of civilization.

In no way does reverence for life allow the individual to give up interest in the world. It is unceasingly compelling him to be concerned about all the life that is round about him, and to feel himself responsible for it. Whenever life whose development we can influence is in question, our concern with it, and our responsibility for it, are not satisfied by our maintaining and furthering its existence as such; they demand that we shall try to raise it to its highest value in every respect.

The being that can be influenced in its development by us is man. So reverence for life compels us to imagine and to will every kind of progress of which man and humanity are capable. It throws us into a restless condition of ever imagining and willing civilization, but as ethical men.

Even a not yet deepened world- and life-affirmation produces this imagining and willing of civilization, but it leaves a man to exert himself more or less without guidance. In reverence for life, however, and the will, which accompanies it, to raise men and humanity to their highest value in every respect, he possesses the guidance which leads him to complete and purified ideals of civilization which with full consciousness of their goal struggle to come to terms with reality.

Defined from outside and quite empirically, complete civilization consists in realizing all possible progress in discovery and invention and in the arrangements of human society, and seeing that they work together for the spiritual perfecting of individuals which is the real and final object of civilization. Reverence for life is in a position to complete this conception of civilization and to build its foundations on what lies at the core of our being. This it does by defining what is meant by the spiritual perfecting of man, and making it consist in reaching the spirituality of an ever deepening reverence for life.

In order to give a meaning to the material and spiritual progress which is to be made actual by the individual man and mankind, the ordinary representation of civilization has to assume an evolution of the world, in which such progress has a meaning. But to do so, it puts itself in dependence on a play of phantasy which reaches no result. It is impossible to depict an evolution of the world in which the civilization produced by the individual man and mankind has any meaning.

In reverence for life, on the contrary, civilization recognizes that it has nothing at all to do with the evolution of the world, but carries its meaning in itself. The essence of civilization consists in this, that the reverence for life which in my will-to-live is struggling for recognition does get stronger and stronger in individuals and in mankind. Civilization, then, is not a phenomenon of any world-evolution, but an experience of the will-to-live within us, which it is neither possible nor necessary to bring into relation with the course of nature as we know it from outside. As a perfecting of our will-to-live it is sufficient for itself. What the development that takes place in us means in the totality of the development in the world we leave on one side as inscrutable. That, as a result of all the progress which men and mankind can make, there shall exist in the world as much as possible of will-to-live, putting reverence for life into practice on all life which comes within the sphere of its influence, and seeking perfection in the spiritual atmosphere of reverence for life: this and nothing else is civilization. So completely does it carry its value in itself, that even the certainty of the human race ceasing to exist within a calculable period would not be able to disconcert us in our efforts to attain to civilization.

As a development in which the highest experience of the will-to-live lives itself out, civilization has a meaning for the world without needing any explanation of the world.

* * *

The will-to-live which is filled with reverence for life is interested in the most lively and persevering way that can be imagined in all kinds of progress. Moreover, it possesses a standard by which to assess their value correctly, and can create a state of mind which allows them all to work in with one another in the most effective way.

Three kinds of progress come within the purview of civilization: progress in knowledge and power; progress in the social organization of mankind; progress in spirituality.

Civilization is made up of four ideals: the ideal of the individual; the ideal of social and political organization; the ideal of spiritual and religious social organization; the ideal of humanity as a whole. On the basis of these four ideals thought tries conclusions with progress.

Progress in knowledge has a directly spiritual significance when it is moulded by thought. It makes us recognize, ever more completely, that everything which exists is power, that is to say, will-to-live; it is ever making larger the circle of the will-to-live of which we can form conceptions by analogy with our own.

What importance it has for our meditation on the world that we have discovered in the cell an individual existence, in whose faculties, active and passive, we see repeated the elements of our own vitality! By our ever-widening knowledge, we are roused to ever greater astonishment at the mystery of life which surrounds us on every hand. From naïve simplicity we arrive at a more profound simplicity.

From our knowledge comes also power over the forces of nature. Our powers of movement and of action are increased in an extraordinary way. There comes about a far-reaching change in the circumstances of our life.

The progress which accompanies it, however, is not to the same extent an advantage for the development of man. By the power we obtain over the forces of nature we do indeed free ourselves from nature, and make her serviceable to us, but at the same time we thereby also cut ourselves loose from her, and slip into conditions of life whose unnatural character brings with it manifold dangers.

We press the forces of nature into our service by means of machines. There is a story in the writings of Chwang-tse of how a pupil of Confucius saw a gardener who, to get water for his flower-beds, repeatedly went down to the spring with his bucket. So he asked him whether he would not like to lessen his labour. "How can I?" replied the other. "You take a long piece of wood for a lever," said Confucius' pupil, "weighted behind, but light in front; with this you dip for the water and it comes up without the least trouble. They call this device a draw-well." But the gardener, who was something of a philosopher, answered: "I have heard my teacher say: 'If a man uses machines, he carries on all the affairs of life like a machine; whoever carries on his affairs like a machine gets a machine-like heart; and when anyone has a machine-like heart in his breast, he loses true simplicity.' "

The dangers that were suspected by that gardener in the fifth century B.C. are active among us in full force. Purely mechanical labour has become the lot of numbers among us to-day. Without houses of their own or any ground of their own which might feed them, they live in a depressing, materialist state of serfdom. As a result of the revolution which machines have brought about, we are almost all subjected to an existence of labour which is far too much governed by rule, too limited in its nature, and too strenuous. Reflection and concentration are made difficult for us. Family life and the upbringing of our children suffer. We are all more or less in danger of becoming human things instead of personalities. Many kinds of material and spiritual injury to human existence form therefore the dark side of the achievements of discovery and invention.

Even our capacity for civilization can be questioned. Claimed entirely by so severe a struggle for existence, many among us are no longer in a position to think about ideals which make for civilization. They cannot reach the objective mood which is necessary for it. All their attention is directed to the improvement of their own existence. The ideals which they set up for this object they proclaim to be ideals of civilization, thus causing confusion in the general conception of what civilization is.

In order to be a match for the state of things produced by the results of these achievements of discovery and invention which are at the same time beneficial and injurious, we must think out an ideal of humanity and wrestle with circumstances to make them hinder as little, and help as much, as possible the development of man up to this ideal.

The ideal of civilized man is none other than that of a man who in every relation of life preserves true human nature. To be civilized men means for us approximately this: that in spite of the conditions of modern civilization we remain human. It is only taking thought for everything which belongs to true human nature that can preserve us, amid the conditions of the most advanced external civilization, from going astray from civilization itself. It is only if the longing to become again truly man is kindled in the man of to-day, that he will be able to find his way out of the confusion in which, blinded by conceit at his knowledge and pride in his powers, he is at present wandering. Only then, too, will he be in a position to strive against the pressure of those relations of life which threaten his human nature.

Reverence for life demands, therefore, as the ideal of the material and spiritual being of man, that with the completest possible development of all his faculties and in the widest possible freedom, both material and spiritual, he should struggle to be honest with himself and to take a sympathetic and helpful interest in all the life that is around him. In earnest concern about himself, he must ever keep in mind all the responsibilities which are his lot, and so, whether active or passive, preserve in his relation to himself and to the world a living spirituality. There should ever be before him as true human nature the duty of being ethical in the profound world- and life-affirmation of reverence for life.

If it is recognized as the aim of civilization that every man shall attain to true human nature in an existence which is as fully as possible worthy of him, then the uncritical overvaluing of the external elements of civilization which we have taken over from the end of the nineteenth century can no longer prevail among us. We are forced more and more into reflection which compels us to distinguish between the essentials and the unessentials of civilization. Senseless pride in civilization loses its power over us. We dare to face the truth that with the progress of knowledge and power civilization has become not easier, but more difficult. We become conscious of the problem of the mutual relations between the material and the spiritual. We know that we all have to wrestle with circumstances on behalf of our human nature, and make it our concern to transform the almost hopeless struggle which many have to carry on to preserve their human nature, into a contest which offers some hope.

As spiritual aid in this struggle we offer them the way of thinking which will allow no man ever to be sacrificed to circumstances, as if he were a mere human thing. Formulated by so-called thinkers and popularized in all possible forms, the conviction is general that civilization is the privilege of an *élite,* and that man in the mass is only a means for realizing it. At the same time the spiritual help to which they are entitled is denied to these men who have a hard struggle to preserve their human nature. That is the effect of the sense of reality to which we have surrendered ourselves. But reverence for life rebels against it, and creates a way of thinking in which there is offered to every man in the thoughts of others the human value and the human dignity which the circumstances of life would deny him. The struggle has thus lost its extreme bitterness. Man has now to assert himself only against his circumstances, and no longer against his fellowmen as well.

Further, the spirit of reverence for life helps those who have to struggle hardest on behalf of their humanity by keeping alive the conception of human nature as the value which must be preserved at any price. It keeps them from going astray with one-sided aims in their struggle for the diminishing of their material bondage, and bids them bethink themselves that much more of humanity and freedom of soul can be combined with their actual life-circumstances than they actually secure. It leads them to preserve equanimity and spirituality when they have hitherto given them up.

There must come about a spiritualizing of the masses. The mass of individuals must begin to reflect about their lives, about what they want to secure for their lives in the struggle for existence, about what makes their circumstances difficult, and about what they deny themselves. They are wanting in spirituality because they have only a confused conception of what spirituality is. They forget to think, because elementary thought about themselves has become unfamiliar. In what is in our day cultivated as spirituality and practised as thought, there is absolutely nothing that comes directly home to them as necessary for themselves. But if it comes about that the thoughts suggested by reverence for life become common among us, there will be a mode of thought which will affect us all, and spirituality will become general and active. Even those who are engaged in the hardest struggle on behalf of their human nature will then be led to reflection and inwardness, and will thereby obtain powers which they did not before possess.

Though all of us are alike aware that the maintenance of civilization is dependent first and foremost on the gushing forth of the fountains of spiritual life which are in us, we shall nevertheless zealously take in hand our economic and social problems. The highest possible material freedom for the greatest possible number is a requirement of civilization.

The recognition that we evidently have so little power over economic relations does not discourage us. We know this to be to a considerable extent a result of the fact that hitherto facts were contending with facts, and passions with passions. Our impotence comes from our feeling for reality. We shall be able to deal with things much more effectively, if we resolve to try to solve our problems by a change in our way of thinking. And we are at length ready for the recognition of this. The efforts for control which were made on the strength of economic theories and Utopias were in every respect inexpedient, and have brought us to a terrible state of affairs. There remains nothing for us to do but to try a radical change of policy, that is to say, the solution of our problems in an appropriate way by means of helpful understanding and confidence. It is reverence for life alone which can create the disposition needed for this. The understanding and confidence which we mutually accord to each other with a view to what is most purposive, and by means of which we obtain the utmost power that is possible over circumstances, can be enjoyed only if everyone can assume in everyone else reverence for the existence of the other and regard for his material and spiritual welfare as a disposition which influences them to the depths of their being. Only through reverence for life can we attain the standards of economic justice, about which we have to come to an understanding with each other.

Will it be possible to bring about this development? We must, if we are not all to be ruined together, materially and spiritually. All progress in discovery and invention evolves at last to a fatal result, if we do not maintain control over it through a corresponding progress in our spirituality. Through the power which we gain over the forces of nature, in sinister fashion we get control as human beings over other human beings. With the possession of a hundred machines a single man or a company is given a supremacy over all who work the machines. Some new invention may make it possible for one man by a single movement to kill not merely a hundred, but ten thousand of his fellow-men. In no sort of struggle is it possible to avoid becoming ruinous to one another by economic or physical power. At best the result is that the oppressor and the oppressed exchange rôles. The only thing that can help is that we renounce the power which is given us over one another. But that is an act of spirituality.

Intoxicated by the progress in discovery and invention with

which our age has been flooded, we forgot to trouble ourselves about men's progress in immaterial matters. In the absence of all thought we slid unawares into the pessimism of believing in all sorts of progress, but no longer in the spiritual progress of the individual and of mankind.

Facts call us now to bethink ourselves, just as movements of their capsizing vessel drive the crew up on to the deck and into the rigging. Belief in the spiritual progress of the individual and of mankind has already become almost impossible for us, but with the courage of despair we must force ourselves to that belief. That we shall all unanimously again will this spiritual progress and again hope for it: that is the reversal of the helm which we must succeed in making, if our vessel is at the last moment to be brought once more before the wind.

Only through thoughtful reverence for life shall we become capable of this achievement. If that reverence begins anywhere to work in our minds, then the miracle is possible. The power of the elementary and living spirituality that is to be found in it is beyond calculation.

* * *

State and Church are only modalities of the organization of men towards humanity. The ideals of social-political and religious organization are therefore determined by the necessity of these entities being made effective aids to the ethical spiritualizing of men, and to their organization towards humanity.

The fact that the ideals of State and Church among us are not in power in their true form is due to our historical sense. The men of the "Aufklärung" assumed that State and Church had come into existence by reason of estimates made of their usefulness. They sought to comprehend the nature of these two entities by means of theories about their origins, but in this proceeding they did nothing but read back their own view into history. Not feeling the least reverence for any natural historical entity, they found it easy to approach them with demands suggested by a rational ideal. We, on the contrary, have such a measure of this reverence that we feel shy of wishing to transform in accordance with theoretical ideas what had a quite different origin.

But State and Church are not merely natural historical entities; they are also necessary entities. The only way in which reflection can deal with them is to be always at work, transforming them from what they are as received, into organisms which are in accordance with reason and effective in every respect. Only in this capacity for development is their existence fully apprehended and justified.

The natural historical entity presents us always only with initial facts which lead on to corresponding further happenings, but never with facts in which the nature of society, that is to say the way in which we are to behave towards it and to belong to it, can be determined. If one allows that in the conception of the natural entity there is also given one of a self-determined purpose, there arises a fundamental confusion in people's notion of the organization of society. The individual and humanity as a whole, which are just as truly natural entities as the two historical ones, are robbed of their rights and sacrificed to the latter. The increased understanding with which we now study the natural policy of societies with historical origin can therefore not alter at all our demand that State and Church shall direct their course more and more with reference to the ideals of man and of humanity as their natural poles, and be obliged to find in them their higher effectiveness.

Civilization demands, then, that State and Church become capable of development. This presupposes that the relations of influence between the collective body and its individual members will become different from what they have been. In the last generations the individual confronted with State and Church has surrendered more and more of his spiritual independence. He received his way of thinking from them, instead of the attitude of mind that was growing within him working as a formative influence upon State and Church.

This abnormal relation was unavoidable. The individual had, of course, nothing in which he could be spiritually independent. He had, therefore, no spirit and temper in which he could come to terms with the entities of real life. Nor was he in a position to think out ideals which could affect reality. There was no course left for him but to adopt as an ideal an idealized reality.

But in the world- and life-view of reverence for life he obtains the means to a firm and valuable self-determination. It is with a will and a hope which he carries ready shaped within himself that he faces reality. It is to him self-evident that every society that is formed among men must serve towards the maintenance, the advancement, and the higher development of life, and the growth of true spirituality.

That which is decisive for the commencement of a development of State and Church which has civilization for its object, is that the mass of men belong to these two entities in the attitude of mind of reverence for life and the ideals which grow from it: when that is the case there arises in States and Churches a spirit which works for their transformation into ethical and spiritual values.

A forecast of the course this process will take cannot be made, nor is one needed. The mental attitude of reverence for life is a force which works effectively in every respect. The important thing is that it shall be present with a strength and constancy which will suffice to bring about the transformation.

* * *

If the Church is to accomplish its task, it must unite men in elementary, thoughtful, ethical religiousness. This it has hitherto done very imperfectly. How far it is from being what it ought to be was revealed by its absolute failure in the war. There devolved on it the duty of summoning men out of the struggle of national passions to reflection, and of keeping them in the spirit and temper of the highest ideals. It was not able to do this, and indeed did not seriously make the attempt. Only too completely historical, and too well organized, and too little a directly religious association, it succumbed to the spirit of the time and mixed up with religion the dogmas of nationalism and pragmatism. There was only one tiny church, the community of the Quakers, which attempted to defend the unconditional validity of reverence for life, as it is contained in the religion of Jesus.

The spirit of reverence for life is able to work for the transformation of the Church to the ideal of a religious association, because it is itself deeply religious. In all historically formulated belief it seeks to bring into general acceptance as the elemental and essential constituent of piety the ethical mysticism of oneness with the infinite Will, which experiences itself in us as the will to love. By putting in the very centre of things the most living and universal element of piety, it leads the different re-religious associations out of the narrowness of their historical past, and paves the way for understanding and union between them.

But this attitude of mind does even more than that. Besides bringing the existing historical religious associations out of their historical existence into a development towards the ideal of religious association, it operates also where they can do nothing, namely in the sphere of non-religion. There are many non-religious people among us. They have become so partly through thoughtlessness and absence of any world-view, and partly because as a result of honest thinking they could no longer be content with a traditional religious conception of the universe. The world- and life-view of reverence for life enables these non-religious minds to learn that every philosophy of life which is based on sincere thought necessarily becomes religious. Ethical mysticism reveals to them the necessity to thought of the religion of love, and thus leads them back to paths which they believed they had abandoned forever.

Just as the transformation of the religious association must be the result primarily of a change of heart, so also must be that of the social and political community.

It is true, indeed, that to believe in the possibility of transforming the modern state into the civilized state is a piece of heroism. The modern state finds itself to-day in an unprecedented condition of material and spiritual penury. Collapsing under the weight of debts, torn by economic and political conflicts, stripped of all moral authority, and scarcely able any longer to maintain its authority in practical matters, it has to struggle for its existence in a succession of fresh troubles. In the face of all these things whence is it to get power to develop into a truly civilized state?

What crises and catastrophes the modern state is still destined to go through cannot be foreseen. Its position is further endangered especially by the fact that it has far overstepped the limits of its natural sphere of operation. It is an extraordinarily complicated organism which intervenes in all social relationships, which tries to regulate everything, and therefore in every respect functions ineffectively; it tries to dominate economic life as it dominates spiritual life; and for its activities over this extensive field it works with machinery which in itself at once constitutes a danger.

At some time and in some way or other the modern state must emerge from its financial trouble, and reduce its activity to a normal standard, but by what methods it can ever again get back to a natural and healthy condition remains still a riddle.

The tragic thing is, then, that we have to belong to the unsympathetic and unhealthy modern state while cherishing the will to transform it into a civilized state. There is demanded from us an all but impossible achievement of faith in the power of the spirit. But the ethical outlook on the world and on life gives us strength for the task.

Living in the modern state and thinking the ideal of the civilized state, we first of all put an end to the illusions which the former cherishes about itself. Only by the majority of its members taking up a critical attitude towards it can it come to itself again in reflection about itself. The absolute impossibility of the continuance of the state in its present condition must become the universal conviction before things can become in any way better.

But at the same time, through meditation on the civilized state, the perception must become common property that all merely external measures for raising and making healthy the modern state, however expedient they may be in themselves, will have only a quite imperfect result unless the spirit of the state becomes quite different. Let us, then, undertake to drive the modern state, so far as the power of our thought reaches, into the spirituality and the morality of the civilized state as it is to be, according to the idea contained in reverence for life. We demand from it that it shall become more spiritual and more ethical than any state has hitherto been expected to become. Only with efforts to reach the true ideal do we get progress.

The objection is raised that, according to all experience, the state cannot exist by relying merely on truth, justice, and ethical considerations, but in the last resort has to take refuge in opportunism. We smile at this experience. It is refuted by the dreary results. We have, therefore, the right to declare the opposite course to be true wisdom, and to say that true power for the state as for the individual is to be found in spirituality and ethical conduct. The state lives by the confidence of those who belong to it; it lives by the confidence felt in it by other states. Opportunist policy may have temporary successes to record, but in the long run it assuredly ends in failure.

Thus ethical world- and life-affirmation demands of the modern state that it shall aspire to making itself an ethical and spiritual personality. It presses this obstinately upon the state, and does not let itself be deterred by the smiles of superior persons. The wisdom of to-morrow has a different tone from that of yesterday.

Only by a new attitude of mind ruling within it can the state attain to peace within its borders; only by a new attitude of mind arising between them can different states come to understand each other, and cease to bring destruction upon each other; only by treating the overseas world in a different spirit from that of the past and of to-day can modern states cease to load themselves in that connection with guilt.

Such moral talk about the civilized state has often been heard in the past. Certainly it has. But it acquires a special tone at a time when the modern state is perishing in misery, because it refused in the past to continue to be in any way spiritually ethical. It possesses a new authority, too, to-day because in the world- and life-view of reverence for life there is revealed the significance of the ethical in its full extent and its full profundity.

We are therefore freed from any duty of forming a conception of the civilized state which accords with the specifications of nationalism and national civilization, and we are at liberty to turn back to the profound *naïveté* of thinking it to be a state which allows itself to be guided by an ethical spirit of civilization. With confidence in the strength of the civilized attitude of mind which springs from reverence for life we undertake the task of making this civilized state an actuality.

Feeling ourselves responsible to the civilized way of thinking we look beyond peoples and states to humanity as a whole. To anyone who has devoted himself to ethical world- and life-affirmation, the future of men and of mankind is a subject of anxiety and of hope. To become free from this anxiety and hope is poverty; to be wholly surrendered to it is riches. Thus it is our consolation that in a time of difficulty and without knowing how much we may still experience of a better future, we are paving the way, solely by our confidence in the power of the spirit, for a civilized mankind which is to come.

Kant published, with the title *Towards Perpetual Peace,* a work containing rules which were to be observed with a view to lasting peace whenever treaties of peace were concluded. It was a mistake. Rules for treaties of peace, however well intentioned and however ably drawn up, can accomplish nothing. Only such thinking as establishes the sway of the mental attitude of reverence for life can bring to mankind perpetual peace.

INDEX TO PART II

P9-BHT-571

ETHICS FOR AN INDUSTRIAL AGE

Ethics for an Industrial Age

A CHRISTIAN INQUIRY

By Victor Obenhaus

AFTERWORD BY F. ERNEST JOHNSON

HARPER & ROW, PUBLISHERS

NEW YORK

FIRST EDITION

LIBRARY OF CONGRESS CATALOG CARD NUMBER: 65-21020

K-P

Contents

Foreword

BY CHARLES P. TAFT
Chairman of the Commission on the Church and Economic Life

This book is the final volume in a larger study of Christian Ethics and Economic Life which was begun in 1949 by the Department of the Church and Economic Life of the Federal Council of the Churches of Christ in America. At the beginning of 1951 the Federal Council was merged with other interdenominational agencies to form the National Council of the Churches of Christ in the United States of America, made up of thirty-four Protestant and Orthodox church bodies within the United States.

In recent years religious leaders have recognized that the ethical problems of economic life have become increasingly urgent. The ethics of everyday decisions and practices in economic life, both private and public, are matters of wide concern. We need to go behind individual acts and group pressures for a deeper understanding of the motives underlying what people do in their economic activities, of how the system fits together, of how close our preconceived ideas are to reality.

Change is dominant in our national life and perhaps nowhere so much so as in its economic aspects. During the past half-century our ways of life and work have undergone a vast alteration. The change has been accomplished without violence, but with increasing if not always obvious upset, and the tempo of its pace is revolutionary. Certainly if people whose span of life was in the nineteenth century could see what we see in everyday life, they would hardly accept any word but revolution for the process that has brought it about.

This accelerated change demands that all thoughtful people understand its effects upon ethics and human values. How shall we deal with the dynamism in our economic life so as to preserve and extend the dignity of the individual, respect for the rights of minorities, sensitivity to the public welfare, and free discussion and peaceful persuasion? We cannot rely upon business statistics to measure these intangibles. Judgments of even the best qualified individuals about actual or impending changes, affected as opinions are by individual temperament, vested interests, or political partisanship, are also inadequate if considered separately. The fullest use of all our resources for information and face-to-face discussion is required for sound progress toward solution of our complex problems.

There is no vital threat to our inherited and cherished values either in the status quo as such or in change as such. We cannot separate ethics from practical economic concerns. What is needed is a better understanding both of economic facts and of those ethical convictions and values which have special significance in the meaning and direction they should give to economic activity.

In many parts of the world we find a fanatic cynicism or a false philosophy in opposition to the foundations upon which Western society is based. What earlier generations took for granted, such as the value and integrity of the individual, the character of government as a means for service of the people, the capacity of human life for essential decency and justice—these are now challenged by conflicting assumptions also claimed to be moral or at least essential for an efficient society.

Here lies the real crisis of the second half of the present century. We must meet this challenge, in so far as it is evil, and clarify in relation to our own institutions the basic ethical affirmations which we support.

The Federal Council of Churches conducted for many years, and the National Council of Churches has continued, an educational program on the ethical issues involved in economic life. Many denominational bodies have likewise been active in this field. It became clear, however, that we needed a more careful and realistic investigation of economic life and its relation to spiritual and moral values in a Christian frame of reference. We needed to make use of the capacities of social scientists and theologians, in close association with other persons drawn from many occupations.

Accordingly, a study was begun in 1949 under a grant from the Rockefeller Foundation and continued under further grants from the same source in 1952 and 1959. The Foundation has not sought to exercise any supervisory control over the study and does not assume responsibility for any of the findings. The results of the study so far are presented in ten volumes: *Goals of Economic Life, The Organizational Revolution, Social Responsibilities of the Businessman, American Income and Its Use, The American Economy—Attitudes and Opinions, Christian Values and Economic Life, Social Responsibility in Farm Leadership, Social Responsibilities of Organized Labor, Responsibility in Mass Communication,* and *The Church as Employer, Money-Raiser, and Investor.*

This final volume in the series subjects to further analysis and interpretation some of the major economic issues of the study as a whole in their relation to the concern of the churches in social education and action.

Gratitude is due to the several authors in the entire series for their devotion and creativity in the writing of these books. In all the volumes of the series the authors have been free to write as they wished and to accept or reject suggestions or criticisms; each book is the responsibility of the individual writer.

Others have made valuable contributions to the total study effort of which this volume is an important part. The Reverend Cameron P. Hall, executive director of the Department (now Commission) of the Church and Economic Life, has given the project his unfailing and effective administrative support. Dr. Howard R. Bowen, former economic consultant to the study, made an invaluable contribution in the formulation of the project and aided also in criticism of manuscripts. The Reverend A. Dudley Ward served as director of studies from the beginning in 1949 unitl the fall of 1953. He carried out his responsibilities as organizer and coordinator with imagination and efficiency, and also gave help after he had left for other important work. Since September 1953 Dr. F. Ernest Johnson has been in charge of the studies. His long experience in research and education, with the Federal Council and in other connections, has made him exceptionally qualified for this service.

A study committee of the department, including both lay and

clerical members and representing a variety of occupations, has reviewed the program of the study at various stages. Dr. Roy Blough, professor of international economics at Columbia University, has chaired the study committee since 1958 and given close supervision to its work. The late Charles H. Seaver served as editorial consultant and secretary of the study committee and carefully edited most of the manuscripts.

The National Council of Churches has taken no official position and assumes no responsibility regarding the content of any of the volumes. In no sense, therefore, can or should any statement in the series be regarded as an official declaration of the National Council of Churches or any of its units.

Preface

It is taken for granted that religion and culture are closely intertwined in American life. This is not different from other types of society since religion in most areas of the world is an integral part of the culture which prevails. Economic life is also an integral part of culture.

In many areas of the world primitive economic life and religion have been closely related. In the Middle Ages they were indistinguishable. In some parts of Colonial America and some immigrant and utopian communities they were intimately connected. With expanding industrialism, the relationship has become increasingly ill-defined. Attempts have been made, both in Europe and the United States, to indicate the desirable correlation of these two facets of culture necessary to the health of each. America's most impressive contribution to this correlation was the Social Gospel. Regardless of one's theological persuasion the problem remains inseparable and the viability of any religious emphasis is tied to the manner in which it relates our means of livelihood and our faith.

Despite the pluralistic nature of our present society a marked homogenization has been occurring. "Americanization" has blurred many hitherto observable differentiations. What is "American" has superseded what is "Christian" or "Jewish" and what is American has come to mean what is identified with business or economic life. By this process the role of religion in economic life has been diminshed or obscured.

A fundamental thesis of this volume, and of the entire Series on The Ethics and Economics of Society, is that economics and religion cannot be divorced without peril to society. That they have been separated in the minds and actions of very large numbers is painfully obvious. The indifference of nominally religious people to the economic activities which may be undermining their faith represents a defaulting of their whole religious heritage. This is why the volume begins with a chapter on "Roots of Religious Concern for Economic Life." It is a further hypothesis of this volume that only as the relation between religion and the various forms of economic expression is realized can there be genuine health in either religion or economics. At present there is much in industrial life to impair that relationship.

Each of the areas dealt with in this volume involves profound ethical issues. Obviously there are no simple solutions. One's religion and his faith cannot provide formulas for the quick resolution of these issues. Nevertheless, there are criteria in the religious heritages of each of us which raise fundamental questions concerning the values which are served or sabotaged by current practices. I have, therefore, attempted to lift up a few of the major economic issues of our times and present them as areas for consideration in the light of the values and standards inherent in our faith. No doubt readers will feel some very important ones have been omitted. It was necessary to be selective. In each of the issues chosen it is possible for religiously motivated people to engage in constructive action. In many instances action in concert with sympathetic-minded people is essential; in others, independent action is possible.

This volume is intended for those who are or might become seriously concerned with the relation between religious faith and economic issues. In other volumes of this series fuller theological and philosophical treatment of ethics and economics has been provided. My purpose here has been to portray some of the problems in both their historic development and their present-day implications. Many of the changes which have occurred are coincident with the development of industrial life. This does not sanctify them or make them inevitable despite a widely held assumption that economic practices are validated only in a world of their own. Inherent in the entire presentation is the conviction that not only are religiously-sensitive people not helpless before these changes but that in their heritage is a mandate to alter what stands in violation of faith's demands. Thus, though this volume is not intended as a technically comprehensive resource for the expert in the areas discussed, it is hoped that religio-ethical implications would be apparent. For the greater body of nonexperts it is hoped that the documentation of the issues would serve to illustrate and clarify what is for religiously-sensitive people an inescapable relation between religion and economics.

As is always the case, an author is indebted to far too many people to be able to mention them all and give proper credit. In this instance the author is indebted above all others to Dr. F. Ernest Johnson, editor of most of the volumes which comprise the Series on the Ethics and Economics of Society. He patiently and painstakingly reviewed and helped in the development of the entire volume. Out of a rich wisdom and long experience in the total area of ethics and economics he gave sage counsel. It is fitting he should provide the "Afterword" which concludes both this volume and the entire series. To Professor Roy Blough, chairman of the Study Committee, is owed a profound debt of gratitude. He has not only read the contents but has made invaluable suggestions out of his own extensive professional skill in the areas he knows best and has given counsel in organization of other materials. Dr. Cameron Hall, director of the Commission on Church and Economic Life, after aiding in the initiation of the volume has followed each step of its development and has given helpful implementation at many points. Miss Elma Greenwood, associate director of the Commission, in her quiet and efficient way has similarly facilitated the progress of the volume. A committee of specialists representing some of the areas dealt with in the volume, each a member of the Commission on Church and Economic Life, gave much help along the way. However, the author alone must assume responsibility both for the form and content of the pages which follow. Complete authority was given to the author to develop what he thought would be the needed treatment of the over-all theme. John Loeschen, a student at the Chicago Theological Seminary, was most helpful in the gathering of materials and in making useful suggestions. To Mrs. Frances Ritsch is owed a special debt of gratitude for serving as typist for each of the many editions. Finally, as is so often the case, an author's debt to his family is unlimited. They listened to or read many sections and suffered numerous inconveniences during the writing.

V. O.

Chicago, Illinois
July 1965

1

Roots of Religious Concern for Economic Life

To separate the spiritual aspects of Hebrew-Christian religion from the economic is impossible, for all of life is one piece. It is summed up in the affirmation, "Hear, O Israel, the Lord thy God is one God; thou shalt love the Lord thy God with all thy heart, and soul and mind, and thy neighbor as thyself." This declaration is the basis of a most profound and at the same time ever-continuing revolution. The earliest Hebrews understood this, and they knew that whenever they had departed from it, their personal and national life had lost something of its purpose and true dimension. Embedded deeply in the individual and collective life of this people was a conviction that religion could be expressed fully only when it incorporated responsibility to both God and man. The love of God and the love of neighbor inescapably involved man in economic relations.

The seminomadic people delivered from Egypt by God through Moses lived in an economy of grain cultivation and sheep herding. The social structure which held that order together was a patriarchal society with each local unit dominated by the head of the family and the larger clan governed by a cluster of heads of families. Responsibility for members of the families resided with the leadership. Such a pattern was not confined to the Hebrew tribes and their families; any difference from other nomadic tribes derives from the manner in which the family and the clan regarded themselves in relation to their God. Economics, worship, family ties, and communal relationships were woven together into a common fabric; but the unifying factor was a conviction that their ultimate obligation was to a God who had a special concern for the well-being of His people. Only out of such a communal conviction can the powerful affirmations of the Hebrew prophets be understood.

Moving into a new land following the departure from Egypt, the Israelites found it necessary to establish property regulations in which dividing lines had to be established and the inheritance of land made integral to the national and communal life. Land was conceived not as being owned outright but as being held under a stewardship, a conception of property which has never been disavowed by those who inherit the Hebrew-Christian tradition. The combination of the Israelitic conviction that the land belonged to God, the subsequent corruption of this belief in personal and family life, the conflict with other cultures which maintained no such ideas of property, occasioned protests and indictments on the part of sensitive religious leaders. This line of judgment and the theological-economic insight run from the middle of the eighth century B.C. to the middle of the twentieth century A.D.

To say that the Hebrew prophets were primarily interested in the economic question is of course a distortion, for the simple reason that the economic question is fundamentally a part of the larger issue of the nature of man and his obligation to the God, who is both Creator and Redeemer. It was the Hebrew prophets who confronted men with the fact that the distortion of their relation to God often came at the point of communal irresponsibility and the blindness fostered by pride. They recognized that perversions which led to individual arrogance and acquisition constituted a form of false worship. Other neighboring religions found no difficulty with property arrangements which provided for individual appropriation. Therefore, the struggle against false gods was focused, in part at least, on the problems of land ownership. The issue at stake is God's sovereignty as seen in the acts of His creation and the subsequent stewardship of creation by those who held it in trust. Stewardship is corroded by pride, and the Hebrew prophets understood this.

So axiomatic is the corrosion of ownership through pride that wealth was suspect and often regarded as synonymous with failure to abide by God's commands. The rich are identified with the wicked, while the poor are more nearly capable of qualifying as God's children. "And they made his grave with the wicked and with a rich man in his death . . ." (Isaiah 53 : 9).

The messages of the prophets bear down on the pride of possession as well as express the conviction that all property belongs to God, the Sovereign. "Take heed . . . lest when you have eaten and are full, and have built goodly houses and live in them, and when your herds and flocks multiply, and your silver and gold is multiplied, and all that you have is multiplied, then your heart be lifted up, and you forget the Lord your God. . . . You say in your heart, 'My power and the might of my hand have gotten me this wealth.' You shall remember the Lord your God, for it is He who gives you power to get wealth . . ." (Deut. 8 : 11–18).

Despite the belief that virtue is materially rewarded, the delicate balance of possession and stewardship created the dilemma in which disobedience is punished through property loss. The resolution of this dilemma lay in the recognition that wealth belonged not to an individual but to a whole family or community, which in turn derived its possession from God, the Sovereign.

Man's defection from his true heritage is seen in his disregard of the rightful claims of God upon him, especially as they are manifested in his communal and personal relations. Amos points the finger of judgment at those who take advantage of others: "You who trample upon the needy, and bring the poor of the land to an end, saying, 'When will the new moon be over, that we may sell grain?'" (Amos 8 : 4).

The corrosion of justice has gone so far that Amos complains, "The end is come upon my people Israel" (Amos 8 : 2). And Jeremiah asks, "Can the Ethopian change his skin or the leopard his spots? Then also you can do good who are accustomed to do evil" (Jer. 13 : 23). Isaiah condemns those "who join house to house, who add field to field, until there is no more room, and you are made to dwell alone in the midst of the land" (Isaiah 5 : 8).

Standing in judgment against all such injustice and the selfish use of economic power, the Hebrew prophets saw a Sovereign God whose will for His people included justice in economic arrangements and the proper subordination of human pride. Willful exploitation and manifestations of personal aggrandizement could be nothing but an affront to this true Sovereign of the nation. Such willfulness could only be regarded as sacrilegious. Not even by a king of Israel could the deeply rooted and elemental rights be abrogated. Property a man needed to provide for his family was guaranteed to him against the personal desires and acquisitiveness of even the most powerful force in the land. When Ahab, unable to secure Naboth's vineyard by persuasion, secured it through trumped-up charges and murder, he was indicted by Elijah, and an ignominous fate is foretold. The king and his greedy queen, Jezebel, sought the land to satisfy pride. For Naboth it was an extension of himself, satisfying his need for existence. In its truest sense the earth belonged to the Lord, but within that ultimate ownership individuals held rights of use which were subject to criteria of need. Property might be privately held, but ownership was not absolute or without judgment from a higher source.

The idea of land held in trust or under stewardship was embodied in the institutions of the sabbatical year and the year of jubilee. It was expected that by lying fallow in the seventh year, the land would benefit the poor. Similarly, in the seventh year a slave was freed from bond service (Ex. 21 : 2) and debt was to be forgiven (Deut. 15 : 1). The year of jubilee brought recovery of liberty throughout the land for everyone at intervals of fifty years. At this time land reverted to its original owner. "The land shall not be sold in perpetuity, for the land is mine; for you are strangers and sojourners with me" (Lev. 25 : 23).

When Nathan charged the great and popular King David with the usurpation of property rights in the stealing of another man's wife, he knew he had behind him the full force of a just God. Ostensibly he presented his case in the form of a tale involving the stealing of one little lamb (II Sam. 12 : 1–14). Revealed in this tale is the deep conviction that not even temporal leaders may violate the more basic rights and human justice granted by a Sovereign God.

The Old Testament principles concerning property, says Charles

L. Taylor, "can be summarized as, (1) the ownership of God; (2) the goodness of God's gifts by which He shares Himself; (3) the community of rights and responsibilities in which there must be justice; (4) the unremitting condemnation of the use of property for selfish advantage; and (5) an awakening appreciation of service and sacrifice."[1]

The Hebrew people sense realistically that economic relations constitute one of the means by which spiritual values find expression. Any spirituality devoid of fruitage in human relations was truncated and false. Man's inclination to self-justification in the acquisition of possessions stood constantly under the judgment of a God whose worship included economic justice to one's fellow men.

The New Testament and Property

There is no major emphasis on the economic theme as such in the gospel message, certainly not in primary focus as in the case of the prophets. Nevertheless the Gospels are saturated with implications for economic life. Jesus' life and message, though concerned primarily with the kingdom of God, have economic implications largely for the same reasons that actuated the prophets. Primary preoccupation with goods and things can serve to dilute, if not actually obliterate, the awareness of man's ultimate obligations and commitment; for example, ". . . take heed, and beware of all covetousness; for a man's life does not consist in the abundance of his possessions" (Luke 12 : 15), or "for where your treasure is, there will your heart be also" (Matt. 6: :21).

The purity of heart which enables one to seek the pearl of great price can be destroyed by preoccupation with possessions. The parable of the servants and the talents, like almost all of Jesus' parables, makes use of an economic framework understood by listeners to illustrate a more profound insight than the economic facts narrated. Scarcely any phase of Jesus' ministry is without reference to common experience and ordinary human need. From the parables and the accounts of His association with those about Him it is apparent that He was concerned with these elemental needs by which life was sustained. A hungry multitude must be fed before they could hear and understand His message. His special solicitude for the poor, whose lives were not yet distorted by possessions, attests sensitiveness to economic differences. Hunger and poverty must be alleviated, but unless their alleviation is achieved with something more than a mere change in physical condition they have missed the purpose of life itself. Finally, in one of His last acts together with His associates, Jesus had arranged for a common meal. There He used the most common components of a meal, bread and wine, to symbolize the reality of His own relation to all men. They were not ends in themselves, but rather, as was and is true of all economic realities, they pointed to and were a part of life's more profound meaning.

Possessions are intended to be instruments for the service of God, but instead they can become man's master. Jesus' life served as the best example of the command "Do not lay up for yourselves treasures on earth . . . but lay up for yourselves treasures in heaven . . ." (Matt. 6 : 19–20). Or again, "No servant can serve two masters. . . . You cannot serve God and mammon" (Luke 16 : 13). Jesus confronts men with the hard fact that money can become their god or it can be utilized in the service of God. A large part of Jesus' teaching dealt with wealth and possessions, not because they were significant in themselves but because of their consequences to persons. Of prime importance was the intent behind the acquisition of wealth. Its disposition revealed what the temporary owner regarded as first in importance.

The kingdom of which Jesus spoke so frequently and which constituted so all-penetrating a part of His message was both "at hand" and was "coming" in the not distant future. Concern with physical arrangements, legal actions, and specifications were of secondary importance in the face of the demands of the God who was establishing the present and coming kingdom. Presumably, economic arrangements would be consummated in the light of the all-consuming purpose claiming the attention of Jesus' followers. In spite of this great concern with the kingdom there could be no mistaking Jesus' intention that personal relationships, including economic activities, must be subjected to the supreme demands of the One whose kingdom it is to be.

In the centuries following the life, death, and resurrection of Jesus Christ, innumerable groups have sought to incorporate the principles and admonitions of the Gospels into their common life. Many have done this on the assumption that they are recapturing the spirit of the first-century Christians, those who knew the disciples or who were influenced by the Apostle Paul. We are told that some members of the early church liquidated their possessions in expectation of the early return of Christ. Both because of the expected return and because of the close relationship among those who held this expectation, there was disposition to sacrifice for each other and to share their worldly possessions; ". . . and no one said that any of the things which he possessed was his own, but they had everything in common" (Acts 4 : 32).

This desire to share with others who are bound together in common ties of devotion to one God and one Lord has had numerous manifestations throughout the generations. But no small part of the inspiration and authority of such ventures derives from the biblical narrative describing the life of Jesus and the experience of first-century Christians. The primary citizenship of the members of these colonies is in Heaven, according to the Apostle Paul, and his letters contain frequent admonitions concerning the conduct of the members while they wait to take up their full membership in the new life. Paul's concern with property and economic matters is therefore not spelled out in detail. There are general suggestions for individual and social conduct; "Each one must do as he had made up his mind, not reluctantly or under compulsion, for God loves a cheerful giver" (II Cor. 9 : 7). The political conditions of the time were hardly such as to warrant specific suggestions for economic reorganization.

Property and ownership were not a concern of the Apostle Paul for the simple reason that the ultimate concerns of man were for him always dominant. The latter could be seen in their proper relationship only when the primary concern of the individual was understood; that primary concern was Christ. "For me to live is Christ . . ." (Philip. 1 : 21). "The colonies of Heaven" which Paul visited and to which he wrote, were thus bound together by a common hope and a conviction of one common ultimate purpose. An act of sharing worldly goods among fellow believers was not an act of religious communism so much as an act of common faith inspired by mutual devotion. St. John could write, "But if anyone has the world's goods and sees his brother in need, yet closes his heart against him, how does God's love abide in him? Little children, let us not love in word or speech but in deed and in truth" (I John 3 : 17–18). Since the church was but an "earnest" of the final age, there was little point in challenging the present age.

With the passing of the disciples and the Apostle Paul from the active life of the early church congregations, the spiritual direction of these small but growing clusters of devotees of the new religion came from a group of individuals widely scattered geographically but united in the fellowship of the church and contributing to its emerging tradition. This group would include such figures as Clement of Alexandria, Origen, Cyprian, Ambrose, and Chrysostom. To this list of church fathers must be added the name of the one who influenced the life of the church most pronouncedly for a thousand years—Augustine, bishop of Hippo. With the emergence of the church as an institution there came a marked separation in the roles of church and state, particularly as they are reflected in relation to property. The world of the church and the world at large developed their own spheres of influence. The distinctiveness of the church required a separation in areas of authority but gave encouragement to the conviction that economic activity on behalf of the church merited a special place in the decisions and aspirations of its members. Clement of Alexandria argued, "What we are called on to surrender is not necessarily property as such, but excessive attachment to it; this is the danger of the wealthy but also of the poor—in fact, the anxious desire for what one lacks may be as soul-destroying as undue interest in what one has."[2] One outcome of the early church's attempt to find a solution to the difficult problem of economic life was the monastery. Here, under the aegis of the church, it was possible to govern all economic activities and to direct them toward the ends which were not as attainable in the world outside the church.

This partial answer served the church for more than a millennium. With numerous variations and deviations the principle behind the monastic society has found expression up to the present day.

The Middle Ages

There are many people in our own time who long for the reputed harmony and seemingly well-structured society which characterized the Middle Ages. It is believed that in the preindustrial era when life was administered by the church, the kinds of infraction which later came to disrupt society were unknown. If only we could get back, they say, to that well-ordered era, many of the tensions and competitive aspects of an industrial-technological society could be eliminated.

What were the distinctive features of economic life in the Middle Ages? The establishment of the church as integral and official in the life of the state by Emperor Constantine placed it in an ambiguous position. It was official and therefore had to represent the state, but at the same time it inherited the traditions and affirmations of the prophets, of Jesus, the first-century Christians, and the early church fathers. Augustine had provided a partial resolution of the church-state dilemma by confronting the church with its sacred objective to make the world into the City of God. Such an ideal could be held persistently only by a small group or a monastic order. The two levels of society had to be maintained side by side. A. T. Mollegen says: "Augustine achieved a catholic synthesis of sect and church outlooks by posting a higher order, the kingdom-life on earth, which has its highest expression in monastic asceticism where the counsels of perfection were obeyed; and a lower order of kingdom-life in general human society, that is, in the family, the city, the state and the world, expressed in the Christianization of natural life where the *precepts* were obeyed."[3] It was held that all of life had been created by God, but its purity had been corrupted by human sin. Since men, because of their sin, could not be counted on to conduct their relations in a manner consistent with the pure order God had intended, regulations had to be imposed. Private property, for example, though its protection is a responsibility of the state, is not sacrosanct, and its possession is dependent upon the use to which the property is put. "It is clear that St. Augustine regarded private property as being normally a creation, not of the divine, but of the positive law and as subject to the determination of the state, and limited by the degree of its utility."[4] All of this becomes more comprehensible when we recognize that possession did not have the same meaning in the Middle Ages as the modern use of the term implies. Personal and household goods could be regarded as property, but land was held under a tenure arrangement with the justification for its use dependent upon the degree of social obligation accepted by the manorial lord or overseer of the land.[5]

By the thirteenth century, Thomas Aquinas had introduced some refinements in the concept of ownership. For him there is a moral difference between the acquisition of property and its use. Under this theory an individual is justified in taking another man's possessions if he himself is starving, but it may not be designated as theft.[6] Such a theory of property finds expression even down to recent years, in the encyclicals of the late nineteenth- and early twentieth-century popes. They derive from an Aristotelian affirmation that "things should be held privately but should be public in their use."

When we refer to the economic life of the Middle Ages, we are not looking at a well-ordered system, even though it is operated under the combined aegis of a church and a state. As Tawney says, "All that we call the economic system was not a system but a mass of individual trades and individual dealings."[7] What gives uniqueness and distinction to the economic life of the Middle Ages, however, is the fact that "economic interests are subordinate to the real business of life which is salvation and that economic conduct is one aspect of personal conduct upon which, as on other parts of it, the rules of morality are binding."[8]

Lacking formal rules for determining the size of one's income or the ethics of his relationship to those with whom he had commerce, the individual could but be reminded of the consequences resulting from the sin of avarice and therefore was subject to condemnation by ecclesiastical authorities. Charging interest for the loan of money created a problem which taxed self-restraint, but ecclesiastical needs rendered less severe the condemnation of those who were actually or potentially benefactors of the church. Usury, i.e., taking money for the "use" of money, was prohibited, but the line between usury and interest donated to the church was difficult to establish. This remains one of the unresolved and contentious issues in the church's attempt to cope with emerging economic practices.

From the combined church-state domination of all life, wherever that relationship prevailed, there emerged another concept correspondingly difficult to define but representing an attempt to avoid the harshness and injustice of an unregulated economy—the "just price." Where this was exceeded, restitution must be made to society in the form of almsgiving. To guide the seller in the establishment of his price, public agencies were given authority to establish rates which would restrain the negotiator and conform more nearly to the social ideal. Where private conscience was an inadequate control, a collective appraisal was more effectual.

Through the monastic order the Middle Ages sought to build a church impelled to the creation of a city of God, the elimination of avarice, the sensitizing of conscience to care for the needy, and the establishment of regulations for commerce, and also the endowment of posterity with incentives for the application of religious norms in economic life. Though inadequate for the new type of life which was emerging, they were valuable as reminders of the ultimate ends toward which all life, including its economic aspects, is directed.

The Reformation

Great new forces were being unleased in the land, and such cohesiveness as the feudal system and the church could give was not sufficient to withstand them. The resultant of these forces is well known by all—expanding commerce, a money economy, discovery of new sources and markets, a rising merchant class with its allies, the bankers, and new colonial empires—all of these and many more elements rendered obsolete the economic structures which had prevailed in the Middle Ages. Concomitant with the economic changes and contributing to them was the intellectual reconstruction identified with the Renaissance. John Herman Randall, Jr. has commented that "if the roots of the new world of the Renaissance are to be sought in economic conditions, its justification and its means are to be found in the new spirit and knowledge that destroyed monasticism and Aristotelian science as capitalism was destroying feudalism and the guilds."[9] It was within this atmosphere that the Protestant Reformation emerged.

Max Weber, Ernst Troeltsch, Richard Tawney, and many others have made twentieth-century Christians sensitive to the fact that Protestantism was powerfully influential in reshaping medieval attitudes toward property and economics in general—in addition to the fact that the intellectual and economic forces were also contributing to the shaping of Protestantism. The two figures who have left their imprint on Protestant economic thought with such forcefulness that their interpretations still shape the convictions of contemporary Christians and non-Christians, are, of course, Martin Luther and John Calvin.

It is understandable that Luther, steeped in the experience of the medieval church, thought in terms of a church which encompassed the whole of society. Though he departed from the one all-inclusive church of his own experience, he did not disavow the authority of the church in areas of its rightful supremacy. Yet it was just on the issue of the rightful areas of the church's supremacy that he defied the church in whose service he had been a devoted monk. From the New Testament he learned the distinction between the church as a spiritual reality where men love each other because they are loved by God, and the requirements of the church as an institution. Yet love finds expression in all of life and is not divided between the life of the individual and the life of the church. The church, therefore, was not the final arbiter of the way in which man's love shall find expression; it, too, stood under the judgment of God. And when faith fails, it is God alone who grants forgiveness to a repentant individual and a repentant church.

Dependence of the individual conscience upon the church and

its claims being replaced by personal loyalty to God does not, however, make the individual autonomous and independent in his political life as well. The state has its own existence, and it is the duty of the Christian to serve as a Christian within its confines and under its obligations. He may defy that state only when it commands him to contravene the will of God as he discerns it. In his personal relationships and in the life of his church he thus acts from the motive of love and assumes that others do likewise. The state, being composed of fellow citizens similarly motivated, may be trusted.

All of this has profound implications for economic life. Both Calvin and Luther evolved a doctrine of vocation recognizing that the way a person engaged in his labors and disposed of his earnings constituted an index of the ultimate authority for his life. In Luther's view, man served in his work to give evidence of his faithfulness; for Calvin, man worked as an earnest of his conviction that the work he performed and the society of which he was a part reflected as best he knew how the intended order of God's creation. In the instances of both the reformers, man stood in a relationship of need for justification and under judgment in the totality of his life. Since man's economic life constituted so large a part of his existence, it was inescapable that its correlation with the divine purpose be examined.

These two systems led for centuries to varying interpretations of man's obligations to the economic order. Now with the fuller implications of the trends which were first observable in the destruction of feudalism becoming clear, the fundamental question to which the reformers sought an answer confronts us with new clarity. It has become increasingly apparent that the problems of property, of earning, of disposition of earnings, have implications for the totality of society and can no longer be regarded solely on an individual basis.

Love for one's neighbor and love for God are given expression in Luther's concept of vocation, *Beruf*. A man's calling, then, is the means whereby he participates in economic life and in response to God's claims upon him works in faithful obedience. The kind of work one does in his calling is not the primary consideration.

Formerly there prevailed a hierarchy of importance by which the spiritual quality of work was rated; now, presumably, any work one does as an obedient Christian is sanctified.

With the state freed from ecclesiastical control, it could proceed to set up its own ethical and economic norms. This created for the Christian a new set of complexities whose validity the church's demands did not clarify. Since the state had become the ultimate arbiter of economic life, the Christian was at a loss to know what God required of him. For the followers of Luther the resolution of the dilemma would lie primarily in the performance of their tasks as Christians, the decisions of the economic order being left to the state. Thus Lutheranism offered its adherents insufficient guidance for adapting to the type of economy coming into existence through the trade, manufacturing, and financing innovations which swept over the lands where the religious impact of Luther had been dominant.

Men turned to Calvin more than to any other theologian for an explanation of the release of the feudal mind from the restrictions of an ecclesiastically dictated economy. Calvin also stressed the ultimacy of a calling, but with marked differences from Luther's position. Calvin believed that man served God through his calling rather than simply in it, as Luther had contended. Serving God through one's calling makes it necessary for the individual to raise fundamental questions about the thing he is doing. A man's calling, for Calvin, was accepted and pursued with diligence as a means of qualifying for his "election" to salvation. He had no way of knowing whether he was one of the elect, but at least by vigorous pursuit of his calling he would be ready if it turned out that he were one of the elect. Such a condition impelled man to labor within society, but inevitably he was forced to raise the question whether his activity could truly be thought consistent with God's requirements for man and society. This was less of a problem for Luther, because men were saved individually by God's love even though the world around them remained evil. For the Calvinist the rectification of the evils of the world itself became an integral part of the fulfillment of his calling. As Paul Lehmann expresses it, "Vocational faithfulness was for Calvin a matter of working *against* (i.e., in anticipation of) the day of deliverance rather than working *until* the day of deliverance. When you are working *against* the day of deliverance you are more likely to work so hard as to find the material well-being the mark of piety; whereas if you are working *until* the day of deliverance you are more likely to find contentment with whatever favors have fallen to your lot as the surest clue to pious duty."[10]

All of this inspired the followers of Calvin to labor with vigor to create the kind of society which God had intended for man and which would in turn glorify God. Calvin sought to subject all forms of human activity to God's sovereignty and thus to re-establish a life world reflecting the society described in the Old Testament.

The new dynamic in this situation, the subjection of all forms of life to the sovereignty of God, lent itself to the new types of political and economic life which were beginning to find expression in the breakup of the feudal order. The norm by which the Christian is regulated, then, is not some dictate of an ecclesiastical organization but is rather his personal responsibility to the sovereign Lord of man and history. Individual obligation and self-examination, plus the counsel of one's peers, serve to keep in check the inordinate striving for wealth which might destroy the zeal to labor against the day of deliverance. The time was not far off, however, when the acquisition of goods could be regarded as one symbol of God's favorable attitude toward one who labored so zealously.

Unimpeded by restrictions imposed by church authorities, the seeker for deliverance could look with openness on the new patterns of economic life which were becoming available: the acceptance of profit, justification for interest on money loaned, the increased opportunities for private property, etc. This does not assume that Calvin approved high rates on loans, for in fact he laid it upon the heart of the lender to keep his demands within modest limits and according to conscience.

Along with the obligation to work diligently in a manner acceptable to a sovereign God, another key to Calvin's interpretation of Christian life in the economic realm is the idea of stewardship.

"We are not our own . . . we are God's: toward Him, therefore, as our only legitimate end, let every part of our lives be directed. There cannot be imagined a more certain rule or a more powerful exhortation to the observance of it than when we are taught that all blessings we enjoy are divine deposits committed to our trust on this condition that they should be dispensed for the benefit of our neighbors. Whatever God has conferred on us which enables us to assist our neighbors we are stewards of it and must one day render an account of our stewardship."[11] The very fact of possession is an indication of the Creator's benevolence. If one accepts all that is temporarily his as held in trust, he acts toward it in a different way than he would if he assumed it all to be solely his own. Here is the check on man's egoism and on his temptation to arrogance through the exploitation and exhibition of possessions. Likewise, if all possessions are held in stewardship, his neighbor has a partial claim upon them, and his act of generosity or consideration toward his neighbor becomes another evidence of his comprehension of the meaning of stewardship. In its political application, this could make possible regulatory activities causing the possessions held in the name of the state or under private stewardship to be allocated to the needs of others. By the same token the temptations to arrogance would be restricted in the name of the body politic and because of the mandate of stewardship.

Both Calvin and Luther maintained the conviction of the rightfulness of private property. Their difference from a more strictly interpreted capitalism would be: ". . . according to the Reformation, the right to use determines the right to possess; whereas the capitalist doctrine is that the right to possess determines the right to use. Rightly understood possession is an order to use and is not an order to possess."[12]

The full import of the Reformation is not embodied in the life and thought of Luther and Calvin. They do, however, represent the principal lines of conviction and the emerging trends. Economic life is thus held under judgment of a sovereign God who seeks that men shall love each other and live in harmonious community because they are children of one father. Earthly possessions are held not as solely private but under stewardship wherewith man serves his fellow men since all that he possesses has been entrusted to him; and through or in his vocation he attests his acknowledgment of God's benefactions to him, and he labors to be worthy if salvation should be granted to him. For those in the Lutheran tradition the political and economic orders of the state are presumably under the direction of men who love God, and therefore their actions will reflect this devotion. The inheritors of the Calvinist tradition are less trusting of man's propensity or capacity to live in loving relationship with his fellow men, and so they assume a greater responsibility for shaping the nature of the society in which man must live out his days.

England: Economics and the Reformation

The scientific discoveries of Newton along with the writings of Locke and Hume released a flood of scientific and intellectual curiosity in the seventeenth century which prepared the mind of the educated Englishman for the acceptance of innovations in economics, government, and religion. "Men saw in the world no more chaos, no more confusion, but an essentially rational and harmonious machine. This was an intoxicating discovery."[13] The Reformation and the Renaissance on the continent were bearing fruit in the lessening of limitations formerly placed by institutionalized religion on the human spirit. As individuals were released from the requirements based upon supernatural obligations, it became possible to develop the implications of scientific discoveries in the form of industrial life and the kind of economy which best accompanied it. Thus came about the industrialization which transformed a rural England into the foremost processing and manufacturing center of the world.

Three hundred years after the Protestant Reformation, with the Industrial Revolution in full force in England and increasingly in evidence on the continent, it became apparent to religious leaders that the benefactions of the new order were not wholly constructive. Under a combination of Lutheran, Calvinistic, and Arminian influences John Wesley brought to a disintegrating social life his passion for man's redemption. Industrial society had taken its toll of the spiritual vitality of the English people, and forces of violence were gathering. Wesley brought to this situation a reawakening to man's spiritual heritage and destiny, and set them over against the forces of secularization which in his judgment and that of many others were corrupting church and nation. Within the framework of his spiritual message he uttered the famous mandate "Gain all you can, save all you can, give all you can." It was a reaffirmation of the stewardship principle, plus an exhortation to the diligence by which acquisition and integrity could be used as witness to faith. This was no solution of the economic problem, but it fostered a new sense of responsibility within the then existing economic order.

Christian Socialism

Still another manifestation of protest against economic ills came almost a century later, with the Industrial Revolution now in full swing, in the development of Christian socialism. Since the beginning of the nineteenth century there has been a small but steady stream of activity on the part of persons who identified themselves as Christian socialists. Their purpose was to bring the Christian witness to bear upon and reform economic practices in general and upon the activities and programs of socialism in particular. Among the earliest of the religious leaders to adopt a Christian approach to socialist activity was a French Catholic priest, de Lamennais. For him a function of the church, in addition to its traditional religious role, was to be the heart and soul of economic life as well. In his primary concern for the workingman, he pleaded with the Roman hierarchy, including Popes Leo XII and Gregory XVI, to share his opposition to the stratified and crystalized economic system supported by the temporal leaders.

Best known of the Christian socialists in the Protestant tradition, however, were Frederick Denison Maurice, John M. Ludlow, and Charles Kingsley. Maurice and Kingsley were clergymen, Ludlow a lawyer. They all agreed that all of life derived from God's creation and beneficence, but that it had been distorted and partially defeated by human selfishness.[14] It is more than mere coincidence that the thinking of these men found expression at the same time that Marx and Engels wrote the *Communist Manifesto*. There were forces giving rise to many different kinds and degrees of socialism untempered by the restraining qualities which these three leaders and others associated with them felt were the contributions a Christian society should exhibit; only in this way could socialism be rescued from its tendency to reduce man to his lower instincts. Maurice wrote: "We are teaching true socialism, true liberty, brotherhood and equality—not the carnal dead-level equality of the Communist, but the spiritual equality of the church idea, which gives every man an equal chance of developing and rewards every man according to his work."[15] In their journal, *The Christian Socialist*, under Ludlow's editorship, it was contended that "socialism without Christianity on the one hand is lifeless as the feathers without the bird, however skillfully the stuffer may dress them up into an artificial semblance of life."[16]

The period of prominence for the Christian socialist movement as such, in England at least, was a brief one; it had come to an end by 1855. But in the meantime it had strongly influenced both clergy and laity, for whom the idea of a Christian society expressing itself in the economy of the times was substantially novel. Though the life of the movement was brief, a seed had been sown which produced innumerable outcroppings of the same purposes throughout the following century. Christian socialism was not restricted to England; similar expressions were formed in Germany, Austria, France, Belgium, and other countries.

The interest in Christian socialism in England found later expression in the Christian Socialist League, which incorporated participation by representatives from other denominations as well as from the Church of England. As part of its goal it states: "The League will work in close connection with the labor and socialist movements. It believes that the necessary transformation of our social order requires a change of heart and mind and will and a corresponding change of political and industrial arrangements; substituting mutual service for exploitation and a social democracy for the struggle of individuals and classes."[17]

Though there are few definite recorded consequences of the interest in Christian socialism in England, it is generally felt that it gave substantial impetus to the cooperative movement as an economic expression of Christian concern. Toyohiko Kagawa could insist, on one of his visits to the United States, that the cooperative movement was the kingdom of God in action and must therefore merit the full-fledged support of Christians. Christian socialism sensitized the Christian conscience of the community, especially of those who were not themselves members of the underprivileged class. This characteristic may in some measure be responsible for the brevity of the movement's life. It was never able to come to grips with the deeper problems of those constituting the "lower" class. Its closest approximation to the working economics of the latter was its support of the cooperative movement to which many of them had turned.

For reasons worth exploring, there has never been a strong Christian socialist movement in the United States. Though there have been organizations incorporating the name "Christian" and "socialist" and containing some powerful intellectual and religious leaders, they have been few and for the most part without great influence. Possibly the closest approximation in America to the Christian socialist movement in England has been what is commonly designated the Social Gospel movement, a few of whose leaders eagerly welcomed the designation "Christian socialist" while others carefully avoided that title.

The Social Gospel

America's most distinctive contribution to the relation of religion to economics comes from what has been very broadly designated as "the Social Gospel." The Social Gospel involves no clear-cut theological or belief system. It takes its name from the conviction that an individualistic religion preoccupied with personal salvation to the neglect of any implications for society was leaving untouched the forces which were shaping the lives of people in an industrializing culture. As America changed from a rural to an urban nation, from agriculture to industry as the dominant element in the economy, it became apparent that the concentration of power in financial and industrial centers and the concentration of people in the cities created problems of justice, equitable distribution of goods, and other problems resulting from people's living in greater propinquity and dependence upon regularity of employment and an adequate living base. Irregular and inadequate income brought deprivations for which charity resources were inadequate, and suffering was widespread. The result for many was disintegration of life and a measure of hardship destructive of both health and morale.

A great host of religious leaders, representing many denominations and many sections of the nation, were convinced that these conditions were inconsistent with the ideals of Jesus' life and message and were making difficult the presentation of the Christian gospel. There followed an intensive study of the Hebrew prophets, the life and teachings of Jesus, and of current social conditions. The latter study sent many ministers into the field of sociology. Another factor intensifying the social concern on the part of ministers was the development of a scientific study of biblical sources and of the conditions prevailing at the time when biblical materials were in preparation. A correlation between the social concerns of the Hebrew prophets and of Jesus served to deepen the sense of responsibility for the then current situation in the United States. One of the consequences of this interest was the staffing with clergymen of several newly formed departments of sociology in colleges and universities. In addition the new sociological concern and the new-found relation between the life and teachings of Jesus and the prophets on one hand and the current economic situation on the other stirred a number of economists to bring their talents and skills to bear upon the situation. The result of this total combination was an impetus to the social sciences and an attempt to use these new disciplines for the alleviation of suffering and maladjustment in society at large.

Prominent among the leaders of the Social Gospel movement were George F. Peabody, Washington Gladden, George D. Herron, and—best known as the intellectual and spiritual leader of the entire movement—Walter Rauschenbusch. The writings of the latter are by far the most widely known among the clergy and theological students of that period and of a generation thereafter. It is likely that he influenced more ministers in his time than any other contemporary theologian. Many of the major seminaries affiliated with universities became strongly committed to the underlying purposes of the Social Gospel movement. Close association with departments of economics, sociology, and related social sciences stimulated the intellectual pursuit of the causes and conditions of social degradation and deprivation.

Few of the adherents of this undefined but nevertheless evident movement identified themselves with political socialism or even with an American version of English Christian socialism. The same reasons that deterred Walter Rauschenbusch from identifying himself with political socialism served as a deterrent to many others. He believed that political and economic socialism failed to take account of the spiritual factors which ultimately must shape human purposes and directions, and he himself never lost sight of the fact that man's ultimate end was not economic but spiritual.

What is said to be the most widely published book in history with the exception of the Bible is a product of Christian concern with economic issues, emerging in the era of the Social Gospel's greatest strength. It is Charles M. Sheldon's *In His Steps*, which is based upon a set of imaginary responses to the command to live like Jesus in our time. The story is a series of incidents relating to the way in which people—a newspaper man, a railroad man, a singer, and others—fulfilled their understanding of this commandment in their respective types of work. Whether they would designate this self-consciously as their Christian vocation is doubtful; neither the theology of Luther nor that of Calvin, at least in its vocational emphasis, was widely familiar at the time. Nevertheless, consciously or unconsciously this was a manifestation of the Christian doctrine of vocation. That the book had a profound effect is attested by the widespread attempt to live in this same fashion by thousands of others who undertook similar experiments.

Much more significant as a product of the Social Gospel is the development of support for the labor movement and for attempts to secure justice for agriculture and to alleviate misery through social service activities and political action. Not least among its accomplishments was the incentive to collective activity on the part of certain denominations when it became apparent that the economic forces determining many of the conditions in American life were too powerful to be met by single denominations. An indirect consequence was the formation of the Federal Council of Churches, and a direct consequence was the establishment of a working relationship between religion and labor within the Federal Council of Churches. This movement led to the Department of Church and Economic Life of the present National Council of Churches, and coincidentally to the series on Ethics and Economic Life of which this volume is a part. More will be said of the activities of this department in later chapters.

By the time of the first World War it was becoming apparent that the broad and multifarious concerns and points of view incorporated in the Social Gospel were inadequate to offset the forces which were shaping and disturbing the life of the time. The roots of change lay much deeper, and the Social Gospel was unable to cope with so profound and far-reaching a debacle as the Great Depression. Some of its leaders may have been naïve enough to expect that devotion to Jesus and his principles would suffice to rectify economic injustice; others were not so sanguine. They realized also that the root of the economic problem lay much deeper than anything which could be remedied by good will and the application of the love ethic as it was currently understood. Instead, the great contribution of the Social Gospel was its quickening of human sensitivity to injustice and its use of new resources both from sociology and theology in the attempt to understand the social and especially the economic life of the nation in which the Social Gospel found its warmest reception. Prominent in its concerns was the question of war and its hostility to all that war involved. For some of its adherents this meant fostering the development of a militant pacifism. The assumption was that war was a force which could be dealt with by itself. The infinitely more complex aspects of war—its psychological, theological, as well as economic components—had not been sufficiently explicated or comprehended. These factors will be considered in further discussions in this volume.

2

Industrialism as Our Culture

> Many of the members were left with the impression as voiced by one of them, that modern industrial society is radically reshaping human personality and life in directions opposite to that transformation intended by the Gospel, and that consequently most of our mission program ad methods appear to be utterly theoretical and irrelevant. This realization makes us humble and penitent and it moves us to a searching re-valuation of the aims and methods of the mission now employed in the ministry of reconciliation in Jesus Christ which God has committed unto us.[1]

The bewilderment and anxiety thus expressed in a world missions seminar reveals the apprehension and confusion on the part of many others besides world mission exponents over the extension of the industrializing process. For good or ill, industrialization is the dominant phenomenon of our era, as it has been for more than a century.

In the preceding chapter Christian socialism and the Social Gospel were portrayed as attempts of religiously sensitive people to provide remedies for the hardships and inequities caused by the emerging industrial society. It was not apparent to most of those seeking resolution of the social disharmonies and injuries to human life created by its emergence that the real problem lay in the industrialization process itself. As was described in that chapter, economists, sociologists, and clergymen sought to remedy the evil consequences through pressure for humanitarian measures and an appeal to religious sanctions for a more just consideration for one's neighbor. It had not yet become apparent that growing technological competence and the very expansion of education, both technical and humanistic, were themselves giving an impetus to an industrializing phenomenon from which there was apparently no retreat. It is no wonder that entire religious organizations and diversely stationed individuals looked longingly to the "holistic" society which was reputed to have existed under the medieval synthesis. In fact, however, it became increasingly apparent that the gains in education and science and the transformation in ways of living, enjoyed by beneficiaries of the technological-industrial era, were not going to be relinquished but instead increased and accelerated. Efforts of humanitarian leaders to rectify the abuses of the all-engulfing industrial system were directed toward the evils causing blighted lives and loss of personal freedom. Many of the specific evils could be remedied, and were, through the formation of the labor movement, whose historic trilogy, "wages, hours, and working conditions," became the battle cry for the war to eliminate the sordid and injurious conditions under which many persons were required to work. Interestingly, a century later the same objectives exist, but with varying emphasis, as will be indicated subsequently. With the sweat shop and the other labor conditions leading to human disintegration all but eliminated in modern industrial life, however, the industrializing process itself continues with increasing acceleration. Many of its injurious aspects have been eliminated, at least in the more advanced nations, but new and unforeseen consequences have take their place.

Under industrialization and its economy we have moved almost overnight from a condition of scarcity to one of abundance and surplus in the advanced nations. All of this has placed us in a climate for which previous economic systems, philosophies, and religious formulations have not been prepared. We have not been without seers and prophets, but a world which has lived in an economy of scarcity cannot quickly adjust its thinking to a basis so radically new. It is therefore not surprising that religious institutions and their leaders could not visualize the type of society which industrialization has created. In the total span of the life of mankind only the last few minutes, figuratively speaking, represent the industrial era as contrasted with the agricultural era.

Industrialism's Nature and Requirements

Possibly industrialism began with the use of the lever and the wheel, but this is an historical question we need not debate. Suffice it to say that wherever the benefits resulting from labor saving and new forms of energy have been appropriated, industrialism has been fostered. Industrialization involves the full utilization of the resources of science to make any products which people can or will use. It means the willingness to explore every possibility for production and then in turn to find or create a market for acceptance of its products. Science inevitably leads those engaged in industry to find all possible means for the utilization of new and potentially less expensive forms of energy to replace manpower and outmoded mechanical devices. Industrialism makes use of manpower, of course, but only to the extent that machines cannot perform the functions now or at any time undertaken. It means capital for the development of new instruments and for the marketing of the products and research for the finding of new means of creating and distributing. More will be said later of its characteristics and consequences. In short, it means the use of every available means for creating products and meeting needs in so far as available scientific resources make this possible. The manipulation and direction of human energy is integral to industrialization. Management of those who are responsible for the oversight and operation of machines is indispenable to the total system; the respective and interrelated roles of management and labor result.

Ramifications of this phenomenon lead into the problems of urbanization and larger collectivities of people within reach of the place of work.

The evolution of the various means of production from the lever and the wheel to nuclear fission has been too well documented to need amplification here. What have not been so well portrayed are the consequent beliefs and attitudes resulting from this transition. For modern man the most significant development in the use of new energies is the industrial system itself with its organization of production and distribution, the social life emerging around that process, and the cities and even small communities whose life and thought have been shaped by all that underlies and finds expression in industrialism. If there is one phenomenon that stands out more clearly than any other in modern times, it is the fact that personal, national, and international life are being dominated by the concept of industrialism, and are in a large measure the achievement of industrialization. Some have called this urbanization, and we are witnessing a major attack on the consequences of urban living. But behind urbanization lies the development of technology and the industrial-economic thought pattern which creates it.

Though Karl Marx understood the fact that a revolution in thought processes and the organization of society was taking place because of the growth of industrialism, he erred in assuming that freedom could somehow be channeled to support a set of values for the kind of society which was being produced. He did not understand that if the resources of technology were to be fully utilized, they must be permitted development and application wherever, whenever, and in whatever way their discoverers performed their tasks. Now after forty years of experimentation with a system which, if it is to be effective, cannot be thus curtailed, the USSR has had to grant permission for collaboration and cooperation in free research with those who represent a diametrically opposite type of political system. Freedom in scientific research cannot be hampered without destruction or deterioration of the industrial process, and the success of the Soviet experiment hinges on its superiority in the development of technology and industry.

The enterprise-capitalism system, which evolved with industrialism and was founded on the premises of freedom and the rights of individuals to explore and express themselves as they wish, finds itself in a similar dilemma. In addition to realizing that the research of its scientists must go on in cooperation with those of a rival political system which it disavows, the capitalistic system has had to face the fact that the range and scope of scientific discovery and technological development is greater than can be contained in the backroom laboratories of individual scientists. The day of making scientific observations from the falling apple or a set of test tubes and beakers may not be wholly past, but the vast network of interrelated team research, 85 per cent supported by the Federal government, attests what has occurred. If the process of industrialization is to expand—and it is—it is dependent upon research so vast in scope that only the taxpayers' money and unified authorization by a national government can make it possible, objectors notwithstanding. The result of all this is that in the forty years since the Russian Revolution of 1918 the inexorable forward movement of industrialization has forced a modification of some of the fundamental tenets of that revolution, and on the capitalistic side has forced a corresponding modification in a direction contrary to some of its fundamental tenets. "In our times it is no longer the specter of communism which is haunting Europe, but rather, emerging industrialization in many forms that is confronting the whole world. The giant of industrialization is stalking the earth, transforming almost all the features of older and traditional societies."[2]

Marx saw capitalism as the demon restraining man's attainment of his full potential, and so he insisted that the class struggle was responsible for the impairment of human opportunities. The problem was one of property ownership and the control of one life by another or many lives by one. What he could not foresee was that under a system of free access to ideas, including the ideas by which technology is advanced, human beings may not be enslaved but may actually be made freer of drudgery and have freer access to the products of industrial technology. He was not sufficiently aware of human psychology or of the nature of man, as it is understood in the West at least, to believe that human rights would ever transcend property rights. The irony of all this, of course, is that the system which Marx espoused, though it has given impetus to the most rapid industrial development in any country in history, has, in contrast to the system he denounced, precluded opportunities for the expression of freedom and the achievement of fuller human potential. Even with the rapid increase in communication in our time it may be another generation before both sides of this ideological argument can be freed sufficiently from the pseudo fears and the false convictions built up by each system, and both recognize that if industrialism is to be maintained, it will be only after both ideologies have given up the luxury of their obsessions.

Psychologists and sociologists long ago discovered that the transition from a rural to an urban society involves more than adopting technology and its skills. It involves a traumatic experience and a major revolution in cultural outlook. A family accustomed to cooperative work arrangements and a common schedule with a recognized hierarchical structure can no longer be maintained. The family in urban society, as we have now come to recognize painfully, is a very different social unit from that which prevailed in the rural setting. But almost as profound is the change in outlook on life for those who remain in agriculture, at least in the highly commercialized type of agricultural life. Primary attention is focused on the markets and the use of laborsaving, cost-cutting machinery. In industrialized nations the rapid decline in the numbers engaged in agriculture indicates the measure of that nation's industrialization.

While this volume was in preparation, large-scale campaigns were being waged to convince both young and old that new skills will be required to meet with the ever-changing needs of industrial society; this means education of a type and to a degree not heretofore attained. High premium is increasingly being placed upon ability to read instructions and to make calculations. All of this requires more education.

Free public education has become the great leveler and the instrument for upward mobility. Without universal education the industrialization process is hamstrung; separate industries are imperiled, and the total life of the industrialized nation is restrained. National policy cannot permit these restrictions on its development; and so government enters the picture with increasing vigor to force a wider availability of education and an intensification of training in industrial skills. In the process traditional class structures are undermined. So irresistible is the demand for industrialization that even traditional societies, steeped in religiously dictated class structures, eventually yield. The alternative is extinction.

"The industrial society," Clark Kerr and his co-authors contend, "is an open community, encouraging occupational and geographical mobility and social mobility. In this sense, industrialism must be flexible and competitive; it is against tradition and status based upon family, class, religion, race or caste."[3] If the society is to remain competitive and if the individual is to be mobile, he must possess the facility to adapt himself to varieties of situations. The new complex of forces, with the realignment of labor-management relations, necessitates the entrance of government into the field as the initiator and the preserver of actions designed to protect "the public" as well as to guarantee justice for the participants in industrial conflicts. Special attention will be given to the increasing role of government in industrial society. Suffice it for the moment to suggest that all the changes indicated above involve a measure of governmental participation, far greater than anything at least some parts of the free society have heretofore known.

Some Consequences of Industrialization

In another inaccurate projection into the future Marx, unable to foresee the fuller consequences of industrialization, misjudged the future role of classes. Not only did he fail to credit the elements of human equality and justice which would reduce the crystalization of the classes, but he could not foresee the heightened demands for skilled workers and the education which would support the possibilities for their development. Widespread general education and technical competence would increase the importance of the worker and render him indispensable to the processes of production, where the line between owners and workers would become less distinct as each became increasingly dependent upon the other.

The result is that religious sanctions go by the board. This is the meaning of India's eagerness to press for new steel mills, electronics factories, and all the other symbols of an industrializing nation. Under this pressure there is no place for caste and class systems, whose justification is the traditional religious life and whose stronghold is the small rural communities which have harbored the traditional systems. "Similarily, the Muslim religion has not interfered with the industrial development of banking, trading, or commercial and industrial institutions in Egypt. Traditionalist religious values do not seem to have been as serious an obstacle to economic thought in the long run as some anthropologists have thought."[4]

The obliteration of class sanctions is not the only result of the industrialization process. Community government, the type of education required, physical factors such as highways and shopping centers, the concomitant shift in purchasing times which keeps stores open nights and Sundays—all these things have wrought changes in the thinking of people who occupied the same communities in what were less revolutionary times. Small and seemingly quiet rural communities have become, in many instances in less than five years, booming industrial towns with the advent of one or more new factories. In days prior to the availability of rapid transportation the advent of industrialization in a single community brought a concentration of people in types of residence throwing together large numbers heretofore unacquainted with and unprepared for communal living. Practically every great metropolitan center has been the victim of this process, most notably in England and in the older cities of the United States. There are very few large communities which have come into existence since the achievement of rapid transit and the automobile; Los Angeles, of course, is the major exception. Its problem, however, is compounded by the desirability of establishing new industries, both because of seemingly felicitous climatic conditions and because of a market prepared by those who had moved into that area in such large numbers for purposes of retirement, recreation, or some specialized form of productivity.

The new conditions of living which confronted migrants from more stable and established backgrounds, whether in the rural or urban life of Europe or from the rural hinterlands of the United States, have been expressed in the discomfiture and anguish of those whose roots had been torn up before new ones could be established. Families which moved to a new and industrializing country did so with their own roots deep in the "stem-type" family, the great family where care was assured and where age was respected. For many who moved to the United States in the period of its greatest influx of immigrants the stem-type family could still be held in esteem and respect, so long as the family, whether with all generations or a single generation, worked on the land. It was not until a later period, when the land could no longer support the diverse generations, that the ones who were forced to move to the city found themselves creating a nuclear family in which individual effort counted rather than the teamwork of the agricultural background. Meanwhile, the immigrant to the city, though attempting to maintain roots in the stem-type family, found even more quickly that the nuclear family was the only type which could maintain itself in urban and industrial life. In each case, the religious backgrounds represented were based on the life of the family and that of the total community, often with major emphasis on the life of a single parish. A common background of work made possible a genuine community of interests, but unless all the members of the now nuclear family were related to a single plant to which their destinies were tied, there was little sense of community. Added to this is the fact that the type of work done in plant and the new social arrangements based upon skill rather than familial or hierarchical status further served to fracture the homogeneity of social life. Religious sanctions based upon the class structure and the family system of a rural or common community background in the Old World could no longer be maintained. The work ethic and its production demand have created new alignments of class, and the controls once so commonly accepted no longer have meaning. Recreation, long tied to the rural pattern of life and the sanctity of the seventh day of rest observed in rural society, placed its stamp temporarily on the industrial portion of the nation's life. Finally, however, either pressures of work made laboring on the Sabbath necessary, or the longer weekend and a means of faster travel gave incentive to foresake the familiar places of worship on the traditional day. Industrialization has thus brought about a large-scale revolution in the traditional observances of religion and in the instruments which have historically served to reinforce religious objectives.

A dilemma fraught with both philosophical and economic factors in the advancement of industrialization is the problem of labor surpluses. Through all human history until recent times the production of food and the cultivation of land have taken all the available manpower. Few facts are better known in the leading industrial nations than those which contrast the numbers employed in agriculture and required to feed persons not specifically engaged in work on the land with the small number now required to feed a much larger population occupied in industrial activities. At present no viable large-scale options for utilizing the mounting surplus of labor have appeared, except in programs of public works and the increase of service activities. The problem for our times is high-lighted by the widespread concern for the high school dropout, for those released from the trades or skills by which they formerly earned a living and which have been since eliminated, and for those adults and young adults for whom unskilled manual labor is simply unavailable. All of this is further complicated by the failure of birth rates to decline appreciably in industrialized nations and the actual increase in population through improved health and the decline of infant mortality in the nations now anxiously seeking to industrialize. These are the nations which W. W. Rostow describes as being in the traditional or take-off stages.[5]

Welfare's New Importance

Industrialization and welfare economics are coordinate phenomena. Partly for reasons indicated above and partly for reasons inherent in the industrializing process itself the welfare aspects of industrial society have to match the progress of industrialization. A fuller treatment of this theme will appear later, but here it must be indicated as an integral aspect of industrial society. The growth of the profession of social worker parallels the growth of the professions of scientist, technologist, and industrial manager. In turn the political scientist and the politician are called upon to convince the individuals and forces fostering industrialization that a substantial portion of their earnings must be used to provide for the temporarily unusable member of the labor force or those who are rejected because of the advances in technology. The politician may not understand the reasons for the close relation between industrialization and welfare, but he is caught between the managers and those responsible for the financial welfare of industry, and the ever-increasing numbers for whom at least a minimum living standard must be provided and who in addition possess voting strength.

Debate as to whether people are assuming sufficient responsibility for their own well-being or are taking advantage of the welfare programs as a form of escape from the exercise of initiative, will go on endlessly so long as individuals are differently constituted. The number of the dishonest or the shiftless may in the aggregate appear large, but the evidence points to the fact that there are many more who would like to take responsibility for their own well-being, particularly at the point of finding work.

From the standpoint of health services still another factor enters. It is the provision of health resources, which Peter Drucker has discussed in various writings.[6] The organization of these resources—the modern hospital in particular—has adopted the techniques and philosophy of the industrializing process. Though techniques for diagnosis and restoration of health have been inexpressibly improved, they have also involved commensurate costs. These in turn have made maintenance and restoration of health beyond the personal financial resources of a great many people. One consequence has been the burgeoning of insurance plans, such as Blue Cross and Blue Shield, to spread the costs more equitably. Industries have protected themselves against losses in time and costs by providing as a "fringe benefit" various types of health insurance. To all this are added, of course, welfare benefits provided through taxes, especially in terms of medical services made available at minimal cost for the indigent. But topping all others and symbolic of the welfare requirements both created and made possible by industrialization, has been the vast social security enterprise of national governments. We have come to take for granted, though not without a struggle, that a society which rests on an industrial basis must include in its costs the casualties which are incident to it. Transition from dependence upon the great family to dependence upon the great society with its great government and the great semipublic agencies for health and economic undergirding is a phenomenon less than a century old.

Specialization of Skills

Running like a thread through all the manifestations of the advance of industrialism is the role of the innovator and the expert. Mass movements cannot decide the direction of industrialism, hence the decline of ideologies. The internal rationale of industrialism lies in the advancement of technical knowledge and the means for adapting it to the needs and capacities of the individuals affected. Mass movements may call attention to inequities and violations of human well-being, but they cannot formulate the technical structures required to produce the devices for reducing labor or increasing production. These are the products of individuals or groups technically competent to foster such developments. Here is a dilemma in which the labor movement has increasingly found itself. Its more astute leaders have equipped themselves to meet the technical competence of industrial managers or have provided a philosophical counterbalance to the objectives and directions which management has pursued. In the industrializing process it has been necessary for labor organizations to develop persons competent to cope with the technological advances of their respective industries. Mere protest is obviously no longer sufficient, and significantly in the major industrialized nations labor groups, recognizing the futility of opposing scientific developments, have become increasingly cooperative with the advances of the industry itself.

Another way of saying all this is to recognize that the role of the technically qualified manager has become the primary role in industrialization. This does not mean that he is solely concerned with the sciences of physics, chemistry, and mathematics, etc. A science of adapting individuals to suitable work or changes in work and the investigation of work qualification has been evolving. All of this is of a piece with the total managerial role. This has meant specialization, with the highest rank going to those who know how to appropriate the talents of other specialists and coordinate clusters of specialists toward the advancement of the industry or organization. Related to the specialization within industries and between industries is the task of evaluating the total potential of a department or a product and making the allocation or withdrawal of financial support. Specialization in the management of money relative to the industrial development is a coordinate function of industrialization.

Included in the general catalog of consequences of industrialization are also suggestions of the continuing requirements made mandatory in an industrializing economy. Among them is the new type of leadership, which Kerr et al. designate as the elites, the individuals who singly and collectively foster the advancement of industrialization, who are thus both a consequence and an ever-expanding requirement of the process. As Kerr points out, however, the problem is not whether elites will emerge; that is a foregone conclusion. The real question is which one will come to dominate the life of a given nation. Different types of societies will be dominated by different types of elites. They are designated as (1) the dynastic elite, (2) the middle class, (3) the revolutionary intellectuals, (4) the colonial administrators, (5) the nationalistic leaders.[7] From these vividly descriptive titles one can readily surmise the roles they perform and the sources from which they emerge.

Still another consequence and requirement is the type of personality at home in the industrialized culture. Max Weber has been vigorously attacked but possibly even more vigorously supported in his thesis that Protestantism rendered its adherents more comfortable than Catholicism in the capitalist-industrial evolution. The fact that industrialization has proceeded furthest in the nations which departed earliest from the strictures and controls of a hierarchically dominated religion has been viewed by some as the justification for Weber's contention. Others have attributed the disposition toward industrialization and the economy which accompanied it to climate, diet, and other correlated factors. Yet one social analyst, Gerhard Lenski, has contended that even now the residual influences of an authoritarian religion serve to restrict the ambitions of its people to a greater degree than is the case with those who are inheritors of the Protestant tradition.[8] Whether the findings of his study can be universally applied is open to question, but at least the data he acquired in Detroit, one of the most industrial of all cities, seem to bear out the Weber thesis. Another study conducted in an industrializing rural area reveals the fact that among those who have lived a generation or more in this region there remain no appreciable differences in ideologies or social attitudes relative to issues which have been markedly affected by industrialization, e.g., welfare, approval of labor organizations, and international relations, etc.[9] A common technology and its concomitant patterns of living make for uniformity of ideas, whatever the variation in work incentives.

Emotional Adaptations

We are not adequately fortified with records of mental ailments during the medieval period, and thus we cannot assume that the high incidence of mental breakdown characteristic of the industrial society is actually any greater than that which prevailed in a simpler and more cohesive economic and social existence. We do know that as the profession of the social worker has mounted in importance with the increase of industrialization, so has the importance of the psychologist and psychiatrist. It would seem that psychological security and a sense of what is of ultimate importance have declined with the advance of technology and the independence of man from the religious cohesiveness he knew in another era. The result is a new type of person, more insistent upon experiencing the full limits of existence within the type of life which unlimited productivity and its satisfaction of wants is attempting to provide.

Opponents of industrialism and those who long for the simpler society have pointed to its evil consequences and gloried in the more wholesome order of an earlier day. In answer to this a United Nations study suggests that industrialism may appear to breed wretched working conditions, starvation wages, child labor, broken families, overcrowding, filth and sordidness in slums, delinquency and corruption of youth. But these agonies are not a necessary consequence of industrialization; they may simply represent evils of poverty and overcrowding that are independent of industrial growth; they represent a rapid transfer of rural misery to an urban setting where it is more conspicuous. What is needed in such cases, the UN study observes, is not less but more industrialization.[10]

The patterns of living required by industrialization have exacted their toll in the readjustment of human relationships, but they have also brought a measure of freedom from drudgery which modern man prefers to the reputedly well-ordered life of another era with all of its discomforts. The disruption of his security, his being cut loose from long-established mores and customs, have created a new frontier for religion.

There is strong agreement concerning one consequence of industrialization and the culture which it has created. This is that disintegration of the homogeneous community, the almost complete elimination of the stem type family and corresponding threat to the nuclear family, and the disappearance of unchallenged religious authority, have caused participants to ask fundamental questions about themselves: What is my ultimate destiny? By what regulations, if any, shall my existence be governed? Is the objective of my work deserving of the full expenditure of my energy? These are modern versions of the question which emerged in the Reformation, asked by Luther, Calvin, and many others: What is my calling? Thus to enable people to find meaning for their lives in a type of society which is increasingly able to provide their physical comforts, the proponent of religion has asked more fundamental questions than he as industrialized man has thus far been able to answer. Many of these questions have to do with the quality of interpersonal life which is possible in the new era, the obligation one may have to work in the interest of his neighbor, whether he be in the same production plant or in another hemisphere. In the same vein he is forced to ask whether the destitution and deteriorated lives of even a small percentage of people in industrialized nations, in addition to the very large percentage of those in lands undeveloped industrially, can be justified.

Industrialization and the economy which accompanies it are as much a part of twentieth-century man as breathing. The changes they have produced in cultural patterns of work and leisure and the life style of those dependent on them have effected profound modifications in attitudes, beliefs, and aspirations. It is in industrialized society where religious attitudes, beliefs, and aspirations must also find expression. If they are relevant, there results a harmony of man and his world; if not, either the beliefs or the economic practices must be relinquished. The fundamental issue is thus the relevance of faith to the economic life of industrial man.

3

Issues Challenging Industrialism

It is a basic assumption of this capstone volume in the Series on Ethics and Economics of Society that industrialism shapes our culture but that it now confronts some profound problems. There are those who contend that automation, instead of freeing society from wide discrepancies in income, for example, will actually accentuate these differences and begin a return to the type of differences in wealth prevailing in the Middle Ages. Despite fears that increasing concentration of ownership and control may lead to a reversal of the trend of the past century which gave the widespread benefits from increasing technology, this reversal seems unlikely. Nevertheless, in the processes of humanization fostered by our almost universal education, a free press, and rational control of communication instruments, many in our society have become convinced that unless the economy which undergirds our industrial and business order can provide adequately for people, it must be modified.

Until now the increase of real income for workers has proved Marx wrong, i.e., that their position would deteriorate. There are some who believe that the accelerated use of laborsaving devices and the necessary concentration of ownership of these instruments may well reverse the trend. Hitherto it has been beneficial to both owner-manager and worker to make certain that the fruits of industrialism be widespread. It is no foregone conclusion today, however, either that the benefits of automation will or that they will not be widely spread; neither is it inevitable that the humanitarian concern of the Hebrew-Christian tradition, that all human systems allow man to fulfill his ultimate destiny as a creature of God, will be realized.

The suggestion that some other pattern of socioeconomic arrangement might come into being is not made with intention to disturb, but rather to take account of the fact that there is no guarantee that the present formulas and generally accepted philosophy of economic structures will prevail. Nor should there be. To insist upon such a guarantee would involve us in the establishment of a legal framework and a set of regulations too complex to administer.

Our economic system is undergoing constant modification. At stake is the issue of the direction being taken and the objectives of those most responsible for that direction. Obviously lines of least resistance or short-term goals cannot provide adequate justification. Inherent in this volume and all the others in the series is a conviction that the purposes and goals delineated for man in the Hebrew-Christian heritage constitute the desired objective of our economy. We think it imperative, therefore, that modern man come to know the essentials of that heritage.

Industrialism will always have unfinished business if it is allowed to develop. It cannot be rigidly structured, for its very essence is unrestricted recourse to change in whatever direction new developments and discoveries may dictate. As vast programs of research go forward, however, there are warning signs pointing to immediate, unfinished business, neglect of which could injure if not kill the advances of industrial life.

Unemployment

One sign suggested in the preceding chapter is the increasing ratio of the unemployed and the (under present conditions) unemployable to the number actually employed. A volume of unemployment in excess of 5 per cent of the available working population may not be statistically alarming to some people, but in those numbers are persons who cannot be readily retrained for other kinds of work and who are potentially permanent relief recipients.* There are school dropouts who fall steadily behind the procession (we shall discuss them in greater detail below), and the aged, of course, for whom little or no employment is likely, and the large number, both white- and blue-collar, for whom some kind of adequate retraining program has not been found. And compounding all these issues is the fact that despite the increase of educational opportunities for the rest of the nation, a group that comprises more than 10 per cent of the total population, the nonwhite, is steadily falling further behind in the ability to make a useful contribution to the total economy. Here the principal handicap is not inherent in the persons concerned; it is simply the handicap of color. Though the civil rights law of 1964 will hopefully go a long way toward making job opportunities accessible to this large segment of the population, the necessity for beginning at such low levels due to heavy educational limitations and correspondingly limited accomplishment places a majority of those included in this 10 per cent of the population under an oppressive and frightening handicap.

The Dropout

The term "dropout" (from school) has become a symbol of our unemployment dilemma. Though it is not an economic problem by itself, it is integral to the ability of our industrial economy to provide employment or to make provision for all who need it. The dropout is so distinctive a type that special comment concerning him is in order. One-fourth of all the unemployed in America are teen agers. In 1962 the number of jobless teen-age boys averaged 472,000, and the number increased in 1963 and again in 1964 by more than 100,000. The tragedy lies not simply in their present state of unemployment but in the fact that the dropout is making a move that will affect all the years of his active life. Of youth 14 to 24 years of age (1962) out of 14,772,000 not in school, 1,212,000 were both out of school and out of work; and

* In this number, too, are those unemployed for short periods and the "hard core" of unemployables, i.e., those physically or mentally incapable of employment.

of these, 338,000 were described as "not even looking." In every category the per cent for nonwhites is higher than for whites. And as might be inferred from previous figures, the dropouts constitute a steadily decreasing percentage of the work force. In 1940 the number of dropouts was 68 per cent, in 1962 only 46 per cent of the active work force. Every indication points to a continuing decline in the percentages. As is true for the economy as a whole, low-skilled jobs are drying up.[1]

There are no simple solutions or easy adjustments which would accommodate these young people in the work force. Some see this problem as "structural." Basically it is a question of how the nation's resources available for production are allocated. For example, it has been pointed out that 2.7 billion dollars spent in producing the TFX airplane would finance the creation of something like three hundred thousand jobs; the same amount spent on urban renewal would create three million jobs.[2] Behind the decision to allocate is the question whether a concern with defense shall have priority over the elemental needs of the population. This is more than an economic question in the strictly technical sense, since it involves us in a problem of human values.

Poverty

On March 16, 1964 President Johnson said in a message to Congress:

We are citizens of the richest and most fortunate nation in the history of the world . . . the path forward has not been an easy one. There are millions of Americans . . . one-fifth of our people . . . who have not shared in the abundance which has been granted to most of us and on whom the gates of opportunity have been closed. . . . The war on poverty is not a struggle simply to support people, to make them dependent on the generosity of others. It is a struggle to give people a chance. . . . Our fight against poverty will be an investment and the most valuable of our resources . . . the skills and strength of our people. . . . If we can raise the annual earnings of ten million among the poor by only $1,000 we will have added fourteen billion dollars a year to our national output. . . . Because it is right, because it is wise and because for the first time in our history it is possible to conquer poverty, I submit for the consideration of the Congress and the country, the Economic Opportunity Act of 1964.

The President then went on to indicate what he believed the measure would do and some of the activities that would necessarily be undertaken by the government to provide those opportunities.

It is safe to say that never before has the attention of this nation been as heavily concentrated on the subject of poverty. (A possible exception is the period giving rise to Franklin D. Roosevelt's oft-quoted description "one-third of a nation ill-fed, ill-clothed and ill-housed." The circumstances however were substantially different at that time. The entire nation was in the depths of a depression and was concerned not primarily with poverty as a social phenomenon nor with the ability of the economy itself to meet the needs of an industrial society. The chief concern was with the relief of suffering.) The very fact that the President of the United States is free to talk about poverty and to expose it as vigorously as does his message, indicates more than merely a concern with poverty itself; it reveals the belief that poverty need not exist to the degree that his announcements indicate, and that it is not a political liability to acknowledge so great a weakness existing in the nation's life. That poverty can be eliminated with the resources of our economy and that it shall be eliminated because it is a drag upon the rest of the nation as well as because it is injurious to persons affected reveal the dual emphasis underlying the reasons for attempting to cope with it.

As President Johnson spoke, four-fifths of the nation were enjoying the highest measure of prosperity the world has ever known. There was little doubt that the economy through which this prosperity had been achieved was basically sound. Thirty-five years of watching an alternative system in the Soviet Union had disillusioned many who had entertained the notion that a totalitarian society under a Marxist-Leninist economy could provide both goods and freedom. Thus the deliverances of Presidents Roosevelt and Johnson came under vastly different circumstances in the nation's life and the life of the world.

Poverty is a relative thing. A movie portraying the poverty of

Appalachia makes an ex-coal miner and his family the central figures. They are poor because there is no more opportunity for mining coal. Other forms of energy have supplanted the "black gold" under the hills of Appalachia. But the family still had an automobile and was making payments on some very modern electric appliances.[3] However only a small fraction of the 20 per cent of Americans classified as poor are as well off as this ex-mining family. Only two out of every five nonwhite families live in sound structures with running water and a flush toilet. The figures are even worse in the South, where 60 per cent of the nonwhites still live.

Some may say, "What's all the excitement about? Things are getting better all the time, aren't they? We have moved from one-third of a nation in poverty to one-fifth in a single generation. At this rate it will be down to an infinitesimal percentage in a comparatively few years." The National Policy Committee on Pockets of Poverty answers that "unless remedial steps are undertaken, there will be considerably more poor even with a more affluent America." The circumstances which made possible the remedy of some of the conditions deplored by President Roosevelt can no longer be relied upon. The acceleration of automation has injected a virtually new feature into the economic scene. It is very doubtful that a stepped-up economy can of itself absorb the numbers of people who are being displaced economically by advancing technologies.* What the National Policy Committee says in reference to people in the Appalachians could equally apply to others who are being divorced from the benefits of our economy. It will not do to argue, as most policy makers and economists do, "that poverty will be done away with by policies aimed at bringing about full employment."[4]

A special assistant in the President's program against poverty, Daniel P. Moynihan, contends:

The central fact about poverty in America is that it is a political problem. This is a fact we must face. . . . Consider that in the last three

* And considerations of regional poverty must of course take into account the fact that there are always those who will not leave a familiar locus, even preferring deprivation to the difficulties and uncertainties of departure.

years, 1961, 1962, 1963, our gross national product grew by one hundred billion dollars. This is considerably greater than the entire GNP of Great Britain. Yet nowhere in the United Kingdom will you find the extensive areas of massive poverty such as you find here in our urban slums and rural wastelands. Having reached the point of something very much like mass affluence we remain one of the few great industrial nations of the world to retain within its borders mass poverty. Half as many people live here in poverty as live in all the United Kingdom. . . . Everyone says we have the opportunity to be the first nation in the history of mankind to eradicate the scourge of poverty from our borders. That is no longer true. It is too late for us to be the first to do this; other great nations have in effect done so. . . . To a great extent it is our size, our diversity and our lack of homogeneity that have produced our situation. To a great degree poverty in America is the aftermath of a hard-driving exploitation of men and materials which has also been one of the causes of today's economic affluence. The poor are left-over miners; the used-up coal and iron rangers; the small-skill southern white farmers eking out livings on used-up land; Negroes living in the aftermath of three centuries of the utmost exploitation; the Indians driven off the best land.[5]

Michael Harrington in *The Other America* has focused the attention of an entire nation on a comparatively recent aspect of the problem of poverty. Though there are still large areas such as Appalachia where the poor may be seen (as they were by John F. Kennedy when he went to West Virginia to campaign for his nomination), the fact remains that much of current poverty is what Harrington designates as invisible. It includes those who have been provided for in a minimal way by public housing and relief checks, the rapidly increasing number of persons over sixty-five who are living on one of several forms of government assistance,* and the minorities who because of prejudice are being afflicted with increasing handicaps. It includes people who follow the crops and who for a fraction of the year appear to be adequately employed but who for the remainder of the year live in abject poverty and out of the mainstreams of society.

Poverty's consequences have been so vividly and voluminously described that it is hardly necessary to amplify them here. Harring-

* At the time of this writing 9 per cent of the American population is over 65 and the Department of Health, Education, and Welfare estimates that in 1975 nearly 10 per cent will have reached that age.

ton, in his moving documentation of the fact of poverty and its consequences, conforms with many other conscientious students of society who have confronted us with the incontrovertible facts. Collectively they have pointed in prophetic fashion to the consequences for American life in particular when poverty becomes accepted as all but inevitable. Among such consequences is the mental and emotional distortion which racks the bodies and minds of individuals and exacts a terrifying price from the community at large. Commenting on one study of this factor, Harrington writes: "The stress factors listed by the Cornell Study are the very stuff of the life of the poor: physical illness, broken homes, worries about work, money and all the rest. The slum with its vibrant dense life hammers away at the individual. And because of the sheer grinding, dirty experience of being poor, the personality—the spirit—is impaired. It is as if human beings dilapidate along with the tenements in which they live."[6]

A conference on the Churches and Persistent Pockets of Poverty in the U.S.A., sponsored by the Division of Christian Life and Work and the Division of Home Missions of the National Council of Churches of Christ in the U.S.A., concluded:

> Today for the first time in human history the great productive potential of our economy and the creative imagination of our citizenry provide the means to eradicate poverty and alleviate its evil consequences. In view of the rapidly increasing economic interdependence of our world, America's plans for the elimination of poverty can no longer be nationalistic or isolated. They must take account of the tragic depths of poverty which characterize wide stretches of the globe.[7]

The conference report suggested as the consequences of poverty:

> There can be no question that material want, not voluntarily chosen but externally imposed, places severe pressures upon individuals, families, communities, the nation and the church.
>
> Among the injurious effects of poverty upon *individuals* are: physical dangers in terms of poor health, inadequate medical care, malnutrition, poor housing, severe crowding; sometimes forced intimacy with its moral dangers; cultural deprivations in terms of interrupted schooling and underdeveloped capacities, restricted opportunities; psychological damage, resulting in frustration and resignation or resentment and rebellion, possibility of antisocial attitudes leading to crime and

delinquency, mental breakdown, the undermining of initiative, and a sense of isolation or rejection. . . . Poverty puts severe strain upon the family, already threatened by rapid changes of modern life.

Poverty means deprivation for the community; poor schools and high dropout rates, the social costs of bad health and crime, the thwarting of human capabilities and the loss of their potential contribution. . . . Poverty means trouble for the entire *nation;* class divisions lead to class conflict; attenuation of educational and cultural services; the weakening of economic growth, national security, democratic processes and political stability. . . . Poverty also has serious consequences for the *church.* Its outreach is seriously restricted in depressed areas. Some churches and church programs, while rendering important service, often tend to reinforce separation of rich and poor, white and non-white, both in the community and in the household of faith. . . .[8]

Though we are profoundly concerned with and disturbed about the consequences of poverty, the principal focus of concern lies in its economic and social causes. The conference cited above suggested that though physical and mental handicaps, chronic ill health, and false value orientations uncongenial to economic advancement are significant as causes—

Far more influential factors, especially for explaining pockets of poverty, are to be found in the structure of our society and in the lags in adjustments to far-reaching and fast-moving technological, economic and social changes. Illustrations include: (1) lack of opportunity for general education and/or vocational training; (2) discrimination in employment on grounds of age, race, nationality or sex; (3) lack of employment opportunities due to cyclical or structural factors; (4) part-time employment and under-employment in industry and other occupations; (5) employment in traditionally low-wage jobs; (6) under-employment in agriculture due to a lack of adequate land, tools or capital; (7) exploitation of seasonally employed farm labor under chaotic systems of farm labor utilization; (8) exhaustion of resources in an area; (9) population pressure on resources in an area; (10) relative immobility of people and resistance to change; (11) inadequate rate of economic growth; (12) absence of collective bargaining power through lack of organization.[9]

Professor Oscar Ornati in a panel as a part of the same conference stated: "The American economy is now so productive as to have passed the cross-over point. It is clear that while in the recent past this was not so, now the Ameican economy is producing enough to do away with poverty."[10]

He went on to comment on the absence of precise data even though the phenomena are very evident. Precise data are of inestimable value and an absolute requirement for facing the problem fully. However, many facts concerning the extent and nature of the phenomenon of poverty are readily at hand.

It is not possible to charge poverty against industrialization or technical change. The phenomenon of poverty existed long before these aspects of society were prominent. Neither is it justifiable to contend that poverty in its continuing form is a product of inadequate economic growth. What Professor Ornati and his colleagues are contending is that the problem runs deeper than mere tinkering with present economic and industrial schemes can affect.

Economic Growth

If we have assumed that natural growth in our economic welfare will automatically take care of these conditions, some hard facts are in order. Fifteen years ago 20 per cent of the population with the lowest income received 5 per cent of our national income. Fifteen years later the 20 per cent with the lowest income still receive 5 per cent. The problem is simply not being solved.

Roy Blough is pointing to the same facts from another statistical perspective when he comments that the average annual rate of economic growth between 1909 and 1960 was 2.9 per cent in real terms; this was also the average rate for the periods 1909–1929 and 1929–1960. Technological progress has resulted in rapid economic growth with rising employment, civilian employment increasing from approximately twenty-seven million in 1900 to sixty-six million in 1960. From the standpoint of personal consumption expenditure per capita there was an increase between 1939 and 1962, based on 1962 prices, from $1,072.00 to $1,912.00, 2¼ per cent a year in real terms. Despite all this, as Professor Blough points out, there were many who did not share in the increases of income or shared so little that their condition can still only be described as very severe or even desperate poverty.

"Clearly economic growth in the past has not eliminated hard-core poverty and there is no reason to expect it to do so by itself in the future."[11]

Underdeveloped Nations

However significant the gap between the rich and poor, the privileged and the underprivileged in the United States, it is less significant for the world at large than the gap between the rich and the poor nations. America's poor are much better off in physical comforts and diet than the great majority of people in the underdeveloped nations of Africa, Asia, and South America; not much sympathy from the latter can be expected for their counterpart in the United States. It is the poor of the underdeveloped nations who present to industrialism and its economy its greatest challenge. The contrast in relative per capita output, which in 1960 was $2,800.00 for the United States and $75.00 for South Asia, $135.00 for Africa and $250.00 for Latin America, tells the story.[12]

People in developed nations may wonder why the underdeveloped countries cannot grasp the fact that economic development is not something to be achieved quickly. For the latter, political freedom was reached in a comparatively short time after momentum in that direction was initiated. The ideals of liberty, equality, and brotherhood are slogans of political emergency which fire the imagination and instill hope. But here is one of the paradoxes of the technological revolution: in the widespread knowledge of possibilities of enhancing human freedom resulting from technological advances in communications, the psychological and philosophical, or in other words, the intellectual resources for freedom become available; but the educational disciplines and the educational system required to provide the benefits of technology quickly dampen the hope burgeoning in the hearts of those who still live in what is termed traditional society. And with the experience of the new freedom it becomes apparent that the material resources for freedom, the foundation of industrialism, remain almost a mirage. Describing millions of those involved in such a situation, Gunnar Myrdal says: "Above all they are poor, mostly illiterate and backward, and they are being made conscious of it. The important thing is that they are not satisfied with liberty but demand equality of opportunity and common brotherhood as well. They describe themselves as underdeveloped with the clear implication that they should have economic development and a fuller share of the good things of life."[13]

Underdeveloped nations and their people are given encouragement when they look upon the accomplishments of the Soviet Union, and they cannot but be receptive when the latter offers them technical assistance and material resources for quick industrialization. It is understandable that they do not question immediately the obligations and commitments in which they become enmeshed. Sugar-coated promises of industrial expansion have to be matched with a frank appraisal of what is to be expected. "Financial aid the Soviet Union can supply, she can also supply technicians. But she cannot supply an example of a free and functioning industrial society. Russian communism denies that such a society is possible, that its problems exist and are real. It must deny this or else give up the beliefs in its own tenets and especially in the dogma that all social and economic problems are automatically solved by the mere establishment of the dictatorship of the proletariat."[14] Honest protagonists of industrialism thus become the true servants of the only viable option for giving freedom from misery as well as enslavement to the people of emerging nations.

Population

Inseparable from any discussion of underdeveloped nations is the ominous problem of population. Underdeveloped countries have historically maintained a balance between birth rates and death rates (35–40 per 1,000), but improved technology has sorely disrupted this balance. Its first consequence is the reduction of the death rate, particularly infant mortality; then follows a sudden population increase. With the incidence of disease no longer as high and with insufficient means of communicating to illiterate people the necessity for reducing birth rates, the peril mounts.

Not until sufficient numbers have been drawn into industrial communities where the implications of high birth rate become apparent is there a noticeable tendency to curtail family size.

India, for example, as a national policy has sought to find means of acquainting its millions of small village people with the fact that if it is to be a nation capable of holding its own in the world of nations, it cannot have its strength vitiated by a population which it cannot feed and which in turn lacks the strength to provide for itself through industrial production. Egypt, in attempting desperately to industrialize, finds it similarly difficult if not impossible to restrict its population increase so that it will not become such a drain upon the productive capacities of the nation. Even with all the assistance from many other nations, Egypt faces disaster unless through its rapid industrialization it can reduce the force which is undermining its national expectations. What is true of India and Egypt is similarly true of China in its powerful drive toward industrialization. Now new African nations eagerly striving to come into the main stream of human history are beginning to face the same issue. However, "if raising the standard of living is a prerequisite for reducing the birth-rate, therefore, the problem of surplus population and surplus labor is likely to persist for many years in most of the under-developed countries."[15] With two-thirds of the world's population now in the process of industrialization or eagerly anxious to participate in it, any rationale for industrialism must carry with it the capacity to indicate to underdeveloped nations and their peoples the imperativeness of population control.

Education

Among the most obvious and oft-repeated facts coincident with the rise of industrialism is the necessity for an educational system commensurate with, but also creating, the advancing requirements of an industrialized society. In one major segment of the world's population, the U.S.S.R., education has been vigorously supported because it contributes to the industrializing process itself. In what is generally designated as the free world the function of education is to develop the whole being with full consideration of the individual's needs in relation to his fellow man. This philosophy places demands upon the industrial system and determines the economy which shall prevail within it. Thus industrialism and its economy are not regarded as autonomous forces, but are subject to the requirements and objectives of man.

Rightfully, much is being made of the disparity of opportunity for advancement between whites and nonwhites. In the southern segment of the United States, for example, agriculture has provided the economic base from the nation's beginning until the middle of the twentieth century. Unskilled labor could provide in the form of "field hands" all that was necesesary for that economy. Besides the few skilled artisans needed for the plantation houses of the Old South, training for advanced skills or education beyond minimum requirements for communication was unnecessary. Mechanization of agriculture and increasing industrialization of southern cities, however, made new requirements. The availability of communication resources—television, radio, the press—placed an increasing premium on literacy, and excited interest in and demand for the products so glamourously presented by the advertising specialists. The demand for education increased in geometric ratio. Gunnar Myrdal relates that when he was conducting his now famous study *An American Dilemma*, he asked Southerners what whites were going to do when the education being provided for Negroes caused them to insist upon the same rights and opportunities as whites. He attests that the question produced animated response, to the effect that the "mores" would be unaffected.

An industrial society cannot have widespread discrepancies in educational opportunities, or its potential markets are curtailed and the progress which is mandatory on a technological society is reduced in its rate of acceleration. In 1961 President Kennedy's Council of Economic Advisors estimated that if the education and training of the Negro population were utilized, it would increase the income of the nation by thirteen billion dollars a year.

Education of the nonwhites, however, is but one part of the

total problem. The real issue is whether an industrial society can take from its earnings or create sufficient earnings to provide the kind of education required by everyone who would live adequately in that kind of a society. This means minimal competence in reading instructions, of course, but even more it means capacity to comprehend the very nature of the social system, the government, and the type of demands a free society places upon individuals. Thomas Jefferson saw this even before an industrial society had shaped the life of this nation. Industrialism in a free and democratic society must run the risk of its people making demands on the economic system, which demands may even go counter to certain concepts of property fostered by that system. Though this could be detrimental to the ownership patterns and economic concepts held by some people, it has the salutary consequence of making it possible for free citizens to understand the nature of the economy of which they are a part and from which they derive their livelihood. It could enable them to assume responsibility for directing that economy. The alternative is a system where responsibility has been abdicated and is conducted by those who through power, however achieved, essay to govern the lives of others according to their own personal desires. This is the paradox of unrestricted education in and for a free industrial society. Some would contend, of course, that so few are capable of grasping the importance of assuming responsibility for the life and work in our economy, that it is necessary for an elite to exercise the paternal or dominant role. This is obviously the risk which the Soviet Union is unwilling to take and yet which a free society, if it is to be fully free, must assume.

We are discussing here not simply the formal educational institutions of all levels, public and private, but the manifold variety of other educational instruments through which one discovers his role in relation to the rest of society and the necessity for responsible action in it. Countervailing forces are present in every form of social organization, but there are special reasons for their vitality in a free society committed to the use of all instruments and resources for its enhancement. Too great conservatism in economics may serve to restrict the forward movement of technology and the industrialism which utilizes it. If it is restrained, for example, by the suppression of new inventions, this may cause special advantages to accrue to those who benefit from monopoly of idea or ownership, to the detriment of the majority. On the other hand, widespread availability of discoveries and innovations can bring benefit to the population at large. Our patent laws have provided protection for the innovator, and they have benefited the rest of society as well by limiting the length of time a person's discovery or creation may be controlled, whether by an individual or a corporation. Behind this governmental action lies a theory that a government representing its people has the wisdom to decide whether and how long a needed instrument shall be preserved for limited benefit. At the other extreme is the disposition to share the discoveries relative to nuclear fission with any others who indicate willingness to accept responsibility and to use the discovery in accordance with mutually agreed regulations. The widespread mutual sharing of information relative to the most basic scientific discoveries attests both their universally valid nature and the mutual trust of those who are engaging in fundamental research. There is no private ownership of the profoundest wisdom of the universe.

The discovery of nuclear energy and the sharing of basic scientific knowledge parallel and symbolize the role of education at all levels in society. If industrial society is to advance in keeping with the essence of its own life, it is axiomatic that its fundamental tenets, its organization, and its regulations become a part of the common wisdom of as large a percentage of its beneficiaries as are capable of appropriating them. This means both unlimited access to all the facets of industrial society and a willingness to use an adequate portion of its benefits to encourage all who will do so to extend their general education.

4

Automation—Cybernation

The editor of the *Saturday Review,* Norman Cousins, has contended that two fears are stalking America: automation and peace. The first fear stems from the fact that automation could take over the tasks of more than half our labor force. The second from the fact that peace could bring economic disaster to an economy heavily dependent upon military preparation. That the two fears are related becomes obvious. We have become dependent on the national defense program for maintaining present levels of employment; but at the same time we are insistent upon the use of every means available for increasing efficiency and cutting costs. For our economy this has come to mean automation.

Our concern with the burgeoning phenomenon of automation derives from its implications for the kind of life it will make possible or necessary rather than from its contribution to industrial efficiency, important as the latter may be; it is with its significance for society and the individual who, theoretically at least, is intended to benefit from the automation process.

Whether automation is a new phenomenon or merely a continuation of other forms of mechanization is not important, despite the heat engendered by the discussion of the question. What is important is whether our competence in dealing with the products and instruments of industrial revolution as we have known it, has equipped us to cope adequately with what has been frequently termed "the second industrial revolution." In automation we are confronted with machines which are very much like the human brain, and thus we are faced with a revolution not only in economics but in philosophy as well.

The situation and conditions created by automation present philosophical and theological problems. Automation is a technological problem, of course, and its processes are beyond the range of theological concern; nevertheless the extent of its use and the rapidity of its adoption as a process, having run far ahead of our capacities to adapt to its consequences, have profound theological implications.

What Are Automation and Cybernation?

The general facts concerning automation stagger the imagination of those reared in a less complicated industrial society, and these facts have become widely known. Data relating to computers, transfer systems, the uncanny skills coincident with cybernation, the numbers disemployed in various types of plants, etc., are all subjects of everyday conversation. Many popular journals and weekend magazine sections have carried articles describing the consequences of this rapidly spreading phenomenon. A few of them have attempted to be reassuring and suggest that despite temporary discomfort things are going to be much better in the future.

Definitions of automation are almost as numerous as their authors, but basically they incorporate similar underlying components. They range from Peter Drucker's "the use of machines to run machines" to A. H. Raskin's "automation is the harnessing of the electronic brains to mechanical muscles" to those which incorporate the manifold processes involved in the broad gamut covered by the theme. Such definitions would include the integration of automatic machinery with automatic materials-handling equipment, the development of electronic computing machines capable of storing, counting, recording, surveying and selecting data, and the capacity to perform simple and highly complex mathematical operations with great rapidity. These capabilities all involve the use of "feed-back" control devices to supervise and control the process flow. Because it incorporates this feed-back process, automation is more than mechanization.

The U. S. Department of Labor defines automation as "the partial or full replacement of workers as a source of energy and/or control by machines." Automation is a way of thinking as much as a way of doing; it has become a way of organizing and analyzing production, and has heightened concern with the production processes as a system.

Cybernation involves attaching a computer to the automated machine, thus making possible the storing and evaluation of data and a corresponding expansion of the automated machine's function.

Implications and Benefits

So much has been written about the dire consequences of automation that its benefits have tended to be obscured. High on the list of beneficial consequences is the potential for dignifying human life. The human machine is much too valuable to be wasted on some of the processes to which it has been applied. Human dignity, which in theological terms is the product of God's creation and can be expressed in the poetic biblical affirmation "Thou hast made him little less than God" (Ps. 8 : 5), can be greatly enhanced by the much-feared phenomenon of automation. Surely anything which assists man in achieving the fuller dimensions of which he is capable must be in keeping with the Creator's purpose. Can it be anything but destructive to have a potentially active mind dulled into inactivity by a routine action involving no decisions or judgments?

One finds abundant basis for identification with either camp, both with those fearful of large scale unemployment and economic slump and with those who regard with optimism the increasing adoption of automated methods. If there is one aspect which can be beneficial to both sides of the argument, however, it is the assurance that whatever direction the economy takes, there is going to be information available at a rapid rate, which will better enable us to plan policies and thus mitigate the danger of a slump. Capacity to amass the necessary data can give direction to whatever course is needed, and thus constitutes one of the plus factors in the emergence of the whole phenomenon of automation.

Another implication of the growing acceptance of automation is the impetus accorded the development of increased accuracy and clarity of both thought and action. We are referring here not only to the consequences for the advanced nations but also to those for the less developed nations as they attempt to leap over centuries of experience of industrialized nations. For both, however, the hit-or-miss, trial-and-error process which has been accepted as a part of the earlier industrializing experience is no longer a viable option where more reliable resources are available. Accuracy in machine operations and computations is indispensable in a technical society. This means the ability to read and make mathematical calculations. Hence for the less developed nations, already handicapped through inadequate educational programs, the need accelerates and the pressure mounts. If they are to compete in a world increasingly technological, traits and values evolved through centuries must quickly be replaced or modified. Thus automation, the newest symbol of the technological society, forces the reorganization of national life.

A concomitant benefit may be the fact that workers will be encouraged to think of the plant as a whole, to see the correlation of their participation more readily than has been possible heretofore. Social gain could be the result. Teamwork assumes increased importance, and the results of coordinated activity supplant those of individuals. In many industries teamwork is already indispensable under present arrangements, but automation promises to increase the practice. What the long-term consequences of this trend may be cannot be fully foreseen, but it seems likely that attitudes of both management and labor toward the whole production process will be altered. "A new work morality may arise in place of a morality based on unit worth concept. . . . Worth will be judged on the basis of organization and planning and the continuously smooth functioning of the operation. As the individual worker loses his importance and is replaced by the team greater value is placed on the operating unit as a whole. The traditional individualism of American society may soon be replaced."[1] One man's contribution is still important, but it is submerged in the cooperative action of the larger producing unit. Thus whether the worker philosophizes or not over the meaning of his new relationships, he is compelled to know something of the meaning of mutual dependence and responsible coordination.

The father of the term "automation," John Diebold, in taking account of the fact that heretofore machines had to be designed within the limits of the operator's potential skills, says: "With the introduction of the new concept in technology of self-regulating systems it is no longer necessary to design the production process around the limitations of human skills."[2] The undulating curve of human capacities, fatigue or freshness, no longer need determine the planning for production, and the factor in labor thus diminishes in importance. The fact that productive processes can be maintained continuously with predictable regularity has other significance besides the easing of human strain. It means that the shift system, with occasional breaks in the operation where one or more shifts are "down," becomes even less economical due to the heightened expense of the machinery and the necessity for deriving maximum performance from it.

Social Costs

What is being said here is that it is easier, perhaps, to extrapolate the benefits than the social costs of automation. Much of the anxiety about automation is based upon the scale of threatened unemployment. Many economists believe that we actually have nothing to fear "in the long run."[3] Ultimately, they say, more jobs will be created, as has been the case with other innovations in the industrial revolution preceding the present one. This optimistic expectation seems to overlook the fact that the kinds of jobs being created require on the part of a very large percentage of our work force a level of skill necessary to earn a living in an automated society which they will not be able to achieve in the forseeable future. No one can predict how many people are going to be needed for the work force in twenty years, but all present statistics indicate that jobs are being eliminated faster than people can be trained for new work and faster than the economy can accommodate the numbers of young people coming into the labor market. It is this piling up of excess labor, both from those "disemployed" and those who are unemployable because of age or insufficient training, which creates for an industrial nation a philosophical, moral, and ethical problem.

While it is recognized that any figures relating to employment are liable to quick change and may subject the written record to the charge of being outdated, it is nevertheless estimated that during the 1960s twenty-six million new young workers will need to be absorbed into the employment rolls.[4] A drop of 10 to 15 per cent in the wage force in steel, autos, transportation, and of course even more than that in coal, has not been offset by increased employment in the automated industries which are expanding most rapidly. It is this "short-run" situation which is the special concern of organized labor and which constitutes a serious dilemma for all who are concerned with opportunities for work. And who isn't? At this writing (1965) about 5 per cent of the labor force is unemployed, and something approximating this figure has been the unemployment rate for an extended period.

One of the basic differences of the present period from the past is the rate at which human effort is being displaced. Earlier forms of mechanical progress downgraded the job and created a large number of semiskilled functions to which existing human capacities were readily adapted. Automation eliminates manipulative tasks and transfers the direct human control functions to an intermediate and higher order. Machine operators are displaced by the technician and the engineer, making it difficult for a large number of workers to adapt to the new job situation. The result will be a serious downgrading of those workers into residual low-order jobs. Some individuals can be retrained for the more complex types of manipulation. For many in our society, however, a new set of values will have to emerge. We say "many" because there are some who have long contended that human need and the provision of humane services are primary concerns of society itself. In another era, as an earlier industrial revolution was in sight, John Stuart Mill, one of the most perceptive political economists in the western tradition, commented: "There cannot be a more legitimate object of the legislator's care than the interest of those who are thus sacrificed to the gain of their fellow citizens and posterity—those displaced by changing methods of production."[5]

Grounds of Concern

Some would contend that whatever the consequences, the victims of any down-turn need not be as badly damaged as were the victims of the earlier industrial revolution. The existence of supplemental unemployment benefits, the thirty-hour week, retraining programs, minimizing of accidents, better health resources, etc., have cushioned the shock of the industrial revolution in our period. Equally beneficial supports will presumably be made available as automation expands. The combination of humanitarianism, efficiency, and the need for stability will serve beneficially. They may provide poor consolation for those already suffering the ill effects of automation, but the extent of suffering may not be as great as that which characterized other innovations.

Organized labor has been profoundly exercised and anxious concerning the extension of automation in industries now substantially organized and also in those not yet organized. Management contends that the introduction of automated processes is required for efficiency and is the only means of remaining competitive. Organized labor naturally looks at the issue from the viewpoint of the numbers disemployed. The bargaining which ensues does not deal with the question of increased efficiency but with that of the human consequences. In the dispute over dismissal of firemen on diesel locomotives, for example, there was little disposition to deny the disposability of the fireman's role except as a safety factor. Major attention was focused on what would happen to the thousands of men then employed who in many instances could not be trained for other kinds of work. The railroad dispute also brought into focus other issues in addition to the problem of income maintenance for dismissed firemen. It caused the industry and the nation at large to look at the entire industrial complex and to ask where responsibility lay for the major changes required by the introduction of laborsaving machinery. The introduction of the diesel engine may not be exactly described as a part of the automation process, but it symbolizes the direction taken and decisions required where large scale disemployment has occurred. It has become possible and necessary for labor and management to look at the consequences of the production process of which they are both a part. This new labor-management relationship will be discussed in a later chapter.

Erich Fromm is but one of many who fear that automation tends to isolate man psychologically from his colleagues. He contends that there is loss of companionship and camaraderie on the job, which affects those workers who are reduced to a "push-button" existence. Another analyst of automation, James Bright, says: "I do not find that the upgrading effect has occurred to anywhere near the extent that it is often assumed. On the contrary I find that automation has reduced the skilled requirements of the operating force and occasionally the entire factory force including the maintenance organization."[6] To this we may add Bruno Bettelheim's comment that the modern workman in a rapidly changing technological social order is very much like a prisoner in a concentration camp who is told daily that he may be thrown at any moment into the yawning mouth of the giant rock crusher he is required to feed with the labor of his bare hands.[7]

It is not without significance that one of the most optimistic advocates of automation, Paul Einzig, concludes his glowing praise of its possibilities with these words: "It will be perhaps the most difficult of all the difficult problems arising from automation to insure that mankind in its impatient drive for material betterment does not lose its soul."[8]

Consequences to Value and Belief Structure

As suggested earlier, some of the most pronounced effects of automation will be on the values and beliefs currently held in much of our society. An individualistic religion is confronted with the fact that only a corporate solution is possible for attaining the well-being which a healthy society requires. The processes of automation require an integration of manufacturing organizations, of community life, of buying practices and of many current patterns of life. These forces cannot be allowed to proceed unguided and independent of the common good. Government action becomes an increasingly necessary consequence. Undoubtedly the charge of socialism will be leveled, but the very term itself becomes irrelevant and inconsequential in the face of the fact that an ever-increasing centralization in industry makes necessary a corresponding action on the part of government to deal with the consequences of centralization. The implications of increased concentration of government power for providing balance and giving a direction to the integration of the total economy increase proportionately the necessity for participation in government on an intelligent basis; the alternative is abdication to the world of George Orwell's 1984. Whether a heightening of educational reorganization and redirection can occur in time is a speculative question. We are thus faced with moral and educational issues involving society in a reorientation of its traditional values.

This is not a matter of concern to any one nation alone. Automation merely reflects what is occurring on a worldwide scale and gives accelerated impetus to the process of world unification. Of this process Gustave Weigel says: "As Teilhard de Chardin supposed, our evolution at the present time is to an ever greater solidarity of mankind. We are moving to become a single species-subject of action. Individuals can no longer consider themselves in isolation in the stage of evolution which we have entered. All individuals become closer in action and —belong to all other individuals."[9] It would appear that the technology of automation is proving to be one of the major factors in fostering the solidarity which Teilhard de Chardin predicted.

The problem of leisure will be dealt with more inclusively in chapter 12, but since the processes of automation contribute increasingly both to the opportunities and to the problem of leisure, we take note of that fact here. Whether automation provides opportunities for increasing dignity and fulfillment of man's creative purpose constitutes one of the major philosophical and ethical issues of our time. The biblically oriented culture under which most of us have been reared and which has been (correctly or incorrectly) designated by Max Weber "the Protestant ethic" insists that work is an essential part of human existence. Traditionally, we have been taught that the pain of work brings the pleasure of rest and accomplishment. We have become imbued with the conviction that our reward is to come as the result of the sweat of our brow. Only if one works hard may he enjoy rest, leisure, and pleasure. Now we have a society in which extended hard manual or clerical labor will be unlikely for an increasing number. It becomes apparent that many will have to be rewarded for not working hard or for working in ways which are not traditionally regarded as work.

What this possibility would seem to suggest is that work may not be identified with earning, but that there are other forms of reward, for example, the earning of time to do the things one much wants to do. The increase in wisdom, the capacity for creativity, will increasingly have to be developed for their own sakes because the very nature of the human psyche requires development to prevent disintegration. Those who are responsible for the increase of automation or are caught in its seemingly inevitable extension are thus rediscovering a fundamentally spiritual problem with which the writers of the creation story in the Garden of Eden dealt.

Earlier it was stated that we are finding ourselves plunged into the necessity of devising or discerning a new set of living standards. We have become able to produce enough food, shelter, clothing, and medicine for all, even though we have not achieved an acceptable standard for distribution. But automation is pressing us at the distribution level as well. It is true that at the moment we have some thirty to forty million people living below what is a commonly accepted standard of decency, but this deficiency has now been lifted to the level of a national concern. Either the needs of all will be met, or the automation process itself will be challenged. The facts that the process of automation is capable of providing those minimal requirements and that the other four-fifths who are living above the minimal standard and profiting from the contributions of automation will probably not seek to curtail it place the total society in a new frame.

The compounded effect of this greatly improved capacity for production may be the complete triumph of the enterprise and may at the same time contain the disavowal of some of the very values which created it. This, it seems to some, is ironically the era into which we are moving. A *Reader's Digest* article on the consequences of automation says: "The new automation of the intelligent machine is a benefactor that will help us grow and help our way of life to survive."[10] If the writer means by "our way of life" an adequacy of goods, he may be right; but the structure of society under which those goods are produced will be greatly changed, and marked by sharp deviations from what we think of as our way of life.

Religious and ethical pioneers have long wrestled with the problem of distributive justice. The industrial revolution made necessary the breakup of a feudal society which placed a premium on class and disparity of income. Industrialization, with its concomitant necessity for spreading buying power, and the emergence of democracy fostered a measure of egalitarianism, partly in self-defense and partly as a result of an awareness of the biblical commands for sharing, mutual aid, etc.

With automation the concept of buying power takes on substantial new importance. Not only will some people probably have to be paid though not "working," but the gains from automation will have to be spread much more widely as a means of guaranteeing the continuing use of machines which cannot be laid off without serious harm of the economic structure itself.

Frictional unemployment will have to be reduced through a series of regulatory actions by central decision-making agencies. It seems inevitable that an automated economy will increasingly approximate one integrated output plant. Centralization of decision-making is one of its concomitants; and thereby comes the correlative expansion of bureaucracy. This is affirmed on the hypothesis that the efficiency required by automation—the continuous flow of raw materials and finished product—cannot be assured in any other way.

In rethinking the values for our society as influenced by automation, an allocation of resources to service industries, to health, education, highways, and many other components would seem to be called for. There is no surplus of workers in the areas of social service, where the remedies of society's ills are most required. Whatever our apprehensions about machines taking care of machines, etc., automation cannot take care of children and those who are sick, for example; it may, however, help diagnose their ailments and reduce the incidence of disease.

Presumably no extensive apologia is needed for including the theme of religion and automation in a discussion of ethics and economics. Whatever affects human life is included in the concern of religion. We have not attempted to formalize the theological implications of automation but rather to indicate some of its consequences to persons and to society. Justice, freedom, and order have been central concerns of the more thoughtful and religious-minded persons in our day. The attainment of these ends has been both accelerated and jeopardized in industrial society. Freedom to learn has enabled men to discern societal structures which enhance concern for justice and order. If automation releases man still further with freedom from drudgery and enables him to create an order which is equitable and just, it will have helped provide him with a new dignity. Within this dignity he may better realize the potential given him by his Creator.

5

Welfare and Our Industrial Economy

The evolution of welfare* is an index of our industrial economy, each stage of it emerging as an outgrowth of industrial development. Poverty and calamity to individual and group life were at least as severe in preindustrial periods, but not until the advent in industry of advanced technology was welfare organized in a systematic way. Whereas in an agrarian society poverty and calamity were met by the family or the community, from the resources of the soil and out of a bond of mutual obligation, industrialism altered and in a large measure removed both the resource and the bond.

Poverty is not the only cause for welfare activities, but the two are so inseparable that it is mandatory for a consideration of the change in welfare to follow a chapter contending that reduction of poverty tests the validity of our industrial economy.

Every modern nation has become a welfare state. Despite the attempt of some people to blame this upon socialism or communism, the fact remains that it is impossible to have a modern industrial state without its becoming at the same time a welfare state. Communist welfare had its inception in the theory of society which underlay the Marxist-Leninist experiment in the Soviet Union. The state from the beginning was the guarantor of minimal decency, even though in the process it was necessary to deprive the beneficiary of the opportunity to express his convictions to the rest of the body politic in the form of a voting

* As used here the term connotes the meeting of needs for which individuals and groups cannot of themselves make adequate provision. This would include concerns related to mental and physical health, income maintenance, family, employment, care of children and the aged, etc.

franchise. For those nations whose economy is designated as capitalist, on the other hand, the provisions for the well-being of its citizens derive from the very individualism which is at the heart of the capitalist theory. For generations it was assumed that a person in need had only himself to blame; but the humanitarianism stemming from Hebrew-Christian origins still extended compassion toward the injured or deprived. Eventually it became clear that many thus affected were the victims of circumstances over which they had no control. This is presumably the meaning of that major watershed in American life known as the Great Depression. We finally awakened to the fact that industrious, hard-working, aspiring, virtuous people could be trapped and mangled in economic circumstances not of their own making; capitalist welfare thereby came into being.

Origins of Present Welfare Situation

A seemingly endless and inexhaustible new continent afforded the American people the luxury of Darwinian and Spencerian presuppositions about man's ability to survive. This thesis did not go unchallenged through the series of depressions which periodically deflated the buoyancy of America's industrial economy, but not until the greatest depression of them all, beginning with the stock market crash of 1929 and running through most of the decade of the 1930s, were Americans convinced that the very system which was providing for them so abundantly could not, unchanged, guarantee its working population the ability to purchase the abundant products of its fields and factories. It is more than coincidence that the most comprehensive welfare act in American history, the Social Security Act of 1935, and the National Labor Relations Act became law in the same year. The enactment of these two pieces of legislation was a recognition of the fact that only some form of income maintenance provided by the federal government could stabilize the economy, and that labor should be guaranteed the right to bargain collectively on behalf of income maintenance for its members. Both of these actions were designed to stabilize incomes and to reduce the vagaries of factors which disturbed the regularity of income; and although both enactments were the products of industrialism and its economy, they became the foundation stones of a national welfare program.

The process by which an agricultural nation became industrial is too well known to require repetition here. Almost equally well known are the adaptations made necessary for first-generation immigrants coming from Europe directly to industrial plants, or second-generation immigrants coming off the farms into industrial employment. The history of welfare in the United States parallels the evolution of the city as an industrial center, at least until the decade of the 1930s made it finally apparent even to rural America that its surpluses were no longer temporary and that it could no longer accommodate the population then hoping to make its living from the land. The farm produce and population surplus became acute following the mighty efforts to increase production for World War I; the agricultural depression thus antedated the industrial by almost a decade. For a short period during World War II there was again prosperity in agriculture; thereafter the long decline continued, interrupted briefly by the Korean War. Local aid had long since been exhausted, and the federal government by means of the Social Security Act and a long series of agricultural stabilization programs has maintained minimum adequacy of income for a high percentage of persons living on the land.

The immigrant settling in the cities faced a different but related problem. The factory, unlike his rural European family, offered no guarantees of protection, and his community security was undermined. Other factors were similarly important, however, in changing his way of life: regimentation and discipline created a stress; the tools which he used were not his own, and he became subject to the direction and control of others, including the very machine to which he was tied; and finally, his very place of residence became uncertain because of variation in the need for workers. Such elements combined to cause traumatic experiences for those who had come out of a totally different type of existence. Both at the time and in retrospect it seemed the newcomers were subjected to excessive hardships. In reality this was true, but when compared with their former state, for many at least the contrast was not unfavorable. "When we think of the transition from European peasant to American industrial worker, we are often comparing a run-down rural economy with an expanding industrial economy. It is surprising that life in the urban industrial setting did not seem wonderful by contrast."[1]

A good deal of anguish has been expressed over the physical and psychological consequences of this transition from a rural "mind-set" to that of urban existence. The pain of adjustment was real, and undoubtedly much more could have been done to ease the transition had we comprehended its nature and causes. At the same time it must be recognized that the experiences were a part of the metamorphosis of our industrial economy itself. Philosopher Charles Frankel says: "A great many of the problems that face our welfare programs arise as the result of the migration of rural people to the cities. . . . Successive waves of immigrants, almost all of them with rural backgrounds, have made the history of our cities. Now it is the Latin American and the Negro; a generation ago it was the Italian. Only the Jew on the whole has brought an urban background with him. Most of the problems of urban welfare programs arise in that context. This fact is not a fault in our system. It is the sign, the symptom, and the consequence of the industrial growth of our system and of its creation of increasing opportunity. Adjustment to urban life is a problem, in other words, like the problem of education, not like the problem of crime."[2]

New Circumstances Bring Adaptations

Income insecurity and psychological adjustments to new types of work were only two problems confronting the industrial worker, whether a recent immigrant or a native reared in the industrial milieu, between World Wars I and II when we shifted from an agricultural to a predominantly industrial economy. Among the other experiences tending to strain, confuse, disturb, or warp the new urban worker was the uncertainty about the type of work to be expected of him regardless of whatever he may have done before. No longer did his position in the community depend upon his skills, for these may be only temporarily demanded; tradition became of little significance, while change has become omnipresent; family stability has become uncertain and the nuclear family—parents and children—increased the ease of mobility. Being less and less in demand for industrial productivity, youth are increasingly rejected and are finding it more difficult to earn even supplemental income for recreation; marriage for many is thus necessarily postponed. In an aging population in which the number of those over 65 has quadrupled since 1900, the people who must be taken out of the work force to make room for younger workers but who yet have substantial productive capacity constitute one of the most pressing problems. Another is the broken family which cannot be supported by the parent in whose custody the children remain. Here the problem is obviously not simply the custody and support of children, enormous though this problem be, but the accessibility of divorce where cohesiveness of family life is not a requisite as in agricultural living. Still another is the exhausting pressure of the assembly line, the pace of the machine and the herding effect on multitudes of others regimented by the demands of production schedules. And the list could be greatly amplified. The most important thing is that counterinfluences were set in motion, and welfare programs designed to offset each deleterious phase were instituted.

Wilensky and Lebeaux contend that "the central theme running through our picture of urban industrial America is this: we can perhaps view most of the targets of complaint as transitional, passing results of industrialization under 19th century conditions. Coercive recruitment and painful transformation of peasant immigrants into urban industrial workers; the insecurities of the factory system; the uncushioned impact of the dilution and obsolescence of skills; the de-humanization of work (whether through back-breaking labor or machine-paced repetitive routine); class polarization; community disintegration—these decline as economic growth continues. A new welfare bureaucratic society emerges —more stable than its early form suggests, richer and more varied than men had dreamed when they observed the harsh, initial development period."[3]

It is popular in some circles to bemoan the suffering and agony accompanying the readjustments which technology forces upon individuals, families, and communities. Because society has not traveled this way before, there are few built-in protective devices; they have to be constructed after the ailments, agonies, and misfortunes occur. The very existence of such problems often induces effective and constructive social change, since activities on behalf of their improvement become integral parts of the system which caused them. This has apparently not been the attitude either of those most basically involved in developing a technological society or, sad to note, not always the attitude of those engaged in ameliorating the consequences of industrialism.

As Charles Frankel suggested, our inability to see the larger process of welfare as a sign of the success of the industrial system rather than as an evidence of its failures, is one of the obtacles to the advancement of human welfare.[4] This is not to condone its ills, but to accept them as a part of the price to be paid for innovations. The tragedy appears when people refuse to face the fact that the disorganizing and destructive elements can be remedied within the framework of the same society which created them, and *mirabile dictu* the same forces of technological progress are capable of providing an economy within which its casualties can be rescued.

We might use as illustrations of our capacity to adapt constructively to a problem created by our society the development of treatment for the aged, or the broken home, or of the rising incidence of mental disease resulting from the individual's inability to find his place in a fast-shifting culture. Juvenile delinquency illustrates the total situation with special aptness. It is a far cry from the day when small children tended spools in cloth mills, providing the cheap labor on which fortunes were made and funds accumulated to invest in enterprises in other lands. Not only were the warped bodies and minds of children the reason for eliminating this condition, but industry required more sophisticated skills, which in turn required training programs and an educational system adequate to provide both technical and managerial direction. Juvenile delinquency and its coordinate condition, the high school dropout, present our generation with a situation paralleling the attack on child labor a century ago. Not only are lives being corroded through inactivity and the lives of still others endangered through the misdirected activity of youth out of school and unemployed, but in addition society as a whole is losing the potentially constructive contribution of these young people. Given the requisite training and the assurance that they can make a useful contribution, they are capable of being responsible producers and consumers in our society. All of this places upon us the obligation to create and conduct the institutions and programs which can foster successful adaptation of teen-age youth into the total economy. As public education became a requirement of a democracy and a great gamut of public services emerged to provide for the needs of people gathered together in new forms of communal life, so is our type of urban society now required to find a solution to the unused talents and potentially destructive forces let loose where human energies are unchanneled. Instead of such a solution being a grudging concession to troublesome youth, it becomes a primary mandate of the modern era.

A corollary of the contention that many forms of casualty attendant upon industrialization are the result of its successes and therefore are remediable, is our acceptance of the fact that such casualties no longer are branded as personal failures. In an era of burgeoning industry, of at least periodically unlimited markets and enough mouths to consume all agricultural products, there were jobs enough to go around. Adjustments to a new country and irregularity of employment created only temporary casualties. Meanwhile, there was a growing disposition to express in formal institutions a belief inherent in the American ideal that individuals were entitled to a minimal standard of living as a part of their citizenship. What Locke and John Stuart Mill had affirmed in the eighteenth and nineteenth centuries, and what Augustine and Aquinas had contended centuries earlier, had now become a reality because for the first time an industrial economy could make it possible. On this issue Thomas Gladwin comments: "Obviously the right to a decent manner of life remained an academic issue until sufficient goods were available to supply the needs of the bulk of the people. However, a high rate of productivity does not in itself guarantee that those who remain poor will be considered to have a right to expect the help of others not so poor. As we watch the steady rise of a standard of living in the United States it is easy to forget that for many years this rise was not accompanied by an attitude we now take as axiomatic: that anyone who is really willing to work has a right to share in the general affluence."[5]

This extraordinary combination—a common respect for humanity born of the Hebrew-Christian tradition, the Renaissance, the Enlightenment, and the democratic tradition—has helped to bring about and is itself brought to flower by a society capable of providing for that need. Gradually but firmly the realization penetrated Western life and America in particular that the unfortunate things occurring to men, inhibiting their opportunities for the good life, were not necessarily their own fault. The poor had known this but had lacked the organization for demanding and the articulateness for expressing it. Now for the first time the middle class became aware of the fact, and thanks to widepread education and a grounding in the traditions of a democratic society and an ethical religion, they refused to remain inert. The result was the burgeoning of welfare programs, for the most part instituted within the lifetime of those born before World War I.

The evolution of welfare and its history is a rich and wholesome phenomenon in the life of this and other Western nations. Our concern however, is not primarily with its history but with the modifications required as it kept pace with the emergence of our industrial economy.

One consequence of the shift in attitude toward welfare is the confusion centering about the word itself. For many people it connotes relief, the elimination of suffering and the provision of minimal sustenance until such time as the recipient can "get on his feet again." Obviously, this is a carry-over from the era when it was expected that one should by his own efforts transcend temporary mishaps or misfortunes. For others it may connote social security, supplementary unemployment benefits, and the pension funds of corporations which benefit both management and labor.

It is significant that today labor-management controversies center increasingly on the extent of those benefits rather than primarily on wages. The pension factors and the various forms of government assistance designed to provide income maintenance have become so extensive that in a comparatively short time the latter came to be considered less as "welfare" than as a "right" of the citizen.

Changing Concepts of Welfare

One of the consequences of large-scale support and insurance programs, whether privately or publicly initiated, is the blurring if not elimination of distinctions between what is welfare and what are the standard programs for meeting common needs. In a single generation governmental agencies have not only been initiated but have become accepted as a permanent and normal part of ongoing life. Such has been the rapid evolution in our acceptance of the welfare principle. What was born of an emergency now continues because the emergency itself is permanent. No index of this phenomenon is more striking than the proliferation of schools of social work in most major public universities and many private ones. Almost within a generation a new and highly self-conscious profession has come into being; its standards have been articulated, and its place as an integral part of a technological society has been established.* Although the private agencies, called into existence originally by the phenomenon of immigration and the casualties of individual and family life in an urban society, still remain highly useful and frequently pioneer in special kinds of work, for the most part welfare has become predominantly a public responsibility. The scale of this evolution has greatly contributed to the obsolescence of the old concept of welfare. "It seems likely that distinctions between welfare and other types of social institutions will become more and more blurred. Under continuing industrialization all institutions will be oriented toward and evaluated in terms of social welfare aims. The 'welfare state' will become the 'welfare society' and both will be more reality than epithet."[6]

Government Role

Special attention will be given later to the increasing role of government in our economy, but nothing illustrates this trend

* There are 96,696 persons indicated as "Social and Welfare Workers" in the United States. (Source: Statistical abstract of the U. S., 1963, p. 232)

more vividly than increasing governmental involvement in welfare. We are here using the term "government" in its inclusive sense, designating all local, state, and national units concerned with public welfare. Space permits no complete listing of welfare areas in which government is involved, but even a partial list is indicative of the scope: old age and survivors' disability insurance, public assistance, child welfare, vocational rehabilitation, public health, veteran's services, unemployment insurance and employment service, federal court social services and federal correctional system, Indian welfare services, housing programs and income security programs for railroad workers.

Each of these agencies and programs is dependent upon tax support and federal participation. Many of these programs parallel or are conducted in relation to the state governments, which in turn may have their own programs supplemented by federal funds. The compounded effect of governmental participation in welfare at all levels results in an expenditure of approximately 11.5 per cent of our gross national product. "Even where private charity is involved directly with the poor," says Edgar May, "frequently much of the cost of that involvement is paid by the government. For example, I was surprised to learn that in my own state, New York, of 57 million dollars spent in 1961 by private institutions for children and by child-caring agencies, 42 million dollars came from taxpayers. I wonder if most people realize this."[7]*

No small part of the welfare costs of our time result from technological changes. In the long run those changes may be beneficial in the sense that they create new jobs in types of industry perhaps not even envisaged now. Who should bear the transitional costs? Roy Blough says that an "approach to reducing the rate of labor displacement is to place more of the social cost of a technological change on the benefiting employer than is the case when he bears none of the cost of unemployment or the obsolescence of skills. . . . This would encourage the employer to find ways of keeping on the worker, would result in socially more accurate balancing of

* Social Welfare Expenditures 1961–62:
Total public (federal, state, local) .... $62,496.7 mill
Total private (health, medical care, income maintenance and welfare) .... 33,418 mill
(Source: *Social Security Bulletins,* Vol. 26, No. 11, Nov. 1963)

the benefits and costs of technological progress. . . ."[8]

Attempts have been made to estimate the extent of returns from welfare programs. It is not solely a drain on the taxpayer, as some have implied. Consequences in the form of stabilization of the economy and maintenance of the health of present and future workers are obviously incalculable, as is also the reduction in disease and in the costs of crime. That the latter is very great is incontestable, but that it might have been infinitely greater is also a very real likelihood. High on the list of factors justifying the welfare programs now extant are the minimization of public restlessness and the reduction of turmoil and revolt. This was a conscious aim of one of the earliest major welfare programs, that of Germany under Bismarck. It probably forestalled a Marxist revolution; there is good reason to believe that the seething and incipient revolt in the United States during the Great Depression was deterred or deflected by the programs of WPA, PWA, and others initiated during the administration of Franklin Roosevelt and conducted by his trouble-shooting social worker, Harry Hopkins.

Though education is not a part of welfare in the sense in which it is used here, it is appropriate to include a short reference to it because of its implications for welfare. In our society it is almost axiomatic that education is the means for elevating a person and those dependent on him. By this means likelihood of having to depend on others is presumably lessened. In recent years the importance of education as a means of facilitating job adjustments, transfers, and training has mounted greatly. This we have come to accept. Not so well known or understood is the benefit to society at large through reduction of the drain on the public finances where education has been made more widely available. Professor Theodore W. Schultz in his study *The Economic Value of Education* indicates how education provides both psychological values to the individual and serves to reduce "the inequality in the personal distribution of income."[9] A concomitant of active participation in the educative process is the benefit to the economic growth of the nation. Schultz's study and the others upon which it draws conclude that for its own health and welfare the nation cannot skimp its support of public education.

Expanded Private Concern

No discussion of welfare in our economy would be complete without taking substantial account of the programs of both management and labor. Whatever the reason for management's introduction of extensive welfare activities, they have provided manifold benefits. Some have been initiated at the instigation and insistence of labor and others—voluntary in many instances—by the companies themselves. The latter's objectives have been: to increase the tenure of the workers, to reduce absenteeism, and to heighten loyalty to the employing organization. And like other programs of welfare emanating from government sources, they have served to stabilize the economy by providing income maintenance.*

Sharp contests have arisen over the administration of these funds, the charge being made by labor that when they are administered by management, they may be used as instruments of pressure to inhibit resistance from the employees in the event that the labor organization decides forceful action against the company to be in order. Unions have preferred that the pension and welfare funds be independent of management.

One of the paradoxical phenomena of our time is the extraordinary financial power developed by unions in the administration of their own pension, strike, and welfare funds. The size of these funds has approached dimensions sufficient to influence the stock or bond market in which they have been invested, and misuse of some of them has created sensational court cases. Management of the funds has contributed to the rapid metamorphosis in union leadership. Obviously labor organizers are rarely if ever qualified to invest and manage these large sums of money themselves, so that financial specialists become indispensable auxiliary aids of the unions. It is not surprising that some unions have become protagonists of a conservative philosophy, since future income of their

* Pensions, sick pay, hospitalization, sabbatical leaves, insurance programs, and many other benefits traditionally identified with welfare have entered the employer-employee relationship, both to stabilize conditions within the organization and to assure continuity of purchasing power. The concept of welfare and purchasing capacity or income maintenance has become one of the newer phenomena whereby industrialism seeks to guarantee the stability of its economy.

retired workers is dependent upon both the rate of investment and their hourly wage.

Emerging Nations and Welfare

The distance from the highly developed welfare programs of industrial nations, with their guarantees of minimal existence for all, to the nations emerging from agricultural life or tribal customs is to be reckoned not in income per capita but in the centuries to be hurdled. Emerging leadership in the underdeveloped nations must give promise of greater physical advantages and security.

Instead of waiting for the evolutionary process by which industrially advanced nations developed their welfare programs, they seek to institute them earlier. They have the advantage of perspective and the experimentation of the "developed" nations.[10] The Soviet Union has capitalized on this necessity for providing minimal security, even though by the standards of underdeveloped nations it is among the most advanced. Here, however, a factor has to be reckoned with which is less evident in some developing nations. In conversation with Russian people one hears repeatedly the statement "Though we do not have all that we would like, it is so much more than we formerly had that we are grateful for the gains made." It has also been hypothesized that the Russian people for centuries have lived in an atmosphere of expectation, dominated by an eschatology which assured something good eventually. The great cost in suffering and sacrifice by which the nation carried through its industrialization program could be borne because of the history of suffering which was at long last to be relieved. Nations which have lived adjacent to or under colonial domination by other industrialized nations may have a better idea of the cost to be incurred in their development before the full welfare program can be assured them.

The new nations so recently elevated to self-consciousness may appreciate less well the cost entailed in achieving a level where the state can guarantee freedom from poverty and want. One demand characterizes the populations of nations at either end of the scale, whether the most advanced or the most primitive; it is the insistence that at least minimal opportunities for making a living or maintaining existence shall prevail.

Gunnar Myrdal contends that concern for achieving the welfare society has been a factor in heightening nationalistic awareness and preoccupation.[11] Each nation desires to preserve the levels of individual security achieved by its welfare programs. Citizens suspect that assistance to other nations might (a) reduce the benefits already available at home, (b) impair the nation's economy, and (c) aid a potential competitor. Paradoxically, at the very time when nations are being brought into greater proximity through faster means of communication, they are drawn into greater self-centeredness. Determination to preserve all the advantages accruing from their economy tends to render them increasingly insensitive to the needs of other nations which would like to become welfare societies also. This theme of Myrdal will occupy our attention more extensively in a later section on foreign aid. We cite it here, however, because of this puzzling paradox. Understanding the human propensity toward self-preservation can quickly explain this national phenomenon. Yet the ironical fact is that the ability to maintain the level of welfare experienced by advanced nations hinges in large measure upon their capacity to raise the levels of well-being on the part of aspiring and less developed lands. But a nation is not an individual, and its collective sense rarely coincides with the enlightened understanding of its more sensitive and comprehending constituents. Nations do not voluntarily relinquish the advantage of their advanced welfare stage, partly because the impairment rarely falls equally on the total citizenry. At the same time, nations currently emerging from a stage of tribalism can hardly comprehend the costs and the generations of time required to move into industrial society. Neither can they grasp what is involved in achieving a level of welfare in which such humane provisions as characterize modern "welfare states" have been attained. Nevertheless the harmonization of these divergent understandings and contrasting economies is a mandate upon the industrialized welfare society.

6

U. S. Agriculture in Domestic and World Economy

Next to defense the largest Congressional appropriations are for agriculture. For more than forty years agriculture has been one of the most consistently aggravating domestic problems confronting those who are responsible for achieving economic stability. The irony is that its magnitude is the result of the success and efficiency of the agricultural enterprise which industriousness, technological advancement, and all the forces we think of as related to progress have accomplished. What gave the stamp of industry to our culture has done the same thing for agriculture, with the result that the two are inseparably interrelated. Compounding the irony is the fact that if the American economy and the related world economy are to remain healthy, agriculture must become even more successful both at home in the United States and abroad.

The fortunate geographic situation of the United States and its combination with a political philosophy which has been consistently favorable to the farmer and agricultural producer have had felicitous results. Because Thomas Jefferson and others associated with him had a profound respect for those who worked on the land and for the consequences to them as a result of their intimate association with the soil, this nation has experienced a long history of friendliness toward the agrarian. Only in recent years has the political center of gravity shifted from the rural areas to urban centers. The most recent evidence is the Supreme Court's decision of 1964 requiring the realignment of voting units for state legislatures. Despite the trend in political power to urban centers, the nation as a whole is deeply sensitive to the welfare of those living on the land and to the even greater number whose economic life is substantially affected by the welfare of those making their living on the land. The ever-increasing integration of agriculture and industry explains some of the reluctance of urban-based legislators to discriminate more vigorously against the claims of rural people who are not their constituents.

The Farm Problem

There was a time when the slogan "depressions are farm-fed and farm-led" was taken seriously, but that time has passed. There is little temptation, however, to discount the close relationship between the agricultural economy and the economy of the nation as a whole.

The term "agribusiness" has been coined to express the combination of all production work on the farm, the manufacture and distribution of farm supplies, and the processing and distribution of farm commodities and items made from them. Agribusiness employs around 40 per cent of all the people that work in the United States and supplies the commodities which account for about 40 per cent of total consumer expenditures. Agricultural production supplies over 60 per cent of the value of raw materials consumed in the United States.

Of the 65 million people employed in the United States, about 25 million work somewhere in the agricultural industry: 7 million work on farms, 7 million produce for and service farmers, and 11 million process and distribute farm products. In addition, a half million scientists and technicians directly or indirectly serve agriculture.[1]

Though the population now residing on farms represents a very small percentage of the nation's population, they, together with the people whose economic life is tied to agriculture, constitute a portion of the total populace sufficient to influence its total health. It is for this reason that even the most urban of legislators have come to accept the fact that farm price stabilization is a permanent part of our economy.

The fact is that so long as the farmer's capacity to produce far exceeds the demands of his markets, he cannot expect to achieve stability of income and an equitable share of the nation's prosperity unless (1) the producers of the various crops develop bargaining power in the market place as other industries in our free enterprise economy have done . . . or (2) the government by various devices subsidizes farm income to make up the difference between what the farmer receives in the market place and a reasonable income in representing the investment, management, skill and labor he invests in the production of food and other farm commodities.

In the ten years, 1953–62 inclusive, although all of the segments of the economy have been booming, the net income of agriculture was $21 billion less than in the previous ten years, 1943–52 inclusive. Meanwhile the Department of Agriculture spent for all purposes in those ten years, $35 billion more than in the previous ten years. The costs from 1953 through 1962 were almost $20 billion more than all expenditures of the Department in the previous ninety years of its history. However, it must be noted that a great part of the expenditures of the Department of Agriculture in recent years have been primarily for the benefit of consumers and for aid of distressed people in other countries.[2]

Whatever may have been the basis of the general disposition toward agricultural people until now, and however convinced we may be that the economy is so closely integrated that agriculture may not be allowed to suffer impairment, the fact remains that it is not possible to consume in the United States the full production of agriculture's efforts. Meanwhile, surpluses greatly in excess of requirements for drought insurance or even for military exigencies are being accumulated. To complicate matters, there is every assurance that production could be increased from between 50 to 100 per cent through utilization of knowledge and skills already available.

At the very foundation of American agricultural life is a magnificent program of technical education designed to increase the total output of agriculture. Research activities in dozens of land-grant colleges and in government research centers have enabled the American agricultural producer to achieve results which are the admiration of all who know of them. All of this lies behind the steadily mounting surpluses which correspondingly account for the steady decline in agricultural income. Wheat, for example, has increased from 11.2 bushels per acre in 1938 to 26 bushels in 1961. Corn has experienced a comparable increase from 22 bushels per acre in 1933 to 61 bushels in 1961.

Is there no likelihood of these mounting surpluses being utilized in the domestic life of this nation? Undoubtedly improvement in the inadequate diets of an estimated one-fourth of the nation now living at a poverty level could absorb much, but not all, of the available surplus food resources. One might sensibly ask why the farmer does not curtail production when prices go down and his income shrinks. This question has been asked times without end. The plain fact is that the farmer cannot shut down his plant as the manufacturer normally does when his costs exceed his income. The farmer increases his effort and his use of fertilizer and hopes to beat the price decline by increased volume, thus adding still further to the surpluses and price impairment.

We have been presenting the farm problem in terms of surpluses. D. Gale Johnson places it in another context, though with the same implication. "Stated simply, the farm problem is the result of the employment of more labor in agriculture than can earn as large a real income as the same labor could earn elsewhere in the economy. . . . This simple statement of the nature of the farm problem is not universally accepted. Some economists argue that no conceivable reduction in the number of farm workers could result in a significant improvement in the real income position of those remaining in agriculture. . . . Those who argue in this way tend to believe that the solution to the farm problem lies in increasing the bargaining power of farmers, the effective restriction of output and marketing, and, in some cases, the withdrawal of land from agricultural production."[3]

Whether the problem is too many workers—which is undoubtedly an important part of it, or even the major issue as Gale Johnson contends—or whether it is the matter of mounting surpluses which have accompanied increasing efficiency and might even be accelerated with yet greater efficiency, the fact remains that the problem is taxing both the intellectual resources and the patience of all who are concerned with it, and directly and indirectly that means everybody in the country.

Agriculture and Efficiency

Before turning to some of the proposals for resolving the dilemma, the question must be asked whether agriculture, in spite of its historically privileged position, has now become so patently a part of the industrial complex and culture that it can no longer be regarded as meriting distinction because it is "a way of life," that is, seeing the farmer as a modern version of the traditional yeoman.

Iowa State University has established a Center for Agricultural Adjustment and more recently a Center for Agricultural and Economic Development, and it is noteworthy that so large a percentage of the themes discussed in three major conferences dealt with the philosophical, cultural, and even theological problems created by the new agriculture. The titles of the books containing the addresses and discussions are revealing: *Problems and Policies of American Agriculture* (1959), *Goals and Values in Agricultural Policy* (1961), and *Farm Goals in Conflict* (1963). It is safe to say there are no three contemporaneous books containing a greater wealth of material dealing with the cultural aspects of American agriculture and their consequences for the economy of the rest of the world. There have been many conferences on many continents dealing with the problem of technology in agriculture and its implications for the types of society prevailing on those continents. Nowhere, one suspects, has so much attention been paid to the underlying causes and consequences of technology and the industrialization process for the agricultural and allied economies as are there treated. It is hardly coincidental that there should be such a plethora of profound and penetrating analyses at this particular time. If anything, they are long overdue. In a humorous vein, nevertheless weighted with astute insight, economist Kenneth Boulding suggested in one of the forums that universities such as Iowa State have contributed to the dilemma by their very efficiency. But the universities which have helped so magnificently to increase food production have been primarily commodity-centered and have not given adequate attention to the consequences of their efforts on people. He goes on to suggest abolishing the Department of Agriculture, along with several others, and suggests substituting in a department of science and research a unit on poverty and economics.[4]

For many years in the reports of the Department of Agriculture there appeared charts indicating the mounting use of tractors as against the numbers of horses and mules. These no longer elicit response. We take for granted the mechanization of agriculture. We are now more impressed with the charts on farm mortgages, increase of land values, increase of farm size and corresponding decrease in number of farms, the use of land credit, productivity per capita in agriculture vs. industry, the corporate structure of the agricultural enterprise, etc. The term "agribusiness" is all but universally acceptable and is an accurate description. A few remain who are zealous that agriculture as a way of life be maintained, but if they are farmers themselves, they also have one eye cocked for the market. With the exception of a few pockets, such as the Amish in eastern Pennsylvania, technology has been thoroughly accepted in American agriculture; the findings of research on crops, fertilizers, animal husbandry, and all the rest are being adopted almost as rapidly as their counterpart discoveries in urbanized manufacturing centers. Perhaps all of this is symbolized in a study which reports that 23 per cent of Wisconsin farmers carry union cards. They move with ease between the industrial and the agricultural plant.[5] These part-time workers in agriculture point to another of the increasingly obvious problems in agriculture—the decline in numbers of those required for work on the land. Either they must find part-time work in industry or leave agriculture altogether.

Agricultural Employment

No statement concerning U. S. agriculture would be comprehensive which failed to include reference to one of the most difficult and trying problems confronting the agricultural economy—the migrant worker. Those who follow the crops, working when harvest time for each arrives and then enduring unemployment between seasons, represent a gross weakness in what is vaunted as an otherwise efficient system. Disruption of family life, low wages, inadequate care of the sick, absence of protection for industrial workers, reduced educational opportunities—these and many other harmful aspects mark the experience of many whose work is necessary for the harvesting of food. Granting of security to those "industrial workers in agriculture" has thus far been successfully resisted. Mervin G. Smith states: "Many farmers find it impossible to make the adjustments required by the continual adoption of new technologies and therefore they have low incomes. Since farm land is limited it is only as some farmers leave farming that others nearby can enlarge their farms for efficient operation. Many farmers do not have this immediate possibility since nearby land is not for sale. Even though they may have changed the combination of their resources by investing in labor-saving new technology, they have not been able to enlarge their farms. This has left them with excess labor (including their own) and sometimes with too much equipment. Some have then obtained another job and become part-time farmers to improve their incomes."[6]

It is estimated that 38 per cent of all Ohio farmers are employed at least one hundred days per year in off-farm work. In other industrialized states the figures would probably not differ greatly. The significant thing here, however, is not simply the number who are occupied part-time in industry but the fact that even with their spending a substantial portion of their working hours away from the farm, agricultural productivity continues to mount. We are facing here the same problem presented in the discussion of industrialism earlier and in the discussion of automation. Technology is creating for agriculture, as in other phases of the total economy, the very efficiency which compounds its dilemma.

Illustrative of the coordination of technology and business in agriculture is "vertical integration." Most notably adopted in the chicken business, it has now spread to other animal production, especially hogs and cattle. Its process is simple: a feed company places its animals in the custody of the farmer who nurtures them from infancy to market, using the company's feeds and finally selling them at the company's direction. The farmer's role is that of custodian and overseer, while technical and financial aspects are directed by the initiating organization.

From its earliest beginnings, in the northern part of this country at least, farming has been centered in the "family farm." Much of the current anxiety over agriculture in the United States stems from the fear that something inherently valuable for our national life will be lost if this historic keystone of agriculture and national stability disappears. Now the entire question of family farming is being reappraised in the light of the new situation. A comment by Emerson Shideler reflects the opinion of many others. "We are now capable of producing sufficient quantities of goods and fiber quite independent of family farming as such. But we are still arguing that in order to preserve stability of the family it is necessary to keep these families in a business that is no longer necessary as a business. We need to re-examine the relationship between these two values."[7]

All these facts together plus a vast complex of statistics related to many other phases of these and other problems combine to create what has been designated as "the farm problem."

Some Proposed Solutions

Belatedly but effectively, agriculture learned the lessons taught it by the expansion of industry. Giant pressure groups emerged in the form of the American Farm Bureau Federation, Farmers Union, the Grange, and more recently, the National Farmers Organization. The latter has taken a leaf out of the notebook of industry in its program for withholding produce and livestock from the market until prices can be brought to an optimum level. Each of these organizations develops its corresponding pressure programs, filling legislative halls with lobbyists seeking to obtain for agriculture what industry long ago learned to secure for itself. The pattern of industry is to be found perhaps even more directly in the development of the farmers cooperative organizations, whether for marketing or for production. Through them the farmer has learned to acquire economic power and to influence, in some measure at least, the price factor. A nation historically kindly disposed toward agriculture has willingly encouraged the development of such self-help enterprises to the point where they have become themselves economic giants capable of competing on finance row, in the research laboratory, and in the legislatures.

The so-called "farm problem" was beginning to make itself known prior to World War I. Its seriousness was temporarily delayed and then greatly aggravated by that war when American grain and foodstuff became necessary as a part of the war effort itself. Large areas of land which we now know should never have been used for grain production were plowed under; farmers were encouraged to produce to the fullest of their ability, and they then found it difficult, if not impossible, to cut back production when the needs subsided. A result was an agricultural depression ten years before the world-shaking economic collapse and industrial depression following the crash in 1929. From that day to the present each administration has proposed programs designed to provide income stability for agriculture and a harmonization of agricultural-industrial-financial situations for the nation and consequently for the rest of the world. At the time of this writing, a new program is in the offing, but probably such a statement could be made at the time of any writing in the foreseeable future. A delineation of those programs makes fascinating study and reveals much about the political and economic temper of this nation for the period of their acceptance or rejection. Because a portrayal of those plans would involve us in too extensive a digression, we will forego the temptation except for a quick review of the positions of the major farm organizations. Thus at one time it is possible to indicate varying programs and something of the pressure groups behind them. Since the differences become apparent in the areas of support prices, land use, production payments, the positions for our purposes are confined to these areas.

The American Farm Bureau Federation states:

> A major objective of farm bureau policy is to create conditions whereby farmers may earn and get a high per family real income in a manner which will preserve freedom and opportunity. We firmly believe that this objective can best be accomplished by preserving the market price system as the principal influence in allocating the use of farm resources and in distributing farm production.[8]

The Farmer's Union believes: (1) the efficient family farmer should have full parity of income, returns on labor, management and capital invested in comparison with returns to comparable resources invested in nonfarm enterprise; (2) the preservation of the family farm is in the national interest; (3) farmers must acquire more bargaining power in the market place.[9]

The Grange:

The primary goal of Grange farm program policy is the re-alignment of these established and fully accepted government provided protective devices so as to supply equitable income opportunities to farmers. This re-alignment must include programs necessary to give agricultural producers an opportunity to earn and receive for their labor, management, risk and investment a return reasonably comparable to that provided by those same factors in their best nonfarm employments.[10]

The National Farm Organization:

First, farmers must organize, because there is no substitute for organized strength in an organized economy. If farmers want to price their products, they must go to the market place with equal or greater strength than those that buy their products. Therefore, they cannot solve their problems and then organize. They must organize to solve their problems. . . . Secondly, farmers must bring together enough of the total production so that the present marketing system cannot fulfill their needs from other sources. . . . And how do you make your bargaining power felt? By the use of holding actions. There has never been a commodity or a service priced in America on which the holding action has not been used.[11]

Such statements are but small sections of the full policy statements and are included here primarily to give the "flavor" of the organization's position. Nor are these the only organizations which have agricultural programs. They are, however, the major farmers' organizations seeking to influence total agricultural policy formation at the national level.

Agricultural economist Walter Wilcox, reviewing various price stabilization programs, comments:

Government farm price stabilization activities probably have become a permanent part of our economic system. Those who would abolish all these programs are in a distinct minority. Farm leaders find there is widespread disagreement, however, on: (1) the level of supports that should be maintained in relation to long-run normal free market prices; (2) the number of commodities that should be included in the group having mandatory supports; (3) the restrictions that should be placed on the use of diverted acres when marketing quotas and acreage allotments are in effect; (4) the restriction of the conflict between domestic price stabilization and freer international trade; (5) the distribution of benefits among farm families.[12]

There may be disagreement among farm leaders on many parts of the total farm situation, but there is no disagreement on the fact that the farm population is shrinking, that farm technology has made unnecessary a large percentage of those now engaged in farming, that agricultural supplies and production are greatly in excess of what could be consumed in the United States even with a massive reduction in poverty, that there are values inherent in the production of agricultural supplies which contribute to the life of individuals, families, and communities, and that programs must be devised which will preserve the best in agricultural life and at the same time not impair or penalize the rest of the economy.

These areas of common agreement, though they are American in their present setting, have implications for the life of many other nations, both because of the necessity for using American agricultural surpluses for the creation of stable world relationships and because many other nations will face similar problems as they also move from agricultural to industrial predominance. A clue to this latter situation is in the description of European agricultural changes by the Dutch rural sociologist E. W. Hofstee: "What has been said will probably be sufficient to demonstrate that agricultural and rural life in Europe are in a serious crisis which will demonstrate itself in the years to come still far more clearly than it has already. As far as history can tell us, the European countryside faces the most important and the most sudden change of its existence. Even the existence of a class of farmers as a separate group with its own social, cultural and economic characteristics is at stake."[13]

It is the difference between the situation in the United States and that in most of the other countries of the world which not only creates the problem but also may hold a partial key to its solution. "The United States," says agricultural economist Earl O. Hardy, "has a farm problem only because it is wealthy and has progressed far up the path of economic development. In contrast, many other nations have problems of agriculture because they are poor and economic progress has been tardy. Because we are so far advanced in over-all national economic development, we perhaps have 10 to 20 years of slack ahead of us, during which we can adjust toward any more effective use of resources needed in the long-run. It will take longer than this for the other nations with large populations and resource bases to catch up in level of economic development and potentiality in production."[14]

Is there a solution? Not in a great increase of consumption in the United States at least, for demand elasticity is low. Undoubtedly there could be greater food consumption on the part of those at the lower end of the economic scale. Estimates vary greatly as to the amount which could be consumed, were all residents of this nation capable of receiving a balanced and adequate diet. This would, however, be no permanent solution to the problem of agricultural surpluses. Undoubtedly, too, chemistry will find new uses for products of the soil, and further reduction in surpluses will be made during the next decade, providing additions are not made to the surpluses by policies which encourage increased production. The devices we have employed thus far—price supports, soil bank, acreage reserves, conservation reserves, and a variety of income-supporting programs—have served to stablize the income of agricultural producers and have made it possible for many families to remain on the farm when they would otherwise have been pressured off. If the benefits had accrued only to the family-type farm, hostility to the programs on the part of some urban people might have diminished. Well known, however, is the fact that very large farm operators have been the recipients of government benefits, in some instances approximating a million dollars per operator. Sociologist Robin Williams contends: "There is a limit to the subsidization of comparatively well-off commercial farmers that will be politically tolerated in an urbanized democracy. There is a limit to the acceptability to the conscience of the public of the mass misery of migratory farm workers or of the rural slums of stranded populations."[15]

As indicated earlier, a great many people have gotten into the act of making proposals for the resolution of the "farm problem." Another analysis of the situation which has received wide attention because of the competent and distinguished panel producing the proposals is that of the Committee for Economic Development. Their proposal, comprehensive in scope, can be stated in their own words in a single paragraph:

The programs we are suggesting would result in fewer workers in agriculture, working a smaller number of farms of greater average size and receiving substantially higher income per worker. . . . There are two ways to reduce governmental agriculture outlays without great losses to farmers. One is to tighten controls of production and marketing enough to reduce farm output to the point where all output will sell at the higher prices. This will make consumers pay more for farm products and let the government pay less. The other way is to attract and assist enough farmers out of farming so that farm income per farmer will be sustained without rising farm prices despite a decline in government spending on agriculture.[16]

Another popular and widely discussed analysis of the farm problem suggests:

There is no solution which will not hurt some farmer and benefit others. Even to abandon all farm programs would be a boon to some agriculturists and a catastrophe to others. Like everyone else in a dynamic society, farmers are changing as the economy changes around them. . . . Now that farm subsidies run around $5 billion a year instead of .3 billion as they did in 1952, the taxpayer is entitled to believe that the point of diminishing returns has been reached. . . . The end of a process, however, does not mean an end to all evolution. To the contrary, as far as American agriculture is concerned perhaps the end of big government spending will mark the beginning of new and more intensive efforts by farmers to manage their businesses and seek their personal fortunes in more sophisticated ways.[17]

Here the solution, though bound to injure some, is to recognize that farming is itself primarily a business and must henceforth be treated in what the author calls "more sophisticated ways." This does not mean the end of the family farm, but asks that farming as a family occupation accept the criteria of efficiency without demanding of other taxpayers a subsidy for their continued operation disproportionate to any other segment of the economy. It does not take into account the fact that industry in a very large measure is dependent upon taxpayers' support in the form of payment for defense costs, which are approximately ten times greater than the current outlay for agriculture. Presumably, however, it is reasonable to expect that an increasing resolution of the world tensions will make possible a steady diminution in the taxpayers' outlay for defense purposes. We have no illusions that this will occur without great hue and cry from those who are now subsidized through defense outlays, as the response to modest cut-backs in the current period already presaged.

It becomes increasingly apparent that the defense aspects of the economy, the projected and hoped-for projects of foreign aid, the massive attacks on the poverty situation, are all tied together in a common bundle including the agriculture problem.

Our Surpluses and World Needs

American surpluses in agricultural production have provided a political and economic headache for the nation as a whole, but they also present a bright aspect. Our program of storage and reserve fulfilled its initial purpose in periods of drought and in times of dire need coincident with World War II and the Korean conflict. But a succession of highly productive years has again brought surpluses to a size beyond any immediately foreseeable domestic needs.

"What we need now," says Byron Johnson, "is an affirmative program that will bring our domestic agricultural policy into harmony with our foreign policy. The world needs our food but the problem domestically is the cost in allocating this food to places where need exists and the problem of placing the food in such spots of need without disrupting the economy of the country receiving it or of other nations which might reasonably expect to sell their own agricultural products to the needy nations."[18]

It is of this that Charles M. Hardin is speaking when he says: "We must radically change our Agricultural Trade Development and Assistance Act and really insure that our overseas disposal programs make a net addition to consumption and not to a replacement of what would otherwise move in world trade."[19]

The problem is greater than simply that of designating surplus foods for hungry people in other parts of the world. Food, we recognize, can be an instrument for strengthening the bodies of those in recipient nations and thereby can contribute to building up the productive capacities within the receiving nations. Harvard's John D. Black suggests disposal of agricultural products "as an assistance to a backward or undeveloped country in carrying out a program that will increase its ability to feed itself. Such programs and assistance need to be planned carefully because: (1) There is danger that the productivity will not be built up faster than the increased supply of food checks the death rate, so that if the food assistance is cut off at any time, the people of that country will be worse off than before."[20]

Our national policy of food distribution has been characterized by considerable ambivalence. We have not been fully certain that the use of our food resources is primarily intended to strengthen our relationships with other countries and ultimately to contribute to a greater degree of interdependence between nations. We have been inclined to regard the distribution of food and agricultural products as a part of the farm support program, which indeed they were; but to regard them primarily in this fashion is to miss a major opportunity. "On the national and international scene many forces are working together to demand a fresh and bold program. Specifically the U. S. and the UN-FAO have launched a Freedom from Hunger campaign; the U. S. did invite the world and the UN agreed to join in making the 1960's a UN decade of development. In order to deal with the emerging regional economic groupings in Europe and Latin America, the U. S. has strengthened its trade policy through the Trade Expansion Act. Finally, fundamental criticisms of the U. S. farm program at home as well as abroad have underlined our need for a basic revision of the program."[21]

The Food and Agriculture Organization has already designated 100 million dollars to be used for placing foods where most needed. The U. S. has assumed a major role making these funds available and thus participates in an international venture whose long-range outcome will benefit the economy of the whole world.

A program of wise allocation of American surplus foods, in conjunction with other nations similarly blessed, could both strengthen the receiving people and make for a far more comprehensive appreciation of the interrelatedness of the world and its resources. This would not relieve United States agriculture of the necessity for devising programs consistent with the evolution of agriculture's technology, but it would place the total problem in a new context. "We cannot, we must not, turn our backs upon the world. We can, we must, and therefore we will, prepare to cooperate hereafter so that more people are better fed, with fewer workers engaged in agriculture and with better incomes for all. . . . This is our opportunity."[22]

It has become apparent that there are basic differences in the goals of those who seek to improve the overall agricultural situation in the United States. There is no such thing as *the* agricultural position. Even though rural and urban interests may be in conflict in some phases of the political scene, they are very much dependent upon each other in other ways. Willard W. Cochrane, former director of agricultural economics in the U. S. Department of Agriculture, says:

"The only conceivable way of resolving this conflict between our historic commitments to both commutative and distributive justice for farm people is to *limit total farm output* to a level that will bring to agriculture as a whole a fair return and all farm operators of inadequate farms to achieve efficient sized farm units. . . . But this method of resolving the conflict between commutative and distributive justice throws our historic premiums on technological advance and entrepreneurial freedom into opposition and conflict at another conceptual level. This is true because limiting the total output of farm units prevents operators from using new and available technologies in whatever ways they may desire.[23]

This, however, is only a part of the area of conflict and of the difference in goals maintained for agriculture. There are regional differences, differences due to type of agricultural products (e.g., cottonseed oil vs. soybean oil), and fundamental ideological differences over supporting a segment of the total population for the purpose of stabilizing the economy as a whole. Robin Williams contends that entrepreneurial freedom is incompatible with several of the other important goals and values desired by farm people; "because we want several incompatible things, the agricultural programs of the future will continue to represent complex compromises among different values and goals." He adds that "the only hope for an effective agriculture and an enduring rural life is in selective change and adaptation to new conditions. There is no simple panacea."[24]

Conflicting farm interests have also found expression in terms of contradictory national and international political ideologies. Economist T. W. Schultz states:

Farmers in the United States have had a large hand politically in developing our welfare state, long before the New Deal and McNary-Haugenism. The earlier agrarian movements protested strongly against the doctrine of laissez faire not because farm leaders had been schooled in European socialism or in Marxian thought. Their protests were a direct indigenous response to the raw industrialism of the post Civil War decade and to the long decline in the general level of prices. More recently, mainly after the first World War, farmers turned to the Federal government to intervene in their behalf in adjusting agricultural production and in supporting particular farm prices in what John D. Black called "assisted laissez faire." Despite the strong political influence farmers have had in the developing of our welfare state, they have not acquired many of the social services that it renders unto others in society. The puzzle is why? . . .

The combination of the political influence of Southern tradition, the conflict of interest among farm families, the fact that farm leaders are not conversant with the ideas, the philosophical basis and the historical process of which modern agriculture is an integral part and the extraordinary commitment to having the government enact and administer production-price programs, represent a formidable barrier to welfare. It is a high wall against the social services of the welfare state. This wall will not come tumbling down until this combination is undermined. Until then the U. S. welfare state cannot serve the welfare of farm people adequately.[25]

Economist Walter Wilcox contends that the problem is, in part at least, the result of misplaced emphases:

One hears repeatedly that we cannot make progress in adopting more desirable farm policies because of conflicts in goals and values among farm and nonfarm groups. In my opinion, a more accurate statement would be that because of mistaken beliefs about the nature of the economic consequences of alternative policies, groups fail to discover their common interests. Most of the group conflicts as we know them today in the farm policy field are the result of mistaken beliefs regarding the effects of existing policies and expected effects of alternative policies. And we should ask ourselves: Why is this situation so prevalent today?

Why is such a small part of the research and educational resources in agricultural economics devoted to obtaining a better understanding of these policy issues? Why do our brightest graduate students work on the more concrete but less important problems of farm and industry efficiency under static conditions of equilibrium?[26]

Belatedly, perhaps, but nonetheless seriously we have begun to analyze the agricultural dilemma where it is the result of vigorous but noninclusive considerations. We can hope that the kinds of considerations elicited by the Iowa State University Center for Agricultural Economic Adjustment portend further treatment of this vast and complex theme.

As is true of each of the areas dealt with heretofore and of those which follow, differences in policy and their attendant programs cannot be resolved at the level of economic theory, at least in its limited sense. Each of these issues involves fundamental philosophical problems, and many, including myself, would contend that there are theological considerations involved as well.

Since its inception in 1950 the National Council of Churches, as was true of the Federal Council of Churches which preceded this organization, has been deeply concerned with the problem of agricultural policy. This is not by any means solely a Protestant concern. *Mater et Magistra*, an encyclical of Pope John XXIII, has sometimes been referred to as the "agricultural encyclical." The National Council of Churches' statement on "Ethical Goals for Agricultural Policy" was designed with the United States" situation primarily in mind, though it has implications for world agriculture as well. This statement adopted by the General Board of the National Council of Churches comes as close to being an official statement of Protestant position as anything could be, considering the structure of cooperating Protestant organizations. "A Christian ethical approach to agriculture begins with the acknowledgment that 'the earth is the Lord's and the fulness thereof.' God, the Creator, has given man a special position in the world, with specific responsibility for the fruits of the earth and towards all living things. This is the stewardship of the earth's resources for the nourishment and the enrichment of human life. Thus the production of food and fiber—the primary task of farmers—becomes a service to God and man."[27]

Carrying the theme beyond the specifically domestic scene is a resolution approved by the General Assembly of the National Council, titled "Ethical Issues in the International Age of Agriculture." It states: "God's concern for the needs of all His children for nourishment, both of body and soul, is revealed in His act of creation and in the gift of His Son, Jesus Christ. Our Lord made perfectly clear that man's duty to God includes the production and sharing of the material necessities of life. He described the conditions of salvation at the ultimate judgment to include the fact that we did—or did not—'feed the hungry and clothe the naked.'"[28] The implications of such a commission include (a) sharing our food supplies, (b) sharing technological knowledge and experience, (c) sharing economic aid for agriculture and food production, (d) role of religious and other voluntary organizations, (e) a major global program. The last commends for support by governments and people of every nation the world-wide five-year Freedom from Hunger campaign of the UN specialized agency, the Food and Agriculture Organization. In both purpose and scope this program is commended to our churches and their members. National and international church organizations thus lend their support to individuals, to national and international political agencies contending that America's temporary embarrassment can be a boon to world development. And through this use of her resources the long-run purposes of the nation itself are best served.

7

*The Consumer—Power or Pushover?**

When President Johnson established a President's Committee on Consumer Interests and made Mrs. Esther Peterson the Special Assistant for Consumer Affairs, responsible directly to the White House, a half century of work on behalf of consumers' interest was crowned with success. This act may not guarantee the full realization of the ends desired by those who have championed the cause of the consumer, but it does represent an advance toward their objectives. The irony of this accomplishment lies in the fact that every one of the 195 million persons in this country, as well as the 3.5 billion persons in the rest of the world, is a consumer. Why has it taken so long for the interests of the consumer to be recognized as an important part of the structure of government? One answer is that we assume a free market and a free choice on the part of the buyer. He—or more likely, she—exercises freedom of choice in purchases and thereby determines what products shall be produced and the price that shall be paid. This in itself, it is hypothesized, should provide protection. What the champions of the consumer have been trying to say for at least half a century, however, is that freedom of choice does not exist and that the consumer is in need of protection against those who can control the market and, through devices of their own construction, beguile the buyer into accepting inferior products at dishonest weights and measures. There is much evidence that were he not protected by government-established health standards, his life itself could be

* I am especially indebted to Dr. Leland Gordon for his excellent paper on "The Role and Responsibility of the Consumer," prepared for the Fourth National Study Conference on the Church and Economic Life (November 1962).

in danger. Quickly it must be added, however, that devices to protect the consumer are also valuable in protecting the preponderance of honest manufacturers and distributors who hold high standards of integrity and public service.

The Economic System and the Ultimate Consumer

The economic system exists to provide goods and services for the satisfaction of human needs and wants. Within that system the consumer theoretically determines what is produced and the price paid. If the costs exceed the value to him, he declines to buy; if the return is too low, the producer declines to produce. This seems to be an almost ridiculously simple explanation for an economy which also spends almost 50 billion dollars a year for armaments. In our economic system we assume that if the consumer did not feel this was justifiable, he could, so the free-choice theory goes, decline to spend his money in this way. By contrast, for example, the Communist system needs no such justification or endorsement. Its directors have determined that a specified percentage of their national income must be used for defense purposes, and in response to their judgment the Russian consumer seems to go along. (Of course, the Russian expenditures, too, are justified in their minds by the fact that the American consumer has endorsed the expenditure of so large a sum for "defense." And so the escalation continues.)

Freedom of choice for the consumer is not a uniform condition. Again, under the Russian system, overseers of the economy have determined that capital goods (producers' goods) take precedence over consumer wants, as a means of building up the capacity for industrial productivity. In the United States productive capacities have long since exceeded what the consumer desires, and the result is the well-known surpluses in grain and "inventories" in automobiles, refrigerators, and many other things. The exception, of course, would be in what is called the public sector—schools, roads, housing, and health resources. But here again the consumer has presumably voted, consciously or unconsciously, that his funds in the form of taxes shall go for space exploration and defense.

Meanwhile, the Russian consumer is informed that in the near future his productive capacity will have reached the desired stage and that consumer goods will soon become available.

Theoretically, then, part of the difference between the "free" and the regulated economy lies in the extent to which the consumer is permitted to use his earnings in the satisfaction of his wants.

On the face of it, it would appear that the consumer in a free economy exercises his freedom under the direction of a balanced judgment which comprehends total needs and what is best for himself and his dependents. He will secure what is ultimately best for his welfare in a way that the Russian consumer is not able to do. One quick look at the imbalance between the things that are purchased and the needs that exist would indicate that in the minds of many, at least, there is no unanimity of judgment in this matter of purchases. "Do all consumers know what goods and services will promote their welfare?" asks Leland Gordon. "If all of them know, does it follow that they will consume only those goods and services which are beneficial? Are consumers able to judge the quality of the thousands of items they find in the market? Everything consumers buy is priced on the basis of weight, measure, or numerical count. To what extent are consumer buyers able to check the quantity measurements of their purchases? Can consumers know whether prices are really competitive? To what extent are the prices of some goods and services determined by the collusive action of the sellers? . . . To what extent are consumers rational?"[1]

If the consumer were truly rational, would it make any difference in the allocation of his expendable funds? Our liquor and tobacco bill per capita is only slightly less than our outlay for public education.[2]* At present this is the way the consumer chooses to have it under the freedom accorded him in our kind of system. ". . . High expenditures for tobacco, alcoholic beverages, soft drinks and movies, for example, by families with 'inadequate' diets, 'substandard' housing, and 'insufficient' medical care have been taken by some people as evidence that consumers cannot be expected

* Expenditures per capita in 1963 for public education, $116; tobacco $42.70 (approximately); liquor $60 (approximately)

to choose wisely. Some proposals have seemed to imply that decisions as to what kind of consumption is more important should be left largely to specialists who have greater knowledge and wisdom concerning consumer needs. This tendency is at variance with the deep-rooted conviction in the American society that individuals should be free to explore and to decide what is best for them, and that consumer education to improve free choice is a sounder way than decisions by experts to direct the course of future consumption."[3]

The American consumer, collectively speaking, has a voting power of approximately 410 billion dollars (1964) which represents his disposable income. His government, using his taxes, makes an impact on the economy to the tune of 110 billion dollars—purchases which are also dictated by this same consumer. The question of primary concern, then, is: On what basis the consumer, either himself or through his government, makes the judgment as to what is best for him and for the country as a whole? There have been instances in which the consumer vote made profound changes necessary. For example, when the Food and Drug Administration was created, it was no longer possible for "patent medicines" to be distributed with advertising which claimed benefits the medicines could not provide. More recently, after long and bitter debate between "specialists" it was finally concluded that cigarettes were a factor contributing to cancer. The consumer, through a tax-supported agency, forced public recognition of the cigarette as a menace to health—although judging from cigarette sales, this public action has as yet had little effect.

What the Modern Consumer Assumes

Before looking at the forces bombarding the consumer, shaping his thought and conditioning his purchasing, it is necessary to consider a whole world of influences which shape the thinking of the consumer almost without his awareness. These lines are being written during the longest period of continuous upward movement of economic indices in modern times. But whether such a setting is the one best known by the consumer or not, the state of the economy in which he happens to be living affects the degree of confidence or pessimism he reveals. I recall spending an evening with a small-town banker whose bank remained solvent during the Great Depression when others all about him collapsed. His conservatism and stability were household words in his own county and far beyond. Then came World War II and the backlog of buying potential, which fooled many economists and business leaders whose memories of postwar situations told them to expect a collapse. A minor collapse came, but much later. Through all of this the small-town banker remained conservative and admonished his customers to do likewise. Everywhere the expansion-minded were making remarkable headway, and the conservatives, including this banker, were left behind. This practice was not, however, confined to small-town bankers, merchants, and farmers. A famous case is that of a world-renowned mail-order house whose leadership operated on the same principles, until they were outdistanced by competitors and a change-minded board of directors switched management. The psychology of confidence or the expectation of retrenchment is a powerful factor in shaping the decision of the consumer.

Affecting both the small consumer and the buyer of giant proportions are certain major economic changes which have become commonplace in the consumer world and whose influence is widely if not universally felt, even though the consumer may not be constantly reminded of their presence. We shall consider these one by one.

The first of these changes is the emergence of powerful corporations determining the welfare of their industry, their employees, and in varying degrees those who buy and sell their product. Where they have been efficient—and except for the jerry-built structures designed for quick profits by speculators, they have been efficient—they are able to market their products at an advantage over the smaller operator who cannot take advantage of the economies in large-scale purchases and distribution. But the strictly economic factor may not be the dominant influence of these giant corporations; for they require a bureaucratic structure. Individually and collectively they shape the mentality of whole communities and their institutional life. Though they stress the necessity of their employees fostering the image of community concern, their own principal objectives are not primarily the welfare of the consumer but the operation of the market. The giant corporation begets its opposite number in the giant union organization. They are dependent upon each other and in collusion may take such action as will enhance profits and wages irrespective of the public welfare. What is true for the giant corporations has its parallel in all other large-scale enterprises, whether in agriculture or in medicine. We accept these great combinations as an inevitable part of the American system.

Second, whereas a generation ago military expenditures were very modest, we take it for granted that they have now become an all-encompassing factor in our economy, as has been indicated earlier. But here again the major factor may not be merely the size of the portion the military represents in the economy but the impact on the mentality of the people who are themselves products of its training.

Third is the rapid change that has occurred in the method of merchandising, as we moved from the store salesman or door-to-door salesman to the presentation of goods in picture form in unlimited variety in one's own living room. Value and quality are not the primary concern of the agencies who secure extrance to whatever part of the house we use to watch television or listen to radio. The objective is attractiveness and capacity to lure the potential buyer without opportunity for comparison with other "makes and models."

The fourth revolutionary change, which has come unheralded but nonetheless has taken possession of the mind of the modern consumer, is the consciousness that somehow spending is a patriotic duty and that everyone is under obligation to serve the economy. The nation's well-being depends upon keeping the economy healthy. The important thing is not the merit or quality of what is purchased but that production shall go on so that employment be maintained.

Related directly or indirectly to these four major changes which have occurred within a generation are others which call for some special mention. Rare is the person reared in another day who does not shake his head perplexedly when the question of installment buying arises. Expectation of continued prosperity has lifted the private debt of this country from 60 billion dollars to almost 400 billion dollars in less than a quarter century. Financial analysts are constantly being interrogated, and their answers headlined, on the question whether we have reached a saturation point in personal credit. We have come to assume that both fiscal and monetary policy can be brought into action quickly enough to curtail excesses if such seem to be emerging. Young people do not expect to start a home with the limited equipment of their parents. With an easy credit situation they can enjoy a measure of comfort comparable to that of a generation of others who own similar gadgets and conveniences after a lifetime of saving. This has given rise to such a large business of loaning money for installment purchases that some merchandising establishments make more money in the loaning of money on time payments than on the sale of the merchandise. The convenience of having the equipment transcends anxieties over future capacity to continue payments. It adds up to the expectation of a plane of living equal to the best, at least in the areas of household equipment and automobiles.

Many who have come to maturity during the current period cannot remember the time when healing drugs were not available, so commonplace have they become. With them has come the resultant expectation of less serious illness or even the prevention of illnesses which at one time were a common dread. So gratified are consumers that these drugs can be readily obtainable, that there is little disposition to ask whether they are available at a price commensurate with their costs. The Congressional hearings on drug costs, chaired by the late Estes Kefauver, shook the drug industry with its sensational findings but apparently elicited no great public indignation.

What is true of drugs is perhaps even truer of food. Frequently have we been reminded that food takes a lesser percentage of the American budget than is the case in any other country, and therefore we do not ask the question whether it could be available even more cheaply.* The convenience of ready-prepared foods, so beneficial to the household where time for preparation is at a premium, has minimized the inclination to inquire about the costs of the food itself and the processing which makes it available so quickly. The facts that, though food is in great abundance, its cost continually rises and the farmer receives a steadily declining proportionate return for what he has produced, constitute one of the paradoxes of our time. Only recently has there been emerging at Congressional level the demand for a major analysis of this dilemma.

To any list of commonplace assumptions would have to be added the expectation of obsolescence. A productive society capable of manufacturing more than can be consumed must foster a disposition to purchase new models and to discourage repairs. The automobile industry is a major example of this encouragement of artificial obsolescence. Until recently there has been little serious resistance to the manufacturers' policy, but the importation of some durable foreign-made cars seems to have induced a disposition to concentrate on quality in the domestic automotive industry.

Nevertheless the widespread misgivings concerning doubtful claims for many products have undermined public confidence in many types of advertising. Noteworthy efforts have been made to achieve and maintain standards of integrity in offering certain goods and services, but that deviations are frequent is widely apparent. The current trend in self-regulation as observed in the area of cigarette advertising compares with the regulations resulting from the false claims at one time made for "patent medicines." Medical facts plus public indignation have combined to curb dishonesty. With so many reputable producers using honorable means to portray their products, it may seem harsh to concentrate on those who practice deception. As in every profession or type of work, it is the latter who bring discredit to the work of others. One of

* E. g., comparing Moscow work time as a percentage of New York work time in 1959: butter, 900 per cent (21 min. *vs.* 3 hrs. 4 min.); eggs, 800 per cent; beef, 400 per cent; milk, 400 per cent. (Source: The Conference Board Road Maps of Industry, No. 1275.)

the major frontiers of ethics in our time lies in the promotion of integrity in advertising.

Influencing the Consumer's Judgment

As a nation we believe so thoroughly in the old slogan "it pays to advertise" that we are willing to spend 12 billion dollars, or 2.8 per cent of our national income, for that purpose. This can hardly be condemned as an exorbitant expenditure toward keeping the economy healthy. With considerable truth the defenders of advertising contend that this very large business makes a substantial and necessary contribution to our economic well-being.

In any area of life involving so great a sum of money it would be strange if there were not a proportionate measure of chicanery and outright fraud. Techniques for manipulating the minds and dispositions of others are a constant temptation to dishonesty and give rise to profound ethical problems. In a free economy, where the market is presumed to determine prices, those who practice the science of influencing purchasing decisions can assert with some reasonableness that "no one has to buy," that individuals are still free and can judge for themselves whether they are getting "value received." As was stated earlier when we were discussing the increasing importance of the three big components in our economy—government, labor, and management—it has become apparent that "the sovereign importance of the market is a thing of the past. Even if it were to furnish a perfectly equilibrated price structure the market would resolve few if any of our fateful dilemmas."[4] Also at the level of the individual consumer the market has a diminishing significance. This is not to say that changes do no occur because of changing tastes. Rather it is to suggest that tastes themselves can be created and also that in gratifying these tastes individuals can be induced to buy goods which are, if not inimical to their best interests, at least of poorer quality than others which they might purchase.

Caveat emptor—"let the buyer beware"—has been a cardinal feature of the free-choice system. Presumably, if the buyer has been deceived enough, he will change his purchasing habits. The burden, therefore, has traditionally rested with the buyer. When federal and state governments entered this arena, it was charged that this was interfering with the sovereign right of the buyer and also that of the enterprising producer. A higher standard was resorted to in this controversy—the standard of the well-being, the wealth of society, or what has come to be known as the commonweal. Regulatory agencies having jurisdiction over quality, contents, and weights and measures were set up to give protection to the buyer who himself could not know the content of foods and medicines or judge honest weights. Thus he became protected, in part at least, against the attractiveness of word and picture with which the advertiser confronted him.

Leaving the health aspect aside—for few would argue in this day that government should not protect its citizens against physical injury from food and drugs—the question still remains whether the buyer should not have the privilege of being fooled if he so wishes, or of satisfying his own personal desires as they have been stimulated through advertising media. If he chooses not to be a rational buyer, is not that his privilege? The answer would necessarily be yes if first the individual has been apprized of all the factors which enter into the purchase. If he knows he is getting less than his money's worth, it is certainly his privilege to pay as much as he wishes over and above the actual worth of the product. But if he has insufficient means for discovering the difference between the value of the product and the price being charged, whose responsibility is it?

This difference between cost and value of the product comes out with special clarity in the whole matter of packaging. The issue is stated in the report of a Senate hearing on the subject:

> In our modern society good packaging meets many consumer needs, among them convenience, freshness, safety and attractive appearance. But often in recent years, as the hearings have demonstrated, these benefits have been accompanied by practices which frustrate the consumer's efforts to get the best value for his dollar. In many cases the label seems designed to conceal rather than to reveal the true contents of the package. Sometimes the consumer cannot readily ascertain the net amount of the product, or the ratio of solid contents to air. Frequently he cannot readily compute the comparative costs per unit

of different brands packed in odd sizes, or of the same brand in large, giant, king size, or jumbo packages. And he may not realize that changes in the customary size or shape of the package may account for apparent bargains, or that "cents off" promotions often do not mean real savings.

Misleading, fraudulent or unhelpful practices such as these are clearly incompatible with the efficient and equitable functioning of our free competitive economy. Under our system, consumers have a right to expect that packages will carry reliable and readily usable information about their contents. And those manufacturers whose products are sold in such packages have a right to expect that their competitors will be required to adhere to the same standards.[5]

For many years Congressional leaders, social workers, and all who have a concern for the problem of individual bankruptcy have been pressing for a "truth in lending" bill. In one year (1961) 150,000 families declared themselves in bankruptcy, a rate ten times that of a decade ago. A person buying on credit may pay anywhere from nothing to 275 per cent for the privilege. Cash loans secured through commercial loan companies, or as a part of the criminal "juice" racket, range from 4 to 2000 per cent! Commercial banks and credit unions charge 12 per cent, while consumer finance companies get anywhere from 30 to 42 per cent. An informed borrower could calculate the rate of his loan, but the tragic fact is that many are unable to make this calculation and respond to the blandishments of those exacting inordinately high rates under the happy expectation of paying off all their bills in one lump sum or of taking a vacation free of worries. It is understandable that those in the business of exacting such rates of interest, including automobile financing agencies whose income from the time-payment sale of an automobile is greater than the profit from the sale itself, are vehemently opposed to "truth in lending" legislation.

Trading stamps have become as much the symbol of the American economy as the supermarket. They are also a symbol of joyous self-deception. Everyone (well, almost) "knows" that everything he receives with the trading stamps he has already paid for with the initial purchase.* There is the possibility of a slight bonus

* The price increase ranges between one and two per cent, depending on which of the fifty-odd trading devices is used.

here; the people who do not pick up the goods to which they are entitled through trading stamps leave just that much more in the treasury of the trading stamp company and may add a little to the value received by others who do. This gigantic scheme for "kidding oneself" that he is getting something for nothing seems to be a part of the economic atmosphere of our time. It is a painless and euphoric device to avoid having to make evaluations and to shop discriminately.

Manufacturers in a free-choice economy have tried repeatedly and with some success to institute "fair trade" laws by which their products could not be sold below a stipulated figure without penalty to the seller. Some manufacturers hope that prices would be increased and their standards maintained by legislation better than by the competition of the market. Small merchants find this practice desirable as protection against big merchandisers and discount houses whose greater volume give them advantages. As a protection for the small businessman there is something to be said for the idea. Its major weakness lies in the fact that the free economy is disrupted because costs to the consumer should be going down as improved and more economical methods of production are adopted. When the manufacturer is able to protect himself against giving the benefit of these lowered costs to the consumer, he is less inclined to seek better means of production. The National Recovery Administration fostered price-fixing on a national basis, but it was declared unconstitutional. Then state laws were enacted which supported prices, but before they had been fully tested the World War II created a scarcity which temporarily eliminated the need. From 1941 to 1961 the consumers price index rose from 62.9 to 127.5. This included the years of wartime control. But from 1955 to 1960 the index continued to rise at the average rate of 2.6 points per year. Thus competition even in times of great surplus has not consistently kept prices down. One qualifying comment should be made, however. Hopefully there had been a measure of quality increase which is an offsetting factor and which would have added something to the rise in the index.

The consumer is thus embroiled in endless gamesmanship. There is a way of winning, but he may not want to condition himself for the fray. The producers, processors, and distributors, on the other hand, do not take the game so lightly. They spend millions of dollars to analyze the tastes of the consumer, which they have every right to do, providing they have not indulged in outright fraud. Unfortunately the record indicates a great deal of fraud. The labeling which says "ten cents off" doesn't indicate what it is "off of." The label which says "serves eight" may really mean that it serves four. In the Senate hearings on this kind of fraud, Senator Hart commented: "That is a sign of moral deterioration. . . . You wouldn't want your children to adopt a philosophy like that. There's nothing good about this attitude."

Whether the total fraudulence in packaging and advertising is any greater than the collusion which marked the scandal involving the foremost producers of electrical appliances and equipment is beside the point.* It is all part of the same moral deterioration of which the consumer is a victim and to which he has wittingly or unwittingly contributed. It is also of a piece with the collusion between public officials and the suppliers of road materials and highway equipment to the states and the federal government; the collusion between Billy Sol Estes and the financing companies, which dare not expose him for fear their own houses of cards would tumble; the widely exposed cheating in television, bringing distinguished and honorable names into discredit; and on and on.

Ultimately it is the consumer who must bear the costs of the deception, chicanery, and corruption. Some of it is overlooked on the ground that people really don't mind being fooled. They enjoy the little game, and what little they lose they may get back

* The reference is to the collusion between General Electric, Allis-Chalmers, Westinghouse, and others in the sale of equipment both to private firms and to the government from 1951 to 1960. Government prosecution charged prices were raised as much as 900 per cent on some equipment and 446 per cent on other types. Rigging of prices produced hundreds of millions of dollars in excess profits. The companies were declared guilty by a federal court on February 6, 1961. Seven executives were given jail sentences, others were given suspended sentences, and twenty-nine corporations were fined $1,787,000. Subsequently $7,460,000 was repaid to the federal government and additional sums to others who had been injured by these unethical practices.

in excitement or pleasure. This same rationalization, of course, lies behind the pressure for legalized gambling, currently highlighted with the sanctioning of lotteries by the state of New Hampshire. The justification offered is that ultimately it doesn't cost anybody very much and the schools will be the better for it in terms of modernization of plant and improved salary scale. Whether it is the pay-off of legitimate businesses to the crime syndicate, or legalized gambling at race tracks, or the statewide saturation with gambling in Nevada, the implications are basically the same. The question fundamentally is whether the article bought is contributing something substantial to the physical and spiritual life of persons, and whether the money spent therefore contributes to useful labor. This is the ethical problem confronting the consumer. Whatever forces are playing upon his attitudes in one way or another, they must finally come under judgment as to their social usefulness.

Resources for the Consumer

Leland Gordon, out of his wealth of experience on behalf of consumers, contends that: "Consumers need to know their part in the economy. The motivation and operation of the economic system must be explained. Consumers must be acquainted with its virtues as well as its defects. They must understand that the persistence of fraud, misrepresentation, and other undesirable practices is possible because of their own lack of organized resistance. They need to realize the importance of substituting reason for emotion in the marketplace."[6]

Fortunately there is a very wide spectrum of resources available to the consumer in our time, illustrated by President Johnson's appointment of a Special Assistant for Consumer Affairs, referred to earlier. The manufacturer and distributor have vast resources to help them prepare for their market and to render the consumer more kindly disposed toward their product. Who is doing anything comparable for the consumer, enabling him to select wisely, thus increasing, in effect, his own income and benefiting the total gamut of the consumer's life? These are some of the resources available to the consumer:

1. Foremost are the standards established by many departments of the federal and state governments. At the federal level the Sherman Antitrust Act, the Clayton Antitrust Act, the Federal Trade Commission, and the Food and Drug Administration are instruments for his protection. Not only is health protected, but weights and measures are continually checked against deception. "U. S. Government Inspected" has come to be a symbol of integrity within the range and purpose for which products are appraised. Where health is involved, there is little temporizing. Though the cigarette-smoking contribution to cancer was long in testing, there were strong forces extending every effort to prove cigarettes uninjurious. Similar state and federal legislation to protect borrowers of money has not thus far been as uniformly successful, but gains have been made at state levels even though at this time federal support of "truth in lending" still has not been legislated.

2. The schools have been efficient teachers of making money but less diligent in training for intelligent consumption, which is a necessary part of the learning process.

3. One hundred or more cities have Better Business Bureaus through which the honesty of advertising can be checked and claims investigated. Fraudulence is thereby reduced and the scope of public conscience is enlarged.

4. Seventeen million members of labor unions represent approximately that number of household buying units. Labor organizations long ago realized that one way to increase family income was to encourage intelligent purchasing. To that end some labor journals have introduced sections designed to sensitize their members and families to ways of extending their earnings. Constructive guidance is also available from the American Home Economics Association, the American Dental Association, and the American Medical Association, which in their respective areas, serve to provide better diet and improve oral health and general physical well-being.

5. The foremost nongovernmental agency or movement in the nation concerned with the consumer is the cooperative movement. No other organization or cluster of organizations has done as much for the welfare of the consumer. Starting with the primary assumption that the role of the consumer is of first importance, the

consumer himself devises the kinds of organizations which will assure that his interests are protected. The result is too well known to require recounting here. Out of consumers cooperatives has arisen a host of producer cooperatives owned by those whom they serve. Members of consumer cooperatives have developed confidence in the quality and standards of the products for which they are primarily responsible. If there are deficiencies, there is immediate access to the source.

6. The phenomenal growth of consumer testing agencies, such as Consumers Research or Consumers Union, each independent of any advertising or product dispensing, has given to the buying public a yardstick for quality upon which it can confidently depend. With millions of people basing purchases on their advice, producers have now learned to keep one ear open for the voice of these testing agencies.

Increasingly widespread are the consumer-centered movements dealing with burial practices, life insurance, discount stores, weights and measures, health and medical care, and many other common needs. Central consumer information agencies are available for counsel on these and many other practices. This is but a small fraction of the great wealth of resources available to consumers who desire to know ways of using their incomes wisely and of enriching the life of the economy.

8

Organized Labor's Role

> The American people do not like things that are too big. Our people have always restrained business when it would grow too big. And now they are face-to-face with an organization more powerful, more merciless, and more dangerous than anything that has ever existed in this country—the American Federation of Labor.
>
> —Samuel Harden Church, President, Carnegie Institute, former official of the Pennsylvania Railroad[1]

Little did the gentleman whose quotation appears above realize that he had either misread the signs of the times or misunderstood the American people, or both. Labor and management and government have, in their respective spheres, become bigger and more powerful both in themselves and in their relationships with each other, and short of stopping the whole technological development, there is even more bigness ahead. No responsible analyst of society dares to predict that there will be technological restraints and curtailment of bigness.

Though both labor and management face large and highly complex problems, we shall deal here primarily with the issues confronting labor as they arise in relation to management and to the whole of society. Though management also has serious problems in relation to its employees, it has many other concerns as well—sales, financing, stockholder relations, and all those decisions relating to the continuance and expansion of the business itself. But in many of these decisions there is increasing coordination with labor, so that actually most discussions of labor carry implications for management.

The labor union movement in the United States has never been a vehicle for class struggle in the Marxist sense. There have been unions which attempted to voice class differences and to represent economic ideologies, but they have been few and do not represent the mainstream. This is not to say, however, that there have been no protest movements; actually they have been numerous. But none of these protest movements developed into a major labor movement with sufficient strength to incorporate large blocs of working people. The Industrial Workers of the World (IWW) was strong enough to harass some communities and stir up strife, but there was neither consistently strong leadership nor sufficient ideological conviction to guide a major segment of labor through both prosperity and depression. Attempts to coordinate farm and labor protests have served to challenge financial power centers and secure public sympathy to the extent that political changes were forthcoming. This latter fact is possibly the key to the failure of numerous radical movements in this country. The American people have maintained a sympathy for genuine protest movements resulting from injustices. It is a well-attested fact that the political power which has been available to those working toward economic reconstruction and a steadily rising standard of living have served to remove the frustrations of oppressed groups that believed they had no escape from their economic and social strait jacket. (Such a statement would have needed modification until recently, but dramatic and far-reaching actions affecting the Negro in this country bear out the statement.)

Samuel Gompers, though a product of ideological movements in Europe, had the extraordinary insight to recognize that such patterns would not be effective in the United States. As one of the founders of the American Federation of Labor and its president (except for one year) from 1886 to 1924, he convinced his co-workers that the future of the labor movement in this country depended upon adherence to three fundamental concerns: wages, hours, and working conditions. Other organizations, notably the Knights of Labor, had diluted their effectiveness by pseudoreligious objectives and a broad front of economic concerns. The times simply were not ready for so inclusive a range of economic changes as the Knights espoused.

A program that is right for one period is rarely adequate, in its initial form at least, for subsequent times. After enduring bitter and bloody hostility from management over many years, with the courts sustaining management on theories of property ownership and power, labor finally developed enough strength to challenge the combination of economic and political power exercised by the owners and managers, and a modification resulted. The history of the labor movement has been recounted so fully and in so many ways that it is not essential to repeat it here. We would simply reaffirm the fact that it was around the focus of the three cardinal features—wages, hours and working conditions—and its function of providing members insurance that the strength of the labor movement developed. This fact and the necessity for changing it became of great significance in later periods as labor reconsidered its role and policy.

The story of the development of the labor movement would be incomplete without an account of cooperation with labor on the part of nonlabor groups. In no small measure can the vitality of the Social Gospel movement be identified with its concern for labor. Numerous organizations were formed within Protestant denominations and across denominational lines as a result of the convictions that power was being unjustly wielded by owners and that individuals were being deprived of their God-given rights through excessive burdens and long hours which taxed physical and spiritual resources. One of the most notable instances of the combined effort of the churches on behalf of oppressed labor was the entrance of religious leadership into the 1919 steel strike. The results and the settlement of that strike represented a watershed in industrial relations. Intervention by religious leaders was bitterly resented; but the eight-hour day was established in the steel industry, and the combined influence of labor organizations and religious leadership was made apparent. Though full strength of the labor movement in steel was almost twenty years away, a principle had been established.

Roman Catholic support of labor found its most substantial expression in an encyclical of Leo XIII, *Rerum novarum* (1890), and forty-one years later in another powerful plea for economic justice, *Quadragesimo anno* by Pius XI. Since so large a number of those arriving in this country and becoming employees of a burgeoning industry were Roman Catholics, this concern of their church for their welfare had far-reaching significance.

Any history of the movements supporting labor and its purposes would be incomplete if it failed to recount the work of the League for Industrial Democracy, which, though unrelated to any religious body, included within its ranks large numbers of churchmen and nonchurchmen alike. It has been a militant voice in behalf of justice to labor. Still another agency has been the National Religion and Labor Foundation (more recently, the Religion and Labor Council), whose purpose has been to acquaint seminary students with labor's history and objectives. These organizations and many others came into existence during the times when the labor movement was fighting for its life.

Traditional concepts of property and ownership included neither the formal obligation to provide continuity of work opportunity for the laborer nor the obligation to provide conditions of work which would be safe and wholesome. To these faults labor began to address itself with new zeal and power. The history of resistance to its efforts is now a part of history that will not readily be forgotten and of which many of us are properly ashamed. The record includes the bloody Homestead Strike, the Haymarket Riot, the May 30 Massacre in Chicago, and many others.

Union Strengths and Weaknesses

Thus the Wagner Act of 1935 came after a long history of hostility on the part of industry in particular and the public in general. A depression, a lessened confidence in business leadership, and a political administration sympathetic to labor's purposes wrought a major change in the nation's attitudes. Union membership soared, reaching its highest peak up to that time during the period of World War II. With the war over the pendulum began to swing in the other direction—this time producing the Taft-Hartley Act and subsequently the Landrum-Griffin Act, both designed to reduce the power that labor unions had acquired in the period of their greatest influence. At first there was deep resentment on the part of labor against the new legislation curbing union expansion. But as time went on, the consequences of the new legislation proved to be not as restrictive as anticipated, and labor learned to live with the new regulations, not happily but with acceptance. In spite of the hostility in the period from 1947 to 1951, unions won 97 per cent of 46,146 elections held for the purpose of securing union-shop provisions in contracts. The favorable response to unionism was so great that some firms, it is reported, did not even bother to enter into an election.

Money poured into the coffers of many unions, making possible an investment program which has been both a source of strength and a gross temptation to racketeers. At the present time (1965) union assets exceed 670 million dollars. At a meeting of the AFL-CIO Executive Committee in August 1964 a mortgage investment trust involving pooling of union funds for investment in government guaranteed mortgages was readied for functioning with "a number of millions of dollars" already committed.[2] Many of these funds were accumulated to provide a cushion in time of strikes; but where strikes did not occur, the funds piled up. Others are pension and insurance funds. "Business unionism" took on a new meaning. It had heretofore meant simply taking care of the business affairs of the union, making certain that dues were paid and that membership was intact, and negotiating contracts with employers. Now a new facet of the movement appeared: the need for professionals to handle the intricate business affairs of the unions. Among them were persons competent to invest the union's funds. A labor organizer does not necessarily make a wise investor, any more than the investor possesses the technical and legal skills to enter into intricate negotiations. Unions have had to become profession-conscious in order to secure the caliber of representatives who could attend to the complicated new areas of union business. The abuses of some of these funds have made front-page stories in the daily press, but Clair Cook, himself a labor union member and a clergyman, has commented: "The intensive probing by the McClellan Committee turned up a figure of $10 millions in union money misused for personal gain or stolen outright over the last fifteen years. That last year alone employers illegally kept $250 millions withheld from wages for income taxes and social security, failing to turn it into the federal government after they were entrusted with it."[3] *Life,* in appraising the ethical climate of business, estimated that 5 billion dollars annually is the toll for bribes, kick-backs, and other unethical business expenses.[4] The labor racketeering and misappropriated funds, though bad enough are small by comparison with the scope of corruption in other phases of our national life.

A slackening of pace in the labor movement's expansion and aggressive action cannot be attributed primarily to its increased economic security as indicated by its investments. Having won its right to exist and having demonstrated that harmonious and helpful relations can exist between labor and management, each has come to accept the other (in the major industrialized areas at least). Now they can fulfill their respective functions without having to spend energy in securing general recognition of those functions. It must be added that clean-cut definitions of those respective functions will probably remain elusive. For the time being, with its major objective—recognition—attained, the sense of mission and need to survive is less intense.

One of the reasons American labor has been unreceptive to political ideological programs conflicting with the enterprise system can be seen in the vast program of welfare activities conducted under the auspices of labor unions. The list is much too long to incorporate into this brief space, but it includes housing projects, total health coverage, vacation opportunities, and insurance programs of a wide variety. Many of these programs are in addition to similar programs of the corporations and supplemental to government programs. All of this is in addition to the principal functions which the labor union was originally designed to serve. With all these benefits compounded, one might be inclined to ask why all persons thus eligible for participation in labor unions have not eagerly accepted the opportunity of doing so; for the fact remains that less than 20 per cent of all workers are enrolled in labor organizations.

Some of the reasons for nonparticipation can be seen as a result of the very success of the labor organizations themselves. Having achieved security—in many parts of the country, at least—the sense of being a movement has steadily declined. Since, as we have seen, unions have themselves become major businesses, a criterion for remaining in office is the capacity to operate the business successfully and with a minimum of friction within the organization. Eric Sevareid, no hostile critic of unions, says:

> There is today, among some labor bosses, the same child-like fascination in finance, in deals, in handling big chunks of money that was true of successful businessmen in the booming wonderland of the 1920's; Beck and Hoffa are prime examples of wide-eyed wonder at the reproductive capacity of money. . . . Little of political ideology remains to organized labor; the goals are almost exclusively material in nature and limited in degree. It is a vast, vested interest, the other side of the identical coin of capitalism. . . . Little wonder that the public talk today centers on labor's responsibilities to the general society. Little wonder that the same laws that gradually regulated the once unregulated power of business are slowly creeping up on organized labor. . . .[5]

In consequence there is lessened anxiety over the large number of those not enrolled in unions. To compound matters for those responsible for conducting the business of the union, there is the fact that because of automation unions have been declining still further, as was pointed out in Chapter 4.

Another factor contributing to labor's declining sense of mission is, for good or ill, its collaboration with industry's objectives. To maintain themselves with the minimum of internal disorder, unions of many different types have entered into close relations with employers, who formerly were their opponents. In steel, electric power, and coal, for example, unions have supported the companies in their development programs, many of which would make necessary increased prices to the public. One paradoxical result has been the unofficial support of private power programs while the official position of the union supported public power.

As job opportunities contract and the peril of losing out in the business administration of the union looms larger, any expression of opposition to the organization becomes suspect and unions think they must be curtailed. Some labor organizations, historically democratic in their roots and committed to a theme of human brotherhood, feel themselves under the necessity of suppressing all opposition. The result has been a tendency toward self-appointing hierarchies, with all the temptations accompanying such practices.

Under a system of self-defense and the maintenance of the *status quo*, it is hardly to be expected that unions will become the champions of long-range plans and committed to the development of programs designed to protect the consumer and foster the far-reaching purposes of the nation as a whole in its total economic outlook and its world obligations. Yet it must quickly be said that there are labor leaders capable of this sort of leadership and that they have made a contribution in the nation's life far in excess of what could be expected from their constituency. They have run the risk of being in the forefront and thereby endangering their own support. To their great credit it must be asserted that they have labored diligently to arouse the interests of their fellow members in plans and programs whose ultimate ends are in the best interest of the nation as a whole while in the short run they are less desirable.

Because of Congressional hearings and widespread dissemination of information in the nation's press, labor unions have come into serious condemnation for their seemingly rigid insistence on certain archaic work practices. The sin of which they are guilty, in the public mind at least, is that they are placing an undue burden upon the economy by demanding wages for work not done and thus imperiling the economic health of the industrial organizations forced to continue these dubious practices. "Feather-bedding" aptly illustrates one of the fundamental dilemmas of the economy and of the role of labor unions. As technological improvements are made, certain jobs become unnnecessary. There has been emerging over the generations a reluctant acceptance of the fact that a person has an equity in his job. Unions have fostered this conviction and have won new recognition for this right. Where a job is to be eliminated in a society where other work is unobtainable, unions have stressed the responsibility of the eliminator to give assurance that the worker's livelihood will not be destroyed.* The insistence upon job protection or compensation for job loss constitutes one of the major contributions of labor unions in a period of adjustment. Because some unions have had greater success in defending their members' rights to their jobs than others, the issue has been lifted into full view.

Public indignation has also been aroused over the feather-bedding charge because of a suspicion that the unions fostering the practice are not willing to share the responsibilities for technological changes. Because unions have been in a position to protest job changes, the onus of the defense has fallen on them. Unorganized workers, suffering similar work modifications, have lacked equally vigorous defenders. Behind the charges and countercharges is the preservation of jobs. The rapid disappearance of jobs, with other work unavailable, has caused unions to stress the retention of jobs. Devices to retain jobs and keep members employed have included deliberate inefficiency and "slow-downs," not because of a depreciated sense of quality, as had occasionally been charged, but because it is the most available means of making the work "go around." From the workers' point of view the the slow-down is not loafing; it is a modification in the unit of work, designed to help guarantee a job.

Labor's New Problems

A part of the genius of the labor movement has been its ability to adapt to the shifts in the industrial situation. By concentrating on wages, hours, and working conditions, labor was able to make gains proportionate to the expanding economy and the requirements for added workers. Its strength has always been among those classified by the census as "blue-collar workers." At one time they were the majority of employees, but during the past decade a major shift has occurred, and as has been noted earlier, today the white-collar workers predominate. With them the labor movement has been singularly unsuccessful.

* The result of the arbitration process involving the railroad firemen and the operators, with encouragement from the White House, would indicate at least tacit acceptance of this idea.

The reasons for labor's inability to organize the growing number of white-collar workers are not unrelated to the role of labor itself and the image it has projected—that of a worker with hands and tools rather than with pencil, cash register, or typewriter. Even though labor has never identified itself primarily with a socialist ideology and has itself noticeably gone up the economic scale in an open society, there still remains the class stigma and the aversion of white-collar workers to identification with an historically lower-class movement. It may well be that as white-collar workers discover that they are in need of the kind of job security which helped to give impetus to the labor movement itself, there will be an increasing disposition among them to look favorably on organizations for this purpose. Already there is strong indication that AFL-CIO and unaffiliated unions are mounting major efforts in this direction.

The greatest increase in the labor movement's membership was reached just prior to the passage of the Taft-Hartley Act. Since then a leveling off has occurred, with a slight decline in the early 1960s.* Present membership may represent a more stable constituency than the swollen roster of members who joined the unions during and following World War II. But the leveling off and decline are not simply the defection of lukewarm members; automation is a more serious "culprit." Figures change so rapidly that they are out-of-date before the ink is dry. The fact of the serious decline in membership of major unions does not change, however, and every indication suggests that the decline will continue. It may be offset in part by new members recruited from white-collar ranks, but technological developments in many types of industries will account for further reductions in some unions. The issues presented by automation are not those which can be resolved through collective bargaining. No one can reasonably expect management to continue employing unneeded workers, but neither can one reasonably expect unions to concede that they and their members have become superfluous. What about those disemployed? Who will absorb the costs of moving and retraining them? The workers themselves? Management? Who? "And so the problem of automation and particular unemployment cannot

* The AFL-CIO reported a gain of 360,000 in the first six months of 1964.

be kept inside the confines of traditional collective bargaining; the government must share the responsibility for its solution, and perhaps assume the major share. True, machines have made workers unemployed before but it has never happened at such a rate."[6] An electric coal shovel doing the work of one thousand coal miners in a Kentucky strip mine is a vivid illustration of technological advances in steel, autos, meat-packing and many other areas. In an earlier era the Luddites and their counterparts in other times and places smashed the machines which took their jobs. Today the stripping-machine digging coal for TVA power is not opposed by the United Mine Workers. The machine pays a levy to the union treasury, benefiting welfare funds of union members as well as those unemployed, but the levy does not equal the union dues or put a thousand men to work.

Industry-wide bargaining has been a moot point with labor and management for many years. Management opposes it. Labor once saw advantages in a uniform scale, but now it is unsure. The necessity to abide by a single decision applicable to diverse situations can both create confusion and possibly work hardships. It is easier to confront management with the specific problems of a given plant than to have to abide by an action covering a multiplicity of plants. Unions would rather negotiate with one railroad at a time than with the entire railroad industry. Efficiency might dictate changes in work practices applicable on a nationwide basis, but efficiency as the principal criterion would work havoc in job security at a local level.

Organized labor contends that one of its strongest contributions is its support of democratic principles. But the question widely asked is: Can democracy and efficiency be reconciled?

The essence of technological change and the justification for acceptance of its consequences is the concept of efficiency. But efficiency and job security are largely mutually exclusive. The rapid acceleration in automated activity is justified on grounds of efficiency, while job security disappears. Fundamental to the democratic principle is the right of the individual to exercise some control over the political and economic processes in which he has a large stake. While industry was expanding and there were jobs enough for almost everybody, insistence on democratic practices and rights seemed reasonable. But now there emerges in the name of the sacred concept "efficiency" a set of requirements which call for the reduction of jobs and the minimizing of the democratic process. For this labor has been for the most part unprepared. It should be quickly added, however, that labor is not alone in its unpreparedness. There is apparently in process as these lines are being written a diminution in the ranks of middle management in even greater porportion than the losses in labor ranks. Efficiency is no respecter of status, collar, or color.

Securing and protecting the right to organize and negotiate has long been a justification of labor's participation in politics. New conditions have made political action continually necessary. Length of the work week and minimum hourly rates are established by legislation. Since one obvious and available means of providing jobs or spreading the work is the shortening of the standard work period, labor believes it should use its influence on legislatures to secure this benefit. The same is true for accident and employment compensation, and a wide range of activities in which labor has been interested for itself and the community at large. Recently a concern for retraining of workers has emerged as a necessary service. Probably no group would be more sensitive to this need than organized labor. Political action is required to institute and finance such programs.

Labor's formula of "reward your friends and punish your enemies" has paid off well in the political scene. Labor has learned the necessity of making its wishes known at the national political level as well as the local. A new phase of government relationship has come into the scene, however, complicating life for both labor and management. It is the fact that much of the new work now employing hundreds of thousands of workers is government-supported but privately operated. Contracts are made with private corporations, but the work being performed is government-initiated and in most instances fully government-sustained. Much of the work being performed is authorized by the Department of Defense, and therefore a controversy over wages confronts labor with the delicate question of conflict with our national security and possibly at the same time impairing the relationship of good will with the taxpayer. Nothing illustrates more sharply the intricacy of current economic life than the total dependence of large brackets of industry upon government support and the anomalous, if not paradoxical, relationship of labor as both taxpayer and employee. Traditional collective bargaining takes on new meanings and renders old patterns obsolete. Issues involved here cannot be resolved by traditional bargaining relationships between labor and management. The key is held by government, and each of the other parties is beholden to the "third force," government, for its very livelihood. No amount of brave proclamations about the enterprise system or the rights and dignity of labor against a tyrannically oppressive management can bring a solution to this vast and growing problem.

Closely related to the problem of labor-government relations is the tough and increasingly troublesome problem of our national relationship to foreign markets, balance of payments, tariffs, and the health of our own national economy. The statesmen among labor leaders know that there is no future wholesomeness for American economic life without increasing correlation with the economies of other nations, and now particularly with the "Inner Six" and the "Outer Seven," the European Common Market and those nations most closely related to Britain. Will the rank and file of labor which ultimately elects these statesmen among their leaders understand when concessions in tariffs are made which may further shift employment in our own country? Though American industry has faced this problem before, it has never been under these conditions and under the pressure of the competition of other nations' mounting efficiency.

New Roles for Labor

Economists may disagree over the contribution labor organizations have made to the improvement of working conditions and the rights of working people. Albert Rees in his *Economics of Trade Unions* contends that "the studies to date must be regarded as highly inconclusive; no union effect on labor's share can be discovered with any consistency. . . . By far the most fundamental point, however, is that a successful union will not necessarily raise labor's share even in its own industry." Then he adds: "There are many other aspects of union activity yet to be considered, and an economy has other and perhaps even more important goals than the most efficient allocation of resources."[7]

Possibly the most recent and also the most definitive study of the subject to date, that of H. G. Lewis, estimates that "the average union/non-union relative wage was approximately 10–15% higher than it would have been in the absence of unionism." The author comments further: "These figures imply that recently the average of union workers was about 7–11% higher, relative to the average wage of all workers, both union and non-union, than it would have been in the absence on unions. Similarly, the average wage of non-union workers was about 3–4% lower relative to the average wage of all workers than in the absence of unionism. . . . I conclude tentatively that unionism has had a small impact on the relative inequality of the distribution of wages among all workers. The direction of the effect, on presently available evidence, is ambiguous."[8]

Some economists have gone so far as to suggest that wages have actually been kept lower in certain completely unionized work than might have been the case had they been free from contract arrangements. Whether this is true or not does not constitute our principal point of interest. Possibly labor's greatest contribution to the life of this nation and subsequently to many others as well lies in the achievement of a standard of decency and justice for wage earners. What is of primary importance is the distinctive contribution which labor has made to the well-being of its own people and many others who have no specific identification with the labor movement.

The fear of bigness, which is another way of expressing a fear of power, as indicated in the quotation at the beginning of this chapter, stems from apprehension over the misuse of power. But the very term "misuse of power" is one which does not readily lend itself to clear analysis. Usually it means the way in which the other person is using his power against me. From this perspective labor has been feared by management, and the entire history of the labor movement gives evidence that labor has had just cause to fear the power of management. Now within a comparatively short period of history labor has emerged as one of the major power configurations on the American scene able to provide a check against business maltreatment. In its capacity as a defender of human rights it has served as one of the major instruments for ethical achievement, and in this function it has contributed richly to the physical and spiritual well-being of an entire nation. Coincidentally, it is significant that the areas of the nation where labor has been unable to organize and make itself felt are the areas of greatest poverty, where human welfare is held most cheaply.

With their history of contribution to both the ethical and economic life of a people, the question must now be raised whether labor organizations in their individual or federative forms have a function to perform in the present situation of this nation. It is recognized that the geographic areas referred to still need the kind of humanizing and experience of justice which labor has brought to the more highly industrialized areas of the land, but with the legal and moral protection which has already been built into the economy of the major parts of this industrialized nation, is there still a function for labor organizations?

Business unionism, as indicated above, has obviously become highly successful. Union leadership is a matter for professionals and is no longer the prerogative of those who were most effective with the brass knuckles in a day when force had to be met by force. Children of union leaders and of the rank-and-file are encouraged by the unions themselves to move up into new brackets of economic and educational attainment. Labor journals delight to picture the children of their members who have earned Merit Scholarships and Phi Beta Kappa keys. An open society has made possible upward mobility, and the same talents which make for dynamic leadership in the union are also praised when they lead the second generation into other forms of leadership in society. The assumption behind all of this is that labor leaders—and, by imputation, labor itself—are not simply concerned with their own rights and prerogatives. To the extent that it is an ethical movement concerned for the opportunities of all people, labor has an obligation to share with society at large the convictions it holds or has held about the worth of man and the kind of a society he must build.

If such a picture of labor's expectations seems naïve and over-idealistic, one does not have to go far back into the history of the labor movement to discover a large element of this kind of emphasis. Has business unionism undercut the far-seeing intentions of those who in another generation saw the labor movement as primarily an instrument for human betterment? Obviously there are many in the impressive ranks of labor who still regard labor as a movement and conceive of it as a continuing instrument for society's welfare. Having won earlier battles to bring labor to its position of relative security, many of its more thoughtful members are asking whether its work is over or whether there are frontiers as demanding in this period as those which characterized earlier days. One world-renowned labor leader, when asked on the occasion of an anniversary of his leadership of the organization what the greatest thing he had accomplished for his union was, pointed to the bank which had been formed by and for that union.

Solomon Barkin, who writes from the inside of a labor organization (he is the Director of research in the Textile Workers Union), but who also has maintained a high degree of objectivity about the role of unions, comments that "few social thinkers would now look to unions for the leadership needed to revitalize our economic and social system."[9] Barkin is writing primarily from the standpoint of the ability of unions to offset communist influence and of the decline in general respect which liberals have expressed toward labor as it became so heavily preoccupied with itself and its privileges.

The incontrovertible facts remain that there are still vast areas of injustice in American life and that there are the problems of national and international relations upon which hangs the future health of our own economic existence. Unemployment has been hovering at or above the 5 per cent figure for several years. No other major group is going to speak on behalf of the unemployed, unless militant organizations are formed around the interests of that group alone. No single body, however, has as much knowledge of organization and as much wisdom about the nature of the economy itself as the combined forces of the international unions. With 108 research directors (at last official count) hired by these unions they have at their fingertips data in a quantity equaled only by the federal government itself. Seeking justice for those who are without adequate voice and pressing for the rights of all who may be disadvantaged do not necessarily involve the kinds of organizational procedures upon which labor itself originally came to power. Today its position of eminence on the national scene as a respected wielder of power gives it a leverage in the national political picture second to no other major pressure group. This is not to say that whatever labor wishes can be brought to pass. Obviously the record of labor's advocacy of various measures belies such a claim. But in terms of the actual numbers potentially involved and the record of concern for the totality, the power for civic good on the part of the collective labor organizations in the AFL-CIO is unexcelled.

No longer, however, are contracts limited to wages, hours, and working conditions. Many of the bargaining activities in the current period are less concerned with wage increases than with "fringe benefits." It is these that provide a stability and security which wage contracts alone have been unable to provide. They include such items as life insurance, accidental death and dismemberment insurance, job accident and sickness or disability payments, hospital care, surgical care, obstetrical care, home and office medical expense, and pensions. Most of the contracts negotiated in our times provide for these benefits. Approximately 12 million of the 17 million members of labor organizations are covered by plans including many if not all of these items. This is a phenomenon primarily achieved in the past decade.

During the World War II decade much attention was given to the guaranteed annual wage. Widely publicized plans were developed in a few industries (shoes, soap, meat, etc.). With the advent of unemployment insurance and the large-scale demand for universal income maintenance there has been less pressure for the guaranteed annual wage as such in separate industries. In its place supplemental unemployment benefits have been instituted to cushion the severance from employment. The amounts available vary according to the kind of settlement negotiated with the respective unions.

Illustrative of a technique for labor's securing of advantages in the area of pensions through political activity is the experience of the United Automobile Workers in requesting further assistance in pensions. Management replied that pensions were a state function. When the UAW attempted to get further assistance at this point, management lobbyists registered vigorous opposition on the assumption that the increased taxes would be too burdensome. Shortly labor sought a minimum monthly pension of $100 with the companies paying the difference between social security and that amount. Industry's opposition to the tax increase ceased.

Collective bargaining, which involves the long-range future of both labor and management and ultimately of the economy as a whole, cannot be left to amateurs. A major contribution from all three of the leading parties in this triumvirate would now require that participants take account of the total welfare as the only sure means of protecting the best interests of each one of the participants. Any catalogue of major areas of service for labor in our time would include its concern for sound justice. The record to date is both good and bad. Industrial unions have been opener and readier to include all races. The craft and railroad workers have a less honorable history in this regard. It must be credited to the national federation that officially it has attempted to open the ranks of its international union constituents to all qualified candidates. The fact remains that at the time of this writing there are craft unions and railroad brotherhoods which could greatly strengthen their contribution to the forward thrust of American life by changes in their racial policies.

No single idea can incorporate the full range of possibilities for labor union contributions to the national life. One objective, however, encompasses so broad a scope of possibilities that it deserves special mention. It is an area in which labor has already made a rich contribution to society at large: its sense of obligation to the community. For many years union leadership has recognized that good will is a prime asset of both local unions and the national organization. Community specialists thus became an integral part of locals, if they were strong enough, or of the central organization for the larger area. Membership in community fund organizations and on school boards symbolized this sensitivity to good will. But essentially more than that was involved. What affected the community affected union members, and vice versa. With a background of organizational know-how and a collective body capable of exercising pressure, the unions stood in the advantageous position of being able to secure benefits for the community at large. Here is a vast area of union contribution which fulfills the long history of union objectives for welfare and gives the union a usefulness far beyond the plant and its own membership. At an AFL convention prior to the merger with the CIO the executive council reported to its delegates that it had been "mindful of the responsibilities that American labor must meet in this critical period of world history. Today our duty goes far beyond the building of a powerful trade union movement in our own country. Today our tasks go far beyond those of strengthening our trade union movement as a dynamic voluntary organization, as a pivotal force in, of, and for our free society and American way of life."[10] Then at the 1955 convention of AFL-CIO actions were called for which "include support of child labor laws and other measures in the interest of childhood and youth; federal aid to medical schools, hospitals, and medical research; health insurance; improved facilities for the handicapped; federal aid to education; revision and liberalization of the McCarran-Walter Immigration Act; amendment of the Refugee Relief Act to insure admission of the full number of refugees authorized in the law; provision for federal flood insurance; enactment of a fair employment practices law; approval of the Supreme Court ruling on segregation in schools; and provision for peacetime use of atomic energy."[11]

Indications of labor's commitment to a wider range of community and social involvement is indicated by the changing structure of the AFL-CIO itself. Recent among these indications are the additions of such departments as social security, international affairs, community service, civil rights, and political education.

The life of communities and of the nation includes broader

issues than those which have traditionally been labor's immediate concern. Alert union leaders have long since recognized that gains made in the plant can be wiped out by forces determining the life of their workers in their community and family spheres; for utility rates, rents, housing, and the cost of living are just as important as wage contracts and sanitary washrooms. "To give the worker more than make-believe protection," says Gus Tyler, "a modern union must be concerned with influencing the legislation that goes to make up our legislated economy."[12]

Anyway you look at it, the American labor union has been and will undoubtedly continue to be a powerful force in the economic life of this nation and consequently in other nations as well. Though the record contains both good and bad, the destructive factors are infinitesimal as against the vast good accomplished by all of the bodies related to organized labor. Throughout its history the principal function of organized labor has been collective bargaining, and this will continue to be its major activity. But organized labor, too, will increasingly face the fact that its collective bargaining must take place within a setting even larger than the plant where decisions are being reached through bargaining.

Today adversaries sitting across the table from each other, engaging in what is traditionally known as "labor-management relations," have suddenly found themselves in a strange new world. Where government at one time had to wheedle and cajole to secure a settlement, it now has become involved in a large portion of the economy, and it has become the determiner of policy for an even larger part. To this anomalous situation is added the fact that the welfare of the citizenry is intimately identified with the decisions made at a national level by a central government in relation to other governments and their economic life, upon which we are dependent and which in turn are dependent upon this nation. It is in such a situation that labor organizations through their rank and file and their leaders are compelled to make judgments and arrive at decisions harmonious for numbers far in excess of their own membership. The reality of the integration of ethics and economics has become clear for all but those who will not see.

9

Disarmament and the Economy

The Problem

The expression "having a bear by the tail" aptly describes the situation of the United States and its armaments program. We lay claim to a capacity to "overkill" every Russian industrial metropolitan area 1,250 times, with an estimated one-tenth of the labor force or approximately seven and one-third million engaged in military or related activities in 1965. Moreover, one-tenth of the U. S. production of goods and services is allocated to defense.[1] Yet we continue to increase military production. Jitters in the stock market follow an official suggestion that it might be advisable to reduce the flow of military hardware or atomic fission supplies, both of which are in great oversupply. At the same time the United States Arms Control and Disarmament Agency recognizes the danger of a decline in defense expenditures impairing the long-term stability and growth of the economy, even though present defense expenditures appear to be far in excess of strictly defense needs.

Heavy commitments have been made to our gigantic commercial industrial plant in the form of large allocations of both personnel and equipment. Much of it has been moved to new locations, resulting in the establishment of entire new communities with all the institutions and activities attendant on the formation of a community. Disruption of these arrangements would inevitably work hardships for the persons involved, necessitating readjustments in employment activities as well as closing down manufacturing and research facilities until their services could be put to civilian use.

Comments from members of Congress and the executive branch and the Congressional voting records indicate little if any disposition to attempt seriously the conversion of any military production activities to civilian use. Repercussions from constituents whose livelihoods depend either directly or indirectly on the military production program quickly discourage legislative representatives from any inclination they may have toward economy or converting unneeded military production to the provision of some of the many dire needs required by a wholesome civilian economy.

Whatever may be one's attitude toward the defense program, there can be no denying that as a nation we are deriving substantial economic benefits from the arms race, and our participation in it has stimulated the national economy. In addition, there are many indirect and beneficial effects of this research upon the economy. As Emile Benoit says:

> Most of the important technological break-throughs of recent years have originated in defense research, including radar, atomic energy, jet engines, and space exploration. These in turn have had important effects on the development of new civilian products and services. For example, space research has yielded improvements in basic materials, in water purification, and in techniques for the automatic measurement of body changes. A major drug for the treatment of emotional depression was developed from one component of a rocket fuel.[2]

The question is inevitably asked, "Why rock the boat? We have a very gratifying state of prosperity, don't we?" Unquestionably the economic indices do reveal a recognizable state of prosperity. What they do not indicate, however, is that fact that so large a percentage of the products whose creation accounts for that prosperity are without any use or benefit to this nation or any other, once full capacity for protection has been achieved. No representative of the legislative or executive branch of the government could deny that we already possess many times over the capacity for deterrence—which is the basic reason for our military production in the first place. In sum, the warfare state has become our national condition, and for the time being at least we are both unwilling and unable to reduce our dependence on an economy sustained so largely by military defense.

Scope and Consequences of Defense Economy

The 46 million dollar budget for defense represents approximately 9 per cent of the Gross National Product (GNP). In view of the total production, this may not be unbearable, and if it were required by a genuine need for defense, it could be wholly justifiable. As Benoit points out: "The burden is, of course, only a fraction of what it was during World War II or the Korean War. While defense expenditure absorbs resources which would otherwise be available to the civilian economy, it also contributes importantly to that economy."[3] In comparison with other nations Yugoslavia, England, and France have defense burdens of 7 per cent of the national production and come closest to that of the United States. For the most part, in other nations the figure is nearer 4 or 5 per cent. The reason for the greater U. S. percentages is obvious.

The problem is not only the size of the defense budget but also its allocation. Uneven placement of defense contracts, made possible because of superior jockeying and pressures from Congressmen and/or advantages because of geographical and climatic conditions, have produced temporary benefits for some sections of the country but at the same time have contributed to potential disruptions and complications. In 1959 San Diego, for example, had 82 per cent of its manufacturing employment in aerospace production; Wichita, 72 per cent; Seattle, 53 per cent; and the Los Angeles-Long Beach area, 27 per cent. Fourteen states are included in a bracket "above average dependence on major procurement for their employment, and nine additional states with exceptionally heavy dependence on Department of Defense payrolls to sustain their income."[4] Out of a total of 22 billion dollars of industrial orders placed by the military in 1960, the preponderance went to five states.[5]

The day of reckoning for such heavy concentration and for the failure to anticipate transition to civilian production is typified by the experience of the Republic Aviation Corporation on Long Island, when it was contended that this plant was no longer necessary. Involved were 13,000 jobs and a trail of 990 subcontracting firms, with a total loss of employment of 80,000 to 90,000 jobs.[6]

Not only have industries been meshed into the total military production program, but universities have likewise become dependent on the military budget. A combination of direct payments to universities by the Department of Defense, the Atomic Energy Commission, and the National Aeronautics and Space Administration (NASA), plus funds received from manufacturers engaged in military production, brought the total of defense-supported and aerospace research activity to more than 50 per cent of university research work in 1960–1961.[7]

Since Sputnik we have been voluble in our discussion of the need for training scientists, though our concern hardly began at that point. We simply became more highly aware of the need. Whether to attribute it largely to the danger, real or imagined, created by Sputnik, the fact remains that from two-thirds to three-fourths of all American scientists and engineers are at present engaged in work related to military and defense activities. Redirecting the activities of these highly skilled and useful individuals constitutes one of the major problems in converting to civilian activities.

Few people are aware, for example, of the extent of the atomic installations alone, as one part of the total military production program. Fred J. Cook reports: "The five nuclear installations (Oak Ridge, Hanford, Paducah, Portsmouth, Savannah River) together form the nation's largest consumer of electricity, coal and water; they require more machine tools than General Motors, Ford and Chrysler combined. The Savannah plant (more recent than Oak Ridge and Hanford) cost $1.5 billion, four times the cost of the Panama Canal. It uses more electricity than the entire state of Delaware."[8] The Atomic Energy Commission consumes between 5 and 10 per cent of all the electrical energy produced in the United States. Were any of its plants to cease its contribution to the defense program, it could bring increased tragedy in unemployment and hardship to communities around it and to far-flung points of supply which are dependent on the defense program in the plant.

Not all of the productivity of these plants, to be sure, can be attributed to immediate defense needs. There are health-producing concomitants and contributions to the civilian life which can go on regardless of the defense program. But without the defense program nothing like the present size of operation would be required.

Paralleling and closely tied to the development of fissionable materials and our capacity for overkill is the size of our aircraft industry. In 1964 there were in service 1,855 commercial planes, and approximately 30,000 military planes. Any curtailment in defense production would cause serious dislocation and hardship for many who have identification with aircraft manufacturing.[9]

The program of Research on Economic Adjustments to Disarmament (READ) sponsored by the Center for Research on Conflict Resolution at the University of Michigan estimates that net displacement might amount to between 500,000 and 600,000 employees per year during the first stage of disarmament. It expressed the belief that this would not be unmanageable but that it would increase pressures on a labor market already in difficulty because of large numbers entering that market for the first time and because of technological displacement.[10]

The extraordinary increase in defense appropriations and the manufacturing plant which came into existence out of defense needs is not the result of any sudden or crash program; it has been evolving steadily. "Expenditures of the Department of Defense have risen from $19.8 billion in fiscal year of 1951 to $43 billion in 1961, or by over 100%, a growth rate far in excess of that of any other major area of the American economy. At the present time, Defense Department purchases of goods and services are equal to almost one-tenth of the gross national product. The proportion reached peaks of 48% during World War II and 12% during the Korean War, but was, of course, lower during the interwar period. . . . An abrupt change in the nature of the external threat would probably cause another major shift in the proportion of the country's resources devoted to armaments."[11]

With the capacity to more than match anything that any potential enemy might do, there is ironically not now, nor is there likely to be in the immediate future, a scaling downward in defense resources in terms of plant, highly trained engineers, skilled technicians, or office force required to keep the enterprise in motion.

Resistance to Disarmament Conversion

The Arms Control and Disarmament Agency Report expresses the apprehension that the chief danger of a steep decline would be psychological. Adjusting to a series of defense cuts over a period of a decade would confront us with a situation unparalleled in our history.[12] There have been other experiences of adjustments following wars, but none in which the economy of the nation became so dependent on war and defense preparations. After World War I, for example, business was eager to get back to a peacetime basis; after World War II there were great peacetime needs to be met by a civilian production program. Today those needs have been met, for a large part of the population at least, and we have not yet envisioned the ways in which our economy can meet the very real but insufficiently defined needs of the new industrial society.

It is all but inevitable that as a part of the psychological consequences a stock market decline would accompany any major diminution in government support of military manufacturing. Ironical though it be that stock market enthusiasm is dependent upon artificial and unneeded production, the fact remains that the fear of inability to convert, or in some cases to reconvert, to civilian production would have depressing consequences. As many economists and social analysts working on this problem contend, however, such consequences are not inevitable. With adequate preparation for transfer to other types of manufacturing and production, there is little likelihood that a decline and subsequent pessimism would result.

Social psychologists and anthropologists will, no doubt, engage in extensive studies in years to come to determine why so high a degree of resistance to conversion to a peacetime economy marked the attitudes of the American people in the mid 1960s. Irving Horowitz asks: "Why should it be the case that, in the midst of this intellectual know-how, there is such a paucity of activity oriented toward the realization of that long-postponed and ephemeral phenomenon—a peacetime economy?"[13] He suggests the prospects for such a conversion remain dim because of social and political considerations, prominent among which is the fact that there exists so little awareness of the dangers involved in a military economy. On the other hand, such satisfying conditions already prevail in our economy that it would be inadvisable to introduce major alterations.

The inability of the general public to understand the nature of this problem is not alleviated by the attitudes and actions of Congress. Sluggishness of Congressional hearings reduces the tempo of public awareness and reinforces Congressional actions which perpetuate the *status quo*. Especially in a time when the economy is regarded as generally satisfactory, it is unlikely that lawmakers would approve actions which might even temporarily reduce the over-all contentment. Any extensive program for conversion must be soft-pedaled lest it imply that the present state carries any marks of impermanence. Some of the opposition to the test-ban treaty is undoubtedly (1) resistance to peacetime conversion, and (2) apprehension over Communism. Some opponents have not been above branding advocates of conversion as unpatriotic; because initiative for conversion must come in large measure from government sources, it has been labeled socialistic. The scene of an industry, wholly dependent upon government, caustically calling all attempts to foster greater civilian participation socialistic takes on an element of the ludicrous.

Among other factors influencing the reluctance to provide adequate offsets to defense cuts is the fear of inflation. The question becomes whether producers would be under such pressure to increase their production costs during a transition to nondefense economy that they would unwittingly create a spiral of inflation.

Traditionally we have been taught to abhor personal debt, and this attitude has carried over into our national patterns as well. We dislike budget deficits and feel compunction to reduce national debt. To that end there is strong pressure within the nation to achieve a budget surplus. Espousal of such a program makes election to office somewhat easier. At least the economic stability prevailing under a total program which includes armament costs can be recognized. Whether a similar degree of stability would exist if the armaments were reduced and a public works program were to replace it is uncertain. In the transition period it is doubted that incomes would be equally sustained. This uncertainty probably accounts for no small measure of the reluctance to support a major shift to public works programs. Also, opposition to government spending is deeply grounded in the public mind. Even the suggestion that the spending might be for the benefit of the citizenry is not enough to outweigh this reluctance to increase the public debt. This may be due to a suspicion that such spending implies a trend toward socialism or represents a national conservatism where public debt is involved.

A survey conducted by the University of Michigan Survey Research Center found that this general attitude toward debt was reflected in a strong disposition to using defense savings for national debt reduction.[14] Thus even the continuation of a doubtful defense program would be preferable to extending the national debt, if such became necessary, during periods of transition from defense production to civilian programs. We had such an experience between 1954 and 1960: "By reducing expenditures and holding up taxes, the Federal government, in four out of seven years from 1954 to 1960, inclusively, took more purchasing power away from private consumers and businesses than it restored to them by its own expenditure and benefit programs (that is, it ran a 'budget surplus on income and product account'). With the resultant deflationary impact, unemployment more than doubled, and the industrial output rose only 18% in the period between 1953 and 1960—in marked contrast to the 54% rise in industrial output and the reduction in unemployment achieved in the seven preceding years."[15] While the volume of government spending and taxes was by no means the only factor affecting the economy during this period, its impact was an influential one.

The cold war has become institutionalized, and institutions rarely liquidate themselves. Instead, they find new reasons for their existence and rationalize their continuance. Anticommunism has become a major "cause" for a very large number of Americans, though the "thaw" has undermined its vigor in some quarters. The study of the true sources of support for the anti-Communist crusade has yet to be made, but one does not have to look far for likely sources of its spiritual and financial assistance. The areas of the nation which received the largest measure of government assistance in the form of defense programs are at the same time centers for the most vigorous anticommunism campaigns. That there is a connection does not require super-sleuthing.

Lacking a forward-looking national purpose in the period following two world wars and being confronted with an ideology which momentarily at least seemed to have its people on the march, it is understandable that the American people should have settled for an anticommunist rationale as its own national purpose. It paid off in the form of vigorous scientific-industrial activity, but the result was that the ideology against which it had been generated was itself similarly consumed by fears of opposition and kept from the advances it also might have been making in civilian progress. By a creeping fear that democracy was not capable of organizing itself adequately for civilian pioneering, our nation has been moving from the enterprise system in economics toward a military-dominated centralization.

Happily some of the participants in the total defense program who are most aware of its crippling consequences to democratic life and the freedom of the human spirit, have been most vigorous in urging that the nation recognize the import of the direction in which its policy is pointed. "The increased demand of nuclear scientists for freedom of movement and less secrecy is an indication that one major veto group is cognizant of the relation between secrecy and coercion."[16] What these men, in addition to some economists, philosophers, theologians, and others, have been contending is that the consequences of the excesses of the defense system are destructive to more than economic life, that they inhibit the freedom of the spirit, making its own forward movement less likely. These are results of preoccupation with defense economy, and behind their supporters lies the resistance to its conversion to constructive peacetime ends.

Proposals for Modification and Their Consequences

Central to any viable suggestion for scaling the defense economy downward is the proposal contained in the Arms Control Disarmament Agency's report: "To do the most good, therefore, offsetting measures should, if possible, be initiated at the very time that defense contracts are cancelled and before defense expenditures—not to speak of actual production and employment—begin to drop."[17] The report goes on to suggest the necessity on the part of the Congress to grant the executive branch authority to initiate measures which would accomplish the desired end, especially in the form of stand-by public works or tax reduction. In view of the public misunderstanding of the function of tax reductions, there is little likelihood that such authority will be readily given to the executive branch. The fact that tax reductions would have to be in an amount greater than the reductions in government expenditure complicates the problem of public acceptance; but only reductions of these dimensions would accomplish the desired purpose.

Getting down to specific proposals in terms of adjusted appropriations, Benoit explains:

> Our disarmament model involves a reduction over the full twelve-year period of United States defense expenditures from $56 billion estimated for 1965 to $10 billion estimated for 1977. Offsetting this would be a rise to $7 billion for the United States contribution (assumed to cover one-third of the total) to the annual current costs of the judicial, administrative, inspection, police, and deterrent functions of a World Peace Authority. . . . It is also estimated that the NASA space program, and the civilian Atomic Energy programs (both of which have been closely associated with the defense program) will rise from $4 billion to about $11 billion over this period. Thus the net cutback of all security expenditures (taking account of these offsets) would be from $60 billion to $28 billion—or about $32 billion. Of this total, however, over $21 billion is estimated to occur in the first three years. It is during this period that the maximum economic impact will presumably be felt.[18]

Reductions of such magnitude are not made simply by decree. Curtailment of defense spending and corresponding tax reduction call for a vast array of projects in both the public and the private sectors. Specifically involving the latter is the need for the replacement of more than 10 million substandard dwellings. In the former, the public sector, we are short some 600,000 classrooms; every major city is calling for a solution to its transportation problem; the steady and rapid urbanization of the nation has placed a strain on the available water supply which is bringing some communities to the brink of anxiety. Projects such as these and many others cannot be left to small or segmented planning. They will necessitate a scope comparable to that involved in the development of the TVA, the MVA, or the unifying of resources such as was required in wartime.

Resistance to centralized planning and execution of plans adequate to offset the temporary impairment from defense conversion is probably inevitable. Political capital is to be made of the charge of centralization, even though the defense program itself is more highly centralized than the program which might be substituted for it. Melman suggests that appropriation of funds from national sources could be made with full consideration of local needs. It is possible to avoid the dangers of centralization, he contends.[19]

In the general range of large-scale attacks on the total problem, it would be essential to devise fiscal and monetary policies capable of influencing aggregate demand but sufficiently flexible to affect allocation of resources among competing needs. The ACDA report proposes that "the balance struck between tax reduction and increased Government spending will be governed by the relative importance accorded to private demand for such goods and services as food, clothing, housing, recreation, health, higher education, machine tools, research, and development—as against public demand for school construction, teacher training, roads, space exploration, urban renewal, area redevelopment, public health, and social services."[20]

Even such large-scale proposals as tax reductions, fiscal and monetary policies, assistance to both public and private sectors, will not of themselves be sufficient. There still remain a large number of other possibilities, such as lowering the retirement age, raising the age at which youth undertake jobs, increasing vacations, and other programs specifically designed to influence the working arrangements of individuals. Uniform requirements in such areas as those mentioned could, in the aggregate, make possible a large number of additional jobs. Nevertheless, with the increasing utilization of automation it is unlikely in the immediate future that jobs will be found for all of those who are released from defense production. It is to these that reference is made in Chapter 3, where it was suggested that in an economy capable of providing for all of its people, without all of them having to work full time, there will be many for whom new types of creative expression will have to be found in lieu of the traditional concepts of constructive work.

Despite the complications and dangers involved in a positive effort toward disarmament, there is much that is hopeful in the picture, too. Kenneth Boulding has convincingly contended that the military organization ("milorg") does not make for increase in civilian common markets. It only stimulates its opposite number in some other nation. Therefore if the civilian economy is to thrive, there must be free activity on the part of the business firms and those organizations which exist by serving all of society.[21] With the diminution of the milorg and with various efforts to meet the civilian requirements, full employment is not an impossibility.

Analyses looking toward the reallocation of workers from defense-related activities to civilian production have already been undertaken.[22] Such proposals must necessarily be inconclusive until serious effort has been made on the part of all of the various industries involved to ascertain what other types of activities they might undertake as a part of the civilian production program. Less vague, however, is the insistence of the planner for conversion that, instead of individuals being transported to jobs created for them or available to them in other areas, it is far more satisfactory both from the standpoint of the industry and of the workers that industry wherever possible be brought to the communities which have been reducing their defense activities. Uprooting and dislocating families has social consequences and long-term deleterious effects for the life of individuals, communities, and the nation.

Not least among the consequences of disarmament adjustment will be the reassignment of the large army of scientists and engineers whose services have been available to the many phases of the defense effort. About one-half of all our scientists and engineers engaged in defense work are involved in research and development. "Although scientists and engineers will probably be harder hit by arms reduction than any other occupational group (save military people), it is not likely that unemployment of scientists and engineers will be more than a very short-run problem."[23] In view of the vast needs in the civilian economy the talents of these highly skilled individuals can be adapted with facility to other than defense activities. Thus presumably the 97,000 engineers now employed in government-supported electronics work would be available for work of civilian importance.

Finally, the ACDA proposes some particular programs upon which a start can be made in the near future. They would include: strengthening of our system of employment offices and the unemployment insurance program, a workable retraining scheme, and government attempts to influence industry to provide more liberal pension rights, group insurance, hospitalization, and similar perquisites, and to provide employees with company-wide rights of transfer, etc.[24]

The discussion of the theme "Disarmament and the Economy" began with using the figure of the perplexed person who had a bear by the tail and dared not let go. A person who has possibly done as much as anyone in our time to study the intricacies of this complex problem is Emile Benoit, to whom, as is obvious, we are deeply indebted for much of the foregoing material. He asks the question in another way: "Can we have roast pig without (at the least risk of) burning down the house?" He answers in the affirmative, providing we not only organize "a 'moral equivalent of war' but an 'economic equivalent of defense.' "[25]

From the standpoint of those responsible for this volume the disarmament issue is a profoundly spiritual as well as a technical economic problem. Here our concern has been not primarily the problem of disarmament itself. That is of course a deeply ethical issue. As has been noted, however, our concern is with the significance of disarmament for the economic life of this nation and inevitably for other nations as well.

We believe it is basically unwholesome for a nation's people to live in an atmosphere of suspicion and in expectation that its unprecedented power may be used whether in retaliation or in warding off anticipated blows. The piling up of defense materials in excess of any use to which they could possibly be put constitutes unjustifiable and deleterious action by any nation or people. Its consequences cannot but be inimical to the nation's well-being, and it will serve to delay facing the nation's fundamental needs. Returning to a wholesome civilian economy presents vast and complex problems, but the sanity of the world requires it. Economic considerations, in the traditional sense of the term, are not likely to provide resolution to our dilemma. In its larger sense, implying the fullest meeting of man's needs, there is more reason for confidence. Hence I included this theme in the roster of areas for which a dimension of faith is essential.

10

International Trade and Aid

Two conditions transcend almost all others in their implications for the immediate future of our world: (1) the fact that two-thirds of the world is hungry, and (2) the economic strength and stability of the United States. That these two conditions are closely related constitutes the basis for much of the foreign and domestic policy of the United States, the other industrialized nations, and also the lesser developed nations. Nowhere are those policies more effectively revealed than in the areas of international trade and aid. In them are to be seen both the ethical values of the nations most involved and the way in which their economic life is conceived.

From the days of the Apostle Paul, those in the Hebrew-Christian lineage have recognized that their responsibilities do not end at the nation's boundaries. All persons everywhere are God's children and our brothers. But the limitations of our human vision cause us to have a descending degree of concern as our thought moves outward from those closest and dearest to us. To most of us, foreigners are "they and theirs" as distinguished from "we and ours." The main reasons for this feeling probably are that for the most part *they* have different languages, attitudes, and cultures and live at greater distances from us, and that *they* are subject to other governments and legal jurisdictions.

The foreign missions movement rested on and stimulated a powerful vision that helped Christians overcome these parochial limitations. Businesses, too, have been interested in other peoples, but the chief motivation has been that of economic gain. Governments also have international interests. In part these have been to support the work of the missionaries and businessmen. In part the national economic interest is involved. Also, there are political and security interests to be defended and promoted through the exercise of persuasion and power and through alliances and international organizations.

Our approaches to our responsibility to people in other countries involve all aspects of human relations. The two principal economic concerns are international trade—including investment—and foreign aid.

International trade consists of the exchange across national boundaries of goods and services. Foreign aid is the provision of assistance by the government or people of one country to those of another. Except from a short-run point of view foreign aid has an important aspect of mutuality, benefiting the providing country as well as the receiving country. Seen in the longer perspective, as Paul G. Hoffman has pointed out, "the term 'foreign aid' is illusory. It is neither 'foreign' nor 'aid.' Realistic appraisal of the forces stimulating revolutionary change, and of United States' vital interest in orderly progress suggests that what we really mean by the term is 'mutual development.' "[1] Thus while designated as "aid," its fundamental purpose is to strengthen the governments, economies, and morale of the new nations so that they may more readily rise to that position in the world of nations where interchange and cooperation may go on without condescension and with mutual benefit. Foreign aid, therefore, though it does have a strong humanitarian implication, is fundamentally a preliminary step toward the achievement of dignity and self-support by both individuals and nations.

International trade is of vital importance for many industrial nations in order to supply the goods and services that they could not produce except at relatively great cost, if at all. Even as self-sufficient a country as the United States finds in international trade a source of great economic benefit. International trade is particularly important for the less developed countries, as a source of earnings to finance the importation of capital and other requirements for industrialization and economic development. Foreign aid is a supplementary source of finance for the less developed countries which cannot earn enough through trade.

International Trade With the Industrialized West

In its trade with the industrialized countries of the free world the United States is unusual in being a major exporter both of temperate-zone agricultural products and of finished manufactured goods, many requiring a high level of technology. Its imports from these countries are predominantly manufactured products. Despite the mutual economic benefits flowing from international trade, most industrialized countries place some restrictions or burdens on imports, usually by levying customs duties (tariffs) and sometimes by imposing quotas. Perhaps the most common reason for this is the clamor of certain domestic industries to be protected from foreign competition, but the maintenance of industries that are deemed to be of key importance for national defense also is frequently given as the reason. In some situations, moreover, restrictions on imports may be used as a method of holding imports in balance with exports to avoid disruptive deficits in the country's balance of payments.

After a half century or more when its dominant policy was the protective tariff, the United States in recent years has been promoting agreements with other countries for the mutual reduction of tariffs and other trade restrictions. This effort to liberalize trade was supported by the Section on the World Economy of the Fourth National Study Conference on the Church and Economic Life, which affirmed: "We agree unanimously that the engagement of the United States in a program of mutual development and trade involving the whole world (eventually including the Soviet bloc as soon as international conditions permit), is irrevocable and full of promise, despite the risks it brings to some sections of our economy. The consequences of withdrawing from freer trade with the industrial nations of the European Community (The Common Market) and the British Commonwealth, or of failing to cultivate the development of other nations by trade and aid would be disastrous and unthinkable."[2]

International Trade With the Less Developed Countries

Traditionally the less developed countries have produced and exported agricultural products and raw materials and used the proceeds to buy manufactured goods from the industrialized countries. The pressure of rapid population growth, the high rate of unemployment and underemployment, the failure of the markets for their products to expand with sufficient rapidity, and the "demonstration effect" of economic development in other countries have brought great pressure in the less developed countries for rapid economic development and particularly for industrialization. This has placed a heavy financial burden on these countries to pay for the machinery, equipment, and other resources for industrialization. To some extent the burden is being carried by private foreign investment; to some extent it must be borne by foreign aid, as we shall see. For the most part, however, dependence has been on international trade.

The trade policies of developing countries are protectionist, aimed at helping infant industries develop substitutes for foreign imports. The special need for such protection has been recognized in general by the industrially advanced countries.

As Chase Manhattan Bank economist William Butler writes:

How important international trade is for the less developed nations is indicated by the fact that it frequently accounts for 20% or more of their total economy as against 8% for the economy of the United States. Indeed, trade is much more important to them than aid. Total exports of the less developed areas amounted to $31 billion in 1960 while the total flow of financial assistance from the industrial nations (including private foreign investment) amounted to $8 billion. For all these reasons it would appear that one of the major economic objectives of free world nations should be to promote an expanding volume of trade between the industrial and less developed nations. . . . Their share in world exports has declined steadily from 31.5% of the total in 1953 to 24.7% in 1960. Since 1956 total exports of less developed areas have been growing only 2% per annum as against 6.5% for the industrial areas. The lag has been particularly severe in the case of Latin America where, excluding Venezuela, exports have been rising only at one half of 1% per year.[3]

International Trade With the Communist Bloc

The long-continued emphasis on economic autarchy in the Soviet Union, on the one hand, and the difficulties of carrying on trade with Communist economies, on the other hand, have kept down trade between the industrial West and the Communist East. In addition, the United States has largely boycotted trade with a number of Communist and Communist-oriented countries, including China and Cuba, and pressured its allies to refuse to sell military equipment and certain high-technology machinery and products to the Soviet Union and the Communist countries generally.

The relaxation of East-West tensions in the 1960s, the competition for markets among the Western industrialized countries, and the recognition that the restrictions were no longer achieving their goal of weakening the defense potentials of the Communist world, have resulted in a movement for increased East-West trade which seems likely to continue. On this Roy Blough has commented: "Whether any useful economic purpose is served in further efforts to keep communist countries from Western trade is very doubtful. After all, trade has advantages for us and our friends, as well as for the communists. We have forced the communist countries to become self-sufficient in some commodities when we might have served our security interests better by keeping them dependent on Western supplies."[4]

Issues in International Trade

Much of the American misgiving centering about our foreign economic programs stems from a fear that any resulting imbalance might be injurious to this nation's economic welfare and that we cannot stand the persistent strain. The ideal arrangement would be to effect a proper balance through exchange of raw materials or finished products. The sooner the use of goods can replace the cash outlay, obviously, the sooner the healthy state of genuine trade can be attained. And not the least of the gains recorded thereby will be the national self-respect achieved by the nation which has been on the receiving end.

The need for initiative and constructive action is not confined to the economically advanced nations. Generosity and good intentions on the part of organizations and governments of industrially advanced countries have met with uncooperativeness and injury in developing countries so frequently that caution to the point of wariness attends consideration by the "have" countries of new trade relations. Instability or even hostility on the part of resentful political groups has jeopardized many good intentions. A primary condition for facilitating stable trade relations is the willingness of the nations seeking investments in its productive facilities to encourage the ventures and to understand both the problems of the investors and the need to assure stability. There may be years of chaos before the developing nations can meet the need for that stability which alone can bring economic benefit to their people. Freedom from disruption and unnecessary loss is a *sine qua non* of wholesome trade relations.

Relieving the hunger and overcoming the economic weakness of the world are of course not solely the responsibility of the United States. As a result of the extraordinary recovery after World War II (due in large measure to the Marshall Plan) nations which had been decimated by war now enjoy a prosperity exceeding that of their most satisfactory prewar years. Because of this prosperity they are able to share in alleviating want and helping to build the domestic economies of the less developed nations.

Foreign trade inevitably involves an attempt to bring exports and imports into favorable balance. With industrialized countries it means the ability to sell finished products; for the lesser developed countries it means selling raw materials. Herein lies a dilemma for the United States, since it has both manufactured products and agricultural products which must be sold if its own economy is to remain stable. But hunger and need in the less developed countries require that agricultural products be consumed at home, and so there is less credit for buying the industrial equipment to enable them to become industrial nations and to give their population more productive employment than substitution for beasts of burden in agriculture. According to economist Egbert De Vries,[5] means must be found whereby those countries can expand imports to 50 billion dollars. An import program of those dimensions means, of course, an export program which is commensurate, and it cannot be in soft currency valid only within its own boundaries, for world trade must be conducted on a currency basis which permits transfer of credit.

The conditions under which agreements for trade liberalization can be negotiated have been greatly modified in recent years by the emergence of several new intergovernmental organizations. Most notable and far-reaching, both for their economic and political significance, are the European Coal and Steel Community, the European Atomic Energy Community, and particularly the European Economic Community,* which bring together, in commerce and manufacturing, nations which had but recently been at war with each other. So recent is this development that it cannot be said that all difficulties in relations with nations not in the EEC have been harmoniously resolved. Each nation in the EEC had its own internal arrangements, with special consideration for coal miners or farmers or other types of producers, or for merchants. Internal political stability depends upon maintenance of these established agreements. To break them would mean the downfall of the very governments which entered into this imaginative collective venture at the international level. And not only is there the necessity for reconciling differences within the EEC but also for an attempt to arrive at harmonious relations with the nations outside it which have done business with its members or would like to do so. For the British Commonwealth, the Scandinavian countries, and the United States, therefore, whose economic health depends upon ability to trade with the EEC nations as well as others closer at hand, there are delicate issues portentous of trouble as well as promising benefit.

The formation of such organizations as the European Economic Community and the European Free Trade Association presents the United States with a brand-new situation. Since the emergence of the United States as a dominant world power during the early years of this century, no single nation or combination of nations presented serious competition. Now suddenly powerful trading blocs emerge to challenge United States preeminence. The nations participating in these blocs have been strengthened by the same forces of industrialism which underlay

* This is usually referred to as the Common Market.

the growth of the United States into a world power. They have been the beneficiaries of scientific and technological advances, and their people have demanded ever higher living standards. But the smaller ones among them—Belgium, the Netherlands, and Luxembourg—could not within themselves support the total fabric of resources, trade, mutual benefit, and economic defense which a larger collectivity of nations would make possible. To this consideration must be added the fact that the nations individually, and now collectively in their respective trading blocs, must constantly face the fact of the massive economic and military establishment of the United States. These nations have been protected or opposed by American military and economic resources in two world wars, but after what had been defeat for some of them, they have sought to put aside centuries-old differences and to develop a common power which no longer left them feeling inferior. The fact that they have become bound together in a pact of mutual defense, the North Atlantic Treaty Organization, does not obligate them to include in their economic structures all of the nations comprising NATO. As of this writing the EEC (France, Italy, Germany, Belgium, the Netherlands, and Luxembourg) have not included in their roster the United Kingdom or the Scandinavian countries. The group outside is known as "the Outer Seven" and the EEC as "the Inner Six." But as John W. Hight of the Committee for a National Trade Policy has pointed out: "Any union has two aspects; it brings the participants closer together while it pulls them away from those outside the union. One effect of the European Economic Community has been to cause consternation in the other countries of Western Europe over the prospect of losing non-discriminatory access to the markets of the Six. This, of course, led in the beginning to the creation of a loosely-structured European Free Trade Area, spearheaded by Britain and Sweden and designed to act as a countervailing force to the Six."[6]

Development of the EEC has implications for other nations than its European neighbors. The United States, for which European nations have provided mutual trade relations, is forced to make serious adjustments also. Charles P. Taft stated in 1962:

"In the case of Europe we face the immediate danger of exclusion from a market just as large again as our own U. S. market. This concerns only $6 billion of our exports and a gross national product of $550 billion, but it happens to be a critical $6 billion. It includes $1.3 billion of agricultural products and $800 million of that last are subject to variable levies."[7]

This combination of trade organization and nation cooperation created for the United States a totally new confrontation with which it had to deal in such a way as to avoid injury to itself as well as to its former allies. The General Agreement on Tariffs and Trade (GATT)* forms the foundation for mutual trade action by all the nations involved. The United States Trade Expansion Act (TEA) of 1962 hopefully has paved the way for negotiations in GATT that will liberalize trade relationships between the United States and the European blocs. It delegates to the President of the United States the power to make adjustments without Congressional ratification, within limitations fixed in the Act.

What has occurred in Europe in the establishment of combinations of nations for mutual support in trade and defense has been paralleled by the initiation of the Central American Common Market and the Latin American Free Trade Association, and the prospects are that still other blocs for similar purposes will be formed in Africa, the Far East, and the Middle East. Until now the preponderance of United States trade has been with Canada, the European nations, and Latin America, but the new combinations of nations bid fair to change the patterns of trade.

Foreign Aid

Economic aid and technical assistance are today going only to the developing countries. These countries have vast needs that are not being met. A great new field for trade expansion lies in

* All the principal non-Communist trading nations are members of GATT. Its members have agreed to give to all other members equal consideration in tariffs except when such organizations as the Common Market require otherwise.

the economic potential of those nations, many of which are new, which are to be classed as the "less developed" or "developing" nations. This takes us from the question of trade to the complicated and puzzling problem of aid. Here a new factor has been emerging in recent years: nations lately in need of an economic "shot in the arm" are themselves now able to use their resources for cooperative investments in lands which are just beginning to enter the industrial era.

If aid to the less developed nations were simply a matter of giving funds or materials, the process would be greatly simplified. The fact is, however, that benefactions from nations with surpluses can leave the receiving nation in a penurious condition forever, unless some portion of the benefits are utilized to build self-supporting instruments in the developing nations.

The problem becomes that of finding the kinds of manufacturing which are most suitable to the newly developing nation and which can be sold to the benefactor nation at a price which does not make the sale primarily a charity transaction and which in turn enables the selling nation to invest in further expanding means of production. The word "charity" is used here in an ambiguous sense, for in all probability it will become necessary for the advanced nations to make concessions both as to price and as to product, even though its own production resources and personnel are temporarily impaired. This, of course, is one of the most delicate and difficult decisions for an advanced nation to make. Here the problem is twofold: (1) whether the developing nation can sell its product at a price which yields a profit, especially when the developed nation with higher efficiency in its manufacturing can produce the same article for less, and (2) whether the developing nation may have so low a wage scale that it will impair the economy of the purchasing nation which has made an original investment in the developing country. It is axiomatic that those who are disemployed because of favor shown a nation which needs to expand industrially are not going to be kindly disposed toward the party in power which makes such a decision.

The Fourth National Study Conference on the Church and Economic Life issued the following statement:

In the face of some doubts about the effectiveness and value of aid by the United States government to develop countries we would like to assert the conviction that it is and must be a lasting part of the responsibility of an economically developed country for nations less advanced in this respect. . . . We cannot shirk this burden because other industrialized nations are not doing as much as we think they ought. Foreign aid is necessary in order that aided countries may develop the capacity to support themselves by their own industrial and agricultural production and make their contribution to the world economy. It can be justified by a long-range view of the self-interest of the giving country, for a developed economy is a good customer and a satisfied people contributes to world peace. But this rationale will always need the support of a particularly Christian perspective which emphasizes that we are responsible for our neighbor's welfare as far as we can serve him regardless of the reward we may receive.[8]

There is no hiding the fact that a substantial measure of American support for foreign aid derives from the conviction that this is the means for containing the expansion of communism among nations which in the years ahead could provide trade opportunities but which, if communism were to prevail, would in all probability not exist. American foreign aid, therefore, is compounded of a genuine idealism and also what some might term "hard-boiled realism," the guaranteeing of future trade opportunities. It is the contention of a large number of sensitive, ethically minded people that these two elements are not mutually exclusive. Relieving hunger and at the same time guaranteeing that a whole nation shall not be permanently trapped in an international web whose purpose is to serve one principal nation and its ideology can be ethically realistic. However, effecting these policy objectives is much more difficult than appears on paper. While cooperation may be possible, unforeseen problems have arisen at both ends to inhibit the success of the aid program.

The fundamental problem is hunger. Beyond assuaging hunger lies the need for constructive action to prevent hunger and to begin establishing a decent standard of living. Hungry people cannot put their minds to work at learning the skills and techniques required to eliminate hunger, but unless educational levels rise and skills increase, hunger will not be alleviated. So at the heart of all aid programs in the developing nations is improvement of agriculture, with the subsequent reduction of the numbers engaged in agriculture; thereby an adequate supply of industrial labor can be freed to make the products that will increase the national income and with it the standard of living. This is not usually a politically acceptable conclusion in the developing country, where the pressure is for rapid industrialization and agriculture tends to be neglected.

The fact remains, however, that "one-half of the world's people live in countries where the average per capita income is less than $100 per year. In contrast the 15% of the world's people who live in the United States, Canada, Western Europe, the United Kingdom, Australia and New Zealand, enjoy about 75% of the world's income. The United States alone with 6% of the world's population, enjoys more than 40% of the world's income."[9]

Paul Hoffman's *World Without Want* is a documentation of the plight of nations whose people know "the eternal compulsory fast and where misery and squalor are the accepted, though resented, conditions." In this emotion-arousing portrayal of the tragedy of living in underdeveloped nations, Hoffman discusses some of the agencies working to eliminate the conditions now endured with bitterness because the people know they are no longer inevitable. He admits that mistakes have been made in the decade of experimentation: one was to assume that benefiting these nations through assistance programs constituted a program of charity or "give away."

> Development programs are investments in people and prosperity—and investments in peace and freedom as well. They benefit both the giver and the receiver. . . . Closely allied to the charity mistake has been the continuance of the "donor country-recipient country" point of view. These terms were perfectly acceptable in describing international relief programs, but they outlived their usefulness when attention shifted from relief to recovery and then to development. As this change occurred the relationship between the nations changed into a partnership—a partnership in an international joint venture to relieve human misery and expand the world economy.[10]

To catalogue here the great variety of forms of aid and the manifold types of projects sponsored by aid-giving countries and agencies is not possible. For the most part, however, they come under these general categories: (1) disaster relief, (2) aid to shore up countries which are not stable in their own economy but must be fortified against communism, and (3) long-range aid. Under both of the latter two, aid may be extended through technical assistance, loans, or grants, or even a combination of all three. In any event, the nation extending the aid is primarily concerned that the result shall be an increase in the ability of the recipient nation to sustain itself and to increase its own capacity for trade. Here again the economic stability of the assisting nation, if it is the United States, is of ultimate importance. "A recession in the United States and Western Europe during 1957/58 depressed the demand for and the price of such products as coffee, tea and cocoa. This decreased the export earnings of the under-developed nations by some 7%. Since the prices of manufactured goods continued to rise the under-developed nations lost about $2 billion in import capacity. This was almost as much as all the economic aid they received during the recession year."[11] The sum total distributed under the Mutual Security Program of the United States is unquestionably very large. Nevertheless, the fact remains that in no single year has our participation in the development of other nations amounted to as much as one per cent of our national production. Those who contend that even the one per cent of our gross national product is more than we should allocate to other nations must realize that the recipient countries spend 80 per cent of their aid money in the United States. Actually, increase in aid would even put some of our own unemployed to work.

Resistance to participation in aid programs has come from those who felt that this nation was bearing too high a proportion of the total costs and that much of the giving, whether in the form of goods or cash, went into the hands of individuals who fattened their own incomes and whose funds subsequently found their way to Swiss banks. Where money and goods in such large quantities have been hastily poured out, there has undoubtedly been opportunity for corruption. This does not minimize the need or the ultimate goal. It makes mandatory more careful supervision and intelligent allocation.

That there are insufficient funds to meet the needs of every developing nation is obvious. Some selection must be made, but in doing this international feelings are bruised among both the giving and receiving nations. Even with the best of criteria there remain some who doubt the wisdom of sending assistance outside the country when there are still those within it who are themselves in need. There can be no end to this argument, since there will be at least relative need in our own country as far into the future as anyone can see. The question is rather whether the proposed aid will serve to lift the level of competence and capacity for self-support on the part of the receiving (or partner?) nation. All of this requires a capacity to sense and weigh the respective needs both of other nations and of one's own and to envision potential future relationships. It is the failure to think inclusively which gives rise to Gunnar Myrdal's thesis that as nations become welfare-minded, they decline in their acceptance of international responsibility and become instead increasingly nationalistic. This is the ethical and spiritual dilemma of the nations which are already advanced and capable of doing more for their own citizens than can the nations which are still in the "traditional," or at the "take-off," stage. Confronting its own citizens with this fact constitutes one of a government's primary responsibilities.

A nation's life transcends that of its citizens. The future well-being of a whole nation may depend on the mutual trade relations beginning with an act of beneficence. Speaking of this in reference to the delicate problem of increasing exports in the developing nations, even at the cost of embarrassing and disrupting imports, William Butler suggests that "painful though they may be, such adjustments work in the long-run interests of the industrial nations, which will be able to obtain consumer goods at lower costs, while shifting their production to the more highly technical products where their international advantage is greater."[12]

U. S. foreign aid from July 1, 1945, through June 30, 1962, totaled approximately 97.1 billion dollars. This includes 30.7 billion dollars in military assistance and 66.4 billion dollars in grants and loans to 112 foreign countries, territories, possessions, etc. Of the amount of economic aid, some 31.5 billion dollars went to Europe and Japan, and 31.5 billion dollars to the underdeveloped countries. Through the year 1963 the grand total was 101.1 billion dollars. In allocations of such magnitude it is almost inevitable that there should be certain failures, and they cannot easily be tossed off. There has not been time to develop a large and tested staff of administrators, rich in wisdom and experience in the nations to which allocations have been made. This fact does not excuse the failures, unless there has been a little learning and constructive experience while nations and people have been relieved, in some measure at least, from want and given hope for future development. To give aid to less developed nations means inevitably some form of interference with their political, economic, and social life, but to insure that the interference is constructive and designed for the best interests of that nation requires specialists who understand the life, customs, and needs of the developing nation. Only thus will viable economies emerge and future harmony with the contributing nations be assured.

Out of the welter of new experience has emerged a single organization responsible for most of the civilian operations in providing both relief and solid instructive programs, the Agency for International Development (AID). Its structure and program have become well known both in our own nation and around the world. One indication of its extent is the fact that it is manned by some 13,000 workers, more than 6,000 of whom are United States nationals overseas.

The American people have been bombarded with a wide variety of arguments relative to foreign aid. A U. S. Senate special committee to study the foreign aid program reported that "foreign aid has been justified at one and the same time as the answer to the prevention of further Communist expansion; as a key to the national defense; as a lid to cap explosive political situations like that in the Middle East; as a vehicle for the expression of our friendship and our humanitarianism; as a means for keeping or winning the less developed nations to freedom; as a principal bulwark of world peace; as a stimulator of trade, investment and free enterprise throughout the world; as the answer to the problem of agricultural surpluses and other lesser economic dislocations in this country."

The committee goes on to suggest that this confusion "has resulted in distortions to the purposes, cost and potentialities of particular types of aid. This misconception was bound to lead, as it has led, to increasing disillusionment and hostility toward foreign aid in this country."

John Nuveen, investment banker and former U. S. minister and chief of this country's economic mission in Greece and Belgium during the Marshall Plan period, commenting on the consequences for communism under the Marshall Plan program in Europe, says that in Belgium there were forty Communists in the Parliament prior to the Plan. In 1950 there were ten, and by 1958 three. True, this was the nation which had known a healthy economy and cannot be compared accurately to the developing nations. But as Nuveen goes on to point out, after eliminating military aid figures, the United States is attempting to cure the economic anemia of the underdeveloped countries with one-sixtieth of the strength (on a per capita basis) which produced results in Europe.[13]

Communist competition has loomed large in the justification for foreign aid, and correctly so. The well-being of the people of an emerging nation may be the concern of the people of nations providing assistance, but at the national level the expectancy of future trade benefits constitutes the principal rationale. Potential exclusion from the benefits of trade confronts nations which must project their life long into the future with the possibility of impairment in economic relations. Evidence of Communist gains already made justly give rise to apprehension.

> The increase in Communist aid to the under-developed countries has been matched by an increase in Communist trade. The Soviet Union itself has been taking the agricultural surpluses of those countries—Egypt's cotton, Burma's rice, Uruguay's wool—and sending in return, arms or capital goods and raw materials needed for development. Between 1953 and 1956 the Soviet Union nearly doubled its imports from the under-developed countries and increased its exports to more than five-fold. Other members of the Communist bloc—Poland, Czechoslovakia, and more recently, Communist China—have also increased their trade with the under-developed countries though by lesser amounts. By the end of 1958 Western businessmen were talking about Communist China's economic invasion of Asia and Africa.[14]

The United States' answer to this challenge is first, of course, the maintenance of economic strength and stability in this nation.

But beyond that lie the various kinds of assistance to which reference has been made above. As the people of less developed nations and their leaders discern the fact that assistance from the West carries with it no mortgaging of their future or bondage to a rigid political system, they will evolve in their own self-respect and note in the history of their national life the fact that the aid given them did not carry crippling requirements.

Stipulations as to agencies and specific programs are unnecessary at this writing, for they must change in accordance with evolving needs. The principle underlying participation in economic assistance has not altered nor is it likely to be altered in the foreseeable future. Conditions in developing nations do suggest, however, some variations to be taken into consideration. The development of traditional societies presents different requirements, in contrast to those of the nations aided by the Marshall Plan, and the patterns found so successful immediately after World War II cannot be exactly duplicated. This may be illustrated in the comment of an Indian official: "The Germans have built us steel works but we are the hostages of their technology. How can we get our people trained to replace them, without adequate elementary schools to give any grounding? Give me 10,000 teachers."[15]

Aid in the form of loans, grants, food, schools, technical assistance, and many other forms is indispensable. To these, however, must be added substantial help in the form of control of population growth. As stated earlier, most of the benefits accruing from assistance, however unselfishly motivated, could be minimized if not destroyed by a rate of population growth too great to permit the nation to develop itself for holding its own with other nations in the world of trade. It becomes obligatory upon the assisting nations to find means for convincing the receiving "partners" that extensive measures must be taken to limit their population increase.

No small clue to economic development for the less developed nations lies in the attitude of the American people. Development of living standards in the United States exemplified the forces which have aroused the aspirations of those living in underdeveloped lands, aspirations which can never be quelled. It is difficult for middle-class Americans to understand the realities behind the standard-of-living figures of the nations now seeking an increasing measure of the things Americans take for granted.

U Thant, secretary-general of the UN, says: "The truth, the central stupendous truth, about developed countries today is that they can have—in anything but the shortest run—the kind and scale of resources they decide to have. . . . It is no longer resources that limit decisions. It is the decisions that make the resources. This is the fundamental revolutionary change—perhaps the most revolutionary mankind has ever known."[16] This is the attitude which has permeated the thought of a large percentage of people in the developed nations.

Because the future health of world economic relations depends upon a recognition of both its own fortuitous situation and the possibilities for increasing world economic health, it is recommended that "the United States in cooperation with other rich countries of the world, take an unlimited commitment to provide the developing countries with all the financial resources which they can usefully absorb and which can be effectively used. In other words, the Commission recommends that a lack of financial resources should no longer be allowed to hamper programs of aid to the developing countries."[17] It is estimated that to accomplish this purpose it would require only 15 per cent of the annual increase in income which could normally be expected in the nations participating in the giving.

Finally, it becomes apparent that motives for participation in foreign aid are a compound of genuine generosity and national benefit. There is nothing derogatory or reprehensible in this combination. Here economic well-being of our neighbor is inseparable from the consequences of concern for him as neighbor. In the whole issue of foreign aid the mutual involvement of mankind is illustrated with convincing evidence. As the Fourth National Study Conference on Church and Economic Life stated: "A basic condition of truly effective aid is a sense of mutual purpose and shared responsibility among the countries and people involved."[18]

11

Government Power and the Economy

The proper role of government—the most inclusive of all organizations—has, except in totalitarian states where it is all-embracing, become a major issue in the consideration of problems of economic development.

—William Adams Brown, Jr., in *Christian Values and Economic Life*

If Alexander Hamilton and Thomas Jefferson could witness what has occurred in their country a century and a half after their famous controversy over concentration of government power, they would be surprised to learn that each had won his point: the powers of the central government have increased steadily, and the rights, privileges, and security of the citizens have experienced parallel increase. Thus the fundamental intentions of both men have been realized. The paradox is that it has been the mounting insistence that the federal government provide for the well-being of the individual citizen which has been so largely instrumental in concentrating power at the national level.

Hamilton's interest in a strong central government was hardly motivated by a zeal for establishing a welfare state; in fact, if some historical analyses of that period are correct, the Federalist Party espousing strong centralization went out of existence in part because of its reputation for indifference to the common man. Jefferson's fear, on the other hand, was that artistocrats wielding power would be insufficiently aware of and incapable of protecting the interests of the overwhelming majority, the ordinary citizens. Thus not only did the two men not foresee that the nation would ultimately focus major attention on the welfare needs of its people (and that of other nations as well), but that in consequence the stability of the economy which both men so eagerly desired would be realized.

Government Expansion

Seemingly unlimited opportunities for geographic expansion and a conviction that material salvation was the assured result of hard work spared a new nation the necessity for clarifying its central economic policies. An unlimited frontier could give substance to Horace Greeley's admonition, "vote yourself a farm," at least until the closing of the frontier around 1890. The maxim "that government is best which governs least" had special meaning for all who stood to gain by their diligence or skill in appropriating the resources of the new country. The psychology of the whole nation supported their efforts. Courts, reflecting the dominant tone of expansion and optimism of the nation, upheld their actions and property claims. The Federal Land Policy, expressed notably in the Homestead Act of 1862, likewise reflected the national temper. Land was the symbol of property. Independent and self-reliant citizens would acquire it either for agricultural purposes or for speculation. Government's role was to facilitate the acquisition of land and to foster the type of citizen Jefferson believed was the backbone of the nation.

As the new government sought means of facilitating the nation's expansion, prior to its encouragement of railroads and land disposal, it entered into various business ventures. In 1791 a national bank was established, though later abandoned; canals were dug in many states, and a national road was constructed. State governments also undertook the initiating and operating of ventures designed to increase their own functions and to expand the economy within their borders. In addition to roads, canals, and banks even some manufacturing was undertaken. At least one state, North Dakota, continues to operate banks and grain elevators, not so much, however, to expand the economic activities of the state as to protect its citizens from injury by outsiders.

Then came the greatest decision since the founding of the nation itself. It emerged from a casual land policy and forced a government heretofore unchallenged in its land disposition to decide whether newly opened areas should be operated on a slave economy. A war with England in 1812 united a new nation in the common defense but left unresolved the major question whether the central government had the right and power to coerce its own people into uniformity where a fundamental ideological difference still remained.

With the Civil War issue resolved, at least on the political and legal levels, the rebuilding of a devastated southland and the continued westward expansion of agriculture, transportation, and mining, major government controls were delayed more than a generation. Government resources poured into agricultural production through the land-grant colleges, direct aid to farmers, land gifts to railroads, high tariffs to protect "infant industries," judicial discouragement of labor organizations, and through many other means supporting unrestrained individual and corporate aggrandizement. All this presumed that an ultimate harmony of individual and social needs would result if restraints were minimal. The hypotheses of John Locke, the influence of David Hume and his utilitarian school, and Jeremy Bentham and his laissez-faire philosophy, all of which had so richly informed the thinking of the founding fathers, remained the cornerstones of political and economic philosophy.

But Locke, Hume, and Bentham had not envisioned the misuses to which their advocates might direct their theories. Though the ability of the federal government to maintain the union had met its greatest challenge, there remained the necessity for defending the one group of citizens who benefited from the government policy of land disposition against another group who also benefited but in the form of railroad franchises. The result was "The Green Rising," or Populist Movement. Intimately related to the injuries done the farmer by fraudulent grain-grading programs and excessive and discriminatory charges for hauling of agricultural products was the conviction that the farmer was the victim of money rates and interest charges making it increasingly difficult to pay off land mortgages. This protest produced the beginnings of the farm organization movement which in turn enhanced the power of the agricultural states to secure from the federal government both redress of grievances and a measure of special consideration which has prevailed until very recently.

Industry had experienced no such necessity for securing its objectives; a government already kindly disposed toward manufacture and trade did not have to achieve its end through consolidated opposition to powers already installed. Though labor had long since attempted collective pressure, it had not won the public support and sympathy accorded agriculture. After all, the farmer was an indigenous American embodying the very essence of the American system, the "Protestant ethic"; he worked with his hands, but he was also an entrepreneur, and he represented that pure type which Jefferson thought could be trusted with the destiny of the nation.

Labor, on the other hand, represented massed power, and many of its dissident leaders as well as its rank and file bore names which were other than English or North European. Massed power in the form of labor unions was regarded as a vulgar threat to the persons who, through initiative, diligence, and personal economy, had arrived at their places of distinction. A government traditionally founded on the qualities associated with Calvinistic virtues was not yet disposed to come to the rescue of those who were judged to have failed to exhibit these virtues and to take advantage of the opportunities supposedly available to all. Thus it was no violation of fundamental tenets of American life to organize the forces of government on behalf of its most exemplary citizens, the farmer. By protecting him this same benevolent government was merely extending the action originally taken to provide the nation with a solid core of loyal independent citizens on the land. It is therefore consistent that when this particular exemplary citizen fell upon evil days in the maturing of the total economy, it was around his needs that major rescue programs evolved. They were the forerunners of those systems which ultimately had to be devised by an increasingly centralized government to rescue the entire economy.

A greater factor, even, than the plight of agriculture in creating the necessity for increasing the central power of government was the process of industrialization and technological development. This theme was dealt with more fully in chapter two. Here it must be affirmed that concentration of government power is no more a devious plot than is the centralizing of power by industry and business. It is an inevitable consequence of utilizing the scientific gains whereby efficiency is enhanced and living standards raised. One may question whether the consequences are universally desirable, which introduces a question of relative values. But it can be unequivocally insisted that if we continue the technological advances which have produced concentrations of economic power, a commensurate governmental power becomes necessary and inevitable if a democratic society is to survive. This nation has assumed from its inception that economic enterprise is subordinate to the common welfare and is not, therefore, autonomous. The rapid advances in technology and industry have created the confusion and tension attending the formation of corresponding government responses. Some of this results presumably from sheer resentment against government expansion, but much if not most of it is the consequence of trial and error in ascertaining the most appropriate and effective instruments for government action in our evolving industrial society.

Welfare and Increased Central Authority

Since the founding of the nation there has been no serious denial of the central government's authority to initiate the defense program and to manage the finances of the nation. Protests on either score would hardly be taken seriously. Though there are still a few individuals who would like to have the postal service placed under private management, they attract little serious support. Control over corporation abuses against the populace as a whole has been reflected in "trust busting" activities under the Sherman Antitrust Act; because the scandals of corporate abuse and defiance of public good were so widely portrayed, the public was prepared for the restraining action. For similar reasons, the food and drug legislation found acceptance. Not so readily accepted, however, was the legislation establishing the federal income tax. A wartime income tax of 1861 had been repealed in 1872; another tax levied in 1894 was declared unconstitutional. Finally, in 1913 the income tax amendment was adopted. There was intense opposition to the tax by business and higher income groups who attacked it as being socialistic; small but noisy outbreaks of such opposition continue to exist a half century later.

Support for the nation's citizens whether in need or in return for service rendered their country found no place in the earliest stages of the nation's life. Veterans of the Revolutionary War and the War of 1812 were given grants of land in the newly opened areas of the country, but this was not in the form of continued payments or pensions. The granting of pensions, both to meet actual need and as tokens of gratitude, began after the Civil War. Therewith began the policy of providing through the national government for unmet needs of the nation's citizens.

Private charitable agencies, the traditional method of meeting need in this country, were unable to cope with either the causes or the consequences of unemployment, with hunger and suffering. Public welfare measures were the province of the states, but under the impact of nationwide and world-wide need state programs were inadequate. Not until the depression of the 1930's, however, was the scope of government's role as sustainer of the well-being of its citizens fully realized.

Though the agricultural dilemma had been handled—not wholly successfully, it is true—with proposals for sustaining farm incomes, there was no acknowledgment of responsibility on the part of the federal government to assure income maintenance for individual citizens. Finally, the lag between capacity to produce and ability to purchase the goods produced became a recognized issue in the total economy. A government which heretofore had been responsible for sustaining industries in difficulty because of production costs or inability to sell competitively either in this country or abroad, was now confronted with the fact that millions of its citizens were unable to sustain themselves within the resources of the then current economy. European nations had long since experienced the evolution of "the welfare state." It now became apparent that the same forces which had fostered the sense of governmental obligation in European countries were inevitable and were operative in this nation. Though the range of newly accepted responsibilities is essential documentation, the spate of legislation produced by this new awareness of government responsibility is too well known to rehearse here. Those responsibilities include: (1) alternative action where private resources and enterprise are deficient; (2) establishing levels of decency below which persons shall not be expected to descend and providing them the resources to maintain themselves in dignity when private resources fail; (3) fostering conditions for full employment and, where this is not available, stabilizing the income of those temporarily or even for longer periods forced into unemployment; (4) providing for those whose physical condition no longer permits them to take their full and vigorous part in the life of the economy, i.e., the aged, the dependent, and the ill, so that their well-being becomes a responsibility of the nation as a whole; (5) specifying the conditions of work, lest hazards and unsanitary surroundings impair the physical or mental condition of the worker; (6) requiring a basic education for the entire populace, so that the nation as a whole might be freed from the deleterious effects of illiteracy and hampered in its own opportunities to play an effective role in the world of nations; (7) and finally, taking such steps as may be necessary to give impetus to the total economy, in order that the health of the nation and the well-being of its people shall be assured.

All of this was not a vast movement on behalf of those at the bottom of the economic scale; rather it furnished a broad base for the entire economy. It included in its range the Reconstruction Finance Corporation and such income maintenance projects as the Works Progress Administration. Here was a revolution in assumptions about the role of the state and its obligations to its people.

Would any political party seeking to reverse this trend of federal responsibility for the well-being of its citizens be taken seriously by any appreciable number of voters? Most individuals with sufficient literacy to read a newspaper know that the economy of the nation is increasingly dependent on the kinds of decisions made at its center. No major corporation would expect to go it alone in the economy independently of any and all government coordination. As civilization itself evolves and establishes ever higher minimal standards for human decency, it becomes apparent that some major force must assure those standards of decency, since unconnected and inchoate bodies uncommitted to any common standard are incapable of maintaining such levels.

This is not to suggest that the activity of a central government in devising programs designed to sustain its people and maintain harmony in the life of the state is the product of deliberate intent over an extended period. Many of the devices and instruments established for benefiting the citizens have emerged out of pressures, agonies, and needs occasioned by the exigencies of the times. Only as an accumulation of these needs appears has there arisen the awareness that something much more consistent and comprehensive had to be instituted. But even that may fall short of full and comprehensive organization. As Gunnar Myrdal has expressed it: "In the same way as the 'created harmony' of interest in the welfare state of the western countries was never planned, and thus never created in the strict sense of having been purposively attained, so the actual large-scale planning, which is today a major explanation of the high degree of harmony that actually exists, has remained largely unprogramatic."[1] Relative to the whole concept of the welfare state he adds: "It can even be seen that, to many persons, the term 'welfare state' has negative, not positive connotations—not, of course, because they do not appreciate welfare, but because they are bent upon protecting themselves against realizing that welfare has not come into being by itself, as a result of the unhampered play of market forces, but through public policies which are all under the ultimate sanction of the state."[2]

That a central government does not expect its welfare programs to go forward solely by accident and exigency is attested by the formation of the United States Department of Health, Education and Welfare at cabinet level. It has become accepted in the total national life that health, education, and welfare can no longer be left to mere fortuitous development. The life of a total people is too important to be left to the unregulated activities of an uncertain economy. To this department has therefore been given the commission to engage in the kind of planning over both the short and long future and to assure to the nation that its most humane interests be protected.

The Government and Business

A major product of the technological age is the large corporation. It may be nationwide or, as is increasingly the case, international in the scope of its activities. Oil companies have long operated on a multicontinent basis; more recently the automobile business has extended its areas of sales and manufacture. Because of policy established in the earliest days of the nation, each of these nationwide corporations or international organizations operates under a charter issued by and in a single state, not by the national government. Despite this fact no corporation chartered even in a single state, if doing business in other nations, may act independently of the policies and requirements of its own central government. Thus, though the fiction of responsibility to one of the fifty states is maintained, the ultimate controls over any corporation with international business interests are established by the national government. Many corporation activities even strictly within the national limits must likewise be constantly reviewed to insure compliance with the stipulations of the national government.

As corporations and markets become nationwide, with similar products required or available in diverse areas of the nation, a regulatory body with comparable authority becomes essential. Distances are of little importance with almost instantaneous communication. Thus policies and practices of corporations operating nationwide and affecting the population in many areas require oversight by the one agency responsible to the total population, the national government.

With increasing demands at the national level and the realization of the necessity to preserve common values, not only corporations but also states once regarding themselves as sovereign have faced the need for common controls. "Abdications of power to a central unit are designed precisely to defend all that can be maintained of the autonomy and individuality of the surrendering group. Much of the success of the American federal experiment rests on the aptness of the federal instrument in just this respect. The federal system can recognize, preserve, and defend diverse individual and parochial values at the same time that it unites forces necessary for the common welfare and the common defense."[3]

For each major area related to industrial activity, such as transportation, petroleum, steel, and finally aircraft, there have been brought into being either agencies or major policies for regulation and control to protect the public and to prevent injury to the economy of the nation and to the industries themselves in the process. Here, however, the governmental regulation is both direct and indirect and for a variety of reasons. All of these industries are privately owned and operated, yet their health and vitality is heavily dependent on the federal government. For example, 95 per cent of all aircraft production is sold to the government, and, presumably, the government market for fissionable materials is even higher in percentage than that of aircraft production. While substantial supervision over some areas of industry and technology can be required because they owe a very large percentage of their business to the federal government, this does not constitute the principal reason for exercising control and providing directions. A more fundmental reason is the significance of the operating practices of the industries involved as they bear upon national welfare. Disharmonies through unbridled competition with subsequent personal losses and community injury can and should be avoided. Examples are prevention of profligate waste from undue competition through production quotas (oil) or regulation of monopoly power (public utilities and transportation systems) and, more recently, labor standards of firms doing business with the government. Increasingly it becomes mandatory that a power of adequate magnitude shall enter into the decisions of organizations whose activities deeply involve the national welfare.

A. A. Berle contends that five hundred corporations control

two-thirds of the nonfarm economy of this nation; and of those five hundred corporations a comparatively small group determines the major policies of each. This, Berle says, is the highest concentration of economic power in recorded history. "Since the United States carries on not quite half of the manufacturing production of the entire world today, these 500 groupings, each with its own little dominating pyramid within it, represent a concentration of power over economics which makes the medieval feudal system look like a Sunday School party. In sheer economic power this has gone far beyond anything we have yet seen."[4] Ownership and control of these corporations represent one of the major confusions of our society. It is illustrated by the historic remark of a General Motors official who, on being asked to open the books of the corporation to a labor union, remarked, "We don't even show our books to our stockholders." The agonies through which some stockholders have had to pass in order to get changes made in the management reveals the slight and often unimportant role of the theoretical owners.

Kenneth Boulding points out that there are some corporations which are larger and affect the lives of more people than many of the nations of the world.[5] Many of these corporations in their local units determine the existence of whole communities, while collectively they influence the lives and destinies of more people than some of the fifty states in the United States.

Almost any time in the last half century it could be reported that a plant had closed and moved to another location, bringing despair and economic tragedy to a whole community. More recently it could be added that where a plant had chosen to move to another community for purposes of tax advantage and lower labor costs, a federal court has intervened on behalf of the workers. In at least one instance such a move was not permitted, and in a number of others the government ordered compensation for those who could not move and other jobs made available to those who would be willing to accept employment in the new location. At this writing there is no uniform policy, but both practices have been recorded.

In the field of communications a single industry, the American

Telephone and Telegraph Company, so penetrates the life of the nation that it enjoys a status tantamount to a public agency under private ownership. What is true at A. T. & T. is also true, even though in lesser degrees, of many corporations which do not enjoy such a near monopoly. It is no longer possible to make clean-cut distinctions between public and private agencies. Even privately owned corporations not enjoying those concessions made by a central government which are necessary for utilities are under such a measure of public jurisdiction and the consequent necessity for maintaining the public good will that they must presumably conduct themselves with a high degree of circumspection. The broad field of communications—radio, television, newspapers, wire services of many sorts—has been increasingly recognized as enjoying special governmental privileges, though without the more rigid regulations of public utilities, and is therefore under the obligation to conduct itself in a manner evidencing consideration for the national well-being.

The operation of these semipublic and private corporations may not be as intimately related to the health of the economy as, for example, would be the operations of fiscal and monetary policy, but there can be no doubt that with the total harmony of national life and the stability of individuals and organizations at stake, each of these corporations has an intimate tie with the total economy. Thus, much of the insistence upon authority and control over the public and private corporations has arisen for reasons which are at the same time economic and ethical.

Government and the National Economy

Earlier it was suggested that a watershed in the role of government was reached during the great depression, when the nation first realized that the welfare of its people was a national concern and that only measures taken at the national level could guarantee proper subsistence. Functions of a government are never isolated from each other, and however much one would like to have the welfare aspects of government identifiable and operated strictly within their own range, they cannot be separated from the forces which affect the total economy.

Fiscal and monetary policy* have a direct bearing on the problem of employment, gross national product, expansion or growth in the economy, and everything else affecting economic life.

National monetary policy in the United States may be said to have had its principal development with the passage of the Federal Reserve Act in 1913. Fiscal policy, however, was an activity that began with the depression in the 1930s. Because industries lacked the liquid resources and could not secure funds at a sufficiently low level of interest to launch major expansion programs, the federal government undertook the now famous pump priming program under the Works Progress Administration, Public Works Administration, Reconstruction Finance Corporation, any many others. Under a monetary policy of reduced interest rates and more adequate supply of funds through the Federal Reserve Board, encouragement was given to industries to start expansion. The income maintenance provisions of the social security programs not only protected individuals and families but served to increase effective demand. However, during the first few years of the decade repeated efforts were made to balance the budget by increasing taxes, always without success. Influenced largely by the British economist J. M. Keynes, the Roosevelt administration after 1937 moved toward the policy of federal spending as a positive means of accelerating the economy's growth. Meanwhile, taxes were not further increased lest this should offset the stimulating economic impact of the increase in expenditures. The result was a moderate increase in the national debt, a fact reluctantly accepted as a necessary consequence of the other steps. Major developments in the use of fiscal policy were made during and after the war.

Obviously, such actions can be taken only at the national level, for the integration of the economy is so complete that only nationwide use of governmental expenditures, taxation, and interest rates can have the necessary impact. It is significant in this instance that through the exercise of both fiscal and monetary policy the results could be felt immediately not only by those at the lowest

* Fiscal policy is designed to influence the economy by changing the volume of demand in the economy through measures of taxation and government expenditure, including deficit spending. Monetary policy is designed to influence the volume of demand and accordingly of economic activity by changing the supply of money and its cost to the borrower.

level of income but also by the most powerful corporations in the nation. It was total economic therapy.

That not everyone is pleased with the use of fiscal and monetary policy as means of stimulating the economy is revealed by vigorous opposition to tax reduction as a means of putting more money to work in the expansion of plant and increase of buying power on the part of individuals. So accustomed are we to thinking of the finances of the federal government in terms comparable to the finances of a family that it is difficult to make convincing argument that going further into debt as a means of stimulating economic life is at times justifiable. In 1963 former President Eisenhower said: "I say that the time-tested rules of financial policy still apply. Spending for spending's sake is patently a false theory. No family, no business, no nation can spend itself into prosperity. Any way you look at it, a nation is nothing more than a collection of families—about 47 million of them make up the United States—and it is their money that the government is spending."[6] Nevertheless a year later a government which had witnessed the longest continued span of prosperity in many years voted a large tax reduction as a means of assuring the continuance of what appeared to be a healthy economy. This was done with the encouragement of the President's economic advisors and large sections of the financial and industrial leadership of the nation.

In addition to the protest against a "spending for prosperity" theory there should also be mentioned the objection to the use of taxing powers for the general distribution of wealth. This is regarded by many individuals as "socialism."

Fiscal and monetary policies are tools to be used in promoting the growth and stability of the internal economy. Their use is determined or stimulated by many factors, among which is the balance of payments with the rest of the world. Paradoxically a deficit in balance of payments may result from rising internal demand achieved by successful fiscal and monetary policy. Its remedy may come from still further changes in those policies, through, for example, the deflation of demand and the increase of interest rates. Doing so may, however, cast a cloud over the economy's health, as a reduction of levels in business and employment may result. Obviously, the making of fiscal and monetary policies is an extremely delicate matter and, to be effectively applied, requires the utmost in governmental responsibility. The point being made here is not a defense of or an opposition to the practices described but a warning that in so complex a matter as the total economy of the nation only a central administrative force can exercise the initiative and fulfill practices required to meet what are deemed the fundamental needs of the nation.

Emerging Government Functions

At this writing the federal government, in fulfillment of its mandate to provide for the general welfare, has envisioned a vast program for the reduction of poverty. In magnitude it is comparable to some of the programs initiated during the depression, though the circumstances are by no means identical. We are mindful of the paradox that extensive poverty exists when the economy is enjoying a degree of health unknown before and unparalleled in its duration. Not only are public works being initiated to provide employment, but also retraining programs made necessary by the obsolescence of certain industries and types of work are under way. Responsibility for implementing programs designed to strengthen the economy does not lie solely with the federal government; nevertheless much of the difficulty can be overcome where government exercises such initiative in cooperation with private agencies.

Roy Blough proposes some measures to speed readjustment in the economy impaired or inhibited by technological, psychological, or cyclical factors: "One positive approach is to take the kinds of steps that will speed the necessary re-adjustment to technological change. Among these are maintaining a high level of general economic demand, improving labor mobility, enlarging and improvising educational programs, and encouraging the development of new industries."[7] He goes on to discuss proposals that have been made for government programs to support employment, shorten hours, and share work, which make for wider and more nearly equal distribution of income. Again, though these are not entirely a government responsibility, they can be substantially implemented through joint government-private agencies or institutions. "The imaginative creation of new institutions and relations between governments and private groups is a critical need of our time."[8]

No full classification of central government actions or responsibilities is here intended or possible. What have been suggested above are essentially illustrations of the fact that government action is necessary to assure national viability. In his *American Capitalism: The Concept of Countervailing Power* John Kenneth Galbraith developed the thesis now popularly identified with him. The power structures in contemporary life are so great that there must be a comparable force to provide checks against misuse of power. Such countervailing powers tend to come into being to meet great power structures, but when this does not happen, the duty rests on government to perform the restraining function of countervailing power. Thus labor unions have become a countervailing power to management, but the power of government sometimes must be exerted to restrain the overzealousness of both labor and management. It was on a similar thesis that the founding fathers established a government with three major centers of power and control, each capable of correcting the excesses of the others. It must be pointed out that in the present period of history the defense aspect of the government looms so large, both as strictly defense activity and because of its increased involvement in the total economy, that it has come to be the most significantly determining influence in the total life of the nation. The countervailing power in this situation is obscure. Labor, management, and the legislative and the executive branches of the government are so much under the pressure of the reputed defense requirements that they are apparently reluctant to exercise their countervailing competence. As will be explained later, this phenomenon has found its rationale in the need for maintaining the stability of the economy. The thesis being put forward here, however, is not impaired by this phenomenon. It simply exhibits even more pointedly the role of the federal government in its maintenance and regulation of the economy.

Inherent in all of the functions to which reference has been made is a phase of their existence which perhaps is taken for granted but which is increasing in scope and intensity; it is the area broadly designated as planning. When the Beveridge Plan came into prominence in Britain at the conclusion of World War II, substantial resistance was recorded in the United States, because planning, as implied in the Beveridge Report, was taken to mean socialism. The emergence of the National Planning Association has met with approval by many organizations and individuals that might have been alienated by the imputation of socialism, since the roster of those identified with the NPA constituted the bluebook of American industry.

Countervailing power of itself is inadequate to give balance and to provide direction for the life of the economy. Earlier in our history much that characterized the relationship between government and business was the result of a policy or the product of a theory that things would work themselves out satisfactorily. Obviously that day is gone. "More and more we are asking," says W. H. Ferry, "whether it is possible to organize matters better—perhaps with planning as a central means—to serve the ends of a liberal republic. More recent concern with what these ends may actually be is exemplified by the appointment of a Presidential Commission on National Goals."[9]

Every organization making significant headway has a planning body within it, analyzing its past and projecting for its future. All corporations have such units in their structure if they expect to survive. The State Department has a policy planning staff, and unions, educational organizations, professional groups, and many others have come to realize that planning is indispensable.

One concomitant of the development of planning programs is the realization that such brand names as socialism and capitalism have become outmoded. The enterprise system is dependent upon planning in the organization of its life for the long pull. Capitalism, having long since departed from its original laissez-faire ideology, accepts the role of government supervision and coordination as integral and essential to its existence. Meanwhile, the public as a whole may not be as kindly disposed toward the term "welfare state" as it has been ready to accept the changes involved in order to maintain the enterprise system. It is the same desire for the over-all well-being of the nation which has produced acceptance of the fundamental necessity of basic planning. Apprehension over increasing power of centralized government has provided a rallying point for one major political party in our time and is a source of concern to many individuals, whatever their political affiliation. We have come to accept the fact that only confusion and anarchy would result if central planning in many aspects of the nation's life were to be abandoned. One issue seems to be whether a responsible citizenry will undertake at local levels those activities which can best be effected there and thus help determine the range and areas of national action.

The central objective of planning is to make certain that the best interests of the whole society are preserved, and this means increasing responsibility of the actions of government at all levels. This does not necessarily mean that governmental intervention as such will need to increase.

Planning is needed to make consistent and effective use of intervention. To some authors, notably Gunnar Myrdal, an objective and hoped-for achievement of planning in the welfare state is to simplify the character of intervention and to reduce the need for it. Under this conception planning would seek to substitute a few general policies for a growing mesh of detailed and specific ones, and in particular would restructure the national economy to the end that for the most part cooperation and collective bargaining would determine the norms for people living together.

There is fear on the part of some individuals that in the process of planning, power may be used for the purpose of manipulating the lives and interests of persons irrespective of their own best interest. This is indeed a risk, but there are options open to a responsible electorate for its protection. Willy-nilly, we will have some kind of government. The question is simply whether it will be a humane government, sensitive to the interests of its people or responsive to the will of those who may stand to gain most for themselves. David Bazelon puts the issue thus:

An advancing technological society cannot exist ungoverned; without more coherent government than we now have we will end up crushing each other—eventually physically, as now psychologically. With more and more people living together in increasingly complicated and inter-dependent patternings made possible and imperative by the technology and its astounding historical pace, fewer areas of social life can safely remain free of governing. Each time we wait for problems to solve themselves we deny the probable world around us, thus seeking a disaster we must ultimately find. Health, education, employment and organization of our living and working areas along with the development of the scientific technology which is the source of all our blessings and troubles—all these require some decisive support or control by the national government, some positive use of central power.[10]

The suitable figure of speech for the kind of society which has been emerging in the United States and in many other nations of the West is not that of a pendulum swinging from the extreme of corporate domination to the opposite extreme of consideration for individual welfare. Perhaps a better figure would be the circle including within it both the welfare of the component economic units and the rights and well-being of individuals. Whether this is to be called the welfare state or the security state or the enterprise-economy state or what-not is immaterial. Sidney Hook has suggested that whatever may be our attitude toward the name and the direction in which it has been moving, "it's only alternative is the ill-fare state."[11]

Conclusion

Thomas Jefferson's misgivings about concentration of power in the hands of a few stemmed from his misgivings about the ability of a people to resist their oppressors once power was concentrated in them. If we do not fear the state as oppressor in this country, it is for reasons which can be identified with historic ideological roots, religious origins, and the opportunities for personal and economic developments provided by a beneficent continent. A free public school system has taught the people of the nation that no class is superior and that power may be exercised only by those who earn the right to use it in the free market place of ideas.

The result is that despite abuses of this option and occasional distortions of freedom resulting in malevolence, government is regarded as man's servant and not his master.

Throughout this discussion of government power it may seem to be implied that power will be used impartially and beneficially. The record should disabuse us of such a notion. But even where such an application of power as is conceivably possible has been effected, there are some individuals who are restricted and whose intentions are frustrated. In our immediate period of history the conflict over civil rights has intensely illuminated this problem.

The rectifying of many decades of economic and political disadvantage inevitably impinges on practices and customs which under canons of human decency should never have come into existence. Regional regulations obviously cannot be counted on to protect human rights, hence only the larger power of a government serving the entirety of a nation can be efficacious. Where regional courts cannot be relied upon to administer justice, a court with nationwide responsibility is utterly essential.

The ethical use of power cannot be decided by majority vote, but fortunately, with respect to deprivation and injury because of race, the majority has, though belatedly, made progress toward ethical goals. Ethical norms in a pluralistic society cannot be posited upon the standards of a single religion. They can, however, find opportunity for expression if freedom in the market place of ideas is assured. Here government has dual involvement. It can be the defender of such freedom and at the same time can become the instrument and trustee of increased power. It is in this way that it functions constructively in the economy.

12

The New Meaning of Leisure and Work

Books, studies, and articles about leisure are, like spring, "busting out all over." Our accelerated interest in the subject parallels in rate the changes resulting from technology; it is almost a one-to-one relationship for the very obvious reason that it is technology which is increasing the measure and availability of leisure.

Leisure was a subject of debate even in the time of Aristotle. Greeks who lived on a slave economy had time to ask themselves why they were permitted the experience of leisure as against the experience of the toiling masses of slaves who made such leisure possible. Now with mechanical slaves many who are not philosophers have a degree of leisure comparable to those who in earlier periods had time to ponder the question. Consequently the meaning and role of leisure has once again emerged as a subject of discussion.

Observers of developments in industrial society foresaw the changes which were to result in increased leisure long before cybernation alerted us to them with new clarity. In 1880 the Presidential candidate James A. Garfield, addressing an audience at Lake Chautauqua, proposed that human history could be divided into two major parts. "First the fight to get leisure; and then the second fight of civilization—what shall we do with our leisure when we get it?[1]

WHAT IS LEISURE?

We have chosen to link work and leisure together because leisure is a corollary of work. It is a state of existence which results from work and which can be enriched by work. Though in a work-oriented society they are often confused, leisure should be more than idleness; idleness may be destructive or disintegrative of selfhood, whereas leisure can be constructive. This creates for our generation one of its most fundamental problems: whether shortened hours of work will produce only idleness, or hours free from work will make possible a health-giving leisure?

"Not everything one does in one's free time qualifies as leisure," says Robert Lee. "Of course, free time may be converted into leisure. Hence, free time is only potentially leisure time. Non-committed or free time may well be idle time. The mood of leisure is affirmative whereas the mood of idleness is negative. . . . Leisure need not be viewed as subordinate to work or as a restorative for work but may be seen as an end in itself, something valued for its own sake."[2]

A debate on the nature of idleness and leisure could be interesting, but it is not our fundamental purpose. We will settle for the fact that free time is becoming increasingly available and that the use made of that time is an all-important question for industrial civilization. It is with the use of that time that we are primarily concerned. Marion Clawson says: "By leisure we mean all time beyond the existence and subsistence of time . . . so defined leisure closely resembles discretionary income, a concept which economists find very useful even though there is some ambiguity about some items that might be included in it. Leisure has well been called 'choosing time' because one can choose what to do with it. . . ."[3] Our concern, then, is with what is in fact chosen to constitute the substance of leisure activity.

Many people are compelled to work at tasks which are not their first choice as a way of living. Thus what they do in their free time becomes of great importance. It is during the period of leisure that they can become what they really are. This is the time when they may be at their best and fulfill their true potential as human beings, but there is also the alternative option of using that time at a level lower than one's potential.

Some fortunate people find their work more interesting than anything else they could do, and would do it even if it were not necessary for their livelihood. For them idleness is no problem; they are the ones whose work time is increasing while the hours spent at remunerative labor for most others is decreasing. Scientists, some individuals engaged in what are commonly termed professions, and independent creative workers will be unaffected by the forced free time of the rest of society, though even they must have respite from a too steady occupation at a single task. What they do by way of diversion may also contribute to their general well-being. Of greater concern, however, are those whose educational equipment, training, or background does not prepare them to take advantage of the increased leisure forced upon them. It is they whose idleness can be most destructive to themselves and to the rest of society, and for them increased free time can only create a downward spiral of disintegration.

Those deprived of education are not the only ones for whom forced idleness can be disintegrative. In 1900 the average life of a retired person was three years beyond retirement. At present it is somewhat over six years, and in another third of a century the average is expected to be nine years. Will the time be spent in vegetating, or will it add richly to the potentially "golden years"?

The established fact is that the shift from a production to a consumption economy, with an increasing number of workers available for a productive process requiring fewer and fewer man-hours, is confronting mass society with the problem of a constructive use of its leisure to a degree of breadth and importance unparalleled in history. With more free time available a very large percentage of the population is, paradoxically, subject to pressures demanding or coaxing them to utilize what free time they have in a manner primarily beneficial to others, who have a stake in their choice. The term "choosing time" therefore takes on added meaning. It is not simply the time one chooses not to work but the time in which he decides for himself what he wants to do.

Extent of Leisure

During World War I steelworkers in the United States worked 84 hours per week, and paid holidays were few. Not all industries were on the twelve-hour day, but the 70-hour week was normal less than a century ago. Now we take for granted the 40-hour week, and the 30- to 35-hour week is no longer idle talk. since in some industries this has already become a reality. It was estimated by the U. S. Bureau of Labor Statistics in June 1961 that the average hours of work per week per employee in 1976 will be 35.4, that the average paid vacation will be 2.8 weeks, and that the average number of holidays will be 8.5. When the increase in life span is added to these figures, the total is 22 more years of leisure in an average individual life, 1,500 free hours per year, or some 33,000 additional free hours for a lifetime.[4] Of course this is not universally applicable throughout the country. People who are in a position to determine their own hours of work and who may be engaged in service activities or creative work of many kinds will actually be under pressure to *curtail* their disposable leisure because of demands made upon them by those who have more leisure!

Anyone who has been on a public highway from Friday afternoon through Sunday evening, or during a holiday, does not have to be told that increased leisure has created whole new industries and expanded others immensely. Boating and fishing equipment and the do-it-yourself trend for home repairs and construction attest a phenomenon unknown a generation ago.

Reduction in the number of hours in a workday and "the long week-end" are but two of the sources of increased leisure. Another is the growing acceptance of and insistence upon designated holidays. Labor Day is now an established day of freedom from work, marking the end of the summer, and for families with children the last free time before school begins. Veterans' Day (formerly Armistice Day) gets increasing attention as a day of respite from work, just as Memorial Day has come to have significance as the end of the spring period and the beginning of summer. The leisure they provide thus carries a dual role. Christmas as a combination of sacred and secular holiday is taken for granted by almost everyone. St. Patrick's Day and Columbus Day have special meaning for certain ethnic groups, involving the closing of some establishments, as is also true of Good Friday in some communities. It is more than likely that observance of some of these now partially observed days will increase and that new ones will be added.

As suggested in the chapter on labor organizations, negotiations center increasingly around free time, both in addition to and as a substitute for wage increases. This does not imply a lack of interest in added income but a realization that wage increases may spiral inflationary movements and thus suggest insensitivity to the economic condition of the particular company or industry. Similarly, shortening hours without decreasing wages would also have an inflationary effect of the "cost push" variety much the same as would result from wage increases.

Shorter hours and additional free time in the form of holidays and earlier retirement represent concessions to a society which already has the minimal necessities, at least in its highly industrialized areas. Free time under these circumstances means a benefit to the worker who prizes it. With his added mobility and increased resources for enjoying free time he prefers the extra hours for personal satisfactions.

Parenthetically it has to be added that not everyone chooses to take this time for purposes of personal enjoyment. Whereas in 1950 approximately 3 per cent of those employed in nonagricultural pursuits were "moonlighting," it is estimated that more than 7 per cent of all nonagricultural workers in 1964 were engaged in one or more jobs in addition to their main occupation. On the long weekends, for example, school teachers, salesmen, and clerical workers may find employment in merchandizing organizations.[5]

The Historical Relation of Work and Leisure

"In the sweat of your face you shall eat bread" (Genesis 3 : 19). In accord with this biblical injunction man for centuries has assumed that his lot is to work in order to sustain himself. But the Bible does not say that man shall do nothing but work. Even God himself, the biblical writers tell us, "rested" on the seventh day, and a "day of rest" has been incorporated in the calendar as an integral part of our routine of life.

When men worked from sunup to sundown, whether in a hunting or agricultural economy, there were times between seasons and even during seasons when they took time out to revere the source of their livelihood. Out of such occasions grew the holy days and subsequently the holidays. When religion and livelihood were inseparably intertwined, secular holidays were unknown. As nations evolved and required esteem and praise, they set aside days for that purpose. The intermingling of sacred and secular holidays rendered some of them indistinguishable. Regardless of the sacred or secular nature of these days of leisure, industrial society, evolving its own rhythms of work, found it necessary to establish times for respite and recuperation.

With the emergence of industry long hours of continuous labor for both children and adults were rationalized on the grounds that busy hands were not engaged in mischief and that the productivity of those hands contributed to the character of the person. This was pleasing to God and at the same time made for economic stability. Max Weber has characterized these qualities by the term most frequently associated with his name, "the Protestant ethic."

As the industrializing nations evolved and extended their influence beyond their own national boundaries, a premium was placed on effort and frugality. Work was characterized as noble because it helped to offset the misuse of time and the consequent injuries to the working powers of those whose labor was needed in the burgeoning industries. This excessive emphasis on the virtue of work has been erroneously branded as a "Puritan" attitude, largely because of the continuous diligence required by Puritans in America, of whom the rigors of existence demanded persistent labor. But it was the Puritan's realistic understanding of himself as a child of God and responsible to his Maker which determined his attitudes toward all of life, his family, his neighbors, and the use of his time in work and leisure—not work for work's sake. Any attempt to comprehend "the Puritan mind" must include his own sense of obligation to his Creator and his desire to be worthy of salvation if such should be accorded him.

Thus periods both of work and of leisure were occasions for glorifying God. But this is vastly different from self-mortification.

It is not difficult to understand, however, why eventually a preoccupation with the virtues of work for its own sake did emerge from a background of Puritan industriousness. A fear that individuals would lack the capacity to use their freedom wisely made continuous labor seem preferable to a leisure which could be misappropriated. Religion came to occupy itself more extensively with the virtues of diligence and work than with training for creative use of such free time as might be provided in a system not so regimented. A "gospel of work" was extolled. It was easier to monitor and regulate life under a work program than to inspire its constructive use outside of work. In either case, the real question was the value of time and the use for which it was employed.

Then there came to our industrial civilization the unprecedented experience of finding it impossible to engage full-time in productive labor even if one wanted to. A society which found its meanings and values for life in productive labor was now faced with the necessity for discerning the fundamental meanings of life in its leisure-time activities. Now, only in their leisure are most people fully able to be themselves. Paul Weiss of Yale has commented that leisure "is a time when men can be at their best, making it possible for them to make the rest of their day as excellent as possible—and thereby discerning a new value and perhaps a new objective to whatever is done."[6]

If leisure is "choosing time" and the period in which the individual can be at his best, the basis for his choice has far-reaching implications. It is here that he gives evidence of his own understanding of himself. In effect he asks, "Is this the ultimate end toward which my life should be directed?" Here he has an opportunity both to discover and to express what is of ultimate importance. Not all persons are able to pursue the type of work activity which most truly fits their capabilities and dispositions. Even though there is greater opportunity for preference in the selection of one's work than was true in some preceding generations, there are still millions who must work at tasks which have little inspiration or appeal. Many such tasks are still necessary. That does not make them exciting or uplifting. Fortunately, however, less and less time will have to be spent in our industrial economy at such tasks. We work at them in order to have the leisure which work affords. This is what makes of vast significance the kind of activities in which we engage during leisure and is actually determinative of the very quality of life itself.

Fortunately people are not without extensive resources for guidance in the wise use of the increasing leisure time available to them. There is a mounting wealth of such resources. Any cataloguing of these resources would be far too cumbersome to include in these pages, but it is significant that educational institutions, foundations, governmental agencies, and institutions of all sorts have turned their attention to this important phase of human existence. One symbol is the comprehensive series of Reports to the Outdoor Recreation Resources Review Commission, surveying the country's outdoor recreation resources and measuring the present and likely demands upon them over the next forty years. It is a report made to the President and the Congress by a Commission staff of the National Planning Association and by the Bureau of Labor Statistics of the U. S. Department of Labor. Never before in history has a people been provided with such resources with which to plan for constructive use of its increasing leisure. Studies 23 and 24 deal with projections in economic growth, population, labor force, leisure, and transportation, and No. 24 also deals with economic studies of outdoor recreation. What these monumental reports and projections do for outdoor activities, other agencies are doing to prepare a total society for a new phase of its existence.

Current Attitudes Toward Work

"Primarily man works in order to live," says Emil Brunner. "The fact that he works in order to live, however, is something by which he knows himself to be a human being. . . . He cannot avoid asking himself whether he intends to work, why he does it, how he will do it, and what he intends to do. . . . All this means that work becomes an ethical question."[7]

Leisure and work are interdependent, but the solution of the one problem does not guarantee the solution of the other. Thus even if the problem of leisure were happily resolved, it would still leave unresolved the problem of the nature of work and its significance in an industrial age.

One overarching fact colors our consideration of work: the gap between faith and work. It is this gap which gives rise to our concern with the nature of work and attitudes toward it in contemporary life. Why, one might ask, cannot work be accepted for what it is, without having to confuse the issue by raising philosophical and theological questions about its ultimate meaning? Work, many assume, is what one does to make a living, and if it provides a satisfactory living and enables one to take care of his family and through insurance, social security, etc. to provide for emergencies and his retirement, is not that enough? Apparently it is not enough, if one is to judge by the very great effort being applied by industries, educational institutions, and government agencies to help men understand what it is that seems to be lacking in the kind of work that many of them are now doing and what would provide greater meaning for themselves and their families.

Industrial culture is dependent upon and shaped by the whole process of work. The basis of living in every industrialized nation is determined by the kind of work its citizens do and the meaning they find in doing it. If work is devoid of any significance in itself and is only meaningless drudgery, the whole life of society is conditioned by this fact and is thereby devoid of significance for a large number of its people during half of their waking hours. Even the reduction in working hours cannot reduce that fact. Fortunately for a substantial portion of our population, work is not as barren or bankrupt of meaning as the previous statements might imply. This is not to say, however, that there is rich significance in what they are doing. For most people the meaningfulness of their work ranges between the total commitment of a thoroughly dedicated worker and the vacuousness of one who goes through the motions simply for the paycheck.

There probably never was a time when everyone's work was religiously motivated, but there have been periods when many felt their work had some significance beyond themselves, that it contributed something to the total welfare of the tribe, community, or nation, and that in some sense it had religious meaning. The industrial revolution did more than rearrange populations, develop new governmental forms, and utilize new sources of power. It reduced the sense of meaningful work and in the process changed the relationship between the individual and his community. Early in the industrial age it was still possible for some people to acquire special abilities and to enjoy a status in their community as a result of their craftsmanship and skill. Many studies of industrial relations and the role of the individual in industrial society point to the change in that situation. Increasingly the individual becomes subordinated to the machine instead of the machine being subservient to the direction of the individual. In the automated industries he becomes an extension of that machine.

Contrasting again with an era in which the individual felt his work could be performed as a service to God, the industrial age places primary emphasis on the fact of work itself rather than its objectives. It is by participating in the act of work that one gets what is needed for himself and his family, and any other ends which may have constituted a part of the motivation of other generations become of lesser significance. Thus work has tended to displace an attitude of grateful response to a God who was the Creator and Sustainer of life.[8] Religion for such a worker is less likely to provide the integrating factor in his life. He is simply a worker earning his livelihood and maintaining himself as best he can from the results of his work.

When work alone becomes the objective, a new set of criteria for personal and social existence enters the picture. Craftsmanship may still be a factor for some who manipulate the machines still responsive to individual skills. But even for these persons, without a sense of meaning beyond the satisfaction of their own physical wants, preoccupation with work for its own sake eliminates any reference to the value of their work to society as a whole. Their objectives become those of status and prestige accorded them by their neighbors and devoid of any sanction or judgment by religion. For them and for most of our society it is not expected that religion will have anything significant to say about the nature of work, its importance, and its ultimate meaning.

But meaningless work is not simply a concern of religion but also a profound problem for the industrial system itself. Where meaninglessness prevails, it not only reduces the significance of the person but it is fraught with unfortunate consequences for the productive process itself. The rapid rise of organizations whose primary purpose is to offset the depersonalization which industry fosters, reveals the growing concern for this entire situation. Religion, having become widely discounted by industrial society for its inability to provide an alternative to this depersonalization, finds its place, temporarily at least, occupied by the industrial relations departments, human relations experts, and the numerous studies dealing with the impact of industrialization on the human self. Similarly, religious agencies, uncertain as to the role they should play in offering alternatives to the current emptiness of industrial life, have seen the initiative taken by a proliferation of secular organizations, notably labor unions and fraternal groups, which, though they may not have significant bearing on the nature of the industrial process itself, at least offer complementary or offsetting experiences. The attention to the individual which has been steadily disappearing from the industrial scene finds its support in those groups which fill the time of the worker outside his hours of employment. Thus the depersonalization of industry elicits other forms of activity which partially fill the vacuum caused by the meaninglessness of much of the work industrialism offers.

Are these fraternal groups, social organizations, extrawork fellowships, the only resource available to supply meaning to existence where it has been limited, if not eliminated, by the work experience of our times? Or is the concept of a divine calling to life itself so totally irrelevant that it cannot be considered seriously? This presumably is a fundamental question for religious institutions in an industrial era.

The Christian Meaning of Work

Work is dealt with often in the Bible, but in these few paragraphs it will be possible to present only in bare outline the essence of the biblical interpretation. The fundamental fact is that what is most important is not work but the person who engages in the work. This fact has far-reaching implications for what is considered the hierarchy of jobs in modern society. The important thing, then, is not what kind of a job one has but how each person conceives his relationship to God in the fulfillment of any job. Just as in the case of Adam, the primary fact of whose existence was his relation to God, so every one of Adam's descendants can fulfill his role in life only as he too understands that his primary obligation is to God as Creator and Sustainer and ultimately as Redeemer of man. The significance, then, of any job stems not from the way in which men regard it but "from its bearing on God's overarching purposes."[9]

The Bible's primary concern is the relationship between God and man, and the final criterion of man's life is the degree to which work is an instrument for the glorification of God. As Giver of life there is no phase of that life which God does not penetrate. The realization of that fact and the way the worker adjusts himself to it determines the ultimate meaning of life for him. This, then, makes requisite a consideration of what that life is; for it cannot be simply adopted and lived out apart from honest inquiry as to its purpose. Modern man may be freer of the necessity of asking such a fundamental question because he seemingly can sustain himself apart from any reference to life's ultimate significance. But eventually death comes to him, and in some measure, whether superficially or profoundly, he confronts the real issue of the purpose of that life which has been his.

The biblical interpretation says to the seeker after life's meaning that there is a harmonizing of God's work and man's work in which man can fulfill his true role. This understanding may come to him from a variety of sources, but significantly the individuals who shared this wisdom throughout the biblical record were often people who themselves were engaging in some kind of common and essential work, whether it was dressing sycamore trees, herding livestock, or carpentering. Aside from Jesus himself, the most renowned workman who became a vehicle for interpreting to men their dependence upon God for life and its redemption was the Apostle Paul. He remained a tentmaker so that he might be free to bring the message entrusted to him without being a burden to his hearers and new-found companions in the faith.

The term "vocation" or "calling" for the religious interpretation of labor did not acquire much prominence until the Reformation, but that meaning was there throughout the Old and New Testament periods. Persons and nations were summoned by God to fulfill their destiny in His service, and this calling had bearing on the total range of man's life. Prior to his actions he seeks the wisdom of God and attends to God's commands. These may come to him in an infinite variety of ways, through prophets, family, neighbors, and the far-reaching history of nations. The important thing, however, is that the person be open and ready for God's wisdom because he acknowledges the sovereignty of the Lord. God does not speak in broad generalities to empty spaces and trust to the wind to carry the message; He speaks directly to the hearts of the workers because it is the person who works and not a system.[10]

The Christian lives, as do his Hebrew predecessor and contemporary, to serve a God who Himself serves, and by this manner of life he shares God's way with man and in so doing discovers his own purpose in living. This is the continuing activity of both God and man. It means action, but action with a purpose which is more inclusive than the limited purpose of working only to sustain oneself and one's family. By summons or vocation or any other name, the joyous and willing response of the worker establishes his own identity and lifts his life to an ever higher level. "In this perspective there comes to new expression, with new force, the old Hebrew conviction that human life gets its meaning in and through a 'calling and election' by the Sovereign word of God. For Christian faith, that word is disclosed with new power and wisdom in Jesus Christ—at once a promise and an imperative demand for devotion to God and love to fellowmen."[11]

Stratification is a part of every society. Hebrew and Christian communities knew this fact, and obviously from the record they were not immune to class and status divisions. But basically there is no hierarchy of prestige in useful work, nor is there status to accrue from ecclesiastical affiliation in the true sense of *ecclesia*, the "called ones" who have answered God's summons to loving service. Neither is there a double standard of behavior for those who are professionally identified with the church and for those who are at work in the world. In the history of the relation between God and man and work these distinctions are meaningless, and instead of ennobling they have poisoned the minds of those who have been subjected to their artificial distinctions.

The Apostle Paul, confronted by differences in position and class, used the analogy of bodily interdependence to illustrate the irrelevance of class distinctions in the church. ". . . There are many parts, yet one body. The eye cannot say to the hand, 'I have no need of you,' nor again the head to the feet, 'I have no need of you.' On the contrary, the parts of the body which seem to be weaker are indispensable. . . . Now you are the body of Christ and individually members of it" (I Cor. 12 : 20–22, 27). Though there are diversities of gifts, there is but one Lord, and there are no levels of caste or class in his service.

Monasticism performed a service to humanity of immeasurable proportions as it dignified both manual and mental work and reminded the fellowship that they had one common loyalty and a common call. In the imputed simplicity of a monastic order it may have seemed simple to maintain such commonness of status, but it was discovered that even religious orders could be contaminated with the standards of the world and succumb to the temptations of power and prestige and indolence. If a "religious" organization is not immune, it cannot be charged that industrial society with its hierarchies and status systems are the only offenders and sinners.

From the Hebrew-Christian understanding of the meaning of

life emerged a new interpretation of the function of work. Just as all societies are stratified, feudal society, both in its sacred and secular aspects, reflected both the political and ecclesiastical gradation based on power. But power carries with it the seeds of its own corruption, and even the church fell prey to this common form of deterioration. The noble concept of the dignity of work embodied in the monastic system was not sufficient to maintain ecclesiastical purity. With the abuse of power in the church, a tendency to which no ecclesiastical tradition is immune, a reform movement took root. This was not the sole or perhaps even major purpose of the Reformation, but it was one of its major thrusts. The reformers challenged the power of the ecclesiastical structure in part because it made the ordinary citizen, the worker, if not a second-class citizen at least inferior to the church hierarchy and the nobility. In challenging this system Luther and Calvin, particularly, lifted to new levels of dignity the importance of work and the worker, contending that work done to the glory of God and on behalf of one's neighbor was not inferior to the work done in the church itself. Refinements of the distinctions made by the Reformers relative to man's participation in work are available in such profuseness elsewhere that they will not be delineated here. Suffice it to say that under the impetus of the Reformers a new significance was given to work and the worker. Under their fresh interpretation all men were enabled to realize what the Bible had indicated for centuries, that each man is called by God to work and that any useful work is a form of service to God.

Whatever distortion religious organizations may have perpetrated, the fact remains that for the Christian all work must be judged as it contributes to God's purposes in the world and for the measure in which it reveals our understanding that all of life is lived under trust. Work is service to God and man. The fact that so large a measure of work in modern times causes the question of its usefulness to God and man to be raised constitutes one of the serious dilemmas confronting all earnest people. Each can ask himself only whether his work is performed in order that love may be increased in the world or whether the work he does is inimical to human welfare. The decisions may not be as simple as it seemed to be in a preindustrial era, but this does not invalidate the question. The earth is still the Lord's.

Making Work Meaningful

Since work has become meaningless or of very limited significance for so many workers, the question must be raised: what made it meaningful at any other time? The answer is twofold. First, the work was needed by one's immediate community as well as oneself. This would include family, neighborhood, and possibly a recognizable community even beyond the range of neighborhood. We are, of course, here using the term community in its broad sociological sense as that body of individuals to whom one has a political or moral responsibility or both. Secondly, the conviction that one's life and the way it is used is of importance both to the community and to the Source of life itself. These two factors are not unrelated. It is the sense of responsibility to a power beyond oneself which gives meaning and vitality to the human community as well as to the individual. Work, then, becomes meaningful as it is performed in relation to both of these objectives.

When absenteeism and indifference in war production was undermining production schedules, human relations experts conceived the idea of revealing to workers the indispensable nature of their jobs and the tragic consequences where work was not fulfilled on time and with quality workmanship. Absenteeism dropped perceptibly. The same principle has been widely publicized in relation to the Western Electric studies by Elton Mayo and his colleagues.[12] Other studies of similar nature have been undertaken on the same theory, that individuals must know their work is important to someone and that they themselves have importance.

Cameron P. Hall states, "Through work our lives become involved with those of others. We work for and with, under and over, alongside of and—at times—against others. Each of these prepositions means that our lives are part of the lives of others. Together they add up to a relatedness which is complex and far-flung. The spirit and attitudes men bring into their work relationships are vital to the welfare of others, to the creating of community life, and to the inner strength of democracy. How an individual acts toward others is, likewise, central to Christian living: 'This is my commandment, that you love one another even as I have loved you.' "[13]

Work will become meaningful when (1) the significance of the human community is rediscovered and (2) as the source of the human community itself is recognized. Only then will the spiritual meaning of work be fully established. Surely there is a sense of calling in fulfilling one's obligation and performing useful work on behalf of the community around him, but the authenticity of that call or summons still lacks what in biblical history has brought a full and complete response unless the Source of the call is acknowledged.

Reference was made earlier to the declining importance of the individual in the industrial era. Paradoxically while the importance of the individual was declining because of his decreasing significance as a worker in the industrial complex, there was emerging an increasing insistence upon the importance of the individual in political and social life. Growing sensitivity to the importance of the human spirit gave impetus to political safeguards and the type of legislation which reduced human suffering. Now comes a whole new era for the significance of the individual. The alternative to the disappearance of individualism is the increased meaningfulness of the individual himself. This is a spiritual problem and one which industrial society is just beginning to comprehend.

Because community has been understood in too limited terms, there has been procrastination in discovering the significance of the individual himself within it. It was this awareness which the Social Gospel Movement, described in chapter one, attempted to explicate, but the sociological and theological tools were insufficient at the time. Today that excuse is no longer available. The total environment conditions the life of the individual and in turn enhances his sense of meaningfulness.

Finally, however, it is not the community which makes work meaningful. It serves principally as the tutor and the interpreter.

Meaningfulness is an intensely personal experience and understanding. It is sustained and nurtured by faith, again not a community possession but something deeply personal. Here then is the key to meaningful work—a faith in the source of the human community and of the lives which comprise it. It is expressed in acts of gratitude and love out of appreciation for the gift of this life which one lives in community. Such expenditure of effort out of gratitude and a love for God and neighbor gives a whole new meaning to the useful activities we designate as work.

Conclusion

Leisure and work constitute aspects of man's life experience in which his real self can be expressed, in which some of his fullest satisfactions may be known. Many kinds of work in industrial society make satisfaction unlikely if not impossible. Creativity, the satisfaction of performing a needed task or the achievement of a skilled accomplishment, may be denied in the very nature of required tasks. Fortunately an increasing measure of time, "choosing time" it has been aptly termed, is becoming available in a society wherein fewer hours are required to meet physical needs. It is this time of leisure which can be used to bring added enrichment and personal fulfillment. The use of that time carries with it profound ethical and spiritual significance for individuals and society.

13

Status and Stratification in Industrial Society

> The large complex society requires a system of prestige standards which can measure differences and achievement with some uniformity, measurements which can be clearly understood by the entire population so that all can appreciate the claims of persons not personally known to them. . . . Economic objectives and motivations are only one, though a very important group, among the large number of value areas which go to compose such a prestige system.
>
> —Clarence A. Danhof in *Goals of Economic Life*

"Why," the reader may ask, "even a brief treatment of status and stratification in a volume dealing with the role of religion and ethics in industrial society?" The answer for the Christian lies in the very essence of his way of life. God took the form of a servant to reveal Himself. "He that would be greatest among you let him be servant of all." Jesus insisted on washing the disciples' feet.

In all forms of society role and rank are important. In industrial society status based on power and position is apparently of utmost importance. The devices used to attain rank may vitiate or supersede what the Christian gospel supports. In the end the motivations of economic life in general and industrial society in particular may, unless replaced by nobler purposes, come both to dominate the individual and warp the life of the very institution whose mission it is to make men servants of their fellow men, as was their Lord. The matter of status and stratification is thus a fundamental even if painful concern of the individual Christian and the church as a whole.

There is probably a correlation between the mass of literature and scientific studies relating to status and stratification in the social sciences and the rediscovery by contemporary theologians of pride as the foremost sin. Technology is forcing a readjustment in stratification, along with closer cooperation and coordination in society as a whole. These facts are demanding a reconsideration of human prestige systems.* The problems of status and human pride are basically the same, and they find expression in every age from nomadic to nuclear. Plato dealt with the problem of status in a slave economy; Jesus and the early Christian interpreters dealt with it in both its rural and preindustrial urban setting; Karl Marx sought to cope with it as industrialization threatened to crystallize the class system into two main divisions, the proletariat and the *bourgeoisie*. Each one suggested resolutions to this, one of mankind's most vexing issues. Plato's insistence that each man shall do what he was best fitted to do provides a partial answer. Jesus' conviction that all men are children of a common Father and that their role is to serve each other presents a thesis never fully accepted or renounced.

Karl Marx's theory of a rigid two-class industrial society has in the century since the *Communist Manifesto* been very effectively discredited. The division of all individuals into proletariat and *bourgeoisie* failed to take account of the rapid emergence of a large middle class, sharing in the gains in productivity and in social welfare. This does not, however, exclude the possibility that under the newer and rapidly accelerating forces of modern industrialism a new configuration may take place which can prove Marx more nearly right than some present-day facts would indicate.

Every society has its own form of stratification and status. It may be based on physical prowess, hereditary position, or the measure of one's possessions. Feudalism with its lords, knights, and vassals provided a complete form of social structure with each

* Community studies reflecting this development and achieving wide recognition are: Robert and Helen Lynd, *Middletown;* James West, *Plainville, U.S.A.;* W. Lloyd Warner and Associates, *Yankee City* and *Democracy in Jonesville;* Alison Davis and M. R. Gardiner, *Deep South;* and the "Rural Life Studies" of the Division of Farm Population in Rural Welfare of the USDA. In the field of theological writing no one has done more to sensitize this generation to the role of pride in individual and group esteem than Reinhold Niebuhr.

person contributing his part to the maintenance of that order. The lord of the territory, his status symbolized by his castle, held his property either under his personal ownership or as representative of some other political power above him. He, however, insured the safety of those who served him and worked on his lands. They in turn provided the maintenance and income for their lord in return for their peace and protection. The place of each was well defined and reasonably secure. The rudiments of this system were in evidence in biblical times, as is indicated by Jesus' reference to the evil and faithful stewards. The significant element inherent in the feudal system based on agriculture was the mutual dependence of the participants and their reciprocal obligations. This is not to say that everyone was happy under these arrangements. Peasant revolts were apparently not numerous, but as the feudal era was challenged by the emerging commercialism and the beginnings of industry, dissatisfaction with the lot of those coerced into the stratification of the system became so unbearable as to demand major revisions.

Industrialism could not provide the protection from want which the feudal order seemingly gave. The resulting protest challenged the status orders and the rights of those who claimed to govern their employees but who did not assume the responsibility for their total life requirements.

Despite its feudal roots England was more successful than some other nations in coping with the class struggle and its status structure because it allowed its newly emerging industrial leaders to participate in the political leadership of the nation. With political controls available the rigidity of class structure was less offensive and destructive of self-respect. Despite the fact that English life has not been an "open society" in the sense in which we apply the term to America, it has possessed the safety valve of eligibility for governmental office and therefore to business controls, making possible entry of lower status persons into the upper classes and even to the status of peerage or knighthood. Also significant is the fact that the British people, and the Scottish in particular, have traditionally been highly literate. Their familiarity with the biblical heritage, the partial regulation of their lives by biblical standards, and the capacity to relate their personal, religious, and political life freed "the People of the Book" from some of the restrictions imposed in certain areas of Europe. These biblical standards, too, served to modify some of the class hostility in other countries.

The earlier settlers came to the American continent out of societies free from some of the more vicious forms of class restriction. When still others, fleeing rigidities of class structure in their own lands, arrived on these shores, they found a system of openness which made unnecessary the kinds of protest they had known in their former countries, in some of which status was still ascribed by various forms of nobility and property transmission.

As Max Weber has contended, most forms of power rest on economic foundations. Property and lack of property are the elemental categories of class situations.[1] On arriving in the new land many immigrants were quick to realize that they were no longer bound by the status and class requirements prevailing in their former homeland, and that they themselves might now achieve a measure of distinction undreamed of in their former home. They recognized for themselves one of the fundamental insights which Weber has explicated, that a contrast in life's chances can be the result of the distribution of property or the structure of the economic order. In the acquisition of property a reshuffling of status occurred. It was no surprise, therefore, that the New England Yankees who had acquired real estate or were developing small businesses found offensive the questionable status of those who came to administer their affairs and make demands under their new rights. The continuing availability of property rendered the immigrant unreceptive to Old World types of formal society and rendered meaningless the authority such a society sought to exert. This manifestation of openness reduced the likelihood of class warfare and provided the foundation for a new social stratification, later to be challenged. Similarly, when rigidities of economic structure reinforced by class stratification made for violent protest in Europe, corresponding manifestations did not emerge on this continent except in very limited form, because of the opportunities available for challenging existing stratification.

Status in Contemporary Industrial Society

Status is the relative position a person holds within his class as a result of the esteem in which he is held. This, of course, may range all the way from very high to very low. Sociologists have long struggled to devise adequate definitions for the terms "status" and "class," but we will forego the more definitive analysis of those terms. For our purposes the term "class" is that company of people who have approximately the same life chances as a result of somewhat similar economic interests. Hence, the conclusion that in the United States the great body of the population belongs to the middle class. The upper class would comprise approximately 3 to 4 per cent of the population and the lower class the remaining per cent of the population.* A major factor in determining class membership is goods possessed, access to them, or reasonably justifiable expectation of having them. Status, however, is not the same thing as class. One's status is his position within a class. It is with status that we are primarily concerned, since in the American system of social life the overwhelming preponderance of individuals either place themselves or are placed by others in that broad band occupying most of the continuum and designated as middle class.

By contrast with the more or less open society of the United States, there are societies in which position is not determined by any amount of effort or diligence. In them position is ascribed rather than earned, which presumably is the case in the more nearly open type of society. This is not to say that there is no such thing as an ascribed position in American life. Obviously being born with a prestigious family name immediately begets a position of prestige. The important thing, however, is that others are not denied any position if they can fulfill the requirements for attaining it, and in American society one of the recognized means of attaining such position involves the acquisition of property.

* This very general division is derived from a synthesis of several polls in which individuals were asked to place themselves in one of these three classes.

As reading almost any newspaper or magazine will quickly reveal, status is not limited to birth or possessions. Robin Williams suggests that there are six kinds of criteria by which an individual's status may be recognized and his position in the stratification order documented: (1) birth, (2) possessions, (3) personal qualities, (4) personal achievement, (5) authority, (6) power.[2] Each of these may be facilitated by membership in a family or identification with a particular group, but with the exception of birth all of them can depend to a greater or lesser degree upon the motivation and effort of the person himself. Even so, there are obviously large handicaps which some people must overcome. Being born into a family where educational interest is low and incentive to get out of a particular level of life is minimal is a deterrent and a handicap. For one very large segment of the population, the nonwhite, the handicaps are greater than those suffered by others with the same economic or physical endowments.

It would be inaccurate to say that class distinctions do not prevail in the United States. We have had evidences of vicious distinctions, and in some instances class hatred growing out of those distinctions. The early period of the growth of the labor movement, the open warfare which prevailed in the anthracite regions, the Homestead Strike, and the Memorial Day Massacre in Chicago were all manifestations of deep class hatred as well as a demand for labor's rights and were in turn fed by the flames of resentment. The protest movements in the United States, whether in agriculture, mining, manufacturing, or processing, have had within them elements of class resentment. But they have been modified and the tension has been reduced because embedded in American cultural life is an equalitarianism which provided release through political remedies and exercise of alternative mass power which was available to the protesting bodies and movements. By this process forces making for resentment have been modified and temptations to use power and brutality have been restrained.

Most poignant of all illustrations of class antagonism and lack of mobility in the United States are the Negro, the Indian, and more recently the Puerto Rican. During the current decade we have seen the most massive eruption of movements growing out of protest against forced class subordination. Color alone has been the excuse for keeping almost one-tenth of the total population in the lowest class stratum. Despite repression many within the ranks of the Negroes have risen above their original class identification, achieving in many instances highest distinction for intellectual, professional, and economic attainments. Today the range of class and status among Negroes parallels that in all segments of society, though their movement into higher strata has been greatly limited by restrictions imposed from the exterior. Fortunately those limitations are being removed. As this takes place, however, it is unlikely that the patterns of class and status will differ from those within the society within which they are being increasingly integrated. The same elements which determine the status composition of the rest of industrial society will be evident among newly emerging groups.

Industrial society has traditionally implied manual labor. Within a decade this nation has moved from a preponderance of manual labor ("blue-collar") to a preponderance of white-collar work. Despite the attractiveness of white-collar work it does not inevitably bring superior economic rewards, since there are many blue-collar jobs which pay better than many white-collar occupations. Some of those blue-collar tasks involve very substantial skills, and the rewards are commensurate. For others the premium remuneration may be the result of pressure groups and a type of organization which keeps its ranks from being diluted and its wage scale reduced. By this process added status is attached to some kinds of manual activity which are more or less unattractive but which nevertheless are high in public recognition. Regardless of this fact, however, the evidence points strongly to the upward mobility of the children of high-pay, blue-collar workers.[3] Their parents' income is frequently sufficient to provide them with the quality of education which could make unnecessary their continuance in the blue-collar jobs and in many instances enable them to equip themselves for one of the recognized professions. The point we are making is simply that status, stratification, and vertical mobility are widely recognized social phenomena in this highly industrialized nation. What is true of this nation is also characteristic in varying measure of other industrialized countries.

Forces Reorganizing Status

Few facts are as visible in industrial life as the change in status of many industrial workers. Scarcely had we become adjusted to the shift from skills based on land labor to those involving hand-directed machines when cybernation rendered obsolete many of the skills so recently acquired. While we are still amazed by them, we have become accustomed to incredibly superior precision instruments producing a hundred or more times in volume what single individuals did formerly. Extraordinary as the production figures may be, their concomitants in the reorganization of status and the stratification of society are equally impressive. To neither of these phenomena are we reconciled nor adjusted.

Changes in the order of stratification are expected and accepted in industrial society, and the movement is not only in one direction. The slogan "Shirt sleeves to shirt sleeves in four generations" has its parallel in other nations and cultures. The implications have special meaning in the United States, a society which represents the ultimate in industrialism. Behind that slogan is a portrayal of industriousness on the part of the first generation and a decline of the third, as it fails to exert commensurate zeal in labor and acquisition. Thereafter comes the fall to the level of deprivation experienced before the original exercise of zeal. Behind the moralism of the cycle indicated in the slogan is the assumption that rising status is possible, if only the proper conditions are met. Sloth and carelessness account for the decline. Now, however, there comes into the scene a situation of which sloth and carelessness are not the cause. The acceleration of technology has simply been too great for most people to comprehend, let alone appropriate.

Increasing accessibility of education is a major factor in the upward mobility of whole masses of people. The change has taken place almost within a generation. Of those 65 years of age or older only 10 per cent had collegiate experience and only half graduated, while among the 25–30 year age group 25 per cent went to college and half graduated. In other words, higher education among the population has increased 150 per cent within thirty years. The figures for high school completion are even larger.

Education in an open society has permitted advancement on the part of many who in other countries would have less opportunity for status elevation. The British system, for instance, which makes a sharp division between individuals based on general intelligence as revealed at the ages of 10 to 11 years, has removed from possibilities of advancement through education large numbers who in the American scene would still have open to them channels for status development and higher rating on the stratification scale. British children may still have access to education, but the processes of division presuppose an elite group more likely to provide the leadership required in a less open society. The type of education required or made available in each nation indicates much concerning its status concepts and the function which education may be expected to play in reinforcing the stratification of society. It thus is either the great leveler, in the form of providing opportunity for all, or it helps to keep closed a society of privilege for a few.

In addition to higher wages for their parents rapid technological changes also decrease the likelihood that children will follow their parents' occupation, particularly in areas of manual labor. The unavailability of agriculture as a vocation for sons of farmers has been axiomatic, evidenced by the steady decline in agricultural courses offered in rural high schools. Sons following in fathers' footsteps in manual occupations were one of the sources of stability in society. Just as in agriculture, industrial occupations now suffer the same reduction in opportunities for livelihood. What does it mean to be a skilled coal miner when other forms of power have eliminated coal or when mechanical instruments can replace a thousand miners, as was suggested in a previous chapter? Obviously more is involved here than simply a reduction in numbers of those employed. It involves a major revision of the status of individuals in their home communities.

To all other factors is now added that of physical mobility. It is this which has made possible a substantial measure of social mobility as well. Park Forest, Levittown, Drexelbrook, and many other new communities owe their existence to the combination of physical mobility and social mobility. The pattern of movement required by corporations on the part of their executives at many levels makes necessary a type of living arrangement which corresponds to the short residence to be established in connection with a training period or testing period in the corporation. William F. Whyte has documented the implications of physical and social mobility in his classic, *The Organization Man,* which contains a study of one of these communities (Park Forest). The rapid changes in location, the "bucking" for position in the organization, the pressures for results on the part of the corporation, the evaluation of wives' as well as husbands' accomplishments—all constitute a part of the total complex whereby status and stratification are established and reorganized. These color the total life of a community.

We have been suggesting that the larger forces, such as technological change, new patterns of business organization, accessibility to educational resources, etc., are the influences contributing to the reorganization of status. It is apparent that no one of these is separate and distinct. They and all the allied forces around them are closely intertwined and interdependent. Similarly the individual who is subject to change in his status is not only the victim of this complex of forces but contributes to them as well. Witness the way in which physical mobility has accentuated social mobility. According to Lipset and Bendix's statement, "a person who moves up in the social hierarchy will tend to change his friends, join new organizations, move to a new neighborhood; perhaps he will even change his religious affiliations; in some instances he will change his name; often he will alter his political attitudes."[4] Each of these factors may be conditioned by others, but they also contribute to the shaping of the new status.

Probably no single factor has been more responsible for the over-all change in status and stratification than the rising income level of the population as a whole. Since 1947, for example, the level of income has been raised from about $5,300 per family to about $7,050 per family.* The ability to procure the gadgets and comforts which have become symbols of middle-class living have both reduced the pressures of protest and accorded to their possessors a sense of satisfaction. Thus the rising level of productivity which finds expression in increased consumption has steadily raised the living standards and income of most of the population. The resultant satisfaction in the realization that "progress" or advancement has been made provides assurance that mass improvement in status has been achieved. Though there may be marked differentials and discrepancies, they become less noticeable in the uniform elevation of most of the society. Weber contended that status groups are stratified in relation to their consumption of goods as represented in their styles of life. Where life styles are steadily improving, there is less resentment against others who may be improving even more.[5] Where general improvement in consumption levels and corresponding styles of life are occurring, there is general feeling of good will, even though interrupted by protests from special interest groups who desire additional advantages in the over-all development. The significant thing, however, is the fact that such development in style of life keeps attention from being called to crystallization or rigidities effected in the total stratification picture. To paraphrase Weber again, it is when there is a slowing down of economic development that the status structures and forms of social honor become intensified. It is to these that protest is made and against them resentment is expressed. Hence the importance of a steady rise in productivity and a corresponding increase in levels of income. Though Weber wrote before the Nazi era, he correctly designated the fears in loss of status on the part of the German people as their levels of productivity declined, and the massive protests of resentment took the form of Hitler support.

There are forces which are steadily altering the status and stratification picture. Some individuals are moving upward and others in reverse direction. Fortunately the total picture of pro-

* *Road Maps of Industry,* Nos. 1440, 1273.

ductivity is such that a general feeling of upward movement is experienced by the population as a whole, reducing potential resentments against the distinctions and levels of stratification even in an open society.

Significance of the New Stratification

New lines of stratification follow lines of power. For centuries power has meant property and its control. In the rapid evolution of industrial society a new form of power is emerging. It is not unrelated to property, but it does not of itself involve property ownership. The kind of power which Adolf A. Berle, Jr., has been describing in his *Power Without Property—A New Development in American Economy* implies a control over the property of others. It is the new managerial competence for which property owners are willing to pay the highest salaries in history (General Motors, Bethlehem Steel, Standard Oil of New Jersey, et al.). In a business and industrial society the highest rewards are accorded those who can guarantee that the productivity for which they are responsible can be continued with the desired profits. (Of those being paid for services performed, they are surpassed only by a few entertainers.) The managers may not be the recipients of the greatest personal incomes, since those for the most part go with inherited wealth, but it is the inheritors of wealth who are willing to pay to the managers of their resources the kinds of salaries which indicate their appreciation of the managerial skill involved. Thus in the stratification of industrial society the manager of other people's money is near the top of the pole. Significantly, however, the very top of the status scale does not go to the managers. It goes to those who ultimately can decide on the rectitude and legality of the manager's actions, namely, the members of the Supreme Court.[6] It must be added that managers in the categories referred to above were not included in the list which was presented for ratings. Bankers as a class rank in the top ten, whereas the small store managers rate in the bottom half. Members of boards of directors of large corporations and nuclear physicists have the same rating in the top one-fifth. It is probably safe to surmise that with the mounting importance attached to space science more recent polls would record increasing prestige for those responsible for nuclear and space engineering.

Too much attention should not be given to the rank order of the various occupations, for much depends on who does the ranking. Presumably there would be differences by regions and by economic levels. Our principal reason for including the reference at this point lies in the fact that even though the major rewards of society go to those who are most effective in the production and distribution of goods, a high degree of importance is attached to those who engage in service to society. Next to the Supreme Court justices in rating is the physician, followed by governor, cabinet member, diplomat, mayor, college professor, and scientist. Judges, clergymen, and lawyers differ from the above by almost negligible amounts. For the present, at least, even in a highly technological era the serving professions and those which minister to the basic needs of individuals in this kind of a society are deemed to belong high in the stratification rating.

Without discounting unduly the fact that some professions have a higher status accorded them for historic reasons, may it not be inferred that in a society where status and stratification are subject to constant revision, recognition for distinction will be accorded to those persons who can bring to the lives of people an interpretation of their individual worth and significance in a way that enhances human dignity? With increased leisure and lessened importance in his work the individual thus affected seeks for the means whereby his own life and purpose take on significance to himself and his neighbors. The loss of position resulting from the elimination of his skills must be compensated through other and perhaps hitherto unknown experiences and interpretations. Discovering a useful contribution he can make, he is bolstered in his own self-esteem—a prime requisite for valid status with his fellows. At the same time the person who enables him to discover his innate dignity becomes a figure of major importance to the entire status structure of society.

Two polar forces, both the product of technological advances, are producing major tensions in this rapidly evolving industrial economy. One is freeing man from burdensome physical labor, which historically has given him his self-respect and status among his neighbors but which now threatens to place him in a position where nothing is substituted for the sources of his earlier self-esteem. The second force is making for closer integration of society and the mutual dependence of men, intra- and internationally. It carries possibilities for greatly enhanced human dignity and self-esteem. Technological gains may be utilized to increase the measure of harmony and coordination, or they can concentrate ownership and control in the hands of an ever smaller group, with others dependent on the bounty and generosity of the owners and managers of the new techniques. The issue of status and stratification in industrial society will be profoundly affected by the way this problem is resolved.

It is obvious that with controls residing in the hands of those who have paid for the major advances in the new technology, namely, the entire citizenry, this nation has committed itself to the retention of these fundamental controls. The contest for those controls is not yet over, but unless major reversals occur, they will continue to reside in the hands of all. Because there is at stake the management of ever increasingly powerful centers of control, the Christian cannot but ask the pointed questions "To what end are these functions directed?" and "What are the objectives of those who make the basic decisions?" If the replies, however subtly couched, reveal self-aggrandizement and acquisition of personal power, they may defeat the church's age-long concern for freedom for all men. Herein lies the contemporary test for the openness of our society, and at the same time it provides a clue to the status and stratification systems industrialism fosters.

If ours is to remain an open society, then the channels by which human dignity may be attained cannot be closed through artificial status, class, and stratification devices such as economic manipulation may provide. Opportunity to contribute usefully to the lives of one's neighbors becomes a first requirement of the economy and the institutions which serve it.

14

Ethics and Business

When Chief Justice Warren stated that "in civilized life, Law floats in a sea of Ethics,"* he stimulated sharp reaction from persons who pointed to illustrations seemingly contradicting his affirmation. The General Electric, Westinghouse, et al. collusion for which some executives went to jail, the Billy Sol Estes incident, the Bobby Baker case, rigged TV programs, the Hoffa scandal, and on and on could give the impression that American life floated on a sea of corruption. The cases mentioned and many others are significant, however, not because they illustrate corruption but because they were brought to the bar of justice. When an industrialist, then president of the National Council of Churches, J. Irwin Miller, was asked, "How serious do you think the ethical problem is in the American business community? If something has gone wrong, why?" he replied: "I don't think anything has 'gone wrong.' I've talked a good deal to my father and great uncle about what business competition used to be like. Today we would be genuinely shocked at some of the normal competitive practices existing in the days when Theodore Roosevelt thought it necessary to start 'trust-busting.' Business ethics and moral responsibility have improved substantially since that time. I feel your question really is: 'Has the improvement in business morality been as fast as it is necessary that it be?' "[1]

In the Middle Ages men were concerned about "the just price." It was a function of the church to alert its members to

* Earl Warren, Chief Justice of the U. S. Supreme Court. From a summary of Remarks at the Jewish Theological Seminary of America, Nov. 11, 1962.

the meaning of that term and to judge them when they defaulted. Though the church collectively in its manifold form says little about the just price in the twentieth century, it has had a good deal to say about the social responsibility of the businessman and the ethical role of the corporation. The church is not alone in these emphases; they have come in great volume from secular sources accompanied by philosophical and even theological interpretations. No single denomination is responsible for emphasizing this new concern, though many speakers on behalf of business ethics attest the fact that their interest and concern are motivated by a grounding in Hebrew-Christian foundations. Almost plaintively, it should be added, they ask for clarification and re-enforcement from religious leaders. In almost every chapter of a study reporting ethical issues in a number of occupations, the participants voiced their longing for ethical guidance in their particular vocational problems and lamented the lack of help from their respective churches.[2]

The series which the present volume concludes was initiated because of a deep concern for the level of ethics in our American business society. The late Chester I. Barnard, formerly president of the New Jersey Bell Telephone Company and later of the Rockefeller Foundation, discussing the origin of the Ethics and Economics Series, told the Department of Church and Economic Life that his interest in this theme stemmed from a conviction that the most fundamental problem confronting our civilization was the relevance of the Christian faith to economic life. He felt its relevance had not been made explicit, and it was essential that it should be. Impelled by that conviction he urged and assisted in initiating this series.

An ever-rising level of education and increasing freedom to ask fundamental questions has enabled individuals, whether in or out of business life, to evaluate economic practices as evidenced in modern business. Even more influential, presumably, have been the scientific and technological advances which have placed a premium on size and efficiency. A few giant corporations, dominating individual industries and collectively controlling a large part of the production and the corporate assets of the nation, give rise to questions of their responsibility to the nation as a whole and to those who are employed by them. Decisions made by a relatively small number of individuals affect the personal lives of millions. The question is inevitably asked: by what authority do these individuals possess such power and what are the controls under which they operate?

As industries and businesses increased in magnitude, their leaders found themselves in an equivocal position. Their prime functions were to expand the industry and to continue it as a profitable enterprise. But at the same time an ever more close-knit and interdependent society began to hold those leaders responsible for a contribution to society, and they naturally wanted to become known as accepting that responsibility. Thus a measure of conflict inevitably arose between the immediate requirements of the enterprise they served and the wider ranging claims of responsible citizenship. The two sets of claims are not easily reconciled. The dilemma of the business leader became the dilemma of his organization, the corporation, which also had to recognize its twofold responsibility. Not all of the business organizations which faced this profound issue were large ones, nor were all of the large ones asking such questions. Enough of both types, however, have become involved in this very basic inquiry so that industry and business are presumed by many thoughtful citizens to have a genuine concern for the ethical implications of their operations.

Schools of business connected with universities have served to inspire their students with a professional consciousness. One of the marks of a profession is its ethical criteria and standards. Bernard D. Nossiter, commenting on Adolf Berle's *The Twentieth Century Capitalist Revolution*, contends that corporations are leading the way to a modern "city of God," because their managers are tending to respond to the promptings of conscience or some inchoate higher law.[3] The university school of business finds itself the institution where the dilemma of the corporation and its leadership is most clearly defined. A part of its appeal lies in the fact that it can enable its students to provide substantial economic resources for themselves and their families, but at the same time the very business of the university is to enable its students to see the more comprehensive meaning of life in its totality. These two factors, though not necessarily mutually exclusive, are the source of an uneasy tension. "No one can serve two masters." If the purpose is self-aggrandizement, then the purpose of the university is defeated. If the student is interested only in the philosophical view of the business life, his place is not in the executive suite. The resolution of this ambivalence is an ethical, a philosophical, or, if you will, a theological problem.

The ethics of business must, therefore, include responsibility toward employee, stockholder, and consumer. The businessman becomes a steward of concerns far beyond what was conceived to be his field of responsibility even a half century ago. As Howard Bowen expressed it in another volume in this series: "The first and most essential condition, if social responsibility is to become a more effective force, is that businessmen must acquire a strengthened sense of vocation. They must accept the social implications of their calling. They must recognize that ultimately business exists not for profits, for power, or for personal aggrandizement, but to serve society."[4]

Unethical Practices

In his much-discussed study "How Ethical are Businessmen?" Raymond C. Baumhart, S.J., concludes that "four out of five executives giving an opinion affirm the presence in their industry of practices which are generally accepted and are also unethical."[5] Then he lists some of the practices which executives believe illustrate those categories: (1) seeking preferential treatment through lavish entertainment; (2) kick-back to purchasing department employees; (3) pay-offs to government officials; (4) price-rigging between supplier and contractor varying prices through favoritism; (5) collusion in contract bidding, underbidding with substitution of inferior workmanship or materials, etc.

Similarly, in his contribution to the group reports in *On The Job Ethics* William H. Cohea, Jr., finds parallels in the labor movement to the situations Raymond Baumhart reports from executives in industry.[6] In each of the other five reports of occupational groups similar ethical dilemmas are narrated by bankers, building contractors, business executives, personnel managers, and public relations consultants (in addition to labor unionists).

It would not be difficult to fill a book with instances of dishonesty and venality in business, labor, church, school, medicine, government, and every form of economic activity. Immediately it must be countered that just as quickly, if not more so, could a volume be compiled of honest, gracious, ethical actions by which man's spirit has been ennobled and whole communities have been elevated. The problem, however, is not to catalogue the diseases or glorify the state of health to the exclusion of all other realities. The problem is to examine the circumstances which give rise to destructive and injurious processes and which encourage decency and integrity.

While business ethics is so closely related to other forms of social life, it is impossible to consider business independent of all phases on which it impinges. For our purposes we shall limit consideration to the problems of business itself. Our culture is predominantly a business-industrial culture, and the standards which prevail in it are likely to influence strongly the qualities of the rest of society. This, presumably, is what underlies Chester Barnard's concern for the relevance of Christian ethics to business, indicated above.

Crudely but frankly stated, the express goal of business is to make a profit. But this is not its sole function or even its most important one, for it exists primarily to provide goods in response to human needs. But the individual economic incentive for providing those goods is the anticipated margin of profit by which the producer knows whether his product is in demand and is satisfactory to the consumer. Thus the quality of his workmanship, the attractiveness of the price, and the circumstances under which he makes his product available determine whether he stays in business. The producer and the distributor are rewarded, theoretically, according to the degree to which they meet those criteria. This is a grossly simplified picture of the "enterprise system," which is fraught with potential dangers and abuses, but which we in the West at least consider less vicious than those which attend a totally regulated economy where choice is limited and where caste distinctions are based upon political favoritism or conformity to an established ideology. (We have our ideologies, too, as will be shown shortly, but they are malleable rather than fixed in legal, creedal form, as Communism requires.) "Indeed, in America," says economist Harold L. Johnson, "corporate executives and the enterprises which they coordinate are expected to pursue profit goals, efficiency, innovation, and cost minimization. These items are key elements in the pattern of American business. There are nonprofit aspects to the business role, but in an enterprise system, strong emphasis remains on pursuit of profits, economy with scarce resources, and watching the dollar."[7] Business executives are not rewarded primarily for their civic-mindedness or their participation in nonprofit activities, though these may add to the public esteem of the executive. His primary function is to administer the work for which he is responsible in a way which is profitable to the total enterprise. If he can do this and contribute to the general well-being of his community, he may come to be regarded as a statesman. In the growing professionalism of business this designation becomes increasingly important. But it is not in the "statesman" areas of his activities where the ethical problems emerge primarily; it is in his profit-making activities.

The manager's ethical problem is compounded by the fact that his value to the corporation depends upon his ability to assure the continuity of the organization with an adequate profit rate. But what rate is proper? If it is too low, the company is imperiled and so is the manager's job. If it is too high, it has failed to distribute its earnings equitably among its stockholders and workers and is held to have taken advantage of customers and competitors. The dangers from the latter are less than the former, but nevertheless where social responsibility is taken seriously by the company, it must answer in good conscience for its earnings. Relative to the corporation's survival, management consultant and former Sears-Roebuck executive James Worthy comments: "Unfortunately this relationship between profit and survival is not generally understood. The social stake in profits is heavily obscured by the implicit equating of profit with self interest. This confusion of the two concepts is not only inaccurate; it places the business system in a vulnerable moral position and seriously weakens the claims of business for social policies that will foster its efficient performance. A more realistic and more defensible doctrine of profits will have to be built around the survival needs of the enterprise as an instrumentality of social service."[8] There is no formula for resolving this issue. The consciences of the managers and directors guided by their sense of responsibility to society and to the company for whose continuance they are responsible are the only criteria of decision.

The businessman and everyone else in his business relationships are confronted by the tension between self-interest and the values which might bring superior benefits to others. Writ large, this is the problem of the corporation as well. In both cases, whether individual decisions or corporate action, there may be a deep underlying conviction that what serves the best interests of the individual and the corporation in the long run may also be the best thing for society as a whole. This is the contemporary application of Adam Smith's "invisible hand" theory. Too simply stated, it is this thesis which underlies the American business creed, which will be discussed later. It provides self-justification for actions which "keep the economy going" even though they may have dubious ethical aspects. If rationalization is needed, it can be provided by the fact that profit-seeking can thus produce benefits to others through fostering the very system by which all may gain.

Numerous studies have revealed the fact that increased income or larger profits are not the only or in some cases even the most powerful incentive for activity in business. Though this may be true, there is enough evidence that economic gain has motivated many individuals to participate in ethically questionable activities. The bank clerk living beyond his means, though in the public eye he is a model citizen, provides a story which can be duplicated in almost any city. But this juggling of the books is hardly in the same category as collusion in the rigging of prices on the part of major corporations. We are merely contending that in both instances the incentives may be the same: the desire for self-enhancement or esteem either by the community or by the company which rewards accomplishment on the part of its employees.

In the corporation employee status may depend on many factors—the "right" school, friendships, personal attractiveness. Nepotism may also play a part and influence choices of many others. But fundamentally usefulness to the business depends upon capacity to increase profits and to extend the life and range of the company or corporation. Under such circumstances it is all but inevitable that the individual will do whatever is possible within the range of commonly accepted practices to foster his own present and future security in the organization. All of this is perfectly human, we say, and is no different from what prevails in every other walk of life. The difference, if any, lies in the fact that business is primarily engaged in the making of profit, and therefore it brings into clearer focus the consequences and temptations of profit-seeking. In the face of this fact the marvel would seem to be not that there is so much unethical conduct but that the forces in society at large and the consciences of individuals have created a climate with so high a degree of ethical quality.

The Changing Climate of Ethical Attitudes

Debate over the source of industry's increasing sensitivity to ethical values may be interesting but not particularly helpful unless it adds to the present discussion, i.e., whether that sensitivity derives from a growing ethical consciousness of individuals or whether the nature of business itself makes increased ethical demands in our society. In the long run this question will have far-reaching implications. If, for example, the increasing cohesiveness of society is compelling men to conduct themselves with greater consideration of the rights and privileges of others, it may be that "secular" forces are accomplishing what religious morality and idealism have striven for much less successfully. For our purposes, however, the primary question is not who is more responsible for bringing this about but rather the implications of what is commonly accepted as an increasingly ethical climate in business.

For many years the corporation was a person in the eyes of the law. This fiction was slow in dissipation despite the inconsistency, if not ludicrousness, of attempting to regard the United States Steel Corporation, for example, as a person, where its self-perpetuating board of directors makes decisions and its independence in practice from its numerous stockholders renders it (and most other corporations) something quite different from an entity expressing the personal wishes of its owners. Whether person or not, however, the corporation, whatever its size, has gained a new role of responsibility in the life of the nation and more recently on the total world scene. As a legal person the corporation may have maintained the aura of privacy, but few corporations which seek support from a large investing public any longer regard themselves as solely private agencies. Every major corporation has become an institution with public responsibility and dependent upon public acceptance. Any distinction between public and private is at best inexact. This much is said concerning the corporation and its ethical role for the obvious reason that business standards are established and most visibly maintained by the large organizations. There are, of course, individuals in the smaller organizations who are keenly sensitive to ethical values and who may shape the patterns of their organizations more nearly in keeping with their personal ethical standards. The public, however, is more aware of the standards of A. T. & T., General Motors, Standard Oil, Sears-Roebuck, Swift & Company, and International Harvester as the determiners of ethical standards for industry and business. The emergence of the public relations profession, if it can qualify as a "profession," is intimately related to the desire of each industry to convince the public that it is honorable and ethical.

Having attained positions of eminence where their "image" is of great importance to themselves and to the public, corporations have learned what individuals who have been catapulted to great prominence have also had to learn, namely, that their objectives and standards are no longer merely their own but are made in part by their public and that it is of utmost importance that those standards be maintained. From the standpoint of business ethics, business leaders have discovered the truth of a comment made by the French sociologist Emile Durkheim more than a half century ago: "When one starts with a maxim that there are none but economic interests, one is their prisoner and cannot rise above them." This has been one of the most fundamental mistakes of Marxism, and accounts for a high percentage of the difficulties confronting the Russian economy in our period of rapid change. In its maturation American industry has had to discover that its interests have to transcend the limited meaning of "economics" and face its fuller meaning —the welfare of the entire "house." To the extent that American business has failed to comprehend the necessity for its own adaptability and responsiveness to public requirement, it has suffered and brought calamity to itself and those dependent upon it. Where this has been the case, the industry involved was guilty of the same rigidity that characterizes the Russian system. Ironically the latter theoretically forced a standard of equalitarianism upon its people but in practice provided differential rewards greater in some cases than exist in enterprise economies. Thus in an effort to rectify an unethical condition they created a new imbalance and a warping of creativity. The American system in its evolution as a product of industrial technology and grounded in Hebrew-Christian ethics was slower to coerce ethical equality, but by being free to respond to the trends in industrial society's evolution it has voluntarily created a situation infinitely more conducive to human creativity and mutual consideration.

Much of the grumbling that business does about government interference stems from its apprehension over fears of increasing control. Separating regulations from control in the minds of those who are actually or potentially subject to either makes for ambivalence. Regulation has served to protect industries from dangers in the conduct of their operations and has made for public confidence. But because the line between regulation and control is not clearly defined, the benefits of regulation are accepted with mixed feelings, tempered with the fears of possible control. This attitude toward government has become symbolized in the political party structure. The fact that the Republican party has consistently been supported by the majority of business leadership requires a more comprehensive explanation than simply to suggest that business has apparently had greater freedom from control under the Republicans. There are obviously ethnic and regional factors involved here also. The historic tie of labor (but not all labor) to the Democratic party may account in part also for management's identification with the Republicans. The point we are making here, however, does not deal with political preferences so much as with the reasons for hostility toward government on the part of a large segment of the business community.

It was stated above that the goal of business is to make a profit. The conditions under which that profit is made affects more than the business or industry involved. A government representing all people must be concerned with the balancing of benefits and injuries for the protection of all affected. Only thus can the private profit system be assured continuance. Thus despite restrictions and curtailment of opportunities for gains made against the long range of public interest, business realizes the need for government interference as a means of its own self-protection. It is to this situation that Secretary of Commerce Luther Hodges spoke when he stated: "If you studied the origin of these agencies (Federal regulatory bodies) you will have to draw the conclusion that all these things, troublesome and expensive as they may be, become necessary in modern, thoughtful government because a minority of people in professions, businesses and other groups act unethically, act illegally, or fail to do what the public—and responsible businessmen—regard as the correct and proper thing to do."

Regardless of how much times have changed and the public disposition to criticize business ethics has increased, it is extremely difficult for individuals and organizations engaged in business to regulate themselves in the interest of society at large. This is not a matter of human sinfulness and self-aggrandizement alone

—or even primarily. In a complex society there is insufficient wisdom in individuals or collectivities to inform and effect wise decisions concerning all those who are subject to those decisions. Allocation of wave-lengths to radio and TV stations is a case in point. The personal integrity of those seeking rights to the air is an insufficient guide to the granting process. And thereafter the judgment of what is good for viewers and hearers cannot be left entirely to the probity and wisdom of the station managers. Obviously there is more involved here than just competition. These are business-ethical decisions for which philosophical and/or religious values are required.

Though capitalism has historically espoused competition and gained its strength from the competing forces within it, the nature of our economy has become such that, for much of American business, competition is no longer the basic pattern. Technology has made competition of the traditional type difficult and perhaps impossible in whole areas which are now assumed to be effectively determined by it. The much-reported electrical industry scandal was a vivid illustration of the reluctance of giants in the electrical industry to engage in competition. The reluctance was in part a consequence of the nature of the industry.

Despite support of the competitive system competition between businesses is not viewed with enthusiasm. The situations anonymously related in the reports from the building contractors group in *On The Job Ethics* is a moving tale of the dog-eat-dog existence when open competition prevails. It is not difficult to understand why under these circumstances manufacturers enter into agreements with each other. Collusion or agreement on prices can enable some businesses to stay alive which would otherwise be forced out of existence.

The government has for many decades sought to promote fair competition by outlawing agreements in restraint of trade and unfair competition. The Sherman Antitrust Act, the Clayton Antitrust Act, the Federal Trade Commission, and the Robinson-Patman Act are some of the instruments which have been created to accomplish this end. The fact is that the problem is an enormously difficult one because of the very nature of competition itself and the necessity for maintaining the maximum of justice for all concerned.

Reluctance to face realistically the problem of government regulation may account for the fact that business administration, now being vigorously publicized as a coming profession, has been among the slowest so to regard itself. A characteristic of a profession is its capacity to evaluate itself and to justify itself in the mores and customs of society and to abide by the standards which that society espouses. Until recently business has been highly suspicious of intellectuals and therefore has produced comparatively few business philosophers. That condition is obviously changing. Some business leaders have recognized that their functions and the public weal must be in harmony. The rapid change going on in the technological aspects of society have confronted them with new ethical perspectives. Possibly because they have been powerless to halt those technological developments, they have resented those intellectuals both in government and in the university who have pointed to the inevitability of those changes. Meanwhile, the "statesmen of industry" face realistically the fact that a steadily rising set of ethical standards is demanded in the area most typical of modern existence—business and industry.

There is evidence that a new generation of business leaders is emerging, leaders who have been trained to take into account a wide spectrum of factors as they make decisions relative to company and community. Kenneth Underwood, out of extensive association with business leadership, contends that a new social ethic is to be observed in the health and growth of the corporate enterprise, based on the fulfillment of its useful function in society.[9]

If the level of ethical practices is steadily rising, one could ask, why become exercised? Will not the rational process of society's improvement take care of things? The incontrovertible fact is that man must ever be protected against the human propensity to seek one's own advantage. It is at this point that the forces of religion and ethics make their contribution to the well-being of society. As is indicated in the chapter on the consumer, producers and distributors need to be checked in their temptation to take advantage of the buyer. False and erroneous advertising and packaging are a constant temptation. When the public ire has been roused or conscientious individuals have protested a violation of good practices, a modification sometimes occurs. It is almost axiomatic that this has been the result of pressures from society instead of from a stirring of conscience. It is at this point that religious ethics speaks both to producer and consumer, seller and buyer, professional and client. The complexities of a technological society do not diminish the need. They require new adaptation in ethics.

The realization that no single formula is adequate to resolve the moral and ethical dilemmas created by the business activities of this generation constitutes a distinct gain. One of the dilemmas created for honest men has been the assumption that in the realm of religion there was a formula which, were it only to be known, could be applied. Failing to discover this, men have been disillusioned and disaffected from any attempt to discern the contribution of religious faith to business ethical dilemmas. The issues in business ethics require a grounding in the economic and social needs of society, but also an awareness of the depths of human involvement in the total range of life's resources such as the Christian gospel provides. The dimensions of man's relationship with God include a scope of human experience infinitely more extensive than those apparently inherent in normal business experience. For the Christian it is when these are brought to bear on the business decision that new ethical resources become apparent.

Resources for Business Ethics

"Even an ethical businessman of 1900 might be deemed unethical by today's norms," says Theodore L. Thau. "Conversely, an unethical businessman of today might well have been judged wholly normal in his conduct fifty or sixty years ago."[10] Earlier in this chapter it was recognized that just such changes have taken place. There followed some proposed explanations for those changes. It is axiomatic that changes in customs, mores, ethical practices and the like are effected only where demand for them has been great enough to warrant modification. If it is true, and we believe it is, that great improvements have taken place in the ethics of American business practices, one cannot but ask what the criteria are by which new patterns are established. When Secretary of Commerce Luther Hodges summoned a group of twenty-six businessmen, educators, clergymen, and publishers to form the Business Ethics Advisory Council, it was apparently assumed by the Secretary of Commerce and President Kennedy, who backed this venture, that the time was ripe for clarifying the objectives of business and reviewing the ethical criteria applicable in the second half of the twentieth century.

Many professions and business organizations have codes by which they and the public may evaluate their performance and which give bases for judgment of any proposed movements, experiments, projects, etc. When the moving picture producers were under fire for questionable practices and substandard productions regarded as offensive to the public moral standards, a code was established and an administrator, generally well regarded, was selected to administer the code. This practice has become common where an industry is sensitive to its reputation. Codes spell out explicitly what the industry regards as commendable. For the most part they constitute a "floor" of ethical practice. Since they rest on voluntary acceptance, the ones to whom they apply may be casual about their acceptance, as the public has come to experience. It is probably easier for a corporation dispensing a tangible product to hold itself and to be held accountable than for those identified with the entertainment industry, where art forms are less capable of appraisal and judgment. The Crown Zellerbach Corporation code may illustrate a statement of one industry's standard.[11]*

* 1. To regularly produce from our forest resources the highest quality lumber, cellulose, and chemical products at the lowest possible cost —and, while doing so, to maintain our plants in the highest degree of efficiency and safety.
2. To regularly sell such products to the most people at fair prices and with reasonable profits.
3. To regularly provide jobs at fair wages to as many people as we can gainfully employ.
4. To regularly pay a fair return to our shareholders on their invest-

The Business Ethics Advisory Council, concerning itself with the total gamut of business ethics in the United States, expresses itself in less specific but more inclusive terms. "We therefore now propose that current efforts be expanded and intensified and that new efforts now be undertaken by the American business community to hasten its attainment of those high ethical standards that derive from our heritage and traditions. We urge all enterprises, business groups and associations to accept responsibility—each for itself and in its own most appropriate way—to develop methods and programs for encouraging and sustaining these efforts on a continuous basis. We believe in this goal, we accept it, and we encourage all to pursue its attainment."[12]

More inclusive than codes of individual firms or corporations, though perhaps less idealistic than the hopes expressed in the Business Ethics Advisory Council proposal just quoted, is the blanket standard, undefined and unspecific but nevertheless intensely realistic, "The American Business Creed" which Francis Sutton and his colleagues have explicated in the volume by that name.[13] The authors contend that business ideology has no formal document or official line by which it lives. But that does not mean that it is not governed by standards and concepts which are just as vivid as those written into the Marxist doctrine for Communists. "Briefly, our thesis is that the content of the business ideology can best be explained in terms of the *strains* to which men in the business role are almost inevitably subject. Businessmen adhere to their particular kind of ideology because of the emotional conflicts, the anxieties, and the doubts engendered by the actions which their roles as businessmen compel them to take, and by the conflicting demands of other social roles which they must play, in family and community."[14] The Creed is explicit in the standards it expects of its adherents as they relate themselves to the life of their communities and in their personal conduct. All of this becomes apparent as one lives

---

ment in our business and to protect and safeguard such investment.
5. To always be a good citizen in the communities in which we operate.
6. To discharge our responsibilities to society by maintaining our business in a manner that will earn continual public trust and confidence.

and works in the milieu of American business. He may not have had a course in business ethics or conduct, but the standards about him and the norms observed by his peers tell him that there are criteria which stand over against any actual or proposed conduct on his part or that of his organization. The American Business Creed is a constantly evolving set of standards, raising its levels as the level of society itself rises. It has to be reckoned as one of the available resources for the establishment and the maintaining of ethical attitudes.

In the reports from the Occupational Ethics Groups and from Father Baumhart's study another resource comes to the fore with regularity and prominence. When an employee is confronted with an ethical decision, his guide for resolving that dilemma is probably his superior in the organization or the standards of the individuals who are the company's principal officers. The Baumhart formula is: "If you want to act ethically, find an ethical boss."[15]

In one Occupational Ethics Group men reported they had never been asked to do anything which the superior officers of the firm would not approve. No violation of conscience had ever been required. The quality of leadership in the firm determines the ethical standards all down the line.

Because a major consideration of the theological aspects of economics and business ethics has been included in the current volume, the implications of theology for ethics in business are treated here in only a limited fashion. In one of the Occupational Ethics Groups the members were told that the subject they were discussing had theological implications, and a member asked whether it wasn't in order to discuss those at that time. The reply from another member was: "Good Lord, no—things are bad enough without getting them mixed up with theology." Theology deals with the nature of man and his relation to God and the consequences to society because of that relationship. Religion brings into the consideration of business ethics a dimension which it cannot possess, namely, ultimate loyalties above those of one's community or one's business organization. It raises the question of one's final responsibility, whether it is to the company of which he is a part or whether to the well-being of other persons who are also fellow creatures of a common Father, of a God who is both Creator and Redeemer. The religious dimension greatly complicates business ethics because there is no absolute and final rightness in many decisions. They have to be made out of consideration for both the ongoing life of the institution and for society at large, whose concern is just as much that of God as is the more immediate set of loyalties in the company. To the Christian the ultimate standard of action is love, but rarely can one fulfill the full requirements of love in a business transaction. He must, therefore, act with the freedom with which he has been endowed and serve what, in the light of the circumstances at hand, most truly represents what he believes to be God's will and purpose for that situation.

15

The Role of the Church

How often is the cry heard, "Why doesn't the church do something about that?" Or perhaps even more frequently, "What business has the church got meddling in that situation?" There was a time (the Middle Ages) when neither of these questions was being asked, when no one, openly at least, questioned the propriety of the church's activities in any sphere and everyone took for granted that if anything was needed, the church would attend to it.

The explanation of the vast change from the day when the church was responsible for everything to the present day when its very relevance to social matters generally and to economics in particular is questioned, constitutes a fascinating study in culture, mores, political and scientific history, and the changing attitudes which have resulted in our present expectations of the church's role. Ernst Troeltsch, R. H. Tawney, and many others have described the process by which the power of the church declined in relation to economic processes, and there are many who bemoan this lessening of hegemony over the business and cultural life of society. We will not join in that dirge, not simply because it is "spilled milk" and there is no use crying about it, but because the separation is by no means all loss. One contemporary commentator states: "Today the marriage of the church and society is fast dissolving, brought on by the growing secularization of the West itself and by the challenge to western hegemony put by the peoples of Africa, Asia, and Latin America not only in political and economic affairs but in the realm of ideology."[1] Undoubtedly this is true, but it can hardly be contended that the marriage was of a sacramental nature to begin with, and it was certainly never by mutual consent. The parties had simply grown up together and had had insufficient opportunity to see what matrimony over the years might bring.

The simple fact is that neither the church nor the economic order has had the opportunity under modern conditions to explore their mutual contributions and their mutual dependence. There are many who would contend that there is no mutual dependence; they have full right to make as valid a case for their beliefs as possible. On the other hand, those who believe that the church has a function to perform in the contemporary world in relation to economic life likewise have a valid right to make a claim. It is the fundamental conviction of this writer and of most of the contributors to the Series on Ethics and Economics in Society that the church has something of utmost significance to contribute to economic thought. Likewise economics, serving as it does our industrial society, has much to contribute to religion and its potential for serving an industrial economy.

It is no accident that the subject discussed more than any other in theological circles in this generation is the nature and relevance of the church. Encylopedias are required to do justice to the total gamut of that study. We will make our affirmations in terse and condensed form. The church derives its existence from the fact of the life, death, and resurrection of Jesus Christ. Those who have been influenced through the centuries by the events surrounding the central figure of the Christian faith have found themselves bound together both by a common devotion and by an institutional life. However great they may be, revolutionary events require historical forms to perpetuate them. So the church developed an institutional form in order to convey to its people and to interpret to those who were not a part of it the central fact of its faith. Down through the ages the church has remained a community bound together in large measure by a devotion to the God who is the God and Father of our Lord Jesus Christ. This community has been bound together in many institutional forms, but what is significant is that the church has had strength and continuity only where it had some institutional structure to undergird it.

As James Gustafson has expressed it, this institution has become a community of faith and a community of deed.[2] Neither is sufficient without the other. The supreme test of the church's faith has always been its giving itself to mankind as the continuing embodiment of its Lord, who was "the Man for others." It has been concerned for the welfare of people of all ages, but particularly of those who were least able to defend themselves—children, the aged, and the infirm. It has sought to alleviate injustice and injury because these were destructive of the human spirit and were in violation of God's will for man as seen in the life of our Lord.

In the minds of its most sensitive adherents the church was commissioned by its Lord to be a model of the new community which God desires among men. William Temple, who did much in his time to clarify the meaning of Christianity for the whole of society, contended that it was the purpose of the church to provide the earthly counterpart of the "City of God" which Augustine had portrayed.[3] It was not possible for man to achieve fully the City of God, but he could seek to bring the "City of Man" closer to that ideal.

As times and social environment changed, men who earnestly sought to fulfill their roles as part of the new community of Christ, a community without division, as the Apostle Paul vigorously insisted, were called to find ways in which their devotion to God as known in Christ could fulfill the obligation to create this City of Man. It was one thing to care for those who were in dire need in the years immediately after Jesus' departure from their midst; it was something else to translate that action into care for those who were the victims of economic and social systems whose power was too great and too remote to be reached and modified. While this has been a continuing dilemma for devoted Christians for two thousand years, it has increased since the Industrial Revolution. Those who have profited substantially by absence of interference from others who desired to create the City of Man after the pattern of the City of God, have resisted mightily attempts to modify their practices. Even some acts of private charity have been engaged in for this purpose. Such is man's propensity toward self-righteousness that he resists criticisms or modifications, however just their claims may be.

The Christian knows that the church in its institutionalized form and the world are indissolubly related. However impressive have been the attempts of a few to live apart from the world, their example does not contribute much to the life of our times, for their very existence has been largely dependent upon the willingness of others to live "sinfully" in the world and thus to free ascetics from its demands. Today we accept the fact that if the church is to be relevant to the life around us, it is out of a genuine desire to create the City of Man after the pattern for human life revealed in the Gospel and in the kingdom of Jesus Christ. When men have abandoned the ideal of living a life of justice and compassion for the welfare of others, the results have been chaotic and disintegrative to the human spirit. This we saw with terrifying force in the emergence of a brutal totalitarian regime under the Nazis in Germany and under the tactics of a Stalin in the Soviet Union. We saw it in the brutalities of the slave trade and in the exploitation of human life during the early stages of the Industrial Revolution.

It became apparent that the church was more than a soul-saving station. If each church itself was a colony of heaven, and if the total church was commissioned to become an instrument for achieving the ideal City of Man, it would require concerted action, voluntarily initiated and accepted. Oversight and control from a vast central source such as characterized the church of the Middle Ages could no longer be relied upon. Parenthetically it should be added that the break-up of that power did not begin with the Protestant Reformation; its roots anteceded 1517 by many years, but the Reformation was a protest against the continuing ineptitude and corruption of the church in its totalitarian form and its failure to support the values of human dignity which the new commercialism and the Renaissance with its new learning had inspired.

In England the state church, which understandably took its

pattern from the ecclesiastical body which preceded it, and the new "gathered" church composed of those inspired by familiarity with "the Book" and its description of the early church, both came to regard themselves as responsible for the quality of life around them. But an inevitable dualism arose. Those who were primarily concerned with individual salvation naturally came to expect it in whatever form of church existed. Those who regarded the church as a collective body responsible both for individual and communal life saw in the church an instrument for social reconstruction. The church has come to mean both of these things, sometimes emphasizing one to the exclusion of the other. In all periods there have been those who felt that the principal function of the church was to assure the eternal salvation of their souls. The English Reformation illustrated this dualism. It was no accident that in the Cromwellian Revolution the church was considered an instrument for implementing its ideals for political organization and public morals. Similarly, it was understandable that the church became the nerve center and inspiration for labor unions and cooperatives in England. The point is that the church has always had this dual role.

A look at the history of the church, however, reveals that its dual role has not been uniformly accepted, and the reasons are not far to seek. They lie in the differing understanding of the gospel's function, as interpreted by the two most influential figures in Protestantism, Martin Luther and John Calvin. (This difference was spelled out more fully in chapter one.) Luther's emphasis was primarily on the individual righteousness of the Christian deriving from God's gracious love for him. Presumably the Christian would do that which was good and just as the free response to God's love. Calvin was not so trustful that the free person would live righteously because of devotion to his Maker and Redeemer. Calvin's more explicit development of the positive function of law helped remind the faithful of their obligation to the total community of Christians and helped to prevent those who were not so committed from injuring others. While those in the Lutheran tradition contended that Christian social action should be expressed through the instrumentality of the state, those of Calvinist persuasion conceived the church's social role as that of a countervailing and coordinating force. Under the latter institutional framework the church has seen its role as helping to create the kind of society which would make it more truly the ideal City of Man. It is understandable, therefore, that the immigrants from England sought to establish on the new continent a new holy commonwealth, and their descendants—physical and spiritual—have been much more interested in political and economic institutions than have been the immigrants who came from lands influenced primarily by Martin Luther.

In addition to their differing views concerning the church's relation to the state another factor which influenced the modern complexion of the church was the differing importance attributed to precise theological accord. The Lutheran concern for proper doctrine hindered cooperation with other denominations in concerted social action, while the Calvinists' emphasis on the committed life, as distinguished from strict doctrinal correctness, allowed them to engage more freely in such action. It is therefore understandable that such organizations as the National Council of Churches, the World Council of Churches, and the local church federations have almost uniformly been the result of original instigation on the part of individuals and groups whose roots were in the Calvinistic tradition. It is equally significant that today the leadership for many of these organizations is now coming in increasing volume from the denominations which had their origins in continental Europe.

The denominations originally formed on European soil have, as has every other part of Christendom, been shaken to their roots by the diabolical emergence of Nazism. As the Evanston Report of the World Council meetings states in discussing the European churches: "It has been shown in many studies how, as a result of this period of discovery for the churches, 'some of the narcotic effects of their silent alliance with the world were at last shaken off. The realities of the situation became clear. The churches found out that they had to fight or die. . . .' "[4]

But Europe was not alone in the "narcotic effects" of the alliance with the world. The life of the churches and the life of the world are for many church members indistinguishable. Church membership has not been based primarily on devotion to the gospel or commitment to its Lord. To a very large extent, church membership has been the product of the same type of sales program which business utilizes. It is hardly to be wondered, then, that the churches have not taken seriously their mandate to view the world in the light of a Christian view of man and society. Thus when church members "in good standing" raise the question "What business of the church is it to meddle in these economic matters?" it represents a complete unfamiliarity with the whole history and purpose of the Christian faith in its personal and communal forms.

This challenging of the church, in protest against its assuming responsibility for social life in general and economic life in particular, has had a beneficial chastening effect. The terrible catastrophe afflicting the German people came in part as a result of unfamiliarity with this basically indestructable relationship between faith and all forms of personal and social life. Awareness of this profound relationship has forced the German people and those of every other nation with Christian people to a rediscovery of their own roots. It has led to a large-scale pursuit of theological and biblical study.

The emergence of the World Council of Churches is testimony to the realized need for a rediscovery of our spiritual roots. The development of the ecumenical movement is a by-product of that discovery, but perhaps even more is it responsible for fostering that study. In the Oxford Conference on "The Life and Work of the Church" in 1937 and the Edinburg Conference on "Faith and Order" in the same year, with the dark clouds of totalitarianism rising over the world, it became apparent that the divisions in Christendom were cutting its vital nerve and rendering it less effective than it might be in a world where other values than the sacredness of human life were becoming dominant. Churches which became accustomed to aloofness from the forces that shape society realized when facing a common enemy that they had weakened themselves by insisting on their own little private bailiwicks and prejudices under the guise of the sacredness of their institutional forms. One of the miracles of modern times is the speed with which the churches united in the realization of their common sources and common purpose, when they faced realistically the disintegrative and destructive forces undermining the all-important work to which the churches were historically committed.

Now the circle is completed. It is the industrialization process and its economy which made possible the massing of great forces of evil as well as of good. The primary emphasis on power and the utilization of all the new-found sources of power have placed the industrial and economic institutions in the role of first importance. The key to their success is efficiency. Fascist nations became the tools of persons who had discovered that efficiency and the control of central power were to provide the only possibility, so they thought, for their expansion and domination over others. To all of this the church was and is now called on to present an alternative to sheer "efficiency" and power, based on its convictions about the nature of man and his purpose in living. This is the inheritance of the church and its mandate for appraising all systems and institutions.

So it is not meddling when the church enters into the discussion of economics or any other forms of human endeavor. In fact, if it did not participate in such activities and judgments, it would default on its commission. Because it has defaulted from time to time, the world is poorer. On the other hand, when its people have assumed magnificently the responsibility of bringing the light of the Christian gospel to bear on human activities and institutions, the world is greatly enriched. This does not mean that the church is qualified to speak for God. There is no absolute and final form which embodies the church—it can but say that in the light of its fullest comprehension and analysis of what God requires of man this is the best judgment available at the time. Obedience to the gospel and its Lord is the only source of its authority, and every decision must be held under that mandate. So with humility but with firmness the church must make its judgments relative to economic matters as in every other aspect of human life.

Specific Functions for the Church

The principal function of the church can be expressed in many ways. Cunliffe-Jones states it very aptly. The task of the church, he says, "is to make plain for man's thinking the intimate relation between the fact of God and the personal life of man in himself and in community."[5] For the Christian the reality of God and the personal life of man can never be divorced. Out of his devotion to God, a test of which is also the measure of man's love for his neighbor, stem all of the beneficent forms, agencies, and institutions which man contrives. The church, then, is the community of those who readily ask that their devotion be tested by their love for God and neighbor. It is constantly on the alert for ways to enrich the community of neighbors, and by the same token it is on the alert for anything which injures the life of man in community.

The life of man in community is not his total life, but nearly everything he does is in part a product of community. His very existence is due to the union of others, and we know full well what warping and disintegration follow from the failures of society to accept man's basic needs for wholesome life in community. Hospitals, jails, and corrective institutions of all sorts owe their populations more to the deprivations and distortions of community life than to physical disabilities. And we know that many of the latter are also the product of injury in the limitless areas of human intercourse.

The church's concern for physical and mental welfare has centuries of experience behind it. Jesus' parable of the good Samaritan has inspired untold millions to care for the needs of others. Those communions and denominations with Lutheran backgrounds have, as was the pattern of the Roman Catholic Church which preceded their existence, a special concern for those afflicted by illness or too young or too old to provide for themselves. This story is eloquently and sensitively told in a volume prepared for the First National Conference on "The Churches and Social Welfare."[6] Alleviating the ill effects of industrial society, however, was not enough; it became apparent that much could be done to forestall the accidents and calamities which injured lives. Out of such a concern began to emerge movements and organizations designed to inspire, influence, and restrict the kind of society at whose core was a concern for the very nature of man himself. Here was a reaffirmation of one of Augustine's concerns expressed more than a thousand years earlier, namely, human rights should have precedence over property rights. Economics in its limited sense is primarily concerned with things—goods—in other words, wealth and its distribution. But unless the circumstances attending the acquisition of wealth and the distribution of goods are beneficial to society at large, they can be corrosive and destructive. It is for this reason that the church has contended with increasing vigor that the only economic practices it can approve are those which truly promote the general welfare and which are totally responsible in their administration and operation. From time to time, churches have erroneously identified themselves with particular economic systems. Disillusionment has followed the too-sanguine endorsement of political or economic systems, for none of them is to be trusted as a vehicle for expressing the basic needs of human life. Instead, the function of the church is to deal with "ends, in the sense of long-range goals, standards and principles in the light of which every concrete situation and every proposal for improving it must be tested."[7] At the same time the church realistically recognizes that ends and means cannot be separated. It is equally concerned with the manner in which the ends are attained.

The church itself is not a political or an economic instrument, even though it may carry weight in regard to political and economic issues and give encouragement to the institutions which are the vehicles of both. It is the role of the church to sense the needs of man whatever his place or affiliation, and where possible to initiate or encourage the giving of the cup of water or the loaf of bread wherever there is need. In comparatively recent years we have seen a vast amount of alleviation of suffering conducted in the name of the church and given in the spirit of Him who admonished man to minister to human need. However this is not the church's principal function. By ministering in this way it performs a function which in many instances can be better conducted by other agencies; for the church is not called—nor does it have the machinery—to serve the complete welfare need in a society which is otherwise equipped to perform such functions with greater efficiency. To the everlasting credit of the churches it must be said, however, that where efficiency and service needed to be combined, the human and mechanical facilities were often co-ordinated to that end and human suffering was alleviated.

An industrial society must inevitably place a high premium on its efficiency in production. Productivity has become the most sought for and honored criterion of industrial life. Surely this is good for the most part, but productivity itself is not the total end or objective of man's life; it is of very great importance that the things which he produces be useful and beneficial. If they are destructive, they must be restricted; if there are unmet needs for which production has not yet been sufficient, these must be lifted up. Here is another basic function the church must perform. It evaluates the whole productive process, including the efficiency ideal, and insists that a failure to serve these ends is a failure in efficiency. It is at this point that tension has arisen between those who have held such high purposes for the life of the church and those who believed that productivity in itself is a sufficient criterion. "It is good for the economy" has become a criterion. On this basis even gambling has been justified. The church can give no commendation to the gambling activities, however magnificently they may appear to benefit the public agencies. What adds nothing to the health of society at large must be renounced by the fellowship of those whose purpose is to foster a quality of life that is consistent with God's creation of man.

John C. Bennett effectively makes this point when he states: ". . . No degree of justice in the organization of economic life can compensate for failure to be efficiently productive, for on this depends the capacity to provide adequately the food, the clothing, the shelter, and other goods which are required by the community. Those who represent Christian theology and ethics are tempted to underestimate the significance of this test of effectiveness in their concern to apply ethical tests, just as economists have often shown an opposite kind of one-sideness and have declared the independence of economics from ethics."[8]

Implementing the Church's Functions in Economic Life

For reasons which are rooted in the historical development or its ethical concerns, the church in recent times has paid more attention to economic life than to political action. Possibly because the consequences of economic life were revealed in industrial activities and the communities which reflected them, the ills were more apparent and seemed more readily dealt with. Long before international affairs attracted the attention of the sensitive and far-ranging minds of some Christians, there had been developed organizations to modify the harshness of the industrial order. Such organizations as the Church Association for the Advancement of the Interests of Labor, the Society of Christian Socialists, Walter Rauschenbusch's Fellowship of the Kingdom, and more recently Christian Action were formed to espouse, among other things, economic justice. One by one the objectives of these organizations have become embodied in political forms sustained and regulated by government activities or have become the concerns of larger secular bodies. Significantly many of the movements initiated by the church have become embedded in the total life of our society.

Following World War I increasing attention was paid to international affairs, world peace, and race. The pseudo prosperity of the 1920s culminating in the 1929 crash reduced concern for economic problems. The Great Depression evoked interest in schemes designed to reconstruct our economic system, with many conscientious individuals looking wonderingly at the Soviet Union to see whether its program held substantial bases for hope. Increasingly it became apparent that the Marxist-Leninist-Stalinist "solution" overlooked or rejected some of the most elemental considerations which must be taken account of in any realistic approach to economics, and its attractiveness waned. Meanwhile, the "enterprise" economy evolved some correctives, and gains were made in economic welfare. A series of major innovations became established in American life.

If this is so, one asks, what then is there left to do, since the National Labor Relations Act, the Social Security Act on behalf of all levels and ages, child labor legislation and minimum wage legislation, Workmen's Compensation and many others, now provide safeguards which were not available during the lifetime of many people now living? The answer to this question is presumably to be seen in the continuous discovery of new areas of need by interdenominational church bodies, in some instances, by church agencies and of course by secular and governmental agencies. A list of the activities of the Department of Church and Economic Life of the National Council of Churches would be highly revealing, but too long to be included in these pages. Simply for illustration mention may be made of the Conferences or Consultations held on Peacetime Uses for Nuclear Energy, Agricultural Policy, the Ministry of the Churches to Labor and Management, the Christian Conscience and an Economy of Abundance, the Churches and Persistent Pockets of Poverty, the Economic Practices of the Churches, Ethical Implications of Rapid Economic Change in the U.S.A., and many others.

Illustrating a role the church may play in a situation obviously needing ethical judgment and clarification was the investigation of the steel strike in 1918. The cooperative efforts of leaders in many denominations were brought to bear on some tragic conditions. Happily major recommendations of the churchmen were adopted, and their efforts are credited with ultimately influencing the elimination of the twelve-hour day and the recognition of the right to organize for purposes of collective bargaining.

Forty years later, at the time of another bitter and extended strike, a special committee under authorization by the National Council of Churches dealt with the critical issues which closed mills and put five hundred thousand people out of work. The specific issues were different, but the fundamental problems were related: the use of power by big industrial organizations and its impingement on human freedom. Both labor and management were censured for their irresponsible use of power. The committee held that false claims and propaganda by both parties were designed to deceive the general public. The representatives of the churches then pointed to such profound and unresolved issues as a fair wage, a just price, adequate profits, and the definition of "public welfare" as questions inescapably related to Christian values. All of this was posited on "the basic conviction that Christians must be responsible for the quality of the social order in which they live."[9]

The Ethics and Economic Life Series which this volume concludes represents another major emphasis of the Department of Church and Economic Life. It embodies the attempt to cope realistically with the issues of economics in a Christian context.

Increasingly the churches in their cooperative endeavors have been finding readiness and even enthusiasm for cooperation on the part of so-called "secular forces," whether in government, in the universities, or in the multiplicity of private agencies operating for socially constructive ends. Often their immediate objectives are identical, though there may be fundamental differences in the philosophical or theological background of those engaged in these reconstructive activities.

The massive attempt currently being undertaken by government to overcome poverty was anticipated by several years on the part of cooperative church bodies which held a consultation among leaders of many denominations to discern possible lines of approach to the elimination of poverty in this seemingly affluent nation. Similarly, as national forces began to converge on the problem of school dropouts, the churches, through the National Council of Churches and working in cooperation with governmental and private agencies, sought to find means whereby the churches might give vigorous support to the movement, urging young people to prepare themselves in school for the kinds of earning opportunities our economy will be providing in the years ahead.

Not limited to the problems of economics, but designed to further the work of the church as it meets needs in many areas of life, has been the impressive increase in research functions, both within the individual denominations and in cooperation. The research program of the churches is turning to the unmet needs of human beings in many forms of individual and communal life.

The expressions of the life of the church as briefly portrayed above are, however, actually only a small part of the total action of the church as it seeks to minister to human needs in an industrial society. The spectacle of substantial portions of the church capitulating to the nationalistic interests of the nations in Europe—and, we must confess, to a less sensational degree but perhaps nonetheless also in the English-speaking world as well—has produced the realization that some of the forms of the church we have known may be inadequate. As Franklin H. Littell has so aptly portrayed, out of the ashes of this tragedy has come the realization that new forms of church life and new ways of expressing the Christian faith are required.[10] Small groups of searching Christians have sought means of relating their faith to the economic problems of their day. In these smaller groups, often assembled because of common vocational or professional interests, there has emerged the concern for the meaning of work in industrial society. With development of the Evangelical Academies in central Europe, and of Iona in Scotland under Sir George McCleod, and many other such experiments, it has become apparent that the church is not limited to its traditional forms of parish life in order to perform its role. In some of these new forms of parish life the real life issues are more readily dealt with. Those issues may center about the ethical dilemmas of the industrial society in whose midst the "parish" exists.

Reluctant though we be to relinquish so time-honored an institution as the parish church, there are evidences from all sides that the church should not be confined to any single form and that its very existence depends upon imaginative ways of relating the gospel to the needs of all men wherever they may be. "The picture of the local church," says Martin Marty, "is so powerful, it tends to exhaust the definition of the church."[11] We understand Marty's meaning when we realize how restricted have been our imaginations at the point of discovering new ways of bringing the witness of the church to bear on our common life. Such a useful little book as *Your Church in Your Community* by Huber Klemme is representative of many other volumes of this sort now coming to the fore that describe the ways in which parish churches, or perhaps more accurately, small groups within parish churches, have sought to make the witness of the church known in uncommon ways.[12]

Apparently the answer to the church's effective witness in an industrial society lies both in the forms of collective action cited above and in the action of small and committed groups whose members have sensed a need and have sought to minister to it. In the process they have called the attention of the larger church to similar concerns and needs. One such demonstration is the East Harlem Parish in New York and its spreading counterparts in many industrial cities. The most recent outgrowth of such interest is the formation, in process at the time of this writing, of the Urban Training Center in Chicago, whose purpose is to prepare church leadership for the unresolved needs of urban society. Likewise, out of unmet needs in town and country life there has been created and put into operation in Merom, Indiana, the Ecumenical Center of Renewal and Planning on behalf of town and country churches.

It has always been true that "new occasions teach new duties." Our times are experiencing a wealth of new illustrations relating the church to economic life in industrial society. None may contend that it is the only true expression of the church. The final test is its faithfulness to the healing ministry of Christ, that no injury be done "to the least of these" and that all men may be free to attain the measure of the full stature which they were intended to attain.

16

Spiritual Foundations

The first chapter of this book presented a brief historical survey of the relation between religion and economic life. That survey concluded with a characterization of the Social Gospel, America's most distinctive and imaginative contribution to religious thought. It was this nation's first comprehensive attempt to bring the resources of religion to bear on some of the issues related to industrialism.

In Europe prior to the twentieth century Roman Catholicism, with its ties to the feudal order, its leaders in government and economic life committed to more authoritarian structures, was losing its working people. It had not accommodated itself to the new industrial scene. Pope Leo XIII's encyclical *Rerum novarum* sought to remedy this situation. Likewise, Protestantism in Europe, with much of its ecclesiastical life still resembling the Roman Catholic patterns it had sought to rectify, found itself unable to cope with the major reorganization of thought and institutional life accompanying industrial changes. England, as noted earlier, with its roots deeper in democratic processes, witnessed the emergence of small clusters of persons determined to bring the humanizing and ameliorating influences of the Christian religion to bear on their social and economic problems.

American Religion and Economic Justice

A new continent, holding new expectations and unrestricted by ecclesiastical forms and theologies of the Old World, developed unconsciously but persistently a fresh approach to political as well as religious life. For many in the new land the new freedom for individuals had a religious rootage even though the official documents of the nation avoided specific mention thereof. Instead of seeking to develop a "Christian socialism" they accepted religious values as inherent in the common life and as standing in judgment of it. No single theological framework implemented this conviction. It was simply assumed by many to be built into the American way of life. The Social Gospel provided both the analytical tools and the ideal norms with which to confront some of the unchallenged assumptions of American life. It must be added that any realistic confrontation of the contemporary ethical problems will have to build on the pioneering of this religious emphasis. Utilizing the rapidly emerging social sciences as instruments for analyzing both individual and social life, it could delineate the evils and point to the good. The natural sciences too, newly spurred by Darwin, were quickly appropriated. All new learning, in so far as it was gained in a genuine search for truth, was a potential contributor. And by no means least in importance was the new emphasis on a study of the social and economic conditions lying behind the biblical record, based on belief that they might throw light on the knowledge derived from the study. In this atmosphere large and influential groups of both economists and sociologists joined in the efforts to remedy the ills which were evident in the industrial economy. With these resources, knowledge, and expertness a substantial number of men and women, both lay and professional, sought to bring religious convictions to bear on conditions within the emerging industrial society. Richly informed by familiarity with the life and teachings of Jesus—the Sermon on the Mount, in particular—they were moved by a profound conviction that there could be created a social order more nearly resembling what Jesus portrayed than the existing one. That determination has not disappeared, but some of the same disciplines used in the study of our own society and in the study of the biblical record have revealed that there were deeper forms of resistance to be overcome than might have been inferred at an earlier time.

Ethically responsible behavior rests on two foundations. One is factual and analytical, the other is spiritual. The factual and analytical foundation is the understanding of what the consequences of action, whether taken individually or through groups, will be for all persons affected by them. The spiritual foundation is the pattern of attitudes and values held by persons, which determines how they will act in view of the anticipated consequences of their action. Neither foundation alone will achieve ethical behavior. A sadistic person may fully understand the harmful consequences of his cruelty but may revel in them. A person who is completely pure in heart may cause equally harmful consequences by uninformed or ill-informed acts. Good intentions are necessary but not sufficient to assure ethically responsible action.

The individual person is not only responsible for his own actions but must share responsibility for those taken by groups of which he is a member. As industrial society has grown in complexity, the acts of the individual have had a wider and wider span of consequences, and the importance of the actions taken by groups has greatly increased. The factual and analytical foundations have accordingly become more difficult for anyone to gain empirically through personal experience and observation. Despite these difficulties we know more about the consequences of individual and group behavior than ever before, thanks to the development of the natural sciences, and particularly of the social sciences, and their application in careful and objective studies. Such studies are most likely to be relevant and fruitful for ethical behavior if they are carried on by persons who are concerned with ethical problems. The highly productive work of the Department of the Church and Economic Life of the National Council of Churches is evidence for this conclusion.

In addition to the growing complexity of industrial society is the fact of rapid social and economic change. In many economic relationships the consequences of personal or group actions, including the actions of government, that we concluded were true a generation ago cannot be counted on as being true today. Moreover new kinds of problems and new relationships are continuously coming into existence, or at least into importance. Hopeful progress has been made in building into the life of Western society moral standards derived from Hebrew-Christian ethical ideals. Our laws reflect this progress. For example, child labor in industry is for the most part eliminated, and social security and aid to dependent children have been provided by law for the aged, widows, and the fatherless. Safeguards in industry have been made mandatory by legislation, by the demands of labor and by the humanitarian concern of employers. The list is long and impressive, and each of these protective instruments has come about as a result of needs emerging in a particular time and place.

But now more new problems have emerged, and the solutions of earlier periods are not adequate to meet them. All of this change and complexity poses puzzling dilemmas for persons in economic life today. If the author may draw upon his experience with a number of business and industrial groups, it has been apparent that their members feel that the major brutalities of industrial and economic life have been refined and are no longer to be feared. At the same time there is almost complete agreement that religion in general and the church in particular are offering little help with the kind of dilemmas confronting industry in this generation. Those dilemmas have to do with such ethical questions as the necessity for increasing productivity in order that the economy may continue to expand, the contribution of labor organizations to the economy and the potential danger inherent in their power, the power concentration in industry itself, the role of salesmanship and advertising, collusion in bidding, and many others. The ethical formulas of another day offer little reliable guidance for such problems as these. Nevertheless there is widespread longing for just such reliable guidance. This does not insure that the guidance would be accepted even if it were available, but there is a deep surmise that there are norms for guidance somewhere and that the church with its roots in the Christian faith ought to be able to provide competent counsel.

It should be obvious that because of complexity and change in economic life the longing for definite answers, for a handbook available for quick consultation, or for a formula or formulas that can be readily applied, is not going to be satisfied. The approaches that are actually feasible have already been indicated. They are on the one hand the application of scientific study to determine the social consequences of actions, and on the other hand the strengthening and purifying of the ethical posture or stance of the individual as he faces up to those consequences. Here we see joined together in determining ethical behavior both science and religion, science supplying the knowledge of the consequences of our actions and religion supplying the pattern of values by which we decide our actions in the light of those consequences. Much of the discussion in the preceding chapters has been devoted to laying the foundations for analyses of the consequences of individual and group action. It will be the purpose of the present chapter to examine in summary form the major aspects of the spiritual foundations of ethical behavior in economic life.

Since this study is intended to present a Christian approach to ethical problems, emphasis will of course be placed on what is relevant in Christian teaching. Such emphasis is in no way intended to suggest that other religions, as well as persons who profess no religion, do not recognize ethical problems, or that many great truths about man's relations to his fellow man and his position in the universe have not been revealed by religious faith generally. In particular it is not intended to discount the implications and contributions of Hebrew thought and belief to the ethics of industrial society. The Jewish religion, grounded in the Torah with its commandments, prophets, and teachers, confronts the same ethical issues. Many common values and objectives would characterize the solutions to economic problems as sought by thoughtful Jews and Christians. Though the Christian has the same historical roots in the Old Testament, he has a special problem in the confusion of interpretations which have centered around the person of Jesus Christ. It is because of this confusion that there have been sharp differences among Christians as to the way their faith relates to economics. The Jew faces less ambiguity in the authoritative requirement, at least, of his faith. This is one reason we have attempted to deal primarily with the implications of the Christian faith. At the same time we realize that there would be a high degree of harmony among faithful adherents of both inheritors of the Hebrew-Christian religious foundations as they arrive at similar or identical solutions.

After two millenniums it might be thought that the institutional life of the church would be a safe guide for our ethical attitudes. The church as the custodian and exemplar of the Christian ethic should supposedly present such a clear example of high-minded business practices and attitudes toward economic life in general that businessmen would find in it a criterion for many of their own business practices. In fact, however, church leadership and membership often reflect the status drives and jockeying for position which are taken for granted as a part of the business world. Business practices of the churches have not differed so noticeably from business practices at large that they can stand as reminders of a standard of economic conduct higher than those which prevail around them. A study of business practices in the church reports: "A major finding of the study is that to a disturbing extent the churches and their various agencies take less seriously their corporate responsibilities than their official pronouncements on social and economic problems give the community a right to expect."[1] In its practices the church may have offered comfort and absence of criticism for those who are not overly sensitive to the application of Christian ethical ideals.

Economic Relevance of Theological Presuppositions

For the Christian the person of Jesus Christ throws light on the meaning of human existence in society, including the very large part which is economic life. Because of His death and resurrection men have been made aware that God entered into human existence in an unprecedented and incomparable fashion. The narrative of Jesus' life as told in the Gospels has moved countless millions to faith and compassion. God's revelation of himself in human history, giving evidence of his great compassion for his world, is for those who accept the Christian faith the most revolutionary event of all time. But to comprehend its significance requires a measure of depth for which the mind seeking easy answers is not prepared. The self-giving of God in Christ is for Christians the ultimate criterion of social existence, and the most durable element in human society is self-giving love.

Although economic life as we know it has never been fully conducted on this basis, every economy stands under the ultimate criterion of self-giving love as we find it in the total experience of Jesus as the Christ. The person who really accepts the criterion of Christian social life as the expression of self-giving love toward his neighbor cannot but conduct his social relationships in a manner different from that of one who believes that the purpose of life is to live only for himself and those closest to him. A society moved by the latter motivation can scarcely understand the divine purposes for man and the world; it has been immunized against the true meaning of existence. The first need, then, of the Christian community is a broader understanding of Jesus, not merely as a model for conduct and an ethical teacher but as the Incarnation of the eternal God. "The Word was made flesh."

Also basic to our attitudes in economic behavior is the acceptance of God as the ground and the source of all life and also the source of its redemption. This acceptance is difficult to achieve because it involves an intellectual and spiritual depth of probing and discovery for which the mind is seldom equipped and against which it has been insulated by most of the life around it. Today men tend to be no longer afraid of what the church can do to them by way of consigning them to punishment. They accept the view that life's rewards and punishments are in the here and now. Earlier generations, raised on a doctrine of punishment after death and a God who keeps some kind of a score, may have lived better lives out of a fear of consequences after this life. However with expanding education has come a lessening of concern over punishment in the hereafter. Such consequences were assumed to have been initiated by a God who acted as a personal judge and to whom the individual was personally responsible. This kind of God many men today feel they can well do without. The problem is that for many no adequate theological conviction, no profound sense of obligation has been substituted.

So long as God was "out there," there was no sense of immediate obligation or likelihood of retribution, and man felt himself free. The conventionally religious person may conduct himself in no significantly different way from the person who finds himself with no theological framework. For him there is a gulf between man and such a God. This gulf permits the kind of inconsistency which rationalizes racial conflict and justifies discrimination. The economic life of contemporary man will not be seriously or effectively modified through religious beliefs which posit a God who is primarily "out there" and is not deeply involved in man's relations with his fellow men—an "absentee God," to borrow a crude expression.

Some of the most truly constructive actions being taken in our time make no reference whatever to any theological foundations. By its very definition that which fosters the goodness of life and cooperates with the created universe as it has been given to us is in harmony with the Creator and Redeemer of life. Why, then, cannot all actions be entrusted to the common-sense ethical purpose of individuals and thus not be modified or complicated by theological formulas? An answer lies in the observation over the centuries that men become more responsible and more consistent in their responsibility once they have realized that their own lives and the life of all society are held together in a common bond of creation and of redemption. As they have comprehended the depth of their obligation to this source and have expressed their gratitude in lives of love and compassion, a meaning and cohesiveness appear which they had not recognized before.

It would be most extraordinary if traditional religious phrases, heard from infancy and often quoted by rote, did not lose some of their initial meaning. To offset such experience philosophers and theologians have sought to devise new and fresh terms from time to time to encompass the great and moving ideas which have engaged the thinking of all generations. In large measure the historic phrases have been found adequate and not readily replaceable.

No single word has been found more capable of bearing the original meaning than the word "creation," and no single phrase has been found more serviceable in expressing God's continued responsibility for the object of creation than the Psalmist's words: "The earth is the Lord's." For the person of Hebrew-Christian heritage, on this simple phrase hinges all forms of relationship between man and man and between man and the earth which is his home. In their search for reality men throughout history have again and again arrived at the same conclusion, that the real world is a creation of God and that the only possible assurance of a consistent and meaningful existence within it is found in living as a "tenant of the Almighty." It is presumably something of this response which Dietrich Bonhoeffer is expressing when he says: "I never experienced the reality of God without the reality of the world or the reality of the world without the reality of God."[2]

Many persons have paid little attention to the implications that follow from this revolutionary proposition that the earth is not man's but God's. Whether it is the brevity of man's life that urges him to secure for himself and his family the most that is possible in so short a time, or whether man's incapacity for grasping the nature of the created order has rendered him unresponsive to so far-reaching and profound a meaning, we of course cannot know. It remains very obvious, however, that a large part of mankind has not accepted seriously God's prior "ownership" and responsibility for the world. Instead of accepting the assumptions of biblical and theological thought "the secularist" feels that his patterns of thinking are more dependable, especially since he doubts the validity of restraints which come from religious sources. The panoply of forces attempting to provide man with his existential needs cry out that the biblical interpretation of the world complicates matters and inhibits many of the practices and desires which have been fostered by man's own man-made worldliness. So the secular world provides, he assumes, the only acceptable framework. But, comments Gayraud S. Wilmore, what we call secularity "is only the moralistic and ideological consensus of the American middle class or of those who aspire to that class, carefully prodded and patronized by businessmen and politicians, and made slightly aromatic by the illusive perfume of Christianity."[3]

Another of those phrases so frequently quoted that their meanings may have been reduced to only antiquarian value is: "None of us lives to himself, and none of us dies to himself. If we live, we live to the Lord, and if we die, we die to the Lord; so then whether we live or whether we die, we are the Lord's" (Rom. 14:7–8).

Affirmations and explanations are conditioned by time and carry meanings for one generation which are not the same for another. To many contemporary persons that affirmation of the Apostle Paul contains little meaning. Those phrases convey insight only if one accepts the assumption that the earth is God's kingdom. Expressing the same conviction in another phrase, Paul admonishes ". . . whatever you do, do all to the glory of God" (I Cor. 10 : 31). The reasoning is the same—that all that man is and has is held as a gift from God, and his total life has meaning only to the extent that he lives it as an expression of gratitude for that gift.

In a mass society moving with inexorable force toward further urbanization it becomes increasingly difficult to comprehend or accept the significance of individual lives. In the Hebrew-Christian foundations the Hebrew people were important as a nation because they gave evidence of collective devotion to their God, but it was the individual who in his devotion, compounded at the national level, bore the responsibility for the only quality of life which could survive. The importance of the individual, in Western society at least, can be attributed in large part to these biblical roots elevating the importance of the person because of his importance to God. As suggested earlier, much of the protective and welfare legislation of industrial society owes its origin to the deep-grounded religious foundations concerning the worth of the individual.

We have now come to a point in the industrialization of society where neglect of the individual can no longer be permitted. A spurious individualism, we can now recognize, is endangering society as a whole. The consequences of neglect are embarrassing to those more fortunate; more to the point, they threaten the entire social fabric. In the reputedly affluent American society the "pockets of poverty" become a hazard to the plateaus of prosperity because of neglect of community. It is insufficient that we have compassion for a few selected persons whose welfare holds special interest. All persons are of equal worth to God. Person-to-person measures of charity are commendable, but only constructive measures through collective action can be adequate. Individualism here takes the form of responsible action in concert with others of like mind and spirit. This is responsible individualism.

Doctrines and their Application

Out of awareness of his own origins and the source of his sustenance, of the mutual dependence of man upon man and upon the earth which sustains him, emerged the doctrine of stewardship, the most meaningful explanation of man's relationship to the life about him. He is not owner, he is not its creator or source. He is, however, responsible for what has been given to him.

It is understandable that man should look upon life around him, particularly the artifacts, systems, and institutions which men have created, and assume that these things are his, at least to the extent that he has had any part in them. He has been led to believe that in some vague way he is a "steward" of them. Here is another of those words which come easily to the lips when we attempt to portray the nature of responsibility for the life of the world. Stewardship has become too readily identified with the "every member canvass," connoting the giving of money. This is a serious belittling of its true scope and meaning. A faithful steward makes the best adjustment possible under the circumstances. Nor are the areas of decision related only to money. They may involve personnel—a school board decision on transportation, the preservation of land for recreation, or the choice of a political candidate. A faithful (and wise) steward goes into action on the trouble fronts, working for the best possible solution—and not being disillusioned if he and his cause do not win total victory.

In an economy which has traditionally placed a high premium on individual initiative, the importance of genuine stewardship has been delimited. This has been especially apparent in the stewardship of our natural resources. Too frequently they have been treated as personal possessions, subject only to the dictates of their "owner." Belatedly a nation—or a world—facing shortages of food, fiber, recreation space, and even room for family and community life, finds itself injured by the failure of men individually or collectively to acknowledge their stewardship. Too late it is recognized that they had defaulted on a trust involving resources they did not create.

The Christian doctrine of man includes, among many other things, the belief that he is responsible to the God who is his Creator and Redeemer and is responsible to his fellowmen who are held in a similar relationship. Because of this responsibility he stands under the judgment it imposes upon him. It is a personal judgment even though he may share it collectively along with others. Men have always preferred to avoid any judgment placed upon themselves by their fellow men, but even more have they resented the assumption that they stand under judgment for the way in which they have fulfilled their stewardship.* The responsible Christian must know that no one can avoid judgment upon himself either as an individual or in his collective relationships. This is true not only because of what one actually does. Failure to act when action is required can be even more self-corrupting than some negative actions. Literally, then, under no circumstances is a man able to enjoy the smugness of self-gratification. Reinhold Niebuhr has commented: "It is well to know that God judges all men and that in His sight no man is justified. But we are men and not God. We must make historic choices."[5] It is for those choices that the Christian seeks a wisdom grounded elsewhere than in his ever-present self-interest. Only a consistent awareness that his own life is bound by ties of gratitude to the Source of his being protects him from more impermanent and more partial answers. Man cannot understand his relationship to his Creator and Redeemer unless he holds in love the rest of mankind. ". . . For he who does not love his brother whom he has seen, cannot love God whom he has not seen" (I John 4 : 20).

We like to entertain the belief that our decisions are our own and that our beliefs have been arrived at through the exercise of sound thought and judgment. Calm analysis of the facts reveals this to be erroneous. Group or national interests have dictated

* In a study conducted by the author and a colleague, an attempt was made to ascertain the extent to which individuals acknowledge any judgment upon them for their actions in our society and its economy. An almost negligible number indicated that their understanding of God included a judgmental relationship. This was true regardless of denomination.[4]

mass opinion, and individuals have either accepted them unthinkingly or have rationalized their judgment. Mass convictions have rarely if ever been the result of careful thought. In modern mass society this condition may be more prevalent than previously for the obvious reason that the instruments for influencing opinion can reach so much larger audiences with the same ideas. It could be argued that with rising levels of education and more people having access to the means for making decisions the likelihood of more balanced judgment would follow. Such apparently is not the case.

In an economy increasingly dominated by ever larger units and the availability of resources to influence opinions and judgments of increasing numbers the question of individual and mass decision takes on greater significance. Large economic units are in position to bring pressure to bear on employees, communities served, and auditors or viewers of their message. Their objectives may or may not be meritorious. The same is true for causes and movements of all descriptions. The instruments for influencing judgment can be utilized for good as well as for evil. Of primary importance is the fact that decisions and judgments in our economy are likely to be influenced by forces determined on, or skilled in, securing their own desired ends. Within this framework the conscientious religious person has to operate.

In the last analysis, however, all decisions are personal, though they may be influenced by mass acceptance or action. It is through personal decision alone that love finds expression either in person-to-person relationships or where larger groups of one's fellow men are involved. Acting responsibly and out of gratitude for the life given him it is the individual who expresses in love what is called for by the circumstances in which he finds himself. Out of his love and gratitude to God he brings to the situations of his life a similar quality. This is no sentimental outburst or whimsical self-gratification. It is the most powerful element in existence—it is the adhesive which makes for the fullest humanity possible. In its simplest form it demands justice in human relationships. There can be no love without justice. The responsible person, then, knows that his return of God's love for him in all forms of human relationship is tested at the primary level in its fulfillment of elementary justice. Paul Tillich has commented: "It is regrettable that Christianity has often concealed its unwillingness to do justice or to fight for it by setting off love against justice and performing the works of love in the sense of 'charity' instead of battling for the removal of social injustice."[6] Love, then, which incorporates justice is the most distinctive element in all Christian ethics. Every economic system and every personal justification or rationalization must meet the test of this all-engulfing quality. It is the ultimate criterion by which all of man's actions are judged by God.

Sensitive and responsible persons know full well that they cannot carry fully to completion most, let alone all, of their noble objectives impelled by love and responsibility to God. No matter what vocation a person may follow, he is continually pressed into making partial and unsatisfactory decisions. Undoubtedly there are kinds of work which try one's soul more severely than others. The expectation that only perfection will be accepted has driven many individuals to find their fulfillment in isolation outside the range of ordinary human life. This is no solution for most people. All men are sinners, but to the extent that they are sinners and seeking forgiveness for their sinfulness, it is readily and freely given, and it is this which makes it possible for conscientious and responsible individuals to go on.

Briefly in the first chapter reference was made to the emergence of the Christian doctrine of vocation. A genuine difference in the appropriation of this doctrine was expressed by the respective followers of Luther and Calvin. A century ago greater differences could be discerned between the types of work chosen by them. The fact that the followers of Calvin believed their role was to serve God through their work inspired many to ask whether the work itself was truly a form of worship and glorification of God. The Lutheran adherent asked whether he might serve God in his work, with less concern as to whether the work itself contributed to this service. Today it seems that such differences are largely erased. The Christian doctrine of vocation has come into fresh prominence with the insistent pressure from many sources to discern whether one's work or prospects for work contribute meaningfully to the life of man. The certainty of personal summons may not be as great as we are led to believe some "calls" were in earlier times, but surely the meeting of a genuine human need is no less convincing as an indication of call.

Out of frustration over inability to make ideal and perfect choices some people, in disillusionment, may have ceased trying. It requires spiritual maturity to accept the fact that the faults of the economic order can be overcome only relatively, since in so large measure even benevolent human actions must leave some phases of life unaffected or even harmed. The test of one's integrity as a Christian, or of whatever religious persuasion, is the sincerity of intent to serve one's fellow man and to utilize all available resources toward that end. He seeks the good in so far as his understanding and resources permit. To him the admonition "Thou shalt love the Lord thy God with all thy heart and soul and mind, and thy neighbor as thyself" becomes not a counsel of perfection or one which is designed to leave man in disillusionment. It is not a counsel of perfection in the ways and works of man. It does provide a standard by which to appraise one's own integrity whether in person-to-person relationships, in family, in the community at large, or in economic relationships.

The Economy and Community

There is something fallacious in a discussion of the spiritual foundations of the Chirstian faith which separates individual concerns from the welfare of the community. If such a treatment has been apparent in this discussion, it is due solely to organizational requirements and the need for clarification in the meaning of terms. Certainly there is no such division in the Christian faith itself, as has been stated in several ways above. The Gospels make no such artificial division. The Old Testament and especially the prophets presume a cohesiveness of man and society. The early church and every valid demonstration of religious life down through the centuries have assumed that man and his community, his brother, or his neighbor are inseparable. Each man may have to do his own dying, as Martin Luther insisted, but while he is alive, he is an integral part of the whole human fabric.

Little is to be gained by discussing the various meanings attached to the word "community," that is, whether it is primarily a theological or a sociological term. Events of recent years graphically and frequently with chilling force point to the interdependence of all mankind. So we use the term "community" here in the sense of connoting the interrelatedness and interdependence of human beings.

In the light of such a consideration of the term "community," we are compelled to ask in what way the forms and institutions men have devised are consonant with the most fundamental understandings of human society. Against such ultimate and fundamental considerations the varying economic systems that men have contrived must be evaluated. It is apparent that no system of "pure" individualism or of collectivism (in the sense in which that word is most commonly used—to refer to communism or socialism) can beget the unqualified support as being "Christian."

Hopefully the Christian has matured in his theological and economic thinking to the point where labels are not determinative. Of primary importance is the question of the quality of life which is possible under whatever type of economy is chosen. For Western nations three criteria have stood above others. They are freedom, justice, and order. Does the economic system adopted permit a degree of freedom which assures the maximum of opportunity to all, with the fullest consideration of the rights of each individual in relation to others? Is each person or group assured recourse to a rule of law by which favoritism is denied and justice is attainable? And is provision made for a maximum of continuity and harmony in the carrying on of the activities needed for the preservation of society?

None of these conditions is peculiarly Christian, yet they are qualities that a mature Christian desires to see actualized. These standards are a common denominator of society's ethical ideals. A Christian is committed to constant pursuit of them. For that reason he evaluates economic conditions, programs, and proposals in the light of these three criteria. They are the minimal requirements for community, for only under them can the individual have opportunity to be wholly an individual.

Because these are minimal conditions for society in general and its economy in particular, the Christian will support in the economy that which gives promise of providing them. This would include all measures which enhance human dignty. Long before public support was attained for aid to children and the aged, for slum elimination and maintenance of income for those afflicted in a variety of ways, for the right to organize and bargain collectively, for using our resources to relieve misery and build wholesome life in other lands, and for many other economic activities, members of churches and synagogues were engaging in activities of this kind and persuading others to do likewise. With much of this now embodied in our national policy the consistent Christian will direct his attention to the central economic issues of our own times, recognizing their spiritual import.

All men are equally the object of God's love despite the fact that they are not equally endowed either physically or mentally. Divisions which have been created because of inequalities in native capacities have always been used as rationalization for taking advantage of others. By this process community has been fractured and men have been alienated both from themselves and from the source of their being. The chief end of man is, as is stated in so manifold a fashion through the whole biblical record, the love of God and neighbor. It is the very simplest form of expressing the fact of human community. In the framework of that simply expressed but incomprehensibly magnificent conception the economic life of man is experienced. Jesus as the Christ, revealing the nature of God to man, confronts man with the basis for realization that all men are one in God.

Our immediate period in history is witnessing the tragic consequences of a flagrant denial of this profound truth in the form of racial tensions. Centuries of refusal to acknowledge the community of man as God's irreducible minimum has warped the minds and robbed the well-being of countless millions. Slowly some of those who perceive the magnitude of the losses to man's economic life are attempting to bridge the gap which poison has corroded. Is it not ironical that one of the most influential forces in restoring community is the awareness of economic loss? Understandably estimates vary and are at best inaccurate, but the loss to the economy due to racial discrimination could approximate 10 billion dollars annually. This is not mere money-consciousness. It is another indication that essentially economic life can itself be healthy only when it serves the total needs of the human community.

The human community is thus seen for what it truly is—a spiritual matter whose essence is portrayed in those affirmations —perhaps over-familiar—concerning the ultimate ownership of the earth and the interrelationship of man, his Creator, and his fellow man. This message comes to persons both in their solitude and as members of communities, as they realize at the same time that no person lives only in solitude or only in the midst of others. Under both circumstances, whether alone or actively engaging in the communal life about him, a man is experiencing a part of his relationship to God. From this fact he can never fully escape. When he attempts to do so, it results in peril to himself and to the society around him.

In the preceding sections of this book there have been briefly delineated some—not all, by any means—of the critical areas related to industrial society. No one conversant with the issues and with the "human factor" could have illusions as to the immediate resolution of those issues. Christians have just reason to ask, however, whether the purposes underlying present practices give promise of furthering the well-being of society. In this book we have tried to take into account the fact that few if any decisions can incorporate the full range of what is good. There remains the timeless question concerning man's awareness that his decisions and actions stand under the judgment of Eternal Wisdom.

There is rich substance for the conviction, in the face of the evidence of faith and the situation of our times, that man's role in his brief and perplexing life is to serve the Lord of creation who is also the God and Father of our Lord Jesus Christ. For all who accept this truth all economic and political systems will be ultimately judged by it.

AFTERWORD

Reflections on Ethics and Economics

BY F. ERNEST JOHNSON

When planning this concluding volume of the series on Ethics and Economic Life the Study Committee of the Department and Dr. Obenhaus invited me to write a section dealing with some of the major fundamental and continually recurring issues that have arisen during our protracted inquiry. It was thought that, as Study Consultant to the project from 1953 on, I might contribute something to an understanding of its nature and significance. It has been a task that I relished; inevitably what I am offering is a rather highly personalized account.

At first glance the various topics discussed may seem to the reader to have been arbitrarily chosen, and presented without due regard to sequence. This would be a mistaken inference. To be sure, the breadth and depth of the subject itself have made necessary a degree of selectivity and may also have caused some abruptness in transition from one section to another. However, the selection of topics was deliberate and purposeful, and the sequence was designed.

The reader may be disposed to ask at the outset why so much attention is given to ethics *in general*—that is, to issues that are no more relevant to economics than to other areas of human interest and action. For example, the nature of moral decisions, the relation of moral "principles" to objective analysis of the situations in which the issues arise, the age-old problem of "means and ends," the distinction between compromise as moral *surrender* and compromise as moral *strategy*—why have these, and some other issues dealt with in these pages, been considered to require attention in a short essay on ethics in the sphere of economics?

This question goes to the heart of the matter. Underlying the entire discussion is a concern for the restoration in economic theory and practice, of a centuries' old belief that economics is not an autonomous, self-contained discipline, built upon a "business-is-business" philosophy, but a sphere of life in which ethics is a major factor. Hence the stress on the interplay of these disciplines, and upon the necessity of achieving and maintaining a moral consensus in the conduct, at all levels, of economic affairs. And, it must be added, the discussion that follows seeks to show that the present all-pervading anxiety over "rapid social change" cannot be allayed without a deepening of the conviction that social stability and social justice are two sides of one shield.

Since economic life is a conditioning factor in all phases of our culture and, conversely, since the community as a whole is the ultimate arbiter of economic disputes, everyone of us is among those "for whom the bell tolls."

"Ethics" and "Morals"

Let us now clear the air as to the meaning of the words "ethical" and "moral." Some scholars make a rather sharp distinction between ethics and morals—using the former word to characterize a philosophic and religious discipline and the latter to denote what its etymology suggests, namely, a set of behavior patterns, socially inherited, and imbedded in the "mores." This may explain why so many writers in our time have made a virtue of nonconformity and acquired something akin to contempt for the "conventional wisdom" that prevails in contemporary life. I have even been challenged by a graduate student in a class in educational philosophy, who contended that the words "moral" and "morality" connote a spurious ethics!

The distinctions just referred to are not without significance, but I am disposed to regard the words ethics and morals—one of Greek and the other of Latin derivation—as having virtually equivalent meanings in the context of this discussion.[1] Yet the word moral, through common usage, has come to connote an approved pattern of individual behavior which, while not unrelated to virtue, may leave much to be desired. This fact should be kept in mind as a corrective of the current mind-set against "conformity." Riesman's contention for "inner direction" of personality is no doubt sound in the intended context, but like all such generalizations it needs a sprinkling of Aristotelian wisdom: "nothing too much." For it hardly needs saying that the tendency to conform is the foundation of all communication, social activity, and group effort. Moreover, the "inner" self in large measure reflects the social environment. The phenomenon of leadership—that most important though elusive concept in the lexicon of democracy—demonstrates a type of rational, noncompulsive conformity.

Probing further, we discover that many scholars—notably those known as "positivist" in philosophy—are disposed to regard right and wrong as mental "constructs," having no ultimate significance. According to that view the statement "This is right" is to all intents equivalent to "I like it." Here we have a virtual identification of "ought to be" and "is," where the moral judgment has no more than descriptive significance. Now the descriptive phase of ethics—seeking to discover and interpret human behavior in value terms and to find the "springs" of moral impulse and action—is of great importance. But descriptive ethics is important for the very reason that it is an aid to normative ethics —the discipline concerned with analysis of behavior in terms of right and wrong, good and evil.

I hope it will be apparent that by "normative" I do not mean "authoritatively prescriptive," in the sense of seeking to bring all people to acceptance of a common mode of thought and behavior. Individual differences, which psychologists and anthropologists have taught us to take very seriously, stand in the way of any such endeavor. However people of serious mind and generous impulse are concerned with building "community." Such a concern indicates a large measure of like-mindedness, what we may call the "universal human"—essential postulate of any scheme of social order. It seems safe to say that there will always be enough in the way of individual differences to keep humanity interesting if there is enough shared conviction and purpose to keep the human adventure alive!

The perspective of such a study as we have been engaged in is, of course, sharply at variance with the positivist contention. We regard "ought" and "is" as distinct categories.[2] As descriptive, ethics may be properly called a science—a study of objective facts concerning human behavior in relation to values. As normative, it prescribes what its formulators believe to be "right"—that is, what "ought" to be done, and what is "good" as opposed to "evil." What is right is, by definition, also good, from the standpoint of the decision maker; but his value judgment may be in error as judged by his family, his community, or his church. In the last analysis he is obligated to obey his conscience in spite of adverse judgment from any source. This I understand to be in accord with Catholic and Jewish as well as Protestant teaching. But in the field of social ethics, where our inquiry lies, the individual himself is obligated to take serious account of the moral consensus of the community to which he belongs. He may then ally himself with the common judgment or oppose it by word or act. As will later appear, the matter of "moral consensus" is basic, in this writer's view, to all thinking about social ethics within a growing pluralist culture.

"Principle" and "Situation"

Here, however, a further problem arises—one with which some of our theologians have been wrestling in recent years. How should a person in the exercise of his freedom make up his mind on an issue of right and wrong about which people of high repute differ sharply? Where can he find guidance when confronted with a "forced option"—when either public duty or moral self-respect or both may compel decision? It is quite natural to all of us to reach out for explicit and trustworthy directions—partly because of a genuine yearning to "know and do the right," but partly because of a sense of insecurity. William James, one of America's truly great philosophers, spoke of the type of insecure person who wants to get a firm grasp of something that is "true, no matter what"! But truth and right are not matters for simple prescription. They do not exist "out of all relationship" but as accompaniments of intensive spiritual discipline, dedicated moral striving and—not least—intensive application of critical intelligence. They are profoundly personal.

Some Protestant theologians are now engaged in controversy over what are called the "principles" approach and the "contextual" (or "situational") approach to the making of ethical decisions. This problem is of the essence in social ethics and is at the root of much ethical turmoil in economic life; but I think it has been unhappily confused. The two "approaches" are not antithetical. On the contrary, close inspection will show them, I believe, to be inseparable authentic parts of a complete act of ethical decision.

It is a deceptively simple matter to apply what are called "general principles" to particular situations without analyzing the latter to discover the foreseeable consequences of a given course of action. This is not authentic ethical method. Rather it is an attempt to embody the "universal" in the "particular," whereas universal imperatives, such as the Decalogue embodies, can never be wholly contained in a particular case. Fitting a given principle to a particular situation may make sense with respect to "Thou shalt not covet," but doing likewise with respect to "Thou shalt not kill" has given rise to sharp controversy throughout the religious world. "Love thy neighbor as thyself"—a counsel of perfection, to be sure—is no doubt applicable to social situations generally, but it furnishes insufficient guidance in terms of practice. It gives no blueprint of what neighborly relations should be. The ethical demands in specific economic relationships present perhaps the most thorny questions of all. The "good life" cannot be determined by the number of ethical principles one has accepted for guidance, without reference to the quality of one's aims and the depth and breadth of the wisdom and courage that inform his decisions.

Responsibility for Consequences

At the heart of the matter is the relevance of probable consequences of alternative decisions on moral issues. Recently I heard one of the most eminent Protestant leaders in Europe say that the challenge to resolute action in a moral crisis is altogether independent of anticipated consequences; that one abdicates morally when he allows such considerations to influence his decision. The statement had reference to the challenge of Hitler's genocidal program to the Christian conscience. There is, of course, an authentic ring in such a statement. It recalls the declaration that faith is not "believing against the evidence, but living in scorn of consequences." If what was meant is that one should not decide a moral issue on the basis of consequences to himself, the churchman's statement readily commands assent. But the matter of foreseen consequences in their entirety is inevitably a datum for ethical judgment. As a matter of fact, great weight is given to anticipated consequences in all institutional policy and planning—religious and secular alike. How could it be otherwise?

Contemporary political conflict over "right-to-work" laws and the "right to strike," especially on the part of public employees, has intensified the "rights" issue in this country. A serious aspect of the unending controversy over the rights of labor and those of management is the fact that absolutist claims by either side can be made with deceptive plausibility. Employers tend to regard the demand for "union security" through the union shop as patently a violation of the right not to belong to a union. Labor leaders look upon "right-to-work" laws as an infringement of the right of a union member to work alongside his fellow unionists.

There could be no better illustration of the ethical confusion that results from seizing upon a single "principle" and giving to it a sort of "eminent domain" which takes precedence over all other factors in the working situation. Indeed, solutions in this kind of controversy can seldom be arrived at by "yes" or "no" decisions. As a contemporary writer has said, there is too much "gray" area—neither black nor white—to admit of such a facile judgment.

This matter is so important as to warrant more specific illustration. Take the prevalent attitude of union labor toward "crossing a picket line." It is a valid attitude for union labor and for the public in general—provided the cause that gave rise to the strike is a valid one. It can be argued that where the grievance against which the union concerned is protesting is a real one, and if there is reason to believe that the union strategy is well conceived—if these considerations have been met, then the public may be under ethical obligation to give the strikers moral support and perhaps to join them in making the strike effective. But there are some strikes that lack moral and economic justification, and it may happen that conscientious citizens will feel obligated to throw their influence on the other side and ignore the pickets.

Something should be said—and done—about absolute prohibition of labor strikes, which many people would like to see enacted into law. This is "extremism." Henry Ford II should have had an "Oscar" for his recent statement on the subject as reported in the press: "There seems to be a widespread assumption that government and public opinion will no longer tolerate strikes in major industries and therefore that a real strike in the automotive industry is out of the question this year. I am convinced that responsible bargaining is most unlikely if the very possibility of a strike is ruled out from the beginning. . . . The best and probably the only effective way to prevent [one party's] over-reaching is to preserve the possibility that a strike may occur." Elementary, as Sherlock Holmes might say.

As for prohibition of strikes by public employes, the state of New York has its Condon-Wadlin Act, which has been virtually a dead letter from the beginning. There is much to be said for its purpose, but it should be clear by now that unless the workers are convinced that ample compensation in pay or in some other form is given them for surrender of a "right" that other workers enjoy, the problem has not been solved. It is essential to a working principle of ethics or equity that it shall not violate the common man's conception of "fair play"—a common denominator of all successful social engineering.

By the same token labor's traditional, unconditional rejection of compulsory arbitration is an example of making an excellent working rule into an absolute principle—in spite of the obvious fact that in cases of nationwide involvement this could lead to industrial paralysis and national catastrophe. To repeat, nothing is more hazardous than the attempt to make a universal principle yield an authentic specific directive for ethical action, without regard for presumptive consequences in a particular situation.

To be sure, I have known a devout and renowned Christian leader to declare that God will never allow a person who trusts in him to be confronted by a situation so morally ambiguous that some absolute principle cannot be invoked to resolve it. This is surely a lamentable illusion. God summons the intellect as well as the conscience. How vastly more placid this life would be if its ambiguities could be so simply resolved! But would we still be men?

Means and Ends

The age-old problem of "means and ends" confronts us here. "The end justifies the means" is not a mere worldly maxim, as is often assumed. Strictly speaking, nothing but the end can validate the means. After all, what does "means" mean? Whatever is designated as "means" is a path leading to some end. The means can, of course, be so evil in itself as to "corrupt the end." But a means can be qualitatively validated only by reference to an end. "Doing evil that good may come" is really a self-contradictory formula: if predominantly good results flow from a deliberate deviation from an accepted moral code, a reappraisal of the code is in order. This is one way in which ethical progress comes about.

The controversy in the soft coal industry in the 1920s which resulted in a stoppage of work and other similar controversies have amply illustrated the confusion that may arise when an ethically ambiguous situation confronts a person, a group, or an organization with a forced option. We all probably have been involved in such situations. The mandate that usually emerges is "choose the lesser of two evils." But does not this miss the point?

The person involved is not so much "choosing" the one as avoiding the other. Perhaps the reason why many very conscientious people reject the "lesser evil" principle is that to "choose evil" is prima facie an unsanctifiable act. What is of paramount importance is to escape the unacceptable alternative of doing nothing. It seems to me that our moralists sometimes induce in inquiring minds a sort of emotional paralysis.

To put the whole matter in extreme form for emphasis, what guilt can possibly attach to the physician who closes his ears to a pitiful emergency call because he is hastening to another emergency case where the patient hovers between life and death? The very formulation of such a question seems childish. Yet if we insist on making the words "evil" and "sin" interchangeable, do we not thrust ourselves into a logical—and ethical—impasse? Life itself drives us to the recognition that ethical decisions are relative —or better perhaps, relational—in a prevailingly gray world where black-and-white contrasts are seldom encountered. But to affirm this does not negate principles, even absolutes. My duty to put forth my best effort to be of some use in the world admits of no diminution; it is absolute. "We have an absolute duty to do our relative best." Just as infinity is an indispensable concept in mathematics, so the unattainable ultimate is indispensable in ethics. Man's reach must "exceed his grasp." And concern with the ultimate is a distinguishing mark of religion at its highest level.

What Is a Principle?

To say all this is, of course, to invite the question, what precisely is a principle? In the view I am presenting and in the context of the above discussion a principle is a generalized statement of a moral value that we hold to be ultimate. Incidentally, a useful distinction with respect to the use of the word "value" was made by a noted educator some years ago: there are technical, economic values that are thought of as things one can enrich himself with by possessing—things one can have; but values that are thought of as improving what one will be, are in the moral category. This is a useful distinction. A principle derives its force from the value consensus behind it. But it stands in contrast to a rule, which is specific and explicit in what it enjoins.

To illustrate, a well-known company in the clothing industry many years ago experienced no little embarrassment over a clause in its union contract which stipulated the right of the employer to introduce labor-saving machinery. Although the union accepted it in principle, trouble arose when the company disclosed its intention to bring into the plant a machine that would eliminate a whole department! The union spokesmen, when the company cited the permissive clause in the contract, said, "Sure, we agreed to introduction of machinery, but we never meant anything like that!" The "impartial chairman" held up the company's proposal on the ground that it was likely to put too great a strain on the agreement. He knew that the letter of the contract was less important than keeping the structure of labor relations intact. A sound principle was involved, but it could not be translated into a specific, uniform rule of action without reckoning with conditioning factors in the situation that affected the requirements of equity.

A grievous industrial conflict in the soft coal industry into which I was once drawn made a lasting impression on my mind because the labor union, which had the stronger case in contractual—abstractly moral—terms, was on the weak side in economic terms. The industry was in the doldrums. The existing agreement was quite out of line with market conditions, but the union officials were disposed to focus attention on the one fact that the operators had gone back on the agreement to maintain the specified wage scale. That is to say, the mines were opened after many miners had begged for work on the company's terms, and the strike was broken. I spent hours one day discussing the matter with a union official, who began by unconditionally condemning the company for a palpably immoral act. But after an hour or so he said, "It seems that the more we talk about this, the more ethics moves into the background, while economics comes into the foreground." The real point, as I saw it, was that consideration of the context changed the nature of the ethical issue itself.

The lesson I drew from all this was that no working agreement that is out of line with economic realities—like an international treaty that is out of line with political realities—will prove viable. Hence it rests on a shaky moral foundation. Keeping one's word is indeed an indispensable condition of integrity and moral prestige. But if the conditions of fulfillment are lacking, the element of obligation calls for reassessment.

It is important to note, on the other hand, that those who seem to have become preoccupied with "situational ethics" to the point of relative unconcern with principles are also unrealistic. Principles, I have said, are generalized statements of moral values, which means that when appropriated by an individual, they have a dispositional effect that determines what kind of person he is. They become a wellspring from which he draws sustenance. The late John Dewey, America's foremost exponent of the pragmatic philosophy—in which the truth of a proposition is defined by the consequences of its acceptance for action—once wrote an impressive passage (which I suspect many of his students and followers have not read) that strikes me as embodying an important insight. I quote it here:

> We are sure that the *attitude* of personal kindliness, of sincerity and fairness, will make our judgment of the effects of a proposed action on the good of others infinitely more likely to be correct than will those of hate, hypocrisy, and self-seeking. A man who trusted simply to details of external consequences might readily convince himself that the removal of a certain person by murder would contribute to general happiness. One cannot imagine an honest person convincing himself that a disposition of disregard for human life would have beneficial consequences. It is true, on one hand, that the ultimate standard for judgment of acts is their objective consequences; the outcome constitutes the meaning of an act. But it is equally true that the warrant for correctness of judgment and for power of judgment to operate as an influence in conduct lies in the intrinsic make-up of character; it would be safer to trust a man of a kind and honest disposition without much ability in calculation than it would a man having great power of foresight of the future who was malicious and insincere.[3]

Here we have the two aspects of the moral life shown in relation to each other: (1) concern for the consequences of one's decisions, which impels him to a searching analysis of the situation calling for a moral judgment; and (2) a character structure, a basic disposition, a discipline of the spirit, that will "weight" one's moral decisions on the side of the best in his cultural tradition—in other words, on the side of principle. Exclusive dependence on the foreseen consequences of a decision opens the door to expediency and "rationalizing." And since there are always contingencies involved in a forecast of consequences, the "probable error," as the statisticians say, in this process is more formidable. But what person of mature mind does not realize that there is an ineluctable element of tragedy in human life? Martin Luther's agonized cry when he made his momentous decision is a classic example of the birth pangs of a moral judgment that will have unpredictable consequences: "Here I stand. I cannot do otherwise. God help me. Amen."

Crucial moral decisions are made under pressures from without and from within. When subsequent events validate them, they become a part of our cultural heritage, of our wealth in terms of moral principle.

Ethics of Compromise

What has just been said bears directly on the much-debated issue of compromise—a matter that surely needs clarification. The ambiguity is the result, I suppose, of our making one word do the work of two, for compromise has two distinct meanings. Compromising a principle is, of course, a moral fault, indicating cowardice or hypocrisy. On the other hand, compromising disputed claims in business, industry, or politics may be a valid and wise choice of "half a loaf" as an alternative to "no bread." This is implied in the familiar saying that "politics is the art of the possible." Compromise in this sense underlies the enlightened and growing practice of arbitration in the business world.

But difficulty arises when it is said that a compromise of this second kind is morally justifiable, and even "the will of God," and it is then added that nevertheless it is sinful. This seems to be carrying authentic paradox into outright contradiction! If a well-motivated decision leads to results that are, and were foreseen to be, in part bad but nevertheless the best that could be obtained, the person making this compromise has a deep moral need to feel that he is not fractionally right, but unexceptionably right—in this particular instance. The situations that life confronts us with are ambiguous enough, at best, and the inner impulsion to possess what the Latin poet Virgil called a *mens conscia recti* (a clear conscience) is, I must contend, unassailable. A morally right decision is certified as such not merely by the quantitative results to which it actually leads but by the intention it embodies and the plus value that it represents. One must bear responsibility for the consequences of his acts; this is a requirement of justice. But to be limited in foresight is often an inescapable human predicament. Paul Tillich has dealt with this point in an impressive paragraph:

> We may ask . . . whether a moral decision can stand under an unconditional imperative if the decision is a moral risk—the "risk" implying that it might prove to be the wrong decision. The answer to this question is that the unconditional character does not refer to the content, but to the form of the moral decision. Whichever side of a moral alternative might be chosen, however great the risk in a bold decision may be, if it be a *moral* decision it is dependent only on the pure "ought to be" of the moral imperative. And should anyone be in doubt as to which of several possible acts conforms to the moral imperative, he should be reminded that each of them might be justified in a particular situation, but that whatever he chooses must be done with the consciousness of standing under an unconditional imperative.[4]

A striking brief statement on compromise is found in John Morley's essay bearing that title. He holds that the issue "obviously turns upon the placing of the boundary that divides wise suspense in forming opinions, wise reserve in expressing them, and wise tardiness in trying to realise them, from unavowed disingenuousness and self-illusion, from voluntary dissimulation, and from indolence and pusillanimity." *Multum in parvo!*

I said earlier that the "principle" and "contextual" aspects of decision making are inseparable parts of a complete ethical act. The ethics of compromise shows the reciprocal relationship strikingly. The art of political compromise can avoid the abyss of hypocrisy and shallow expediency only by keeping the ethical principles involved continually in mind. Only so will the boundaries of legitimate, objective compromise remain clear.

But what I have just written leaves out of account something that classical Christian theology holds essential, namely, the sinfulness of human nature at its best—in theological language, original sin. This term is puzzling to laymen. (A nationally known churchman and business executive who participated actively in the study that we are now bringing to conclusion once said to me, "I have read and reread Niebuhr's *The Nature and Destiny of Man,* but I don't believe in original sin!") What is the meaning of the biblical account of the human predicament "original righteousness," the "fall," and the consequent unfitness to dwell in the garden of God? Realistic theologians have utilized the category of myth to designate materials that have come down to us in narrative form but whose meaning is manifestly symbolic rather than historical. But no amount of critical analysis or interpretation of scripture can dissolve away the moral facts of experience on which man's need of salvation is predicated. These facts of experience have taught man that in the process of evolution he has changed from an unmoral being to a being equipped with a conscience and prone to make wrong decisions. That in our day this is thought of as a "rise" rather than a "fall" is beside the point.

It is therefore quite true that the conscious rectitude which a person is entitled to feel and needs to feel, with respect to a particular moral decision, would be vitiated by complacency and pride that obliterate the consciousness that the human condition is one of standing under the judgment of God. This, it seems to me, may be taken as a fitting commentary on the Scriptural confession, "We are unprofitable servants; we have done only what was our duty to do." That paradoxical cry embodies both a vast humility and the spiritual satisfaction of having rendered obedience.

I am contending for a resolution of this paradox, not by looking upon an ethically imperative compromise as infected with sin—which seems to me an egregious error and a counsel of moral despair—but rather by continual awareness that sincere acts of moral decision, though "reckoned unto us for righteousness," do not cancel out smugness and pride, to which Christian saints through the centuries have felt themselves prone. Nor does rendering a decision that is a morally necessary coming-to-terms with ugly realities lighten the burden of responsibility for doing something toward destroying the evil that frustrates the nobler strivings of which human beings are capable.

Is There a "Christian Social Ethics"?

In the course of this study we have heard from time to time the troubled inquiry, "What is distinctively Christian in what you are writing?" It is a serious and important challenge, which must be dealt with. My own answer is that we are dealing with public problems confronting a pluralist society and attempting to give some guidance to Christians with respect to issues whose resolution requires cooperation on the part of citizens belonging to different faiths or professing no religious faith; and that we are aiming at a moral consensus that is authentically but not exclusively Christian. An undertaking of this sort is inevitably concerned with "contextual" analysis of ethical problems whose impact is virtually the same on all citizens who have equivalent moral sensitiveness, regardless of religious affiliation. Not only so, but the body of moral "principles" generally recognized among us is basically a Judaeo-Christian heritage.

There is a Christian social ethics in the sense that Christians witness to the lordship of Christ and seek in the Christian *koinonia* (spiritual fellowship) distinctive ways of "practicing the presence of God." But in a pluralist society in which a biblical, Judaeo-Christian tradition is recognized, an effective moral consensus is essential for conceiving and implementing ethical ends. In such a society the moral consensus so seriously needed cannot be built on a foundation that is the exclusive possession of one faith group.

Nevertheless the question raised in the above caption is important. In his *Ethics in a Christian Context* Paul L. Lehmann, of

Union Theological Seminary, presents a systematic exposition of *koinonia* ethics, that is, the ethics that grows out of the experience of fellowship and work in a Christian community.[5] This *koinonia* ethics contrasts sharply with traditional ethics, which is in the philosophical tradition. In general, ethics is taught as a philosophic discipline. Every student of ethics must have been impressed by the fact that the various "schools" of ethics deal with much the same subject matter. The *koinonia* ethics is constructed on a different pattern. It is contextual in the sense indicated above, and existential in its approach to ethical issues. Its focus is on the concrete Christian community. This is to the good: "Nothing is real until it becomes local." But it is also true that nothing of basic spiritual importance is "real" until it transcends the local and the particular.

Years of fruitful cooperation between Christians and Jews in this country have set a pattern for interfaith efforts in the field of social ethics. We have long been impressed with the parallel between the social teachings of the Old Testament prophets and the teachings of Jesus. For many years leaders of the several faiths worked together in the pattern set for Protestants in the "Social Ideals of the Churches," or equivalent declarations.

I have tried to make clear that the contextual or situational approach to a working ethics has characterized this study; otherwise we would have been content with cataloguing the "principles"! Indeed, I would call the adherence to contextual method a "first principle" of such inquiry. I have always emphasized it in my efforts to teach ethics. There is a polarity between universal and particular, between "principle" and context. And I venture to suggest that when terms are fully defined, the area of conflict among students of ethics is much reduced. Consider the following passage in Lehmann's book:

> A contextual ethic deals with behavior basically in *indicative* rather than in imperative terms. This does not mean that there are no ethical demands. It means that such ethical demands as are authentic acquire meaning and authority from specific ethical relationships, and the latter constitute the context out of which these demands emerge and which shapes the demands. This is why the definitive

question with which Christian ethics has to do has been formulated, not as "what *ought* I . . . ," but rather as "what *am* I, as a believer in Jesus Christ and as a member of his church, to do?"[6]

This, it seems to me, means that the "ethical demands"—which constitute our "principles"—"acquire meaning and authority" only as their relevance to specific situations is established. Only so can the question "What am I . . . to do?" be answered. It seems to me also that the "imperative" is not wanting in this ethical framework but is implied in the urgent inquiry "What ought I . . . ?" The indicative—the "what" of that question—emerges as a result of an inner compulsion to respond to the challenge of an actual situation. John C. Bennett's discussion of this subject has impressed me so much that I am prompted to quote rather extensively from it.[7]

The trend toward contextual ethics has many sources. One is the recognition by students of Christian Ethics of the complexity of the factors that enter into our concrete decisions. All of us agree that there is no direct line from Christian ideals to these concrete decisions, that they involve many technical judgments concerning which there is no distinctively Christian guidance, that there are judgments of strategy in relation to the use of power which belong to a different world from that of abstract Christian principles, that many of our choices are difficult, indeed agonizing, choices between evils, no one of which fits ideal prescriptions. The "existentialist" mood of the times casts discredit on universal ethical judgments. Many of our most influential theologians have sharply challenged any Christian ethic that is based upon principles.

Here it is appropriate to notice the "existentialist" element in contextualism. The late H. R. Niebuhr made a revealing statement in his *Christ and Culture*. Of the decisions Christians have to make "in the midst of cultural history" he said:

They are existential as well as relative decisions; that is to say, they are decisions that cannot be reached by speculative inquiry, but must be made in freedom by a responsible subject acting in the present moment on the basis of what is true for him. Kierkegaard, to whom belongs the honor of having underscored and ministered to this existential nature of the irreducible self more than any other modern thinker, can be something of a guide to us in our effort to understand how, in facing our enduring problem, we must and can arrive at our answer, rather than at *the* Christian answer.[8]

Returning to Bennett's comments, we find an illuminating passage:

Sometimes the contextual emphasis is presented in such a way that it seems to provide a religious short-cut to wisdom about the situation because of the language that is used. We are exhorted to respond to what God is doing in the situation. . . . To determine what God is doing in the situation is no easier than it is to decide what we should do, though exhortations of this kind often seem to assume that what God is doing is an obvious matter.

Bennett makes this specific comment on the *koinonia* ethic:

There is a special problem in connection with "koinonia ethics." When Christians make decisions about matters of public policy, they must usually think and act with non-Christians and so there must be some common moral convictions which guide them. These convictions may be derived from revelation ultimately in a society which is strongly influenced by Christianity but even so they can still be defended by considerations which have a broader base than the Christian revelation. There is operating here at least an equivalent of the idea of "natural law," if that phrase seems to represent too rigid a pattern to be useful.

I think an especially valuable contribution to this entire discussion is Bennett's emphasis on "what Christians bring to the situation." Even though an interfaith group, including perhaps some secular humanists, may find their substantive contributions to the analysis of the situation calling for decision quite similar, there are sure to be significant elements in the discussion which grow out of the several religious and ethical traditions. To bring these out is a major purpose of "dialogue."

It interests me in this connection that H. R. Niebuhr in his book *The Meaning of Revelation* says that revelation should be understood as confessional, that is, as having particular relevance to distinctive elements in the prevailing tradition.

It seems strange that a distinction well established in the Scholastic theology has not been capitalized in Protestant theology.

Two Greek words (found in an English dictionary) distinguish the two phases of moral decision making. *Synteresis* (conscience, in the general sense of recognizing moral obligation) corresponds to "principle," as I have used it in this discussion. *Syneidesis* is the denotative term, expressing a particular judgment as to what the moral imperative demands in terms of action in a particular situation. The second of those moral categories is the realm of casuistry, in the valid and useful sense of that term.

I don't expect these classical terms to find their way into Protestant theological discourse, but what they stand for would be helpful in Protestant thinking.

The Quest of Certainty

The preceding discussion almost inevitably raises the question of moral certainty as prelude to decision. A troublesome question arises between morality and religion on the one hand and science on the other, concerning the ultimate test of "truth." The late Edmund W. Sinnott of Yale, a noted scientist, forcefully and impressively defended the claim of religion to be regarded as a source of truth, parallel with that of science. He said that "most of our attitudes and reactions are not the result of reason, of taking logical thought about them, but spring directly into consciousness through the natural qualities of our minds, molded by conditioning and experience. . . . These deep, instinctive feelings, coming directly from living stuff itself, just as the still more primitive physiological reactions do, and without the mediation of conscious mind, may be our closest contact with reality. This is the province of the human spirit."[9]

Nevertheless, is there not a harmful confusion in identifying truth, in the sense of correspondence with factual reality—which science undertakes to establish—with the kind of validity and worth which the religious seer or moral philosopher feels he has established in his own way? I was struck by a remark made to me by an eminent and scholarly Jewish rabbi: "You Christians think differently from us on theological matters. You think *propositionally*." His point was sharpened by what another learned rabbi said to me: "Any statement in the form 'God is . . .' is untrue; we can't make factual, existential statements about deity." Such statements suggest the existentialist slogan *Wahrheit ist Begegnung* (Truth is Encounter).

They also call to mind that the original name for the Apostles' Creed was the Old Roman Symbol and that in the theological curriculum the study of creeds was once known as "symbolics."

In a recent book John Herman Randall, Jr., one of our foremost American philosophers, discusses the scope and limits of "knowledge" and "knowing." He concludes: "It is well to keep 'truth' for the knowledge that is science, with all its complex procedures and criteria for verifying propositions that can be stated in words."[10] He discerns, however, in the scientists' own current vocabularly a tendency to employ such terms as "warranted assertibility" instead of "scientific truth" where the latter would imply finality of empirical inquiry and intellectual grasp. And he adds: "Perhaps, after all, we have at last come the full circle. Perhaps it is now the visions of the unified possibilities of the world—of the Divine, of the 'order of splendor'—that we are once more permitted to call 'true.'"

This is a rugged road for mental travel, but we may find on it guideposts to what Felix Adler called "the knowledge and practice and love of the right." Also it somehow calls to my mind that simple, nontheological, now centuries-old Christian classic, Brother Lawrence's "Practice of the Presence of God."

Economic Change—Cultural Lag

Since our protracted study was begun, this country has become greatly concerned over "rapid social change." The intensity of this concern was inevitable because of the profound influence that the "technological revolution" has already had on our culture. To say this is not to embrace a philosophy of economic determinism but only to recognize the obvious effects of economic patterns and levels of life upon an industrial society.

But there is an aspect of this subject that I think has not had sufficient attention. It has to do with the concept "cultural lag," which claimed the attention of sociologists a few decades ago. In other words, it has to do not with the over-all facts of social change but with an ominous differential between the rates of change in different parts of our culture. I will try to show that this fact is of great importance for the ethical progress of the nation. As elaborated by an eminent American sociologist this phrase expressed the characteristic difference between the rates of growth in the "material culture" and the "adaptive culture."[11] For example, the factory system came into being long before workmen's compensation for injuries was established and before industry recognized the evils of child labor. Automobiles and airplanes filled highways and skyways with almost incredible rapidity while society groped for methods and measures that would bring the new monsters under rational human control. Today automation confronts us with the same problem in a new dimension: can social invention—the development of new services and new ways of employing time in creative fashion—keep pace with our galloping technology in pursuit of the goal of full employment? In other words, can the adaptive phase of our culture be made to keep abreast of the material, mechanical phase?

No one is able to answer this question unless he is ready to assume an improbable lowering of living standards. My concern here is less with the answer than with the nature of the problem. It seems clear to me that the main reason why society is so tardy in adapting itself socially and politically to the brisk march of technology is that the financial rewards afforded by material progress are so great in comparison with those of activities in the nonprofit area, particularly in what is commonly designated the "public sector" of the economy. A conspicuous example today is the plight of public education. It should be obvious that the need for school plants, equipment, and personnel increases as the tempo of social change is stepped up and the functions of citizenship become more complicated and at the same time more vital. Incidentally, if this country should actually find ways to recruit, train, and maintain a body of teachers adequate for the nation's needs, a very considerable part of its unemployment problem in this area of automation would be solved.

Profit System and Profit Motive

Much ink has been spilled in controversy over the profit motive, as if it were necessary to make a virtue of it in order to defend the profit system. Such discussion misses the point. Indeed, there is a rather surprising correspondence between what some of our realistic theologians have written about the sinfulness of man and what defenders of the classical economics have had to say about the necessity of the profit incentive because of the self-interest inherent in human nature. One can be as critical of the motive of private profit as any economic radical, yet defend the profit system as the only demonstrated way to accumulate and conserve the social surplus. Not only so, but one may consistently contend for a rigorous discipline of the profit motive as essential to the continued workability of the profit system. The making of profit is essential to the survival of economic enterprise, regardless of whether it accrues to individual owners, is shared with employees, is "plowed back" into plant and equipment as capital, or—one may add—used to compensate management for what the income tax has taken out of their salaries! In any case, there is good reason to think that whatever may have been true in the past, the "maximization of profit" as an end in itself is far from being an exclusive concern on the part of business and industrial management. The late John Maurice Clark, one of the most far-seeing and ethically sensitive among American economists in this century, had this to say on the point:

> Corporate business must still consider profits, and it has an obligation to do as well by its equity investors as it reasonably can. But when economic theorists describe business as "maximizing profits," they are indulging in an impossible and unrealistic degree of precision. The farther a firm's policies extend into the future, the less certain can it be just what policy will precisely "maximize profits." The company is more likely to be consciously concerned with reasonably assured survival as a paramount aim, and beyond this, to formulate its governing policies in terms of some such concept as "sound business," usually contributory to healthy growth. . . .
>
> Where there is this margin of uncertainty as to precisely what policy would "maximize profits," there is room for management to give the benefit of the doubt to policies that represent good economic citizen-

ship. And it seems that an increasing number of managements are giving increasing weight to this kind of consideration.[12]

The reason for the well-known opposition of the early church to the taking of interest seems to have been the strong belief that only effort can earn—that money is "sterile" as far as creating wealth is concerned. Profit in the strict sense was unknown in those early days, it came into being along with the "entrepreneur." He was the person who organized the establishment; he was the enterpriser. Theoretically he went into the capital market for the needed money and into the labor market for workers, rented the required land, erected plant, equipped it, and began to manufacture or to buy and sell goods. Against the proceeds he charged wages for labor and management including his own, "ground rent" on the land, and interest on invested capital. The balance, if any, was his profit.

Today the distinction between interest and dividends has been blurred, but the essence of the matter has not changed. That is to say, profit is the excess of earnings over all fixed or legal charges. This is why critics of the profit system call profit "something for nothing," that is, for no physical or mental labor, since all work at every level is rewarded in the wage category. As already said, the question of legitimacy of profit would seem to be one of the over-all utility of private profit as a means of conserving the "social surplus." In the matter of motive I see no essential ethical difference between profit and earned income—if we assume that the profit justifies itself in the respect just indicated. One can be exploitative in the use of money that comes to him in salary or wages as well as in his use of a dividend check. When the late Stanley Baldwin presented the British government with one-half of his wealth, hoping many other wealthy citizens would follow suit, he was illustrating the fact that one can dedicate his profit as well as his earned income. The hoped for result seems never to have come.

"Consumer Sovereignty"

Much has been written about the "sovereign" role of the consumer in the operation of the market. While management, labor, and government exercise "countervailing power," consumers are in general not in position to use economic power to equivalent advantage. Leland Gordon, an authority on this subject, has written:

> The concept of consumer sovereignty has persisted 180 years. Among businessmen it is still popular. Defenders of the *status quo* pay it faithful lip service. Operating within the social and economic institutional framework of the United States, the traditional function of the consumer has been to guide production. Responding to his wishes, producers produce only those goods and services consumers want, according to this concept. The consumer expresses his wishes by casting dollar votes. Everytime he spends money in the market place, or fails to spend, he "votes." Producers fit their actions to his wishes. By ordering only what he wants, by rejecting inferior quality and insufficient quantity, and by paying only a fair price, the consumer determines what shall be produced, what shall not be produced, and at the same time eliminates the unscrupulous producer.
>
> A serious defect in the concept of dollar voting lies in the fact that income is unevenly distributed. Consumers with many dollars can cast many votes, while those with few dollars have correspondingly few votes. Like corporation stockholders, consumers vote according to the number of dollar "shares" they have in the economy. Obviously such a system of voting gives some consumers more influence.[13]

Toward a Moral Consensus

This discussion is not designed to be a defense or a rejection of any "system." Its main purpose is to direct attention to a cultural situation in America—a situation in which it is very difficult to find a "moral consensus" concerning national goals. In brief, I mean the seeming predominance in our culture of divisive over integrative forces. To be sure, most of us would doubtless agree that our economic system contrasts favorably with the crude mercantilism which it displaced. Also we are probably agreed that what we were taught to call "laissez-faire" economics has been greatly modified. Altered patterns of economic power in America under the impact first of the Great Depression and then of World War II have gone far to make the term "welfare state" a recognized descriptive phrase instead of "fighting words."

In spite of all this there goes on among us what may perhaps be called an economic "cold war" between some of the greatest of our corporations and the federal government—both its executive and judicial branches. And the sharpest encounters are over violations of a fundamental tenet of the classical economics: "free competition." "Big Labor" now and then enters the same arena in defiance of government and in spite of public protests. Indeed, a significant aspect of this situation is the nonexistence of definitive public opinion because there is no such entity as the "general public" in relation to particular issues and events. Rather there are variant *ad hoc* "publics" which take form in response to fortuitous and unpredictable developments.

There is nothing really novel about this. It stems from the fragmentizing of the culture politically and religiously with the transition from the medieval to the modern era. The most significant feature of that transition is, I think, the acquisition by the economy of an autonomous status—in sharp contrast to the medieval system which preceded it. "Business is business" sloganizes this modern philosophy.

It will, I think, clarify and fortify this discussion to present here two illuminating descriptive accounts of the bearing of ethics and religion on economic life at the close of the medieval period. The first is by Ernst Troeltsch, in his monumental two-volume work *The Social Teachings of the Christian Churches*. Concerning the ethics of the age in its economic aspect, Troeltsch says:

> The whole spirit of this way of thinking on economic matters may be summed up thus: property and gain are based upon the personal performance of work; goods are exchanged only when necessary, and then only according to the principles of a just price, which does not give an undue advantage to anyone; (this 'just price' is best regulated by the Government), consumption is regulated (a) in accordance with the principle of moderation, which only permits the natural purpose of the maintenance of existence to be fulfilled, and (b) which makes room for a generosity which takes the needs of others into account; at the same time great differences in social position and in fortune, and therefore in the exercise of liberality, are fully recognized.[14]

The second passage is from the pen of the late R. H. Tawney in his well-known book *Religion and the Rise of Capitalism*.

The criticism which dismisses the concern of Churches with economic relations and social organization as a modern innovation finds little support in past history. What requires explanation is not the view that these matters are part of the province of religion, but the view that they are not. When the age of the Reformation begins, economics is still a branch of ethics, and ethics of theology; all human activities are treated as falling within a single scheme, whose character is determined by the spiritual destiny of mankind; the appeal of theorists is to natural law, not to utility; the legitimacy of economic transactions is tried by reference, less to the movements of the market, than to moral standards derived from the traditional teaching of the Christian Church; the Church itself is regarded as a society wielding theoretical, and sometimes practical, authority in social affairs. The secularization of political thought, which was to be the work of the next two centuries, had profound reactions on social speculation, and by the Restoration the whole perspective, at least in England, has been revolutionized. Religion has been converted from the keystone which holds together the social edifice into one department within it, and the idea of a rule of right is replaced by economic expediency as the arbiter of policy and the criterion of conduct.[15]

The disposition, of course, to glorify the Middle Ages because of this "mediaeval synthesis" of all aspects of life, built upon a common faith, reflects a superficial view of that era, but the historical significance of the latter, as Tawney depicts it, is beyond question. The task with which it confronts us is not that of turning back the clock but of building out of an ample heritage a value structure that will bear the weight of a vast and complex civilization—the "Great Society," as it is being called.

To repeat, we are in a period of rapid economic change, due in the first instance to developments in technology. It sets the pace, so to speak, because it makes possible two coveted achievements: a great increase in productivity and an indeterminate but very substantial reduction in labor costs. This will mean a quantitative, not a qualitative, change in the economic scene, but sheer magnitude may make the difference between the "developmental" and the "revolutionary." Our history indicates that "cultural lag" will widen the gap between lucrative productivity and the social adjustments which that entails. This may be expected to increase the moral ambivalence and confusion on the economic scene, and what I have called the predominance of the divisive over the integrative forces in our national life. To prevent this, it seems to me, is the problem of problems in our time for "general" education on all cultural levels.

"Natural Law"

Walter Lippmann has written cogently on this theme in his book *The Public Philosophy*,[16] by which term he means the "natural law." Now, the "natural law" concept does not, of course, refer to the field of the natural sciences but to the moral law conceived of as given by an all-wise Creator. It was current among American intellectuals in the Revolutionary era, as witness the use of the phrase "the laws of Nature and of Nature's God." Philosophically it is a deistic rather than a theistic formula. Since the time of Jefferson, however, natural law has come to be a familiar term in theological writings.

In spite of what he calls the "semantic confusion" to which this term gives rise and the general neglect of the idea of a "public philosophy," Lippmann defends it emphatically. "If," he writes, "the discussion of public philosophy has been, so to speak, tabled in the liberal democracies, can we assume that, though it is not being discussed, there is a public philosophy? Is there a body of positive principles and precepts which a good citizen cannot deny or ignore? I am writing this book in the conviction that there is. It is a conviction which I have acquired gradually, not so much from a theoretical education, but rather from the practical experience of seeing how hard it is for our generation to make democracy work." He says further: "Except on the premises of this philosophy, it is impossible to reach intelligible and workable conceptions of popular election, majority rule, representative assemblies, free speech, loyalty, property, corporations and voluntary associations. The founders of these institutions, which the recently enfranchised democracies have inherited, were all of them adherents of some one of the various schools of natural law."

Mr. Lippmann sees a progressive alienation of the citizenry from the public philosophy, on which their own institutions were founded. He is not calling for a return to the Middle Ages, but he asks the startling, "poignant" question whether modern men can recover contact with the lost traditions, and if so, how. If I understand him, he is in search of a way to insure the ascendancy of the integrative forces in our culture.

Protestants have had much difficulty with the "natural law" concept as Roman Catholic writers have freely used it, because they believe that it encourages an artificial, stereotyped casuistry and freezes patterns of moral behavior for which authority is claimed. It will be evident to the reader that in terms of the preceding discussion Lippmann, who is highly esteemed as a social and political analyst, is arguing for the indispensability of principle in relation to situational context.

"Legitimate Power"

Let me put alongside the Lippmann analysis some statements by Peter Drucker, one of the most perceptive contemporary students of our industrial society. In this book *The Future of Industrial Man*[17] he examines the nature and locus of power in our society and distinguishes two types, "legitimate" and "illegitimate." His definitions are intriguing and, I think, bear significantly on the argument I am trying to sketch. "Legitimate power," he writes, "stems from the same *basic belief of society regarding man's nature and fulfillment* on which the individual's social status and function rest. Indeed, legitimate power can be defined as rulership which finds its justification in *the basic ethos of the society*" (my italics). In contrast, "illegitimate power is a power which does not derive its claim from the basic beliefs of the society. Accordingly, there is no possibility to decide whether the ruler wielding the power is exercising it in conformity with the purpose of power or not; for there is no social purpose." By its very nature it is irresponsible, since "there is no criterion of responsibility, no socially accepted final authority for its justification."

But alongside this somber picture we may place a more encouraging prospect. Ernst Troeltsch has said of Thomism, "the great fundamental form of Catholic social philosophy," that "alongside of the ordinary secular institutions an idea has arisen, an idea which will certainly never be allowed to die out, a universal, ethical, and religious idea, the idea, namely, of personality united with God, and of human society united with God, and this idea is struggling to create a society which will accord with its point of view, and it must aspire to carry out those ideas into the life of the whole, far beyond the circle of the particular religious community."[18]

Here we have a prefiguring of the vision which the Social Gospel movement long afterward undertook to fix in men's minds. Also the words "a universal, ethical, and religious idea . . . of a human society united with God" express the goal toward which this essay is pointed.

Ethics of Democracy

Reference was made by Walter Lippmann to the problem of "making democracy work." Even the basic concepts embodied in that word—equality, liberty, universal suffrage, popular sovereignty, and so on—call insistently for scrutiny and definition today. Equality is admittedly not a matter of fact in any general sense, yet we cannot escape it as ethical mandate. Liberty—the word is politically oriented—is thought of as absence of restraint, and as such it is a bedrock concept, for it stands between the person and the political state. In ethical terms it means freeing individual persons for voluntary dedication to self-chosen ends. Freedom means obedience, as Saint Paul insisted—obedience not to a tribunal but to a divine imperative that engages conscience. When a person is consciously committed to the "more excellent way," he feels free. Liberty has to be defined and assured by government. Freedom is won in voluntary commitment.

> Our fathers, chained in prisons dark,
> Were still in heart and conscience free.

We have stressed the different rates of change between the "material" culture and the "adaptive" culture and the further widening of the gap which automation may be expected to bring about. It is not a bright picture, if one takes seriously what I have tried to set forth—with the aid of wisdom borrowed from others—concerning the imperative need of a moral consensus among the American people. The lack of such a consensus needs no proof.

Let us take a close look at what we may call the democratic situation. The word "democracy" seems not to be in as high repute among us—except at celebrations—as we assume in dialectic. I was shocked on the occasion of a college dinner to hear the head of the institution, a prominent educational leader, declare in a formal address that he had discontinued use of the word "democracy." He thought it had lost meaning. Even more impressive to me was the fact that he "got away with it." I never heard a criticism from a member of his audience of educators.

The relatively low status of the democratic idea is, of course, due in part to a certain vagueness that envelops it and in part to an unhappy connotation of ineptitude and even corruption that is often found in a formally democratic political regime. The latter seems to have been the chief reason for Plato's skepticism concerning democratic rule. The late Harold Laski was fond of saying that he knew no political argument for democracy that he could not refute in ten minutes—and then adding that he knew no alternative to it that would last five!

It is significant that in Lincoln's Gettysburg Address he declared that this nation was "*dedicated to the proposition* that all men are created equal." He did not base that declaration on accomplished fact. To him it was a proposition to be validated in the course of the nation's history. The outlook for political democracy was dim in 1863. But "dedicated to a proposition" is a formidable cluster of words. The substance of the proposition, taken literally, is palpably untrue: there is no sense in which the equality of all men can be called a fact. Inequality lends itself more readily to factual statement. When we say that all persons are equal, we often add "before the law" or "in the eyes of God." This is not very helpful, since we cannot see with the eyes of God and positive "law" often fails to implement democratic principle.

A teacher of mine—later a colleague—once said, "Democracy means an opportunity for every person to be all that is in him to be, and recognition of every person for all that he is." I think most of us would settle for that as a statement of the ethical meaning of democracy as a way of life, but functional problems remain. I have found a measure of satisfaction in this form of the statement: I am ethically bound to accept an obligation to do all in my power to see that all persons have equal opportunity to become all they have the potential to become. This affirms, not a "fact," but an ethical imperative.

Many years ago I was impressed by a statement about men and government by an outstanding sociologist. He was quite ready to grant that the mass of citizens were incapable of making decisions on many policies and measures on which lawmaking bodies must act. But, said he, the people can do the necessary thing—they are wise enough to select leaders who can represent their interests in government.

That sounded good to me. Incidentally, it was very like what Walter Lippmann said years ago in *The Phantom Public.* But as years passed, the names of certain notorious "leaders" who enjoyed appalling political longevity became household words of opprobrium. It was a sobering spectacle. We seem to have demonstrated in our national history that the rank and file of our people are not politically minded. They are better as humans than as citizens. When a national campaign is approaching, large numbers of people never think of studying issues; many of them are quite unprepared to vote either on issues or on candidates; many do not go to the polls at all; and many who do vote are actuated by superficial motives—perhaps having been shamed into doing so by "bring-out-the-vote" crusades. It does not seem to occur to the zealous citizens who persist in such efforts that voting in order to get it off one's conscience or in response to an appeal to "vote, no matter how, but vote" is not an exercise in good citizenship but an assault upon it. Unhappy thought though it is, I strongly suspect that the results of some of our elections would be more useful if men and women who are not prepared to vote intelligently stayed at home. There is no duty to vote, period; there is duty to be informed, to arrive at convictions, and then to vote.

With every year that passes economics and politics become

more closely bound together. Not only so, but a major goal—a vastly improved nationwide program of general education—will not be reached except through very extensive cooperation by the federal government and the states. Thus the problem becomes a political one. Indeed, practically every issue discussed in this book has a national political outreach. I cannot put too strongly the need for a cultural "leap forward" that will measurably overcome cultural lag and will contribute heavily toward making the integrative forces in the nation predominant over the divisive forces. To the probable rejoinder that cultural leaps are not easily made and that they usually "come high," one can say only that the time is past when America can regard herself as a pocket of safety in a world that is in revolution. We are in an economic and cultural crisis—the kind that will not just "go away."

In spite of all this we should be reassured by the fact that "rapid social change," which is the highest common denominator of present concern and discussion, is after all not the most pervasive social fact. Continuity bulks larger than change. Our language, our institutions, our susceptibilities, and our conscious elemental needs do not change rapidly. Nostalgia we may feel, and frustration we may suffer, but the way ahead is open.

Moreover, change is not only inevitable: it is salutary in a way we seldom allow ourselves to think about. A revolutionary period in history is not a time of altogether essential novelty; revolutionary stirrings spring from a sense of having lost something. The rising demand for civil rights is in reality a harking back to the vision—however imperfect—of the founding fathers. A discerning look backward gives us a direction forward.

Democracy and Human Nature

There seems to be an unfortunate confusion in our thinking about the implications of the rise of modern democracy concerning human nature. As a secular phenomenon it certainly has emphasized the essential goodness, the indeterminate "perfectibility" of mankind. This does not mean that "progress" is automatic, though it cannot be denied that much of the literature of democracy has conveyed that idea. Indeed, it has been said that in the eighteenth century man became convinced that "by taking thought he could add a cubit to his stature," and in the nineteenth century he was convinced that "a cubit would be added whether he took thought or not"! Certainly there is a broad streak of "Enlightenment" optimism in secular democratic "ideology."

In the realm of classical theology, however, the emphasis is in sharp contrast to the "melioristic" view of man. Casserley has expressed this well: "The great difference between the interpretations of democracy provided by secular humanists and the interpretation of democracy put forward by the Christian theologian is this: the secular humanist tends to understand and defend democracy in terms of a romantic belief in human perfectibility, whereas the Christian theologian prefers to understand and defend democracy in terms of one of his basic Biblical conceptions, the doctrine of original sin." And again: "It is because men are everywhere corruptible and always corrupted that no single man or group of men can be trusted with too much power, indeed with any power at all that is not in some way balanced and checked by the power of other men."[19]

Reinhold Niebuhr, in a widely quoted aphorism, has brought these ideas into polar relationship: "Man's capacity for justice makes democracy possible; man's inclination to injustice makes democracy necessary." There is a world of difference between "necessary" and "automatic." But if the "liberal" emphasis on the improvability of human nature points to a "built-in" tendency, so do the immortal words of Augustine: "Thou hast formed us for Thyself, and our hearts are restless till they rest in Thee."

Ethics and the Law

Commonly heard is the saying "You can't make people good by law." This is so broadly and significantly true as to obscure the very important limits of its application! Behavior most certainly has been improved by law, for everybody knows that food and drug laws can greatly reduce addiction and can protect the community, in large measure, from dangerous poisons. Traffic laws are a necessity and in large measure effectual in checking murderous recklessness on the highways. Not only so, but a statutory requirement or prohibition—in the nature of a building code, for example—may be the initial stimulus to the growth of social responsibility.

I believe there has been some criticism overseas of the "American faith in law as an educational instrument." We have had abundant proof that such a faith may be, so to say, "more than the traffic will bear." Yet our history has demonstrated that the American people can assimilate political experience pointing to higher and more consistent moral living, though the amount of lawbreaking and evasion is shameful. We can learn by failures as well as through successes, though the immediate results of majority rule are often disappointing. Democracy has "growing pains," but it does grow. It is typically in some sense experimental and exploratory, never quite sure of itself.

A troublesome issue arises as a result of this experimental character of legislation, combined with our doctrine and practice of "judicial review." This is the power and assumed duty of the federal courts to pass on the constitutionality of an act of Congress, or of one of the states, which has been plausibly challenged on constitutional grounds. Since it is substantially accepted that "the Constitution is what the judges say it is," it follows that a statute that remains in doubt while the case that raised the issue is pending may enjoy many months, or even years, of spurious validity. It is not strange that interested parties should withhold compliance in the interim, yet it must put an ethical strain on individuals or corporations to find themselves in defiance of the lawmaking body, thus appropriating an advantage in ways that may presently be found criminal.

All this is said not by way of disparaging "judicial review," as many have done. A nation like ours, which embodies a federal system and has a written constitution, could scarcely maintain political and economic equilibrium without provision for judicial review, culminating if necessary in decision by a tribunal of last resort. Indeed, the recent revival of attacks on our Supreme Court reflects, it seems to me, an ominous regression to provincialism that could become a grievous hindrance to national unity.

The particular point I wish to make here is that what we may call an ethical gap exists between the enactment of a law affecting business procedures, possibly in a vital way, and the final judicial determination as to its constitutionality. A negative decision means that the "law" is not and never was really a law at all, and government has no sanction to invoke for its enforcement. It would seem that in the case of a law that has wide legislative approval and a substantial popular sanction, all parties concerned have a prima-facie duty to comply rather than to enjoy the possible fruits of immunity during a succession of court procedures that may continue for years. "Assumed to be innocent until proved guilty" is held by all of us to be a basic principle of justice in criminal law. May it be that "valid until authoritatively pronounced invalid" would be a wholesome standard for business, industry, and labor when confronted by legal requirements which are regarded as unfair? Is not pressure for judicial review consistent with observance during the time required for that process? It should go without saying that genuinely conscientious withholding of obedience to a law, such as the military draft, is a quite different issue, which our government has recognized.

No theoretical fixing of a boundary to legislative action in relation to moral conduct, individual or corporate, can stand up against popular indignation at gross defiance of the public will and the public interest. The first responsibility of government is to govern—to maintain order and the conditions of wholesome living. The widely publicized violations of law by persons of high standing in the business and industrial world has doubtless seriously affected our national unity and impaired America's influence abroad.

I know of no more striking statement of business practices at their worst than the following, by Chancellor Louis Finkelstein of the Jewish Theological Seminary of America, published a few years ago in *Fortune*:[20]

The most casual observer is aware of the transgressions that go on daily in the American business community. He hears of tax returns that are outright perjury; he hears of purchasing agents who are taking bribes from suppliers, of businessmen offering bribes for false testimony or for police protection of some dubious enterprise. He reads of industries attempting to suborn state legislators for favorable legislation. He reads of businessmen bestowing favors on government officials to win special privileges. Even in my ivory tower on Morningside Heights, I have been urged by businessmen to accept a gift for the Theological Seminary in return for admitting a student—and have been threatened by withdrawal of contributions to the school if I failed to do so.

We hear of businessmen using wire taps to obtain information about their competitors, of management acting in collusion with racketeers, of men using prostitution to promote the sale of their goods. We hear of businessmen violating the most elementary requirements of city building codes and profiting from rat-infested tenements.

It would be less than fair to let that stand without quoting Rabbi Finkelstein's further comment:

Business leaders who generously advised me in the preparation of this article said, "The majority of the American business community are not evil men, and want to do right. Let us say we admit the indictment and accept our responsibility—what can we do?"

Ethics of Collective Bargaining

Let us look now at a major problem of democracy that is organized labor's most distinctive function and prime concern—collective bargaining. Many of us are sympathetic with the criticism that "bargaining" has an unfortunate flavor of hostile encounter—which has often been an accurate designation of what goes on at the bargaining table. I must say first, however, that it is better to be realistic about this institution than to perpetuate the fiction that "the interests of labor and capital are identical." That statement is perhaps no more fictional than the declaration in the Clayton Antitrust Act, on behalf of the unions, that "labor is not a commodity." Everybody knows that what makes bargaining possible in labor-management relations is the fact that both sides have a financial stake in the contract negotiations. Union labor considers wages as the price put upon its work. It should be said, of course, that what presumably was really meant by the slogan written into the Clayton Antitrust Act is that the laborer himself is not to be treated as a commodity. That, of course, should go without saying.

While the 1964 contract negotiations in the automobile industry were in progress, the *New York Times* in a leading editorial (Mar. 28, p. 18) said:

> The initial wage proposals offered by the automobile industry's big three and their immediate rejection by the United Automobile Workers follow a traditional and dreary ritual. Both management and the union possess responsible and imaginative talent that is equipped to exercise creative leadership on the economic and technological problems confronting industry, but they are put into the back seat at contract time. . . .
>
> The bargaining-as-usual attitude displayed by both sides reflects a dodging of the real issue. It is clear that business is far better than usual, with an excellent chance that consumer demand will remain strong for an unprecedented fourth year in a row. It also is clear that a simple dividing up of the cake of increasing productivity between shareholders and workers is contrary to the public interest. With its huge profits, the big three could absorb a substantial rise without any increase in prices.

The bedrock trouble here seems to be that this incomparably huge industrial society, the United States of America, has no adequate constitutional government for its industry. We are rightly, as a nation, opposed to the "omnicompetent state" and devoted to free initiative, in principle, but we have no constitutional provision for balancing economic power—no stable policy for preventing recurrent crises resulting from economic strife. An Industrial Councils plan has been advocated by the Roman Catholic Church—a tripartite organization of economic power representing management, labor, and government. It should have more attention.

The burden of all this is that the "common interest" of labor and management is in the maintenance of a profitable and socially wholesome enterprise. One of my most honored professors of philosophy, the late Felix Adler, used to call this shared purpose the "overarching end." He made it the key to a functional reciprocality, applicable to the areas of conflict in human life.

And What of the Church?

We have passed through what is commonly called the "social gospel" era when pulpits and ecclesiastical assemblies often spoke in radical terms on controversial issues, deriving inspiration from some outstanding leaders, chief among whom in the early days was Walter Rauschenbusch. I recall with some wonderment that his books were prominent in reading lists for young ministers during my own "novitiate," though he was a "Christian Socialist" who would probably have encountered vigorous opposition a generation later. It might be instructive to inquire into the reasons for the change in the religious climate during recent decades. Why have our Protestant churches seemed to be moving to the "right" while the Nation has been moving politically to the "left"? The latter observation refers, of course, not to ideology but to the growth of the public sector of the economy, the development of a powerful labor movement, the growth of a sense of managerial responsibility in business and industry, the firm establishment of social security, the civil rights "revolution," and other characteristics of what used to be disapprovingly called the "welfare state."

I think the "social gospel" movement swept over the churches —I should say, *some* of them, for many were apparently little affected by it—as the religious counterpart of a wave of social and political liberalism and, like the latter, subsided, but not until it had left its mark. The social gospel did not vanish when it ceased to be an impressive "movement" any more than the sea vanishes with an ebbing of the tide. To be sure, there was an element of "utopianism" in the literature it produced. But changes in thought and mood seem to come that way, and Utopia has its uses.

Whatever other causes may have been operating to alter the posture of the churches with respect to socioeconomic issues, I think the rapid growth of church membership is one. This has been a major religious phenomenon. More and more the religious population tends to approximate, at the cultural level, the temper and mood of the secular community. In physical science "force" is defined as "mass times acceleration." It is not strange that this should be true—with exceptions—of the churches, that acceleration—drive for needed social change—diminishes as size increases. Historically, it has been only in the smaller religious bodies that religion sharply challenged the community as a whole on any issue, except perhaps Prohibition. It is true, however, that when leaders of great representative religious bodies "take the field" on behalf of minority groups and unpopular liberating movements, the impact is impressive. This has been a striking feature of the civil rights crusade.

A point to emphasize here is that the church—the inclusive church—has two functions, related but distinct. As "the community on its knees," having "some of everybody" in its membership, the church can properly rejoice in seeing "the weakest saint upon his knees." It has its doors open and its altar accessible to all who want to "practice the presence of God." A church that is inclusive, as to race and class, can therefore say to its community, "Whosoever will, may come." But the soul of the church should be a disciplined fellowship, recognizable as an embodiment of the Christian redemptive enterprise always and everywhere.

The great historian Ernst Troeltsch has called the first of these the church-type and the second the sect-type. In a significant passage in his great work already referred to he says:

Very often in the so-called "sects" it is precisely the essential elements of the Gospel which are fully expressed; they themselves always appeal to the Gospel and to Primitive Christianity, and accuse the Church of having fallen away from its ideal; these impulses are always those which have been either suppressed or undeveloped in the official churches, of course for good and characteristic reasons, which again are not taken into account by the passionate party polemics of the sects. There can, however, be no doubt about the actual fact: the sects, with their greater independence of the world, and their continual emphasis upon the original ideals of Christianity, often represent in a very direct and characteristic way the essential fundamental ideas of Christianity; to a very great extent they are a most important factor in the study of the development of the sociological consequences of Christian thought.[21]

Again he writes:

The Church is that type of organization which is overwhelmingly conservative, which to a certain extent accepts the secular order, and dominates the masses; in principle, therefore, it is universal, i.e., it desires to cover the whole life of humanity. The sects, on the other hand, are comparatively small groups; they aspire after personal inward perfection, and they aim at a direct personal fellowship between the members of each group.[22]

It seems quite apparent that the "church-type" is normative for the vast majority of the church-going population. But what is ideally called for is incorporation of the sect within the church. The inclusive "whosoever will" church should foster within itself the growth of self-limiting, self-disciplining fellowships for the pursuit of excellence within their religious tradition. In such groups would be found, as Vida Scudder put it, the "leaven" which causes the "loaf"—the church as a whole—to "rise." The church is loaf, she said, not leaven!

We must never forget that the church is, in the first instance, a religious more than an ethical organization. That is to say, people come to the church to worship, to find comfort, and to have their faith strengthened. Before admission to membership they are examined in one or another manner as to their faith, but seldom as to their works! Ecclesiastical discipline is rarely resorted to in Protestantism, and never, as far as I know, because of practices that violated the "Social Ideals of the Churches." I have known a group of ministers to discuss perplexedly this lack of a membership discipline, but nothing that seemed practicable was formulated. Our churches, for the most part, have theological creeds but few guides to behavior in the field of social ethics. Ethical sensitiveness at the higher levels is not a common denominator of our church congregations. "Straight is the gate and narrow is the way. . . ."

With respect to the decline in issuance of vigorous radical pronouncements on controversial social issues, I think it is on the whole a good omen. We are now having fewer and better social pronouncements. The trouble with many of those earlier resolutions was that they appeared to represent the views of the communion, synod, conference, or other ecclesiastical unit, while as a matter of fact they were minority utterances. This is not to say that they were unbiblical or in any other sense invalid but that they were too often not the voice of the church.

No one should write in this fashion without giving attention to the constructive aspects of the situation he is dealing with. As just intimated, my criticism is not of pronouncements per se; it concerns what or whom they are supposed to represent. In the period when pronouncements were numerous, ardent reform groups were often eager to "put more teeth into it than we did last time" when framing a statement on the social order. And if the assembly—denominational or interchurch—really wanted to pass it after ample debate, the action was valid. But too often, I fear, the study and discussion that should have come first came afterward, and with disillusioning force.

What has just been said does not of course mean that a church body which is small is *ipso facto* liberal with respect to social and political issues. The sect-type religious body, in our time, more characteristically expresses its nonconformity in religious or cultural terms, or in both. The point is that to be consistently and effectually "against the world" a religious body must have a membership consisting predominantly of persons who are ready to challenge the prevailing way of life in some significant respect. Christianity itself began as a sect and behaved as a sect during its early history. When it began to grow, taking into its fellowship persons who lived at peace with the secular world, Christianity became less and less able to challenge the prevailing culture. And it has been well said that the "natural history of a sect is to become a church."

A large church body has been known to take a virtually absolutist stand against war, only to recede from the pacifist position under pressure from its own constituency. The great influence of the Protestant churches in the movement culminating in national Prohibition was preceded by generations of teaching and discipline aimed at "total abstinence." This judgment is, of course, quite independent of any appraisals of the regime thus inaugurated, as a matter of social policy.

If the principle I am trying to state can be put into concise, epigrammatic form, it would be something like this: a church body can successfully challenge the community, at the local or national level, only when it has developed an internal discipline corresponding to its external testimony. Moreover, I do not mean to imply that no utterance on controversial subjects should be made until the members of the "judicatory" body have expressly authorized it. Elected or appointed representatives of constituent groups are not chosen merely to reflect present opinions of the constituency. A thoroughly responsible person, chosen as a representative of a constituency, knows that not just his voice but his brain and his conscience have been laid under tribute to a cause. "Concern" groups should be encouraged to "speak out," but always for themselves—not for the church. Some of our larger communions and the National Council of Churches have been setting a pattern for pronouncements, studies, and problem analyses that meets the issue of representativeness through a process of unhurried, patient study and—especially—of consultation with the most knowledgeable people available and with the parties who have a stake in the outcome.

A similar problem arises, or should arise, with respect to the pulpit. A few years ago many pulpits rang with bold pronouncements about the social order. They bespoke courage, and I suppose that in the main the fighting stance of the preachers was justified and their utterances were biblically wellfounded. But the pulpit is not the church, and some of those utterances would have been more appropriate in the parish lecture hall, where laymen can and should talk back if they are moved to do so. In that case, of course, they should speak as Christian laymen and laywomen, not as representatives of secular interest groups. I am here writing of the denominational bodies whose membership is qualitatively very nearly coextensive with the community. Granted, our pews are in no small part occupied by people whose acquaintance with scripture is not impressive and whose opinions on the social-ethical issues of our time were not molded under sacred auspices! But if they are bona fide members of the church, they are entitled to a voice. I shall not forget a long conversation with a brilliant young minister, typical of the prophetic school at its best. He told me with evident satisfaction of a remonstrance from some of his official members occasioned by a forthright social sermon. "I said to them," he told me, "'Brethren, nobody goes with me into the pulpit, not even my wife. Only God goes with me into the pulpit'." Courageous, yes, but very presumptuous.

Does this limit the prophetic office? Not the real prophetic office. Prophecy is not a lone-star performance. The prophetic voice belongs to a person who is in such intimate relationship with the people he serves that he knows the word that will awaken an authentic response. Prophecy, someone has said, is "reminding people of what they have forgotten—on purpose." The hearer in the pew may at first be resentful and indignant, but sooner or later he is likely to say, "The preacher was right." God speaks to the people, we say, through the preacher. It is equally true that God speaks to the preacher through the people.

Another factor in the situation under discussion is the change in the Protestant theological climate during recent decades. The impact of the "realistic" theology—with its stress on human fallibility and the illusory character of Utopias—has been pronounced. Its corrective influence on superficial ethical optimism should be acknowledged by all of us. At the same time it seems probable that excessive emphasis on human self-regard and profit-motivation which has often characterized the literature of employing interests has in some measure found support in the writings of the theological realists, with their stern emphasis on original sin!

It cannot be too strongly emphasized that the "social gospel," now almost always referred to in the past tense, has continued to be a vital force. The purpose of the movement was from the beginning to apply the Christian gospel to the social structure itself, thus developing a climate in which Christian character can come to flower. As these lines are written, the revised Social Creed of the Methodist Church is being publicized. "We believe," it declares, "that it is our duty not only to bring Christ to the individual, but also to bring the increasingly technological society within which we live more nearly into conformity with the teachings of Christ." This is certainly what the Social Gospel set out to do.

Jewish religious leaders have participated in this social thrust, evidencing kinship in spirit and purpose between the Old Testament prophets and the writers of the New Testament Gospels. The Roman Catholic Church has long been working at this task, especially through its great encyclicals. The realistic theologians themselves, earlier referred to, are for the most part, I believe, committed to this effort. If the movement for social redemption was "dated," was that not, in part, because its main drive—to challenge the social order itself in the name of Christianity—had measurably succeeded? The transformation is, alas, still lagging. The name given the movement is perhaps unfortunate: there is only one gospel in Christianity. But the main contention of those who have sought to interpret the gospel socially is recognized, I believe, by most of our theologians of whatever school.

Just as the important function of myth in the religious sphere as a means of interpreting the past is recognized by theologians of various schools, it is reasonable to grant the validity of what may be thought of as inverted myth in depicting the indeterminate future. "These things shall be" is not predictive so much as imperative! "Thy Kingdom come on earth" is still a valid prayer.

One of the greatest weaknesses in the educational programs of our churches is the neglect of "occupational ethics." Religious vocation commonly means the ministry or some related form of professional religious activity. Quite as important and almost completely neglected is the task of organizing and conducting groups on an occupational basis for the purpose of studying the import of Christian teaching for a particular vocational group. Some useful pioneering has been done, but it is a pity that with thousands of adult classes in the churches so little has been done in the way of teaching what is being called "ethics on the job." Here is a field well suited to exploration, especially by councils of churches.

It seems strange that so limited use is made by the churches of our thoroughly radical doctrine of the stewardship of possessions. Tithing—dedicating a part of one's income "to the Lord"—is a useful device for stimulating giving, but it has little intrinsic relation to stewardship, which rests on the proposition that Christians own no private wealth but hold all their property in trust for almighty God. We all have known persons who approximate genuine Christian stewardship, but total stewardship of possessions is still a vague concept. It could bring economic life to the fore in a religious context, dominating the consideration of family budgets as well as the conduct of business. It would involve families in the solution of a major contemporary problem: how to reconcile an inherited ideal of frugality in spending with the now recognized economic necessity of increased consumption. High priority should be given to the ethics of consumption for a generation nurtured in an economy of scarcity and conditioned by a discipline of frugality.

In planning our long study we were strongly impressed that we should not omit the corporate practices of the church itself. I quote from the volume embodying the results of this phase of the inquiry: "A major finding of the study is that to a disturbing extent the churches and their various agencies take less seriously their corporate responsibilities than their official pronouncements on social and economic problems give the community a right to expect." Also the study revealed "a marked contrast between the way in which a denominational or an interdenominational assembly addresses itself to economic issues and the indifferent attitude —the lack of a sense of involvement—shown by individual churches with respect to such matters in the conduct of their business affairs."[23]

Indeed, it is hardly too much to say that most of the ethical blind spots and most of the questionable practices—barring criminal offenses—that are evident in secular business can be found somewhere and in some measure in the conduct of church affairs. Notable among these blemishes upon church corporate practices in the economic sphere are those having to do with the salaries of church employees; personnel and labor policies in large church organizations; discrimination in employment on the basis of sex, age, and color; use of objectionable methods of raising money; and investment of church funds.

Moreover, I fear there is a too little noted tendency for church policies and practices to share the defects that critics of contemporary society are continually pointing out as accompaniments of "bigness." It seems that the larger an organization becomes, the stronger is the tendency to give priority to its own corporate interests at the expense of individual needs and the claims of human dignity. Big church organizations, like their secular counterparts, often exhibit this fault. Now, I think it wrong to assume that bigness is *ipso facto* and inevitably a corrupter of values; but there can scarcely be any question that the qualities which are assumed to characterize the "organization man" continually threaten the ethical standards of religious organizations as well as those of a secular character. In both types size and corporate prestige may inflate organization loyalty beyond ethical limits.

Earlier, I referred to what has been called "*koinonia* ethics"—the ethos, so to speak, of the living, worshiping, working Christian community as a creative spiritual fellowship. Surely we can all agree that we shall not meet the crisis with which this age confronts us without a new "baptism of the Spirit" that will bring the existential church far closer to its historic ideal as the Body of Christ.

Notes

Chapter 1. Roots of Religious Concern for Economic Life

1. Charles L. Taylor, "Old Testament Foundations," in *Christianity and Property*, ed. Joseph F. Fletcher (Philadelphia: Westminster Press, 1947), p. 30.
2. Edward Hardy, Jr., "The Way of the Early Church," in *Christianity and Property*, p. 59.
3. A. T. Mollegen, "Historical Development of the Christian Testimony Concerning Economic Relations," in *Information Service* (New York: Federal Council of Churches of Christ in America), Jan. 11, 1947.
4. A. J. Carlyle, "The Theory of Property in Medieval Theology," in *Property*, 3rd edn. (London: Macmillan, 1915), p. 131.
5. Frederick H. Smyth, "The Middle Ages," in *Christianity and Property*, pp. 76–77.
6. A. J. Carlyle, *op. cit.*, p. 137.
7. Richard H. Tawney, *Religion and the Rise of Capitalism* (New York: Penguin Books, 1926), p. 30.
8. Ibid., p. 34.
9. John H. Randall, Jr., *The Making of a Modern Mind* (Boston & New York: Houghton & Mifflin Co., 1926), p. 114.
10. Paul Lehmann, "The Standpoint of the Reformation," in *Christianity and Property*, p. 122.
11. H. T. Kerr, Jr., *Compend of the Institutes* (Philadelphia: Presbyterian Board of Christian Education, 1939).
12. Paul Lehmann, op. cit., p. 114.
13. John H. Randall, Jr., op. cit., p. 274.
14. Charles Kingsley, *Letters and Memories of His Life*, p. 250.
15. Idem, *Kingsley Letters*, I, 248.
16. John M. Ludlow, "The New Idea," in *The Christian Socialist*, Vol. I, Nov. 2, 1850; quoted from Harry W. Laidler, *Social Economic Movements* (New York: Thomas Y. Crowell Co., 1946), p. 726.
17. Harry W. Laidler, *Social Economic Movements*, p. 730.

Chapter 2. Industrialism as Our Culture

1. Mimeographed report of the seminar "Christian Responsibility in the Emerging World Situation: The Population Explosion, Industrialization, and

World Mission," the Federated Theological Faculty, University of Chicago, March, 1959. Quoted in Paul Abrecht, *The Church and Rapid Social Change,* (Garden City, N.Y.: Doubleday, 1961), p. 151.

2. Clark Kerr, John T. Dunlop, Frederick H. Harbison, and Charles A. Myers, *Industrialism and Industrial Man* (Cambridge, Mass.: Harvard Univ. Press, 1960), p. 28.

3. Ibid., p. 43.

4. Ibid., p. 89.

5. W. W. Rostow, *Stages of Economic Growth* (Cambridge, Eng.: Cambridge Univ. Press, 1964).

6. Peter Drucker, *Landmarks of Tomorrow* (New York: Harper & Row, 1957), pp. 42–43.

7. Kerr et al., op. cit., p. 47.

8. Gerhard Lenski, *The Religious Factor* (New York: Doubleday, 1961).

9. W. Widick Schroeder and Victor Obenhaus, *Religion in American Culture* (New York: Free Press of Glencoe, 1964).

10. *Business Week,* April 15, 1961, p. 162.

Chapter 3. Issues Challenging Industrialism

1. "Jobs for Youth," Report on a Consultation on the Church and Youth Employment sponsored by the Department of Church and Economic Life, with other units of the National Council of Churches of Christ in the U.S.A. (January, 1964).

2. Eli E. Cohen, "Jobs for Youth," p. 8.

3. "The Captive," Department of Church in Town and Country, Division of Home Missions, The National Council of Churches of Christ in the U.S.A.

4. Dr. Oscar Ornati, "Poverty in America," Report of National Policy Committee on Pockets of Poverty (Washington, D.C., 1964), p. 18.

5. Daniel P. Moynihan, in "Christ in the Technological Revolution," a Presentation to the General Board, National Council of Churches of Christ in the U.S.A., (February 27, 1964), p. 10.

6. Michael Harrington, *The Other America* (New York: Macmillan, 1962), p. 126.

7. "The Churches and Persistent Pockets of Poverty," a report of The National Council of Churches of Christ in the U.S.A. (1962), p. 11.

8. Ibid., p. 10.

9. Ibid., p. 11.

10. Ibid., p. 14.

11. Roy Blough, "Technology and Livelihood," in *Servants of the Eternal Christ,* source book for 1963 General Assembly, National Council of Churches of Christ in the U.S.A., p. 60.

12. William P. Bundy, *Goals for Americans,* the Report of the President's Commission on National Goals (New York: The American Assembly, Columbia Univ.), p. 369.

13. Gunnar Myrdal, *Beyond the Welfare State* (New Haven: Yale Univ. Press, 1960), p. 228.

14. Peter Drucker, *Landmarks of Tomorrow,* (New York: Harper & Bros., 1957), p. 187.

15. Kerr et al., *Industrialism and Industrial Man*, (Cambridge, Mass.: Harvard Univ. Press, 1960), p. 185.

Chapter 4. Automation—Cybernation

1. Automation issue of *Information Service* (New York: National Council of Churches of Christ in the U.S.A.), September 13, 1958, p. 3.
2. John Diebold, *Automation: Its Impact on Business and Labor* (Washington, D. C.: National Planning Association Pamphlet No. 106, May 1959).
3. Typical are: Yale Brozen, Univ. of Chicago, and W. Allen Wallis, President of Univ. of Rochester.
4. Seymour L. Wolfbein, "Automation and Manpower in the 1960s," in *The Ethical Aftermath of Automation*, ed. Francis X. Quinn, S.J. (Westminster, Md.: Newman Press, 1962), p. 29.
5. John Stuart Mill, *Essay on Liberty* (Harvard Classics).
6. James Bright, in *Automation*, ed. Walter Buckingham. (New York: Harper & Row, 1961).
7. Bruno Bettelheim, in *Automation*.
8. Paul Einzig, *The Economic Consequences of Automation* (New York: W. W. Norton & Co., 1957), p. 23.
9. Gustave Weigel, S.J., "Automation in the Life of a Catholic," in *The Ethical Aftermath of Automation*, p. 179.
10. Lester Velie, "Automation, Friend or Foe," in *Reader's Digest*, October, 1962 (repr.), p. 5.

Chapter 5. Welfare and Our Industrial Economy

1. Harold L. Wilensky and Charles N. Lebeaux, *Industrial Society and Social Welfare* (New York: Russell Sage Foundation, 1958), p. 56.
2. Charles Frankel, "Obstacles to Action for Human Welfare," in *The Social Welfare Forum—1961* (New York: Columbia Univ. Press), pp. 274–275.
3. Wilensky and Lebeaux, op. cit., pp. 132–133.
4. Charles Frankel, op. cit., p. 274.
5. Thomas Gladwin, "The Anthropologist's View of Poverty," in *The Social Welfare Forum—1961*, p. 77.
6. Wilensky and Lebeaux, op. cit., p. 147.
7. Edgar May, "The Disjointed Trio: Poverty, Politics, and Power," in *The Social Welfare Forum—1963*, p. 52.
8. Roy Blough, *Servants of The Eternal Christ*, source book for 1963 General Assembly, National Council of Churches of Christ in the U.S.A., p. 68.
9. Theodore W. Schultz, *The Economic Value of Education* (New York: Columbia Univ. Press, 1963), p. 65.
10. UNESCO, *International Survey of Progress of Social Development* (New York: United Nations, Document E/CN5/301, 1955).
11. Gunnar Myrdal, *Beyond the Welfare State*, (New Haven: Yale Univ. Press, 1960), p. 179.

Chapter 6. U. S. Agriculture in Domestic and World Economy

1. Philip F. Aylesworth, *Keeping Abreast of Change in the Rural Community,* (U. S. Dept. of Agriculture, Federal Extension Service, Agricultural Information Bulletin No. 215, October 1959).
2. Quoted from "Food Costs—Farm Prices," a compilation of information related to agriculture by the Committee on Agriculture, House of Representatives, 88th Cong., July 1964.
3. D. Gale Johnson, "The Dimensions of the Farm Problem," in *Problems and Policies of American Agriculture* (Ames, Iowa: State Univ. Center for Agricultural Adjustment), pp. 47–48.
4. Kenneth E. Boulding, *Farm Goals in Conflict* (Ames: Iowa State Univ.), 1963.
5. Don F. Hadwiger, *Goals and Values in Agricultural Policy,* p. 233. Quoted from *Wisconsin Agriculturist* (Iowa State University, 1960).
6. Mervin G. Smith, quoted from a study paper on Agricultural Policy for the Department of Church and Economic Life, National Council of Churches of Christ, in the U.S.A. (1962).
7. Emerson W. Shideler, quoted in Boulding, *Farm Goals in Conflict,* p. 211.
8. Farm Bureau policy for 1963.
9. Gilbert Rohde, "Goals and Values Underlying Programs of Farmers Union," in *Farm Goals in Conflict,* p. 81.
10. Herschel D. Newsom, "Goals and Values Underlying Programs of the Grange," in *Farm Goals in Conflict,* pp. 87–88.
11. Oren Lee Staley, "The National Farmers Organization," in *Farm Goals in Conflict,* pp. 108–109.
12. Walter W. Wilcox, *Social Responsibility in Farm Leadership* (New York: Harper & Row, 1956), p. 32.
13. E. W. Hofstee, "European Perspectives of Agricultural Changes and Societal Adaptations," in *Farm Goals in Conflict,* pp. 204–205.
14. Earl O. Heady, "Feasible Criteria and Programs," in *Problems and Policies of American Agriculture,* pp. 206–207.
15. Robin M. Williams, Jr., "How to Judge Institutional Programs," in *Farm Goals in Conflict,* p. 182.
16. Quoted from "An Adaptive Program for Agriculture," a statement on national policy by the Research and Policy Committee of the Committee for Economic Development (1962).
17. Edward Higbee, in *Farms and Farmers in an Urban Age* (New York: Twentieth Century Fund, 1963), p. 143.
18. Byron Johnson, "Enlarging the Dimensions of the Food for Peace Program," address delivered at Food for Peace Conference, Denver, 1961.
19. Charles M. Hardin, "Economic Adjustment—An Instrument to Political Preservation," in *Problems and Policies in American Agriculture,* p. 163.
20. John D. Black, "Societal Obligations To and Of Agriculture," in *Problems and Policies of American Agriculture,* p. 79.
21. Byron Johnson, op. cit.

22. Ibid.
23. Willard W. Cochrane, "Beliefs and Values Underlying Agricultural Policies and Programs," in *Farm Goals in Conflict*, p. 57.
24. Robin M. Williams, Jr., op. cit., p. 7.
25. Theodore W. Schultz, "Welfare State and the Welfare People" University of Chicago Office of Agricultural Economics Research Paper No. 6406 (Feb. 5, 1964).
26. Walter W. Wilcox, "Policy Conflicts Relating to the Economic Organization of Agriculture," in Hadwiger, *Goals and Values in Agricultural Policy*, pp. 181–182.
27. Statement on Ethical Goals for Agricultural Policy, adopted by the General Board of the National Council of the Churches of Christ in the U.S.A. (June 4, 1958).
28. Resolution adopted December 9, 1960, p. 1.

Chapter 7. The Consumer—Power or Pushover

1. Leland Gordon, "The Role and Responsibility of the Consumer and How He Exercises It," study paper for the Fourth National Study Conference on the Church and Economic Life, National Council of Churches of Christ in the U.S.A. (Nov. 1962), p. 6.
2. Source of tobacco and liquor statistics: *Survey of Current Business*, U. S. Department of Commerce, Office of Business Economics; July 1964, Table 14, p. 16.
3. Margaret G. Reid, *American Income and Its Use* (New York: Harper & Row, 1954), pp. 164–165.
4. W. H. Ferry, *The Economy Under Law* (Santa Barbara, Calif.: Center for the Study of Democratic Institutions, 1960), p. 22.
5. Quoted from *Congressional Record*, April 1961, pp. 4170–4171.
6. Leland Gordon, *The Function of the Consumer*, (Westport, Conn.: Kazanjian Economics Foundation, 1957), p. 35.

Chapter 8. Organized Labor's Role

1. *The New York Times*, Sept. 17, 1922.
2. *AFL–CIO NEWS*, Aug. 8, 1964.
3. *The Adult Teacher*, Nov. 1960.
4. *Life*, Oct. 14, 1957.
5. Eric Sevareid, "The Other Side of the Coin," in *The Reporter*, Sept. 18, 1958.
6. Paul Jacobs, *Old Before Its Time—Collective Bargaining at Twenty-Eight* (Santa Barbara: Center for the Study of Democratic Institutions, 1963), p. 10.
7. Albert Rees, *Economics of Trade Unions* (Univ. of Chicago Press, 1962), pp. 44–45.
8. H. G. Lewis, *Unionism and Relative Wages in the United States* (Univ. of Chicago Press, 1963), p. 5.
9. Solomon Barkin, *The Decline of the Labor Movement* (Santa Barbara: Center for the Study of Democratic Institutions, 1961), p. 27.

10. John A. Fitch, *Social Responsibilities of Organized Labor* (New York: Harper & Row, 1957), p. 153.
11. Ibid., p. 154.
12. Gus Tyler, *A New Philosophy for Labor* (New York: Fund for the Republic, 1959), p. 11.

Chapter 9. Disarmament and the Economy

1. *Economic Impacts of Disarmament* (Washington, D. C.: U. S. Arms Control and Disarmament Agency, Jan., 1962), p. 3.
2. Emile Benoit, "Disarmament in the United States," in *Disarmament: Its Politics and Economics*, ed. Seymour Melman (Boston: American Academy of Arts and Sciences, 1962), pp. 139–140.
3. Ibid., p. 137.
4. *Economic Impacts of Disarmament*, p. 4.
5. Seymour Melman, "Economic Alternatives to Arms Prosperity," in *Annals* of the American Academy of Political and Social Science, Jan. 1964, p. 123.
6. Ibid., p. 122.
7. Allan L. Madian, "The Depletion of Education and the Conversion of University Defense Research," paper read at the Second Annual Conference of Scientists on Survival (New York: June 1963). Quoted in Melman, op. cit.
8. Fred J. Cook, "The Warfare State," in *Annals* of the American Academy of Political and Social Science, p. 105.
9. Figures from Air Transport Assn., Washington, D.C. and *Statistical Abstract of the U.S.*, 1964, p. 264.
10. Adolf Sturmthal, "Measures to Deal With Labor Displacement in Disarmament," in *Disarmament and the Economy* ed. Emile Benoit and Kenneth E. Boulding (New York: Harper & Row, 1963), p. 195.
11. Murray L. Weidenbaum, "Problems of Adjustment for Defense Industries," in *Disarmament and the Economy*, p. 67.
12. *Economic Impacts of Disarmament*, p. 9.
13. Irving L. Horowitz, "Non-Economic Factors in the Institutionalization of the Cold War," in *Annals* of the American Academy of Political and Social Science, p. 111.
14. *Economic Aspects of Disarmament*, p. 11.
15. Emile Benoit, op. cit., p. 146.
16. Irving L. Horowitz, op. cit., p. 117.
17. *Economic Aspects of Disarmament*, p. 12.
18. Emile Benoit, op. cit., pp. 144–145.
19. Seymour Melman, op. cit., p. 129.
20. Emile Benoit, in *Economic Aspects of Disarmament*, p. 14.
21. Benoit and Boulding, op. cit., pp. 9–10.
22. Marion Hoffenberg and W. W. Leontief, "The Economic Effects of Disarmament," in *Scientific American*, April 1961.
23. Richard K. Nelson, "Research and Development," in *Disarmament and the Economy*, p. 125.
24. Emile Benoit, in *Economic Aspects of Disarmament*, pp. 18–19.
25. Benoit and Boulding, op. cit., p. 296.

Chapter 10. International Trade and Aid

1. Paul G. Hoffman, *World Without Want* (New York: Harper & Row, 1962), p. 118.
2. From the report on Topic 6, "The United States Economy and World Economy," in *General and Group Reports,* Fourth National Study Conference on Church and Economic Life, National Council of Churches of Christ in the U.S.A. (Nov. 1962), p. 41.
3. William Butler, "Trade and the Less Developed Areas," in *Foreign Affairs,* XLI (Oct. 1962–July 1963), 373–374.
4. Roy Blough, "International Developments Affecting Business," address at the 77th Annual Meeting of the American Institute of Certified Public Accountants, October 4, 1964, in Miami, Florida, pp. 10–11.
5. Egbert DeVries, Director, Institute of Social Studies, The Hague, Netherlands.
6. John W. Haight, Study paper on "The U. S. Economy and the World Economy" prep. for the Fourth National Study Conference on the Church and Economic Life (1962), p. 3.
7. Charles P. Taft, "The U. S. Economy and the World Economy," address at the Fourth National Study Conference on Church and Economic Life (1962).
8. From the report on Topic 6, Fourth National Study Conference (1962), p. 43.
9. Benjamin H. Javits and Leon H. Keyserling, *The World Development Corp.* (Washington D.C., 1959), p. 3.
10. Paul G. Hoffman, op. cit., p. 118.
11. "Focus on Foreign Aid," Foreign Policy Association, Vol. 5, No. 4, p. 14.
12. William Butler, op. cit., p. 383.
13. John Nuveen, "Foreign Aid Is Like An Elephant," in *The Christian Century,* Nov. 7, 1963.
14. "New Directions in U. S. Foreign Economic Policy," Headline Series, No. 133, p. 23.
15. "Understanding Foreign Aid," Headline Series, No. 160, July 1963, p. 50.
16. Quoted from Draft Reports of the Preparatory Study Commission on Patterns of Economic and Social Change, National Council of Churches of Christ in the U.S.A., p. 21.
17. Ibid., p. 21.
18. From the Report on Topic 6, Fourth National Study Conference (1962), p. 44.

Chapter 11. Government Power in the Economy

1. Gunnar Myrdal, *Beyond the Welfare State,* (New Haven: Yale Univ. Press, 1960), p. 82.
2. Ibid., pp. 82–83.
3. Adolph A. Berle, Jr., "Evolving Capitalism and Political Federalism," in *Federalism—Mature and Emergent* (New York: Doubleday, 1955), p. 79.

4. Adolph A. Berle, Jr., "Economic Power and the Free Society," in *The Fund for the Republic* (1957), p. 14.
5. Kenneth Boulding, *The Organizational Revolution* (New York: Harper & Bros., 1953), p. 35; a book in this series.
6. Dwight D. Eisenhower, "Spending Into Trouble," in *Saturday Evening Post*, May 18, 1963, pp. 15ff.
7. Roy Blough, *Servants of the Eternal Christ*, source book for 1963 General Assembly, National Council of Churches of Christ in the U.S.A., p. 66.
8. Ibid., p. 69.
9. W. H. Ferry, *The Corporation and the Economy* (Santa Barbara, Calif.: Center for the Study of Democratic Institutions, 1959), p. 14.
10. David Bazelon, "Non-Rule in America," in *Commentary*, XXXVI: 6 (Dec. 1963), 439.
11. Sidney Hook, "Welfare State—A Debate That Isn't," in *The New York Times Magazine*, Nov. 27, 1960.

Chapter 12. The New Meaning of Leisure and Work

1. J. L. Hurlburt, *The Story of Chautauqua* (New York: J. P. Putnam Son, 1921), p. 184. Quoted from "Leisure in America—Blessing or Curse?" In the *Annals* of the American Academy of Political and Social Science (April 1964), p. 47.
2. Robert Lee, *Religion and Leisure in America* (Nashville: Abingdon Press, 1964), pp. 28–29.
3. Marion Clawson, in "Leisure in America—Blessing or Curse?" p. 1.
4. Robert Lee, op. cit., p. 37.
5. James C. Charlesworth, "A Comprehensive Plan for the Wise Use of Leisure," in "Leisure in America—Blessing or Curse?" p. 32.
6. Paul Weiss, "A Philosophical Definition of Leisure," in "Leisure in America—Blessing or Curse?" p. 22.
7. Emil Brunner, *The Divine Imperative* (Philadelphia: Westminster Press, 1947), p. 384.
8. Robert S. Michaelson, "Work and Vocation in American Industrial Society," in *Work and Vocation*, ed. John Oliver Nelson (New York: Harper & Row, 1954), p. 119.
9. Paul S. Minear, "Work and Vocation in Scripture," in *Work and Vocation*, p. 39.
10. Ibid., p. 40.
11. Robert L. Calhoun, "Work and Vocation in Christian History," in *Work and Vocation*, p. 88.
12. Elton Mayo, *Social Problems of an Industrial Civilization* (Boston, Division of Research, Graduate School of Business, Harvard Univ. 1945).
13. Cameron P. Hall, *The Christian at His Daily Work* (Department of Church and Economic Life, National Council of Churches, 1951), p. 20.

Chapter 13. Status and Stratification in Industrial Life

1. H. H. Gerth and C. Wright Mills, "Class, Status, Party," in *From Max Weber—Essays in Sociology* (New York: Oxford Univ. Press, 1946).

2. Robin M. Williams, Jr., *American Society* (New York: Alfred A. Knopf, 1960), p. 96.
3. S. M. Lipset and R. Bendix, *Social Mobility in Industrial Society* (Berkeley: Univ. of California Press, 1959).
4. Ibid., p. 6.
5. Gerth and Mills, op. cit.
6. From National Opinion Research Center; reported in Opinion News, Vol. IX, Sept. 1, 1947.

Chapter 14. Ethics and Business

1. J. Irwin Miller, *The Corporation and the Union* (Santa Barbara, Calif.: Center for the Study of Democratic Institutions, 1962); from one of a series of interviews on the American character.
2. Cameron P. Hall, ed., *On the Job Ethics* (Department of Church & Economic Life, The National Council of the Churches of Christ in the U.S.A. 1963); a pioneering analysis by men engaged in six major occupations.
3. Bernard D. Nossiter, "The Troubled Conscience of American Business," in *Harper's Magazine*, Sept. 1963, p. 38.
4. Howard R. Bowen, *Social Responsibilities of the Businessman* (New York: Harper & Row, 1953), p. 135.
5. Raymond C. Baumhart, S.J., "How Ethical Are Businessmen?" in *Harvard Business Review*, July–Aug. 1961.
6. William H. Cohea, Jr., in *On The Job Ethics.*
7. Harold L. Johnson, "Alternative Views of Big Business," in the *Annals* of the American Academy of Political and Social Science, Sept. 1962, p. 8.
8. James C. Worthy, notes on "Business and the Good Society," privately circulated Oct. 12, 1963.
9. Kenneth Underwood, "The New Social Ethic in American Business," in *Christianity and Crisis,* March 5, 1962, p. 23.
10. Theodore L. Thau, "The Business Ethics Advisory Council," in the *Annals,* Sept. 1962.
11. Harold L. Johnson, noted in *The Christian As a Businessman* (New York: Association Press, 1964), p. 71.
12. Theodore L. Thau, op. cit., p. 138.
13. Francis X. Sutton, Seymour E. Harris, Carl Kaysen, and James Tobin, *The American Business Creed* (Cambridge, Mass.: Harvard Univ. Press, 1956).
14. Ibid., p. 11.
15. Raymond C. Baumhart, S.J., op. cit.

Chapter 15. The Role of the Church

1. Arthur E. Walmsley, ed., "The Mission of the Church in the New Era," in *The Church in a Society of Abundance* (New York: Seabury Press, 1963), p. 58.
2. James M. Gustafson, *Treasure in Earthen Vessels* (New York: Harper & Row, 1961), p. 86.

3. William Temple, *The Church Looks Forward* (New York: Macmillan & Co., 1944), p. 3.
4. "The Christian Hope and the Task of the Church," in *The Responsible Society in a World Perspective* (New York: Harper & Row, 1954), p. 28.
5. H. Cunliffe Jones, *Technology, Community and Church* (London: Independent Press, Ltd., 1961.), p. 149.
6. E. Theodore Bachmann, ed., *The Activating Concern,* in Series on Churches and Social Welfare, Vol. 1 (New York: National Council of Churches of Christ in the U.S.A.), 1955.
7. *The Economic Order,* official reports of the Oxford Conference (Chicago: Willett, Clark & Co.; copyright held by Harper & Row, 1937), p. 98.
8. John C. Bennett, "A Theological Conception of Goals for Economic Life," in *Goals of Economic Life,* ed. Dudley A. Ward (New York: Harper & Row, 1953), p. 399.
9. From *Some Ethical Implications of the 1959–60 Dispute in the Steel Industry,* Report of the Special Committee.
10. Franklin H. Littell, *The German Phoenix* (New York: Doubleday, 1960).
11. Martin E. Marty, *The New Shape of American Religion* (New York: Harper & Row, 1958), p. 123.
12. Huber Klemme, *Your Church in Your Community* (Philadelphia: Christian Education Press, 1957).

Chapter 16. Spiritual Foundations

1. F. Ernest Johnson and J. Emery Ackerman, *The Church as Employer, Money Raiser, and Investor* (New York: Harper & Row, 1959), p. 122.
2. Dietrich Bonhoeffer, *Ethics,* ed. Eberhard Bethge (New York: Macmillan Co., 1955), p. 62.
3. Gayraud S. Wilmore, *The Secular Relevance of the Church* (Philadelphia: The Westminster Press, 1962), p. 34.
4. W. Widick Schroeder and Victor Obenhaus, *Religion in American Culture* (New York: Free Press of Glencoe, 1964), p. 138.
5. Reinhold Niebuhr, "Leaves from the Notebook of a War-Bound American," in *The Christian Century,* LVI (Nov. 15, 1939), 1405–1406.
6. Paul Tillich, *Morality and Beyond* (New York: Harper & Row, 1963), p. 39.

Afterword. Reflections on Ethics and Economics

1. Dr. Paul Tillich, in his book *Morality and Beyond,* remarks: "In this study, I use the terms 'morality,' 'morals,' and 'moral' throughout most of the text. And sometimes the term 'ethical' appears. There would be no confusion if, as I now suggest, we defined ethics as the 'science of the moral.' But this is not a generally accepted definition, the chief reason being that the word 'moral,' through historical accidents, has received several distorting connotations" (New York: Harper & Row, 1963), p. 21.

2. "Distinct" here does not mean separate. I am in agreement at this point with James Gustafson that "oughtness" must be "rooted in some ground of 'isness' "; in *Faith and Ethics: The Theology of H. Richard Niebuhr,* ed. Paul Ramsay, (New York: Harper & Row, 1957), p. 120.

3. John Dewey and James Tufts, *Ethics,* rev. edn. (New York: Henry Holt and Co., 1932), p. 265.

4. Paul Tillich, op. cit., p. 231.

5. (New York: Harper & Row, 1963).

6. Ibid., p. 159.

7. In an unpublished ms.; used by permission.

8. (New York: Harper & Row, 1956), p. 241.

9. *Two Roads to Truth* (New York: Viking, 1953), p. 43.

10. *The Role of Knowledge in Western Religion* (Boston: Starr King, 1958), p. 133.

11. William F. Ogburn, *Social Change* (New York: Huebsh, 1922), p. 268 ff.

12. *Economic Institutions and Human Welfare* (New York: Alfred A. Knopf, 1957), p. 218.

13. In C. H. Sandage and Vernon Fryburger, *The Role of Advertising: A Book of Readings* (Homewood, Ill.: R. D. Irwin, 1960), p. 106.

14. I (New York: The Macmillan Co., 1931), p. 320.

15. (New York: Harcourt, Brace & Co., 1926), pp. 278–279.

16. (Boston: Atlantic-Little Brown & Co., 1955), pp. 101–102.

17. (New York: John Day, 1942).

18. Ernst Troeltsch, op. cit., p. 277.

19. Both passages from *The Bent World,* J. V. Langmead Casserley (New York: Oxford Univ. Press, 1955), pp. 85, 89.

20. "The Businessman's Moral Failure," Sept. 1958.

21. Op. cit., p. 334.

22. Ibid., p. 331.

23. F. Ernest Johnson and J. Emory Ackerman, *The Church as Employer, Money-Raiser, and Investor* (New York: Harper & Row, 1959), p. 122.

Index